CARRY ON ACTORS

The Complete Who's Who of the Carry On film series

By Andrew Ross

Foreword by Fenella Fielding

Introduction by Angela Douglas

APEX PUBLISHING LTD

First published in Hardback in 2011 by
Apex Publishing Ltd
PO Box 7086, Clacton on Sea, Essex, CO15 5WN

www.apexpublishing.co.uk

British Library Cataloguing-in-Publication Data
A catalogue record for this book
is available from the British Library

ISBN: 1-906358-95-8 978-1-906358-95-2

Typeset in 10.5pt Baskerville Win95BT

Production Manager: Chris Cowlin

Cover Design: Siobhan Smith

Printed by
MPG Books Group in the UK

For my parents, without whom it would not have been possible

Contents

Introduction

A quick glimpse through the pages of this book will reveal an astonishing array of actors, from the well-known members of the *Carry On* team to the most obscure of character actors and glorified extras. All of those involved in the *Carry On* films – from *Carry On Sergeant* to *Carry On Columbus* – and the television series, *Carry On Laughing*, are included in this reference. I have also included some of those actors whose scenes ended up on the cutting room floor, in an attempt to illustrate the diversity of the series.

The book has been divided into three sections: the main team, supporting actors and production personnel.

For the thirteen main stars of the series I have included short biographies combined with in-depth details of stage, screen and television credits. For the majority of the actors these credit lists are as complete as possible and in most cases the most comprehensive published in one volume. Any omissions or mistakes throughout the book are my own and will gladly be rectified in future editions.

The supporting actors' entries consist of mini biographies and credit 'highlights', as it would be impossible to list complete credits for them all in one volume. *Carry On* roles are, of course, highlighted, and I have tried to include details of performances for which particular actors were best known.

What emerges through this complete reference of *Carry On* actors is an extensive range of performers – many of whom were as equally at home on stage in dramatic roles as they were in film comedies.

Whatever their contribution to the *Carry On* series, I hope this book will act as a tribute to the many actors involved in the film and television productions. Carry On reading!

Acknowledgements

I would like to thank the following actors, agents, authors and agencies for their help in supplying information and photographs: The late Patrick Allen & Sarah Lawson, Robin Askwith, Stephen Atkinson (Rex Features), Lynda Baron, Mrs Kay Beck, Johnny Briggs MBE, Mrs Joan Brody, Brunswick Management, Dora Bryan OBE, CCA Management, CDA Management, June Cann Management (Sydney), Julian Clary, Jennifer Clulow, Martin Clunes, Collis Management, Jim Dale MBE, the late Jack Douglas, Ray Edwards, Brian Ellwood (Barrett & Co.), Kate Feast Management, John Foster, Liz Fraser, Hugh Futcher, the late Barry Gosney, Peter Gilmore, Angela Grant, the late John Hallam, Sheila Hancock CBE, Richard Hatton Management, Melvyn Hayes, Phillip Herbert, Jennifer Hill, Julian Holloway, Laraine Humphrys, Bernard Kay, David Kernan, Bill Kenwright CBE, Burt Kwouk OBE, Rebecca Lacey, Michael Ladkin Management, George Layton, Maureen Lipman CBE, the late David Lodge, Scott Marshall Management, Mahoney Gretton Associates (MGA), Bill Maynard, Media, Entertainment & Arts Alliance (Sydney), Warren Mitchell, Georgina Moon, Massimo Moretti (Optimum Releasing), Milo O'Shea, Richard O'Sullivan, Brian Osborne, Nicholas Parsons, Jacqueline Pearce, Leslie Phillips CBE, Nigel Planer, Joyce Rae (McIntosh Rae Management), the late Andrew Ray, the late Wendy Richard MBE, Luc Roeg, Nicholas Roeg CBE, Lynda Ronan (The Richard Stone Partnership), the late Norman Rossington, Robin Sachs, Shanahan Management (Australia), James Sharkey, Showcast (Australia), Mrs Audrey Skinner, Jack Smethurst, Barry Stacey, Shirley Stelfox, David Stoll, the late Marianne Stone, Frank Thornton, the late Harry Towb, Valerie Walsh, the late Gwendolyn Watts, Richard Webber, David Williams, Richard Wilson OBE, Barbara Windsor MBE, April Young (April Young Management).

Special Thanks

I would like to give special thanks to the following members of the *Carry On* team for their memories and help in supplying information and photographs and answering questions.

The late Terence Alexander, John Antrobus, Vincent Ball, John Bluthal, the late Alec Bregonzi, the late Tim Brinton, Louise Burton, Peter Byrne, Sandra Caron, John Clive, Paul Cole, the late Pat Coombs, the late Brenda Cowling, Bernard Cribbins OBE, Alan Curtis, Alexandra Dane, Larry Dann, the late Claire Davenport, the late Ed Devereaux, Angela Douglas, Shirley Eaton, Heather Emmanuel, David Essex OBE, the late Barbara Evans, the late Hilda Fenemore, Fenella Fielding, Ann Firbank, the late Dave Freeman, Sally Geeson, Mike Grady, Leon Greene, Anita Harris, Julie Harris, the late Donald Hewlett, Michael Hobbs, Bernard Holley, Norman Hudis, Geoffrey Hughes, the late Alan Hume, the late Peter Jones, Vivienne Johnson, Faith Kent, the late Fraser Kerr, Rosalind Knight, the late Larry (Terence Parkes), the late Marjie Lawrence, the late Dilys Laye, Valerie Leon, the late David Lodge, the late Jimmy Logan OBE, Olga Lowe, Don McCorkindale, the late T.P. McKenna, Desmond McNamara, the late Michael Mellinger, the late Norman Mitchell, Trisha Noble, Margaret Nolan, Richard O'Brien, Richard O'Callaghan, the late Bill Owen MBE, Christine Ozanne, Peter Quince, Edmund Pegge, Lance Percival, Bill Pertwee MBE, Jacki Piper, Nosher Powell, the late Brian Rawlinson, Linda Regan, Joe Robinson, the late Peter Rogers, Valerie Shute, Susan Skipper, Madeline Smith, Julie Stevens, the late Ronnie Stevens, the late Philip Stone, the late Eleanor Summerfield, the late Larry Taylor, the late Stanley Unwin, Wanda Ventham, the late Kenneth Waller, the late Molly Weir, June Whitfield CBE, the late Brian Wilde.

My thanks also to the following contributors of *Carry On … Quotes*.

The late Jean Anderson, Renée Asherson, Stanley Baxter OBE, Alan Bennett, N.A.M. Butler, the late Kathleen Byron, the late Judy Campbell, Dame Judi Dench, Jean Fergusson, the late Rose Hill, Mrs Valerie James, the late Rosamund John (Mrs John Silkin), Annette Kerr, Bonnie Langford, Dan Leissner, Virginia McKenna CBE,

Miriam Margolyes OBE, Tom O'Connor, Nicholas Smith, the late Elizabeth Spriggs, Una Stubbs, Sylvia Syms OBE, Josephine Tewson, Angela Thorne, Gudrun Ure.

In addition to the above-mentioned names, numerous people have given help and encouragement in preparing this book. To my family and friends, and in particular the Simpson family (my second family!) for introducing me to the *Carry On's* many years ago, I give my heartfelt thanks.

I am greatly indebted to theatre archivist John Foster for his help in tracing numerous stage credits for many actors featured in this book.

Several members of the *Carry On* team have gone out of their way to provide assistance and I am especially grateful to Alan Curtis, the late Claire Davenport, Angela Douglas (for her touching introduction), Julie Harris, Valerie Leon, the late Norman Mitchell, Christine Ozanne, Jacki Piper, Nikki van der Zyl (for her encouragement and eagle eye!) and June Whitfield CBE for taking the time to meet or talk with me. I am happy to say that friendships have been made along the way, not least of all with that most lovable of characters, the late Pat Coombs.

I owe a huge thank you to my 'first choice', Fenella Fielding, for kindly writing the foreword to this book.

Finally, I would like to give my thanks to Chris Cowlin and the team at Apex Publishing. Their faith in this book and their professionalism has helped to make a dream become a reality.

The Series

The *Carry On* films themselves have already been written about on numerous occasions in recent years, so the following paragraphs serve only as a reminder to fans of the series.

The series began with *Carry On Sergeant* in 1958 and continued with a film a year until *Carry On Emmannuelle* in 1978. After an absence of fourteen years the series was resurrected in 1992 for *Carry On Columbus*, which featured a handful of *Carry On* veterans and a new crew of alternative comedians. In total, 31 *Carry On* films were produced.

Norman Hudis wrote the first six films; innocent romps ideally suited to audiences of the time. Thereafter (until 1974) Talbot Rothwell took on the role of scriptwriter and the series gradually progressed. By the mid-1970s, with Rothwell's failing health and mainstays such as Sid James, Hattie Jacques and Charles Hawtrey no longer appearing in the films, the series quickly declined. Various writers, with limited success, scripted the final films in the series.

The popularity of the series, however, also inspired Christmas television specials and a 13-episode television series – *Carry On Laughing* – in 1975. It featured most of the regular cast, with the notable exceptions of Kenneth Williams and Charles Hawtrey. In the early 1970s there was also a successful stage run, *Carry On London*, starring Sid James, Barbara Windsor, Bernard Bresslaw, Kenneth Connor, Peter Butterworth and Jack Douglas. Further stage productions came in 1976 (*Carry On Laughing at the Slimming Factory*) and 1992 (*Wot a Carry On in Blackpool*). Kenneth Williams and Barbara Windsor also hosted the compilation, *That's Carry On* (1978), and there were a couple of other television specials, again with Williams and Windsor, in the early 1980s.

In 1987, by which time the series had lost three of its main stars, there were rumours of a new *Carry On*. Of course this did not materialise and it wasn't until 1992 that a new film – *Carry On Columbus* - was released. It was panned by critics and fans alike.

In chronological order the films were:
Sergeant (1958), *Nurse* (1959), *Teacher* (1959), *Constable* (1960), *Regardless* (1961), *Cruising* (1962), *Cabby* (1963), *Jack* (1964), *Spying* (1964), *Cleo* (1964), *Cowboy* (1965), *Screaming* (1966), *Don't Lose Your Head* (1966), *Follow That Camel* (1967), *Doctor* (1967), *Up the Khyber* (1968), *Camping* (1969), *Again Doctor* (1969), *Up the Jungle* (1970), *Loving* (1971), *Henry* (1971), *At Your Convenience* (1971), *Matron* (1972), *Abroad* (1972), *Girls* (1973), *Dick* (1974), *Behind* (1975), *England* (1976), *That's Carry On* (compilation, 1978), *Emmannuelle* (1978) and *Columbus* (1992).

Television specials:
Carry On Christmas (1969), *Carry On Again Christmas* (1970), *Carry On Stuffing* (1972), *What a Carry On!* (1973), *Carry On Christmas* (1973), *Carry On Laughing* (13 episodes, 1975), *Carry On Laughing's Christmas Classics* (1983, hosted by Kenneth Williams and Barbara Windsor), *Norbert Smith – A Life* (*Carry On Banging*, 1989, featuring Barbara Windsor, Jack Douglas and Kenneth Connor).

Foreword by Fenella Fielding

Why does everyone love the *Carry On* films? Nearly everybody does. Is it the sauciness, the double entendres delivered so innocently? You're socially safe with innuendo, because you can choose which meaning you prefer. Joan Sims, in *Don't Lose Your Head*, delivered a particular line, and repeated it several times, with such a delicate impudence that I couldn't believe my ears. I'm still not sure if she really said what I thought she had.

The producer and director, Peter Rogers and Gerald Thomas, were a great team, and being clever men, made sure of very good scripts (the first six by Norman Hudis and about twenty after that by Talbot Rothwell) and they cast them really well with brilliant actors and actresses who they knew could deliver the goods. (And preferably, in one take, to keep the costs down!) And, of course, plenty of beautiful girls.

The *Carry On's* were successful from the word go. The critics were scathing but the public loved them. The first, *Carry On Sergeant*, did well, but the second, *Carry On Nurse*, with Hattie Jacques as a prime asset, was such a success that it set the seal on the whole series, which went on for twenty years or so. How could they fail with such a wonderful team as the multi-voiced Kenneth Williams, Joan Sims, who could play anything and with any accent, from glamour to harridan and back, Charles Hawtrey, making it all seem easy, Sid James, the archetypal rascal with-a-heart-of-gold, Jim Dale, charming, versatile and nimble to a degree - I saw him play the hero at the Vaudeville Theatre in *The Drunkard*, a Victorian temperance play, (it was sent up, of course), making a dramatic entrance from the wings, seemingly from mid-air. I asked if he'd had to climb a ladder to make this effect. He was amazed, and said no, he'd just jumped! And he did learn to walk the tightrope when he starred in *Barnum*, the Broadway musical. Then Barbara Windsor arrived on the scene as a sexy nurse of a high order and losing her bra to a round of applause as a Not the Girl Next Door. And Jack Douglas, and so many others.

The only time it stuttered was when it panicked and tried to change its personality to suit the Permissive Era with *Carry On Emmanuelle*. Outrageous naughtiness was one thing, but this was a step too far and its audience withdrew. That was in 1978. It looked like the end of the *Carry On's*.

But you can't keep real comedy down, not comedies like these that are larky and daring and full of cheek and that make your blood run faster. They had to be re-discovered and they were. Audiences have been growing bigger and bigger and with a passion to know more about the *Carry On's*, not just in broad outline but in detail. And that's where the wonderful Andrew Ross comes in.

This amazing book, *Carry On Actors*, really is a Who's Who of *Carry On* films, from the regular stars to the walk-ons, and even how they felt about each other, and all this between these two covers. Andrew Ross, you're a marvel.

Fenella Fielding

Fenella Fielding

Introduction by Angela Douglas

It is with a tinge of sadness that I remember the laughter of long ago. So spontaneous, full and genuine – at times quite hysterical.

The sadness? At the loss of so many of my fellow gigglers ... Sid, Joan, Hattie, Peter, Roy and of course, the great and incorrigible Kenny. It's impossible to explain this laughter to those who were not there but just turn to the last reel of *Khyber* and there's not a serious face on the set! It proved impossible to shoot a close up of me as a waterfall of tears, tears of laughter, spilled down my cheeks.

O Happy days!

Angela Douglas x

Angela Douglas

The Main Team

Kenneth Williams

Kenneth Williams appeared in more *Carry On* films than any other actor. As a result, his public persona became so entrenched in the series that, to many, a *Carry On* film without him was unthinkable. His style and humour were an indefinable and unique part of the series and it was Williams - perhaps more than any other actor - who made the films his own.

Kenneth Williams was born in London on 22 February 1926, the only son of barber Charlie Williams and his wife Louisa (Morgan). Kenneth trained as a lithographer from the age of fourteen. He had been briefly evacuated from London during the Blitz and in 1943 spent some time with an amateur repertory company, the Tavistock Players. At the age of eighteen, towards the end of the war, Kenneth joined the armed forces and was posted with the Survey Section of the Royal Engineers. Stationed in India (Bombay and Ceylon) as part of the map reproduction unit, he subsequently joined the Combined Services Entertainments Unit, making his debut in *Seven Keys to Baldpate* at the Victoria Theatre, Singapore, in 1946. It was during this time that Kenneth met the Scottish comedian Stanley Baxter, who was to remain a lifelong friend.

Following the war, Kenneth spent over a year on stage in repertory before making his London stage debut in a production of *Peter Pan* in 1949. Many stage credits followed, including *Saint Joan* with Siobhan McKenna, and he gained success in revues such as *One Over the Eight* with Sheila Hancock and Lance Percival (both q.v.) and *Pieces of Eight* with Fenella Fielding (q.v.) in the early 1960s. After his first major 'flop' in *Gentle Jack* with Dame Edith Evans in 1963, he largely avoided the stage, disliking what he considered unsociable hours and repetitive work.

At the beginning of his career, Kenneth Williams gained success on radio; a medium to which he would remain loyal for over forty years. He was well known for his many years in *Round the Horne* and *Beyond Our Ken* (with Betty Marsden and Bill Pertwee, both q.v.) and worked with Tony Hancock, Sid James and Hattie Jacques both on radio and television. Kenneth would later have his own radio series, *The Kenneth Williams Show* and *Stop Messing About*.

Kenneth made his television debut in 1952. He gained success on the small screen as a television 'personality' in *International Cabaret*, which led to his own show, *The Kenneth Williams Show*, and specials such as *An Audience with Kenneth Williams*. In later years he became well known as a popular contestant on programmes such as *Give Us a Clue*, with Michael Aspel, and *Whose Baby*?

Kenneth Williams joined the *Carry On* series in the first film, *Sergeant*, in 1958. He could have little idea that twenty years later he would still be working on the films. He remained grateful to Peter Rogers and Gerald Thomas for his role in the series, which gave a regular source of income and many friends, even if, privately, he disliked most of the humour. As well as starring in more *Carry On* feature films than any other actor, Kenneth also appeared in several spin-offs, although, perhaps wisely, he avoided both *Carry On Laughing* (on television) and *Carry On London* (on stage).

The early films saw Kenneth as an intellectual, effete egghead. As James Bailey (BA!) he was cold, acerbic and aloof. In *Carry On Nurse*, for the first and only time in the entire series, he was given a serious romance, opposite Jill Ireland (q.v.), then continued as intellectual characters in *Carry On Teacher* (as English teacher Mr Milton) and *Carry On Constable* (as PC Benson). He was given more comic scope in *Carry On Regardless*, but as the bilingual Francis Courtenay he maintained a certain aloofness.

Following a couple of absences from the series, Kenneth returned with star billing as Captain Fearless in *Carry On Jack*. The following year, in *Carry On Spying*, Kenneth again topped the credit list. Unique among the series, *Spying* can be seen largely as a vehicle for Williams himself, and his persona dominated the film. In the absence of the usual regulars - Sid James, Hattie Jacques and Joan Sims - it was Williams (using his 'snide' voice for the first time on screen) who successfully guided the team through one of the best films in the series. Many of his by now famous catchphrases were employed, in particular his most popular, "stop messin' about!". A notable change in character came with Kenneth's role as Caesar in *Carry On Cleo*, in which he, again, provided one of his finest performances. By now he had fully matured into the sorts of roles that were to continue for the next fourteen years. He still excelled as pompous types, but his characters were altogether more confident and latterly outrageous and sex-starved! Earlier, more romantic roles were completely set aside as his *Carry On* personality became less serious and ultimately rather camp.

Kenneth would continue in leading roles throughout the remainder of the series and was tart, devious and overblown as Dr Watt, opposite

Fenella Fielding (q.v.), in *Carry On Screaming*. Similar roles followed with Citizen Camembert in *Carry On Don't Lose Your Head* and Commandant Burger in *Carry On Follow That Camel*. Comically villainous roles continued in *Carry On Up the Khyber* (as the Khasi) and *Carry On Henry*, in a brilliantly 'executed' role as Cromwell.

Among his many *Carry On* characters, Kenneth is perhaps most memorable for his role as a doctor in *Carry On Doctor*, *Again Doctor* and *Matron*. In *Doctor*, *Matron* and *Camping* he excels as repressed characters, pursued by (and sometimes pursuing) the ample form of *Carry On* Grande Dame, Hattie Jacques. Their scenes together provide truly classic *Carry On* situations.

In *Carry On At Your Convenience*, *Carry On Abroad* and *Carry On Behind*, Kenneth continues in sexually naive roles. As in most of his appearances, he finds a measure of romance, but not before providing unforgettably outrageous scenes.

Kenneth's nude posterior shot in *Carry On Behind*, albeit brief, probably marked the 'beginning of the end' of the series. He again appeared semi nude when he made his final appearance in the series in *Carry On Emmannuelle*, once more as the leading man. Despite his best efforts, even Kenneth's talents were not enough to save a truly sad storyline and script. Over a decade later (in his published diaries), it was clear that Kenneth accepted the role of Emile Emmannuelle purely out of loyalty to Peter Rogers and Gerald Thomas.

Away from acting, Kenneth enjoyed calligraphy, diarising, reading and walking and had a deep interest in music, poetry and literature. From the 1970s onwards he contributed to many newspapers and magazines (including the *TV Times*) and was an avid writer of letters. In 1980 Kenneth published *Acid Drops*, a collection of 'tart retorts', which was followed by *Back Drops - Pages from a Private Diary* in 1983. Both books were well received. *I Only Have to Close My Eyes*, a children's book, was a new venture for Kenneth in 1986. His autobiography, *Just Williams*, was released in 1985, but the best record of his life came in 1993 when his private diaries were published. Meticulously kept, from 1946 until the night of his death, the diaries were suitably edited by Russell Davies, but they remained painfully personal and many questioned the moral dilemma surrounding their release. It seems likely, however, that Williams himself would have been wise enough to expect their eventual publication. Following the success of the diaries, Kenneth's letters, again edited by Russell Davies, were published in 1994.

Following *Carry On Emmannuelle* (his final feature film), Kenneth worked consistently for the remaining decade of his life on television and radio. His *Carry On* persona had, however, become so fixed in the public mind that he would have found it very difficult to pursue a career as a dramatic actor or character comedian even if he had wanted to. Instead, his appearances on television, as so often in the past, were invariably as 'himself' in chat and game shows, where he proved to be a popular, albeit unpredictable, performer. His flair for accents and mimicry, together with his talent as a natural raconteur, made him a welcome guest on programmes such as *Parkinson* and *Wogan*.

Kenneth's voice was undoubtedly his greatest asset, and in his latter years a great deal of his work (and the majority of his income) came from voice-over work for television and radio commercials. In the 1980s he became well known for narration (both seen and unseen) in programmes such as *Jackanory*, *Willo the Wisp* and *Galloping Galaxies*.

With Barbara Windsor, Kenneth had hosted *That's Carry On* in 1978. The pair were largely in *Carry On* 'character' but gave brilliant performances. Kenneth and Barbara were seen again, five years later, in the television special, *Carry On Christmas Capers*. Persistent rumours of a *Carry On* resurrection, shortly before Kenneth's death, were largely unfounded. He was, by the late 1980s, the main surviving cast member, but he had little or no desire to star in another film.

Despite this, however, a decade after his last *Carry On* film Kenneth was still strongly associated with the films and was happy to appear on television with Barbara Windsor, Kenneth Connor and Bernard Bresslaw on *Wogan* in 1987. It was one of his last television appearances. His final work was on radio in *Just a Minute*, to which he had remained loyal for twenty years.

Kenneth's published diaries show that he was a complex, often contradictory character: a scholarly, well-read and articulate man. Among other things, he struggled with his own sexuality, friendships and public recognition. Essentially a loner (with eccentric but well-known habits), Williams nevertheless formed cherished friendships with many of his peers. Dame Maggie Smith and her husband Beverley Cross were loyal 'chums', as too were Stanley Baxter, Gordon Jackson and Rona Anderson. Not surprisingly, Kenneth was good friends with many actors from the *Carry On* films, in particular Hattie Jacques, Barbara Windsor, Kenneth Connor and Bernard Bresslaw. He had a long, though often volatile, friendship with Joan Sims and held high opinions of other stars from the films such as Peter Butterworth, Roy Castle and Angela Douglas. His feelings were evidently easily hurt and his opinions could be scathing. Many leading ladies were the subject of his acidulous comments, including Fenella Fielding. Others earned more lasting respect, most notably Sheila Hancock. His views were rarely stagnant, and after a difficult relationship with Fenella Fielding during their time together in *Pieces of Eight* he seemed genuinely pleased to have worked with her several years later in *Carry On Screaming*. His disdain for Sidney James, however, was a view that was enduring and plainly heartfelt.

Kenneth Williams never married, despite a couple of half-hearted proposals to close friends such as Annette Kerr and Joan Sims. His personality was probably too self-absorbed (and mother-fixated) to have supported such a relationship. His diaries (and letters) were a form of release into which he devoted many hours. They provide a unique record of his life and, not surprisingly, they were both best-sellers.

The final two years of Kenneth's life were overshadowed by ill health, and he had been due to undergo an operation shortly before his death. In 1986 he was diagnosed with a spastic colon and this, combined with a stomach ulcer and back problems, led to deep depression in a man who in private was prone to be melancholy. Kenneth also had the added difficulty of looking after his elderly mother, Louisa (Lou) (1901-91), to whom he was devoted. The pair lived in adjoining flats, but Louisa's failing physical and mental health was an added worry during Kenneth's own final years.

Kenneth Williams died at the age of sixty-two, from an overdose of barbiturates taken with alcohol, at his home in London on 14/15 April 1988. The coroner later returned an open verdict, yet to those who have read his diaries the verdict might seem more obvious. Suicide was a spectre that had followed Kenneth throughout most of his adult life; in the end it appears to have been a welcome final release.

Williams's passing saw national mourning. He had become, in many ways, a comic icon. His fans and friends were shocked at the circumstances of his death. In the immediate wake of the sad event, many believed that because of the sudden circumstances he had died of a heart attack or (given intermittent poor health since 1986) bowel cancer. The truth did not emerge for some time and, even then, it was thought that his death might have been the result of an accidental overdose. It was only when his private diaries were published in 1993 that a partly satisfactory explanation was yielded.

In 1994 Barbara Windsor (with Norman Wisdom) unveiled a Dead Comics' Society plaque in memory of Kenneth Williams at 8 Malborough House, Osnaburgh Street. In April 1998 Barbara again paid tribute to her late friend when she unveiled a British Comedy Society plaque in memory of Kenneth at the home of the *Carry On* films, Pinewood Studios. They remain tributes to a fascinating, multi-talented and much-loved performer.

Carry On … ***Quotes***

What can I tell you about Kenneth Williams that is not already known through articles and TV documentaries? He was a lonely neuter, wonderful company and never embarrassing in spite of the vulgarity of his stories. A real charmer but sad.
Peter Rogers, 1998

All the memories and anecdotes about Ken are in the public domain already in his published letters and diaries. I wish to add no more. I am constantly being asked by TV and radio people to talk about Ken and I always refuse. Just too, too sad a story – best left untold.
Stanley Baxter OBE, 2000

I met Kenneth in a Repertory Company in 1949 and remained close friends until his death. I miss him. He was a complex character and to answer what he was like would take a long time and every person would give you a description with a different facet of his personality. He worked as a draughtsman and was a talented calligrapher (from some of his letters, reflecting his mood, you would not think so!) Joining an entertainment group in the army started his love of theatre and revealed a considerable talent to entertain. There he met similarly talented people who remained friends all his life.
He was a serious reader with a love of history and literature which I share and which formed our friendship. He acquired a lot of knowledge by reading and having a remarkable memory he became very well informed.
In a very popular comedy series on the radio his character frequently used the catchphrase "Oh stop messing about" which became attached to him. If I recount this anecdote you will perhaps see two sides to his character. Returning to his flat from lunch out with him in a taxi (it was raining, otherwise with Kenneth one always walked!) he was telling me about some passage in Gibbon's Decline and Fall of the Roman Empire. *When we arrived and as he paid the driver, he was asked if he would say "Stop Messing About" for him. Kenneth obliged then immediately returned to Gibbon. I was privileged to be invited to his flat - few people were. He was well known for his love of privacy and for his acute fastidiousness.*
Annette Kerr, 2000

Fundamentally a sad man.
Miriam Margolyes OBE, 2003

Carry On **CREDITS 1958-78**

Sergeant (James Bailey); *Nurse* (Oliver Reckitt); *Teacher* (Edwin Milton); *Constable* (PC Stanley Benson); *Regardless* (Francis Courtenay); *Cruising* (Leonard Marjoribanks); *Jack* (Captain Fearless); *Spying* (Desmond Simkins); *Cleo* (Julius Caesar); *Cowboy* (Judge Burke); *Screaming* (Dr Orlando Watt); *Don't Lose Your Head* (Citizen Camembert); *Follow That Camel* (Commandant Burger); *Doctor* (Dr Kenneth Tinkle); *Up the Khyber* (The Khasi of Kalabar); *Camping* (Dr Kenneth Soaper); *Again Doctor* (Dr Frederick Carver); *Loving* (Percival Snooper); *Henry* (Thomas Cromwell); *At Your Convenience* (W.C. Boggs); *Matron* (Sir Bernard Cutting); *Abroad* (Stuart Farquhar); *Dick* (Captain Desmond Fancey); *Behind* (Professor Roland Crump); *That's Carry On* (co-host); *Emmannuelle* (Emile Prevert).

STAGE

1948: Began his professional stage career in repertory in Newquay. 1949: *Born Yesterday* (Intimate). 1952: *Before You Die*. 1952: *Peter Pan* (Scala, as Slightly). 1954-55: *Saint Joan* (Arts & St Martin's, as the Dauphin). 1955: *Moby Dick* (Duke of York's). 1955-56: *The Buccaneer* (Lyric, Hammersmith & Apollo). 1956: *Hotel Paradiso* (Winter Garden). 1957: *The Wit to Woo* (Arts). 1957-58: *Share My Lettuce* (revue, Lyric Hammersmith, Comedy & Garrick). 1958: *Cinderella* (Coliseum, as the Ugly Sister). 1959: *Pieces of Eight* (revue, Apollo). 1961: *One Over the Eight* (revue, Duke of York's). 1962: The Public Eye in *The Private Ear* and *The Public Eye* (Globe, double bill). 1963: *Gentle Jack* (Queen's). 1965: *Loot* (Arts, Cambridge). 1965: *The Platinum Cat* (Wyndhams). 1971: *Captain Brassbound's Conversion* (Cambridge). 1972: *My Fat Friend* (Globe). 1976: *Signed and Sealed* (Comedy). 1979: *The Undertaking* (Greenwich & Fortune). 1980: *Loot* (director). 1981: *Entertaining Mr Sloane* (director).

FILM

1952: *Trent's Last Case*. 1953: *Innocents in Paris*; *Valley of Song* (US: *Men Are Children Twice*); *The Beggar's Opera*. 1954: *The Seekers* (US: *Land of Fury*). 1958: *Carry On Sergeant*. 1959: *Carry On Nurse*; *Carry On Teacher*; *Tommy the Toreador*. 1960: *Carry On Constable*; *Make Mine Mink*. 1961: *Carry On Regardless*; *His and Hers*; *Raising the Wind* (US: *Roommates*). 1962: *Carry On Cruising*; *Twice Round the Daffodils*; *Love Me, Love Me, Love Me* (short, narrator only). 1963: *Carry On Jack*. 1964: *Carry On Spying*; *Carry On Cleo*. 1965: *Carry On Cowboy*. 1966: *Carry On Screaming*. *Carry On Don't Lose Your Head*; 1967: *Carry On Follow That Camel*, *Carry On Doctor*. 1968: *Carry On Up the Khyber*. 1969: *Carry On Camping*; *Carry On* Again *Doctor*. 1970: *Carry On Loving*. 1971: *Carry On Henry*; *Carry On At Your Convenience*.1972: *Carry*

On Matron; *Carry On Abroad*. 1974: *Carry On Dick*. 1975: *Carry On Behind*. 1977: *The Hound of the Baskervilles*. 1978: *That's Carry On*; *Carry On Emmannuelle*. 1981: *Willo the Wisp* (voice only). 1995: *Arabian Knight* (aka: *The Thief and the Cobbler*, voice only).

TELEVISION
Includes:
1952: *Wonderful Visit* (as Angel). 1954: *Misalliance*. 1955: *Moby Dick Rehearsed* (incomplete). 1956: *Hancock's Half Hour*. 1957: *Dick and the Duchess*; *Sword of Freedom* (as Tizio); *The Waxworks Story* (as Plozei). 1958: *Time Out for Peggy; The Noble Spaniard* (as Captain Chalford). *Tonight - Peter Patter* (with Dilys Laye). 1963-64: *Juke Box Jury*. 1964: *Catch As Catch Can* (as Napoleon). 1966: *The Eamonn Andrews Show*. 1966-74: *International Cabaret*. 1968, '76, '80 & '83: *Jackanory*. 1969: *Join Jim Dale*. 1970: *The Kenneth Williams Show*. 1973-74: *Any Questions?* 1973, '77, '81 & '82: *The Michael Parkinson Show*. 1974: *Read All About It*. 1977: *Night of 100 Stars*; *All Star Record Breakers*; *Let's Make a Musical*; *Tonight*. 1979-87: *Give Us a Clue* (appearances). 1979: *Star Turn; Star Signs*. 1979-81: *Willo the Wisp* (voice only). 1980: *Whizz Kids*. 1981: *Does the Team Think?* (pilot); *Ratbags* (Australia); *Saturday Night at Pebble Mill*. 1982: *Choices*; *Countdown*; *The Paul Daniels Show*; *The Gloria Hunniford Show*; *Blue Peter*. 1983: *TV-am*; *An Audience with Kenneth Williams*; *Carry On Laughing's Christmas Special* (with Barbara Windsor). 1984: *Private Lives*; *All Star Secrets*; *Did You See*? *Revelations*; *Looks Familiar*; *Some You Win*. 1984-87: *Whose Baby*? (appearances). 1985: *Child's Play*. 1985-86: *Galloping Galaxies* (voice only, as SID). 1986: *Through the Keyhole*. 1987: *Arena*; *Wogan* (guest host & appearances); *Drop That Name* (pilot); *Cover to Cover*. 1994: *Obituary* (archive footage). 1995: *The Parkinson Interviews* (compilation).

RADIO
Includes:
1949: *Gordon Grantley K.C* (as Edward Buttingham). 1951: *Dunworthy 1313* (as Peter Dorn). 1954-59: *Hancock's Half Hour*. 1955: *A Joke by André Gide* (as Lavignette). 1956: *The Man Who Could Work Miracles* (with Hattie Jacques). 1957-64: *Beyond Our Ken*. 1961 & '87: *Desert Island Discs*. 1961: *The Kenneth Williams Story*. 1965-68: *Round the Horne*. 1966-88: *Just a Minute*. 1966 & '68: *Woman's Hour*. 1966-67: *Call My Bluff*. 1968: *A Bannister Called Freda* (with Joan Sims). 1969: *The Kenneth Williams Spectacular*; *Call My Bluff*. 1969-70: *Stop Messin' About*. 1971-73: *The Secret Life of Kenneth Williams*. 1972: *The Betty Witherspoon Show*. 1973-74: *What's My Line?* 1974, '80 & '86: *Start of the Week*. 1974-75: *Get On with It*. 1975: *Start of the Year - Carry On Surviving*. 1975: *Cold Comfort Farm Morning*

Story; *Read Any Good Books?* 1976: *Signed and Sealed* (as Barillon). 1977: *Quote … Unquote*. 1979: *Augustus Carp, Esq.*; *Medium Dry Sherrin*. 1987: *The Law Game*.

RECORDINGS
1959: *Pieces of Eight* (with Fenella Fielding). 1974: *Nightmare Abbey*. 1978: *The Wind in the Willows* (narrator).

LPs
1976: *Jule and Sand* album. 1981: *Willo the Wisp*.

Joan Sims

(b. Irene Joan Marion Sims)

Joan Sims was the undisputed 'Queen' of the *Carry On*'s. The female mainstay of the series, Joan appeared in twenty-four of the feature films - a close runner-up to Kenneth Williams at twenty-five. However, including *Carry On Laughing* on television, she appeared in more *Carry On* productions (thirty-seven) than any other actor. Undoubtedly, Joan gave some of the finest performances of the series - from glamorous to nagging, but always entertaining.

Born in Laindon, Essex, on 9 May 1930, Joan was a shy, only child of railway worker John Henry Sims and his wife Gladys Marie. Joan won a scholarship and trained at RADA, making her first stage appearances in 1950 at the Repertory Theatre in Chorlton-cum-Hardy and in pantomime at Glasgow's Citizen Theatre. Joan made her first major stage appearance two years later in a critically acclaimed performance in the revue, *Intimacy at Eight Thirty*, which led to several other performances of the same play. This was followed by *High Spirits!*, *Man Alive* and *Breath of Spring*. The stage, however, quickly took second place for Joan as she entered both a screen and television career in October 1952.

Film roles were many and began with *Will Any Gentleman...?*, with George Cole. In the 1950s the pretty and curvaceous young actress remained extremely busy in cinema, not surprisingly mainly in comic roles. The *Doctor* series of films were among her first with *Doctor in the House* (1954) and *Doctor at Sea* (1955), and she was to return to this series three more times over the next fifteen years. In 1959 Joan joined the *Carry On* series in the second film, *Carry On Nurse*, as the accident-prone trainee Nurse Dawson. For the next twenty years she would remain with the series, until *Carry On Emmannuelle* in 1978.

The *Carry On* series not only made Joan Sims a well-known face in the world of cinema but also gave her the chance to play a wide variety of character roles. It saw the actress develop from the age of twenty-nine to forty-eight, and as she grew older her *Carry On* roles obviously changed. The early films saw Joan as a figure of fun, as exemplified by her role as the shapely gym mistress Miss Alcock in *Carry On Teacher*. Never a leading lady in the strictest sense of the word (she lost out in *Carry On Regardless* to the hourglass figure of Liz Fraser, and later Barbara Windsor would be associated with the 'glamour' roles), Joan nevertheless managed to shine through where others could not. In *Carry On Cowboy* as Belle she is stunning in a figure-hugging sequin dress and pearls and completes the film by rescuing her man (in the form of Sidney James) in a quick getaway. As late as 1970 and 1971, as the female lead in *Carry On Loving* and *Carry On At Your Convenience*, Joan played the flirtatious and eye-catching romantic interest of the leading man (again Sidney James, in both cases). These were very much Barbara Windsor roles, but the more mature Sims carried them off superbly. In *Carry On Up the Khyber* (despite suffering from vertigo!), *Carry On Up the Jungle*, *Carry On Henry* and *Carry On Dick* she excelled at her best in buxom, seductive and haughty roles that remain, above all, feminine and dignified. Part of Joan's excellence, evident in many of her *Carry On* roles, is her inevitable slide from eloquent English to broad cockney, always in her light, easily recognisable tones. This is particularly evident in both *Don't Lose Your Head* as Désirée and *Up the Khyber* as Lady Ruff-Diamond.

As the *Carry On* series progressed, Joan Sims was often cast as the nagging wife of the leading man. She tortured Kenneth Williams in *Carry On Cleo*, Harry H. Corbett in *Carry On Screaming* and Sidney James in both *Henry* and *Girls*. One of Joan's final *Carry On* films, *Carry On Behind*, saw her as the nagging mother-in-law of Bernard Bresslaw, but her characters could be less serious, as in the final scenes of *Carry On Abroad* in which she gives one of the most convincing performances of the film, again with Sidney James.

During the *Carry On* years Joan returned to the stage only six times, notably in *Uproar in the House* (with Nicholas Parsons), *The Country Wife* and *In Order of Appearance*. Joan was a key figure in eleven episodes of *Carry On Laughing* on television in 1975, but the final two films in the *Carry On* series saw her cast in cameo roles. In *Carry On England* she played Jennifer Ffukes Sharpe and in *Carry On Emmannuelle* she played Mrs Dangle - giving one of the few funny scenes of the film as she recalls her most unusual amorous encounter (with Victor Maddern).

Joan Sims's contribution to the *Carry On's* was unique, and the demise of the series was a sad loss for the many actors who had remained loyal to the films - in particular, Joan and Kenneth Williams, who had been the most prolific stars. For twenty years the series had provided a regular source of income and numerous friends, and the years preceding the demise of the series were particularly unhappy ones for the jolly actress. In the space of four years, Joan was to suffer the sudden death of four close friends: Sid James in 1976, Peter Butterworth and her agent Peter Eade in 1979 and Hattie Jacques in 1980. Joan Sims had always been close to fellow *Carry On* star Hattie Jacques, who proved a loyal friend to Joan and many other actors. Her sudden and unexpected death in October 1980 was a crushing blow. Not fully recovered, Joan suffered another loss when her beloved mother died in March 1981.

In her autobiography, *High Spirits* - released to coincide with her 70th birthday - Joan revealed her battles with depression, culminating in the early 1980s and late 1990s, and her dependency on alcohol during these periods. Joan's physical and mental reserves were tested to the limit in later years when she became increasingly 'accident prone'. In 1994 she broke several ribs after falling off a bike while filming a tele-movie. Still recovering from this injury, she then fractured her spine in falls in 1997 and 1999 and, after fracturing her hip in another fall, underwent a hip replacement operation in 2000. She later admitted that her injuries made her 'the queen of puddings' and, having long since abandoned all ideas of dieting, her weight increased noticeably in her sixties. Although she was able to overcome her misfortunes and continue a busy career on television and radio, years of personal tragedy, combined with smoking, periods of alcoholism, and a life-long weight problem, were to undermine Joan's health severely in her final years.

Joan also revealed in her memoirs that, despite two long-term relationships in the 1950s (including living with Anthony Baird, q.v.), she chose not to marry quite simply because she never found the right person. She spent her final years living alone in a small rented flat in Kensington. (In September 2002, Barbara Windsor MBE unveiled a Comedy Heritage plaque in memory of Joan Sims at her former home in Thackeray Street, Kensington. The event was also attended by Liz Fraser (q.v.), Eric Sykes OBE and John Inman).

Despite her periods of private grief, together with a certain shyness that lingered from her youth, Joan proved to be popular both privately and publicly, and many in the acting world have told of their friendship with the actress who was well known for her vitality.

When the *Carry On*'s ended in 1978, with the British film industry in decline, television became the main source of work for Joan and provided a wide variety of roles for over twenty years. Comedy, of course, remained the most prominent, but she also made appearances in drama, children's programmes and classics. During the *Carry On* years Joan had appeared in *The Stanley Baxter Show*, spent nine months on *The Dick Emery Show* and made appearances in *Till Death Us Do Part* and *Sykes* (with Hattie Jacques). In 1979 she worked with Dame Thora Hird in the series *In Loving Memory* and, in a memorably chilling performance, played a Victorian murderess in an episode of *The Lady Killers*. Joan also appeared in two series of *Born and Bred* as well as making guest appearances in *The Two Ronnies*, *East Lynne* and *Worzel Gummidge*.

Joan made her radio debut in 1954 and continued to broadcast up until shortly before her death, notably reuniting with Liz Fraser in the series *Bristow* almost forty years after they had appeared together in

Carry On Regardless.

In 1985 she appeared with *Carry On* star Joan Hickson (q.v.) in *A Murder is Announced* and had a cameo role in the American tele-movie, *Deceptions*, with Stefanie Powers. The following year Joan was once more seen in comedy series, this time for Yorkshire television in *Farrington of the F.O.*, with Angela Thorne. In 1987 and 1988 Joan was busy in the children's series *Simon and the Witch*, with Elizabeth Spriggs, and returned to the stage in a successful tour of the Middle and Far East in Derek Nimmo's *Bedroom Farce*. A new project for Joan in 1988 was a pop video for Morrisey's 'Ouija Board', in which she played a medium.

In 1990 Joan made her first feature film since *Carry On Emmanuelle*, in the classic *The Fool*. In the same year she began a successful series with Dennis Waterman, *On the Up*, playing the often tipsy Mrs Wembley whose catchphrase, 'just the one', caught on for three series, ending in 1992.

In 1993 Joan varied her range by appearing in the black comedy *Tender Loving Care*, with Dawn French. The following year she played an amusing cameo role as Betsy Prigg in the classic *Martin Chuzzlewit*, again with Elizabeth Spriggs, and was reunited with George Cole in episodes of his series, *My Good Friend*. Although absent from *Carry On* Columbus in 1992, Joan was seen with Leslie Phillips (q.v.) in the tele-movie *The Canterville Ghost*, thirty-six years after they had starred together in *Carry On Teacher*. From 1994 Joan made guest appearances in the television series *As Time Goes By*, a role that brought her a new generation of fans. Joan's last acting role was a fitting swansong to a fifty-year career. Among an all-star cast (which included her friends Dame Judi Dench and June Whitfield, q.v.), Joan played Betty, a feisty bandleader, in the BBC tele-movie *The Last of the Blonde Bombshells*.

From the mid-1990s Joan Sims saw the *Carry On* series take on a renewed popularity. She was a notable absentee at *Carry On* reunions (including the 40th Anniversary celebrations) but delighted fans in 1998 when she took part in the Carlton Television documentary, *What's a Carry On*? In the summer of 2000 she again broke with custom and gave television interviews (on *This Morning* and Gloria Hunniford's *Open House*) to help promote her autobiography and was last heard on BBC radio discussing her life of 'slap and tickle' later that year.

Joan Sims was always an essentially private person, but in her final years she was quite rightly regarded as one of the country's finest character comediennes. Sadly, however, even at the end of her life she had not received the full recognition undoubtedly due to her.

Joan Sims was admitted to hospital for a 'routine' operation in November 2000, but complications developed and she lapsed into a coma. She died at London's Chelsea & Westminster Hospital on 27 June 2001. (Joan's death certificate states that she died on 27 June, not 28 June as most sources state. The primary cause of death was liver failure and diverticular disease. She was also suffering from diabetes mellitus and chronic obstructive airways disease). The last great *Carry On* star, Joan Sims was seventy-one years old.

Carry On ... ***Quotes***

Joan Sims started in the Carry On's *as a pin-up teenager and ended up as a matron. The transition, of course, was gradual and she took it in her stride. Such is her professionalism. Actually, she can play anything and is a pleasure to work with. I think I have had more laughs with Joan Sims off the set than any other member of the cast. She has had a lot of sadness in her life and she has overcome it. It is always a pleasure for me to see her on television in shows other than the* Carry On's.
Peter Rogers, 1997

The whole cast of As Time Goes By *have greatly enjoyed working with Joan Sims, especially the younger members since Joan is something of a legend from the* Carry On *films. Joan is a very kind, warm person, always cheerful, and we are great friends.*
Dame Judi Dench, 1997

Joan Sims is one of my closest friends and we have endless fun when working together.
Elizabeth Spriggs, 1997

Joan Sims was a gloriously witty, warm, fun-loving person to work with and we had many laughs together. She is a brilliant comedienne.
Angela Thorne, 1997

Tributes to
Joan Sims (1930-2001)

To me she was the last of the great Carry On's. *She was there from the beginning. Her talent was wonderful, she could do any accent, dialect, she could dance, sing, play dowdy and glam. We laughed all the time and giggled a lot. I will sorely miss her.*
Barbara Windsor MBE

I worked with her for the last five years and I got to know her very well. It is wonderful to be able to say that she really did have all the qualities her fans would have wished. She really did have a great sense of humour, a sympathetic and endearing personality, terrific talents and unfailing consideration for others. Everyone who knew her is going to remember her forever.
Richard Hatton (agent)

One of the great comic performers of cinema and television.
Jack Baine

Carry On **CREDITS 1959-78**
Nurse (trainee nurse Stella Dawson); *Teacher* (Miss Sarah Allcock); *Constable* (WPC Gloria Passworthy); *Regardless* (Lily Duveen); *Cleo* (Calpurnia); *Cowboy* (Belle); *Screaming* (Mrs Emily Bung); *Don't Lose Your Head* (Désirée Dubarry); *Follow That Camel* (Zig-Zig); *Doctor* (Chloe Gibson); *Up the Khyber* (Lady Ruff-Diamond); *Camping* (Joan Fussey); *Again Doctor* (Mrs Ellen Moore); *Up the Jungle* (Lady Evelyn Bagley); *Loving* (Miss Esme Crowfoot); *Henry* (Queen Marie of Normandy); *At Your Convenience* (Mrs Chloe Moore); *Matron* (Mrs Tidey); *Abroad* (Mrs Cora Flange); *Girls* (Connie Philpotts); *Dick* (Madame Désirée); *Behind* (Daphne Barnes); *England* (Private Jennifer Ffukes Sharpe); *Emmannuelle* (Mrs Dangle).

STAGE
First stage appearances were made at the Repertory Theatre, Chorlton-cum-Hardy. After a series of plays she made her London stage debut. 1952: *Just Lately* (revue, Players'); *The Belles of St Martin's* (St Martin's); *Intimacy at Eight Thirty* (revue, New Lindsey). 1953: *High Spirits* (London Hippodrome); *More Intimacy at Eight Thirty* (revue, New Lindsey). 1954: *Intimacy at Eight Thirty* (Criterion, with Dilys Laye). 1956: *Man Alive!* (Aldwych). 1958: *Breath of Spring* (Cambridge). 1961: *The Lord Chamberlain Regrets ...* (revue, Saville). 1964: *Instant Marriage* (Piccadilly). 1967: *Uproar in the House* (Whitehall). 1969: *The Country Wife* (Theatre Royal, Bath). 1971: *Good Time Johnny* (as Queenie, Birmingham Rep). 1977: *In Order of Appearance* (Chichester Festival). 1984: *Jack and the Beanstalk* (Richmond, as Sweetcorn, the Vegetable Fairy, with Kenneth Connor). 1988: *Bedroom Farce* (tour, Middle & Far East).

FILM
1953: *Will Any Gentleman...?; Meet Mr Lucifer; The Square Ring; Colonel*

March Investigates; Trouble in Store. 1954: *The Belles of St Trinian's; Doctor in the House; What Every Woman Wants; The Young Lovers* (US: *Chance Meeting*); *To Dorothy a Son* (US: *Cash on Delivery*); *The Sea Shall Not Have Them*. 1955: *Doctor at Sea; As Long As They're Happy*. 1956: *Lost* (US: *Tears for Simon*); *Keep It Clean; The Silken Affair; Stars in Your Eyes; Dry Rot*. 1957: *Just My Luck; Davy; Carry On Admiral* (US: *The Ship Was Loaded*); *No Time for Tears; The Naked Truth (US: Your Past is Showing)*. 1958: *The Captain's Table*. 1959: *Passport to Shame* (US: *Room 43*); *Life in Emergency Ward 10; Carry On Nurse; Carry On Teacher; Upstairs and Downstairs; Please Turn Over*. 1960: *Carry On Constable; Doctor in Love; Watch Your Stern; His and Hers*. 1961: *Carry On Regardless; Mr Topaze* (US: *I Like Money*); *No, My Darling Daughter!; A Pair of Briefs*. 1962: *Twice Round the Daffodils; The Iron Maiden (US: The Swingin' Maiden)*. 1963: *Nurse on Wheels; Strictly for the Birds*. 1964: *Carry On Cleo*. 1965: *The Big Job; San Ferry Ann; Carry On Cowboy*. 1966: *Doctor in Clover; Carry On Screaming; Carry On Don't Lose Your Head*. 1967: *Carry On Follow That Camel; Carry On Doctor*. 1968: *Carry On Up the Khyber*. 1969: *Carry On Camping; Carry On Again Doctor*. 1970: *Carry On Up the Jungle; Doctor in Trouble; Carry On Loving; Carry On Henry*. 1971: *The Magnificent Seven Deadly Sins; Carry On At Your Convenience*. 1972: *Carry On Matron; The Alf Garnett Saga; Carry On Abroad; Not Now, Darling; A Christmas Carol* (voice only). 1973: *Carry On Girls; Don't Just Lie There, Say Something!; The Cobblers of Umbridge* (short). 1974: *Carry On Dick*. 1975: *Love Among the Ruins* (TV); *Carry On Behind; One of Our Dinosaurs is Missing*. 1976: *Carry On England*. 1978: *Carry On Emmannuelle*. 1985: *Deceptions* (TV). 1990: *The Fool*. 1993: *One Foot in the Algarve* (TV); *Tender Loving Care* (TV). 1995: *Arabian Knight (aka: The Thief and the Cobbler, voice only)*. 1996: *The Canterville Ghost* (TV). 2000: *The Last of the Blonde Bombshells* (TV).

TELEVISION

Includes:

1951: *John of the Fair*. 1955: *Curtains for Harry*; *Here and Now*; *London Playhouse – The General's Mess* (as Daffy Lovell). 1956: *The Adventures of Robin Hood* (as Nell); *Colonel March of Scotland Yard* (as Marjorie Dawson); *The Frankie Howerd Show*. 1957: *The Buccaneers* (as Abigail). 1960: *Our House* (series, with Hattie Jacques, Charles Hawtrey, Bernard Bresslaw and Norman Rossington); *A Holiday Abroad*. 1961: *Off Centre*. 1962: *Dial RIX - Nose to Wheel* (as Shirley Rix). 1963: *The Stanley Baxter Show* (series); *A Christmas Night with the Stars*. 1963-64: *The Dick Emery Show* (2 series). 1964: *The Benny Hill Show* (special guest appearance). 1965: *Love in Triplicate* (as Jill Watson). 1966: *Seven Year Hitch* (with Harry H. Corbett); *Call My Bluff* (with Kenneth Williams). 1967: *Sam and Janet* (series, as

Janet); *Before the Fringe* (7 appearances). 1968: *According to Dora* (several episodes); *Beryl Reid Says Good Evening*; *The Eamonn Andrews Show* (guest, with Kenneth Williams). 1970: *The Kenneth Williams Show* (series); *The Odd Job* (as Kitty Harriman). 1971: *The Goodies; Six Dates With Barker; Decimal Five* (voice only); *Father, Dear Father* (as Miss Armitage); *A Christmas Carol* (voice only, as Mrs Cratchit). 1971 & '73: *The Goodies*. 1972: *Carry On Stuffing; Jackanory Playhouse; Till Death Us Do Part* (series, as Gran). 1972-78: *Sykes* (guest appearances, as Madge Kettlewell). 1973: *Seven of One* (series, as Mrs Dawkins); *Ooh La La!*; *Carry On Christmas*. 1974: *Men of Affairs* (as Lady Mainwaring-Brown). 1975: *A Journey to London* (as Lady Headpiece); *Carry On Laughing* – 'The Prisoner of Spenda' (as Madame Olga), 'The Baron Outlook' (as Lady Isobel), 'The Sobbing Cavalier' (as Lady Kate Houndsbotham), 'One in the Eye for Harold' (as Else), 'The Nine Old Cobblers' (as Amelia Forbush), 'The Case of the Screaming Winkles' (as Mrs MacFlute), 'The Case of the Coughing Parrot' (as Dr Janis Crunbit), 'Under the Round Table' (as Lady Guinevere), 'Short Knight, Long Daze' (as Lady Guinevere), 'And in My Lady's Chamber' (as Mrs Breeches), 'Who Needs Kitchener?' (as Mrs Breeches). 1976: *Virginia Fly is Drowning*. 1976: *East Lynne* (series, as Joyce). 1977: *Lord Tramp* (series, as Miss Pratt). 1978-80: *Born and Bred* (2 series, as Molly Beglar). 1979: *In Loving Memory* (guest appearances). 1979-80: *Worzel Gummidge* (as Mrs Bloomsbury-Barton). 1980: *The Ladykillers - Suffer Little Children* (as Amelia Elizabeth Dyer). 1980: *Dick Turpin* (as the Countess of Durham). 1982: *Educating Marmalade*. 1983: *An Audience with Kenneth Williams; Crown Court; Waters of the Moon* (as Mrs Ashworth). 1984: *Foul Pest; Poor Little Rich Girls; Cockles* (series, as Gloria du Bois); *Tickle on the Tum; Hallelujah!* 1985: *Agatha Christie's A Murder is Announced* (as Miss Amy Murgatroyd). 1986: *Movies from the Mansion - 50 Years of Pinewood* (special). 1986-87: *Farrington of the F.O.* (2 series, as Miss Annie Beggley). 1986: *Doctor Who* (as Katryca). 1987: *Golden Gong - 50 Years of Rank's Films and Stars*; *Super Gran*. 1987-88: *Simon and the Witch* (2 series, as Lady Fox Custard). 1988: *Only Fools and Horses* (as Auntie Reenie Turpin); *An Audience with Victoria Wood*. 1989: *Victoria Wood* (as hostel warden). 1990-92: *On the Up* (3 series, as Mrs Fiona Wembley). 1990: *Cluedo: Christmas special* (as Mrs White). 1992: *Tonight at 8.30* (Fumed Oak); *Boys from the Bush* (2 episodes); 1993: *Smokescreen* (series, as Mrs Nash). 1994, '95, '97 & '98: *As Time Goes By* (guest appearances as Madge Hardcastle). 1994 & '96: *My Good Friend* (as Miss 'Pickles' Byron). 1994: *Martin Chuzzlewit* (series, as Betsy Prigg). 1995: *Pie in the Sky* (as Harriet Coverly); *Just William*. 1996: *Hetty Wainthropp Investigates* (as Adele McCarthy). 1997: *Noel's House Party; Spark* (as Aunt Agatha). 1998: *What's a Carry On?* (doc.). 2000: *This Morning* (interview); *Gloria*

Hunniford's Open House (interview).

Additional Credits
Vegetable Village; Iolanthe; And There's More; Blankety Blank; The New Celebrity Squares; Living Life Lately (pilot).

RADIO
Includes:
1954: *Home and Away*. 1956: *The Floggits* (as Emma Steed). 1960: *Something to Shout About* (as Mavis Willis). 1966-68: *Sam and Janet* (as Janet). 1968: *A Bannister Called Freda* (with Kenneth Williams). 1969: *Stop Messing About* (with Kenneth Williams). 1989: *The Life of Kenneth Connor; London Lights; Pigs Have Wings; Sixth Sense; Early Morning; Uncle Silas*; *Wyrd Sisters*; *101 Dalmatians*; *Passport to Pimlico*. 1995: *Paradise Unbalanced* (pilot); *England's Glory; Two Sisters*. 1999: *Bristow* (with Liz Fraser).

Charles Hawtrey

(b. George Frederick Joffre Hartree)

The star of twenty-three *Carry On* films, Charles Hawtrey was one of the series most prolific actors. Often cast as cheery, effeminate scapegoats, he remained an essential part of *Carry On* humour, bringing with him a flawless comic timing nurtured during a fifty-year career.

Charles Hawtrey was born in Hounslow, Middlesex, on 30 November 1914. Throughout his life he claimed to be the son of stage actor and manager Sir Charles Hawtrey (1858-1923), although a recent biography has proven this to be just one of several myths surrounding the comic actor.

A boy soprano, Charles spent three years training at the Italia Conti Stage School and made his stage debut at the age of eleven in *The Windmill Man*. He subsequently went on to build up his experience on stage in plays, revues and pantomime. Among his many theatrical credits during his early years were *Peter Pan* at the London Palladium, with Charles Laughton and Elsa Lanchester, and *The Taming of the Shrew* at the Old Vic.

Charles Hawtrey made his screen debut in *Tell Your Children* in 1922. He went on to appear in several more silent pictures of the 1920s before his career took off in the late 1930s in the films of Will Hay (1888-1949). He was especially memorable as the aged schoolboy in comedy films such as *Good Morning, Boys* (1937) and *The Goose Steps Out* (1942), and in total he appeared with Hay in five screen classics.

During the Second World War Hawtrey again returned to the stage, notably directing several plays at Q Theatre and starring in 300 performances of the revue *New Faces*. He also directed a couple of films at the same time: *What Do We Do Now?* (1945) and *Dumb Dora Discovers Tobacco* (1945).

Throughout the 1950s Charles was kept busy with cameo appearances in a range of screen comedies, including *The Galloping Major, You're Only Young Twice, As Long as They're Happy, Simon and Laura* and *Man of the Moment*. Dark haired and angular, with his famous wire-rimmed spectacles and corncrake voice, he was always guaranteed to stand out even if his appearances were uncredited.

In 1957 (after making his small-screen debut a decade earlier), Charles Hawtrey came to prominence on television as Private 'Professor' Hatchett in the popular sitcom *The Army Game*. Co-starring future *Carry On* actors William Hartnell, Norman Rossington, Bernard Bresslaw and Michael Medwin (all q.v.), the series set the tone for *Carry On Sergeant* in which Charles made his *Carry On* debut the following year.

As the ever cheerful Private Golightly in *Carry On Sergeant*, Hawtrey breezes through the film with scene-stealing performances. His catchphrase – "Oh, hello!" - immediately caught on and was used throughout the series with increasing flamboyance. In *Carry On Nurse* some of his natural love of music emerges as Humphrey Hinton, the hospital patient who spends most of his time in bed with earphones firmly in place. In *Carry On Teacher* the musical influence again continues as he plays teacher Mr Bean, who is left distraught after his piano is wrecked by the unruly pupils of Maudlin Street School.

In *Carry On Constable* his cheery persona is almost unflappable as Special Constable Gorse. In addition to bringing his budgie (Bobby) and a bunch of flowers to the station, he was especially memorable in drag (as Agatha) opposite Kenneth Williams. Later he played more unfortunate characters, including the unforgettable Private Widdle (who has trouble keeping his 'dangler' warm) in *Carry On Up the Khyber* and Mr Potter in *Carry On Camping*.

Not surprisingly, Charles was often the ideal candidate for camp figures of fun, notably in *Carry On Doctor* when he suffered from a sympathetic pregnancy and in *Carry On Again Doctor* when he again made a second appearance in drag (as Lady Puddleton). Occasionally, he was given slightly meatier roles, such as Tonka in *Carry On Up the Jungle*. Although he doesn't appear until three-quarters of the way through the film, he is superb as the unlikely King of the Lubis. In *Carry On Don't Lose Your Head* and *Carry On Henry* he is surprisingly over-sexed as the Duc de Pommfrit and the unfortunate Sir Roger de Lodgerley.

Although never a leading man, Charles was sometimes given 'mock' romances in the series, notably opposite veteran actress Renée Houston in *Carry On At Your Convenience*. He was also given a misunderstood relationship with Hattie Jacques in *Carry On Matron*, notable as a rare occasion when the two actors shared solo scenes together. Several of his appearances were somewhat inconsequential to the plot of the film but remain exceptional, especially as Seneca in *Carry On Cleo* and as Charlie Bind in *Carry On Spying*. Amazingly, given his position as a vital member of the main team, he even made a cameo appearance in one of the films, as cockney lavatory attendant Dan Dann in *Carry On Screaming*.

In *Carry On Abroad* Hawtrey drinks his way through the film as English tourist Mr Tuttle. His scenes (which perhaps mirrored his real-life drink problem) mainly consist of drunken utterances and outrageous antics, but his blissful ignorance of the chaos around him at the end of the film remains unforgettable. It was also notable as his final *Carry On* appearance. His contribution to the *Carry On* series – as its third most prolific star – was a unique one. His comic timing and camp eccentricity made him by far one of the most distinctive actors of the series.

After joining the *Carry On*'s, Charles Hawtrey's additional film appearances became less frequent. He played Arnold in *What a Whopper* (1961) and Joshua Yellowlees in *The Terrornauts* (1967), his screen career reaching its lowest point when he co-starred with James Robertson Justice in the 1969 sex comedy *Zeta One*.

On television he made only occasional appearances. Apart from *The Army Game* he also starred in the 1960 series *Our House* (with many other *Carry On* actors) and later co-starred in *The Best of Friends* (in which he played an insurance office clerk), with fellow comic great Hylda Baker. On radio Charles was well known in the 1940s as Smart in *The Will Hay Programme*.

Charles Hawtrey's private life was by no means a happy one. Like Kenneth Williams, Charles was very close to his mother, and in later years, as recalled by Barbara Windsor, he looked after her devotedly when she suffered from senile dementia. Her death was a blow from which he never recovered fully. Within the acting community Hawtrey was openly homosexual, but in later life he was upset that his sexuality should be broadcast to the public at large, especially his preference for young sailors and working-class teenagers. Unfulfilled, professionally and personally, he sought solace in alcohol.

Sadly, Hawtrey's personal unhappiness has tended to overshadow his remarkable professional career. Away from acting he had a deep interest in music and was a talented pianist. For many years he lived in a terraced house in the coastal town of Deal, Kent, with a multitude of cats. A recluse in the final years of his life, he largely avoided contact with both colleagues and fans alike, becoming increasingly unpredictable and gaining a reputation among landlords of his hometown for drunken, disorderly behavior.

Charles Hawtrey left the *Carry On* series at the end of 1972, following a confrontation with producer Peter Rogers over billing. As the most prodigious *Carry On* actor, Charles believed that he was entitled to 'star' billing in the television Christmas special, *Carry On Stuffing*, but Rogers insisted that this privilege should go to Hattie Jacques. Finally, when Hawtrey refused to take second place, he was dropped from the series to which he had remained loyal since its onset in 1958. It is perhaps surprising that Charles Hawtrey managed to stay with the team for as long as he did. The problem of star billing had been raised over a decade earlier and Hawtrey's drinking problem had been causing difficulties for cast and crew from as early as 1962 when he was dropped from *Carry On Cruising*. Whatever the case, this was to be the final obstacle. It was clear that Charles Hawtrey would never return to the series (even if he had wanted to), although as late as 1987 it was rumoured that he would be welcomed back when ideas of a new *Carry On* surfaced.

After leaving the *Carry On*'s Charles Hawtrey was largely retired from show business for the remaining sixteen years of his life, with the exception of a couple of appearances. Roles in minor pantomime productions did nothing to enhance his morale, and the effects of his drinking made him unreliable as a performer. In 1979 he was reunited with Harry H. Corbett (his co-star in *Carry On Screaming*) in the 'silent' short *The Plank*, looking tanned and relaxed, having changed little since *Carry On Abroad*. In the same year Peter Byrne (q.v.) directed him in pantomime. It was to be Hawtrey's final stage appearance and, at the age of sixty-five, he was described by Peter Byrne as "a shadow of his former self".

Charles Hawtrey gave his last television interview in Roy Hudd's *Movie Memories* in 1981. Following a heart attack shortly afterwards, he was restricted from further work and was seen only once more on television in an episode of the children's television series *Super Gran*, playing the Duke of Claridge. His last years were increasingly unhappy and his health continued to decline as his drinking increased. In 1984 he made tabloid headlines after being rescued from a fire in his home (minus his toupee) while his young lover lingered in the bedroom. The incident was infamously described by Kenneth Williams and later published in *The Kenneth Williams Letters*.

By the late 1980s Hawtrey was in very poor health and more taciturn than ever. In September 1988, by which time he was the forgotten star of the *Carry On*'s, he again hit tabloid headlines (after being admitted to hospital with a broken leg) beneath the banner 'lose your legs or die'. Serious arterial problems - the result of his years of heavy drinking and smoking - had left Hawtrey's doctor with no choice but to amputate both of his legs in order to save his life. He refused the operation.

When the unfortunate fate of the former *Carry On* star became public knowledge, stories from the actor revealed sad and extremely bitter memories of the *Carry On* series. Hawtrey's final outburst consisted mainly of criticism of 'tight' budgets and his own typecasting in the series. Fans were left saddened by Hawtrey's resentment of the films, which had made him famous - if not rich.

Charles Hawtrey died quietly in a Deal nursing home on 23 October 1988, aged seventy-three. Despite his final criticism of the *Carry On* series, he is still quite rightly regarded as one of the finest actors of the series. A decade after his death Charles Hawtrey was honoured with a British Comedy Society plaque (unveiled by Leslie Phillips CBE) at

Pinewood Studios. The institution had forgiven and finally recognised the impeccable comic actor.

Carry On ... ***Quotes***

Charles Hawtrey was a different loner. He was aloof, never mixed and thought himself above his fellow thespians. When he had a boyfriend he was easy to work with, but when he was alone he drank so much he became impossible to work with.
Peter Rogers, 1998

When I was a young actor I took over from Charlie Hawtrey in Will Hay's stage and radio act playing 'Smart', the cheeky boy - this was in 1945. We played in a revue with Nervo and Knox called For Crying Out Loud *at the Stoll Theatre directed by Val Guest, the first post-war Command Performance at the Coliseum and a BBC radio series called* The Dairy of a Schoolmaster.
I directed poor Charlie at the end of his career in a pantomime in Swindon, but he was a shadow of his former self and died, sadly in poverty and alone shortly after.
Peter Byrne, 1999

My memories of Charles Hawtrey are all good, but I can't remember anything specifically except that at the end of the run of New Faces *the recordings made by the BBC were all broken in a taxi accident (it would be more in keeping with the times to say that it was an air-raid, but in fact it was just a taxi!) Charles thought that it was a pity that no recording of me singing 'Nightingale' survived, and together we found a sound recording studio, and for the princely sum of five shillings or so we made a record together, Charlie playing the piano and me singing. It now reposes somewhere in the depths of the BBC Archives.*
Earlier on during rehearsals, I came back from filming one evening to find Charlie doing a point number which was meant for me. Charlie thought that it would be a good idea if he did it in 'drag'. I wasn't at all put out because I had to admit he was a great deal funnier than I would have been. The first two lines,
'Vivandiere, vivandiere, with a barrel of brandy on my derriere.'
You can imagine what a comic triumph he had with it!
It's strange that we all lost touch after the revue came off, but I think it was the war, and when the war ended people went off in different directions. I for

one got married and went to live in the country, and left the stage for three years. I really was truly fond of Charlie, and do wish that I could remember more.
Judy Campbell, 2002

It was lovely that Charles Hawtrey could join us in Super Gran, *just briefly, and he was so funny and a true professional. He had a very special quality and was a joy to work with and witness.*
Gudrun Ure, 2003

Carry On **CREDITS 1958-72**
Sergeant (Private Golightly); *Nurse* (Humphrey Hinton); *Teacher* (Michael Bean); *Constable* (Special Constable Timothy Gorse); *Regardless* (Gabriel Dimple); *Cabby* (Terry 'Pint-Pot' Tankard); *Jack* (Walter Sweetly); *Spying* (Charles Bind); *Cleo* (Seneca); *Cowboy* (Big Heap); *Screaming* (Dan Dann); *Don't Lose Your Head* (Duc de Pommfrit); *Follow That Camel* (Captain Le Pice); *Doctor* (Mr Barron); *Up the Khyber* (Private Jimmy Widdle); *Camping* (Charlie Muggins); *Again Doctor* (Dr Ernest Stoppidge); *Up the Jungle* (Walter Bagley – King Tonka); *Loving* (James Bedsop); *Henry* (Sir Roger de Lodgerley); *At Your Convenience* (Charles Coote); *Matron* (Dr Francis A. Goode); *Abroad* (Eustace Tuttle).

STAGE
Includes:
1925: made his first stage appearance in *The Windmill Man* (Boscombe, as a street Arab). 1927: *Bluebell in Fairyland* (London debut). 1928: *Where the Rainbow Ends* (Holborn Empire, as William). 1929: *Babes in the Wood* (Theatre Royal, Exeter). 1930: *Street Scene* (Globe, as Willie). 1931: *Peter Pan* (Palladium). 1936: *Your Number's Up* (Gate). 1936: *Peter Pan* (Palladium, with Charles Laughton & Elsa Lanchester). 1937: *Bats in the Belfry* (Ambassadors, 178 performances). 1937: *Members Only* (revue, Gate, with Hermione Gingold). 1938: *Happy Returns* (revue, Adelphi). 1939: *The Taming of the Shrew* (Old Vic, as Gremio). 1939: *Printer's Devil* (Q, as Pumble). 1939: *Counterfeit* (Richmond & Duke of York's, as James Brixton). 1940: *Without the Prince* (Richmond, as Robert Weatherhead). 1940-41: *New Faces* (revue, Comedy & Apollo, over 300 performances, with Judy Campbell). 1941: *New Ambassador's Revue* (Ambassadors). 1942: *Scoop* (Vaudeville). 1943: *Old Chelsea* (Princes Theatre, 86 performances); *Claudius the Bee* (Q, with Irene Handl). 1944: *Merry England* (Winter Gardens, as Walter Wilkins). 1944-45: directed several plays at the Q Theatre. 1945: appeared in Variety at Victoria Palace.

1946: *Mother of Men* (Q & Comedy, directed). 1949: *Who's Your Lady Friend?* (directed). 1951: *Frou Frou* (New Lindsey, with Jean Kent). 1951: *Husbands Don't Count* (New Lindsey). 1951: *Young Men's Fancy* (Q, directed). 1952: *Bless You* (Q, as Mr Mitre). 1952: *Husbands Don't Count* (Winter Garden & tour). 1953: *The Blue Lamp* (directed on tour). 1965: *A Funny Thing Happened on the Way to the Forum* (Hysterium & tour); *Dick Whittington and His Cat*. 1966: *Babes in the Wood* (Globe, Stockton-on-Tees). 1968: *The Sleeping Beauty* (ABC, Peterborough, as King Charlie). 1969: *Jack and the Beanstalk*. 1972: *Stop It Nurse* (Pavilion, Torquay, as Doctor Dimple). 1973: *Snow White* (Arts Centre, Basildon). 1974: *No Sex Please, We're British* (Dreamland, Margate). 1975: *Snow White and the Seven Dwarfs* (Pavilion, Weymouth). 1976: *Snow White and the Seven Dwarfs* (tour). 1979-80: *Jack and the Beanstalk* (Swindon, as King).

FILM

1922: *Tell Your Children*. 1923: *This Freedom*. 1932: *Marry Me*. 1933: *The Melody Maker*. 1935: *Kiddies on Parade*. 1936: *Well Done Henry*; *Sabotage* (US: *The Woman Alone*); *Cheer Up!* 1937: *Good Morning, Boys!* (US: *Where There's a Will*); *The Gap*; *East of Ludgate Hill*. 1939: *Where's That Fire?*; *Jailbirds*. 1941: *The Black Sheep of Whitehall*; *The Ghost of St Michael's*. 1942: *The Goose Steps Out*; *Let the People Sing*; *Much Too Shy*. 1943: *Bell Bottom George*. 1944: *A Canterbury Tale*. 1946: *Meet Me at Dawn*. 1947: *The End of the River*. 1948: *The Story of Shirley Yorke*. 1949: *Passport to Pimlico; Dark Secret*. 1950: *Room to Let*. 1951: *Smart Alec; The Galloping Major; Brandy for the Parson*. 1952: *Hammer for the Toff; You're Only Young Twice!* 1954: *To Dorothy a Son* (US: *Cash on Delivery*); *Five Days* (US: *Paid to Kill*). 1955: *As Long as They're Happy; Timeslip* (US: *The Atomic Man*); *Man of the Moment; Simon and Laura; Jumping for Joy; Who Done It?* 1956: *The March Hare*. 1958: *Carry On Sergeant*; *I Only Arsked!*. 1959: *Carry On Nurse*; *Carry On Teacher*; *Please Turn Over; Inn for Trouble*. 1960: *Carry On Constable*. 1961: *Carry On Regardless*; *Dentist on the Job* (US: *Get On With It!*); *What a Whopper*. 1963: *Carry On Cabby*; *Carry On Jack*. 1964: *Carry On Cleo*; *Carry On Spying*. 1965: *Carry On Cowboy*. 1966: *Carry On Screaming*; *Carry On Don't Lose Your Head*. 1967: *Carry On Follow That Camel*; *Carry On Doctor*; *The Terrornauts*. 1968: *Carry On Up the Khyber*; *Carry On Camping*. 1969: *Carry On Again Doctor*; *Zeta One*. 1970: *Carry On Up the Jungle*; *Carry On Loving*. 1971: *Carry On Henry*; *Carry On At Your Convenience*; *Grasshopper Island* (TV). 1972: *Carry On Matron*; *Carry On Abroad*. 1979: *The Plank* (TV, short).

TELEVISION
Includes:
1945: *The Ten Year Plan*. 1947: *New Faces*. 1956: *Tess and Jim*. 1957: *Laughter in Store* (with Charlie Drake). 1957-58: *The Army Game* (2 series, as Private 'Professor' Hatchett). 1960-61: *Our House* (2 series, as Simon Willow). 1963: *The Best of Friends* (series, as Charles). 1969: *Carry On Christmas*. 1970: *Carry On Again Christmas*. 1972: *This Is Your Life* (Hylda Baker); *This Is Your Life* (Patricia Hayes). 1976: *The Prince and the Pauper; Runaround* (as Count Dracula). 1981: *Movie Memories* (interview). 1987: *Super Gran* (as Clarence, Duke of Claridge).

RADIO
Includes:
1944-45: *The Will Hay Programme* (as Smart). 1945: *Just William* (as Hubert Lane); *Ray's a Laugh*.

Sidney James

(b. Sidney Joel Cohen)

Well regarded as the 'King' of the *Carry On* film series, Sid James was a legend in his own lifetime. Through nineteen films, television Christmas specials, four episodes of *Carry On Laughing* and *Carry On London* on stage in the mid-1970s, he was the series's most prominent figurehead. Today, over thirty years after his death, he is still one of Britain's best-known comedians.

Sid James was born in Newcastle, Natal, South Africa, on 8 May 1913. The second son of vaudeville artists Laurie Cohen and his wife Reine (Solomon), his maternal grandmother was music hall performer 'Ma Solomon' (Flora Solomon). Sid's parents toured on stage and he began acting as a child. One of his earliest roles was at the age of sixteen when he starred in an amateur production of *Sleeping Beauty*, playing Prince Charming.

The early years of Sid's life are somewhat obscure and the actor himself claimed to have worked as a coal heaver, diamond polisher and boxer. It now seems more likely that the majority of his time was spent working as a professional hairdresser.

Sid joined the Johannesburg Repertory Players in 1937 and through this company came work on radio with the South African Broadcasting Corporation, with Moira Lister (1923-2007). He worked frequently on stage, notably in *Hoopla* with Olga Lowe (q.v.), before the outbreak of the Second World War. Details of Sid's war service remain vague, although officially he joined the Witwatersrand Rifles in 1940. It is clear that during the war he was a member of the Union Defence Force Entertainment Unit and appeared in concerts, plays and musicals. After being demobbed he returned to work on stage under Dame Gwen Ffrangcon-Davies (1891-1992) before receiving a grant to move to England to study acting.

Sid James and his second wife arrived in England on Christmas Day 1946. Within nine days he had secured a role in the feature film *Black Memory*. Over the next decade Sid worked as a jobbing actor on screen, stage and radio. His early theatre credits included long runs in *High Button Shoes, Touch and Go, Kiss Me Kate* and *Guys and Dolls*. He went on to enjoy further stage successes later in his career with *The Solid Gold Cadillac* (alongside Dame Margaret Rutherford), *Babes in the Wood* (at the London Palladium) and a sell-out Australian tour of *The Mating Season*.

From his screen debut in 1947 until his first appearance in the *Carry On* series thirteen years later, Sid made over 80 film appearances. He graduated from 'walk on' parts to leading roles, and in the course of his career he made over 110 film appearances (or, according to some sources, more than 280!) His highly distinctive crumpled looks did not deter him from playing leading roles, and in his younger days the comic legend, with his trim build, crinkly hair, twinkling eyes and cheeky grin, was often cast for his rugged sex appeal.

Sid's film career took off following his appearance in *The Lavender Hill Mob* in 1951 and he went on to appear in a succession of comedies, including *Lady Godiva Rides Again, The Galloping Major, Miss Robin Hood* and *The Belles of St Trinian's*. Further success came on radio in partnership with Tony Hancock (1924-1968) in *Hancock's Half Hour* (1954-59), with future *Carry On* co-stars Kenneth Williams and Hattie Jacques. The series later transferred to television, ensuring that Sid was one of Britain's best-known comedy actors by the late 1950s.

Sid made his *Carry On* debut in *Carry On Constable* in 1960. With his 'dirty' laugh and working-class persona he was an instant success and would become the leading man of the series over the next fourteen years. He was able to tread a fine line in comic characterisations as a roughish, scene-stealing hero who could be leering but never smutty.

Whether it be as Captain Crowther in *Carry On Cruising* or factory foreman Sid Plummer in *Carry On At Your Convenience*, Sid was invariably seen as the likeable leading man. His favourite *Carry On* role was as the Rumpo Kid in *Carry On Cowboy*, which provided an opportunity for him to display his fine American accent. For once he was cast as the villain, but he still secured the affection of the audience. He was missing from a couple of films in the 1960s (*Carry On Jack* and *Carry On Follow That Camel* especially suffered without Sid as the leading man) and was confined to bed in *Carry On Doctor* in 1967 after suffering a massive heart attack. In 1968 he returned to leading roles as Sid Boggle in *Carry On Camping* and Sir Sidney Ruff-Diamond in *Carry On Up the Khyber* - two of his finest *Carry On* roles.

After over a decade as the series's leading man, Sid continued to delight audiences as he approached his sixties with leading roles in *Carry On Up the Jungle* (as Mr Boosey) and *Carry On Henry* (in the title role). Opposite Joan Sims and Barbara Windsor in both *Carry On Abroad* and *Carry On Girls* he was his old rascally self and he again teamed with Barbara for his final appearance in the title role of *Carry On Dick*. As the Robin Hood-like rector (doubling as 'Big Dick') he gives yet another flawless performance, sedate and dignified as the rector and reassuringly 'Sid' as Turpin!

Having worked on stage in *Carry On London* for almost two years, Sid made his final *Carry On* appearances in episodes of *Carry On Laughing* on television in 1975. Touchingly, his final role was with Hattie Jacques in the episode 'Orgy and Bess' – a final swansong for two of the key players of the *Carry On* series.

Sid's seemingly natural acting style and ability to play 'himself' have often overshadowed his success as a performer. He was in fact an absolute professional, a perfectionist known as 'one-take Sid', who stuck to his lines and expected his co-stars to do the same. Among the majority of his colleagues Sid was regarded as a true professional and gentleman. Fond of gambling and whisky, he was nevertheless a generous and loyal friend. Hattie Jacques described him as a "chivalrous" man who "belied his TV and film image" and, with the notable exception of Kenneth Williams, he appears to have been liked by all of his *Carry On* contemporaries. Vincent Ball (q.v.) remembered Sid as a member of "our long running poker school", while Heather Emmanuel (q.v.) regarded him as "a kind and sensitive person".

On television Sid was best known as Sidney Abbot in six series of *Bless This House*. Co-starring Diana Coupland, Sally Geeson (q.v.), Robin Stewart and Patsy Rowlands (q.v.), the successful sitcom kept Sid busy for five years up until his sudden death. Regular repeats around the world continue to this day. He also starred in the 1972 film version (produced and directed by Peter Rogers and Gerald Thomas), which was dubbed the 'unofficial' *Carry On* of the year given the numbers of actors featured from the *Carry On* repertoire (including Peter Butterworth, Terry Scott, June Whitfield, Bill Maynard and Marianne Stone). Following his first major success on the small screen in *Hancock's Half Hour* he went on to host his own television series and appeared in sitcoms such as *Citizen James, George and the Dragon* (with the formidable Peggy Mount) and *Two in Clover* (with Victor Spinetti).

Sid James married Berthe Delmont in 1936. They had one daughter, Elizabeth (b.1937), but the marriage was short-lived and they divorced several years later. He subsequently married Meg Sergei (née Williams) in 1943 and they had one daughter, Reine Christina (b.1947). The couple divorced in 1952 after a two-year separation and in the same year Sid married for a third time to stage actress Valerie Ashton (née Assan; 1928-). They had two children, Stephen (b.1954) and Susan (b.1957), and remained married until Sid's death.

During the last years of his life Sid's health deteriorated and he suffered from back problems, which often forced him to rely on a walking stick. His hectic work schedule on the set of *Bless This House*, combined with continued heavy smoking and a fondness for Scotch whisky, did nothing to help his already weak heart. His physical health and emotional well-being were also undermined following his affair with

Barbara Windsor, which has been well publicised since his death.

Sid's relationship with Barbara, which formed the basis of the stage play *Cleo, Camping, Emmannuelle* and *Dick* and subsequent TV movie *Cor, Blimey!* (2000), has been written about by both Barbara Windsor herself and Sid's biographer, Cliff Goodwin. Several of his co-stars (including Joan Sims and Angela Douglas) and Sid's widow have publicly condemned rumours regarding his personal life and reported affairs.

Sid James was appearing on stage at the Sunderland Empire on the opening night of *The Mating Game*, with Terry Scott and Olga Lowe (both q.v.), when he suffered a heart attack and collapsed in the middle of the performance. His wife Valerie - who was waiting in the wings - was with him when he died in an ambulance on the way to hospital on 26 April 1976.

The sudden death of the much-loved actor at the age of 62 left an irreplaceable gap in the *Carry On* series and British comedy in general. In the years since his death constant reruns of the *Carry On* films and *Bless This House* have ensured that his profile is as well known now as it was during his lifetime. He has been honoured with a Dead Comics' Society plaque (unveiled by Sir Harry Secombe in 1992) and a British Comedy Society plaque (unveiled at Pinewood Studios in 1998 by Jack Douglas), although his lasting memorial will always be as the 'King' of the *Carry On* film series.

Carry On ... ***Quotes***

Sidney James virtually played himself. He was a terrible gambler, among other things. But a wonderful artist.
Peter Rogers, 1999

I had just lost a baby – was very depressed – Sid and Dick made it their task to give me a laugh a day. Normally they were rather crude (!), but they constantly cheered me up enormously.
Sylvia Syms OBE (co-star in* The Big Job*), 2000

I am of course delighted that the Carry On *film series continues to delight new and existing audiences. I have been approached by new enthusiasts, young teenagers and children, some as young as eight years of age, who tell me how much they enjoy the films and of course the characters played by my late husband, Sidney James, in particular. There can be no doubt he would have been thrilled!*
Valerie James (widow of Sidney James), 2002

Carry On **CREDITS 1960-74**
Constable (Sergeant Frank Wilkins); *Regardless* (Bert Handy); *Cruising* (Captain Wellington Crowther); *Cabby* (Charlie Hawkins); *Cleo* (Mark Antony); *Cowboy* (The Rumpo Kid/Johnny Finger); *Don't Lose Your Head* (Sir Rodney Ffing/The Black Fingernail); *Doctor* (Charlie Roper); *Up the Khyber* (Sir Sidney Ruff-Diamond); *Camping* (Sid Boggle); *Again Doctor* (Gladstone Screwer); *Up the Jungle* (Bill Boosey); *Loving* (Sidney Bliss); *Henry* (King Henry VIII); *At Your Convenience* (Sid Plummer); *Matron* (Sid Carter); *Abroad* (Vic Flange); *Girls* (Sidney Fiddler); *Dick* (The Reverend Flasher/Dick Turpin).

STAGE
1948-49: *High Button Shoes* (293 performances, New Oxford & Hippodrome, as Henry Longstreet). 1950: *Touch and Go* (348 performances, Prince of Wales). 1951: *The Silver Box* (Prince of Wales Cardiff & Lyric, Hammersmith). 1951-52: *Kiss Me Kate* (502 performances, as 2nd Man, New, Oxford & Coliseum). 1953-54: *Guys and Dolls* (as Nathan Detroit, Coliseum). 1954-55: *Wonderful Town* (207 performances). 1962: *Puss in Boots* (Coventry Theatre). 1964: *Babes in the Wood*. 1965: *The Solid Gold Cadillac* (142 performances, as Edward L. McEver, with Dame Margaret Rutherford). 1965-66: *Babes in the Wood* (212 performances, Palladium, as Robber). 1966: *Wedding Fever* (Pier, Bournemouth). 1966: *Robinson Crusoe* (Hippodrome, Golders Green, as Will Atkins). 1968: *Wedding Fever* (Windmill, Great Yarmouth). 1969: *His Favourite Family* (Grand, Blackpool). 1970: *Wedding Fever* (Windmill, Great Yarmouth). 1971: *The Mating Season* (Pavilion, Torquay, as Henry Gillespie). 1973-75: *Carry On London* (Victoria Palace). 1975: *The Mating Season* (Australian tour & Winter Garden, Blackpool). 1976: *The Mating Season* (tour – collapsed on stage on opening night at Empire Theatre Sunderland, 26 April 1976).

Additional Credits
Sid James's early stage appearances in South Africa included productions of *A Bell for Adano; The Importance of Being Earnest; Red Peppers* and *Wind of Heaven*. In England his additional appearances included summer seasons and pantomimes and *Burlesque* and *Men Without Shadows*.

FILM
Select filmography (sources state that Sid may have appeared in as many as 280 films during his career):
1947: *Black Memory; The October Man; It Always Rains on Sunday*. 1948:

No Orchids for Miss Blandish; *Night Beat*; *The Small Back Room*. 1949: *Once a Jolly Swagman* (US: *Maniacs on Wheels*); *Paper Orchid*; *The Man in Black*; *Give Us This Day*. 1950: *Last Holiday*; *The Lady Craved Excitement*. 1951: *Talk of a Million* (US: *You Can't Beat the Irish*); *Lady Godiva Rides Again*; *The Lavender Hill Mob*; *The Galloping Major*. 1952: *The Magic Box*; *I Believe in You*; *Emergency Call* (US: *Hundred Hour Hunt*); *Gift Horse*; *Miss Robin Hood*; *Cosh Boy* (US: *The Slasher*); *Time Gentlemen, Please!*; *Father's Doing Fine*; *The Venetian Bird* (US: *The Assassin*); *Tall Headlines*; *The Yellow Balloon*. 1953: *Will Any Gentleman...?*; *The Wedding of Lilli Marlene*; *Escape By Night*; *The Titfield Thunderbolt*; *The Weak and the Wicked* (US: *Young and Willing*); *Park Plaza 605* (US: *Norman Conquest*); *The Flanagan Boy* (US: *Bad Blonde*); *Is Your Honeymoon Really Necessary?*; *The Malta Story*. 1954: *The Rainbow Jacket*; *The House Across the Lake* (US: *Heatwave*); *Father Brown* (US: *The Detective*); *Seagulls Over Sorrento* (US: *Crest of a Wave*); *The Crowded Day; Orders Are Orders*; *Aunt Clara*; *For Better, for Worse*; *The Belles of St Trinian's*; *The Frightened Bride*. 1955: *Out of the Clouds*; *Joe Macbeth*; *The Deep Blue Sea*; *A Kid for Two Farthings*; *The Glass Cage* (US: *The Glass Tomb*); *A Yank in Ermine; It's a Great Day*; *John and Julie*. 1956: *Ramsbottom Rides Again; Wicked as They Come; The Extra Day; The Iron Petticoat*; *Dry Rot*; *Trapeze*; *The Baby and the Battleship*. 1957: *Quatermass II* (US: *Enemy from Space*); *Interpol* (US: *Pickup Alley*); *The Smallest Show on Earth*; *The Shiralee*; *Hell Drivers*; *Campbell's Kingdom*; *A King in New York*; *The Story of Esther Costello* (US: *Golden Virgin*). 1958: *The Silent Enemy*; *Another Time, Another Place*; *Next to No Time*; *The Man Inside*; *I Was Monty's Double*; *The Sheriff of Fractured Jaw*. 1959: *Too Many Crooks*; *Make Mine a Million*; *The 39 Steps*; *Upstairs and Downstairs*; *Tommy the Toreador*; *Desert Mice*; *Idle on Parade* (US: *Idol on Parade*). 1960: *Carry On Constable*; *Watch Your Stern*; *And the Same to You*; *The Pure Hell of St Trinian's*; *Double Bunk*; 1961: *A Weekend with Lulu; The Green Helmet; What a Carve Up!*; *Raising the Wind* (US: *Roommates*); *What a Whopper*; *Carry On Regardless*. 1962: *Carry On Cruising*; *We Joined the Navy*. 1963: *Carry On Cabby*. 1964: *Carry On Cleo*; *The Beauty Jungle* (US: *Contest Girl*); *Tokoloshe, the Evil Spirit*. 1965: *Three Hats for Lisa*; *The Big Job*; *Carry On Cowboy*. 1966: *Where Bullets Fly*; *Carry On Don't Lose Your Head*. 1967: *Carry On Doctor*. 1968: *Carry On Up the Khyber*. 1969: *Carry On Camping*; *Carry On Again Doctor; Stop Exchange*. 1970: *Carry On Up the Jungle*; *Carry On Loving*. 1971: *Carry On Henry*; *Carry On At Your Convenience*. 1972: *Carry On Matron*; *Bless This House*; *Carry On Abroad*. 1973: *Carry On Girls*. 1974: *Carry On Dick*.

TELEVISION
Includes:
1951: *Here's Television*. 1956-60: *Hancock's Half Hour* (6 series). 1957: *The*

Buccaneers. 1958: *East End-West End* (series, with Miriam Karlin). 1959: *Merry with Medwin* (with Michael Medwin & Betty Marsden). 1960-62: *Citizen James* (3 series, as Sidney Balmoral James). 1961: *The Sid James Show*. 1963-64: *Taxi!* (2 series, as Sid Stone). 1966-68: *George and the Dragon* (3 series, as George Russell, with Peggy Mount). 1969-70: *Two in Clover* (2 series, as Sid Turner, with Victor Spinetti). 1969: *Carry On Christmas*. 1970: *Carry On Again Christmas; Film Night*. 1971: *The Royal Variety Performance; Jokers Wild*. 1972: *Cilla*. 1971-76: *Bless This House* (6 series, as Sid Abbot). 1972: *Carry On Stuffing*. 1973: *Carry On Christmas; Looks Familiar*; *This Is Your Life* (Diana Coupland). 1975: *Carry On Laughing* – 'The Prisoner of Spenda' (as Prince Rupert/Arnold Basket), 'The Baron Outlook' (as Baron Hubert), 'The Sobbing Cavalier' (as Lovelace), 'Orgy and Bess' (as Sir Francis Drake).

Additional Credits
Comedy Bandbox; Juke Box Jury; The Eammon Andrews Show.

RADIO
Includes:
1954-59: *Hancock's Half Hour.* 1956: *Finkel's Café*. 1960: *Educating Archie*. 1961: *It's a Deal.*

Additional Credits:
The Billy Cotton Band Show; Desert Island Discs; The Fabulous Miss Dangerfield; Open House; They Knew What They Wanted; Paul Temple.

Kenneth Connor MBE

An invaluable supporting actor in seventeen *Carry On* films, Kenneth Connor's career spanned over seventy years. His appearances in the *Carry On* series over a twenty-year period included some of the finest moments of the series, from the hypochondriac Horace Strong in *Carry On Sergeant* to Leyland the sex-starved chauffeur in *Carry On Emmannuelle*.

Kenneth Connor was born in London (or possibly Portsmouth) on 6 June 1918. His father was a petty officer on board the Royal Yacht *Victoria & Albert* and often arranged concert parties. It was at one such party that Kenneth claimed to have made his theatrical 'debut' at the age of two, as an organ grinder's monkey. He featured in concert parties with his brother throughout his childhood.

At the age of nineteen Kenneth earned a scholarship to train at the Central School of Dramatic Art, where he won a Gold Medal. He left in 1936 to pursue his career on stage, notably in fifty-five performances of *The Boy David.*

In 1939, shortly after the outbreak of the Second World War, Kenneth joined the Middlesex Regiment. He spent over six years in the army, including time in the Middle East, and toured in *Stars in Battledress*. After being demobbed he joined the Theatre Royal Bristol (Bristol Old Vic) under Hugh Hunt. The next twelve moths afforded him an excellent grounding in classical theatre, with appearances in plays such as *Macbeth, King Lear* and *The Importance of Being Earnest.*

Kenneth made his screen debut in *Poison Pen* in 1939, although his film career did not take off until the mid-1950s when he went on to appear in comedies such as *Don't Say Die* (1950), *Miss Robin Hood* (1952), *There Was a Young Lady* (1953) and *The Ladykillers* (1955). He later continued to appear in comic roles in the *Dentist* series, *Watch Your Stern* (1960) and *What a Carve Up!* (1962). After joining the *Carry On* series, however, his screen appearances became increasingly infrequent, although he was especially memorable as Swallow (opposite Bill Fraser) in *Captain Nemo and the Underwater City* (1969)

Kenneth became well known on radio from the late 1930s, especially after he took over from Peter Sellers in the hugely popular series *Ray's a Laugh*, with Ted Ray (q.v.). He later made guest appearances in some of the *Goon* shows and teamed up with Eric Barker and Deryck Guyler (both q.v.) in *Just Fancy*. It was on radio that Kenneth developed his catchphrase, "Do you mind?", and this (along with "Oh mate!") was frequently scripted into his *Carry On* work. He continued to broadcast until the end of his life, notably with Leslie Phillips (q.v.) in *Mind Your Own Business*.

Kenneth Connor made his *Carry On* debut as the un-aptly named Horace Strong in *Carry On Sergeant*. Small and trim with dark curly hair, the good-looking actor took on the role of comic romantic lead, desperately chased (and eventually caught) by army cook, Dora Bryan (q.v.). While more serious romantic leads were left to the likes of Terence Longdon, Leslie Phillips and Jim Dale, Connor proved adept as jittering, love-struck little characters in the majority of his early appearances in the series.

In *Carry On Nurse*, opposite Susan Shaw (q.v.), he was thoroughly believable and was marginally more confident as boxer Bernie Bishop. This particular *Carry On* remained a favourite for Kenneth since it included a cameo appearance by his real-life son, Jeremy (q.v.), who was then just three-and-a-half years old! Jeremy would later appear in *Carry On Dick*, *Carry On Behind* and *Carry On England*.

In *Carry On Teacher*, *Carry On Constable* and *Carry On Cruising* Kenneth again played nervous, fumbling, love-struck characters who try their best to be dashing, and he was only slightly more assertive in *Carry On Cabby*. He excelled in *Carry On Cleo* as Hengist Pod (inventor of the square wheel), a role that proved the perfect combination of nervous underdog and bumbling anti-hero! His scenes with Jim Dale are among the best in the series and it was perhaps Kenneth's finest *Carry On* role.

Kenneth Connor returned to the stage in the mid-1960s for a successful run in *A Funny Thing Happened on the Way to the Forum*. He went on to enjoy further success in over 400 performances of *The Four Musketeers* and was reunited with Dora Bryan in episodes of her television series.

After a five-year absence Kenneth returned to the *Carry On* series as Claude Chumley in *Carry On Up the Jungle*. Looking much more mature, he was the perfect foil for Frankie Howerd as the two competed for the affections of Joan Sims. By now he had been ousted from the position of romantic comic lead, although his naive, jittering persona was still occasionally glimpsed in his latter appearances in the series.

In *Carry On Henry* he was unusually cast as the sinister Lord Hampton of Wick, which proved to be a rare chance for him to display treacherous villainy in a *Carry On* role. *Carry On Abroad* saw Kenneth as hen-pecked husband Stanley Blunt and his scenes with June Whitfield (q.v.) are superb, particularly after he savours the delights of the dubious Spanish love potion! A year later Kenneth again excelled himself opposite Whitfield when he played the dithering Mayor Bumble in *Carry On Girls*, while in *Carry On Dick* his talent for 'aged' voices allowed him to play to great effect the randy old constable. In his final three *Carry On* films Kenneth appeared in character roles: as the pompous Major Leep in *Carry On Behind*, the unlikeable Captain S. Melly in *Carry On England* and the seedy, sex-starved chauffeur in *Carry On Emmannuelle*.

In addition to leading roles in seventeen *Carry On* films, Kenneth also featured prominently in television Christmas specials and twelve episodes of *Carry On Laughing* on television in 1975 (notably as Detective Punter and the aged Sir Harry Bulger-Plunger). In the mid-1970s he returned to the stage with Sid James, Barbara Windsor, Peter Butterworth, Bernard Bresslaw and Jack Douglas in *Carry On London*. He later starred on stage in *Carry On Laughing at the Slimming Factory* in the wake of Sid James's death in 1976.

Of his *Carry On* co-stars Kenneth was especially close to Kenneth Williams, while his off-screen antics with Joan Sims kept cast and crew constantly entertained. Like Williams and Sims – the series's most prodigious actors – Kenneth saw the *Carry On* series evolve and gradually decline, although he remained loyal to Peter Rogers and Gerald Thomas until the bitter end. His major supporting role in *Carry On Emmannuelle* was his final appearance in the series. In 1992 he turned down a role in *Carry On Columbus*, stating that he preferred to be remembered as a principal player, not a bit-part actor. It was a decision that his many fans could respect.

Following his final *Carry On* appearance in 1978 Kenneth worked consistently for the remainder of his life. He made his final stage appearance (with Joan Sims and Suzanne Danielle, q.v.) in pantomime in 1984 and thereafter worked exclusively on television and radio. He became well known to a new generation of television viewers through his roles in a succession of popular series, including *Rentaghost* and *Hi-de-Hi!*. In 1984 – now white-haired and aged – Kenneth joined the cast of *'Allo 'Allo* as the fragile, elderly Monsieur Alfonse. His superb comic timing enlivened the role of the French undertaker whose 'dicky ticker' was the cause of much concern! He was kept busy as Alfonse for eight years until the series finally ended in 1992.

Among the longest-lived actor of the 'main' team, Kenneth continued to work until the very end of his life. In 1993 he was touchingly reunited with Betty Marsden (q.v., his co-star in *Carry On Regardless*) in an episode of *The Memoirs of Sherlock Holmes*. It was a rare dramatic appearance for both actors and was not screened until after Kenneth's death. He made his final television appearance in Noel Edmonds' *Telly Addicts* just days before his death.

Kenneth Connor was married for many years and he and his wife

Margaret (1919-99), nicknamed Mickey, had two sons, Jeremy (q.v.) and Kevin. Described as an intensely private person, away from acting Kenneth had a passion for the sea and football and enjoyed spending time with his family "drinking endless cups of tea"! He was awarded a well-deserved (and belated) MBE in the New Year's Honours List 1991.

Kenneth Connor died at his home in Harrow, following a short battle with cancer, on 28 November 1993, aged seventy-five. In 2001 the much-loved actor was honoured with a British Comedy Society plaque, which was unveiled at Pinewood Studios in the presence of his family.

Carry On ... **Quotes**

Kenneth Connor was the most reliable professional you could ever meet and could play anything. He always had a fund of funny stories and his son is taking after him.
Peter Rogers, 1998

In Abroad *... The scene started with rain and everyone was pretending they were peeing, including Kenneth Connor, although he was a very good friend of mine and knew I wouldn't laugh ... he always had a lovely habit of smoking from his ear and then from his nose! Oh! He was a lovely man, so kind and considerate ...*
Alan Curtis, 1998

I enjoyed very much working with the late Kenneth Connor. I thought he did the French accent best of all of us. He was great fun. I did work with him once or twice before, once in a revue in London and another time in a TV sitcom.
Rose Hill (co-star in 'Allo 'Allo), 2000

Carry On **CREDITS 1958-78**
Sergeant (Horace Strong); *Nurse* (Bernie Bishop); *Teacher* (Mr Gregory Adams); *Constable* (PC Charlie Constable); *Regardless* (Sam Twist); *Cruising* (Dr Binn); *Cabby* (Ted Watson); *Cleo* (Hengist Pod); *Up the Jungle* (Mr Claude Chumley); *Henry* (Lord Hampton of Wick); *Matron* (Mr Tidy); *Abroad* (Stanley Blunt); *Girls* (Mayor Bumble); *Dick* (Constable); *Behind* (Major Leep); *England* (Captain S. Melly); *Emmannuelle* (Leyland).

STAGE
1936-37: *The Boy David* (55 performances, as Jonathan). 1938: *Treasure*

Island (Savoy). 1939: *Pericles* (Open Air, Regent's Park, as a sailor). 1939-45: Active war service with the Middlesex Regiment; toured in the Middle East in George Black's revue, *Stars in Battledress*. 1946: Joined the Theatre Royal Bristol (Bristol Old Vic). Over the next twelve months he appeared in various plays including *Macbeth, The Importance of Being Earnest, King Lear* and *The Applecart*. 1947: Joined the Old Vic Company and appeared in plays including: *The Taming of the Shrew* (lead role), *Richard II* (as 2nd Gardner/Groom), *Saint Joan* and *The Government Inspector*. 1948: *The Pom Poms*. 1949: *Hamlet* (as 1st grave digger, Richmond). 1949-50: *Queen Elizabeth Slept Here* (350 performances at Strand Theatre & tour, as Mr Kimber). 1951: *Waggonload o' Monkeys* (Pavilion, Bournemouth & tour, as Taffy); *Post Haste* (as Dewsbury); *The Silent Inn* (as Tommy Briggs, Arts Cambridge). 1952: *Just Lately* (revue). 1953: *The Merchant of Venice* (as Launcelot Gobbo, Old Vic). 1954: *Keep in a Cool Place* (Saville & tour, 108 performances, as Basil Selby). 1962: *One Over the Eight* (took over from Kenneth Williams, Duke of York's). 1963-65: *A Funny Thing Happened on the Way to the Forum* (761 performances, with Charles Hawtrey). 1965-66: *Babes in the Wood* (212 performances, as a robber). 1966: *Forever April* (tour, as Walter Price). 1966-67: *Robinson Crusoe*. 1967: *The Four Musketeers* (Drury Lane, 443 performances, as Louis XIII). 1969: *On a Foggy Day* (with Margaret Lockwood). 1969: *Dick Whittington* (Palladium). 1971: *Boeing Boeing* (as Robert). 1972: *Stop It Nurse* (Pavilion, Torquay). 1973-74: *Carry On London* (Victoria Palace). 1975: *No Room for Sex* (tour, as Dr George Garfield). 1975: *Aladdin* (New Victoria). 1976: *Carry On Laughing; Dick Whittington and His Fabulous Cat* (Theatre Royal Norwich, with Bernard Bresslaw). 1977: *Jack and the Beanstalk*. 1978: *Sextet; Forty Love* (tour, as Arnold). 1979: *Jack and the Beanstalk*; *Oh! Sir James!* (with Hattie Jacques & Jimmy Edwards). 1981: *Robinson Crusoe* (Ashcroft, Croydon, with Jack Douglas). 1982: *Aladdin*. 1983: *Cinderella* (Hippodrome, Bristol). 1984: *Jack and the Beanstalk* (Richmond, Surrey, with Joan Sims).

Additional Credits:
My Fat Friend (South African tour in the mid-1970s).

FILM
1939: *Poison Pen*. 1949: *The Chiltern Hundreds* (US: *The Amazing Mr Beecham*). 1950: *Don't Say Die/Never Say Die*. 1952: *The Beggar's Opera; Elstree Story* (voice only); *Miss Robin Hood*; *There Was a Young Lady*. 1954: *Marilyn*; *The Black Rider*. 1955: *The Ladykillers*. 1957: *Davy*. 1958: *Carry On Sergeant*. 1959: *Carry On Nurse*; *Make Mine a Million*. 1960: *Watch Your Stern; Dentist in the Chair*; *Carry On Constable*. 1961: *Carry On Regardless*;

Nearly a Nasty Accident; His and Hers; A Weekend with Lulu. 1962: *Carry On Cruising*; *What a Carve Up!*. 1963: *Carry On Cabby*. 1964: *Carry On Cleo*. 1965: *Cuckoo Patrol; Gonks Go Beat*. 1967: *Danny the Dragon* (voice only). 1969: *Captain Nemo and the Underwater City*. *Rhubarb*. 1970: *Carry On Up the Jungle*. 1971: *Carry On Henry*. 1972: *Carry On Matron*; *Carry On Abroad*. 1973: *Carry On Girls*. 1974: *Carry On Dick*. 1975: *Carry On Behind*. 1976: *Carry On England*. 1978: *Carry On Emmannuelle*.

TELEVISION

Includes:

1956: *A Show Called Fred* (series); *Son of Fred* (series); *The Charlie Farnsbarns Show* (series); *Two's Company* (series); *The Idiot Weekly, Price 2d* (series). 1957: *Man and Music*; *The Dickie Valentine Show* (series); *Torchy, the Battery Boy* (series, voice only). 1958: *My Pal Bob* (series, with Bob Monkhouse). 1960: *Four Feather Falls* (voice only). 1961: *The Sid James Show* (guest appearances). 1963: *Fit for Heroes* (as Corporal Rust, with Deryck Guyler). 1964: *How to be an Alien* (voice only). 1965: *A Slight Case of …* (series, as Mr Coker). 1967: *Room at the Bottom* (series, as Gus Fogg, with Deryck Guyler). 1968: *According to Dora* (appearances). 1969: *The Jimmy Logan Show*; *Carry On Again Christmas*. 1970-71: *On the House* (2 series, as Gussie Sissons). 1972: *The Kenneth Connor Show*; *Carry On Stuffing*. 1973: *What a Carry On!*; *Carry On Christmas*. 1975: *Carry On Laughing* – 'The Prisoner of Spenda' (as Nickoff), 'The Baron Outlook' (as Sir William), 'Orgy and Bess' (as King Philip), 'One in the Eye for Harold' (as Athelstan), 'The Nine Old Cobblers' (as Punter), 'The Case of the Screaming Winkles' (as Punter), 'The Case of the Coughing Parrot' (as Punter), 'Under the Round Table' (as King Arthur), 'Short Knight, Long Daze' (as King Arthur), 'And in My Lady's Chamber' (as Sir Harry Bulger-Plunger), 'Who Needs Kitchener?' (as Sir Harry Bulger-Plunger), 'Lamp-Posts of the Empire' (as Stanley). 1979: *Ted on the Spot*. 1980: *Frankie Howerd Reveals All*. 1982: *East Lynne*. *Movie Memories* (interview). 1982-83: *Rentaghost* (appearances, as Whatshisname Smith). 1984-92: *'Allo 'Allo* (7 series, as Monsieur Alfonse). 1986-88: *Hi-de-Hi!* (2 series, as Sammy Morris). 1986: *That's My Boy* (as Robert Taylor). 1987: *Wogan; BlackAdder – The Third* (as Mossop). 1989: *Norbert Smith – A Life* (*Carry On Banging,* as Greenham Officer). 1990: *Made in Heaven* (as Harry Ingrams); *You Rang, M'Lord?* (guest appearance). 1993: *Telly Addicts* (guest). 1994 (screened after his death): *The Memoirs of Sherlock Holmes* (as Mr Warren).

Additional Credits:
Club Night; The Ted Ray Show; The Black & White Minstrel Show; The Alfred Marks Show.

RADIO
Includes:
1953-57: *Meet the Huggetts*. 1956: *The Floggits; Finkel's Café*; *Ray's a Laugh* (as Sidney Mincing & Harold); *The Goons* (guest appearances); *Just Fancy* (with Eric Barker & Deryck Guyler). 1965-66: *Spare a Copper* (series, as C. Albert Hereward Lamp). 1971: *Parsley Sidings* (series, with Arthur Lowe & Liz Fraser). 1978-79: *Would the Last Businessman ...* (2 series). 1987-91: *Mind Your Own Business* (appearances, as Jenks).

Peter Butterworth

Although a relatively late arrival to the *Carry On* team, Peter Butterworth became a mainstay of the series through sixteen films, various television specials and two stage productions. A popular member of the main team, his contribution to the series has tended to have been overlooked, yet his leading character roles provided some of the most entertaining and memorable moments of the series.

Peter Butterworth was born in Bramhall, Cheshire, on 4 February 1919. During the Second World War he joined the Fleet Air Arm and after being shot down by the Germans was incarcerated as a prisoner of war. Behind the "barbed wire and boredom" of a German prisoner of war camp he became an entertainer after meeting Talbot (Tolly) Rothwell, the future *Carry On* scriptwriter. The pair famously sang a duet together called 'The Letter Edged in Black' in an effort to distract attention while others attempted to escape the camp.

After being demobbed Peter was spotted by Jack Hylton in a Red Cross show at the Stoll Theatre (London). He went on to make his professional stage debut in *Happy Hunting* in the summer of 1946, which he also directed. He subsequently built up his comic experience in pantomime and in plays such as *Odd Man In* (with Janet Brown and David Stoll, q.v.).

Peter Butterworth made his screen debut in *William Comes to Town* in 1948. Over the next thirty years he appeared in more than fifty films, mainly in cameo roles. Among his comic appearances were *Miss Pilgrim's Progress, Will Any Gentleman...?* and *Fun at St Fanny's*, and he also turned up for more serious work including *The Spider's Web* (as Inspector Lord), *Escort for Hire* (as Inspector Bruce) and *Murder, She Said* (as the ticket collector). His film career didn't really take off until he joined the *Carry On* team - almost midway through the series - in 1965. Over the next thirteen years he became a mainstay of the films and a master of bumbling eccentricity.

Peter made his *Carry On* debut as Doc in *Carry On Cowboy*. Immediately, the tone was set for further appearances as nervous little characters that contrasted well with leading actors such as Sid James and Kenneth Williams. In *Carry On Screaming* Peter made an equally impressive appearance as the 'Watson'-like character, Detective-Constable Slobotham. As Harry H. Corbett's sidekick he steals the show, especially in drag as 'bait' for Odd-Bodd Junior! Peter's skills as a comic character actor in his first two *Carry On* films secured his position as part of the main team and, with a couple of exceptions, he went on to appear in every *Carry On* film until 1978.

In *Carry On Don't Lose Your Head* he played the surprisingly perceptive Citizen Bidet, again opposite Kenneth Williams, while in *Follow That Camel* some of Peter's natural good nature was evident when he played Jim Dale's loyal valet, Simpson. In *Carry On Doctor* he played the mild-mannered Mr Smith whose curious (and unexplained) lump remains a cause of concern for his grape-munching wife, while in *Carry On Up the Khyber* he gave another scene-stealing performance as the dubious missionary, Brother Belcher.

In *Carry On Camping* Peter gave perhaps his most memorable film appearance as the aptly named campsite manager, Mr Fiddler. Deftly conning Sid James out of pound notes, it was a wonderful characterisation.

Amazingly, given his prominence in so many of the *Carry On* films, Peter also turned up for bit-part (and uncredited) roles in several of the films, including playing the shuffling, spot-diagnosis patient in *Carry On Again Doctor* and the sinister ('with mushrooms') client in *Carry On Loving*. In *Carry On Henry* he appeared in a cameo role as Barbara Windsor's father, Henry, Duke of Bristol.

Carry On Abroad in 1972 marked Peter Butterworth's return to the series after several absences. He was superb as the Spanish hotel manager, Pepe, desperately trying to please his English guests. Opposite Hattie Jacques (as his fiery wife, Flo), Peter's eleventh appearance in the series was one of his best.

In *Carry On Girls* Peter played the aged, bottom-pinching Admiral, who bites off more than he can chew when he tackles Barbara Windsor! In the following year he was again seen opposite Windsor (and Sid James) as the ever-loyal verger/highwayman, Tom, in *Carry On Dick*. The on-screen chemistry between Sid and Peter is clear in their scenes together - which were especially unique when they both appeared in drag! Peter and Sid also worked closely in the film version of *Bless This House* in 1972.

Peter's last major role in the *Carry On* series was as Joan Sims's long-lost husband in *Carry On Behind*. In a role reminiscent of Mr Fiddler in *Carry On Camping*, Peter played odd-job man Henry Barnes, another bumbling, English eccentric, who manages to swindle both Kenneth Williams and Ian Lavender. In *Carry On England* Peter turned up for a cameo role (again opposite Sims) as Major Carstairs. In his final appearance he played the ancient boot-boy Richmond, whose spectacles shatter as he recalls his most amorous sexual encounter, in *Carry On Emmannuelle*.

Peter Butterworth's position as a valued member of the 'main' team was reassured through his roles in television Christmas specials and nine episodes of *Carry On Laughing* in 1975. He also appeared on stage with Sid James, Barbara Windsor, Kenneth Connor, Bernard Bresslaw and Jack Douglas in *Carry On London*, which ran for over a year. He later delighted audiences as Willie Stokes on stage in *Carry On Laughing at the Slimming Factory*.

Peter's additional film credits included *She'll Have to Go* (1962), co-starring *Carry On* actors Hattie Jacques and Bob Monkhouse, *Doctor in Distress* (1963) and *The Amorous Adventures of Moll Flanders* (1965). After joining the *Carry On* series his screen credits became less frequent, although he remained active in film roles until the very end of his life. He was later seen as the surgeon in *Robin and Marian* (1976), the police sergeant in *What's Up Nurse?* (1977) and Putnam in *The First Great Train Robbery* (1979).

On television Peter's first appearances were with Terry Thomas in his successful series, *How Do You View?* He went on to enjoy personal success in a series of children's programmes throughout the 1950s, often in tandem with his wife, Janet Brown. He was especially popular in *Peter's Troubles*, which kept him busy for almost a decade.

In the 1960s Peter began to move into work in television sitcoms, notably alongside Bernard Bresslaw in *Meet the Champ* and with Donald Churchill, Amanda Barrie (q.v.) and Geoffrey Palmer in *The Bulldog Breed*. He also featured in *The Roy Castle Show* with his *Up the Khyber* co-star Roy Castle (q.v.) and Pat Coombs (q.v.).

By his early fifties Peter was well established as a comedy character actor, and his reputation, enhanced through his work on the *Carry On* films, meant that he was able to pursue a career on the small screen in a succession of series. In the early 1970s (when he was appearing in minor *Carry On* roles) he was busy on TV playing John Le Mesurier's chauffeur in *A Class by Himself* and co-starred with Peter Jones (q.v.) in *Kindly Leave the Kerb*. He also turned up for guest appearances in *Catweazle*.

Peter Butterworth married actress and impressionist Janet Brown (1923-2011) in 1949. In addition to appearing together on television, notably in *Where Shall We Go?* (1956), they also worked together on stage and in the film version of *Bless This House* in 1972. Peter and Janet had two children, Emma (who died in 1996) and actor Tyler Butterworth (1959-), who has followed in his parents' footsteps, appearing in programmes such as *The Darling Buds of May* and *Hetty Wainthropp Investigates*. Janet Brown (who was a special guest at Pinewood Studios in 2001 for the unveiling of a British Comedy Society plaque in memory of her late husband) remained busy on stage and television well into her eighties with final acting roles including appearances in *Midsomer Murders - Dead in the Water* (2004), *Summer Solstice* (2005) and *Hotel*

Babylon (2009). Away from the stage, Peter was a gentle, well-respected man who enjoyed spending his time sailing.

Peter Butterworth was appearing as Widow Twankey in *Aladdin* when he suffered a heart attack while preparing for bed in his hotel bedroom and died on 17 January 1979. His body was discovered when he did not arrive for the matinee performance the following day.

Peter's sudden death, shortly before his sixtieth birthday, was a great loss to the *Carry On* series and British entertainment in general. There have been few character actors since who could so delight an audience.

Carry On ... ***Quotes***

Peter Butterworth was at one time a prisoner of war with scriptwriter Talbot Rothwell. He was an inventive actor but I would never call him outstanding. Adequate and reliable.
Peter Rogers, 1998

Peter Butterworth was a family man and a very nice one.
Josephine Tewson (co-star in* Odd Man Out*), 2002

Peter Butterworth was in Afternoon Off, *playing Mr Bywaters, the manager of a shoe shop ... He was an excellent actor and I'd happily have worked with him again and indeed written for him if it had been possible.*
Alan Bennett, 2002

Carry On **CREDITS 1965-78**

Cowboy (as Doc); *Screaming* (Detective Constable Slobotham); *Don't Lose Your Head* (Citizen Bidet); *Follow That Camel* (Simpson); *Doctor* (Mr Smith); *Up the Khyber* (Brother Belcher); *Camping* (Josh Fiddler); *Again Doctor* (Shuffling Patient); *Loving* (Sinister Client); *Henry* (Charles, Earl of Bristol); *Abroad* (Pepe); *Girls* (Admiral); *Dick* (Tom); *Behind* (Henry Barnes); *England* (Major Carstairs); *Emmannuelle* (Richmond).

STAGE

1946: *Happy Hunting* (& directed); *Dick Whittington and His Cat* (Finsbury Park Empire). 1948: *For Funsake* (Pier Pavilion, Herne Bay). 1949: *High Tide* (Imperial, Brighton). 1952: *After Dinner* (Pier Casino, Shanklin). 1953: *Alice Through the Looking Glass* (Q Theatre, as Mad Hatter/White Knight). 1954: *Star Wagon* (Pier, Eastbourne); *Cinderella* (Opera House,

Blackpool). 1955: *Cinderella* (His Majesty's, Aberdeen). 1958: *Odd Man In* (tour, with Janet Brown & David Stoll); *Goldilocks and the Three Bears* (as Dame, Lyceum, Sheffield). 1959: *Five Past Eight* (later renamed *The Other Show*); *Goldilocks and the Three Bears* (Grand, Leeds). 1960: *Goldilocks and the Three Bears* (Empire, Newcastle). 1961: *Goldilocks and the Three Bears* (Theatre Royal, Nottingham). 1962: *Goldilocks and the Three Bears* (New, Oxford). 1963: *We're Frying Tonight* (Grand, Blackpool); *Sooty's Christmas Party*. 1965: *Who's Been Sleeping?* (New, Bromley, as Philip Wilcox). 1967: *Uproar in the House* (Whitehall, as David Prosser, with Joan Sims); *Aladdin* (Birmingham, as Widow Twankey). 1968: *Merry King Cole* (as Dame). 1969: *Merry King Cole* (Theatre Royal, Nottingham). 1970: *Cinderella* (Opera House, Manchester, as Ugly Sister). 1972: *Goldilocks and the Three Bears* (New, Cardiff). 1973-75: *Carry On London* (Victoria Palace). 1974: *Babes in the Wood* (Princess, Torquay, as Nurse Butterscotch). 1975: *Babes in the Wood* (Congress, Eastbourne). 1976: *Carry On Laughing* (Royal Opera House, Scarborough); *Dick Whittington* (Concert Hall, Lewisham, as Sarah the Cook). 1977: *The Big Show* (Spa Pavilion, Felixstowe). 1978-79: *Aladdin* (Coventry, as Widow Twankey).

FILM

1948: *William Comes to Town*. 1949: *The Adventures of Jane*; *Murder at the Windmill* (US: *Murder at the Burlesque*). 1950: *Miss Pilgrim's Progress*; *Circle of Danger*; *Night and the City*; *Paul Temple's Triumph*. 1951: *Mr Drake's Duck*; *The Body Said No!*; *The Case of the Missing Scene*; *Old Mother Riley's Jungle Treasure*; *Appointment with Venus* (US: *Island Rescue*); *Saturday Island* (US: *Island of Desire*). 1952: *Penny Princess*; *Is Your Honeymoon Really Necessary?* 1953: *Will Any Gentleman...?*; *Watch Out* (short); *A Good Pull-up* (short). 1954: *The Gay Dog*; *Five O'Clock Finish* (short). 1955: *Fun at St Fanny's*; *Playground Express* (short); *Black in the Face* (short); *That's an Order* (short). 1958: *Blow Your Own Trumpet; Tom Thumb*. 1960: *The Spider's Web; Escort Hire*. 1961: *The Day the Earth Caught Fire*; *Murder, She Said*. 1962: *Fate Takes a Hand*; *The Prince and the Pauper*; *Live Now – Pay Later; She'll Have to Go* (US: *Maid for Murder*). 1963: *The Horse Without a Head* (TV); *Doctor in Distress; The Rescue Squad*. 1964: *Never Mention Murder; A Home of Your Own*. 1965: *Carry On Cowboy*; *The Amorous Adventures of Moll Flanders*. 1966: *A Funny Thing Happened on the Way to the Forum*; *Carry On Screaming*; *Carry On Don't Lose Your Head*. 1967: *Carry On Follow That Camel*; *Carry On Doctor*; *Ouch!* (short); *Danny the Dragon*. 1968: *Carry On Up the Khyber*; *Carry On Camping*; *Prudence and the Pill*. 1969: *Carry On Again Doctor*. 1970: *Carry On Loving*. 1971: *Carry On Henry*; *The Magnificent Seven Deadly Sins*. 1972: *Carry On Abroad*; *Bless This House*. 1973: *Carry On Girls*. 1974: *Carry On Dick*. 1975: *Carry On Behind*. 1976: *Carry On England*; *The Ritz;*

Robin and Marian. 1977: *What's Up Nurse?* 1978: *Carry On Emmannuelle*. 1979: *The First Great Train Robbery* (US: *The Great Train Robbery*).

TELEVISION

Over 200 television appearances, including:
1949-52: *How Do You View?* (5 series, with Terry Thomas & Janet Brown). 1950: *Whirligig* (series). 1953-58: *Peter's Troubles* (8 series & 2 specials, & wrote). 1954: *Friends and Neighbours* (series, as George Bird, with Janet Brown). 1955: *Kept In* (series). 1956: *Two's Company; Butterworth Time* (series, with Janet Brown); *Those Kids* (2 series & special, as Mr Oddy). 1959: *The Ann Shelton Show*. 1960: *Meet the Champ* (series, as Sammy, with Bernard Bresslaw). 1961-62: *The Cheaters*. 1962: *Bulldog Breed* (series, as Henry Broadbent); *Dixon of Dock Green; Make Room for Daddy*. 1963: *The Odd Man; Emergency Ward 10*. 1964: *Armchair Mystery Theatre; Just Jimmy; Love Story; The Edgar Wallace Mystery Theatre*. 1965: *Doctor Who* (episodes as the Meddling Monk); *Porterhouse – Private Eye* (as Edwin Porterhouse, with June Whitfield); *Danger Man; Public Eye; The Roy Castle Show* (series, with Roy Castle & Pat Coombs). 1966: *Frankie Howerd*. 1967: *The Informer*. 1969: *Nearest and Dearest* (as Lord Mayor); *Wink to Me Only; The Wednesday Play – The Fabulous Frump* (as Albert Gill); *Carry On Christmas*. 1970: *Catweazle*. 1971: *Kindly Leave the Kerb* (series, as Ernest Tanner, with Peter Jones). 1972: *A Class by Himself* (series, as Clutton, with John Le Mesurier); *Carry On Stuffing*. 1973: *Carry On Christmas*. 1975: *Dad's Army* (as Mr Bugden); *Carry On Laughing* – 'The Prisoner of Spenda' (as Count Yerackers), 'The Baron Outlook' (as Friar Roger), 'The Sobbing Cavalier' (as Oliver Cromwell), 'The Case of the Screaming Winkles' (as Admiral Clanger), 'The Case of the Coughing Parrot' (as lost property attendant), 'Under the Round Table' (as Merlin), 'Short Knight, Long Daze' (as Merlin), 'And in My Lady's Chamber' (as Silas), 'Lamp-Posts of the Empire' (as Lord Gropefinger); *This Is Your Life* (subject). 1977: *Odd Man Out* (series, as Wilf, with John Inman). 1978: *The Dancing Princess*. 1979: *Six Plays By Alan Bennett: Afternoon Off* (as Mr Bywaters); *Give Us a Clue*.

Additional Credits

SS Saturday Special; Disney Land (series); *Danger Man; ITV Play of the Week; The Terry Scott Show*.

RADIO

Includes:
1947: *Leave It to the Boys* (with Michael Howerd).

Hattie Jacques

(b. Josephine Edwina Jaques)

Hattie Jacques will always be lovingly remembered as the 'Grande Dame' of the *Carry On* film series. The star of fourteen *Carry On* films, from *Carry On Sergeant* in 1958 to *Carry On Dick* in 1974, the talented actress of stage, screen, television and radio was also a singer, occasional writer and director.

The daughter of Robin Rochester Jaques and his wife Mary Adelaide, Hattie was born on 7 February 1922 in Sandgate, Kent. Although she had trained as a hairdresser, her duties during the Second World War were varied and she was even a welder in a factory for short time. During the war Hattie also worked as a nurse for the Red Cross.

Hattie made her stage debut at the Players' Theatre in 1944, after being introduced there by her brother. She would return to the same theatre many times over the next fifteen years. Her favourite stage role was as the Fairy Queen, which she first played in *The Sleeping Beauty in the Wood* at the Players' in 1949. She again played the Fairy Queen in *Riquet with the Tuft* in 1952. Her other stage appearances included *Ali Baba* and *The Belles of St Martin's* and in 1955 she directed *Twenty Minutes South*. Not surprisingly, Hattie was to appear as the Fairy Queen in *Carry On Stuffing* on television in 1972.

As well as the stage, Hattie Jacques was a well-known voice on radio from the late 1940s. With actors such as Sidney James and Kenneth Williams she appeared in Tony Hancock's radio series, and she was familiar as Sophie Tuckshop, the greedy schoolgirl, in *ITMA (It's That Man Again)*.

Hattie made her film debut in *Green for Danger* in 1946 and subsequently appeared in classics such as *Nicholas Nickleby* (1947) and *Oliver Twist* (1948). With *Carry On* star Bill Owen (q.v.) she was especially memorable as Daisy in *Trottie True* in 1949. Throughout the 1950s Hattie made numerous film appearances, starring in over twenty films over a ten-year period, including seven films in 1959 alone! Gradually, having proved herself as a capable serious actress, Hattie moved into comedy roles in which she excelled. Besides her *Carry On* appearances, Hattie was notable in other film comedies, particularly *Make Mine Mink* (1960) as Nanette Parry, with Athene Seyler, Terry Thomas and Billie Whitelaw, and *She'll Have to Go* (1962) with *Carry On* actors Peter Butterworth and Bob Monkhouse. Her later film appearances outside the *Carry On*'s were largely cameo roles, such as the lady journalist in *Monte Carlo or Bust*

(1969) and the airport official in *Three for All* (1974).

Like many of her contemporaries, Hattie considered that her film career took off when she joined the *Carry On* series. Already a well-known voice from her years in radio, the series gave her more notable public recognition. Although mainly typecast in the *Carry On* films, because of her size, into bossy figures of authority (she will always be best remembered as Matron in the hospital films), the series did give some scope for the considerable talents of the actress.

Having always been plump, Hattie was naturally sensitive about her size, particularly as it was the butt of many jokes. "When you're my size," she once famously said, "you become conditioned at people making jokes about you. You have to make them laugh with you rather than at you." Over the years, as her weight increased, she eventually gave up on ideas of dieting, although in a television interview in the year of her death she admitted with slight regret that her size had limited her career: "If you're fat, you're funny. It's as simple as that ... all they see is a funny fat lady; no one ever dreams of casting you as just a normal person." While her *Carry On* persona was often fiery, in real life Hattie was an extremely kind and understanding person - a tower of strength to fellow *Carry On* stars, particularly Joan Sims and Kenneth Williams. Indeed, she was adored by all that knew her. Although Hattie would ultimately become a distinguished comedienne, in private she remained a patient and lovable character.

Undoubtedly a highly attractive and elegant lady, with high cheekbones and dark eyes and hair, Hattie Jacques often showed a romantic, glamorous side to the characters she played in the *Carry On* films. In *Carry On Cabby* (probably her finest *Carry On* film) she brings out both the romantic and rebellious sides of her screen character to win back her husband, Sid James. In *Carry On Camping* she plays the love-struck matron who flutters her eyes and finally pounces on the hapless Kenneth Williams. In *Carry On Doctor* Hattie excels, again as the matron. Clad in sexy nightwear, she once again makes a grab (literally!) for her man – once more in the form of Kenneth Williams.

In the later films Hattie created less eager screen characters. Romance, however, was always on the horizon - as in another bedroom scene with Kenneth Williams in *Carry On Matron*. This time their long-running romantic saga is finally resolved in marriage. *Carry On At Your Convenience* saw Hattie as the non-too-proud housewife, Beattie, a delightful supporting role opposite Joey the budgie! Although obviously comic, the depth given in such performances is clearly evident and Hattie Jacques brings out aspects in her *Carry On* characters that could easily have been lost if the roles had been taken by a lesser actress.

Hattie Jacques made her final feature film (and *Carry On*) in *Carry On Dick* - thirty years after her acting debut. Touchingly, she appeared as the rector's housekeeper/organist, still searching for her man - this time in the form of Sid James. In 1975 Hattie made her final *Carry On* appearance in an episode of *Carry On Laughing* – 'Orgy and Bess', giving a grand performance as Queen Elizabeth I, again opposite Sid James. Both Hattie and Sid had been an integral part of the *Carry On* series, which, ironically, quickly declined following their departure.

With the end of her *Carry On* career, Hattie concentrated on *Sykes*, the popular BBC sitcom in which she played Eric Sykes's sister. The series began in 1960 and ran for five years. The humour was ageless and harmless and the series returned again in 1972, running until shortly before Hattie's death. Hattie also returned to the stage, in partnership with Sykes, and was reunited with Kenneth Connor in *Oh! Sir James!* in 1979. In the same year she completed an arduous tour of *Hatful of Sykes* and in April 1980 again worked with Sykes in the short television film *Rhubarb Rhubarb*.

Hattie Jacques married actor John Le Mesurier (1912-83), as his second wife, in 1949. Although the couple divorced in 1965, following Hattie's affair with John Schofield, they were to remain good friends. Not surprisingly, Hattie and Le Mesurier co-starred in several films (although not always in the same scenes), including *Mother Riley Meets the Vampire, Monte Carlo or Bust* and *Three for All*. The couple had two sons, Robin (1953-) and Kim (1956-90), who went on to work in the music industry. In her later life Hattie lived with John Schofield for several years and she was left heartbroken when the relationship ended. The death of her mother early in 1980 was also a grievous blow for the popular actress.

Late in 1973 Hattie Jacques was hospitalised and diagnosed with arthritis. By Christmas of that year she was back to robust health and hosted a New Year's Eve party at her home, but her health continued to give cause for concern during the remaining years of her life. In private the popular actress - known to those close to her as 'Jo' - enjoyed collecting records and old theatre postcards and she was a generous hostess. She also devoted a great deal of time and energy to supporting a variety of children's charities.

A life-long chain smoker, whose weight problems continued into her fifties, Hattie Jacques died suddenly in her sleep at her London home on 6 October 1980. It was later revealed that the fifty-eight year old star had succumbed to a massive heart attack, her body being discovered by her eldest son who lived in her basement flat. British entertainment and the *Carry On* series sincerely mourned Hattie and her memorial service at St

Paul's, Covent Garden, in November 1980 was attended by stars of the series, including Kenneth Williams and Barbara Windsor, and also John Le Mesurier.

On 5 November 1995 a plaque, organised by Comic Heritage chairman David Green, was unveiled in memory of Hattie Jacques at 67 Eardley Crescent, Earl's Court, and in 1998 June Whitfield (q.v.) unveiled a British Comedy Society plaque in memory of Hattie at Pinewood Studios - tributes to a great British actress who is still missed.

Carry On ... ***Quotes***

Hattie Jacques was the Times *crossword expert and somehow mothered the other girls. They were all inclined to turn to her for advice. She was a very quiet, gentle person. As an artist you could not have wished for anyone more reliable.*
Peter Rogers, 1997

Carry On **CREDITS 1958-74**
Sergeant (Captain Clark); *Nurse* (Matron); *Teacher* (Grace Knight); *Constable* (Sgt Laura Moon); *Regardless* (Sister); *Cabby* (Peggy Hawkins); *Doctor* (Matron); *Camping* (Matron Miss Haggard); *Again Doctor* (Matron); *Loving* (Sophie Bliss); *At Your Convenience* (Mrs Beattie Plummer); *Matron* (Matron); *Abroad* (Floella); *Dick* (Miss Hoggett).

STAGE
First professional stage appearances at the Players' Theatre in 1944, in pantomime, plays and revue. 1947-48: *The King Stag* (tour, with the Young Vic Company). 1948: *Sleeping Beauty in the Wood* (Players'). 1949: *The Beauty and the Beast* (Players'). 1950: *Ali Baba* (co-adapted & contributed lyrics, Players'). 1951: *Riquet with the Tuft* (co-adapted, Players'). 1952: *The Belles of St Martin's* (St Martin's, with Joan Sims). 1953: *Cinderella* (Players'). 1954: *The Players' Minstrels* (directed, Players'). 1954: *The Sleeping Beauty in the Wood* (Players'). 1955: *Twenty Minutes South* (Players', directed 101 performances). 1956: *Albertine by Moonlight* (Westminster); *Ali Baba* (co-adapted); appeared at the Royal Variety Performance. 1958: *Large as Life* (revue, Palladium). 1960: *Riquet with the Tuft* (co-adapted, Players'). 1976: *The Eric Sykes Show* (Pavilion, Torquay). 1977: *The Eric Sykes Show* (Winter Gardens, Blackpool). 1979: *Oh! Sir James!* (with Jimmy Edwards & Kenneth Connor); *Hatful of Sykes* (tour).

FILM

1946: *Green for Danger*. 1947: *Nicholas Nickleby*. 1948: *Oliver Twist*. 1949: *Trottie True* (US: *The Gay Lady*); *The Spider and the Fly*. 1950: *Waterfront* (US: *Waterfront Women*); *Chance of a Lifetime*. 1951: *Scrooge* (US: *A Christmas Carol*). 1952: *No Haunt for a Gentleman; Mother Riley Meets the Vampire* (US: *Vampire Over London*); *The Pickwick Papers*. 1953: *Our Girl Friday* (US: *The Adventures of Sadie*); *All Halloween*. 1954: *The Love Lottery; Up to His Neck*. 1955: *As Long as They're Happy; Now and Forever*. 1958: *Carry On Sergeant*; *The Square Peg*. 1959: *Carry On Nurse*; *Carry On Teacher*; *Left, Right and Centre*; *The Night We Dropped a Clanger; The Navy Lark; Follow a Star; School for Scoundrels*. 1960: *Carry On Constable*; *Make Mine Mink; Watch Your Stern*. 1961: *Carry On Regardless*. 1962: *In the Doghouse*; *She'll Have to Go* (US: *Maid for Murder*); *The Punch and Judy Man*. 1963: *Carry On Cabby*. 1967: *The Bobo; The Plank*; *Carry On Doctor*; *The Mikado* (TV). 1968: *Crooks and Coronets* (US: *Sophie's Place*). 1969: *The Magic Christian; Carry On Camping; Carry On Again Doctor; Monte Carlo or Bust* (US: *Those Daring Young Men in their Jaunty Jalopies*); *The Pickwick Papers* (TV). *Rhubarb*. 1970: *Carry On Loving*. 1971: *Danger Point*; *Carry On At Your Convenience*. 1972: *Carry On Matron*; *Carry On Abroad*. 1974: *Three for All*; *Carry On Dick*. 1980: *Rhubarb Rhubarb* (TV, short).

TELEVISION

Includes:

1950: *Out of This World*. 1954: *Happy Holidays* (series, as Mrs Mulberry). 1955: *The Granville Melodramas; Plunder*. 1956: *Pantomania; The Tony Hancock Show.* 1957-59: *Hancock's Half Hour.* 1959: *Eric Sykes' Gala Opening; Cup of Kindness*. 1960: *The Royal Variety Show*. 1962: *A Christmas Night with the Stars*. 1960-65 & 1972-79: *Sykes* (16 series, as Hattie). 1960-61: *Our House* (2 series, as Georgina Simpson, with Joan Sims, Charles Hawtrey, Bernard Bresslaw & Norman Rossington). 1962: *That Was The Week That Was*. 1963: *This Is Your Life* (subject); *The Royal Variety Performance*. 1964: *Miss Adventure* (series, as Stacey Smith); *Blithe Spirit* (as Madame Arcati). 1965: *Cribbins* (with Bernard Cribbins). 1967: *Jackanory* (several episodes); *Theatre 625; Sykes Versus ITV; The Tom Jones Show.* 1968: *Knock Three Times; Never a Cross Word; The World of Beachcomber; Howerd's Hour* (with Frankie Howerd). 1969: *Join Jim Dale; Catweazle* (as fortune teller); *Carry On Christmas*. 1970: *Charley's Grants* (series, as Miss Manger); *Holiday Startime; Inside George Wembley*. 1971: *Doctor at Large* (as Sybil Askey); *Sykes with a Lid Off; Frankie Howerd – The Laughing Stock of Television; Ask Aspel* (interview). 1972: *Max Bygraves at the Royalty*; *Carry On Stuffing*; *Doctor at Large* (as Mrs Askey); *This Is Your Life* (Deryck Guyler). 1973: *Call My Bluff*. 1975: *Carry On Laughing* – 'Orgy and Bess' (as Queen

Elizabeth I); *Celebrity Squares*; *This Is Your Life* (Peter Butterworth); *Wogan's World* (interview). 1977: *The Eric Sykes Show*. 1978: *Multi-Coloured Swap Shop*. 1979: *This Is Your Life* (Eric Sykes).

RADIO

Includes:

1947-48: *ITMA* (It's That Man Again, as Sophie Tuckshop). 1949: *Clay's College* (as student). 1950: *Educating Archie* (as Agatha Dinglebody). 1954: *You're Only Young Once*. 1954-56: *Hancock's Half Hour*. 1956: *The Man Who Could Work Miracles* (with Kenneth Williams). 1961: *It's a Fair Cop* (as Eric Sykes's sister).

Bernard Bresslaw

At 6ft 7ins Bernard Bresslaw towered over his co-stars in fourteen *Carry On* films, five episodes of *Carry On Laughing* and two stage shows. A real-life gentle giant, the versatile actor was often cast as gormless halfwits but also proved adept at more sinister characters, notably as Sheikh Abdul Abulbul in *Carry On Follow That Camel* and Bungdit Din in *Carry On Up the Khyber*.

Bernard Bresslaw was born in Stepney, London, on 25 February 1934. From a working-class background, he decided to take up acting while still a child. He trained at RADA, after gaining a scholarship, and left in 1953 after winning the Emile Littler Award for most promising actor. His first stage role came after he was spotted by Laurence Olivier and cast as an Irish wrestler in *Wrestler's Honeymoon*.

After several years on stage building up his acting experience Bernard sprang to fame on television as the hapless Private 'Popeye' Popplewell in two series of the hugely popular sitcom, *The Army Game*. The series helped to propel him to stardom and also established his life-long catchphrase – "I Only Arsked" - which was frequently used in the *Carry On*'s.

The series co-starred a host of future *Carry On* actors (including William Hartnell, Charles Hawtrey and Norman Rossington, q.v.) and is widely accepted as being the basis for the first ever *Carry On* film in 1958. Ironically, although Bernard appeared in the 1958 feature film version of the series (*I Only Arsked!*), he would have to wait another eight years before joining the *Carry On* team.

Following the success of *The Army Game* Bernard Bresslaw went on to appear in a string of television series and, in addition to his own series (*The Bernard Bresslaw Show* and *Bresslaw and Friends*), he also starred in the sitcom *Meet the Champ*, with Peter Butterworth (q.v.). He also gained fame as a recording artist with his single 'Mad Pashernate Love', which was originally recorded as a joke but reached No. 4 in the charts!

After making his film debut in *Men of Sherwood* in 1954 Bernard appeared in a range of films, including *The Ugly Duckling* (as a descendant of Dr Jekyll) and *Too Many Crooks*. Sadly, he could not maintain his 'star' status on screen and television without being typecast as oversized halfwits. By the early 1960s Bernard had returned to the stage to vary his acting range with work for the Royal Shakespeare Company and he proved himself as a capable dramatic actor. His comic career enjoyed a second flowering in 1965 when he joined the *Carry On* team as Little Heap in *Carry On Cowboy*.

Over the next decade Bernard (known to his friends as Bernie) would appear in fourteen *Carry On* films, thus securing his position as a member of the main team. His characters in the series proved he could never be underestimated, and whether he was playing the aggressive Little Heap in *Carry On Cowboy* or the suburbanised Arthur Upmore in *Carry On Behind* his performances were always faultless.

After his series debut as Charles Hawtrey's non-too-bright son in *Carry On Cowboy* Bernard went on to play the Lurch-like butler in *Carry On Screaming*. His physical size guaranteed that he was perfect for the role and his 'straight' performance opposite an extravagant Fenella Fielding was perhaps his most unusual in the series. In *Carry On Follow That Camel* and *Carry On Up the Khyber* Bernard broke his screen mould by playing decidedly villainous roles to great effect before returning to more lovable characters.

In 1968 Bernard was teamed with Sid James for the first time and proved to be the ideal 'foil' for the King of the *Carry On*'s in *Carry On Camping* (in which he played the kind-hearted Bernie Lugg). They were later memorable together in *Carry On Up the Jungle* (with Bernard playing Sid's loyal sidekick, Upsidas) and *Carry On Girls* (as beauty contestant organisers).

In *Carry On Camping*, opposite Dilys Laye (q.v.) for the second time (they had earlier formed a romantic partnership in *Carry On Doctor*), Bernard established his gentle giant persona, which was also fully displayed in *Carry On Abroad* when his religious beliefs and everyday urges were tested as Brother Bernard. He also proved to be an unlikely drag artist in *Carry On Up the Jungle* (disguised as a Lubi), *Carry On Matron* (as 'expectant mother' Bernie Bragg) and *Carry On Girls* (as Patricia Potter).

In his final *Carry On* appearances Bernard returned to more serious characters, as the aristocratic Sir Roger Daley in *Carry On Dick* and suburban holidaymaker Arthur Upmore in *Carry On Behind*. He also featured in five episodes of *Carry On Laughing* on television in 1975, having made memorable appearances in a succession of *Carry On Christmas* specials. In the mid-1970s he also joined co-stars Sidney James, Barbara Windsor, Peter Butterworth, Kenneth Connor and Jack Douglas in a successful stage run of *Carry On London* at the Victoria Palace.

Aside from the *Carry On*'s, throughout his career Bernard Bresslaw welcomed the opportunity to return to work on stage, often in Shakespearian roles. He also became one of the country's most popular pantomime actors, especially in the 1970s. Although his screen credits became sporadic after joining the *Carry On* team, his additional film appearances included *Spring and Port Wine* (1970), *Up Pompeii* (1971, with Frankie Howerd) and *Vampira* (1974).

Following his departure from the *Carry On* series in 1975 Bernard went on to appear in a handful of other films, including the Disney classic *One of Our Dinosaurs is Missing* (co-starring Joan Sims, Deryck Guyler and Molly Weir, all q.v.), *Joseph Andrews* and *Jabberwocky*. In the early 1980s he returned to film roles in sword and sorcery productions – *Hawk the Slayer* and *Krull* (as Rell the Cyclops). Sadly, his profile to the public at large became increasingly less well known and he seemed to be denied the opportunities that he deserved. Although he turned up for occasional television appearances (notably as a guest presenter of *The Book Tower*) and British Telecom adverts with Maureen Lipman (q.v.), the majority of his later work was on stage, where he became most at home in his final years.

In 1992 Bernard had a cameo role in the feature film *Leon the Pig Farmer*, which was to be his last screen appearance. In the same year he turned down the opportunity to play King Ferdinand in *Carry On Columbus* (the role subsequently going to Leslie Phillips) and instead returned to the stage, with Barbara Windsor, in a successful run of *Wot a Carry On in Blackpool.*

Bernard Bresslaw met his wife, dancer Elizabeth Wright, in *The Sleeping Beauty* in 1958. They subsequently married and had three sons, James, Mark and Jonathan. In private, Bernard was a quiet, studious, well-read man with a deep interest in history, languages and world religions. Proclaimed by all who knew him as a real-life 'gentle giant', he was a treasured friend to other *Carry On* actors, respected even by the notoriously unpredictable Kenneth Williams.

Bernard Bresslaw collapsed and died from a heart attack shortly before a performance at the Open Air Theatre, Regent's Park, on 11 June 1993. The fifty-nine year old actor had received critical acclaim for his role as Grumio in *The Taming of the Shrew* and was due to appear in the musical *A Connecticut Yankee* later in the same season.

Despite being a key member of the *Carry On* team, the British press shamefully neglected the sudden death of Bernard Bresslaw. Several years later, however, the British comedy magazine *COR!* (edited by Robert Ross) was established in his memory, and in 2001 he was honoured with a British Comedy Society plaque at Pinewood Studios, unveiled in the presence of his family.

Carry On ... ***Quotes***

Bernard Bresslaw was a gentle giant. It was impossible not to like him.
Peter Rogers, 1998

I met and became friends with Bernard while playing the pantomime Mother Goose, *starring Stanley Baxter, at the Theatre Royal, Newcastle.*
Bernard Bresslaw was a charming and talented actor, respected and admired by all his fellow artists.
On another occasion, I played the pantomime Aladdin *at the Richmond Theatre. The actors of this particular show included Barbara Windsor, Jack Douglas and Jon Pertwee. Jack was a keen cook and even wrote a cookery book, one of which I have.*
Barbara Windsor was also a pleasure to work with and still looks very good.
Tom O'Connor (Australian percussionist and entertainer), 2000

... highly intelligent – a wonderful family man and a pleasure to work with.
Dilys Laye, 2001

Carry On **CREDITS 1965-75**
Cowboy (Little Heap); *Screaming* (Sockett); *Follow That Camel* (Sheikh Abdul Abulbul); *Doctor* (Ken Biddle); *Up the Khyber* (Bungdit Din); *Camping* (Bernie Lugg); *Up the Jungle* (Upsidasi); *Loving* (Gripper Burke); *At Your Convenience* (Bernie Hulke); *Matron* (Ernie Bragg); *Abroad* (Brother Bernard); *Girls* (Peter Potter); *Dick* (Sir Roger Daley); *Behind* (Arthur Upmore).

STAGE
Includes:
1953: *Wrestler's Honeymoon* (debut, New, Oxford, as Roary Macroary). 1955: *The Big Bad Seed* (196 performances, Aldwych, as Leroy). 1956: *The Good Sailor* (Lyric, Hammersmith, as Jenkins). 1957: *A Hatful of Rain* (92 performances, Princes, with Sally Ann Howes). 1958: *The Sleeping Beauty* (150 performances, Palladium, as Popeye). 1959: toured in Variety; *Aladdin* (Hippodrome, Manchester). 1960: *Master of None* (as Shorty Brown). 1962: *Women Beware Women* (for the RSC, Arts). 1963: *Day of the Prince* (as Bert). 1965: *Twang!!* (with Barbara Windsor). 1967: *A Midsummer Night's Dream* (as Peter Quince); *Two Gentlemen of Verona* (Open Air, Regent's Park). 1968: *Aladdin* (Theatre Royal Brighton, as Wishee Washee). 1969: *Two Gentlemen of Verona* (Open Air); *Aladdin*

(Hippodrome, Bristol). 1970: *Much Ado About Nothing* (Open Air, as Dogberry); *Dick Whittington* (Hippodrome, Birmingham, as Barnacle Bill). 1971: *Rabelais* (as Friar John of the Funnels); *Aladdin* (Palace, Manchester). 1972: *Stop It Nurse* (Pavilion, Torquay, as Felix Ramsey); *Mother Goose* (Theatre Royal Newcastle, as Hector Small). 1973-74: *Carry On London* (Victoria Palace). 1974: *Babes in the Wood* (Princess, Torquay, as Simple Simon). 1975: *Grandson of Oblomov* (Ambassadors); *Mother Goose* (New, Hull). 1976: *There Goes the Bride* (Pier, Bournemouth, as Charles Babcock); *Under Milk Wood* (Plymouth Theatre Company, as 1st narrator); *Dick Whittington and His Fabulous Cat* (Theatre Royal, Norwich, with Kenneth Connor). 1977: *Foxy* (Palace, Watford, as Lion King); *Cinderella* (Bradford). 1978-79: *Robinson Crusoe* (Richmond & Alexandria, Birmingham, as Blackbeard); *Shut Your Eyes and Think of England* (tour). 1980: season at the Open Air – *Much Ado About Nothing* (as Dogberry); *A Midsummer Night's Dream* (as Bottom); *Babes in the Wood* (Richmond). 1981: in repertory: *The Skin Game, The Devil's Disciple, The Cherry Orchard, Dandy Dick*; *Aladdin* (Richmond). 1982: *Robinson Crusoe* (Towngate, Poole). 1983: *Charley's Aunt* (Aldwych, as Stephen); *Babes in the Wood* (Theatre Royal, Plymouth). 1984: *Run for Your Wife* (Criterion, as Det. Sgt Porterhouse); *Cinderella* (Theatre Royal, Nottingham). 1985-86: *Run for Your Wife* (Criterion). 1986: *A Midsummer Night's Dream* & *Arm and the Man* (Open Air). 1987: *Cinderella* (Palace, Manchester). 1988: *Don Juan* (Royal Exchange, Manchester & tour); *Falstaff* (Greenwich & tour, as Sir John Falstaff). 1989: *Twelfth Night* (as Malvolio) & *The Swaggerer* (as The Captain) (both at the Open Air Theatre, Regent's Park); *The Sleeping Beauty* (Theatre Royal, Plymouth). 1990: *Me and My Girl* (Adelphi, as Sir John Treymayne). 1990-91: *Aladdin* (Theatre Royal, Newcastle); *Arsenic and Old Lace* (Chichester Festival, as Jonathan Brewster). 1992: *Wot a Carry On in Blackpool* (with Barbara Windsor). 1993: *The Taming of the Shrew* (Open Air, as Grumio).

FILM

1954: *Men of Sherwood*. 1955: *The Glass Cage* (US: *The Glass Tomb*). 1956: *Up in the World*. 1957: *High Tide at Noon*. 1958: *Blood of the Vampire; I Only Arsked!* 1959: *The Ugly Duckling*; *Too Many Crooks*. 1963: *It's All Happening*. 1965: *Carry On Cowboy*; *Morgan – An Unsuitable Case for Treatment*. 1966: *Round the Bend* (short); *Carry On Screaming*. 1967: *Carry On Follow That Camel*; *Carry On Doctor*. 1968: *Carry On Up the Khyber*. 1969: *Carry On Camping*; *Moon Zero Two*. 1970: *Carry On Up the Jungle*; *Carry On Loving; Spring and Port Wine*. 1971: *Carry On At Your Convenience*; *Up Pompeii; The Magnificent Seven Deadly Sins; Blinker's Spy Spotter*. 1972: *Carry On Matron*; *Carry On Abroad*. 1973: *Carry On Girls*. 1974: *Carry On Dick*; *Vampira* (US:

Old Dracula). 1975: *Carry On Behind*; *One of Our Dinosaurs Is Missing*. 1977: *Joseph Andrews; Jabberwocky*. 1979: *The Fifth Musketeer* (aka: *Behind the Iron Mask*). 1980: *Hawk the Slayer*. 1983: *Krull*. 1989: *Asterix and the Big Flight* (voice only). 1992: *Leon the Pig Farmer.*

TELEVISION
Includes:
1955: *Three Empty Rooms*. 1956: *The Black Tulip*; *The Adventures of Robin Hood*. 1957: *No Shepherds Watched*. 1957-58: *The Vise* (appearances); *The Army Game* (2 series, as Private 'Popeye' Popplewell). 1958-59: *The Bernard Bresslaw Show*. 1960-61: *Meet the Champ* (series, as Bernie, with Peter Butterworth). 1961: *Our House* (series, as William Singer); *Bresslaw and Friends*. 1963: *A Midsummer Night's Dream* (as Snout). 1964: *Lance at Large* (with Lance Percival); *Richard Whittington Esquire*; *The Kathy Kirby Show* (guest); *Sergeant Cork*. 1965: *The Secret Agent; Danger Man; The Stairway*. 1966: *Amerika*. 1967: *Sykes Versus ITV*; *Doctor Who* (as Varga). 1968: *Stiff Upper Lipp* (as Percy); *Mum's Boy* (series, as Leonard Pallise, with Irene Handl); *Tickertape* (series). 1969: *Doctor in the House* (as Malcolm); *Carry On Christmas*. 1970: *Carry On Again Christmas*. 1971: *The Goodies*. 1972: *Clochemerle* (as Nicholas the Beadle); *Carry On Stuffing*. 1973: *Arthur of the Britons; Ooh La La!*; *What a Carry On*!; *Carry On Christmas*. 1974: *Sykes* (guest appearance). 1975: *Carry On Laughing* – 'Under the Round Table' (as Sir Pureheart), 'Short Knight, Long Daze' (as Sir Lancelot), 'And in My Lady's Chamber' (as Starkers), 'Who Needs Kitchener?' (as Klanger), 'Lamp-Posts of the Empire' (as Dr Pavingstone). 1976: *Well Anyway*. 1980: *Sherlock Holmes and Doctor Watson*. 1982: *Terry and June* (as Morris). 1985: *Mann's Best Friend* (series, as Duncan); *The Giddy Game Show* (voice, as Gorilla). 1987: *The Book Tower* (presenter); *Wogan* (guest); *T-Bag Bounces Back*. 1989: *The Russ Abbot Show*. 1990: *Tales of the Rodent Sherlock Holmes*. 1992: *Virtual Murder* (as Lithgow).

Additional Credits
The Saga of Shorty Breath; Meet Your Lucky Stars; Z-Cars.

RADIO
Includes:
Educating Archie. 1963: *Dishonest to Goodness* (with John Bluthal). 1989: *The Life of Kenneth Connor.*

Jim Dale MBE

(b. James Smith)

The star of eleven *Carry On* films, Jim Dale became the likeable leading man in the middle half of the series. In many ways he was a younger, more handsome version of *Carry On* 'King', Sid James. Characteristically Jim would appear as accident-prone underdogs who ultimately came out on top, and over twenty years after his final role in the series he returned in the title role of *Carry On Columbus*.

Jim Dale was born in Rothwell, Northamptonshire, on 15 August 1935, the son of William Henry Smith and his wife Miriam Jean (Wells). Like many of his contemporaries, Jim's interest in the world of acting began as a child, and while still at school he started taking ballet lessons. After leaving school Jim worked for a time in a shoe factory before becoming a Carroll Levis 'discovery'. He went on to work on television and made his stage debut at the age of sixteen as a stand-up comedian. At the age of eighteen Jim joined the Royal Air Force and for the next two years entertained troops in England and Germany. He would go on to become well known on television as a singer before eventually hosting *6.5 Special* in the late 1950s. The programme made him a household name.

Tall, dark-haired and handsome, Jim became the dashing leading man in the *Carry On*'s in 1963. It was a role unoccupied since the departure of Leslie Phillips and Terence Longdon in 1961. Jim had previously worked for Peter Rogers and Gerald Thomas in two of their films, *Raising the Wind* (1961) and *The Iron Maiden* (1962), and joined many of the *Carry On* team in *Nurse on Wheels* (1963). He made his *Carry On* debut as the frantic expectant father in *Carry On Cabby*, opposite Sid James and Charles Hawtrey. In the following year he again turned up in a supporting role as the carrier in *Carry On Jack* before playing Carstairs – the sleek, James Bond-like figure – in *Carry On Spying*.

Jim's first leading role in the *Carry On* series was as Horsa (inventor of the win-dow!) in *Carry On Cleo*. This agile young hero was one of Jim's finest *Carry On* roles, far removed from the more naive characterisations that were to follow. Jim's second major role in the series was as the unforgettable Marshal P. Knutt in *Carry On Cowboy*. As the endearing Sanitation, Drainage and Garbage Disposal Engineer (First Class!) he is mistakenly appointed as Sheriff of Stodge City. The Marshal's innocent charm is seen throughout the film as he kisses a photograph of his mother 'goodnight' and adjusts his 'pinching' gun belt! Teamed with the stunning Angela Douglas (q.v.), Jim eventually manages to 'clean up'

Stodge City with her help.

In *Carry On Screaming* (again with Angela Douglas) Jim was only slightly more worldly when he played Albert Potter. His scenes with Douglas in Oakham Wood are especially memorable. In *Carry On Don't Lose Your Head* Jim was cast opposite Sid James for the second time, to great effect. Their scenes together are rather like watching a master and his apprentice, with Jim as the daring hero and Sid maintaining his position as a lovable rogue. In *Carry On Follow That Camel* Jim was again cast as a bumbling English 'innocent' when he played Bertram Oliphant (Bo). By now he was well accustomed to playing leading, roles and as in his previous appearances he gave a flawless performance.

Jim Dale was the likeable underdog in both *Carry On Doctor* and *Carry On Again Doctor.* As the accident-prone Doctor Kilmore in *Doctor* his chaotic antics (culminating in a daring rooftop scene featuring Barbara Windsor and a love-struck Anita Harris, q.v.) almost end in disaster until his reputation is restored and the conniving Doctor Tinkle (Kenneth Williams) firmly put in his place.

Jim's role in *Carry On Again Doctor* provides one of the all-time classic scenes of the *Carry On* series as he runs through the hospital wreaking havoc in his path. His descent down the hospital stairs on a tea trolley is especially memorable! Once again, as in previous appearances, Jim comes out on top by 'discovering' a weight loss serum – creating priceless *Carry On* confusion in the process. It was to be Jim's final role in the series until he returned to captain the ship in *Carry On Columbus*, twenty-three years later.

As a notable point of interest, the athletic actor performed all his own stunts in the *Carry On* films and actually sustained a serious (and subsequently life-long) back injury while filming *Carry On Again Doctor*. He would later go on to receive an honorary membership of the Association of American Stuntmen.

Jim Dale was due to return to the *Carry On* series as 'Ug Ug' (the Jungle Boy) in *Carry On Up the Jungle* but alas decided to broaden his horizons and left the *Carry On* team in 1969. His departure from the series left many of his colleagues disappointed and, infamously, several years after his departure some members of the *Carry On* team allegedly boycotted his *This Is Your Life* tribute in protest. Jim Dale left a gap that was never adequately filled in the remaining decade of the *Carry On* series. Julian Holloway, Richard O'Callaghan, Kenneth Cope and Patrick Mower all followed in similar roles but with arguably less success than Dale.

After leaving the *Carry On* series Jim went on to pursue a wide variety of roles in everything from Shakespeare on stage to Walt Disney productions on screen.

Jim made his Shakespearian debut in 1966 in an acclaimed performance as Autolycus in *The Winter's Tale*. He would go on to appear in the film version and also wrote the songs for the play. As a pop singer Jim's recording of 'Be My Girl' reached Number 2 in the charts and he also wrote the lyrics for the film *Georgy Girl* (which went on to receive an Academy Award in 1966), the lyrics for *Shalako* (1968) and all the songs for *Twinky* (1970).

Following the success of his role in *The Winter's Tale* Jim went on to star in a variety of stage plays, earning critical acclaim as Barnet in *The National Health*. This was to be his first major triumph after leaving the *Carry On* series, and he also starred in the 1973 film version. Jim then went on to work with the Young Vic Company in performances of *The Taming of the Shrew* and *The Cheats of Scapino*. His role of Scapino took him to Los Angeles and Broadway in 1974, where he received the Drama Desk Award and the Outer Critics Circle Award. From the mid-1970s Jim has largely been based in America, where further stage successes followed throughout the 1980s, with a Tony Award in 1980 for his role in *Barnum* and a Tony nomination in 1989 for *Privates on Parade*.

In the 1970s Jim worked on the Disney productions of *Pete's Dragon* (utilising his talent as a singer) and starred in *The Spaceman and King Arthur*. He was also reunited with *Carry On* co-star Angela Douglas in the 1973 film *Digby, the Biggest Dog in the World*.

In 1992 Jim was one of the few stalwart cast members to return to the *Carry On* series for *Carry On Columbus*. Cast in the title role as Christopher Columbus, the matured Dale coped well with the film, but in spite of a valiant performance even his talents could not save the production, which was panned by critics and fans alike. While the casting of Dale himself (two decades after his final appearance) was something of a surprise, the role was a special one for the actor himself. Jim, along with Joan Sims and Patsy Rowlands, was a notable absentee at the *Carry On* 40th Anniversary Reunion in 1998, although he did take part in the television documentary *What's a Carry On*? later that year.

In recent years Jim has continued his busy stage career, and after an absence of twenty years he returned to London's West End to play Fagin in the musical *Oliver!* The success of the musical resulted in a run of over two years and also saw Jim reunited with his dance partner in *Carry On Again Doctor* – Patsy Rowlands. His most recent work has been recording all of the *Harry Potter* books (by J.K. Rowling) onto audio cassette and CD, and he returned to Broadway as Mr Peachum in *The Threepenny* Opera in 2006 (for which he received a Tony Award nomination). In 2003 Jim was awarded the MBE and in 2010 he was inducted into the

American Theatre Hall of Fame.

Jim was married to Patricia Gardiner for twenty-three years and they had four children - Belinda, Murray, Adam and actor Toby Dale (q.v.). After divorcing his first wife in 1981 Jim married American art dealer Julie Schafler. Now a grandfather, Jim is permanently based in New York but makes frequent trips to the UK. A keen collector of antiques, Jim is currently working on his autobiography.

Carry On ... ***Quotes***

Jim Dale is a surprising artist. He can play anything and is completely unassuming about it.
Peter Rogers, 1998

Carry On **CREDITS 1963-92**
Cabby (expectant father); *Jack* (Carrier); *Spying* (Carstairs); *Cleo* (Horsa); *Cowboy* (Marshal P. Knutt); *Screaming* (Albert Potter); *Don't Lose Your Head* (Lord Darcy de Pue); *Follow That Camel* (Bertram Oliphant 'Bo' West); *Doctor* (Dr Jim Kilmore); *Again Doctor* (Dr James Nookey); *Columbus* (Columbus).

STAGE
Includes:
1951: stage debut as a stand-up comedian at the Savoy, Kettering. 1964: *The Wayward Way/The Drunkard* (Lyric, Hammersmith). 1966: *The Winter's Tale* (Edinburgh Festival & Cambridge). 1967: *The Burglar* (Vaudeville). 1967: *A Midsummer Night's Dream* (Edinburgh Festival & Saville). 1969: joined the National Theatre Company at the Old Vic; *The National Health; The Travails of Sancho Panza*. 1969: *Love's Labour's Lost*. 1970: *The Merchant of Venice; The Cheats of Scapino; The Taming of the Shrew*. 1971: *The Architect and the Emperor of Assyria; The Good-Natur'd Man; The Captain of Köpenick*. 1972: *The Taming of the Shrew* (European tour, as Petruchio). 1973: *The Card* (Queen's). 1974: *The Taming of the Shrew* & *Scapino* (co-directed & wrote music for *Scapino*, New York - Brooklyn Academy, Circle of the Square & the Ambassador). 1977: *The Comedians* (Mark Taper, LA). 1979: *Privates on Parade* (Long Wharf, New Haven). 1980: *Barnum* (Tony Award); *Joe Egg*. 1984: *The Music Man* (as Harold Hill). 1986-89: *Me and My Girl*. 1989: *Privates on Parade* (Tony nomination). 1994: *Travels with My Aunt* (Long Wharf); *The Music Man*. 1995-97: *Oliver!*

(as Fagan). 1997: *Candide* (as Voltaire, Tony Award nomination). 2003: *Comedians* (as Eddie Waters); *A Christmas Carol* (as Scrooge, Madison Square Garden). 2004: *Address Unknown* (as Max). 2006: *The Threepenny Opera* (as Mr Peachum). *Busker Alley* (as Charlie Baxter, with Glenn Close). 2007: *The Oak Tree* (as Father); *Don Juan in Hell* (as The Devil).

Additional Credits
Asprin & Elephants (as director).

FILM
1958: *6.5 Special*. 1961: *Raising the Wind* (US: *Roommates*). 1962: *The Iron Maiden* (US: *The Swingin' Maiden*). 1963: *Nurse on Wheels*; *Carry On Cabby*; *Carry On Jack*. 1964: *Carry On Spying*; *Carry On Cleo*. 1965: *Carry On Cowboy*; *The Big Job*. 1966: *Carry On Screaming*; *Carry On Don't Lose Your Head*. 1967: *Carry On Follow That Camel*; *The Plank*; *Carry On Doctor*; *The Winter's Tale* (& wrote music). 1969: *Lock Up Your Daughters!*; *Carry On Again Doctor*. 1972: *Adolf Hitler - My Part in His Downfall*. 1973: *Digby, the Biggest Dog in the World; The National Health* (aka: *The Nurse Norton Affair*). 1977: *Pete's Dragon; Joseph Andrews*. 1978: *Hot Lead and Cold Feet*. 1979: *The Spaceman and King Arthur* (US: *Unidentified Flying Oddball*); *Bloodshy*. 1983: *Scandalous*. 1985: *The Adventures of Huckleberry Finn* (TV). 1992: *Carry On Columbus*. 1993: *The American Clock* (TV). 1997: *The Hunchback* (TV).

TELEVISION
Includes:
Carroll Levis Discovery Show. 1957: *Six-Five Special* (host). 1959: *Spectacular*. 1962 & 1965-66: *Thank Your Lucky Stars* (host). 1965: *The New London Palladium Show*. 1968: *Rogues Gallery; Ringling Brothers*. 1969: *Join Jim Dale* (host). *Rogues Gallery* (as Lucifer Kane). 1970: *Jackanory*. 1973: *This Is Your Life* (subject). *Sunday Night at the London Palladium*. 1978: *The Dancing Princess*. 1985: *Barnum and Bailey Circus; The Equalizer* (guest appearances). 1986: *The Ellen Burstyn Show*. 1997: *Cosby* (as Gregory). 1998: *What's a Carry On?* (doc.). 2007: *British Film Forever* (doc.). 2007-09: *Pushing Daisies* (narrator).

RADIO
Includes:
1992: *Carry On Up Yer Cinders!*

Barbara Windsor MBE

(b. Barbara Ann Deeks)

A true star in every sense of the word, Barbara Windsor remains the *Carry On* series's most visible figurehead. Her acting skills and sheer presence in ten *Carry On* films ensured her the rare status of leading lady, and almost fifty years after her *Carry On* debut the much-loved national figure is still best known for her work in the series.

Born in Shoreditch, in the East End of London, on 6 August 1937, Barbara spent the war years evacuated to Blackpool. Her parents divorced when she was a teenager, and despite having elocution lessons she retained her now famous cockney accent. After training at the Aida Foster School, with Shirley Eaton (q.v.), Barbara made her first stage appearance at the age of thirteen in pantomime and her professional debut in 1952 in *Love from Judy,* which ran for over two years. Barbara also appeared on television and became a successful singer and cabaret artist, appearing all over the country with numerous bands, including the Ronnie Scott Band. She made her film debut as one of the rebellious schoolgirls in *The Belles of St Trinian's* in 1954.

In 1959, at the age of twenty-two, Barbara appeared in what was probably her biggest stage triumph, *Fings Ain't Wot They Used T'Be*, which ran for over two years. A string of successes followed, including the TV series *The Rag Trade*, and she was the leading lady in the Joan Littlewood film *Sparrows Can't Sing*. The song from the film (sung by Barbara) became a top 30 hit.

Barbara Windsor joined the *Carry On* series as secret agent Daphne Honeybutt in *Carry On Spying* in 1964. With a photographic memory and a cheeky range of one-liners, she was a welcome addition to the series. During the filming of *Spying* in March 1964 Barbara married Ronnie Knight and the couple famously honeymooned in Madeira, with Kenneth Williams and his mother and sister! Following *Carry On Spying* Barbara appeared on Broadway (making her New York theatre debut) in another Joan Littlewood production, *Oh, What a Lovely War!*. Barbara would later work for Littlewood on stage in *Twang!!*, with Bernard Bresslaw (q.v.).

Barbara returned to the *Carry On* series with a vengeance in 1967 and went on to make eight more films. As Babs, the cheeky pupil of Chaste Place in *Carry On Camping*, she played opposite Sid James to great effect. Her genuine cockney accent shines through and her bra-popping scene, with Kenneth Williams and Hattie Jacques, is now legendary. In *Carry*

On Again Doctor she is the romantic interest of Jim Dale (Dr Nookey). As the aptly named Goldie Locks (originally Maud Boggins and finally Melanie Maddocks) she returns to Dale to receive slimming treatment, but ends up with something very different.

In *Carry On Henry* Barbara captured the King's (Sid James) heart, playing Bettina, the daughter of the Duke of Bristol. In *Carry On Abroad* she played twice-married Sadie Tomkins – again opposite Sid James. In *Carry On Matron*, opposite Kenneth Cope, Barbara is more serious and loses less clothes than usual, but she was back to form in *Carry On Girls* as the glamorous Miss Easy Rider, who revels in a catfight (with Margaret Nolan), surprising Sid James as she opens her leather jacket and infuriating Joan Sims! In her final *Carry On* film, *Carry On Dick*, she was cast as Harriet, the rector's maid. 'Popping out' in *Camping* fashion while ringing the church bells, she eventually heads over the Scottish border with Sid James to 'stand and deliver'!

Sensibly, Barbara did not return to the series for the final three films. She did, however, remain a major figure in the *Carry On Laughing* series on TV in 1975 as well as making a brief appearance in *Carry On Banging* on television in 1989. Barbara also appeared on stage in *Carry On London* (1973-75) and *Wot a Carry On in Blackpool* (1992), with Bernard Bresslaw.

Together with Kenneth Williams, Barbara hosted *That's Carry On* in 1978, looking tanned and relaxed and still sporting her hourglass figure. While many other *Carry On* ladies were glamorous, saucy and even seductive, it was Windsor who brought true sex appeal to the series.

Following the *Carry On* films Barbara began once again to pursue her career on television. Her small-screen roles included children's programmes, drama and comedy, and numerous appearances on chat and game shows. The stage also called her back. During the *Carry On* years she appeared in *Come Spy with Me, Sing a Rude Song, Threepenny Opera* (with Vanessa Redgrave) and Kenneth Williams's *Entertaining Mr Sloane* and toured the world with *A Merry Whiff of Windsor*. Equally at home in serious roles, she also appeared on stage in *Twelfth Night*. Barbara has also become one of the country's most popular actors in pantomime, appearing in several versions of *Babes in the Wood*, both as Principal Boy and Fairy Godmother, and numerous seasons of *Aladdin* and *Cinderella*. During the early 1980s she was also kept busy with tours of *The Mating Game* and in 1991 toured in *Guys and Dolls*, with the late Gareth Hunt.

In 1983 Barbara was on television again with Kenneth Williams for *Carry On Christmas Capers*. It was an emotional reunion following the deaths of two more stars since *That's Carry On*: Peter Butterworth and Hattie Jacques. Almost forty years after her final *Carry On* film, Barbara still recalls the *Carry On* 'gang' with great affection. She was especially close to Kenneth Williams (to whom she would unveil the Dead Comics' Society plaque in 1994 and the British Comedy Society plaque in 1998) and was a great admirer of the work of Charles Hawtrey. Always proud of her contribution to the *Carry On* series, Barbara has attended as many celebrations in recent years as her hectic schedule would allow, and she was a major figure at the 40th Anniversary reunion in 1998. In many ways she has willingly become an icon of the series, with her persona firmly entrenched in the *Carry On*'s in much the same way as Sid James and Kenneth Williams before her.

Barbara Windsor's private life has been well documented through tabloid headlines and her own best-selling memoirs: *Barbara - The Laughter and Tears of a Cockney Sparrow* (1990) and *All of Me: My Extraordinary Life* (2000). The early 1980s were a particularly difficult time for the bubbly 4ft 10in actress. She suffered a serious accident, resulting in internal injuries, while filming on the set of *Worzel Gummidge*, and in 1981 her beloved mother, Rose, died. Around the same time Ronnie Knight was involved in police raids and court cases over his involvement in a security express raid in London. He subsequently fled to Majorca, remarried, and was finally jailed for three years when he returned to England in 1995.

The later, stormy years of her marriage to Ronnie Knight are detailed in her autobiographies, as is her brief affair with Sidney James (a relationship that was dramatised in the 2000 TV film *Cor, Blimey!*, with Barbara making a cameo appearance). She also candidly revealed how the stress of years of court cases and police trails (in connection with Ronnie Knight) caused a breakdown of health, resulting in a stomach ulcer. Following her divorce from Knight in 1985 Barbara married Stephen Hollings - a chef nineteen years her junior. The couple ran a pub together, 'The Plough' in Buckinghamshire, before their subsequent separation and divorce. In 1999 Barbara married Scott Mitchell, an actor twenty-six years her junior.

In 1994, amid much publicity, Barbara joined the cast of the popular TV soap opera *EastEnders*. Cast as Peggy Mitchell, the landlady of the Queen Vic, Barbara quickly settled into the series while continuing to attract a great deal of press attention. The episode in which she made her debut was watched by 27.5 million viewers - the show's highest rating in seven years! Barbara's success in *EastEnders* culminated in 1999 when she was awarded Best Actress in the first ever British TV Soap Awards and was made the first ever member of the BBC Hall of Fame. In 2003 Barbara took time out of the series to recover from Epstein-Barr virus and finally left the soap in 2010 and returned to the stage in pantomime.

Barbara Windsor was awarded a much-deserved MBE in the New Year's Honours List 2000 and in 2003 won the Lifetime Achievement Award at the Women in Film and Television Awards. In 2010 she was given the Freedom of the City of London.

For a much-loved actress, who has been described as a national institution, such honours helped celebrate an incredible sixty-year career, which has spanned stage, screen, television and radio.

Carry On ... ***Quotes***

Barbara Windsor does not seem to have changed since she joined the cast. She is always a very bubbly person and is as down to earth as they come. Again, she is a true professional. She has made the characterisation of herself in the Carry On's *a kind of trademark and in this respect is not unlike Kenneth Williams. She is a very serious person.*
Peter Rogers, 1997

Carry On **CREDITS 1964-78**
Spying (Daphne Honeybutt); *Doctor* (Nurse Sandra May); *Camping* (Barbara); *Again Doctor* (Goldie Locks/Melanie Maddocks); *Henry* (Bettina of Bristol); *Matron* (Nurse Susan Ball); *Abroad* (Sadie Tomkins); *Girls* (Miss Easy Rider, Hope Springs); *Dick* (Harriet); *That's Carry On* (co-host).

STAGE
Includes:
1952-54: *Love from Judy* (594 performances, as Sadie Kate). 1954: *Dreamer's Highway* (Grand, Bolton, & tour). 1955: *Happy Returns* (New Watergate). 1958: *Keep Your Hair On* (Apollo, as Marlene). 1959: *The Gimmick* (tour, as Gabby Burton, with Bernard Braden & Barbara Kelly). 1960-61: *Fings Ain't Wot They Used T'Be*. 1964: *Oh, What a Lovely War!* (London & New York). 1965: *Twang!!* (as Delphini). 1966. *Come Spy with Me* (Whitehall, as Mavis Apple). 1967: *The Beggar's Opera* (Worthing, as Lucy Lockett). 1970: *Sing a Rude Song* (as Marie Lloyd); *Cinderella* (Theatre Royal, Norwich, title role). 1971: *The Country Wife* (as Marjorie Pinchwife); *Cinderella* (Royal Court Theatre, Liverpool, as Wicked Sister). 1972: *Threepenny Opera* (Prince of Wales, as Lucy Brown); *The Owl and the Pussycat* (tour); *Cinderella* (Odeon, Golders Green). 1972-73: *Carry On London* (Victoria Palace). 1975: *Carry On Barbara* (New Zealand); *A*

Merry Whiff of Windsor (tour); *Aladdin* (Richmond, title role, with Jack Douglas & Jon Pertwee). 1976: *Twelfth Night* (Chichester Festival Theatre, as Maria). 1976-77: *Aladdin*. 1978: *Dick Whittington* (Ashcroft, Croydon, title role). 1979: *Calamity Jane* (tour); *Dick Whittington* (Richmond). 1980: *Jack and the Beanstalk* (Theatre Royal, Newcastle). 1981: *The Mating Game* (as Honey Tooks). 1981-82: *Aladdin*. 1982: *The Mating Game* (tour). 1983: *The Mating Game* (with Kathy Staff); *Aladdin*. 1984: *The Mating Game; Dick Whittington*. 1985: *A Right Carry On*; *Aladdin*. 1986: *Dick Whittington*. 1987-88: *Babes in the Wood* (as Fairy Queen). 1989-90: *Cinderella* (as Fairy Godmother). 1991: *Guys and Dolls* (tour, as Miss Adelaide); *Aladdin*. 1992: *Wot a Carry On* (Blackpool); *Cinderella*. 1993: *Aladdin*. 1994-95: *Cinderella* (as Fairy Godmother). 2010-11: *Dick Whittington* (Bristol Hippodrome, as Fairy Bowbells).

FILM

1954: *The Belles of St Trinian's*. 1956: *Lost* (US: *Tears for Simon*). 1959: *Too Hot to Handle* (US: *Play Girl After Dark*). 1961: *On the Fiddle* (US: *Operation Snafu*); *Flame in the Streets; Hair of the Dog*. 1962: *Death Trap; Sparrows Can't Sing*. 1963: *Crooks in Cloisters*. 1964: *Carry On Spying*. 1965: *San Ferry Ann; A Study in Terror* (US: *Fog*). 1967: *Carry On Doctor*. 1968: *Chitty Chitty Bang Bang*. 1969: *Carry On Camping*; *Carry On Again Doctor.* 1970: *Carry On Henry*. 1971: *The Boyfriend*. 1972: *Carry On Matron*; *Carry On Abroad*; *Not Now, Darling*. 1973: *Carry On Girls*. 1974: *Carry On Dick*. 1978: *That's Carry On*. 1986: *Comrades*. 1987: *It Couldn't Happen Here*. 1992: *Double Vision* (TV). 1994: *The Steal*. 2000: *Cor, Blimey!* (TV & consultant). 2010: *Alice in Wonderland* (voice only).

TELEVISION

Includes:

1954: *Dreamer's Highway; The Jack Jackson Show; 6.5 Special*. 1958: *On with the Show* (guest appearances). 1963: *The Rag Trade* (series, as Judy); *The Wind in the Sassafras Trees*. 1964: *The Hen House* (as Cynthia Spooner). 1967: *Before the Fringe*. 1969: *Wild, Wild Women* (series, as Millie). 1969: *Carry On Christmas*. 1970: *Carry On Again Christmas; Up Pompeii!* (guest appearance). 1972: *Carry On Stuffing*. 1973: *Wot a Carry On; Carry On Christmas; This Is Your Life* (Jimmy Logan). 1975: *Carry On Laughing* – 'The Prisoner of Spenda' (as Vera Basket/The Grand Duchess Ingrid of Coronia), 'The Baron Outlook' (as Marie), 'The Sobbing Cavalier' (as Sarah), 'Orgy and Bess' (as Lady Miranda), 'The Nine Old Cobblers' (as Maisie), 'And in My Lady's Chamber' (as Baroness Lottie Von Titenhausen), 'Who Needs Kitchener?' (as Baroness Lottie Von Titenhausen), 'Lamp-Posts of the Empire' (as Lady Mary Airey-Fairey).

1977: *Come Spy with Me*. 1980: *Worzel Gummidge* (2 series, as Saucy Nancy); *The Mike Walsh Show* (Australia). 1983: *Carry On Laughing's Christmas Classics*. 1984: *Whose Baby?* (with Kenneth Williams). 1986: *Movies from the Mansion - 50 Years of Pinewood* (special). 1987: *Super Gran* (as Ethel); *Wogan* (guest appearances); *It's a (Royal) Knockout; Filthy, Rich and Catflap* (as mum). 1988: *The Management* (as Aunt Vicky). 1989: *Norbert Smith - A Life (Carry On Banging)*; *Bluebirds* (series, as Mabel); *Sticky Moments with Julian Clary*. 1990: *Tales of the Rodent Sherlock Holmes; The New Celebrity Squares*. 1991: *That's Showbusiness; You Rang, M'Lord?* (series, as Myrtle). 1992: *This Is Your Life* (subject). 1994: *The South Bank Show* (Kenneth Williams, Obituary); *One Foot in the Grave* – 'The Affair of the Hollow Lady' (as Millicent); *Joan Littlewood's Lovely War* (doc.); *Noel's House Party*. 1994-2003, 2005-10: *EastEnders* (serial, as Peggy Mitchell/Butcher). 1995: *The Mrs Merton Show*. 1996: *Stop Messin' About – The Very Best of Kenneth Williams* (doc.); *Jim Davidson's Generation Game*. 1998: *Babs* (doc.); *A Perfect Carry On* (narrator); *What's a Carry On?* (doc.). 1999: *It's Only TV – But I Like It*. 1999: *Parkinson* (interview). 2000: *Barbara Windsor: BBC Hall of Fame. 2001: The Royal Variety Performance; You Only Live Once – Barbara Windsor; The Kumars at No. 42* (guest). 2005: *Disaster Masters* (narrator). 2006: *Doctor Who* (as Peggy Mitchell). 2010: *Piers Morgan's Life Stories: Barbara Windsor* (interview). 2011: *A Comedy Roast: Barbara Windsor. Come Fly With Me* (as herself).

Additional Credits
Numerous guest appearances on television chat & quiz shows.

RADIO
Includes:
1964: *Two Plus Two* (series, as Louella, with Patsy Rowlands); *Open House*. 1986-89: *Living with Betty* (series, with Rosalind Knight). 1992: *Carry On Up Yer Cinders*. 1994: *Carry On Carrying On!*

CD
1999: *You've Got a Friend* (reissued 2002, as *Smile*).

Patsy Rowlands

(b. Patricia Amy Rowlands)

Patsy Rowlands became a member of the 'regular' cast halfway through the *Carry On* series, a supporting actress in nine films and one episode of *Carry On Laughing*. A talented comedienne, Patsy became a figure of fun in the films and, despite an often dumpy exterior, her comic skills could never be underestimated.

Born in Palmers Green, London, on 19 January 1931 (Patsy Rowlands's death certificate states that she was born in 1931, not 1934), Patsy Rowlands was educated at a succession of convents. She won a scholarship at the age of fifteen and trained at the Guildhall School of Music and Drama (London).

At the age of seventeen Patsy made her first major stage appearance in the chorus of a tour of *Annie Get Your Gun*. Following in the footsteps of Hattie Jacques, she became a member of the Players' Theatre, and her big break came when she was spotted by Vida Hope and subsequently cast in *Valmouth*.

Patsy Rowlands made her film debut in 1960 and her subsequent screen appearances included *Tom Jones, Deadline for Diamonds, Joseph Andrews* and *Tess*. Patsy joined the *Carry On* team in 1969 in *Carry On Again Doctor*. Immediately she made a distinct impression as Miss Fosdick, a willing guinea pig for Kenneth Williams. After dancing cheek to cheek with Dr Nookey (Jim Dale) Miss Dempsey ends up as 'Saturday', the wife of Gladstone Screwer (Sidney James) in the tropical Beatific Islands.

Patsy's next *Carry On* appearance gave more scope for her comic ability. Cast as the dowdy Miss Dempsey, Mr Snooper's (Kenneth Williams) housekeeper, she transforms herself when female competition - in the form of Hattie Jacques - forces her to reveal her true feelings for her employer. She gallantly protects Snooper from wrestler Gripper Burke (Bernard Bresslaw), but in true *Carry On* form she ends up with a face full of custard pie! The following year Patsy was again teamed with Kenneth Williams in *Carry On At Your Convenience*, as the love-struck Miss Withering. It was one of her most memorable appearances, again playing the worm that turned!

Patsy had cameo roles in *Carry On Matron* (again with Williams, as his secretary) and *Carry On Abroad* (as Miss Dobbs) and was glimpsed only briefly as the unfortunate Queen in *Carry On Henry*. In 1973 she excelled by giving her best *Carry On* performance in *Carry On Girls*, as Mildred

Bumble. Dowdy, dreary and sloth-like, she finally rebels against her husband Mayor Bumble to sabotage Fircombe's beauty contest. It was a superb part for which she was ideally cast. Patsy appeared in a cameo role as the elderly country bumpkin Mrs Giles in *Carry On Dick* and made her final appearance in the series in *Carry On Behind* as Linda Upmore, a major character role in which she tries to keep the peace between her mother (Joan Sims) and husband (Bernard Bresslaw).

Although Patsy Rowlands did not join the *Carry On* films until the second half of the series, her nine appearances quite rightly resulted in her becoming a key member of the 'regular' team.

In the immediate years preceding the *Carry On*'s Patsy Rowlands remained busy, having cameo roles in several films up until 1980, as well as appearances in numerous television programmes. In the 1970s she was especially familiar in the television series *Bless This House* with fellow *Carry On* star Sid James. Her portrayal of Betty, the interfering, nosy neighbour, remains one of her best-known roles. In the late 1970s and early 1980s Patsy made numerous other small-screen appearances, including starring in *In Loving Memory, Hallelujah!* and *Kinvig*.

In the mid-1980s Patsy returned to the stage, where she worked consistently until the end of her career. In 1995 she was reunited with Jim Dale in a highly successful run of *Oliver!*, and she later received critical acclaim for her role in the stage musical *My Fair Lady,* with Dennis Waterman and Martine McCutcheon. On television her latter appearances included roles in *Bottom* (as Mrs Potato), *The Bill, Peak Practice* and *Vanity Fair*. In her final years she took part in several television documentaries, notably *Unforgettable Hattie Jacques* (2002), and she played Miss Millament in the 2001 television series *The Cazalets*.

Patsy was married to Malcolm Sircom and they had one son, Alan (b.1963), before their divorce.

In 1995 Patsy Rowlands was present at the gala screening of *Carry On Up the Khyber* and, although absent from the 40th Anniversary celebrations, she took part in the 1998 documentary *What's a Carry On*? Patsy was a special guest at several *Carry On* events at Pinewood Studios, including the *Carry On Stuffing* (1999) and *Carry On Loving* (2000) celebrations. She also provided commentary on DVD releases of the *Carry On*'s.

Patsy Rowlands was diagnosed as suffering from breast cancer while working on stage in *My Fair Lady*. In 2004 she officially retired from acting, although sadly her illness prevented her from fulfilling plans of becoming a drama teacher. Patsy died peacefully in a hospice in Hove on 22 January 2005, shortly after her seventy-fourth birthday. Her death was announced on the Internet by her son with the following statement:

Dear all,
I think you should all know that my mother, Patsy Rowlands, passed away at 6:20am, Saturday 22nd January 2005. She was never very good with mornings.
She died peacefully in her sleep.
Thank you all for your care, concern and kind wishes.
Alan Sircom

A memorial service for the popular actress was held at St Paul's Church, Covent Garden, on 29 April 2005.

Carry On ... ***Quotes***

Patsy Rowlands is another, painstaking Carry On *artist.*
Peter Rogers, 1998

Carry On **CREDITS 1969-75**
Again Doctor (Miss Fosdick); *Loving* (Miss Dempsey); *Henry* (Queen); *At Your Convenience* (Miss Hortence Withering); *Matron* (Miss Banks); *Abroad* (Miss Dobbs); *Girls* (Mildred Bumble); *Dick* (Mrs Giles); *Behind* (Linda Upmore).

STAGE
1951: First professional appearance in the chorus of *Annie Get Your Gun*. Subsequently appeared in repertory, summer shows and pantomime. 1955: *Beauty and the Beast* (Players'). 1956: *The Three Caskets* (Players', as Nerina); *Ali Baba and the Thirty-Nine Thieves* (Players', as Morgiana). 1957: *Zuleika* (124 performances, as Jessie, Saville); *King Charming* (Players', as Princess Florina). 1958-59: *Valmouth* (102 performances, Lyric, Hammersmith, & Saville, as Thetis Tooke). 1959: *One to Another* (37 performances, Apollo); *One-Way Pendulum* (163 performances, Criterion, as Sylvia). 1960: *Fool's Paradise* (as Ida). 1961: *The Three Caskets* (Players', as Nerina). 1962: *The Oldest Trick in the World* (as Miss Spencer). 1962-63: *Semi-Detached* (137 performances, Saville, as Avril Hadfield). 1964: *The Man Who Let It Rain* (Theatre Royal, Stratford, as Myrtle). 1964-65: *Chaganog* (revue, 57 performances, Vaudeville). 1966: *The Imaginary Invalid* & *The Miser* (double-bill, Mermaid); *Wanted: One Body* (Yvonne Arnaud, as Mabel Middy). 1966-67: *Let's Get a Divorce* (342 performances). 1967: *One In the Eye* (Yvonne Arnaud, Guilford). 1971:

The Licentious Fly (Mermaid, as Alice Ramsay). 1972: *Once Upon a Time* (Duke of York's). 1975: *The Seagull* (Lyric, as Paulina); *The Bed Before Yesterday* (Lyric). 1977: *Shut Your Eyes and Think of England* (Apollo). 1984: *Mother Goose* (Theatre Royal, Plymouth). 1986: *When We Are Married* (Whitehall, as Lottie Grady). 1987: *Pride and Prejudice* (tour, as Mrs Bennett). 1987-88: *The Pied Piper* (Olivier, as Lady Lucy Saveloy). 1988: *Bunter* (Northcott, Exeter, as Mrs Kessle). 1989: *The March on Russia* (tour). 1989: *Cinderella* (Theatre Royal, Newcastle, as Fairy Godmother). 1990: *Jubilee* (tour, as Eileen); *Into the Woods* (Phoenix, as Jack's mother). 1991: *The Wind in the Willows* (Olivier, as Hedgehog). 1994: *Me and My Girl* (tour, as Maria, Duchess of Dene). 1995-98: *Oliver Twist* (Palladium, as Mrs Bedwin). 1999-2000: *Beauty and the Beast* (as Mrs Potts). 2000: *Hard Times* (as Mrs Sleary). 2001: *My Fair Lady* (as Mrs Pearce, Lyttleton, Royal National & Drury Lane).

FILM

1961: *Over the Odds*; *In the Doghouse*; *On the Fiddle* (US: *Operation Snafu*). 1962: *A Kind of Loving; Vengeance* (aka: *The Brain*). 1963: *Tom Jones*. 1965: *Deadline for Diamonds*. 1967: *Switch in Time*. 1969: *Carry On Again Doctor*. 1970: *Carry On Loving*. 1971: *Carry On Henry*; *Carry On At Your Convenience*; *Please Sir!* 1972: *Carry On Matron*; *Bless This House*; *Carry On Abroad*; *Alice's Adventures in Wonderland*. 1973: *Carry On Girls*. 1974: *Carry On Dick*. 1975: *Carry On Behind*. 1977: *Joseph Andrews*. 1978: *Sammy's Super T-Shirt*. 1979: *Tess; The Fiendish Plot of Dr Fu Manchu*. 1980: *Little Lord Fauntleroy* (TV). 1981: *Dangerous Davies* (TV). 1990: *Crimestrike*. 1993: *Femme Fatale* (TV). 1998: *The Cater Street Hangman* (TV).

TELEVISION

Includes:

1959: *Gert and Daisy* (as Bonnie). 1960: *Stuff and Nonsense*. 1961 & 1966: *Danger Man*; *The Charlie Drake Show*. 1962: *The Amazing Doctor Clitterhouse; The Rivals* (as Julia). 1964: *The Massingham Affair* (series, as Georgina Deverel). 1965: *Out of the Unknown*. 1966: *Love Story* (as Pinkie Smith). 1967: *Sorry I'm Single* (as Mrs Budge); *Arthur Through the Looking Glass* (as Alice). 1968: *Public Eye*; *State of the Union* (as Gladys); *The Devil in the Fog* (as Mrs Dexter). 1968-70: *Inside George Wembley* (2 series, as Rosemary). 1969: *The Avengers; The Fabulous Frump* (The Wednesday Play, as Trixie); *The Ugliest Girl in Town; An Extra Bunch of Daffodils* (as Mildred Evans). 1970: *Z-Cars* (as Vera Pye). 1971: *For the Love of Ada; Père Goriot; Doctor at Large; Fathers and Sons*. 1971-76: *Bless This House* (as Betty). 1971: *Tottering Towers* (series, as Miss Twitty). 1973: *Ooh La La!* 1974: *Follow That Dog* (series, as Sgt Bryant, with Norman Rossington). 1975: *Carry On*

Laughing – 'The Nine Old Cobblers'; *Not On Your Nellie; Dawson's Weekly; The Basil Brush Show; A Touch of the Casanovas* (with Frankie Howerd). 1975-77: *The Squirrels* (2 series, as Susan). 1977: *Raven* (as Mrs Young). *Two's Company* (as Lil); *The Dick Emery Show*. 1979: *The History of Mr Polly; George and Mildred* (as Beryl); *My Son, My Son* (as Annie Suthurst). 1980: *The Nesbitts Are Coming* (series, as WPC Kitty Naylor); *Cribb* (as Mrs Body); *Can We Get on Now, Please?* 1981: *Robin's Nest; Juliet Bravo; Kinvig* (series, as Netta Kinvig); *Break in the Sun*. 1982: *Rep* (series, as Flossie Nightingale); *Wilfrid and Eileen; Legacy of Murder* (as Thelma). 1982 & '86: *In Loving Memory* (as Tiger-Lily Longstaff). 1983: *Hallelujah!* (series, as Sister Alice Meredith); *Perishing Solicitors*. 1985: *Super Gran* (as Lady Valerie Glutt). 1986: *Little Princess*. 1987: *Imaginary Friends; One By One; When We Are Married* (as Lottie Grady). 1987-89: *Rainbow* (3 episodes, as Auntie). 1989: *Never the Twain; Young Charlie Chaplin*. 1991: *Gone to the Dogs*. 1992: *Bottom* (as Mrs Potato); *In Dreams*. 1995: *The Bill* (as Rachel Armfield). 1995: *Kenneth Williams* (doc.). 1997: *Get Well Soon* (series, as Mrs Clapton). 1998: *Vanity Fair* (series, as Mrs Tinker); *What's a Carry On*? (doc.). 2000: *Unforgettable Hattie Jacques* (doc.); *Unforgettable Sid James* (doc.); *Peak Practice* (as Grace Page). 2001: *The Cazalets* (series, as Miss Millament). 2002: *Most Haunted; Good Food Live; Heroes of Comedy - Hattie Jacques* (doc.). 2003: *This Is Your Life* (Anthony Andrews).

Additional Credits

Imperial Palace; Mooncat and Company.

RADIO

Includes:

1964: *Two Plus Two* (series, as Maudie, with Barbara Windsor & Norman Rossington).

Jack Douglas

(b. John Roberton)

Jack Douglas joined the *Carry On* series in 1972 as the last member of the 'main' team. He went on to appear in every film during the remaining years of the series, including *Carry On Emmannuelle* and *Carry On Columbus*. His position within the series was further enhanced through television Christmas specials, twelve episodes of *Carry On Laughing*, and *Carry On London* on stage in the mid-1970s.

Jack Douglas was born in Newcastle upon Tyne on 26 April 1927. His connections to the theatre spanned four generations; his grandfather worked in silent films, his father was the late impresario John D. Roberton and his brother was the late stage director Bill Roberton.

Jack began his show business career at the age of eleven as a stagehand and scenic artist. Less than four years later, under his father's orders, he directed his first pantomime. By the age of nineteen Jack was working as a professional stand-up comedian and made his professional stage 'debut' with the Combined Services Entertainments Unit in *Hi There*. During his early stage days he was frequently teamed with Joe Baker (1928-2001), often in pantomime.

Jack Douglas went on to work as a 'stooge' for many of Britain's top comedians, including Benny Hill, Arthur Askey and Bruce Forsyth. Lasting fame came via his comic character Alf Ippititimus. This nervy, twitching, hilarious creation in flat cap and steel-rimmed spectacles secured Jack a long-standing stage and television partnership with Des O'Connor (spanning twelve years and over fifty television appearances). In 1969 the pair stole the show at the Royal Variety Performance and went on to appear on *The Ed Sullivan Show* in America. Ultimately the success of 'Alf' resulted in Jack becoming a member of the regular cast in the *Carry On* series.

Tall (6ft 3in) and dark-haired, Jack made his *Carry On* debut as the Twitching Father in *Carry On Matron*. This classic one-line cameo appearance set the tone for roles throughout the remainder of the series. In *Carry On Abroad* he was seen in a supporting role as the beer-swigging Harry, again in the character of 'Alf'. In the following year he graduated to a character part as William, the hotel porter, in *Carry On Girls*. Once again Alf Ippititimus shines through, with Jack relishing the opportunity for a larger screen role. A notably increased contribution to the series followed for Jack in *Carry On Dick*, playing the surprisingly competent (and awfully named!) Sergeant Jock Strapp. In *Carry On Behind* Jack returned to the cloth cap and steel-rimmed glasses of Alf in a leading role opposite Windsor Davies in *Carry On Behind*. The twitch would continue as he played Bombardier Ready in *Carry On England*.

During 1975 Jack Douglas helped to secure his place in the *Carry On* team with appearances in twelve episodes of *Carry On Laughing*, most memorably as Lord Peter Flimsey, the aristocratic detective, opposite Kenneth Connor. In addition, Jack also appeared in television Christmas specials and joined many leading cast members on stage in *Carry On London* (1973-75). In the wake of the death of Sid James, Jack starred in *Carry On Laughing at the Slimming Factory* on stage in 1976.

In *Carry On Emmannuelle* Jack completely abandoned his Ippititimus creation to play the butler, Lyons. It was his only leading role in the series and he gave an admirable performance in spite of the poor script and storyline. Fourteen years later Jack was one of the few veteran actors to return for an appearance in *Carry On Columbus*. Sadly, he was relegated to a shamefully small cameo role (he can be seen opposite Jim Dale and later in the film with Rebecca Lacey) with only a couple of lines throughout the entire film. For the actor himself it was a distinctly forgettable experience, although for fans it was at least a chance to see the popular comedian on the big screen again.

Following the demise of the *Carry On* series Jack Douglas went on to appear in several television series in the early 1980s, notably *Shillingbury Tales* and *Cuffy*, with Bernard Cribbins (q.v.). However, he found the character of Alf difficult to shake off and in the last two decades of his career the majority of his work was on stage, where he also directed.

In his final years a great deal of Jack's time was devoted to promoting the revived interest in the *Carry On* films. He attended most events associated with the series, including the 40th Anniversary celebrations in 1998, where he unveiled a British Comedy Society plaque in memory of Sidney James.* Despite failing health in the last few years of his life, Jack continued to delight fans with his public appearances, which included final visits to Pinewood Studios in April 2007 (to celebrate his eightieth birthday) and April 2008 (for the 50th Anniversary celebrations). He also provided commentaries for DVD releases of the films.

Jack's first marriage ended in divorce and he subsequently married actress Su Douglas (q.v.). From his first marriage Jack had a son, Craig, and daughter, Deborah, and from his second marriage he had a daughter, Sarah. His final partner until his death was Vivien Howell. In private Jack enjoyed cooking, and after contributing to several magazines his first cookery book *The Whey-Hey Guide to Cookery*, was published in 1997. He was also a DIY expert, and his own experience as a stage carpenter resulted in his own TV series and his self-designed homes featured in several magazines. His other hobbies included jazz and designing his own clothes.

From 1997 Jack Douglas lived in Shanklin on the Isle of Wight. He died there from pneumonia on 18 December 2008, aged eighty-one.

* Some of the celebratory events attended by Jack included:

1992: present at the unveiling of a plaque for Sid James, organised by The Dead Comics' Society.

1994: (with Liz Fraser and Valerie Leon) represented the *Carry On* series at 'Action – British Film Production' at Pinewood Studios.

1995: present at the unveiling of a British Comedy Society plaque in memory of Gerald Thomas at Pinewood Studios. Promoted the *Carry On* film festival – *Carry On* Up the Barbican - and appeared in *The Big City* with Peter Rogers, Fenella Fielding and Nicholas Parsons.

1998: 40th Anniversary Reunion at Pinewood Studios.

1999: special guest at *Carry On Stuffing* at Pinewood Studios

2001: special guest at *Carry On at Pinewood* (Pinewood Studios).

2002: special guest at Pinewood Studios to release his autobiography (*A Twitch in Time*, with Sue Benwell) and celebrate his 75th birthday.

2002: special guest at the unveiling of a Heritage Foundation plaque for Joan Sims.

2007: 80th birthday celebrations at Pinewood Studios (attended by Angela Douglas, Shirley Eaton, Fenella Fielding, Alan Hume, Mrs Valerie James, Valerie Leon, Lance Percival, Jacki Piper, Peter Rogers and Madeline Smith).

2008: special guest at the *Carry On* 50th Anniversary celebrations.

*Carry On ... **Quotes***

Jack Douglas came to the Carry On's *with a cloth cap and a twitch but developed into a serious actor.*
Peter Rogers, 1998

Carry On **CREDITS 1972-92**

Matron (Twitching Father); *Abroad* (Harry); *Girls* (William); *Dick* (Sergeant Jock Strapp); *Behind* (Ernie Bragg); *England* (Bombardier Ready); *Emmannuelle* (Lyons); *Columbus* (Marco the Cereal Killer).

STAGE

Includes:

1946: *Hi There* (King's Palace, Preston). 1949: *Dick Whittington* (as Captain). 1955: *Aladdin* (Empire, Chiswick). 1957: *Showtime* (Alexandra Gardens, Weymouth). 1957: *Dick Whittington* (Alexandra, Birmingham). 1958: *Light Up the Town* (Hippodrome, Blackpool); in variety (Prince of

Wales, London). 1959: *New Look & Jubilee Show* (Palace, Blackpool); *Robinson Crusoe* (Empire, Finsbury Park). 1960: *Let's Make a Night of It* (Pavilion, Weymouth); *Robin Hood* (Bradford). 1961: *Startime* (Royal Aquarium, Great Yarmouth). 1962: *What a Racket* (Pavilion, Torquay); *The Birthday Show* (Coventry Theatre). 1963: *Humpty Dumpty* (Grand, Leeds, with Des O'Connor). 1964: *All In Favour* (Britannia, Great Yarmouth, with Des O'Connor); *Cinderella* (New, Oxford, with Des O'Connor). 1965: *The Spring Show* (Coventry, with Des O'Connor); *Aladdin* (Palace, Manchester, with Des O'Connor). 1966: *Showtime* (North Pier, Blackpool, with Des O'Connor); *Cinderella* (Palladium, as Baron Hardup, with Cliff Richard). 1967: *Showtime* (Pavilion, Bournemouth, with Des O'Connor); *Cinderella* (Palace, Manchester, with Des O'Connor). 1968: *Don't Tell the Wife* (as Alf Willis); *Cinderella* (Hippodrome, Birmingham, with Des O'Connor). 1969: *Don't Tell the Wife* (Windmill, Great Yarmouth, as Alf Willis); *Babes in the Wood* (New, Cardiff). 1970: *Don't Tell the Wif*e (Pavilion, Torquay); *Babes in the Wood* (Royal, Nottingham). 1971: *When the Wife's Away* (Windmill, Great Yarmouth); *Dick Whittington* (as Idle Jack). 1972: *The Love Nest* (Grand, Blackpool); *Puss in Boots* (Alexandra, Birmingham, as Alf). 1973-75: *Carry On London* (Victoria Palace). 1975: *Aladdin* (Richmond Theatre). 1976: *Carry On Laughing at the Slimming Factory* (Royal Opera House, Scarborough, as Jack Hardy); *Jack and the Beanstalk* (Theatre Royal, Newcastle). 1978: *Robinson Crusoe* (Churchill, Bromley). 1979: *Cinderella* (Coventry Theatre). 1980: *The Sleeping Beauty* (Pavilion, Bournemouth, directed & co-wrote with Lance Percival). 1981: *Make and Break* (Royal, Windsor & tour, as John Garrard); *Robinson Crusoe* (Ashcroft, Croydon, with Kenneth Connor). 1982: *A Sting in the Tail* (Yvonne Arnaud, Guildford); *Cinderella* (Alexandra, Birmingham). 1983: *Habeas Corpus* (tour); *Cinderella*. 1985: *Spring and Port Wine* (tour); *Don't Tell the Wife; Aladdin*. 1986-87: *Whodunnit* (tour, as Rear Admiral Knatchbull Folliatt). 1988: *Fur Coat and No Knickers* (tour); *Annie*. 1989: *Up in the Gallery* (tour); *Dick Whittington* (Civic Hall, Guildford). 1990: *Robinson Crusoe*. 1991: *Wife Begins at Forty* (tour, as Bernard Harper); *Cinderella* (Marlowe, Canterbury). 1992: *Cinderella* (Swan, High Wycombe, as Baron Hardup). 1993 & '94: *Cinderella*. 1996: *Cinderella* (Grand, Blackpool). 1997: *Sting in the Tail* (Shanklin, Isle of Wight). 1998: *Babes in the Wood*. 1999: *The Fareham Follies* (Fernham Hall, Fareham). 2000: *Cinderella* (Playhouse, Weston Super Mare). 2001-02: *Cinderella* (Crewe Theatre). 2002-03: *Jack and the Beanstalk* (Pavilion, Rhyl).

Additional Credits
Oliver! (as Fagin); *Treasure Island* (musical, as Long John Silver).

FILM

1962: *Nearly a Nasty Accident*. 1964: *Tokyo Olympiad* (voice only). 1972: *Carry On Matron*; *Carry On Abroad*. 1973: *Carry On Girls*. 1974: *Carry On Dick*. 1975: *Carry On Behind*. 1976: *Carry On England*. 1977: *What's Up Nurse?* 1978: *Carry On Emmannuelle*. 1980: *The Shillingbury Tales*. 1983: *The Boys in Blue*; *Bloody Kids*. 1992: *Carry On Columbus*.

TELEVISION

Includes:

1956-57: *Bold Journey*. 1958: *Ignorants Abroad* (as Jack). 1958-59: *New Look* (2 series). 1963-67 & 1970-71: *The Des O'Connor Show* (over 50 appearances in 7 series). 1964: *Dave's Kingdom*. 1967: *The Good Old Days*. 1969: *The Royal Variety Performance*. 1972: *The Edwardians*; *Carry On Stuffing*. 1973: *Carry On Christmas*. 1974: *The Reluctant Juggler*; *The Goodies*. 1975: *Carry On Laughing* – 'The Prisoner of Spenda' (as Colonel Yackoff), 'The Sobbing Cavalier' (as Sir Jethro Houndsbotham), 'Orgy and Bess' (as Lord Essex & master of the rolls), 'One in the Eye for Harold' (as Ethelred), 'The Nine Old Cobblers' (as Lord Peter Flimsey), 'The Case of the Screaming Winkles' (as Lord Peter Flimsey), 'The Case of the Coughing Parrot' (as Lord Peter Flimsey), 'Under the Round Table' (as Sir Gay), 'Short Knight, Long Daze' (as Sir Gay), 'And in My Lady's Chamber' (as Clodson), 'Who Needs Kitchener?' (as Clodson), 'Lamp-Posts of the Empire' (as Elephant Dick Darcy). 1975: *Not On Your Nellie* (series, as Stanley Pickersgill). 1979: *And the Band Played On*. 1980: *The Allan Stewart Tapes* (series); *The Shillingbury Tales* (series, as Jake). 1981: *The End of the Pier Show* (as Mr Pumphrey). 1983: *Cuffy* (series, as Jake). 1985: *This Is Your Life* (subject). 1989: *Norbert Smith – a Life* (*Carry On Banging*, as Greenham Guard). 1995: *Kenneth Williams* (doc.); *The Big City*. 1998: *What's a Carry On?* (doc.) 2000: *Unforgettable Sid James* (doc.). 2002: *When Louis Met Keith Harris and Orville*.

Additional Credits

The Ed Sullivan Show; *Crackerjack* (regular); *The Jimmy Clitheroe Show*; *Pebble Mill*.

Terry Scott

(b. Owen John Scott)

A gifted comedian, Terry Scott was an invaluable addition to the *Carry On* series, and his seven appearances in the series were enough to secure a place as a member of the 'regular' team. It was a position worthy of his talents.

Born in Watford on 4 May 1927, Terry Scott trained as an accountant, after some pressure from his parents. He served in the Navy during the war and after being demobbed seized his chance to begin a career in show business.

Terry began his career as a stage manager before making his first professional appearance in repertory at Grange-over-Sands. This was followed by many years of work in clubs, pubs, pantomime (for which he was to become noted) and summer shows. In 1956 Terry made his television debut with Bill Maynard (q.v.) in *Great Scott, It's Maynard!*, the first of many successful television series.

Following his small-screen debut Terry spent eighteen months at the Whitehall Theatre, at the invitation of (Lord) Brian Rix. This was followed by another television success, with Hugh Lloyd, in *Hugh and I,* which ran for eight series. Further television triumphs came with *Scott On...* and *Son of the Bride*, a series written for him by John Kane, in which he played the hen-pecked son of Mollie Sugden (1922-2009). Perhaps Terry's most memorable television moments were with June Whitfield (q.v.). The pair had first teamed up in 1974 for the series *Happy Ever After* and later found lasting success in *Terry and June*. Terry Scott played the role of Terry Medford in *Terry and June* for 65 episodes over ten series, despite serious health problems at both the beginning and later stages of the eight-year run. It was arguably his finest television role. Indeed, audiences were so convinced by the performances of Terry and June that many mistakenly believed that the couple was married in real life!

As well as television success Terry Scott was to become a much-celebrated pantomime 'Dame'. His appearances in panto included the Ugly Sister in *Cinderella* and Dame in *Babes in the Wood, Mother Goose* and *Aladdin*. Acclaim also came for his work in *The Mating Game*, in which he first appeared in 1969. In later years he became especially associated with the plays of Dave Freeman (including *A Bedfull of Foreigners*) and Ray Cooney (notably in *Run for Your Wife*).

Plump, brown-haired and adept at blustering roles, Terry made his *Carry On* debut as a young-looking Sergeant Paddy O'Brien in the first film, *Carry On Sergeant*. He returned to the series a decade later with a brilliant portrayal as the bellowing Sergeant Major MacNutt in *Carry On Up the Khyber*. Terry's scenes with Charles Hawtrey provided classic *Carry On* situations. The pair continued their hate/hate relationship in *Carry On Camping*, while Terry also had to cope with an infuriating wife (and her laugh!) in the form of Betty Marsden (q.v.). Terry suffered throughout *Camping* with thistles, raging bulls, gunshot wounds and a burning backside, but ultimately ended up the victor. Terry was also memorable as the bumbling Cardinal Wolsey in *Carry On Henry* and tried his hand at something of a leading role, as Terence, in *Carry On Loving*. Possibly Terry's finest *Carry On* role was as Cecil (Ug Ug/Jungle Boy) in *Carry On Up the Jungle*, a *Carry On* send-up of Tarzan. Here Terry tried to avoid 'concealed trees' and struggled to master the English language. Although his dialogue consisted largely of grunts it was a unique performance. Terry's last appearance in the series was as the sex-mad Dr Prodd in *Carry On Matron*. In the same year he also appeared in the film version of *Bless This House*, as Sid James's pompous neighbour, Frederick. Not surprisingly, as one of Britain's foremost television actors, Terry appeared in two *Carry On* Christmas specials, giving the comedian a total of nine *Carry On* appearances.

Terry Scott brought a very special talent to the *Carry On* series, often fitting into roles that were somewhere between a leading man and a character player. Other leading male actors in the films often had very definite typecasts, which interestingly did not apply to Scott, who was well known in the business as an absolute perfectionist.

Terry Scott was married (secondly) to former ballet dancer and drama teacher Margaret Pollen, whom he met on stage in 1957. They had four daughters: Sarah, Nicola, Lindsay and actress Alessandra Scott. Terry and Margaret were also proud grandparents. Although invariably busy on stage and television and a self-confessed workaholic, in private Terry enjoyed spending time in the garden of his home in Surrey.

In 1979 Terry underwent brain surgery following an aneurysm, from which he successfully recovered. In the mid-1980s came a further setback when he was diagnosed with cancer of the bladder and he suffered a nervous breakdown. Once again Terry courageously overcame his health problems and personal anxiety to continue a busy career on stage and television.

Terry provided the voice of Penfold in the popular cartoon *Danger Mouse* until 1991 and was well enough to undertake a Far and Middle East tour of *Run for Your Wife*, which ran until the beginning of 1992. Terry Scott made his final stage appearance in May 1992, in a short season of *A Bedfull of Foreigners*. Sadly, he was too ill to travel to Pinewood for *Carry On Columbus* later that same year.

Terry Scott died from cancer at his home in Guildford on 26 July 1994, aged sixty-seven. A fine comic actor and *Carry On* performer, he was sincerely mourned and in 2001 was honoured with a British Comedy Society plaque, unveiled at Pinewood Studios.

Carry On ... ***Quotes***

Terry Scott came to us from his own comedy show and stayed until his death. He again could play anything and his comedy timing was perfect.
Peter Rogers, 1998

Carry On **CREDITS 1958-72**
Sergeant (Sgt Paddy O'Brien); *Up the Khyber* (Sgt Major MacNutt); *Camping* (Peter Potter); *Up the Jungle* (Cecil the Jungle Boy/Ug Ug); *Loving* (Terry Philpotts); *Henry* (Cardinal Wolsey); *Matron* (Dr Prodd).

STAGE
Began his career as a stage manager, followed by repertory and work in pubs, clubs, pantomime, summer shows and 18 months at the Whitehall Theatre. 1954: *Into the Sun* (Newquay, with Hugh Lloyd). 1954: *Jack and the Beanstalk* (Connaught, Worthing). 1955: *Out of the Blue* (Pier Pavilion, Southend); *The Sleeping Beauty* (Theatre Royal, Leeds, as the Orphan). 1956: *Out of the Blue* (Spa Pavilion, Felixstowe). 1957: *Out of the Blue* (White Rock Pavilion, Hastings). 1959: *Four Men for the Job* (Palace, Watford); *The Russ Conway Show; Jack and Jill* (Hippodrome, Golders Green). 1960: *Make It Tonight; Mother Goose* (title role). 1961: *One for the Pot* (Whitehall, as Jonathan Hardcastle). 1962: *Babes in the Wood* (Hippodrome, Golders Green, (as Dame). 1963-64: *Let's Make a Night of It.* 1965: *Jack & Jill* (Hippodrome, Golders Green). 1966: *Cinderella* (Palladium, as Ugly Sister). 1967: *I Want to See Musov* (Whitehall & tour). 1968: *Robin Hood.* 1969: *Cinderella* (Theatre Royal, Newcastle, as Ugly Sister). 1970: *The Mating Game* (tour, as James Harris); *Aladdin* (Palladium, as Widow Twankey). 1971: *Cinderella* (Palladium, as Ugly Sister). 1972: *The Mating Game* (Apollo, as James Harris). 1973: *Babes in the Wood* (New, Oxford, as Nurse). 1974: *The Mating Game* (Palladium, Torquay, as James Harris); *Mother Goose* (Richmond, title role). 1975: *A Bedfull of Foreigners* (UK & South African tour & Victoria Palace). 1977: *Aladdin* (Alexandria, Birmingham, as Widow Twankey). 1977-78: *A*

Bedfull of Foreigners (Pier, Bournemouth, & Hong Kong). 1978: *Aladdin* (Congress, Eastbourne). 1979: *Murder in a Bad Light* (tour); *A Bedfull of Foreigners*. 1980: *A Bedfull of Foreigners* (Jersey). 1981: *Jack and the Beanstalk*. 1982: *A Bedfull of Foreigners* (tour, Middle & Far East). 1983: *Run for Your Wife* (Shaftsbury); *Babes in the Wood* (with Bernard Bresslaw). 1984: *The School for Wives* (Churchill, Bromley); *The Wind in the Willows* (Yvonne Arnaud, Guildford). 1985: *Jack and the Beanstalk* (Theatre Royal, Bath, with June Whitfield). 1986: *Run for Your Wife* (Criterion, as John Smith); *Jack and the Beanstalk* (Yvonne Arnaud, Guildford). 1987: *Jack and the Beanstalk* (Ashcroft, Croydon). 1988: *Run for Your Wife* (Criterion). 1989: *The Mating Game* (Bournemouth). 1990: *Run for Your Wife* (Whitehall, Aldwych & Duchess). 1991-92: *Run for Your Wife* (tour, Far & Middle East). 1992: *A Bedfull of Foreigners* (Pier, Bournemouth).

FILM

1957: *Blue Murder at St Trinian's*. 1958: *Too Many Crooks*; *Carry On Sergeant*. 1959: *The Bridal Path; I'm All Right Jack*. 1960: *And the Same to You; Double Bunk; The Night We Got the Bird*. 1961: *No, My Darling Daughter; A Pair of Briefs; Mary Had a Little...; Nothing Barred; What a Whopper.* 1962: *Nearly a Nasty Accident*. 1963: *Father Came Too*. 1964: *Murder Most Foul*. 1965: *Gonks Go Beat*. 1966: *The Great St Trinian's Train Robbery*; *Doctor in Clover* (US: *M.D. Carnaby*). 1968: *A Ghost of a Chance*; *Carry On Up the Khyber*. 1969: *Carry On Camping*. 1970: *Carry On Up the Jungle*; *Carry On Loving*; *Carry On Henry*. 1972: *Carry On Matron*; *Bless This House*. 1982: *The Pantomime Dame*. 1987: *Mr. H Is Late* (TV, short).

TELEVISION

Includes:

1955-58: *Great Scott, It's Maynard!*. 1957: *Scott Free* (series, as Terry). 1964: *Scott On Birds*. 1965: *Scott On Money*. 1962-66: *Hugh and I*. 1968: *Hugh and I Spy*. 1969: *The Gnomes of Dulwich* (series, as Big). 1969: *Carry On Christmas*. 1969-74: *Scott On ....* 1970: *Carry On Again Christmas* (as Squire Treyhornay). 1973: *Son of the Bride* (series); *Robin Hood*. 1974-78: *Happy Ever After* (5 series, as Terry Fletcher). 1979-87: *Terry and June* (10 series, as Terry Medford). 1981-87 & 1991-92: *Danger Mouse* (voice, as Penfold).

Additional Credits

The Good Old Days; The Norman Wisdom Show; Looks Familiar; Whodunnit? ; Saturday Night at the Mill; Celebrity Squares; Give Us a Clue; Vintage Quiz; We Love TV.

RADIO
Includes:
Stand Easy. 1964: *One Man's Meat* (as Terry Binks).

A-Y of Supporting Actors

Jill Adams (b. Jill Siggins)

Light leading lady Jill Adams appeared in a variety of films in the 1950s and 1960s. Regrettably, however, she made just one appearance in the *Carry On* series. She can be seen as the ultra-blonde WPC Harrison (Leslie Phillips's love interest) in the opening and closing scenes of *Carry On Constable*.

Jill Adams was born in London on 22 July 1930 and grew up in Hampshire and Wales. She began her career as a model and worked as a film extra in *The Black Knight* before making her screen debut in *One Jump Ahead* (1954). During her relatively short acting career she appeared in over twenty films, mainly under contract with the Rank Organisation, including *Chance Meeting* (1954), *The Young Lovers* (1954), *The Love Match* (1955), *Doctor at Sea* (1955), *Private's Progress* (1956), *The Green Man* (1957), *Dust in the Sun* (1958), *Death Over My Shoulder* (1958), *The Comedy Man* and *Doctor in Distress* (1963).

She also made sporadic appearances on television, notably as Mary in *The Flying Doctors* (1959). Sadly, the husky-voiced actress was mainly seen as 'decoration' in many of her screen appearances and her acting career ended with her role as Mrs B.M. Von Crispin in *Promise Her Anything* in 1966.

In 1951 Jill Adams married David Adams, an American Navy yeoman, with whom she had one daughter, Tina. Jill married secondly to actor and radio personality Peter Haigh (1925-2001), with whom she had another daughter, Peta Louise. Following her divorce from Haigh, Jill had two long-term relationships. From 1971 she spent her time living in Spain and Portugal running restaurants and pursuing her artistic interests. Her final years, as a mother, grandmother and great-grandmother, were spent exhibiting her paintings and sculptures locally.

Jill died at her home in Clareanse (following a three-year battle with cancer) on 13 May 2008, aged seventy-seven.

Holly Aird

Leading film and television actress, Holly Aird was among the new recruits cast for *Carry On Columbus* when she played the dewy-eyed Maria, opposite Peter Richardson (q.v.).

Holly Aird was born in Aldershot, Hampshire, on 18 May 1969. She trained at the Bush Davis Dance and Education School and made her television debut at the age of ten as the Young Miss Polly in *The History of Mr Polly*. She subsequently went on to receive critical acclaim as Elspeth in *The Flame Trees of Thika* (1981, with Hayley Mills), and by the time she had reached her early twenties she had appeared in a variety of productions including *Affairs of the Heart* (1985, as Rosemary Bonamy), *Double First* (1988, as Ellen Hobson) and Agatha Christie's *They Do It with Mirrors* (1991, as Gina Hudd, with Joan Hickson, q.v.).

By the mid-1990s Holly had established herself as one of the country's leading young actresses, having successfully navigated the path from child star to leading lady. Her television work as an adult has ranged from drama such as *Solider Soldier* (1991-93 & '95), as Nancy Thorpe/Garvey, to sitcoms including *Dressing for Dinner* (1995, as Cara).

A string of film roles followed, including *Intimate Relations* (1996), *Fever Pitch* (1997), *The Criminal* (1998), *Dreaming of Joseph Lees* (1999) and *Possession* (2001), before Holly took on the role of forensic pathologist Frankie Wharton in the BBC series *Waking the Dead* (2000-04), for which she is now perhaps best known. Her recent small-screen credits include *Casualty* (2006), *Torn* (2007), *Monday Monday* (2009), *Identity* (2010) and *The Promise* (2011). She looks set to continue a busy acting career for many years to come.

Holly Aird was married to actor James Purefoy (1964-) and they had one son, Joseph (b.1997). Her second husband is actor Toby Merritt and they have one daughter Nelly (b.2004).

Yemi Ajibade

Yemi played the Nosha Witch Doctor in *Carry On Up the Jungle*. Born in Nigeria, his irregular acting credits have since included the television series *The Black Safari* (1972) and the 1991 tele-movie *London Kills Me*.

Terence Alexander

Among the all-star cast of *Carry On Regardless*, Terence Alexander can be seen as Trevor Trelawney, the harassed husband who calls on the help of interpreter Kenneth Williams to resolve an argument with his fiery foreign wife (Julia Arnall, q.v.)!

A well-known actor of stage, screen and television, and latterly most familiar as Charlie Hungerford in nine series of *Bergerac* (1981-91), Terence was born in London on 11 March 1923. After a brief period as an acting ASM he made his theatrical debut in 1939. His stage appearances over the next forty years would include *Ring For Catty* (1956), *Two and Two Make Sex* (1973) and *Habeus Corpus* (1980).

After making his screen debut in 1947 Terence, with his ready grin and easy manner, became a light leading man in over forty films ranging from *The Elusive Pimpernel* (1950) to *That Englishwoman* (1990).

Terence Alexander made his television debut in 1951 and appeared in countless series, including *Garry Halliday* (1959-62, with Terence

Longdon), *The Forsyte Saga* (1967, as Montague Dartie) and two series of *Devenish* (1977-78, as Hugh Fitzjoy). He also made guest appearances in comedy classics such as *Hancock's Half Hour* and the *Dick Emery Show* and played Sir Greville in four series of *The New Statesman* (1987-92), with Rik Mayal (q.v.).

Terence was semi-retired from acting from the mid-1990s because of failing sight but still did the odd job if it was 'pleasant' into his mid-seventies, with final credits including television commercials in Sweden and a guest appearance in *Casualty* in 1999.

Terence was married to actress Juno Stevas and they had two sons, Nicholas and Marcus, before they divorced. In 1976 Terence married his second wife, actress Jane Downs. After suffering from Parkinson's disease in his final years, Terence Alexander died in London on 28 May 2009, at the age of eighty-six.

*Carry On ... **Quotes***

I fear I can't tell you anything much about the Carry On *films as I was only in one of them,* Carry On Regardless, *and even then, I think, only filmed for abut four days. I do remember talking to Freddie Mills the boxer, who was also in it and who was tragically killed sometime afterwards outside his club in Soho.*
Terence Alexander, 1997

Andrea Allan

Andrea, who was born in Glasgow on 18 November 1946, played Minnie, one of the saloon girls in *Carry On Cowboy*. Her additional film appearances included *The Wrong Box* (1966), *Assignment K* (1968) and a leading role in *Scream and Die!* (1973).

Keith Allen

Now one of Britain's leading character actors, well known for playing a variety of 'menacing' roles, Keith Allen was among a select group of up-and-coming alternative comedians when he played Pepi the Poisoner in *Carry On Columbus*.

Born on 2 June 1953, Keith began his career as a stand-up comedian before making his mark on television in the early 1980s in series such as *The Young Ones*, and he went on to become a mainstay of *The Comic Strip Presents ...*

As recalled by co-star Maureen Lipman (q.v.), Keith is an unpredictable actor "...with an air of barely suppressed danger about him and a tendency to rip his clothing off at the least possible provocation". It has been well recorded that on the set of *Columbus* veteran stars and the alternative comedians like Keith Allen mixed like oil and water. At the end of filming he did, however, endear himself to Lipman as she later revealed in *When's It Coming Out?* (1992).

By the mid-1990s Allen had proved himself to be a capable 'star' character actor and received critical acclaim for his role in the 1994 adaptation of *Martin Chuzzlewit*, opposite Sir John Mills and Paul Schofield. In more recent years Keith has continued a busy small-screen career with series such as *Roger Roger* (1998, as Dexter), *Jack of Hearts* (1999, as Jack Denby), *Bob Martin* (2000, as Vinnie), *Adrian Mole: The Cappuccino Years* (2001, as Peter Savage) and *Bodies* (2004-06, as Tony Whitman), and he played Inspector Graves in *Marple: The Moving Finger* (2006). He gained a new legion of fans as the Sheriff of Nottingham in *Robin Hood* (2006-09) and played *Danny Dixon in The Runaway* (2011).

Keith has also made numerous film appearances over the past thirty years, including *Crystal Gazing* (1982), *The Supergrass* (1985), *Comrades* (1987), *Chicago Joe and the Showgirl* (1989), *Second Best* (1994), *Loch Ness* (1996), *Trainspotting* (1996), *Twin Town* (1997), *Rancid Aluminium* (2000), *The Others* (2001), *De-Lovely* (2004), *The Good Night* (2007) and *A Film with Me in It* (2008).

Twice married, Keith has three children including singer Lily Allen (1985-) and actor Alfie Allen (1986-). His autobiography *Grow Up* was published in 2007.

Patrick Allen

As the voice behind thousands of television and radio commercials and as the narrator of dozens of films, Patrick Allen was often billed as the King of voice-overs. His easily recognisable tones can be heard in *Carry On Don't Lose Your Head*, *Doctor* and *Up the Khyber.*

Patrick was born in Malawi on 17 March 1927 and came to Britain as a child before being evacuated to Canada during the Second World War. In the early years of his career his forbidding good looks saw him cast in leading roles, often as villainous types, and he made over forty film appearances including *1984* (1955), *The Long Haul* (1957), *Dunkirk* (1958), *When Dinosaurs Ruled the Earth* (1969), *The Wild Geese* (1978), *The Sea Wolves* (1980) and *Bullet from Beijing* (1995).

In addition to countless voice-over and narration credits, Patrick also appeared in a variety of television series after making his small-screen debut in 1947, most notably the lead role in *Crane* in the early 1960s. In later years he made guest appearances in *Bergerac, The Black Adder* (1983) and *Andrew and Fergie: Behind Palace Doors* (1994, as Major Ferguson).

Patrick Allen married 1950s leading lady Sarah Lawson (b.1928) in 1956 and they had two sons, Stephen and Stuart. Both Patrick and Sarah were semi-retired from acting from the mid-1990s and enjoyed spending time with their children and grandchildren. Patrick, according to his wife, also spent a great deal of time indulging in his favourite hobby - "his fishing"!

Patrick died on 28 July 2006, aged seventy-nine.

Bart Allison

Bart, who played Grandpa in *Carry On Doctor* and Imogen Hassall's Grandpa Grubb in *Carry On Loving*, had a screen career stretching back to the 1950s. He played the auctioneer in *A Kid for Two Farthings* in 1955 and ended up as the Old Priest in *The Ritz* in 1976. He died in 1981, aged in his 80th year.

John Antrobus

John Antrobus is well known in the *Carry On* world as both a writer and bit-part actor.

As well as writing the film (and play) *The Bed-Sitting Room* (1969), John wrote films such as *Idol on Parade* (1959) and *Jazz Boat* (1960). In the *Carry On*'s he is credited as the writer of 'additional' material for both the first and last films (*Carry On Sergeant* in 1958 and *Carry On Columbus* thirty-four years later), and as a bit-part actor in *Carry On Constable* (as a citizen) and *Carry On Columbus* (as Jim Dale's manservant).

Aside from his screen credits, John has also written for hundreds of television programmes, including *Early to Braden* (1957), *Bootsie and Snudge* in the early 1960s, *That Was The Week That Was, The Dustbinmen* (1970), *Room at the Bottom* (& creator, 1986) and *Get Well Soon* (1997, featuring Patsy Rowlands, q.v.). In addition, he shares numerous writing credits with Spike Milligan, of whom he has also written a book, *Surviving Spike Milligan* (2003).

Born in Woolwich, London, on 2 July 1933, John lives in London with his partner Nicole.

Carry On ... ***Quotes***

After Carry On Sergeant, *Peter Rogers offered me £5,000 to write the next three film scripts. We met at the Dorchester for tea, Gerald Thomas too. But I*

declined, wanting to become a playwright …
John Antrobus, 2007

Mark Arden

Mark Arden, who played Mark in *Carry On Columbus*, was born on 31 July 1956. He made his first appearances on television in the late 1970s and during the 1980s he was a familiar face on the small screen in programmes such as *The Young Ones, Happy Families* and *The Comic Strip Presents….* On television he also played Captain Skip Chip in *Space Vets* (1992) and has also had the occasional dramatic role, including appearances in *Heartbeat* and *EastEnders*.

Mark's screen credits include *London's Burning* (1986), *There's No Business* (1994), *Drunk and Disorderly* (1995), *Charlie* (2004) and *Getting Out* (2008).

Julia Arnall

In her only *Carry On* appearance Julia Arnall played Trudy Trelawney, Terence Alexander's irate foreign wife, in *Carry On Regardless*.

Julia Arnall was born in Austria on 21 November 1930 (some sources say 1931) and began her career as a model. She moved to Britain in 1950 and made her film debut in *Knights of the Round Table* in 1953. After being placed under contract by Rank Studios she went on to appear as a light leading lady in films such as *Value for Money* (1955), *Simon and Laura* (1955), *House of Secrets* (1956) and *The Man with No Body* (1957). After her contract was terminated in 1957 her career floundered, although she made several more film appearances over the next decade including *The Trunk* (1960) and *The Double Man* (1967).

Julia had two sons from her first marriage, which ended in divorce in 1955, and one daughter, Gina, from her second marriage to Robert Ottaway (d.1988), which ended in divorce in 1975. Although still a member of Equity, the actor's union has not heard from the former leading lady since 1984.

Robin Askwith

Now inexorably linked with the *Confessions* films of the late 1970s, Robin Askwith joined the *Carry On* series as Larry (June Whitfield's photographer son) in *Carry On Girls*. He had previously worked for Rogers and Thomas on the film version of *Bless This House*, playing Sid James's son.

Robin was born in Southport, Lancashire, on 12 October 1950. A childhood sufferer of polio, his hopes of studying at university were dashed when he was expelled from school and he 'fell into' films as a teenager, under the guidance of Lindsay Anderson. Since his screen debut in *If* ... in 1968 Robin has made over thirty film appearances, including *Otley* (1968), *Nicholas and Alexandra* (1971), *All Coppers Are* ... (1971), *The Four Dimensions of Greta* (1971), *Horror Hospital* (1973), *Queen Kong* (1976, unreleased), *Stand Up Virgin Soldiers* (1977), *Let's Get Laid* (1978) and *Britannia Hospital* (1982).

On the small screen the sandy-haired, boyishly good-looking actor is best known as Dave Deacon in *The Bottle Boys* (1984-85), and since his teens he has made appearances in various television programmes, including *Beryl's Lot* (1972), *Bless This House, Please Sir!, Infidelities* (1985), *Casanova's Last Stand* (1985) and *Boon*.

Robin's comic talents (and a good deal beside!) were revealed when he was cast in the lead role of *The Confessions of a Window Cleaner* (1974). A further three *Confessions* films followed over the next four years, securing Robin's success as a box-office favourite. Explicitly revealing, the *Confessions* films became the flavour of the late 1970s, and they ultimately sounded the death knell for the *Carry On* series. In 1977 Robin formed The Comedy Company and for a decade toured the world with stage plays based on the *Confessions* films.

In more recent years Robin, who has changed little since his twenties, has re-launched his career with appearances on television and stage and with cameo appearances in films such as *The Asylum* (2000), *UZ-560* (2000), *Evil Calls* (2008) and *Back2Hell* (2010). His autobiography, *The Confessions of Robin Askwith*, was published in 1999 and it seems likely that he will enjoy 'cult' status in years to come.

Away from the stage Robin, who was romantically linked to actress Linda Hayden during most of the 1970s, enjoys long distance swimming and off-shore yachting. He lives on the island of Gozo, near Malta.

Diane Aubrey

A light leading lady of the early 1960s, Diane Aubrey played Honoria, 'Potty Poo's' (Leslie Phillips) friend, in *Carry On Constable*.

Diane, who was born in 1939 and trained at LAMDA, made her television debut in 1954 and also appeared in films such as *Petticoat Pirates* (1961), *The Little Ones* (1965) and *The Wild Affair* (1966). She married writer Troy Kennedy-Martin (1932-2009) in 1967 and had two children before their subsequent divorce.

Nina Baden-Semper

Best known on television as Barbie Reynolds in the 1970s sitcom *Love*

Thy Neighbour, Nina Baden-Semper made a cameo appearance in *Carry On Up the Jungle* as the Nosha girl disturbed by Charles Hawtrey during his 'flashback' scene.

Nina was born in the West Indies in 1945. She made her first professional appearances on television from the late 1960s in series such as *The Corridor People* (1966), *Take Three Girls* (1970) and *Callan,* before gaining national recognition in *Love Thy Neighbour* (1972-76), with Rudolph Valentine, Jack Smethurst (q.v.) and Kate Williams.

Since *Love Thy Neighbour* Nina has continued to work sporadically on television, most recently in *Little Napoleons* (1994) and *Brothers and Sisters* for BBC2 in 1997. She has also been the subject of *This Is Your Life* (1975) and appeared in an episode of *Crossroads* in 2002.

Nina's film credits include *Kongi's Harvest* (1970), *Love Thy Neighbour* (1972), *The Love Ban* (1973) and *Rage* (1999). Nina, who was at Pinewood Studios in 2008 for the *Carry On* 50th Anniversary celebrations, has been married to Rev. Murray Grant since 1973 and they have a son and a daughter.

Andrew Bailey

Andrew played Ghengis in *Carry On Columbus*. His additional screen credits include *Blame It on the Bellboy* (1992) and *Penelope* (2006).

Anthony Bailey

In addition to playing the rider in *Carry On Dick*, Anthony Bailey also appeared in *The Main Chance* (1966), *Captain Nemo and the Underwater City* (1969), *Junior Robin Hood* (1977) and *Hussey* (1996). On the small screen Anthony appeared in television classics such as *Crossroads, Dixon of Dock Green, The New Avengers, The Professionals, Tales of the Unexpected, The Bill* and *Grange Hill.*

Born on 31 October 1931, Anthony continued to act until the end of his life and appeared at the National Theatre in *The Forest* (1998-99). He died in Croydon in 2004.

Anthony Baird

Perhaps best known for his two-year relationship with legendary *Carry On* actress Joan Sims, stage and television actor Anthony Baird played a guard (alongside *Carry On* semi-regular Patrick Durkin) in *Carry On Spying*. It was his only appearance in the series.

Born in London on 11 December 1920, Anthony Baird made his film debut in *Dead of Night* (1945). His subsequent appearances over the next forty years included *The Winslow Boy* (1948), *Reluctant Heroes* (1951), *The*

Iron Maiden (1962) and finally *The Cheetah* (1989).

Anthony's first marriage ended in divorce and in the late 1950s he lived with Joan Sims, a relationship recalled in her 2000 autobiography, *High Spirits*. He died in London on 27 August 1995, aged seventy-four.

Shakira Baksh (aka: S. Caine)

Former Miss World contestant Shakira Baksh played Scrubba, one of Sid James's wives who is suitably slimmed down for Jim Dale, in *Carry On Again Doctor*. She is now best known as Lady Michael Caine.

Shakira was born in Guyana on 23 February 1947 and began her career as a model. At the age of nineteen she was Miss Guyana in the Miss World competition, before making her film debut in *Carry On Again Doctor*. She later made cameo appearances in *Son of Dracula* (1974) and *The Man Who Would Be King* (1975).

Shakira has been married to actor Sir Michael Caine since 1973 and they have one daughter, Natasha. The ever-glamorous Lady Caine can usually be seen at her husband's side at events such as the Academy and BAFTA Awards.

Michael Balfour

With over a hundred film appearances to his name, it is hardly surprising that Michael Balfour should be found among these pages, and with his craggy features he was perfectly cast for the role of Matt in *Carry On Constable*.

Michael Balfour was born in Kent on 11 February 1918. He began his career in repertory in 1936 and from the mid-1940s assumed an American identity in order to gain a part in Garson Kanin's stage play, *Born Yesterday*. So convincing was Michael's adopted nationality that for the next fifty years it was commonly believed that he was American!

After making his screen debut in *Just William's Luck* in 1947 Michael went on to appear in countless films, usually in cameo roles as gangsters, porters, taxi drivers or waiters. Among his credits were appearances in *Stop Press Girl* (1949), *Genevieve* (1953), *The Belles of St Trinian's* (1954), *Quatermass II* (1957), *Make Mine Mink* (1960), *The Fast Lady* (1962), *The Sandwich Man* (1966) and *The Private life of Sherlock Holmes* (1970). From the 1970s he mainly worked on stage and television, although film work never completely dried up, with later appearances including *Joseph Andrews* (1977), *Candleshoe* (1978), *The Prisoner of Zenda* (1979) and finally *The Revenge of Billy the Kid* (1992), with Norman Mitchell (q.v.).

On television Michael played the man in the pub in the 1958 series *Educated Evans* and went on to play Twinkle Martin in *Mess Mates* (1961).

He also made numerous guest appearances, including episodes of *The Avengers, The Persuaders* and latterly *Dempsey and Makepeace* (1986) and *The December Rose* (1987).

In 1958 Michael was a passenger in the car crash that killed actor Bonar Colleano (the husband of actress Susan Shaw, q.v.). His injuries required 98 stitches although he was released from hospital in time for Bonar's funeral. Semi-retired from the late 1970s, Michael worked as a circus clown during the last two decades of his life while indulging his passion for painting and sculpting. He died on 24 October 1997, aged seventy-nine.

Vincent Ball

Australian character actor Vincent Ball brought his talents as a guest actor to two *Carry On* films. As the handsome keep-fit instructor in *Carry On Cruising* he turned the heads of Liz Fraser and Dilys Laye before setting his sights on Angela Douglas in *Follow That Camel*, playing the ship's officer.

Vincent was born in Wee Waa, New South Wales, on 4 December 1923. After leaving school at the age of fourteen he worked in various jobs before joining the RAAF in 1941. Following the end of the Second World War he received a grant and trained at the Whitehall Academy of Dramatic Art (Sydney), where he met his future wife and graduated in 1947. After travelling to Britain aboard the Swedish cargo ship *Yarrawonga,* Vincent secured a role as Donald Huston's stunt double in *Blue Lagoon* (1949) before winning a scholarship and training for two years at RADA (1949-51).

During his twenty-five years in Britain as a 'jobbing' actor Vincent appeared in countless films and a range of television series, including the children's programme *Junior Television* (1954-58), *Compact* (1963-65) and as a semi-regular in *Crossroads.* Vincent returned to Australia in 1973 and has remained busy ever since, latterly in stern patriarchal roles. He has made over a hundred films and continued to act into his eighties, with recent screen credits including *Muriel's Wedding* (1994), *Paradise Road* (1996), *Iliad* (1998), *The Man Who Sued God* (2001), *The Night We Called It a Day* (2003) and *The Cherry Orchard* (2003).

Vincent Ball has been married to stage actress Doreen Harrop since 1949 and they have three children, Catherine, Christian and Jonathan. Vincent also has a daughter, Emily, from another relationship. His 1996 autobiography, *Buck Jones, Where Are You?*, revealed a desire to be a "cowboy on the fillums" and, although this did not transpire, Vincent can now look back on a prodigious career as one of Australia's finest character actors. He lives at Balmoral Beach, Sydney.

*Carry On ... **Quotes***

I don't have many recollections about the Carry On *films, except they were great fun to do and Sid James was a member of our long-running poker school. Sid was a great gambler and I don't think a very successful one – not many people are!*
Vincent Ball, 1998

Peter Banks

Canadian-born Peter made his film debut as Gunner Thomas in *Carry On England* and has since made appearances in a range of films such as *Ellis Island* (TV, 1984), *Death Wish 3* (1985), *Highlander* (as a priest, 1986), *Going Home* (1987), *Soup* (1995) and *Down* (2001) and he played Warnie in *C.S. Lewis: Beyond Narnia* (TV, 2005). Peter now works mainly on stage, recently for the Harrogate Theatre Company in *Insignificance*.

Eric Barker

Eric Barker's involvement in the *Carry On* series was two-fold, since in addition to acting roles in four of the films he is also credited with the original story behind *Carry On Cruising*.

Eric Barker was born in Surrey on 20 February 1912, and after leaving school he spent two years working with his father before earning a living as a novelist and short story writer.

Eric made his stage debut at the age of eighteen in Shakespearian plays at the Q Theatre and in 1933 joined the Birmingham Repertory Company. His subsequent stage appearances included further repertory seasons, vaudeville work at the famous Windmill Theatre, *Where There's a Will* (1954, as Alfie Brewer) and *Midsummer Mink* (1963, with Athene Seyler).

During the Second World War Eric spent five years with the Royal Navy. In the late 1940s his career took off with radio series such as *Merry-Go-Round, Much-Binding-in-the-Marsh* and *Stand Easy*, making him a household name and nurturing his skills as a writer. His superb comic timing was heard to best effect in *HMS Waterlogged* and *Waterlogged Spa* (1948-51), in which he broadcast with his wife, actress Pearl Hackney (1916-2009). By the 1950s he was one of the country's top broadcasters, with later credits including *Just Fancy* (1951-61, starred, created and wrote) and *Barker's Folly* (1959).

Eric made his film debut in *Carry On London* in 1936. From the mid-1950s he became a leading comic character actor, gracing well over thirty films including *Brothers in Law* (1956, for which he received a BAFTA Award), *Happy Is the Bride* (1957), *Blue Murder at St Trinian's* (1958), *Dentist in the Chair* (1960), *Watch Your Stern* (1960), *Dentist on the Job* (1961), *Raising the Wind* (1962), *On the Beat* (1962), *Ferry Cross the Mersey* (1964), *Doctor in Clover* (1966) and *The Great Train Robbery* (1966).

Eric Barker's involvement in the *Carry On* films spanned almost the entire series. He made his debut as the short-tempered Captain Potts in *Carry On Sergeant*, a role that set the tone for further appearances. He went on to play Inspector Mills in *Carry On Constable* and was superb as 'Chief' in *Carry On Spying*.

Eric Barker's small-screen credits, dating back to television's earliest days, included *Eric Barker Half Hour* (1951-53), *Look at It This Way* (1955), *The Dickie Valentine Show* (1957), *Something in the City* (series, 1959), *Lance at Large* (1964, with Lance Percival), *The Avengers* (guest appearance, 1969) and *The Chiffy Kids* (1976).

Eric's career was halted in 1966 when he suffered a serious stroke, which left him semi-paralysed. He did, however, return to acting in cameo roles, notably in *Twinky* (1970), *There's a Girl in My Soup* (1970) and *That's Your Funeral* (1972). He also made a fourth (speechless) appearance in the *Carry On* series, as the Ancient General in *Carry On Emmannuelle*. It was his final screen appearance.

For the last decade of his life Eric was almost completely retired, although he was occasionally heard on local radio. His autobiography, *Hark at Barker*, was published in 1956.

Eric and Pearl's only daughter is actress Petronella Barker (1945-), who went on to marry Sir Anthony Hopkins. They had one daughter, actress/singer Abigail Hopkins (1968-), before their divorce in 1972.

Eric Barker died in Faversham on 1 June 1990, aged seventy-eight.

Lynda Baron

An accomplished comedy actress, Lynda Baron made a brief appearance in *Carry On Columbus* and can be seen offering Jim Dale a much-needed drink (and advice) as he attempts to recruit sailors for his voyage to the New World.

Lynda Baron was born in Manchester on 24 March 1942. She made her professional debut fifty years ago, after training for ballet at the Royal Academy of Dancing. One of her earliest appearances was in the stage revue *One Over the Eight* (1961), with Kenneth Williams. During the early years of her career Lynda also had roles in *Doctor Who* and *Z-Cars* and performed as a singer and dancer in *Not So Much a Programme, More a Way of Life* (1963-66). She later found fame as the buxom Nurse Gladys Emmanuel in five series of *Open All Hours* (1976, '81 & '85), with Ronnie

Barker and David Jason, and in the mid-1990s was well known as Auntie Mabel in the children's series *Come Outside* (1994). Among her other TV credits are *Oh No, It's Selwyn Froggitt!* (1977, as Vera, with Bill Maynard, q.v.), *A Roof Over My Head* (1977, as Sheila), *Grundy* (1980, with Harry H. Corbett, q.v.) and *Last of the Summer Wine* (1983, as Lilly Bless-Her).

In addition to her numerous appearances on television, Lynda has had roles in several films, including *Hide and Seek* (1964), *Mrs Brown, You've Got a Lovely Daughter* (1969), *Hands of the Ripper* (1971), *Trauma* (TV, 1991), *Colour Me Kubrick* (2005) and *Scoop* (2006). Her stage appearances range from *The Bedwinner* (1974, with Jon Pertwee, q.v.) and *Funny Money* (1995, with Henry McGee, q.v.) to *In Celebration* (2007, with Orlando Bloom) and *When We Are Married* (2010, with Maureen Lipman, q.v.). She has also appeared regularly in pantomime.

Most recently Lynda has been seen on television in *Coronation Street* (1997, as Renee Turnbull), *The Mrs Bradley Mysteries* (1998), *Goodnight Sweetheart* (1998, as Mrs Green), *Nancherrow* (1999, as Dashka), *Dinnerladies* (1999, as Carmel), *Playing the Field* (2000, as a stripper) and *Peak Practice* (2001). She gained a new legion of fans as Norma Patterson in four series of *Fat Friends* (2000-05), played Rubes Malone in *Down to Earth* (series, 2005) and Linda Collins in *EastEnders* (2009). In 2010 she played actress Violet Carson in *The Road to Coronation Street*, the TV movie based on the early years of *Coronation Street*, which earned her a BAFTA nomination for best supporting actress.

Away from acting Lynda enjoys homely pursuits - sewing, baking and brewing beer. She is married to John M. Lee and they have a son, Morgan, and a daughter, Sarah.

Amanda Barrie (b. Shirley Ann Broadbent)

Although best known as Alma Baldwin in *Coronation Street*, Amanda Barrie occupies a unique position in *Carry On* history having been immortalised in the title role of *Carry On Cleo*.

Amanda was born in Ashton-under-Lyne, Lancashire, on 14 September 1935. Her grandfather, Ernest Broadbent, owned the local theatre and at the age of three Amanda made her first stage appearance singing and dancing. She soon took up ballet lessons and began work in pantomime. At the age of nine Amanda was sent to boarding school and four years later she moved to London to work on stage for Howard and Wyndham in the chorus of *Babes in the Wood*. She then became a member of Lionel Blair's dancing troupe, before making her West End stage debut. Her many subsequent stage appearances have included *Cabaret* (as Sally Bowles) and Maria in *Twelfth Night*.

Amanda made her *Carry On* debut as Anthea, the seductive, GlamCab driver in *Carry On Cabby*. The following year she played the dotty Queen Cleopatra in *Carry On Cleo* and with her stunning looks and famous brown eyes secured her position as one of the most memorable leading ladies of the *Carry On* series. In addition to the *Carry On* films, Amanda also appeared in *A Pair of Briefs* (1962, with Joan Sims), *Doctor in Distress* (1963), *I Gotta Horse* (1965) and *One of Our Dinosaurs Is Missing* (1975).

Having made her television debut as a teenager, Amanda Barrie's career on the small screen now spans half a century. Her first appearances were as a dancer in the Morecambe and Wise series *Running Wild* and she later became the hostess of the quiz show *Double Your Money*. It is as Alma Sedgewick/Baldwin, however, that Amanda is best remembered and it was a role that kept her busy for over a decade. Ironically, for most of her time in *Coronation Street* Amanda was teamed opposite another *Carry On* veteran – Johnny Briggs (q.v.).

Amanda Barrie's enduring public popularity was evident in 1996 when she revealed that she had lost most of her sight in her left eye due to central retinal occlusion. Despite the condition, Amanda bravely continued her hectic work schedule on the set of *Coronation Street* until finally leaving the popular soap in 2001. After leaving 'the Street' Amanda played Margo Phillips in eight episodes of *Doctors* (2004) and became well known for her role as Beverley Tull in *Bad Girls* (2003-06). She was also a contestant on the first series of *Hell's Kitchen* (2004) and has returned to the stage in pantomime. Her excellent autobiography, *It's Not a Rehearsal*, was published in 2002.

Amanda married actor/director Robin Hunter (q.v.) in 1967, and although they separated in 1980 they remained good friends until his death. Away from acting Amanda enjoys horse racing and riding and collects Victorian toys, especially wooden horses. She divides her time between homes in Covent Garden and Manchester.

Hilda Barry (b. Hilda Mary Barry)

Hilda had an endearing role as Grandma Grubb in *Carry On Loving*, giving a tick of approval to Terry Philpotts (Terry Scott), to the delight of her granddaughter Jenny (Imogen Hassall).

Hilda Barry was a familiar face to cinema-goers over a twenty-year period, appearing as mothers, grandmothers and next-door neighbours in films such as *Tiger in the Smoke* (1956), *Horrors of the Black Museum* (1959), *Poor Cow* (1967), *Fragment of Fear* (1971), *Steptoe and Son Ride Again* (1972) and *House of Mortal Sin* (1976). Her television credits included *Dixon of Dock Green, Z-Cars, The Fenn Street Gang, Our Mutual Friend* and *Angels* (1976).

Hilda's biographical details are somewhat vague; some sources give her date of birth as 1885 or 1896 and date of death as 1977 or 1979. It is more likely that she was born on 9 June 1884 and died in Islington, London, on 29 May 1979, aged ninety-four.

Richard Bartlett

Richard, who also appeared in *The Pink Panther Strikes Again* (1976) and TV series such as *Robin's Nest*, played Gunner Drury in *Carry On England*.

Amelia Bayntun (b. A. Ellen Bayntun)

Through her involvement in five *Carry On* films, Amelia Bayntum became a familiar member of the team's supporting cast. She made her series debut as Mrs Fussey, Joan Sims's mother, in *Carry On Camping* and went on to play one of Joan's corseted customers in *Carry On Loving*, the nosy neighbour in *Carry On At Your Convenience*, the ever-pregnant Mrs Jenkins in *Carry On Matron* and Mrs Tuttle (Charles Hawtrey's doting mother) in *Carry On Abroad*.

Amelia, who was born in Bristol on 31 March 1919, joined Bristol Unity Players in 1936. During the Second World War she was released from the ATS to tour in shows for British forces in Austria and Italy in *Stars in Battledress*. After demobilisation she went on to appear in repertory, scoring notable success as Mary Byrne in *The Tinker's Wedding*.

On stage Amelia was best known as Granny Miggs in *Sparrows Can't Sing* for Joan Littlewood in the early 1960s. Her additional stage appearances included *Sailor Beware!* (1959, as Emma Hornett), *Blitz!* (1962, as Mrs Blitzein), *In Celebration* (1970) and *The Old Ones* (1972, as Gerda, Royal Court).

In addition to her acting credits, Amelia also ran public houses from 1959 and later became the hostess of The Grapes, a hostelry in Great Marlborough Street, London.

As well as work on stage and screen, Amelia appeared on television in a range of series, including *Emergency Ward 10, Dixon of Dock Green, Adam Adamant, David Copperfield, Z-Cars, On the Buses, The Dick Emery Show* and *Edna, the Inebriate Woman* (1971), and she played Mother in the 1972 sitcom *Albert*.

Amelia was married to Ronald McCrindell from 1947. She died in Islington in January 1988, aged sixty-eight.

Susan Beaumont (b. S. Black)

A budding leading lady of the 1950s, Susan Beaumont played Nurse Frances James in *Carry On Nurse*. It was her only *Carry On* appearance in a brief acting career.

The daughter of actress Roma Beaumont (1913-2001) and theatrical producer Alfred Black (1913-2002), Susan was born on 26 February 1936 in South London. She made her film debut in *Man of the Moment* when she was nineteen and went on to appear in a handful of films including *Simon and Laura* (1955) and *The Man Who Liked Funerals* (1959), with Leslie Phillips.

It is likely that Susan would have remained busy with acting roles for at least another decade had she not chosen to retire from the business in 1959.

James/(Jimmy) Beck (b. Stanley James Carroll Beck)

Forever remembered as Private Walker in *Dad's Army*, James Beck played one of Kenneth Williams's clients in *Carry On Loving*. Sadly, his scenes with Williams (and Yutte Stensgaard, q.v.) hit the cutting room floor.

Born in Islington, London, on 21 February 1929, James attended art school from the age of fourteen. Passionately interested in the theatre from an early age, he began his career in repertory (following National Service), where he gained critical revues.

From 1958 until the mid-1960s James was kept busy in the theatre, appearing in more than eighty plays. They included *French Without Tears* (as Hon. Alan Howard), *Jane Eyre* (as Richard Mason), *The Diary of Anne Frank* (as Mr Van Daan), *The Entertainer* (as Archie Rice), *Henry IV Part I* (as Owen Glendower), *Pygmalion* (as Professor Henry Higgins), *Goodbye, Mr Chips!* (as Tibbits & Mr Cartwright) and *Who's Afraid of Virginia Woolf?* (as George).

After years on stage, James achieved national fame on television as Private Joe Walker in *Dad's Army* (1968-73). As the local spiv trading in black-market goods James gained a legion of fans, and thanks to regular repeats of the sitcom he remains a familiar face to television viewers thirty years after his early death. Aside from *Dad's Army*, James Beck's small-screen credits included *Coronation Street* (1964, as Sergeant Bowden), *Z-Cars, Softly, Softly, Trouble Shooter, Taxi, Never a Cross Word* and *All Gas and Gaiters*. In 1973, shortly before his death, he played Bert Jones in *Romany Jones*.

Away from the stage James enjoyed painting and sculpting and he was happily married for many years to Kay. James Beck was taken ill during the summer of 1973 with a suspected stomach ulcer and died from a burst pancreas during surgery on 6 August 1973. He was just forty-four years old.

Diana Beevers

Diana Beevers played Penny Lee, one of the rebellious students, in *Carry On Teacher*.

Joan Benham

A character actress of stage, screen and television, Joan Benham played the 'outraged lady' in *Carry On Emmannuelle*. Twenty years prior to her only appearance in the series she had worked opposite Joan Sims in the stage play *Man Alive*.

Joan was born in London on 17 May 1918. In an acting career spanning thirty years she appeared in numerous television series, including *My Wife and I* (1958, as Evelyn Wright), *Hotel Imperial* (1960, as Kate Brett), *Upstairs, Downstairs* (1971-76, as Lady Prudence Fairfax), *Both Ends Meet* (1972, as Mrs Templeton-Smythe, with Dora Bryan and Wendy Richard, both q.v.), *The Duchess of Duke Street* (1976, as Lady Williams), *Take My Wife* (1979, as Mabel Norrington, with Victor Spinetti), *The Sun Trap* (1980, as Fiona) and *Terry and June* (1981, as Melinda Spry). She also made guest appearances with numerous top comedians, including Ronnie Barker and Dick Emery.

In addition to *Carry On Emmannuelle*, Joan made cameo appearances in *The Pickwick Papers* (1952), *The Man Who Loved Redheads* (1954), *Dry Rot* (1956), *The Bridal Path* (1959), *The V.I.P.s* (1963), *Ladies Who Do* (1963), *Murder Ahoy!* (1964), *The Magic Christian* (1969), *Ooh... You Are Awful* (1972), *Steptoe and Son Ride Again* (1972) and *Rosie Dixon – Night Nurse* (1978).

Joan Benham died in London on 13 June 1981, aged sixty-three.

Peter Bennett

Peter played the pickpocket thief in *Carry On Constable*. He was perhaps best known for his role in the 1956 TV series *The Adventures of Sir Lancelot* but also made the occasional film appearance, including *Tarka the Otter* (1979) and *Lady Chatterley's Lover* (as the butler, 1981). He died on 23 December 1989, aged seventy-two.

Harold Berens (b. Ivan Harold Berens)

Harold Berens holds a unique place in *Carry On* history. At the age of almost ninety he was the oldest actor to appear in the series when he played Cecil the Torturer in *Carry On Columbus*. It was his final film appearance in a remarkable sixty-year career spanning stage, screen, television and radio.

Harold Berens was born in Glasgow on 4 March 1903 and began his acting career in the early 1930s in variety and cabaret. During the 1940s he made over a thousand radio broadcasts and became a national figure in the long-running series *Ignorance Is Bliss* (1945-53), with his catchphrase of "Wot a geezer".

Harold made his screen debut in *Candlelight in Algeria* (1944) and went on to appear in over twenty films, from *The Pure Hell of St Trinian's* (1961) and *What a Whopper* (1961) to *Trail of the Pink Panther* (1982) and *Hear My Song* (1991).

His appearances on television as a comedian and character actor included *It Pays to be Ignorant* (1957, with Michael Bentine), *Crossroads, Dad's Army* and *Are You Being Served?* He also appeared in four Royal Variety Performances.

Harold Berens died on 10 May 1995, aged ninety-two.

Gloria Best

Gloria Best appeared as one of the 'Funhouse Girls' in *Carry On Spying*, a Hand Maiden in *Carry On Cleo* and as Bridget (one of the saloon girls) in *Carry On Cowboy*. She also had an uncredited role in *Goldfinger* (1964).

Tanya Binning

In addition to playing Virginia in *Carry On Cleo*, Tanya also appeared in *Runaway* (1964) and *Don't Let It Get to You* (1966).

Donald Bissett

A familiar face on screen and television and a long-term member of the Royal Shakespeare Company, Donald played a patient in *Carry On Again Doctor.* It was his only appearance in the series.

Donald Bissett was born in Brentford, Middlesex, on 3 August 1910 and during his fifty-year career made appearances in a variety of films, including *Murder in the Cathedral* (1952), *Friends and Neighbours* (1959), *Hide and Seek* (1963), *Eye of the Devil* (1967) and *Warlords of Atlantis* (1978). On television he played the Earl of Surrey in *The Six Wives of Henry VIII* (1971) as well as making guest appearances in series ranging from *Nearest and Dearest* to *Doctor Who*. Donald continued to work well into old age and made his final TV appearance in Catherine Cookson's *The Black Velvet Gown*, as Mr Morgan, in 1991.

He died in London on 18 August 1995, aged eighty-five.

Josephine Blain

Josephine played one of the hospitality girls in *Carry On Up the Khyber*.

Denis Blake
Denis was the man behind the mask of Rubbatiti in *Carry On Screaming*.

John Bluthal
A familiar face on television through his involvement in long-running series such as *The Vicar of Dibley*, John Bluthal appeared in supporting roles in three *Carry On* films.

John was born in Galicia, Poland, on 12 August 1929, and moved to Australia with his family in 1938, where he later attended Melbourne University. After moving to Britain in the late 1950s John began his career on television and radio. He made his screen debut in 1963 and has since appeared in over thirty films, often being cast as dubious foreigners. He made his *Carry On* debut in *Carry On Spying* as the head waiter and went on to appear as Colonel Clotski (opposite Phil Silvers) in *Carry On Follow That Camel*. He returned to the series in a wonderful cameo role as Sid James's tailor in *Carry On Henry*, delightfully using the title of one of his best-known television series as one of his lines. In addition to the *Carry On*'s, John's other film appearances range from *A Hard Day's Night* (1964) and *Help!* (1965) to *The Fifth Element* (1997), *Dark City* (1998) and *Love's Brother* (2004).

On television John is best known as Manny in *Never Mind the Quality, Feel the Width* (1967-71) and, more recently, as Frank Pickle in *The Vicar of Dibley* (1994-2007). He has also made numerous guest appearances, both in Britain and Australia, including *It's a Square World* (1960-64), *The Avengers, Matlock* (1973, Aust.), *The Lives and Loves of a She-Devil* (1986), *Birds of a Feather, One Foot in the Grave, Jonathan Creek* (1996), *Time and Tide* (1999 Australian tele-movie, as Harry), *Blue Heelers* (2003, Aust.) and *Spirited* (2010, as Rocco).

John, whose only marriage ended in separation, has a son and a daughter. He now divides his time between London and Sydney.

Carry On ... **Quotes**

I find it strange that I'm asked so many times about the Carry On *films. My involvement was minimal. One that I do recall with pleasure was* Follow That Camel *(name changed for whatever reason) but it was with all the* Carry On *team and Phil Silvers. I loved being with him in that because he became very friendly with me during* A Funny Thing Happened On the Way to the Forum *(with Zero Mostel and Buster Keaton) so I'm proud to have been in a film with Keaton. Silvers introduced me to Jack Benny and*

Ava Gardner but my favourite (he seated me next to her at a dinner party) was Claire Trevor, who won an Academy Award in Key Largo. *I hardly talked with anyone else that night. She had been a favourite of mine for years.*
John Bluthal, 1998

Bruce Boa

A familiar face in British films and television, actor Bruce Boa was appropriately cast as the American Ambassador in *Carry On Emmannuelle*.

Born in Calgary, Canada, on 10 July 1930, Bruce's other screen credits included *The Man in the Moon* (1961), *The Adding Machine* (1969), *The Empire Strikes Back* (1977), *Octopussy* (1983), *Return to Oz* (1985), *Hawks* (1989) and *Screamers* (1995). On the small screen he appeared in a wide selection of tele-films and series, including *The Avengers* and *Fawlty Towers* and in later years *Lace 2* (1985), *The Forgotten* (1989), *The Bruce Curtis Story* (1991), *A Town Torn Apart* (1992), *As Time Goes By* (1995) and *Kavanagh QC* (1997).

Towards the end of his life Bruce proved to be a popular guest at *Star Wars* conventions and signing sessions. He died from cancer on 17 April 2004, aged seventy-three.

Martin Boddey

Dark-haired, Scottish-born character actor Martin Boddey played the 6th Specialist examining Kenneth Connor in *Carry On Sergeant* and can also be seen in *Carry On Nurse*, playing Perkins.

Martin Boddey was born in Stirling on 16 April 1907. He was over forty before making his screen debut in *A Song for Tomorrow* (1948) but went on to make eighty film appearances, usually in cameo roles as policemen or other 'official' types. Among his many film appearances were *Landfall* (1949), *The Third Man* (1949), *The Magic Box* (1952), *Doctor in the House* (1954), *Up to His Neck* (1954), *The Iron Petticoat* (1956), *I Only Arsked!* (1958), *Idol On Parade* (1959), *I'm All Right, Jack* (1959), *Oscar Wilde* (1960), *The Prince and the Pauper* (1962), *A Man for All Seasons* (1966), *Tales from the Crypt* (1972) and *Dark Places* (1973).

Martin continued to work until the end of his life, making his final appearance as the magistrate in *The Naked Civil Servant* on television in 1975.

Martin Boddey died from a heart attack on 24 October 1975, aged sixty-eight.

Eric Boon

Eric, who died in 1981 at the age of sixty-two, played Shorty in *Carry On Constable* and the 'young man' in *Carry On Regardless*.

David Boyce

David had a minor but memorable role in *Carry On Columbus* as the customer who has his ear cut off by Alexei Sayle. Born in 1945, David has appeared on television for over twenty years, with appearances in *Juliet Bravo, Heartbeat* and *Reckless* (1997). In addition to *Carry On Columbus*, his other screen credits include *The Pope Must Die(t)* (1991) and *Anchoress* (1993).

Josie Bradley

Josie played the pianist in the closing scenes of *Carry On Loving*. Born in 1910, Josie also appeared in *The Mysterious Mr Nicholson* in 1947 and played Mildred Knottage in an episode of the TV series *Detective* in 1969.

She died on 30 December 1984, aged seventy-four.

Wilfrid Brambell (b. Henry Wilfred Brambell)

Immortalised in television history as Albert Steptoe in *Steptoe and Son*, character actor Wilfrid Brambell turned up for a wordless, but memorable, cameo role as a randy patient in *Carry On Again Doctor.*

Wilfrid Brambell was born in Dublin on 22 March 1912. His first stage appearance was at the tender age of two, when he entertained troops during the First World War. After training as a journalist he gained early stage experience in Ireland before moving into repertory theatre at the Bristol Old Vic.

Wilfrid's subsequent appearances in the theatre were sporadic but included *The Shadow of the Glen* and *Riders to the Sea* (both 1950), *Blind Man's Buff* (1953), *Canterbury Tales* (1968), *A Christmas Carol* (1970, as Scrooge), and the role of Badger in *Cinderella* in 1976.

Wilfrid Brambell made his film debut in 1935 and over the next fifty years would make more than thirty screen appearances, mainly in cameo roles, including *Dry Rot* (1956), *What a Whopper* (1961), *Crooks in Cloisters* (1963), *A Hard Day's Night* (1964), *San Ferry Ann* (1965), *Cry Wolf* (1968) and *The Adventures of Picasso* (1978).

After years in minor supporting roles Wilfrid achieved stardom in his fifties as the scrawny, grotesque Albert Steptoe in eight series of *Steptoe and Son*, opposite Harry H. Corbett (q.v.). The series, which today remains as popular as ever, ran for twelve years and also included two feature films.

After *Steptoe and Son* ended Wilfrid went on to make occasional film and television appearances and his later credits included guest appearances in *Citizen Smith* (1977), *High Rise Donkey* (1980) and the 1983 film *Sword of the Valiant*. His final role was on TV in *The Terence Davies Trilogy* in 1984.

Wilfrid Brambell, whose only marriage ended in divorce in 1955, published his autobiography *All Above Board* in 1976. He died from cancer on 18 January 1985, aged seventy-two.

Deborah Brayshore

Deborah featured in an uncredited role in *Carry On Emmannuelle*. She had previously played the 'go-cart girl' in *Confessions from a Holiday Camp* (1977).

Alec Bregonzi

Character actor Alec Bregonzi appeared on stage, screen, television and radio for almost fifty years and is perhaps best remembered for his work with two of comedy's best-known stars, Tony Hancock and Ronnie Barker.

Alec was born in Paddington, London, on 21 April 1930. His acting career began as an amateur before various drama lessons at the City Literary Institute. His first stage appearances were in club (fringe) theatre in 1955 at the Castle Theatre (Farnham) and he went on to tour with the Royal Shakespeare Company.

Alec made his *Carry On* debut as the 1st Storeman in *Carry On Sergeant*, distributing kit to the hapless recruits. Thirteen years later he returned as a photographer in *Carry On At Your Convenience*, although his scenes were cut from the final release. Alec's additional film appearances included *Georgy Girl* (1966), *Cool It Carol!* (1970), *Queen of Hearts* (1989) and *A Royal Scandal* (TV, 1996).

Following his small-screen debut in 1956 Alec worked in numerous comedy series, most notably twenty-one episodes of *Hancock's Half Hour* (1957 & '61), *The Benny Hill Show, The Two Ronnies* and *The Kenny Everett Show*. He has also made the occasional dramatic appearance, including the 1978 mini-series *Edward & Mrs. Simpson*. Alec's later work saw him in episodes of *Hale and Pace, The Brian Connolly Show* and *London's Burning* and he provided voices in two series of *The Treacle People* (1995-97).

In 2001 Alec Bregonzi joined a host of *Carry On* actors at Pinewood Studios for the unveiling of British Comedy Society plaques to many of his co-stars and producer Peter Rogers. Five years later, in March 2006, he made a final public appearance at Ronnie Barker's memorial in

Westminster Abbey.

Alec, who was a bachelor, enjoyed opera, theatre, cinema, gardening and travel. He lived in Wandsworth, South London, until his death from cancer on 4 June 2006.

Carry On ... ***Quotes***

As to the Carry On *films, well I was only filming one day so really have nothing to repeat.* Sergeant *was my first film, so I was very nervous. As one of the storemen, I had a scene with a character who never did another* Carry On, *issuing kit to him. We rehearsed the two shots and as the director moved away the other actor said, "Alec if you angle it like this it'll be better" – meaning better for him, my right ear might have been in shot! Anyhow the director heard and said, "We'll do it exactly as we rehearsed," and so we did! Alas it finished up on the cutting room floor and I'm virtually a walk on as Kenneth Williams is whizzed through. Imagine my disappointment when I saw it locally – quite nice billing and then ...*
I also played a photographer on the pier in Brighton in Convenience *but the entire sequence was cut. So that was the* Carry On *part of my life.*
Alec Bregonzi, 2000

Bernard Bresslaw

(See MAIN TEAM).

Johnny Briggs MBE

Before becoming a celebrated cast member of *Coronation Street* Johnny Briggs made over thirty film appearances. He can be spotted as a Sporran Solider in *Carry On Up the Khyber*, as the plasterer in *Carry On Behind* and, most notably (in his last film appearance to date), as Captain Melly's driver in the opening scenes of *Carry On England*.

Johnny was born in Battersea, South London, on 5 September 1935. He was evacuated from London during the war and in 1947 was accepted into the Italia Conti Stage School, where he trained for six years with contemporaries including Millicent Martin, Anthony Newley and Nanette Newman. Johnny made his film debut at the tender age of thirteen in *Quartet* (1948) and in his mid-teens he worked on stage with a variety of famous names ranging from Audrey Hepburn to Bill Maynard (q.v.). Following National Service in the Tank Regiment Johnny continued his film career, and although too short to be cast in leading roles he proved adept as cheeky cockneys. His film appearances included *Second Fiddle* (1957), *Doctor in Love* (1960), *The Bullldog Breed* (1960), *The Leather Boys* (1963), *Bless This House* (1972) and *Man About the House* (1974).

Before joining the regular cast of *Coronation Street* in 1976 Johnny was already an established television actor, having appeared in over twenty series ranging from *The Avengers* to *Crossroads*, and he played Detective Sergeant Russell in three series of *No Hiding Place* (1964-66). He even made an appearance in 'The Case of the Coughing Parrot' – an episode of *Carry On Laughing* (1975) – playing Norman. As Mike Baldwin, the man everyone loved to hate, Johnny won the TV Times Award for Most Popular Actor in 1983 and received a Lifetime Achievement Award at the British Soap Awards in 2006. He left *Coronation Street* in 2006 amid much publicity when his character died from a heart attack after suffering from Alzheimer's disease. Happily, Johnny has continued to act on television, with recent guest appearances in *Holby City* (2007, as Tom Gibson), *Echo Beach* (2008, as Fin Morgan) and *Doctors* (2009, as John Cotham) and he played Sydney Lumley in *Marple: Nemesis* in 2007.

Johnny Briggs has been married and divorced twice and has a son and a daughter (Mark and Karen) from his first marriage and two daughters (Jennifer and Stephanie) and two sons (Michael and Anthony) from his second marriage. In private Johnny is a passionate golfer. He was awarded the MBE in the New Year's Honours List 2007.

Tim Brinton

Real-life television presenter Tim Brinton featured briefly in *Carry On Emmannuelle* as the second television newsreader, just one year before being elected a Member of Parliament.

Tim was born in London on 24 December 1929. He originally trained for acting at the Central School of Speech and Drama (London) and also gained the London University Diploma of Dramatic Art. Tim began his professional career at the BBC as a general trainee and went on to become a radio newsreader/announcer and later a television director and producer.

In the late 1950s Tim spent two years in Hong Kong as the Head of English programmes, before returning to Britain to become a television newsreader for both the BBC and ITV. He is perhaps best remembered on television as the host of the ITV sports programme *Let's Go*. In addition to *Carry On Emmannuelle*, he appeared in a handful of other films: *Information Received* (1962), *Heavens Above* (1963), *Bunny Lake Is Missing* (1965) and *Man at the Top* (1973).

From the late 1960s Tim Brinton began training courses for business and industry executives and in 1974 was elected a member of Kent County Council. He was elected MP for Gravesend, Kent, in 1979 and was a chairman of the backbench Media Committee for eight years.

From 1987 until his retirement in 1997 Tim continued to present and coach media sessions for senior business executives. He lived in Folkestone, Kent, with his second wife Jeanne, until his death on 24 March 2009.

Carry On ... **Quotes**

The Carry On's *were great fun ... I was but a small bit player in one of the later ones,* Carry On Emmannuelle, *coming to the studio for an hour or so to do a piece of about twenty seconds as a newscaster, which in reality I was between 1959 and 1962. To save money the director filmed me with a frame of a TV set around my seated figure. Nowadays they do it electronically – or should I write digitally!*
Tim Brinton, 2000

Ronnie Brody

Character actor Ronnie Brody gave two distinctive cameo performances in the *Carry On* series. He can be spotted as the 'little man' in the ballroom scene of *Don't Lose Your Head* and was later towered over by Alexandra Dane (q.v.) when he played Henry in *Carry On Loving*.

Ronnie was born in Bristol on 6 November 1918, the son of music hall artistes Bourne and Lester Brody. At the age of fifteen Ronnie joined the Merchant Navy, going on to serve with the RAF (in North Africa) during the Second World War.

Following the war Ronnie joined Ralph Reader's Gang and spent many years in variety, summer seasons and pantomime. Eventually he worked his way into films, with screen appearances and cameo roles in *Help!* (1965), *A Funny Thing Happened on the Way to the Forum* (1966), *Percy* (1971), *What's Up Nurse?* (1977), *What's Up Superdoc?* (1978), *Superman III* (1983), *Little Dorrit* (1988) and *The Fool* (1990).

Ronnie Brody first worked on television as a teenager, when he took part in John Logie Baird's first experiments, and he later appeared in a wide range of series, including *Bold as Brass* (1964), *Fire Crackers* (1964), *The Dick Emery Show, Bless This House, Dad's Army, Are You Being Served?, Home James!* and *The 19th Hole* (1989).

Ronnie was married to former actress Joan Dainty and they had one son, Stephen. Ronnie Brody died suddenly from a heart attack on 8 May 1991, aged seventy-two.

Sydney Bromley

One of the most unmistakable British character actors of all time, Sydney Bromley played Sam Houston in *Carry On Cowboy*. He is also sometimes credited with an appearance in *Carry On Screaming*, although he does not appear in the final film release.

Born in Battersea, London, on 24 July 1909, Sydney was one of fifteen children. He trained at the Italia Conti Stage School and made his stage debut at the age of twelve in *Quality Street,* with Fay Compton. He went on to play Prince James in *Charles I* (1922), Brian (the Earl of Warwick's page) in *Saint Joan* (original production, 1924) and one of the choirboys in Noel Coward's revue *On with the Dance* (1925).

From 1932 Sydney appeared in Shakespearian roles and went on to enjoy a distinguished stage career over the next fifty years. He spent eight years with the RSC in London, Stratford and touring the world, and by the end of his career he had played more than a hundred Shakespearian characters. His final stage appearance in 1984 saw him alongside Sir Alec Guinness in *The Merchant of Venice* at the Chichester Festival, playing Old Gobbo.

In addition to his enviable stage career, Sydney also appeared in over thirty films, usually in cameo roles. His screen career began in Will Hay comedies as an over-aged schoolboy in the 1930s before he moved on to played bearded, toothless eccentrics in a range of films, including *Brief Encounter* (1945), *The Mark of Cain* (1947), *Saint Joan* (1957), *Heavens Above* (1963), *Monster of Terror* (1965), *Slave Girls* (1966), *Smashing Time* (1967), *A Little of What You Fancy* (1968), *No Sex Please, We're British* (1973), *Frankenstein and the Monster from Hell* (1973), *The Prince and the Pauper* (1977) and *Candleshoe* (1977). In 1971 he played the role of Porter in the film version of *Macbeth.*

From the 1950s onwards Sydney played several television roles, including Father in *Quatermass II* (1955) and Purdy in *The Gay Cavalier* (1957). He later played Weary Willie in the popular sitcom *Fire Crackers* (1964-65, with Cardew Robinson, Ronnie Brody and Norman Chappell, all q.v.) and worked with Jim Dale in the children's series *Pet Pals* (1965, as Charlie). Among Sydney's guest appearances on the small screen were roles in *The Pallisers* (1974), *The New Avengers* (1976) and *Dangerous Davies – The Last Detective* (1981).

Sydney continued to work in films and television until the end of his life. Always the scene-stealer, his latter appearances included *An American Werewolf in London* (1981, as Alf) and *Dragonslayer* (1981, as Hodge). He was also memorable opposite Patricia Hayes (q.v.) in *The Never-Ending Story* (1984) and made his final appearances in the 1986 mini-series *Anastasia – The Mystery of Anna* (as Herbert, with Amy Irving) and the 1987 film *Crystalstone*.

Sydney Bromley died in Worthing, Sussex, on 14 August 1987, aged seventy-eight.

John Brooking

John Brooking, who made his film debut in *I Met a Murderer* in 1939, played the Third Sea Lord in *Carry On Jack*. He appeared in minor (and often uncredited) roles in over a dozen films.

John Brooking died on 19 May 1966, aged in his mid-fifties.

Ray Brooks

A popular actor of the 1970s and 1980s, Ray Brooks made a guest appearance in *Carry On Abroad*, playing Georgio, June Whitfield's seductive waiter friend.

Ray Brooks was born in Brighton on 20 April 1939. He began his acting career in repertory in Nottingham in 1957, breaking into films and television in the early 1960s. Among his earliest television roles was that of Terry Mills in Sid James's series *Taxi!* (1963), and he played Reg in the acclaimed television play *Cathy Come Home* (1965), with Carol White (q.v.).

Ray's film credits include *Girl on the Roof* (1961), *HMS Defiant* (1962), *Play It Cool* (1962), *The Knack* (1965), *Daleks' Invasion Earth: 2150 A.D.* (1966), *The Flesh and Blood Show* (1972), *Alice's Adventures in Wonderland* (1972), *Tiffany Jones* (1973) and *House of Whipcord* (1974).

Ray is best known for his work on television, most notably as Robbie Box in the 1984 series *Big Deal*. After a long absence from the small screen he returned to play Terry Marsh in *Two Thousand Acres of Sky* in 2001, before joining the cast of *EastEnders* in 2005, playing Joe Macer, the second husband of Pauline Fowler (Wendy Richard MBE, q.v.), for two years.

Ray has been married since 1961 and has one daughter and two sons. Away from acting he is a keen supporter of Fulham Football Club. His autobiography, *Learning My Lines: An Actor's Life*, was published in 2009.

Wayne Browne

Wayne Browne played the Native in 'Lamp-Posts of the Empire', an episodc of *Carry On Laughing* aired on television in 1975.

Dora Bryan OBE (b. D. Broadbent)

One of Britain's leading comediennes, Dora Bryan played Nora – the love-struck army cook – in *Carry On Sergeant*. It was her only appearance in the series but it left a niche that was filled in most of the later films by *Carry On* legend, Joan Sims.

Dora Bryan was born in Southport, Lancashire, on 7 February 1923. She made her stage debut in pantomime in 1935 and would go on to appear in a diverse range of productions, from the title role in *Hello, Dolly!* (1966-68) to Mistress Quickly in *The Merry Wives of Windsor* (1984).

Dora's instantly recognisable nasal tones, ranging from her natural Lancashire accent to a convincing cockney, were arguably her greatest asset during a career spanning over sixty years. She made her film debut in *Odd Man Out* in 1946 and went on to make over fifty film appearances. In 1961, in a rare leading role, she won the BAFTA Award for Best Actress for her role as Helen in *A Taste of Honey*. Sadly, further screen roles did not make the most of Dora's talents and she largely abandoned the cinema in favour of work on stage and television.

A popular real-life personality, Dora's small-screen credits include several versions of her own show, including *Our Dora* (1956) and *The Dora Bryan Show* (1961 & '64). More recently she appeared in two series of *Frank Stubbs Promotes* (1983, as Molly Bramley), *On the Up* (1990, as Dennis Waterman's mum), *Heartbeat* (1994), *Mother's Ruin* (1994, series, with Roy Barraclough), *Absolutely Fabulous – The Last Shout* (1996, with June Whitfield, q.v.) and *Dinnerladies* (2000, as Jean's mother), and she joined the cast of *Last of the Summer Wine* in 1999 as Ros, a role that kept her busy until her retirement in 2006.

In 1995 she received the Olivier Award and in 1996 was awarded a well-deserved OBE. Dora returned to film work in her eighties, with appearances in *MirrorMask* (2005), *Someone in Particular* (2005) and *Gone to the Dogs* (2006).

Dora Bryan was married to William Lawton from 1954 until his death in 2008 and they adopted two children, Daniel and Georgina, before a second son, William, was born. Dora's autobiography, *According to Dora*, was published in 1987 and a second volume of memoirs, *Dora Bryan's Tapestry Tales - An Anthology of Favourite Pieces*, was released in 2005.

Louise Burton

Television actress Louise Burton featured briefly in two of the final *Carry On* films. She joined the series as Private Evans in *Carry On England* and two years later was seen as the girl in the zoo with Jack Douglas in *Carry On Emmannuelle*.

Born in 1955, Louise began acting professionally at the age of thirteen and after leaving school trained at the Italia Conti Stage School. Among her television credits are appearances in *The Dick Emery Show* and *That's My Dog*, and she is perhaps best known for her role as Mr Grace's secretary in episodes of *Are You Being Served?*

Louise retired from acting in 1988 to concentrate on her family but has recently made a comeback to the profession.

Carry On ... ***Quotes***

I really can't remember the Carry On *films, i.e. the laughs. There were so many, although none that really jump to mind. I just remember laughing from 7 in the morning till 7 at night.*
Louise Burton, 2001

Peter Burton

Born in Bromley on 4 April 1921, Peter, who played the hotel manager in *Carry On At Your Convenience*, appeared in numerous films and television series. He made his screen debut in *The Wooden Horse* (1950) and further screen credits include *What the Butler Saw* (1950), *Betrayal* (1957), *The Night We Dropped a Clanger* (1959), *Sink the Bismarck!* (1960), *The Iron Maiden* (1962), *Berserk!* (1970), *A Clockwork Orange* (1971), *The Bitch* (1979) and *The Doctor and The Devils* (1985). Perhaps his most notable screen appearance was as Major Boothroyd in *Dr. No* (1962), the character that later became known as Q. Peter was unavailable for *From Russia with Love* (1963) and was replaced by Desmond Llewelyn, who played the character until his death in 1999.

Peter continued to work on television until his death in London on 21 November 1989, aged sixty-eight.

Peter Butterworth

(See MAIN TEAM).

Peter Byrne

Best known on television for his twenty-year run as PC Andy Crawford in *Dixon of Dock Green*, Peter Byrne appeared as the amiable bridegroom opposite Sid James and Jim Dale in *Carry On Cabby*. It was one of several cameo roles in Peter Rogers/Gerald Thomas films.

Peter was born in London on 29 January 1928. He trained at the Italia

Conti Stage School and made his theatrical debut playing the Third Elf in *Where the Rainbow Ends* in 1944.

Peter's comic roots stretch back to 1945 when he took over from Charles Hawtrey as Smart - the cheeky schoolboy - in Will Hay's stage and radio act. Ironically, Peter also directed the *Carry On* legend in his final stage appearance in 1980.

Although Peter made his film debut in *The Case of the Second Shot* (1953) and went on to appear in *The Large Rope* (1953), *Reach for the Sky* (1956), *Watch Your Stern* (1960), *Raising the Wind* (1961) and *The Iron Maiden* (1962), he has mainly worked on stage and television.

In the theatre Peter has appeared in a diverse range of productions, including *The Blue Lamp* (1952, as PC Andy Crawford), *Boeing-Boeing* (1966), *There's a Girl in My Soup* (1968-69) and *Move Over Mrs Markham* (1973). He has also toured Canada and has appeared in over twenty pantomimes (eleven as director). Peter's additional stage credits have included the first post-war Royal Command Performance (Coliseum, 1945), *For Crying Out Loud* (Stoll, 1945), *Deadly Nightcap* (1986, Westminster), *The Business of Murder* (1988-90, Mayfair), *The Surprise Party* (1998), Barbara Taylor Bradford's *Dangerous To Know* (1998, with Rula Lenska), *September Tide* (Comedy, 2000) and *And Then There Were None* (tour, 2008).

On television Peter gained national recognition as Andy Crawford in *Dixon of Dock Green* (1955-76), with Jack Warner (1896-1981). Peter subsequently made guest appearances in a number of other series and played Mrs Boswell's secret boyfriend in three series of *Bread* (1986-89). Latterly he has remained busy on stage, notably in *The Mouse Trap* (2001-02), which he has also directed, and he toured the country in *Witness for the Prosecution* for Bill Kenwright's (q.v.) Agatha Christie Company in 2010.

Peter's first marriage ended in divorce and he subsequently married Renee Helen. Peter's hobbies include swimming, astronomy and golf. He lives in London.

*Carry On ... **Quotes***

I was somewhat surprised that you remembered I was in Carry On Cabby. *That was the only* Carry On *I appeared in, although I worked in other Peter Rogers films but in a very minor capacity, e.g.* Raising the Wind, Watch Your Stern, The Iron Maiden, *all directed by Gerald Thomas.* Raising the Wind *was Jim Dale's debut, and he went on to play leading roles, but I opted out when my TV career took off in the '60s. The casting director for Peter Rogers was a lovely lady called Betty White, and she cast me in all of these films because her granddaughter was a fan of mine from TV - so much for talent!*

When I was a young actor I took over from Charlie Hawtrey in Will Hay's stage and radio act playing 'Smart', the cheeky boy - this was in 1945. We played in a revue with Nervo and Knox called For Crying Out Loud *at the Stoll Theatre directed by Val Guest, the first post-war Command Performance at the Coliseum, and a BBC radio series called* The Dairy of a Schoolmaster.

I directed poor Charlie at the end of his career in a pantomime in Swindon, but he was a shadow of his former self and died, sadly in poverty and alone, shortly after.

I was on the set of Watch Your Stern *when Sid James heard the news that Tony Hancock had decided to break up their TV partnership. Poor Sid was devastated, and desperately hurt that Tony hadn't had the decency to tell him personally - Sid had read it in a newspaper that morning!*

Tony's life was one self-inflicted wound, and he treated his friends abominably - when he felt like it he could charm the birds out of the trees, so you forgave him - but what a talent!

Peter Byrne, 1999

Simon Cain

Simon Cain featured in a total of six *Carry On's*: as Short in *Carry On Cowboy*; in an uncredited role in *Follow That Camel*; as the tea orderly in *Carry On Doctor*; as the bagpipe soldier in *Up the Khyber*; as the X-ray man in *Again Doctor*; and as the barman in *Carry On At Your Convenience*.

Gerald Campion

Now forever remembered as Billy Bunter in *Billy Bunter of Greyfriars School*, Gerald played Andy Calloway in *Carry On Sergeant*. Surprisingly, it was his only appearance in the *Carry On* series.

Gerald Campion was born in Bloomsbury, London, on 23 April 1921, the son of scriptwriter Cyril Campion. He trained at RADA from the age of fifteen and served with the RAF (as a wireless operator) in Kenya during the Second World War.

Gerald made his screen debut in *Miranda* (1948) and went on to appear in supporting roles in films such as *The Pickwick Papers* (1952), *Up to His Neck* (1954), *Fun at St Fanny's* (1956), *Keep It Clean* (1956), *Inn for Trouble* (1960) and *Chitty Chitty Bang Bang* (1968).

He was best known on television in the title role of *Billy Bunter,* which ran for nine years (1952-61) and 120 episodes. Although the role made Gerald a television star, it also left him typecast, and he moved away from the acting profession in the late 1960s to run a string of restaurants and West End clubs. He made an unexpected return to acting in the 1980s and worked on television in *Doctor Who, The Six Napoleons* (1986), *The Return of Sherlock Holmes* (1986) and the 1989 mini-series *Great Expectations.* Gerald retired from acting in 1991 due to health problems.

Gerald married Jean Symond in 1947 and they had three children before separating in 1964. After their divorce in 1972 he married secondly Susan Marks.

In his final years Gerald suffered from heart problems, and following surgery he was too frail to return to London for planned 80th birthday celebrations.

Gerald Campion died in Agen, France, on 9 July 2002, at the age of eighty-one.

Esma Cannon

Esma Cannon was undoubtedly one of the most delightful actors to grace the *Carry On* films. Tiny and mischievous, she was the classic little old lady of the series.

Esma made her *Carry On* debut as the lady helped across to the wrong side of the road by Kenneth Williams in *Carry On Constable*. She then went on to play Sid James's loyal secretary, Miss Cooling, in *Carry On Regardless*, before capturing the hearts of *Carry On* fans as the spirited Bridget Madderley in *Carry On Cruising*. Her final appearance in the series was as Flo Sims, Hattie Jacques's sidekick in *Carry On Cabby*.

Esma Cannon was born in Randwick, New South Wales, Australia, on 27 December 1905 and made her first stage appearance at the tender age of four in *Madame Butterfly.* She left Australia in the early 1930s for an intended three-month visit to Britain.

Esma made her London stage debut as the maid in *All Rights Reserved* at the Criterion in 1935. She subsequently went on to appear in numerous stage plays, including *Jack and Jill* (1936, as Mistress Mary), *Society Blues* (1938, as Doris Higgins), *Other People's Houses* (1941, as Diana Jones) and *See How They Run* (1945, as Ida). Esma also worked with future *Carry On* stars Kenneth Connor, in *Waggonload of Monkeys* (1951), and Charles Hawtrey, in *Husbands Don't Count* (1952, as Madame Dubbonet). She also played Aunt Ophelia in 119 performances of *Summertime* (1955) and Miss Prism in *The Importance of Being Earnest* (1957), with Dame Margaret Rutherford.

From the mid-1930s Esma also built up a formidable list of film credits (over sixty in total), usually in cameo roles playing maiden aunts, neighbours and little old ladies. Indeed, she became one of those indispensable character actors, in the same league as Irene Handl. She was especially notable in *Sailor Beware!* (1956).

Esma Cannon was at her busiest in the early 1960s when in addition to the *Carry On*'s she appeared on television in *The Rag Trade* (as Little Lil) and on stage in *Watch It, Sailor!* (604 performances, 1960-61, as Edie Hornett). In 1963, at the peak of her success, she retired to live in France.

Esma Cannon was married to Ernest Littman and had one son born in 1946. Away from the stage she enjoyed interior decorating, cooking and bookbinding. She died on 18 October 1972.

Brian Capron

A busy television actor, Brian Capron played the trumpeter in 'Under the Round Table' and 'Short Knight, Long Daze' – two episodes of *Carry On Laughing*.

Brian was born in Woodbridge, Suffolk, on 11 February 1947. He trained at LAMDA and since the early 1970s he has made numerous television appearances, including *Beryl's Lot, The Sweeney, Full House* (1985, as Murray McCoy), *Never Say Die, Birds of a Feather, Class Act* (1994, as Louis Calvin) and *Crocodile Shoes* (1994). He gained national fame as *Coronation Street* villain Richard Hillman (2001-03), having played Donald Worthington in the serial in the early 1980s. He went on to play Ozias Harding in *Where the Heart Is* (2004-06) and has made guest appearances in *Doctors* and *Midsomer Murders: Shot at Dawn* (2008) and *The Sword of Guillaume* (2010).

Brian's most recent film credits include *Emma* (1996), *101 Dalmatians* (1996), *Still Crazy* (1998) and *Ambleton Delight* (2009). He has two grown-up daughters from his marriage to actress Janette Legge and one son with his current partner, Jacqueline Bucknell.

Jane Cadrew

Jane Cadrew played Sid James's second wife in *Carry On Henry* and went on to appear in a number of 1970s sex comedies, including *Four Dimensions of Greta* (1972) and *The Flesh and Blood Show* (1972).

Patrick Cargill

Patrick Cargill holds a special place in the *Carry On* world. Not only did he guest star in *Carry On Regardless* and *Carry On Jack* but he is also credited with the original idea for one of the most successful films of the series – *Carry On Nurse*.

Born in London on 3 June 1918, Patrick was educated at Haileybury College and the Royal Military College (Sandhurst). After serving with the army in India he began his acting career in repertory at Bexhill. During the Second World War he again returned to the army before resuming his career in repertory, gradually working his way to the West End, with notable success in *Boeing Boeing* (1,500 performances over three years). Among Patrick's other stage credits were *Say Who You Are, Blithe Spirit* and *Dear Delinquent*, and he toured Australia and Canada in the 1970s in *Two and Two Make Sex*. Patrick also co-wrote the West End play *Ring for Catty*, which was adapted into *Carry On Nurse*.

Patrick Cargill (together with Jack Beale) was given credit for the original idea of *Carry On Nurse*, and although he is sometimes credited with an acting role in the film Patrick did not make his *Carry On* debut until 1961. As the Raffish Customer in *Carry On Regardless* he can be seen midway through the film, and three years later he returned to the series to play the Spanish Governor in *Carry On Jack*.

Patrick Cargill made his screen debut in *The Sword and the Rose* in 1953. He then went on to appear in over twenty films, including *Up the Creek* (1958), *Doctor in Love* (1960), *Help!* (1964), *A Countess from Hong Kong* (1967), *Inspector Clouseau* (1968), *The Magic Christian* (1969), *Every Home Should Have One* (1970), *Up Pompeii* (1971, as Nero) and *The Picture Show Man* (1977).

In his fifties Patrick gained national recognition as Patrick Glover in seven series of the popular sitcom *Father, Dear Father* (1968-73). The role, which suited the suave actor perfectly, led to further small-screen success in *Father, Dear Father, in Australia* (1978-80) and *The Many Wives of Patrick* (3 series, 1976-80, as Patrick Woodford). Patrick's additional television credits were wide ranging and included roles in leading series of the 1960s, such as *The Long Way Home* (1960), *The Escape of R.D.7* (1961) and *The Reunion* (1963). He also guest starred in *The Avengers* and *The Prisoner*, as well as more light-hearted material such as *Hancock's Half Hour* and *Ooh, La La* (1968).

After 1980 Patrick Cargill largely disappeared from television screens. One of his final small-screen appearances was in the 1985 pilot episode of *Barnett*, in which he played Clive Parmenter. He did, however, remain active on stage into the 1990s, notably as Sir John Tremayne in *Me and My Girl* (1990). During his final years he lived in Henley-on-Thames, Oxfordshire.

In private Patrick – a lifelong bachelor - enjoyed tennis, motor racing and writing plays, and he had a large collection of exotic pets.

Patrick Cargill never fully recovered from a car accident in Australia in

1995. Later that year he was diagnosed with cancer, and he died from a brain tumour in a hospice in Richmond on 23 May 1996, shortly before his seventy-eighth birthday.

John Carlin

Character actor John Carlin spent half a lifetime in 'camp' roles on screen and television. He made two *Carry On* film appearances: as an Officer in *Carry On England* and as Peter Butterworth's sympathetic French Parson in *Carry On Emmannuelle*.

Prior to his role in *Carry On England* John made his *Carry On* debut in exaggerated roles in six episodes of the television series *Carry On Laughing* in 1975. 'Mincing' his way through roles in 'The Baron Outlook' (as Ethelbert), 'Orgy and Bess' (as Sir Walter Raleigh), 'One in the Eye for Harold' (as Egbert), 'The Nine Old Cobblers' (as the vicar), 'The Case of the Screaming Winkles' (as Major Merridick) and 'Lamp-Posts of the Empire' (as the old man at the club), he secured his place in *Carry On* history.

John's numerous other small-screen credits included episodes of *George and Mildred, Robin's Nest, Keep It in the Family, Bergerac, Boon, The New Statesman* (1987, as Mr Speaker) and *Taggart*, and he played Reverend Spink in *The Darling Buds of May* in the 1990s, shortly before his retirement from the profession.

Apart from the *Carry On* films John also made cameo appearances in *Holocaust 2000* (1977), *George and Mildred* (1980) and *A Ghost in Monte Carlo* (TV, 1990).

Sandra Caron

Best known as the younger sister of singer Alma Cogan (1932-66), Sandra Caron played Fanny – Barbara Windsor's school friend – in *Carry On Camping*. Ironically, the pair had also gone to school together in real life!

Sandra made her screen debut in an uncredited role in *Sea Wife* in 1957 and went on to appear in *The Leather Boys* (1965), *Don't Raise the Bridge, Lower the River* (1968) and *Digby, the Biggest Dog in the World* (1974). She has also made numerous stage and television appearances, both in Britain and America, including an episode of *Charlie's Angels* in 1979. In the 1990s she was familiar as Mumsy, the fortune-teller, in *The Crystal Maze* (1990-94) with Richard O'Brien (q.v.) and toured the country on stage with Adam Faith shortly before his death.

Sandra - who has written a biography of her sister - was unable to attend the *Carry On* 40th Anniversary reunion due to work commitments, but she looks back on her solo role in the series with happy memories. She lives in London and is married to American stage and screen actor Brian Greene.

Carry On ... **Quotes**

Carry On Camping *was one of the most exciting times I have ever had on a film set. Just to be with those wonderful actors was an experience in itself, i.e. Barbara Windsor who I have known since I was a little girl at school, Joan Sims who is a consummate comedienne, Hattie Jacques who was a sweet and lovely lady, but my favourite of all was Kenneth Williams. The stories he would tell at lunchtime at Pinewood Studios are memories I treasure for always. We had six weeks of laughter.*
Sandra Caron, 1997

Edwina Carroll

Edwina played Nerda, one of the Nosha girls, in *Carry On Up the Jungle*. She had previously made film appearances in *A Town Like Alice* (1956, as Fatima), *The World of Suzie Wong* (1960) and *Genghis Khan* (1965) and she played the stewardess in *2001: A Space Odyssey* (1968). Edwina's sole *Carry On* appearance was her last film to date.

Alan Casley

Alan Casley played a sailor in *Carry On Cruising*.

Roy Castle OBE

One of the most enduringly popular figures of British show business during his forty-year career, Roy Castle appeared in a guest role, as Captain Keene, in *Carry On Up the Khyber*. Loved by all, he was a welcome addition to the *Carry On* team.

Born in Scholes, near Huddersfield, on 31 August 1932, Roy was the only son of a railway porter. After National Service he took a job for £10 a week performing in a troupe of clowns, before landing a job as 'stooge' to Jimmy Clitheroe and Jimmy James. By 1953 Roy was a professional entertainer, starring in pantomime and appearing in clubs all over the north of England. He ultimately became one of the last true variety artistes – he could sing, dance, act and play countless musical instruments.

Roy's first big break came in 1958 when he was offered a six-minute slot in the Royal Variety Performance, much to the delight of the Queen! He went on to pursue a singing career (with his album *But Seriously* topping the charts in the early 1960s) and received rave reviews for his role in the Tommy Steele West End musical, *Singin' in the Rain*.

Venturing into films in the 1960s, Roy's screen appearances included *Dr Terror's House of Horrors* (1965), *Doctor Who and the Daleks* (1965), *The Plank* (1967), *The Intrepid Mr Twigg* (1969) and *Legend of the Werewolf* (1975). Lasting success, however, came on the small screen as the host of the TV series *Record Breakers*, which ran for over twenty series (1972-92). In addition to hosting the popular show, Roy also broke numerous records himself, notably as a tap dancer and trumpet player. Roy also had television hits with *The Roy Castle Show* (1965, with Peter Butterworth and Pat Coombs, both q.v.) and *Roy Castle Beats Time*.

In 1992 Roy Castle – a lifelong non-smoker - was diagnosed with lung cancer. He blamed the disease on years of performing in smoky clubs but courageously toured the country to help raise money for cancer research. Despite his health problems, Roy also returned to the stage in the 1993 musical *Pickwick Papers*, with Sir Harry Secombe (the pair had co-starred in the 1966 Broadway version of the musical) and later featured in the same role in the 1993 Royal Variety Performance. Roy was awarded the OBE in the same year.

Roy and his wife Fiona had two daughters, Julia and Antonia, and two sons, Daniel and Benjamin. In private he enjoyed gardening, squash, golf, cricket and sleep! His autobiography, *Now and Then*, was published in 1994.

Roy Castle lost his gallant fight against cancer on 2 September 1994, just two days after turning sixty-two.

Cyril Chamberlain

With over a hundred film appearances to his credit, Cyril Chamberlain became a familiar face to cinema goers over a twenty-year period. He was also a regular performer in the early years of the *Carry On* series, appearing in seven films from *Carry On Sergeant* to *Carry On Cabby*.

Born in London on 8 March 1909, Cyril made his screen debut in *Crackerjack* in 1938. In the space of just a couple of years he appeared in over a dozen films, before active war service halted his career for several years. Returning to the profession in 1945, Cyril went on to play thoroughly working-class roles (usually as fathers, policemen, crooks and hired help) in films such as *London Belongs to Me* (1948), *Here Come the Huggetts* (1948), *Helter Skelter* (1949), *The Lavender Hill Mob* (1951), *Trouble in Store* (1953), *Doctor in the House* (1954), *Doctor at Sea* (1955), *Just My Luck* (1957), *Doctor at Large* (1957), *Blue Murder at St Trinian's* (1958),

A Pair of Briefs (1962), *Sky West and Crooked* (1965) and *The Great St Trinian's Train Robbery* (1966).

Although best known for his film work, Cyril also made numerous stage appearances, including *Julius Caesar* (1932, as Caesar's dresser), *Cut for Partners* (tour, 1932), *Husbands Don't Count* (1951), *The White Sheep of the Family* (1951, 273 performances, as Sam Jackson), *The Long March* (1953) and *Meet a Body* (1954). He also directed several stage plays.

Cyril made his *Carry On* debut as the Gun Sergeant in *Carry On Sergeant*. He was well teamed (as husband and wife Bert and Alice Able) with the equally prodigious Marianne Stone (q.v.) in *Carry On Nurse*, the pair having worked together previously in a handful of films, including *Simon and Laura* (1955) and *Lost* (1956), and his most memorable *Carry On* role was as Alf - the school caretaker - in *Carry On Teacher*. Cyril then went on to play PC Thurston in *Carry On Constable*, the park keeper in *Carry On Regardless* and the likeable Tom Tree in *Carry On Cruising*. His final *Carry On* role was as Sarge in *Carry On Cabby*.

In addition to the *Carry On* series, Cyril proved to be a reliable performer in other Gerald Thomas comedies: *Please Turn Over* (1959), *Raising the Wind* (1961) and *The Iron Maiden* (1962).

Cyril Chamberlain, who was known to his friends as Jimmie, spent the last five years of his life perfecting his craft as an antique furniture restorer. He was married to actress Lisa Lee (1907-2001) and they had one child. Cyril was sixty-five years old when he died suddenly of a heart attack at his home in Wales on 30 April 1974.

Norman Chappell

A familiar figure to television audiences of the 1960s and '70s, Norman Chappell played Allbright in *Carry On Cabby* and the 1st Plotter in *Carry On Henry*. He then went on to secure his place in *Carry On* history with appearances in seven episodes of *Carry On Laughing*.

Born in London in 1929, Norman made appearances in films and on television from the late 1950s. His screen appearances were mainly supporting roles, including Benson in *Crooks in Cloisters* (1964), the conductor in *Love Thy Neighbour* (1973) and the principal in *Intimate Games* (1976). On stage he played Fred in *Make Me an Offer* (1960, in London and on tour) and the Vicar in *The Licentious Fly* (1971, Mermaid).

Norman was best known on the small screen, with appearances in a range of programmes including *Firecrackers* (1964-65, as Leading Fireman Piggott, with Cardew Robinson, Sydney Bromley and Ronnie Brody, all q.v.), *Mr. Aitch* (1967, with Harry H. Corbett, q.v.), episodes of *The Avengers, Bless This House, Man About the House, Some Mothers Do Have*

'Em, Whoops Baghdad (1973, as Imshi), Sez Les (1976, with Les Dawson) and *Rushton's Illustrated* (1980), and he played Mr Window in the 1981 series *Doctor's Daughters*.

Norman also featured in seven episodes of *Carry On Laughing* on television in 1975, playing Lord Burleigh in 'Orgy and Bess', King Harold in 'One in the Eye for Harold', Potter in 'The Case of the Screaming Winkles', the ambulance driver in 'The Case of the Coughing Parrot', Sir William in 'Under the Round Table' and 'Short Knight, Long Daze' and the man on the park bench in 'Lamp-Posts of the Empire'.

Norman Chappell died on 21 July 1983, at the early age of fifty-four.

Ronald Clarke

Ronald Clarke played the 6th Storeman in *Carry On Sergeant*. He also made cameo appearances in *Hell Drivers* (1957), *Up the Junction* (1967) and *The Mackintosh Man* (1973).

Julian Clary

Following in the footsteps of *Carry On* greats Kenneth Williams, Charles Hawtrey and Michael Ward, Julian Clary played the outrageous Don Juan Diego in *Carry On Columbus*. In the tradition of camp *Carry On* characters, Julian gave a delightful and scene-stealing performance.

Born in Teddington, Middlesex, on 25 May 1959, Julian Clary studied drama at Goldsmiths' College, University of London. He began his professional career in cabaret in a double act called Glad and May in 1981, before joining the Covent Garden Community Theatre for a year. He then returned to cabaret as Gillian Pie-Face, later known as The Joan Collins Fan Club. Together with Fanny the Wonderdog (Julian's pet whippet!) he appeared on *Friday Night Live* before gaining phenomenal success on Channel 4 with a string of series, including *Sticky Moments* (1989), *Sticky Moments Tour with Julian Clary* (1990) and his 1991-92 sitcom *Terry and Julian*, all of which he wrote.

In *Carry On Columbus* Julian gave the series its most effeminate male to date. Flamboyantly dressed and made up, his character added new meaning to *Carry On* camp! Indeed, a much more risqué brand of humour emerged from Julian, with classic one-liners updating *Carry On* double entendre. Surprisingly, however, Julian was perhaps the only newcomer truly suited to traditional *Carry On* comedy and his scenes are among the best in the entire film.

In the past decade Julian Clary has appeared in well over fifty television programmes, both as an actor and as a personality. He teamed up with *Carry On* stars Frank Thornton and June Whitfield (who also guest starred in *Terry and Julian*) for two series of *All Rise for Julian Clary*, was the host of *Prickly Heat* (1998) and was the team captain for *It's Only TV ... But I Like It* (1999), and he also featured in *Private Property* (1999) and *Mr and Mrs* (1999). Among Julian's acting roles on the small screen are *Brazen Hussies* (1996), *Hospital* (1997), *Jack and the Beanstalk* (1998, as Tim), *Cinderella* (2000, as The Good Fairy) and *Aladdin* (2000, as the Genie of the Lamp). Most recently he has made frequent appearances on *Have I Got News for You.*

On stage Julian has toured Britain and Australia with his one-man shows, many of which have been released on video and DVD. His best-selling autobiography, *A Young Man's Passage*, which details his early years, was published in 2005 and he has also written several novels.

Julian, who remains one of Britain's busiest entertainers, lives in London.

Tom Clegg

Tom Clegg was a regular cameo player in the *Carry On* series, appearing in a total of six films.

Often called upon for heavyweight roles, Tom made his film debut in 1953 in *The Flanagan Boy* and went on to appear in *Moby Dick* (1956), *Peter Roger's Raising the Wind* (1961), *This Sporting Life* (1963) and *Catherine the Great* (1968).

In the *Carry On*'s Tom played Massive Mickey Magee, the boxer, in *Carry On Regardless*, the doorman in *Carry On Spying*, Amanda Barrie's tongueless Sosages in *Carry On Cleo*, the blacksmith in *Carry On Cowboy* and the boxing trainer in *Carry On Loving*. His most notable role in the series, however, was as Oddbod in *Carry On Screaming*.

Peggy Ann Clifford

A larger-than-life character actress, Peggy Ann Clifford appeared in a memorable cameo role in *Carry On Cleo*, as the ample auction bidder - Wella Claudia - who is willing to pay any price to get her hands on Jim Dale!

Peggy Ann, who was born in Bournemouth on 23 March 1919 (some sources say 1921), made her first professional appearances in repertory theatre and later worked for many years with the Joan Littlewood Theatre Company.

Peggy Ann made her film debut in *Forbidden* in 1949 and went on to make over twenty screen appearances in films such as *Man of the Moment* (1955), *Doctor at Large* (1957), *Happy Is the Bride* (1958), *Sparrows Can't Sing* (1962), *Far from the Madding Crowd* (1967), *Under Milk Wood* (1969),

Voices (1973) and *Murder by Decree* (1978).

She also appeared in a variety of small-screen roles, usually as matronly characters, including *Hancock's Half Hour, Bless This House* (2 episodes), *Our Cissie* (1974), *Are You Being Served?*, *Oh Happy Band!* (1980, as Mrs Tickford), *Alas Smith and Jones* (1984), *'Allo 'Allo* and *Super Gran* (1985, as Baroness Glutt).

Peggy Ann Clifford died in 1984.

Philip Clifton

Philip Clifton had an uncredited role in *Carry On Emmannuelle*.

Zena Clifton

Zena Clifton played Valerie Leon's au pair in *Carry On Matron* and Miss Susan Brooks in *Carry On Girls*.

John Clive (b. John Clive Hambley)

John Clive made his *Carry On* debut as Nicholas in *Carry On Abroad* and also made a cameo appearance as Kenneth Williams's tailor in *Carry On Dick*. He has since gone on to become a best-selling novelist.

John, who was born in London on 6 January 1938, trained at the Italia Conti Stage School and made his first professional appearances as a child.

John's film credits include *Yellow Submarine* (1964, voice only), *Smashing Time* (1967), *The Italian Job* (1969), *Tiffany Jones* (1973), *Great Expectations* (TV, 1974), *Revenge of the Pink Panther* (1978) and *R.P.M.* (1994). He has also made numerous television appearances, including *The Gnomes of Dulwich* (1969, as Old, with Terry Scott), *The World of Cilla* (1973, with Cilla Black), *Tropic* (1979, as Rev. Ivor Boon), *The History of Mr Polly* (1979), *The Nesbitts Are Coming* (1980, series, as PC Harris) and most recently *Young Indiana Jones* and *Casualty*.

In addition to his numerous acting credits, John is a well-known scriptwriter and author whose books have been published around the world. His first novel, *KG 200* (1977), was a number one best-seller and sold more than a million copies in the UK and USA alone. Since then he has written *The Last Liberator* (1980), *Barossa* (1981), *Broken Wings* (1983), *Ark* (1986) and *The Lions' Cage* (1988).

John, who was present at Pinewood for the *Carry On* 40th Anniversary reunion, provided commentary on the DVD release of *Carry On Abroad* in 2003. His only marriage ended in divorce and he has a son and a daughter. John Clive divides his time between homes in Richmond, Surrey, and Spain.

Carry On ... ***Quotes***

... it never ceases to amaze me how popular the Carry On *films are and, although I only did a couple of them, the mail still rolls in.*
It's a long time ago now, but my experience on Carry On Abroad *was a good one, the regular team, particularly Barbara Windsor and Sid James were very friendly, and where I half expected a rough ride from Kenneth Williams, because I was playing a 'camp' role, I only ever got encouragement.*
They were a wonderful bunch of very fine character actors, who deeply understood exactly how far they could go, and played everything with superb timing and delivery. Only now, sadly after most of them have passed on, is it being widely appreciated, which is a shame. Still better late than never.
John Clive, 2000

Jennifer Clulow

In her only film appearance to date, Jennifer Clulow played the 'first lady' listening to the Duc de Pommfrit's tall tales at Sir Rodney Ffing's ball in *Carry On Don't Lose Your Head*.

Born in Grimsby on 30 March 1942, Jennifer began her career on stage with the Royal Shakespeare Company, touring with Paul Schofield. She later had the lead role in the West End musical *4000 Brass Pennies*. Her acting credits on television include appearances in *The Odd Man* (1962-63), *Mr Rose* (2 series, 1967-68, as Jessica Dalton), *The Avengers, Bergerac* and *Keeping Up Appearances* (1993).

Jennifer Clulow has worked for many years as a television presenter and after several series she joined Westward TV as a senior announcer and reporter. Her broadcasts have included interviews and local reporting and she has also worked extensively in voice-overs.

Besides her acting and broadcasting credits, Jennifer is perhaps best known as the lady in the famous Cointreau television commercials, which ran for over fifteen years.

Martin Clunes (b. Alexander Martin Clunes)

Through his role in the long-running television series *Men Behaving Badly* and more recently *Doc Martin* and the remake of *Reggie Perrin*, Martin Clunes has become one of Britain's best-known actors. In 1992 he played Martin in *Carry On Columbus*.

The son of actor Alec Clunes (1912-1970), Martin Clunes was born on 28 November 1961. He made his television debut in four episodes of *Doctor Who* in 1983 and over the past thirty years has become one of the most prodigious actors of his generation, with countless appearances on the small screen. He is, of course, best known as Gary in *Men Behaving Badly*, a role that kept him busy for a decade, and he has played the title roles in *Doc Martin* (since 2004) and *Reggie Perrin* (since 2009). Among his other television credits are *All at No 20* (1988, as Henry), *Boon* (1989), *The Paradise Club* (1990), *Jeeves and Wooster* (1990-91), *Inspector Morse: Happy Families* (1992), *Demob* (1993, series as Dick Dobson), *Harry Enfield and Chums* (1994), *Never Mind the Horrocks* (1996), *Randall and Hopkirk (Deceased)* (2000), *Lorna Doone* (2000, as Jeremy Stickles) and *William and Mary* (2003, as William Shawcross).

In addition to *Carry On Columbus,* Martin has appeared in other films such as *The Russia House* (1990), *Staggered* (& directed, 1994), *Lord of Misrule* (TV, 1996), *The Acid House* (1998), *Shakespeare in Love* (1998), *Saving Grace* (2000), *Gormenghast* (TV, 2000), *Goodbye, Mr Chips* (TV, 2002) and *The Man Who Lost His Head* (TV, 2006).

A well-known supporter of numerous charities, including The Born Free Foundation, Martin was married to actress Lucy Aston. Following their divorce in 1994 he married TV producer Philippa Braithwaite and they have one daughter, Emily. Martin's book, *A Dog's Life,* was published in 2009.

Brian Coburn

Brian Coburn, who played the Scottish highwayman in *Carry On Dick*, was born in Scotland on 15 December 1936. He mainly worked on stage but also made occasional film appearances, including *Fiddler on the Roof* (1971), *Mary Queen of Scots* (1972), *Octopussy* (1983) and *Sword of the Valiant* (1984).

In later years Brian was seen in television series such as *Blott on the Landscape* (1985), *Lenny Henry Tonight* (1986) and *Campion* (1989). He died in London on 28 December 1989, aged fifty-three.

Peter Cockburn

Peter Cockburn was the narrator of *Carry On Camping*.

Paul Cole

Paul Cole appeared in *Dracula* (1958) and *Please Don't Turn Over* (1959) before playing Atkins, one of the cheeky pupils, in *Carry On Teacher*. His additional film appearances included *Next to No Time* (1959) and *The Man on the Moon* (1963).

Paul gave up acting in 1967 when he joined the BBC as a floor assistant. His work at the BBC included *International Cabaret,* where he was remembered by his *Carry On Teacher* co-star, Kenneth Williams.

In 1984 he became a freelance director and since then has directed, written and produced many television programmes, mainly for children. His most recent work includes *The Tweenies* and *The Sooty Show.*

Carry On ... *Quotes*

My memories of Carry On Teacher *are distant but pleasant. We shot it at Pinewood Studios (I have since worked there several times as a director and have always loved it). Kenneth Williams kept us all laughing during the shoot and Gerald Thomas never said cut without a laugh in his voice.*
Paul Cole, 2002

Gary Colleano

Gary Colleano played Slim in *Carry On Cowboy*.

Jeannie Collins

Jeannie played Private Edwards in *Carry On England*. Born in Liverpool in 1952, during her brief acting career she also appeared in *The Confessions of a Window Cleaner* (1974) and *Cruel Passion* (1977).

Laura Collins

Laura played a nurse in *Carry On Matron*.

Marian/(Marion) Collins

Marion made her screen debut in *The Love Lottery* in 1954 and appeared in supporting roles in *Behind the Headlines* (1956), *My Teenage Daughter* (1956), *Them Nice Americans* (1958) and *No Love for Johnnie* (1961). She became a semi-regular in the *Carry On*'s from 1962, playing the bride in *Carry On Cruising*, the bride in *Carry On Cabby* and one of the girls at Dirty Dick's tavern in *Carry On Jack*.

Jeremy Connor

The son of *Carry On* legend Kenneth Connor, Jeremy made his *Carry On* debut at the age of three when he played Kenneth's son in *Carry On Nurse*. He returned to the series at the age of eighteen to play one of the footpads in *Carry On Dick* and was later seen as the college student with the ice cream at Kenneth Williams's lecture in *Carry On Behind* and as Gunner Hiscocks in *Carry On England*. Jeremy returned to Pinewood

Studios in 1998 for the 40th Anniversary reunion and now lives in New Zealand.

Kenneth Connor MBE

(See MAIN TEAM).

Pat Coombs

A much-loved face on television and a veteran radio actress, Pat Coombs made cameo appearances in two *Carry On* films. In *Carry On Doctor* she had a wordless (and uncredited) role as the patient handed a bedpan by Bernard Bresslaw, and in *Carry On Again Doctor* she played the new matron who snubs Kenneth Williams in a most snooty fashion!

Pat was born in Camberwell, South London, on 27 August 1926. She took drama lessons as a teenager, and after a short spell as a kindergarten teacher she won a scholarship and trained at LAMDA. After graduating Pat toured the country in repertory before her first big professional break on radio in *Hello Playmates* (1954, with Irene Handl). She then went on to make innumerable broadcasts with big names from the past, such as Ted Ray, Arthur Askey and Bob Monkhouse.

Pat Coombs made her television debut in 1956 in *Great Scott, It's Maynard!* (with Bill Maynard and Terry Scott, both q.v.) and appeared in dozens of series, including *Hancock's Half Hour, Barney Is My Darling* (1965, with Irene Handl, q.v.), *Beggar My Neighbour* (1966-68, with June Whitfield, q.v.), *Wild, Wild Women* (1969, with Barbara Windsor, q.v.), *Lollipop Loves Mr Mole* (1971) and *You're Only Young Twice* (1978-81, with Peggy Mount).

Often cast as mousy or kind-hearted characters, in addition to the *Carry On* films Pat appeared in *Follow a Star* (1959), the screen versions of *Till Death Us Do Part* (1968), *On the Buses* (1971) and *Dad's Army* (1971), *Cry Wolf* (1968), *Willy Wonka and the Chocolate Factory* (1971), *Ooh... You Are Awful* (1972) and *Adolf Hitler – My Part in His Downfall* (1972).

By the mid-1970s Pat Coombs was one of the country's busiest comediennes as well as being a popular personality in programmes such as *Celebrity Squares*. She was the subject of *This Is Your Life* in 1978.

In the 1980s Pat was seen opposite Patricia Hayes (q.v.) in two series of *The Lady Is a Tramp* (1984-85) and she was also hugely successful in the children's series *Ragdolly Anna*. In 1989 she joined the cast of *EastEnders* as Brown Owl Marge Green and stayed with the serial for over a year. She then went on to play Prudence Prendergast in three series of *Noel's House Party* (1992-95).

In the mid-1990s Pat's career was abruptly halted for some time by the debilitating effects of the brittle bone disease, osteoporosis. In 1997 she revealed her brave fight to readers of *The Sun* and in the following year became a patron of the National Osteoporosis Society, helping to raise £100,000 for their 1998 Christmas appeal. Courageously Pat - known to her friends as Patty - continued to work until the end of her life, and in 1998-99 and 2001-02 she was reunited with June Whitfield in the radio series *Like They've Never Been Gone*. Pat also provided voices for the 2000 cartoon series *Treasure* and made guest appearances in *The Michael Barrymore Show* (2000), *Doctors* (2001, as Irene Morris) and *Heroes of Comedy – Dick Emery* (doc., 2002).

A popular real-life personality, Pat Coombs never married despite at least two proposals. For many years she lived in Harrow with her feline friends, Rudy and Nola, before spending her final years living happily at Denville Hall, the actors' retirement home, in Northwood. There, surrounded by friends - including Peggy Mount OBE (1915-2001), she enjoyed relaxing with a glass of white wine and an endless stream of menthol cigarettes.

Pat Coombs died at Denville Hall on 25 May 2002, from complications arising from emphysema, aged seventy-five.

Carry On ... ***Quotes***

I certainly have some great memories and small though my contribution was I am very proud of being a part of the Carry On's. *Working with the* Carry On *people I can only say my times with them were very short - but I loved each and every one, though I found Ken Williams a bit scary 'cos he was so outspoken!*
Pat Coombs, 1997

June Cooper

Model June Cooper played one of the girls in *Carry On Don't Lose Your Head* and one of the Khasi's wives in *Carry On Up the Khyber*.

Kenneth Cope

A well-known television actor, Kenneth Cope featured in leading roles in two *Carry On* films.

Born in Liverpool on 14 June 1931 (some sources say 14 April 1934), Kenneth began his acting career at the Bristol Old Vic Theatre School in 1950.

By the mid-1950s Kenneth had made his screen debut, and over the past fifty years he has featured in supporting roles in more than thirty films, including *These Dangerous Years* (1957), *Dunkirk* (1958), *The Lady Is a Square* (1959), *The Unstoppable Man* (1960), *Tomorrow at Ten* (1962), *Dateline Diamonds* (1965), *Genghis Khan* (1965), *The Desperados* (1969), *Rentadick* (1972), *Juggernaut* (1974), *George and Mildred* (1980) and *Captives* (1994). In *Carry On At Your Convenience* Kenneth played militant union official Vic Spanner and he was seen to best effect as likeable would-be gangster Cyril Carter in *Carry On Matron*.

Kenneth is best known for his work on the small screen, notably as Jed Stone ('Sonny Jim') in *Coronation Street* (1961-66) and as ghost Marty Hopkirk in the popular series *Randall and Hopkirk (Deceased)* (1969-74).

On television Kenneth has also made countless guest appearances, including *Ivanhoe* (1958), *Shelley* (1979), *Minder, Juliet Bravo, Doctor Who, Rumpole of the Bailey, Bergerac,* Agatha Christie's *Sleeping Murder* (1987), *Casualty, A Touch of Frost* (1997) and *Goodnight Sweetheart* (1997). Kenneth also helped host the popular sixties series *That Was The Week That Was* (1962-63), played Joe Trent in *Change Partners* (1965) and Percy James in *Bootle Saddles* (1984), and featured in the 1990s children's series *Uncle Jack and Operation Green* (1991). Kenneth played Ray Hilton in *Brookside* for three years (1999-2002) and most recently has turned up in episodes of *Waking the Dead, The Bill* and *The Royal*. He reprised his role in *Coronation Street* for several months in 2008. In addition to his numerous acting credits, Kenneth has worked as a scriptwriter on *Thingumybob* (1968) and *A Sharp Intake of Breath* (1977).

Kenneth Cope has been married for fifty years to actress Renny Lister, whom he worked alongside in *Coronation Street*, and they have three children: singers Mark and Nick Cope and actress Martha Cope. In 2008 Kenneth was among the guests at the *Carry On* 50th Anniversary celebrations at Pinewood Studios.

Harry H. Corbett OBE

A well-loved actor, still familiar through regular reruns of *Steptoe and Son,* Harry H. Corbett made a guest appearance in the *Carry On* series as Detective Sergeant Bung in *Carry On Screaming*. The film remains one of the most popular of the entire series and is a fitting tribute to the talented comic actor.

Harry H. Corbett was born in Rangoon, Burma - where his father was an officer in the army - on 28 February 1925. His mother died when he was just three and he was raised by an aunt in Manchester. During the Second World War he served in the Royal Marines, before making his first stage appearance as an understudy in repertory at Chorlton. He then spent ten years with Joan Littlewood's Theatre Workshop Company and throughout the 1950s and '60s was kept busy on stage in parts ranging from Shakespeare to light comedy. Among Harry's many theatre roles were Peter Stockmann in *An Enemy of the People* (1954), Lieutenant of Police in *The Power and the Glory* (1956), Waitwell in *The Way of the World* (1956) and the title role in *Ned Kelly* (1960). He remained busy on stage until the end of his life, with later credits including a tour of Australia in *Last of the Red Hot Lovers* (1972), the title role in *Macbeth* (1973) and Widow Twankey in *Aladdin* (1979).

The dark-haired, bug-eyed comedian made his screen debut in *Never Look Back* in 1958. He went on to appear in more than thirty films, mainly comedies, including *Shake Hands with the Devil* (1959), *Sparrows Can't Sing* (1962), *Ladies Who Do* (1963), *Joey Boy* (1965), *The Sandwich Man* (1966), *Crooks and Coronets* (1968), *The Magnificent Seven Deadly Sins* (1971), *Percy's Progress* (1974), *Jabberwocky* (1977), *What's Up Superdoc?* (1978) and *Silver Dream Racer* (1980).

Harry became famous around the world for his role of rag-and-bone man Harold Steptoe in eight series of *Steptoe and Son* (1964-74), with Wilfrid Brambell (q.v.). The enduringly popular series is still repeated to this day and made Harry a household name. It also inspired two feature films, *Steptoe and Son* in 1972 and *Steptoe and Son Ride Again* the following year. Not surprisingly, Harry found the character of Harold difficult to shake off, although he did go on to star in additional series including *Mr. Aitch* (1967, as Harry Aitch), *The Best Things in Life* (2 series, 1969-70, as Alfred Wilcox, with June Whitfield, q.v.) and *Grundy* (1980, as Grundy, with Lynda Baron, q.v.). He also made guest appearances on television in *Seven Year Hitch* (1973, as Ernest Conway, with Joan Sims), Eric Sykes's 'silent' comedy *The Plank* (1979, with Charles Hawtrey) and *Comedy Tonight* (1980).

Harry, who added the 'H' to his name to avoid confusion with Harry Corbett, the creator of Sooty, was married to South African-born actress Sheila Steafel (1935-) but the couple later divorced. He found lasting happiness with his second wife, Maureen Blott, and the couple had two children, a son and a daughter. Their daughter, actress Susannah Corbett (b.1968) – very much reflecting her father's likeness – is now a successful television actress, familiar through her work in *Peak Practice* and *Dalziel and Pascoe*. Harry was awarded the OBE in 1976.

Harry H. Corbett died in Hastings, after suffering a massive heart attack, on 21 March 1982.

Shane Cordell

Shane, who played the attractive nurse in *Carry On Nurse*, also appeared in *Three Men in a Boat* (1956), *The Good Companions* (1957) and *Girls at Sea* (1958).

Allan/(Alan) Corduner

A busy film and television actor, Allan Corduner played Sam in *Carry On Columbus*.

Born in Stockholm, Sweden, on 2 April 1950, Allan trained for the stage at the Bristol Old Vic Theatre School. His additional screen credits include *The Return of the Soldier* (1982), *Yentl* (1983), *A Business Affair* (1994), *Voices* (1995), *Topsy-Turvy* (1999, as Sir Arthur Sullivan), *Kiss Kiss, Bang Bang* (2000), *The Grey Zone* (2001), *Vera Drake* (2004), *Defiance* (2008) and *Burke and Hare* (2010).

On television Allan has been seen in *Heartbeat* (2007), *Fat Friends* (2000), *Drop the Dead Donkey* (1998), *Nostromo* (1996), *The Last Machine* (1995), *Paris* (1994) and *Nobody's Children* (1994). His earlier small-screen credits ranged from *Girls on Top* (1985) to *Minder* (1993).

Billy Cornelius

Through supporting roles in seven *Carry On* films, *Carry On Laughing* and the film version of *Bless This House*, Billy Cornelius became a familiar member of the *Carry On* team, albeit in a minor capacity.

Billy made an impressive *Carry On* debut as Oddbod Junior in *Carry On Screaming*. The brother of *Carry On* actor Joe Cornelius (q.v.), Billy, who began his career as a boxer and stuntman, went on to play a soldier in *Carry On Don't Lose Your Head*, the patient in plaster in *Carry On Doctor* and a guard in *Carry On Henry*. He had a speaking role as the policeman opposite David Lodge in *Carry On Girls*, played a 'tough man' in *Carry On Dick* and is credited as the man with the salad in *Carry On Behind*.

Born in London in 1934, Billy also worked for Peter Rogers and Gerald Thomas in *Bless This House* (1972), as the police constable (with Norman Mitchell, q.v.), and took part in three episodes of *Carry On Laughing* on television in 1975. Billy's other small-screen credits include *Dave's Kingdom* (1964, with Jack Douglas) and episodes of *Doctor Who* and *The Avengers* in the 1960s. Billy's last screen appearance (to date) was in *The Long Good Friday* in 1980.

Joe Cornelius

Joe, who played the boxer in *Carry On Loving*, also had the dubious role of the 'Missing Link' in *Trog* (1970) - Joan Crawford's final screen appearance. He is the older brother of Billy Cornelius (q.v.).

Eric Corrie

Eric, who played the 4th Citizen in *Carry On Constable*, appeared in a range of films over a period of a decade, including *Fire Over Africa* (1954), *Idols on Parade* (1959), *Watch Your Stern* (1961), *The Iron Maiden* (1962) and *The Scarlet Blade* (1963). He died in Lanzarote, Spain, in 1999 aged seventy-five.

Jenny Counsell

Jenny played the night sister in *Carry On Again Doctor*. She is the daughter of actors John Counsell (1905-87) and Mary Kerridge (1914-99) and sister of actress Elizabeth Counsell (1942-), who is best known for her role as Veronica Bainbridge in the 1980s television series *Brush Strokes*.

Brenda Cowling

A familiar face on television, Brenda Cowling played the hospital matron in *Carry On Girls* and can also be glimpsed as the wife in the audience of Kenneth Williams's lecture in *Carry On Behind*.

Brenda was born in London on 23 April 1925 and trained for acting at RADA with Warren Mitchell (q.v.) and Jimmy Perry. She made her screen debut in *Stage Fright* in 1950.

Over a period of fifty years Brenda made numerous appearances on stage, screen and television. She was perhaps best known as Mrs Lipton in four series of *You Rang, M'Lord?* (1991-93) and she also made appearances in *Dad's Army*, *Fawlty Towers* (as matron), *The Duchess of Duke Street*, *Are You Being Served?*, *In Sickness and in Health*, *All in Good Faith*, *Goodnight Sweetheart*, *Where The Heart Is* (2000) and *French and Saunders* (2004).

Brenda's film appearances were mainly in cameo roles and included *Up in the Air* (1969), *The Railway Children* (1970), *Young Winston* (1972), *International Velvet* (1978), *Octopussy* (1983), *Knights and Emeralds* (1986) and *Room to Rent* (1999).

In 1995 Brenda was at Pinewood Studios for the unveiling of the British Comedy Society plaque in memory of Gerald Thomas and six years later was a special guest at the Kenneth Williams Celebrations. In her final years she also took part in several events to celebrate *Dad's Army*.

Brenda Cowling never married and retired from acting in 2006 following a stroke. After a long illness she died at Denville Hall, the actor's retirement home, on 2 October 2010.

Carry On ... ***Quotes***

As you are probably aware the films were made very quickly in one or two takes for each scene. Those of us who were not in the regular cast, and who were called in for a day or two, had little time to get to know the regulars, unless you were playing a scene with them.
I enjoyed playing scenes with Kenneth Connor who was mayor to my matron in one of the films and who later played several guest episodes in You Rang, M'Lord? *– he was a very funny comedy actor, and easy and pleasant to work with. I also played with Hattie Jacques in the Eric Sykes TV show – another very talented, funny actress.*
Brenda Cowling, 1997

Jenny Cox

Jenny played Veronica in *Carry On Behind*.

Howard Marion Crawford

In his only role in the *Carry On* series, character actor Howard Marion Crawford played the organiser of the wine-tasting session in *Carry On Regardless*.

Born on 17 January 1914, the grandson of writer Francis Marion Crawford (1854-1909), Howard made his screen debut in *The Guv'nor* in 1935, and over the next thirty years he featured in over forty films. Well built and mustachioed, he was frequently called upon to play figures of authority, and his film appearances included *The Rake's Progress* (1945), *Stage Fright* (1949), *The Man in the White Suit* (1951), *Star of India* (1953), *The Silken Affair* (1956), *Foxhole in Cairo* (1960), *Lawrence of Arabia* (1962), *The Brides of Fu Manchu* (1966), *Blood of Fu Manchu* (1968), *The Castle of Fu Manchu* (1968) and *The Charge of the Light Brigade* (1968). Howard had two children from his two marriages, which both ended in divorce. His second wife was actress Mary Wimbush (1924-2005).

Howard Marion Crawford, who also played Dr Watson in the 1954 television series of *Sherlock Holmes,* died from an overdose of sleeping pills on 24 November 1969, aged fifty-five.

Bernard Cribbins OBE

A comedy star, hit singer and latterly character actor, Bernard Cribbins joined the *Carry On* series for two films in the 1960s, and as a well-regarded member of the team he was welcomed back almost thirty years later for *Carry On Columbus*.

Born in Lancashire on 29 December 1928, Bernard began acting at the age of fourteen at Oldham Repertory Theatre. He remained there for eight years before completing National Service with the Parachute Regiment. He made his West End stage debut in *A Comedy of Errors* in 1956. Throughout the late 1950s he gained success in theatre revues and had several pop chart hits, including *Hole in the Ground* (No. 9, 1962), *Right Said Fred* (No. 1, 1962) and *Gossip Calypso* (No. 25, 1962).

Bernard Cribbins made his screen debut in 1957, and a clear talent for comedy saw him cast in films such as *Make Mine a Million* (1959) and *Two-Way Stretch* (1960). He made his *Carry On* debut as Midshipman Albert Poop-Decker in *Carry On Jack*. The following year a combination of the heroic and bumbling set the tone for his role as secret agent 'Blue Bottle' Harold Crump in *Carry On Spying*.

Both characters were set somewhere between those taken on by Kenneth Connor and Jim Dale - an effective combination of hero and underdog.

Bernard returned to the *Carry On* series, an incredible twenty-eight years later, as Mordecai Mendoza in *Carry On Columbus*. Opposite Jim Dale, Bernard excelled and their scenes together can only be described as treasurable.

In addition to his screen credits (including a lead role in *Daleks' Invasion Earth: 2150 A.D.* in 1966), Bernard has made countless television appearances, including several versions of his own show, *Fawlty Towers* (1975, as Mr Hutchinson), *Shillingbury Tales* (1981, as Cuffy), *Dangerous Davies – The Last Detective* (1981), *Cuffy* (1983, lead role), *Tonight at Eight Thirty* (1991) and *Dalziel and Pascoe* (1999). He is also well remembered as the narrator of the popular children's series *The Wombles* and as the voice of Busby (the British Telecom bird), and he is constantly busy with voice-over and narration work for documentaries and television commercials.

Most recently on televison Bernard played Wally Bannister in *Coronation Street* (2003) and Frank Cosgrove in *Down to Earth* (2005), and he gained a new legion of fans in his eighties as Wilfred Mott in *Doctor Who* (2007-10).

A popular addition to the *Carry On* series, Bernard attended the 40th Anniversary celebrations in 1998 and also provided commentary on DVD releases of the series. Away from acting Bernard enjoys fly-fishing, clay pigeon shooting and golf and he is also a prodigious charity worker. He and his wife, Gillian McBarnet, live in Weybridge, Surrey. He was awarded the OBE in 2011.

*Carry On ... **Quotes***

... I can tell you a story about Bernie Cribbins and I in panto. We were in Aladdin *– Bernie was playing Widow Twankey and I was playing* Aladdin. *At one performance we had reached the scene where I was meeting the Princess for the first time. She said to me, "You're the boy from the apple tree." And in the moment of silence before my reply, a small child shouted from the gallery, "No, it's not, it's a girl!" At which point the audience erupted with laughter and Bernie ran on the stage and said, "No, it's not, and I'm his mother!" We could barely continue for laughing!!!*
Bonnie Langford, 2000

My memories of the three Carry On *films I was in are mixed to say the least. Generally pleasant, with a few others which are fading as some things do.* Carry On Jack *is my favourite I think – I remember the sun shone and we played cricket when we weren't shooting. An Oz actor – Ed Devereaux - was a very useful spin bowler (looked a bit like Shane Warne!).* Carry On Columbus *has faded almost completely now - thank God!*
Bernard Cribbins OBE, 2000

Larry Cross

Larry played Perkins in *Carry On Cowboy*. His other screen credits included minor roles in *The Good Companions* (1957), *The Girl Hunters* (1963), *Battle Beneath the Earth* (1967) and *The Wind and the Lion* (1975).

He died in June 1976, aged sixty-three.

Sara Crowe

Forever remembered for her role in the Philadelphia cheese TV adverts, Sara Crowe played Fatima, opposite Jim Dale, in *Carry On Columbus*. Ironically, she went on to become Dale's real-life daughter-in-law!

Born in Irvine, Scotland, on 22 March 1966, Sara began her career on stage where her credits include *Henceforth, Twelfth Night* and *A Woman of No Importance,* with the RSC. She received the Olivier Award for Best Supporting Actress for her role in *Private Lives*, played Marie-Louise in *The Constant Wife* (2002) and starred in *Calendar Girls* in 2009.

From the late 1980s onwards Sara has made appearances in television comedies, including *Alas Smith and Jones, Hot Metal* (series, 1988), *Rory Bremner* (3 series) and *Harry Enfield*. She had the lead role of Max in the 1995 series *Sometime Never,* and in recent years she has made guest appearances in *Born and Bred, The Green Green Grass, Casualty, Mayo* and

Skins (2009).

Sara's most notable screen credit to date has been *Four Weddings and a Funeral* in 1994. Her other film credits include *The Steal* (1994) and *Caught in the Act* (1995). In *Carry On Columbus* she successfully tackled the role of female lead, despite the poor standard of the film in general.

Sara Crowe met her husband Toby Dale (q.v.) on the set of *Carry On Columbus* in 1992 and they married in the same year. The couple divorced in 1998.

Bill Cummings

Bill, who played the 2nd Thug in *Carry On Spying*, has had a long screen career as both an actor and a stuntman. His film credits include *Thunderball* (1965), *The Pink Panther Strikes Again* (1976) and, as stuntman (and co-ordinator), most of the Bond '007' films.

Ian Curry

Born in Northern Rhodesia in 1930, Ian Curry played Eric in *Carry On Constable* and Leonard Beamish in *Carry On Regardless*.

Ian came to England at the age of six and studied Social Sciences at Liverpool University. After working as a teacher in South Wales he returned to Rhodesia and worked on South African radio. After two years he returned to England and spent five years (1956-61) in repertory. On stage he was especially notable as Albert Tufnell in *Watch It, Sailor!*, with fellow *Carry On* actors Esma Cannon, Wanda Ventham, Fraser Kerr and Ann Lancaster (all q.v.) in the early 1960s.

In addition to the *Carry On* series, Ian also appeared in *Sink the Bismarck!* (1960), *Hell Is a City* (1960) and *The Dock Brief* (1962), and he made appearances in more than twenty television series, including *Underground* (1958), *Crime Sheet, Tell It to the Marines* and *Emergency Ward Ten*.

By 1964 Ian was working as a staff announcer for Southern TV, after which he appears to have left the acting profession. He married Jeanette in 1958 and they had two sons, Nigel and Jonsen.

Alan Curtis

Well regarded as the 'King' of English pantomime, Alan Curtis appeared in cameo roles in two *Carry On* films: as the Conte Di Pisa in *Carry On Henry* and the Chief of Police in *Carry On Abroad*.

Alan Curtis was born on 20 July 1930. The youngest of three sons, he made his first stage appearances while at school, which included playing the role of Gwendolyn in *The Importance of Being Earnest*. He began his professional career in repertory in Gloucester in 1947, where at the age of sixteen he designed and painted scenery. Around the same time he also worked as an artist and actor on single frame animation films for the princely sum of £7 a week. He made his professional stage debut three years later and in a career spanning fifty years has appeared in over 600 stage plays, including five separate appearances at the London Palladium (a rare distinction that earned him the 'Brass Plate').

In addition to the *Carry On* series, Alan has made over thirty film appearances including *Ladies Who Do* (1963), *Frenzy* (1972), *Tiffany Jones* (1973), *The Flesh and Blood Show* (1973), *The Prisoner of Zenda* (1979) and *The Vision* (TV, 1987).

On television Alan's most memorable work was with Eric and Ernie in twenty-six episodes of the *Morecambe and Wise* series and he also worked with the famous comedy duo in pantomime on three occasions. Alan's additional small screen appearances included *Doctor Who, Coronation Street, Crossroads, The Avengers, The Saint, Up Pompeii, Whoops Baghdad* (1973, as Captain of the Guard), *Sir Yellow* (1973, as Sir Griswold), *The Howerd Confessions* (1976, as Sergeant Hardiman), *Duty Free* (1984) and *Crimewatch* (1993).

In 1995 Alan suffered a massive stroke, which left him semi-paralysed. He has, nevertheless, continued to work as a director of several companies, and as an avid cricket fan he continues to commentate from time to time. He was present at the *Carry On* 40th Anniversary celebrations in 1998 and was seated in the front row of the official photograph. Away from acting Alan enjoys travel and has visited most countries around the world, including Australia on many occasions. In 2003, having given more than 12,000 individual performances (on stage, screen and television and as a broadcaster), he made a return to acting when he played Alec in several episodes of the TV series *Footballers' Wives*.

Alan, whose only marriage to Yana Guard ended in an amicable divorce in the 1960s, lives in West London.

Carry On ... ***Quotes***

At the 40th Anniversary celebrations I said to Peter Rogers - a very cool, sophisticated man in his eighties - "Peter, I feel a bit of a fraud, I only did two of your films." There was a slight pause and he said, "Umm. You were lucky!" A lot of people did find them a chore - the money was not good. Sid (James) used to get about five or six thousand per film, which was not good money for

a six-week job. It worked out less than 1,000 pounds a week even in the seventies. Good money compared with working on stage but not good for a film. Rogers and Gerald Thomas made a fortune selling them around the world ... We all fumed about it. Always the irate ones were the young actors like Julian Holloway, who saw himself taking over the Jim Dale parts.
Of course the one person who should have been at the reunion was Joan Sims ... a lovely, lovely lady. I did a radio series with her and David Kossof called Sam and Janet *- they were husband and wife. I don't think she ever married - quite a source of disappointment. I last saw her when she did a pantomime near Chiswick ... she did like the fact that she could get home before the pubs emptied at night so missed great crowds of people.*
Apart from Joan they were all at the reunion - Jack Douglas was involved in organising with the crowd at Pinewood. Peter Gilmore (Captain Onedin), Bernard Cribbins, a good actor called John Clive ... A lot of the girls were there, Liz Fraser, June Whitfield and Sylvia Syms - even though she wasn't actually in the Carry On's. *And of course the guy who was the life and soul of the party was Norman Wisdom - he never appeared in the films - but they had done something recently for him at Pinewood and he was invited. Playing by the book he wasn't entitled to appear in the group photograph. I was very honoured to appear in that photograph and because of my disability I got on the front row. Peter Rogers was in the middle flanked by Barbara Windsor and June Whitfield and all the rest of the front row were women apart from Jack Douglas and I and Leslie Phillips at the other. Quite a photograph, taken in the ballroom. There was an auction, a big marquee and we had lunch. The auction raised a lot of money for a couple of charities. Norman Mitchell sat at the same table as me with Liz Fraser and John Clive. Norman is one of the absolute stalwarts of the British film industry. I should think he has appeared in more films than almost any other actor. He has had a great career of various bits and pieces - never got great billing any more than I did, but always had distinguished scenes - constables, publicans, innkeepers. A lovely, lovely man.*
Fenella Fielding and I live quite close to each other. I used her in a couple of shows - one at the Alexandria, Birmingham. She is terrific at these things. She does very childlike poems with deep sexual undertones. She and I did a famous Morecambe and Wise *show together ... everyone loves her voice ... "ooh darling!" She was at the reunion.*
I never did a bill with Hattie Jacques at the Players' Theatre but I had known her for years because she always used to come down to the charity cricket match which Harry Secombe organised every third Sunday in September - a great guest list of actors and cricketers ... all to raise money for the local hospital. I used to meet Hattie there. We were never close friends but I admired her work ...
Gail Grainger was a friend of Leslie Phillips; they were in a show together at

the time of Carry On Abroad - he was doing a revival of The Man Most Likely To. *I would be very surprised if she lasted more than a couple more years in the business. She was a reasonable looking girl, photographed well, but there was no film work for girls like that.*
In some of the early films - they come in clear categories - the first ones they weren't really sure where they were going and the collection of Carry On *characters was got together rather by accident. They had marvellous actors like Bill Hartnell doing the first one … very interesting. Then came the middle bracket, which really were not quite genuine Carry On's, with old Phil Silvers in* Carry On Follow That Camel, *with the* Carry On *title tagged on after it. Undoubtedly* Cleo *was outstanding. All the costumes came from Cleopatra - that nearly killed the British film industry stone dead! I used one of the costumes with Frankie Howerd in* Up Pompeii.
I had to do my horse-riding scene (for Carry On Henry*) the morning after the Royal Variety Performance and I was very hung over! They always have terrific parties after and I met a girlfriend whom I hadn't seen for quite a while and the inevitable happened and I had to get up the next morning and go to Pinewood and get on this bloody horse. The Royal Variety always happens at the end of November so it was cold … The Horseman really cheered me up when he told me that the horse had thrown Julian Holloway earlier in the week and Julian had a bad back for the rest of the film. It was freezing, freezing cold. Peter Rogers shouted at me, "I'm going to do it again. When you come into the courtyard don't look around so much. You look as though you're looking for number 38 Coronation Street when there's only one castle."*
In Abroad *the prison scene was the entire team except Hattie Jacques and Peter Butterworth, who were working in the hotel, and Jim Dale had dropped out by then … the one thing I remember was the fact that they all tried to make me laugh. The scene started with rain and everyone was pretending they were peeing, including Kenneth Connor, although he was a very good friend of mine and knew I wouldn't laugh … he always had a lovely habit of smoking from his ear and then from his nose! Oh, he was a lovely man, so kind and considerate …*
Going back to Abroad, *the girls were new and behaved themselves but the rest of the cast - Bernie (Bernard Bresslaw), Jimmy Logan and Kenneth Williams kept saying, "Ooh! You great big constable you - come on, give us a gesture!" A lot of Americans like the film and remember the gesture. They like the chance to go round and do that!*
Extracts from conversation with Alan Curtis, December 1998

Jim Dale MBE

(See MAIN TEAM).

Toby Dale

The son of *Carry On* stalwart Jim Dale, Toby played Inquisitor No. 5 in *Carry On Columbus*. He is, alas, unrecognisable behind a thick black cloak!

Toby Dale's additional acting credits have mainly been on stage and include the lead role in *Marlowe, Richard III*, Jarvis in *Hungry Ghosts* and Craze in *A Passionate Woman*. He also featured in the 1999 short film *At This Stage in My Career*.

Toby was married to *Carry On Columbus* co-star, Sara Crowe (q.v.) for six years.

Alexandra Dane

Through her involvement in five *Carry On* films, Alexandra Dane became a familiar member of the series's supporting cast and is perhaps best remembered by fans as the aptly named Busti in *Carry On Up the Khyber*.

Alexandra Dane was born in South Africa in 1946. She studied drama at Cape Town University and after moving to England worked on stage and formed her own company (The Cambridge Shakespeare Group).

Alexandra began her screen career as a glamour girl in the late 1960s. Her ample assets were used to full advantage in a variety of publicity stills when she joined the *Carry On* team as the female instructor putting Charles Hawtrey through maternity classes in *Carry On Doctor*. Her most impressive role in the series came when she played Busti, opposite Peter Butterworth and Cardew Robinson, in *Carry On Up the Khyber*. In *Carry On Again Doctor* Alexandra played the 'stout woman' whose exercise routine is sent spinning by the antics of Jim Dale, and in *Carry On Loving* she appeared in another cameo role (with Ronnie Brody, q.v.) as one of the unfortunate clients of the marriage bureau agency. Five years later, in her final *Carry On* appearance, Alexandra's famous cleavage received an unexpected surprise during Kenneth Williams's lecture in *Carry On Behind*.

In addition to the *Carry On* series, Alexandra Dane made appearances in Hammer Horror films and a range of screen comedies, including *Don't Raise the Bridge, Lower the River* (1968) and *Jabberwocky* (1977).

On the small screen Alexandra played Beryl in the 1974 series *Not On Your Nellie* (with Hylda Baker) and went on to appear in *The Melting Pot* (1975), *The Upchat Line* (1977) and various episodes of *Alas Smith and Jones* in the mid-1980s. Since 1981 Alexandra Dane's professional activities have mainly centred on her puppet company – Pom Pom Puppets – which she now runs with her daughter, actress Laura McKale.

Although absent from the *Carry On* 40th Anniversary reunion, Alexandra returned to Pinewood Studios in November 1999 for the *Carry On Stuffing* celebrations. She lives in London and Spain.

*Carry On ... **Quotes***

> Carry On's *were such a long time ago that I don't remember much, except that appearing on them was always a very happy experience – a big happy family and great fun.*
> ***Alexandra Dane, 1999***

Suzanne Danielle

Suzanne Danielle appeared as a guest star in the last of the 'true' *Carry On*'s, playing the insatiable Emmannuelle Prevert in *Carry On Emmannuelle*. It was one of several leading film roles undertaken by the glamorous actress during her brief acting career.

Born in London, on 14 January 1957, Suzanne appeared in a string of film roles from her very early twenties, including *Wild Geese* (1978), *The Stud* (1978), *Golden Lady* (1979), *Arabian Adventure* (1979) and *Flash Gordon* (1980).

In *Carry On Emmannuelle* she proved to be a breath of fresh air, taking centre stage among the middle-aged mainstays, including Kenneth Williams, Joan Sims and Kenneth Connor, and she ultimately proved to be the *Carry On*'s final leading lady.

By the early 1980s Suzanne was an established stage and television actress, and on the small screen she was perhaps best known for her work with Mike Yarwood. The pair featured together in the Royal Variety Performance (1981) as Prince Charles and Princess Diana. She also made guest appearances in *Doctor Who, Hammer House of Horror, The Persuaders* and *Strangers* and played Lola in the 1982 series *Jane*.

In 1983 Suzanne played Kim in the Cannon and Ball film, *Boys in Blue* (co-starring Jack Douglas) and in the following year she was reunited on stage with Joan Sims and Kenneth Connor in pantomime.

For several years Suzanne was romantically linked with Patrick Mower (q.v.) before her marriage to Scottish golfer Sam Torrance (1953-) in 1988. She now devotes the majority of her time to bringing up her three children, having made her final screen appearance in *The Trouble with*

Spies in 1987.

Suzanne was present at both the *Carry On* 40th Anniversary reunion and the 50th Anniversary celebrations a decade later. She has, however, "always made it her policy not to comment publicly about her role in the *Carry On* film" (1998).

Danny Daniels

American actor Danny Daniels played the Nosha Witch Doctor in *Carry On Up the Jungle*. Born in Georgetown, British Guiana on 1 November 1927, Danny made his screen debut in 1958. His occasional credits thereafter included *Prehistoric Women* (1967) and *The Oblong Box* (1969). He continued to act into the early 1970s.

Danny spent his final years living in America. He died from lung cancer at his home in Linden on 6 December 2010, aged eighty-three.

Larry Dann

Larry Dann made his *Carry On* debut as a teenager, playing one of the pupils in *Carry On Teacher*. Almost twenty years later, after cameo appearances in *Carry On Behind* and *Carry On England*, he was cast in a lead role as Theodore Valentine in *Carry On Emmannuelle*.

Born in London on 4 May 1941, Larry's acting career began by "fluke", with a "chance knock at the door looking for kids to work in films". Larry was just five years old when he made his screen debut in *Adam and Evelyn* (1946), with Jean Simmons and Stewart Granger. He continued to gain work as an extra before training at the Corona Academy from 1952.

Larry's first major acting appearance on stage was in the opera, *Wozzeck*, and from 1962 he worked for Joan Littlewood at the renowned Theatre Workshop (following in the footsteps of numerous other *Carry On* actors, including Barbara Windsor). Larry's long association with Joan included *Oh, What a Lovely War!* on Broadway.

Larry's first appearance in the *Carry On* series came when he was cast as one of the pupils in *Carry On Teacher*. He subsequently went on to appear in *The Bulldog Breed* (1960), *What a Crazy World* (1963), *All Neat in Black Stockings* (1968), *Before Winter Comes* (1969), *Thin Air* (1969), *Whirlpool* (1970), *Ghost Story* (1974), *In the Forest* (1978) and *All the Fun of the Fair* (1979).

After a long absence Larry returned to the *Carry On* series as Clive, one of the archaeology students, in *Carry On Behind*. He then went on to play the ever-blinking Gunner Shaw in *Carry On England*, before making his most notable contribution to the series as the naive Theodore Valentine in *Carry On Emmannuelle*. Significantly, Larry's *Carry On* credits spanned almost the entire length of the series, a record matched by only a handful of other actors.

Although Larry considers himself to be mainly a stage actor, he admits that the public best knows him for his work in the *Carry On* series and, more recently, as Sergeant Alec Peters in *The Bill* (1984-92).

One of Larry's earliest television appearances was in the pilot of *Coronation Street* and latterly he has been busy on stage, where his credits include *The Jests of Skoggan* (2001), *Jack and the Beanstalk* (2002, with Jack Douglas) and *The Ragged Trousered Philanthropists* (2010).

Larry, who has also written and directed for television, is married to costume designer Liz.

Carry On ... *Quotes*

The first Carry On *I did was* Carry On Teacher *in which I played the drummer in the orchestra. There was another scene filmed that wasn't shown where we started to play Jazz. It was great fun for me as I was allowed to go berserk and trash the drum kit. Sadly, I never saw it. I suppose it ended up on the cutting room floor and was then confined to the bin. It was many years later that I met Gerry Thomas at a commercial casting. He told me I wasn't right for that particular part but he would remember me for the next* Carry On. *Of course I thought "Oh yes", but he was true to his word and a few weeks later I got the call.*
Then I did the next three: Behind, England *and* Emmannuelle.
My two favourite Carry On *actors were the two Kenny's – Connor and Williams. They were both really great to me, gave me lots of their time and help. Not that the others didn't, but I felt they were special. The other 'special' person was Beryl Reid, who played my mum in* Emmannuelle. *We originally only had two scenes together but they went so well that others were written for us.*
Larry Dann, 2001

Diana Darvey (b. D. Roloff)

Diana, who played Maureen, opposite Jack Douglas and Windsor Davies, in *Carry On Behind*, was born on 21 April 1945 in Cheadle, Cheshire. Her greatest claim to fame was as a glamour girl in two series of *The Benny Hill Show* in the mid-1970s.

Twice married, Diana Darvey died in Redhill, Surrey, following a fall at her home, on 11 April 2000, at the age of fifty-four.

Claire Davenport (b. Claire Bernice Davenport)

Character actress Claire Davenport was ideally cast as Kenneth Connor's most amorous encounter in her only *Carry On* film – *Emmannuelle*. As the blonde in the pub, she is dragged back to her rancid bedsit by Connor, only to justify her reputation as the 'Closet Queen of Camden Town'!

Claire was born in Sale, Cheshire, on 24 April 1933. After training as a teacher she began working as an amateur actor, before gaining a scholarship and training at RADA, with Patrick Mower (q.v.). Her busy acting career began in the early 1960s in repertory and with the John Neville Theatre Company at the Nottingham Playhouse.

Claire Davenport made her screen debut in *Ladies Who Do* in 1963 and went on to make more than twenty film appearances, including *Some Will, Some Won't* (1969), *On the Buses* (1971), *The Return of the Pink Panther* (1975), *The Bawdy Adventures of Tom Jones* (1976), *Rosie Dixon – Night Nurse* (1978), *The Elephant Man* (1980), *The Return of the Jedi* (as Jabba's 'fat dancer', 1983), *War Requiem* (1988) and *Camping* (1990). Her more outrageous performances saw the matronly actress playing a masseuse in *Adventures of a Plumber's Mate* (1978) and a nude model in *The Birth of the Beatles* (1979).

On television Claire was typically cast as Scandinavian characters. She was perhaps best known as Dick Emery's wife in his television series, a role she played for four years. She also became a familiar face to television viewers with other small-screen credits, including *The Rag Trade* (1963, as Myrtle), *Fawlty Towers, George and Mildred, Robin's Nest, Not the Nine O'Clock News, The Frankie Howerd Show, By the Sword Divided* (1984, as Mrs Dumfry) and *In Sickness and in Health.*

From the early 1990s a succession of minor strokes gradually diminished Claire's powers of concentration and eventually ended her acting career. Her final small-screen appearances included the 1992 series *Space Vets* (as Daphne the Bossy Lizard!), *Flush* (1994, as Nursey) and the 1995 Disney production, *Stick With Me, Kid.*

In her final and rather sad declining years the obliging and kind-hearted actress found renewed popularity among *Star Wars* fans and was kept busy with signing sessions for *Doctor Who* and *Star Wars* conventions. She made a final public appearance at the Jedicon Four Festival in December 2001.

Claire, who never married and had no children, enjoyed travel, reading and swimming. She lived for many years in Holland Park, London, and spent part of each summer holidaying in Italy.

Claire Davenport died at Hammersmith Hospital, London, following a stroke and kidney failure, on 25 February 2002. She was 68 years old.

Carry On ... ***Quotes***

Because Barbara Windsor did not want to do the film they sent for me, because the team, and director were always the same for every Carry On *and because they all knew each other well, they made it very quickly with very few takes. They were all great professionals but they did help me and I think I did my best. We laughed a lot when the bed broke. We leapt on it with great joy (and great weight)!!*
Claire Davenport, 1997

David Davenport

David Davenport appeared in three *Carry On* films; as the Sergeant at the Chateau in *Don't Lose Your Head*, as Major Domo in *Carry On Henry* and most notably as the treacherous Bilius in *Carry On Cleo*.

David Davenport was born in Fairhill on 26 December 1921. Unlikely as it may seem - as one of the most imposing-looking actors to appear in the *Carry On* series - he began his career as a ballet dancer, having been introduced to the art by his mother at the age of twelve. After joining London's Cone Ripman Ballet School he went on to dance with the Lydia Kyasht Russian Ballet and in 1942 joined the Royal Ballet. He would go on to enjoy a distinguished dancing career opposite such luminaries as Dame Margot Fonteyn and Sir Robert Helpmann.

David made his stage debut with the New Russian Ballet in 1942, and during the Second World War he was a wireless operator in the RAF, before breaking into film and television. A dependable character actor for over twenty-five years, in addition to the *Carry On* series David featured in films such as *The Challenge* (1960), *That Kind of Girl* (1963), *The Secret of My Success* (1965) and *84 Charing Cross Road* (1986).

On stage David enjoyed a long and varied career, with appearances in *Annie Get Your Gun* (1949), *Oklahoma* (1954), *A Funny Thing Happened on the Way to the Forum* (1965, tour), *Dial 'M' for Murder* (tour, 1972), *The King and I* (tour, 1973) and *Little Women* (tour, 1974). In later years he made numerous appearances in pantomime, including *Jack and the Beanstalk* (1976), *Aladdin* (1982, with Ken Dodd) and *Goldilocks and the Three Bears* (1983, with Frankie Howerd).

David's television appearances included roles in *Dad's Army, Crossroads* (as Noele Gordon's husband) and *All Creatures Great and Small.*

Following stage appearances in *The Secret Diary of Adrian Mole Aged 13¾* (as Bert Baxter) in 1986, David retired from acting due to ill health. He had been due to appear on stage again with Frankie Howerd (q.v.).

David Davenport, whose marriage to Margaret Madison ended in divorce, had one daughter, Amanda (b.1955). He died at St John's and St Elizabeth's Hospice, St John's Wood, on 27 November 1995, aged seventy-three.

Evan David

Evan played the Bridegroom in *Carry On Cruising*.

Windsor Davies

Adept comic actor Windsor Davies featured notably in two *Carry On* films, as Fred Ramsden in *Carry On Behind* and the blustering Sergeant Major 'Tiger' Bloomer in *Carry On England*.

Windsor Davies was born in Canning Town, London, on 28 August 1930, of Welsh parents. He spent his first ten years living in London before returning with his parents to Wales, where he worked as a miner, factory worker and teacher. He was thirty-one when he became a professional actor, having completed a drama course at Richmond College of Further Education.

In *Carry On Behind* Windsor provided an effective double act with Jack Douglas. Stepping into a typical 'Sid James' role, Windsor, as butcher Fred Ramsden, managed to fit in well with the main team. In the following year he was ideally cast in a supporting role as Sergeant Major Bloomer in *Carry On England*, a role similar to his most famous on television. Ironically, Windsor's *Carry On* connection did not end with *Carry On England*. At the age of seventy he played Sir Toby Belch in *Cor, Blimey!* (2000), the television adaptation of Derek Johnson's critically acclaimed stage play based on the love affair between Sid James and Barbara Windsor.

In addition to the *Carry On* series, Windsor's film credits have included *Murder Most Foul* (1964), *The Alphabet Murders* (1966), *Drop Dead Darling* (1969), *Adolf Hitler – My Part in His Downfall* (1972), *The Old Curiosity Shop* (1975), *Not Now, Comrade* (1976), *Confessions of a Driving Instructor* (1976) and *Old Scores* (1991).

On television Windsor became a household name as Battery Sergeant Major Williams in eight series of *It Ain't Half Hot Mum* (1974-81). He followed up this successful role with eleven series of the equally popular *Never the Twain* (1981-91, as Oliver Smallbridge), with Sir Donald Sinden.

Windsor's other small-screen credits include *Probation Officer* (1962, as

Bill Morgan), *Recap, Doctor Who, UFO, Callan, 2Point4 Children, Oh, Doctor Beeching!, Sunburn* and *Casualty*. At the peak of his television success he released two singles: 'Whispering Grass' (1975, with Don Estelle), which reached Number One in the charts, and 'Paper Doll', which reached Number 41 in the same year. In the early 1980s Windsor was a familiar voice to children as Sergeant Major Zero in *Terrahawks*.

Now white-haired and often bearded, most recently he has appeared in scene-stealing dramatic performances on television, playing Lloyd George in *Mosley* (1998), General Tufto in *Vanity Fair* (1998) and Rottcodd in *Gormenghast* (2000).

Windsor Davies is married and has four daughters and one son.

Francis De Wolff

One of the most distinctive actors of his generation, Francis De Wolff appeared in a guest role in *Carry On Cleo*, playing the formidable Agrippa.

Francis De Wolff was born in Essex on 7 January 1913 and trained at RADA. His forty-year screen career began with the 1935 film *Sexton Blake and the Mademoiselle* and he was frequently called upon to play villainous characters in more than fifty screen appearances, including *Adam and Evelyn* (1949), *Trottie True* (1949), *Scrooge* (1951), *Ivanhoe* (1952), *Miss Robin Hood* (1952), *Moby Dick* (1956), *The Hound of the Baskervilles* (1959), *The Two Faces of Dr Jekyll* (1960), *Curse of the Werewolf* (1961), *From Russia with Love* (1963), *Licensed to Kill* (1965), *Sinful Davy* (1969) and *The Three Musketeers* (1973).

On stage from 1934 Francis played the photographer in *The Root of All Evil*, Ajax in *These Mortals* (1935) and Johnson in *Murder on Account* (1936). His later appearances in the theatre included *Diamond Lil* (1947-48, with Mae West), *Robinson Crusoe* (1957, as Bluebeard) and *She Stoops to Conquer* (1966, as Diggory).

Francis also made sporadic appearances on television, including episodes of *Danger Man, The Avengers* and *Doctor Who*. He ended his career playing Simon the Pharisee in the 1976 mini-series *Jesus of Nazareth*, after which poor heath prevented him continuing his career as one of Britain's most successful actors.

Francis De Wolff died at Peacehaven, Sussex, on 18 April 1984, aged seventy-one.

Jeremy Dempster

Jeremy played the 10th Recruit in *Carry On Sergeant*.

Carmen Dene

Carmen Dene played the Mexican Girl in *Carry On Cowboy* and had an uncredited role in *Up the Khyber* as a hospitality girl.

Jerry Desmonde (b. James Robert Sadler)

A popular 'stooge' to some of Britain's finest comedians, Jerry Desmonde appeared among the all-star cast of *Carry On Regardless*, playing randy TV star Paul Martin, opposite Joan Sims.

The son of actor and variety artiste Joseph Sadler, Jerry was born in Middlesbrough on 20 July 1908. He made his stage debut in 1919 and until the age of twenty appeared on stage in an act with his father, elder brother and two sisters. Jerry made his West End stage debut (as James Sadler) in *After Dinner* in 1932. He subsequently went on to work in variety with his brother and future wife.

In 1941, during the dark days of the Second World War, Jerry joined the RAF. He was invalided out after just a year and went on to join Sid Field (1904-50) for an eight-week roadshow. Jerry subsequently became one of the country's finest 'straight' men, and over the next twenty years he would make numerous appearances on stage, screen, television and radio.

Following his successful partnership with Sid Field, Jerry went on to become Sir Norman Wisdom's stooge for over a decade, from 1953, and the pair appeared together in eight films. Jerry made his screen debut in *London Town* (1946) and subsequently made almost twenty film appearances, including *Cardboard Cavalier* (1948), *Trouble in Store* (1953), *Malta Story* (1953), *Follow a Star* (1959), *A Kind of Loving* (1962), *The Switch* (1963), *The Beauty Jungle* (1964), *The Early Bird* (1965) and *Gonks Go Beat* (1965).

A founder member of *What's My Line?* on television, Jerry also gained popularity in television quiz shows *It's the Limit* and *The 64,000 Question*. He also broadcast on radio and to the end of his life continued to work regularly on stage, with final appearances including *Doctor at Sea* (1966, as Captain Hogg) and *One for the Pot* (1966, as Jonathan Hardcastle).

Jerry Desmonde was married for more than twenty years to Peggy Duncan, whom he met in a musical comedy show. The pair later appeared together on stage as a variety act and song and dance team, and they had two children. Peggy's death - following a long illness - in 1966, was a crushing blow for Jerry and he died in London on 11 February 1967, aged fifty-eight. At the time of his death he was about to become an entertainment organiser with a shipping company. Some sources give his cause of death as suicide.

Ed Devereaux

Australian character actor Ed Devereaux appeared in five *Carry On* films – a small proportion of a career that included acting, singing, writing and directing.

Ed was born in Sydney on 27 August 1925. He began his theatrical career in 1930 and by the age of nineteen had joined the Gladys Moncrieff Company, touring regional Australia in musicals. In the same year he made his radio debut and went on to become a band singer for Monty Richardson, notably in *Can You Take It.*

Ed left Australia for Britain in 1950 and worked at the London Palladium and as a band singer for BBC Bands in London and Manchester. He had made his screen debut in *Smithy* in 1946 and went on to make over seventy film appearances. In *Carry On Sergeant* he played Sergeant Russell, and he was seen opposite Bill Owen, as a patient, in *Carry On Nurse*. In *Carry On Regardless* Ed played Mr Panting, Fenella Fielding's (q.v.) jealous husband, and in *Carry On Cruising* he was cast as a young officer. He made his most memorable *Carry On* appearance as the scar-faced Hook in *Carry On Jack*.

Shortly after his final appearance in the *Carry On* series Ed returned to his homeland to play Matt Hammond, in the popular TV series *Skippy* – a role for which he is still fondly remembered. From the 1970s he divided his time and work between Australia and Britain, and his final credits included *Snakes and Ladders* (1989, as Lord Tewkesbury), *Degrees of Error* (1995, as Dr Crane) and *Absolutely Fabulous – The Last Shout* (1996, with Dora Bryan and June Whitfield, both q.v.).

Ed was married twice. His first wife was Irene Champion, who appeared with him for over a year in a variety song and dance act. From his first marriage he had four sons: John, a music composer; Stephen, a former actor/singer turned producer; Timothy, a music teacher; and Matthew, a singer/musician.

Ed, who never retired and believed in the adage that "old actors never die, they just fade away", was still acting into his seventies. He died from cancer in London on 17 December 2003, aged seventy-eight.

Carry On ... **Quotes**

I have done 75 films and can only remember half of them! I started in the Carry On's *in* Sergeant *on a lowly salary of £10 a day and finished up, five years later, in* Jack *on £100 a day, which was a lot of money in those days. When I was a little boy I used to sit on the banks of the creek and dream of*

carrying on and now I Carry On and get paid for it!
Ed Devereaux, 1999

Arnold Diamond

A versatile character actor, Arnold Diamond played the 5th Specialist examining Kenneth Connor in *Carry On Sergeant*. It was just one of more than sixty film appearances in a career spanning over thirty years.

Born in London on 18 April 1915, Arnold began his acting career as an amateur while working as a librarian. During the Second World War he spent time in an Italian hospital for prisoners of war, where he wrote and directed plays. Following the end of the war he trained at RADA and then spent many years building up his experience in repertory.

Arnold made his screen debut in *Cairo Road* (1950). Over the next three decades he made over sixty film appearances, often as foreigners or efficient officials, including *South of Algiers* (1952), *Mantrap* (1953), *The Revenge of Frankenstein* (1958), *The Duke Wore Jeans* (1958), *The Hands of Orlac* (1960), *The Switch* (1963), *The Spy with a Cold Nose* (1966), *The Best House in London* (1969), *All the Way Up* (1970), *Fiddler on the Roof* (1971), *The Alf Garnett Saga* (1972), *Frankenstein: The True Story* (1973), *Don't Just Lie There, Say Something!* (1973), *The Bawdy Adventures of Tom Jones* (1976), *Revenge of the Pink Panther* (1978) and *Omen: The Final Conflict* (1981).

Arnold's career on the small screen was equally prodigious and he turned up for guest appearances in an array of programmes, including *1984* (1954), *The Avengers, Dad's Army* (as Major-General Anstruther), *Not On Your Nellie, Citizen Smith* (1981), *Robin's Nest, A.D.* (1984) and *In Sickness and in Health.*

Arnold remained a working actor well into his seventies, with final appearances including television mini-series Anastasia: *The Mystery of Anna* (1986, as Dr Markov) and *War and Remembrance* (1989, as Mr Stern).

Arnold Diamond died in Bournemouth on 18 March 1992, aged seventy-six.

Peter Diamond

Acclaimed stuntman Peter Diamond had uncredited roles in several *Carry On* films, including *Carry On Cleo* and *Carry On Don't Lose Your Head.*

Born on 10 August 1929, Peter trained as an actor at RADA and went on to become one of the best-known stuntmen/fight directors in the business. His countless film credits included the *Star Wars* series of films, *Bond* movies, *Raiders of the Lost Ark* (1981), *Superman IV: The Quest for Peace* (1987) and *The Princess Bride* (1987). He continued to work as a stunt coordinator on television until the very end of his life.

Peter died in Wakefield, Yorkshire, on 27 March 2004 after suffering a stroke.

Terry Dickenson

Terry played the 11th Recruit in *Carry On Sergeant*.

Monica Dietrich

In addition to an uncredited role in *Carry On Don't Lose Your Head* and playing Katherine Howard in *Carry On Henry*, Monica appeared in *A Dandy in Aspic* and *For Men Only* (both 1968).

Basil Dignam

A character actor with over seventy film appearances to his credit, Basil Dignam played the 3rd Specialist examining Kenneth Connor in *Carry On Sergeant*.

Basil was born in Sheffield, Yorkshire, on 24 October 1905. After many years on stage he made his film debut in *The Lady with a Lamp* in 1951. Over the next twenty years he featured in cameo roles in an array of films, including *Touch and Go* (1955), *Private's Progress* (1956), *Reach for the Sky* (1956), *I Only Arsked!* (1958), *Room at the Top* (1959), *I'm All Right, Jack* (1959), *The Pure Hell of St Trinian's* (1960), *The Amorous Adventures of Moll Flanders* (1965), *Assignment K* (1967), *Battle of Britain* (1969), *There's a Girl in My Soup* (1970), *Young Winston* (1972) and *Soft Beds, Hard Battles* (1973).

Basil Dignam rounded off his long career with appearances in television series such as *The Persuaders, Randall and Hopkirk (Deceased), UFO, Elizabeth R, The Sweeney* and *Edward the King* (1975, as Herbert Asquith).

Basil - whose younger brother Mark Dignam (1909-89) was also an actor - was married to actress Mona Washbourne (1903-88). He died on 31 January 1979, aged seventy-three.

Dominique Don

Dominique appeared in minor roles in three *Carry On*'s – as one of the girls at Dirty Dick's Tavern in *Carry On Jack*, as a harem girl in *Carry On Follow That Camel* and most notably as the girl who lures Sergeant Major MacNutt (Terry Scott) in *Carry On Up the Khyber*.

Robert Dorning

Round-faced character actor Robert Dorning appeared in *Carry On Emmannuelle*, playing the Prime Minister. It was his only appearance in the series.

Born on 13 May 1913 (some sources say 1914) in St Helens, Lancashire, Robert began his career as a musician and ballet dancer, and he played a dancer in *The Red Shoes* (1948), one of his earliest film appearances. He served in the RAF during the Second World War and then resumed his stage and screen career.

During forty years in the business, Robert Dorning made over twenty film appearances, including *They Came By Night* (1940), *The One That Got Away* (1957), *Innocent Meeting* (1958), *Live Now - Pay Later* (1962), *Fanatic* (1965), *Cul-de-Sac* (1966), *School for Sex* (1969), *The Black Windmill* (1974), *The Ups and Downs of a Handyman* (1975), *Confessions of a Pop Performer* (1975), *The Human Factor* (1981), *Evil Under the Sun* (1982), *Pirates* (1986) and *Mona Lisa* (1986).

Robert's television career was equally busy and he appeared in countless comedy series, including *Bootsie and Snudge* (1961-63, 3 series, as Rt Hon. Sec. Hesketh Pendleton), *Are There Any More at Home Like You?* (1965), *Sykes Versus ITV* (1967), *Before the Fringe* (1967), *Turn Out the Lights* (series, as Wally Hunt, with Arthur Lowe), *Charlie Drake Comedy Hour* (1972), *Hogg's Back* (1975-76, as General Balding), *No Appointment Necessary* (1977, series, as Colonel Marshall), *The Dick Emery Special* (1979) and *Can We Get On Now, Please?* (1980, series, as Mr Butterfield JP). Although mainly in character roles, Robert did have a lead role in the one-off sitcom *The Loves of Larch Hill* (1969, as Robert Love). Sadly, a series did not transpire. Robert Dorning also featured in a variety of guest roles on the small screen, with appearances in *Coronation Street, Dad's Army* and several Spike Milligan series.

Robert was married to actress Honor Shepherd (1926-2000) and they had two daughters, Stacy Dorning (1958-) and Kate Dorning, both of whom followed in their parents' footsteps.

Robert Dorning died in London (from complications arising from diabetes) on 20 February 1989.

Angela Douglas (b. A. Josephine McDonagh)

With 'English Rose' looks Angela Douglas was a natural successor to Shirley Eaton in the *Carry On*'s and she remains a beloved figure among fans of the series.

Born in Gerrards Cross, Buckinghamshire, on 29 October 1940, Angela made her stage debut as a teenager before going on to make her professional theatrical debut in *Anniversary Waltz,* as an understudy. After training at the Italia Conti Stage School Angela appeared in television commercials, before making her film debut, at the age of nineteen, in *Feet of Clay*. She has since been seen in supporting roles in a range of films, including *The Gentle Terror* (1962), *The Comedy Man* (1963), *John Goldfarb, Please Come Home* (1965), *Maroc 7* (1967) and *Digby, the Biggest Dog in the World* (1973, with Jim Dale). She returned to film work in the 1990s after a long absence from the big screen and has featured in *Hamlet* (1996), *Shadow Run* (1998), *This Year's Love* (1999), *South Kensington* (2001), *The Four Feathers* (2002), *The Baby Juice Express* (2004), *Stealing Up* (2005) and *Sniff* (short, 2009).

Angela made her *Carry On* debut as Annie Oakley – the stunning heroine - in *Carry On Cowboy*. She made brief appearances in *Carry On Screaming* as Doris Mann before tackling her finest *Carry On* role as Lady Jane Ponsonby in *Carry On Follow That Camel*. In the following year Angela played the perfectly moulded Princess Jelhi in *Carry On Up the Khyber*, her final role in the series.

In the early 1960s Angela caused a sensation by living with Kenneth More, the leading film actor, who was already married and twenty-six years her senior. The couple married in 1968 and their years together prior to Kenneth's death from Parkinson's Disease were beautifully described in Angela's 1983 autobiography, *Swings and Roundabouts*. Following her marriage to Kenneth More (as his third wife) Angela largely withdrew from acting for almost a decade, although she did appear with More on television in *Father Brown* in 1974. In the 1980s Angela returned to the small screen (having previously made appearances in programmes ranging from *The Avengers* to *Coronation Street*), notably in *Give Us a Clue, Third Time Lucky* (1982, as Rosemary), *Sharing Time* (1984) and *Doctor Who* (1989, as Doris Lethbridge-Stewart).

In her fifties Angela happily increased her television appearances, mainly in dramatic roles. In the 1990s she was seen in *Strathblair* (1991, as Marjorie), *Cardiac Arrest* (1995-96, as Isabel) and *Brookside* (1999-2000). Most recently, having aged gracefully, she has been seen in *Deceit* (2000, as Anne), *Peak Practice* (2001), *Heartbeat* (2001, as Sonia Parkin), *Holby City* (2004, as Sally Stone) and *Four Seasons* (2004-08). On the whole, however, her acting appearances have generally been fewer than one would like.

In addition to her autobiography, Angela regularly contributes to newspapers and magazines and she also wrote the craft book, *Present Affairs* (1987).

Angela Douglas, who has provided commentary on DVD releases of the *Carry On* films, has also featured in several television documentaries, notably *What's a Carry On*? (1998) and *Heroes of Comedy - Hattie Jacques* (2002).

Angela married playwright and director Bill Bryden in New York in 2008.

Jack Douglas

(See MAIN TEAM).

Sally Douglas

Sally Douglas was a semi-regular glamour girl in the *Carry On* series, appearing in six of the films during the 1960s.

Born in 1942, Sally made her film debut in *A Weekend with Lulu* at the age of twenty. Her first *Carry On* roles - as an Amazon Guard in *Carry On Spying*, as one of the girls at Dirty Dick's Tavern in *Carry On Jack* and as Mark Antony's Dusky Maiden in *Carry On Cleo*, were uncredited. Her most notable contribution to the series was as Kitikata, Charles Hawtrey's shapely Indian friend, in *Carry On Cowboy*. Sally later played a victim of the Oddbods in *Carry On Screaming* and made a final appearance as a harem girl in *Carry On Follow That Camel*.

In addition to the *Carry On* series, together with a couple of other minor film roles, Sally also appeared on television, notably in several episodes of *Dad's Army* and *On the Buses*. She left show business in the early 1970s to care for her baby son.

Sally Douglas died in September 2001 following a long battle with cancer.

Su Douglas

The former wife of *Carry On* mainstay Jack Douglas, Su Douglas had a cameo role in *Carry On Columbus*. Playing Countess Joanna, she can be seen opposite Maureen Lipman (q.v.) in the early stages of the film.

Born in Nottingham on 8 November 1942, Su attended the Aida Foster School and Pauline Grant Ballet School. She began her career on stage, where her appearances included *The Elephant Man, Don't Just Lie There, Say Something!* and *Sleeping Beauty*.

On television Su has appeared in a range of programmes, from drama to comedy. Her early credits included the prison series *Within These Walls* and appearances in the *Mike Yarwood Show*. More recently she has been seen in supporting roles in *The Ruth Rendell Mysteries, The Upper Hand, Coronation Street* and *Sunburn* (1999). Still a busy stage actress, she toured the country in 2004 in *The Cemetery Club*, starring Edward Woodward, Michelle Dotrice and Shirley-Anne Field.

In addition to *Carry On Columbus*, Su has appeared in a handful of other films, including *Funny Money* (1982), *Boys in Blue* (1983, co-starring Jack Douglas), *Dragonworld* (1994) and *London to Brighton* (2006).

Su's marriage to Jack Douglas had ended in divorce by the time of his death in 2008. She has one daughter, Sarah.

Duncan Duff

Duncan Duff, along with actors such as Toby Dale and Michael Hobbs, had an unrecognisable role in *Carry On Columbus*, playing Inquisitor Number 2.

Since his solo *Carry On* appearance Duncan has mainly worked on television, with guest appearances in *May to December, Hamish Macbeth* (as Doc Brown) and *The Creatives* (1998), and he played Dr Geoff Spiller in the 2000 series *Big Kids*. More recently he has been seen in episodes of *Rosemary and Thyme* and *Doctor Who* (2006).

Lesley Duff

A light leading lady on television, Lesley Duff was just sixteen when she played Norma, one of the pupils of Chaste Place, in *Carry On Camping*. It was her only *Carry On* appearance.

Born in London on 25 April 1952, Lesley studied drama with Beryl Cooke before becoming an ASM in Birmingham. Her early career was spent in repertory at Watford, Derby and Leicester before appearing in West End plays such as *The Philanthropist, Happy as a Sandbag* (and television and radio), *The Bells of Hell* and *Beyond the Rainbow*.

On television Lesley's sporadic appearances included the second series of *Up the Workers* (1976, as Andrea), *Emu's Christmas Adventures, People Like Us, Leave Him to Heaven* (1979), *Doctor's Daughters* (1981, as Dr Lucy Drake), *Streets Apart* (1988-89, as Lyn), *Westbeach* (1993, as Maggie Cromer), *Class Act* (1994), *Castles* (1995) and *Fast Food* (1998, as Scarlet). She left the profession in the late 1990s and now co-runs a casting agency.

Patrick Durkin

Supporting actor Patrick Durkin appeared in four *Carry On* films, covering almost the entire lifespan of the series, from *Carry On Sergeant* in 1958 to *Carry On Dick* in 1974.

As the 6th Recruit in *Carry On Sergeant* Patrick's role was that of a glorified extra, but he made a greater mark as Jackson in *Carry On Nurse*. In the same year Patrick featured (in an uncredited role) in Gerald Thomas's *Please Turn Over*. After a five-year absence he returned to the *Carry On* series to play the 2nd Guard in *Carry On Spying* and made a final appearance in *Carry On Dick*, playing William.

Patrick was born in Middlesbrough on 9 June 1936. After training at LAMDA and making his screen debut in *Carry On Sergeant* Patrick went on to make more than twenty film appearances, featuring in *The Man Who Had Power Over Women* (1970), the screen version of *Love Thy*

Neighbour (1973), *The Big Sleep* (1979) and *Yanks* (1979). His television credits, over a twenty-year period, included episodes of *The Baron, The Professionals, Coronation Street, In Loving Memory* and *Juliet Bravo*.

Patrick continued acting in films and television well into the 1980s, his later appearances including *Raiders of the Lost Ark* (1981), *Britannia Hospital* (1982), *The Supergrass* (1985), *Lionheart* (1987) and finally *Monk Dawson* (1998). A stroke in 2001 forced Patrick to retire from acting, and despite suffering with diabetes towards the end of his life he took on work in clubs in Benidorm and happily met up with fans, making a final public appearance in July 2009 at the London Film and Comic Convention.

Patrick Durkin, who had two children, died in London on 1 September 2009, following a short illness. He was seventy-three years old.

Noël Dyson

A character actress of stage, screen and television, Noël Dyson played the 'vague' woman who calls on Charles Hawtrey to help rescue her cat in *Carry On Constable*. She later appeared in *Carry On Cabby*, as the District Nurse.

Born in Newton Heath, Manchester, on 23 December 1916, Noël Dyson initially trained as a secretary before joining RADA in 1936. During the Second World War she was a nurse and she later worked for ENSA, touring the country.

Noël was in her mid-forties before she secured fame on television as Ida Barlow – Kenneth Barlow's long-suffering mother – in *Coronation Street*. Seen in the first episode of the serial in 1960, Noël's character was killed off (at the actress's request) in 1961, after which she went on to pursue a busy small-screen career.

To the majority of television viewers Noël will be forever remembered as 'Nanny' Matilda Harris in seven series of the sitcom *Father, Dear Father* (1968-73), with Patrick Cargill (q.v.). Noël also played Mrs Chambers in *Whatever Happened to the Likely Lads* (1974) and Aileen Potter in three series of *Potter* (1979-83), and she reprised her role of Nanny in Australia in 1980 for *Father, Dear Father, Down Under.*

In addition to her work on television, Noël appeared in a handful of films, including Gerald Thomas's *Please Turn Over* (1959), *Gutter Girls* (1964), *Mister Ten Per Cent* (1966), *Champions* (1983) and *Super Grass* (1994).

In her later years Noël Dyson was frequently called upon for guest spots in TV series such as *Bergerac, Never the Twain, Executive Stress* and *May to December.* She continued to work until the very end of her life, her final appearances including the role of Dame Helen Mirren's mother in *Prime Suspect* (1990) and *Prime Suspect 2* (1992), and guest roles in *Waiting for God* (1992) and *Heartbeat* (1995).

Noël, who was married to actor Kenneth Edwards (1918-93), died from cancer of the liver in June 1995, aged seventy-eight.

Leon Eagles

Leon Eagles played the 4th Recruit in *Carry On Sergeant*. Born in Cardiff on 6 April 1932, Leon trained for acting at RADA and mainly worked on television, his later appearances including episodes of *Bergerac, C.A.T.S. Eyes, Heading Home* and *The Bill*. Besides *Carry On Sergeant* he also had small roles in *Performance* (1970), *Puppet on a Chain* (1970) and *Frenzy* (1972).

Leon and his wife Mary Preston (who died in 1994) had one daughter. Leon Eagles died on 16 December 1997, at the age of sixty-five.

Susanna/(Suzanna) East

A light leading lady of the 1970s, Susanna had an uncredited role in *Carry On Emmannuelle*. Her additional screen appearances include *Permissive* (1970), *The Fiend* (1971), *Savage Messiah* (1972), *Kronos* (1973) and *Tumbled* (short, 1999). She is still a working actress.

Shirley Eaton

Shirley Eaton was the first leading lady of the *Carry On* series. In her three *Carry On* appearances she presented cool and captivating characters – just as sexy as, if not more than, the more flagrant female leads in the later films.

Born on 12 January 1937 at Edgware Hospital, Essex, Shirley Eaton joined the Aida Foster School at the age of ten. She made her stage debut in 1949 in *Set to Partners* and at the age of thirteen appeared in the successful musical *Let's Make an Opera*, which ran for two years.

By the early 1950s, while still a teenager, the stunningly attractive, blue-eyed blonde had become one of Britain's biggest stars. After appearing in numerous stage productions with Max Bygraves she went on to make solo appearances as a singer and dancer at the Prince of Wales Theatre, and she extended her star output by appearing on television with Bill Maynard and Terry Scott (both q.v.) in *Great Scott, It's Maynard!* and on radio in *Educating Archie*.

Shirley made her screen debut at the age of seventeen in *You Know What Sailors Are* and went on to make over twenty film appearances, including *Doctor in the House* (1954), *The Love Match* (1955), *Doctor at*

Large (1957), *A Weekend with Lulu* (1961), *Dentist on the Job* (1961) and *What a Carve Up* (1961).

Shirley Eaton made her *Carry On* debut as Mary Sage in *Carry On Sergeant*. As Bob Monkhouse's wife she plays the female lead, with a unique combination of both the sexy and demure. The following year she was again cast in a leading role, as the enticing Nurse Dorothy Denton in *Carry On Nurse*. Shirley's roles in the series presented a marked contrast to the comic antics of Dora Bryan and Joan Sims. She nevertheless provided just the right amount of sex appeal for audiences in the late 1950s. In 1960 Shirley made her final *Carry On* appearance as Sally Barry in *Carry On Constable*, showing off her trim figure to full advantage - just five months after the birth of her first son!

In the mid-1960s Shirley's film career noticeably changed direction to include a greater variety of dramatic roles, and she went on to appear in *The Girl Hunters* (1963) and *Rhino* (1963) and took on her most famous role as the girl painted gold in the James Bond classic, *Goldfinger* (1964). Shirley's final film appearance (to date) was *The Girl from Rio*, in 1968.

In 1970, after a hectic twenty-year career, Shirley retired from acting to concentrate on family life. She married building contractor Colin Lenton-Rowe in 1958 and they had two sons, Grant (b.1959) and Jason (b.1966). During her retirement Shirley attended art school, producing numerous sculptures and oil paintings, and from 1987 until her husband's death in 1995 she lived in the South of France.

By 1997 Shirley had once more become involved with the world of show business, attending functions and conventions in connection with her acting career. In 1998 she was present at the *Carry On* 40th Anniversary reunion and she has since taken part in several events at Pinewood Studios, notably as a special guest at the *Carry On* Weekend (1999) and at the 50th Anniversary celebrations in 2008. Exuding a true film star quality, Shirley remains a popular guest at autograph conventions and charity galas.

Shirley, who featured in the 1998 documentary *What's a Carry On?*, lives in Harrow. Her autobiography, *Golden Girl*, was published in 1999 and she released a volume of poetry, *Golden Touch*, a decade later.

Carry On ... ***Quotes***

I do not have any more to say about the Carry On *films, except I am very glad I was part of that historic film series.*
Shirley Eaton, 2000

Eve Eden (aka: Utka Levka)

In addition to playing one of the Khasi's wives in *Carry On Up the Khyber*, Eve appeared in minor roles in over a dozen films, including *Operation Bullshine* (1959), *A Weekend with Lulu* (1961), *Help!* (1965), *Scream and Scream Again* (1969) and *The Oblong Box* (1969).

Ray Edwards

Ray, who began his acting career in 1949, had an uncredited role as 'the man with the water' in *Carry On Behind*.

Born in England, Ray spent fifteen years of his early life living in Australia, where he served in the Australian Infantry in Japan and Korea. In 1954 he was a personal orderly to the Queen during her 1954 Commonwealth tour of Australia and he was decorated three times.

Ray's acting career began in the Antipodes with stage tours of Australia and New Zealand in *Nude with Violin, Oklahoma* and *Brigadoon*. He has since enjoyed a long and varied career on stage, screen and television in Britain, America and Australia.

On stage Ray has toured in *My Fair Lady*, *Pirates of Penzance, Hay Fever* and *The Cocktail Party*. He also worked for the Royal National Theatre in *Front Page* and toured Australia for six years. During the 1980s Ray featured in various runs of *Noises Off* and more recently utilised his military training in *Tosca* (1995) and *Carmen* (1997).

On television Ray has featured in episodes of *The Avengers, The Bill, Casualty, Families* (Aust.) *Neat & Tidy* and *Grange Hill*.

In addition to *Carry On Behind*, Ray Edwards has featured in minor roles in several other films, including *Oh! What a Lovely War* (1969) and *Alice's Adventures in Wonderland* (1972).

Angela Ellison

Angela played the cloakroom girl in *Carry On Spying*. She continues to act occasionally on stage and television.

Heather Emmanuel

Diminutive character actress Heather Emmanuel appeared in two *Carry On*'s: as the plump native girl in *Carry On Again Doctor* and as the pregnant Lubi in *Carry On Up the Jungle*.

Heather trained for the theatre at RADA and Fellow Trinity College, London. Over the past forty years she has featured in over a dozen films and videos, ranging from *Secret of Blood Island* (1965) to *Mama Mia!* (2008). On the small screen Heather has appeared in more than fifty series, including *Andromeda Breakthrough* (series, 1962, as Nurse), *Dixon of*

Dock Green (4 episodes), *Danger Man* (3 episodes), *Family Pride* (11 episodes), *Outbreak of Murder* (6 episodes), *Angels* (3 episodes), *The Doctors* (6 episodes), *Sexton Blake* (6 episodes), *Close* (14 episodes) and *Children's Ward* (2 episodes).

Heather's stage appearances have included seasons at the Old Vic and time with the RSC at Stratford, and she has also run drama workshops for deaf children. Frequently called upon for narration and voice-over work in films and television series, she remains one of the country's busiest voice artists.

In addition to her numerous television credits, Heather Emmanuel has enjoyed an equally prodigious career on radio, having worked on more than sixty programmes, ranging from Schools Radio to *101 Dalmatians*.

*Carry On ... **Quotes***

Many things have been written about Sid James – some not so good. He was a kind and sensitive person. On my first day in Carry On Again Doctor *he saw me looking lost, a mere nobody, took me by the hand and introduced me to all the big stars. When I went back for* Carry On Up the Jungle *he still remembered me – that says a lot for someone who knew and met so many people.*
Heather Emmanuel, 2001

E.V.H. Emmett

A distinctive commentator, film editor, screenwriter and producer, E.V.H. Emmett was the narrator of *Carry On Cleo*.

Born in London on 18 June 1902, E.V.H. was the voice of Gaumont News for over a decade from the 1930s and the voice of Universal News in the 1950s.

In addition to *Carry On Cleo*, former journalist E.V.H. also narrated a variety of other films, including *Wings of the Morning* (1937), *The Lion Has Wings* (1939), *Sailors Three* (1940), *On Approval* (1940), *Easy Money* (1948) and *Invitation to Monte Carlo* (1959).

He co-wrote the 1936 film *Sabotage* (directed by Alfred Hitchcock) and was also credited as a writer (and writer of additional dialogue) for films such as *Non-Stop New York* (1937), *The Worst Case* (1938), *Bothered by a Beard* (1945) and *Dance Hall* (1950).

For four years (from 1946), E.V.H. also produced films at Ealing

Studios, including the 1949 Stanley Holloway film *Passport to Pimlico*.
E.V.H. Emmett died on 7 June 1971.

David Essex OBE (b. D. Albert Cook)

Singing legend David Essex was just twenty-two years old when he played a heckler in *Carry On Henry*. He remains the most famous *Carry On* actor to end up on the cutting room floor.

David Essex was born in Plaistow, London, on 23 July 1947. He began his career as an apprentice electrician, while spending his spare time as a drummer in a band. He shot to fame after auditioning for the role of Jesus in *Godspell*. David then went on to appear in lead film roles in *That'll Be the Day* (1973, with Ringo Starr) and *Stardust* (1974, with Adam Faith). In the 1970s the good-looking singer and actor was a teen idol celebrated in Britain and around the world. His first number one single 'Rock On' in 1973 was followed by more hits, including 'Gonna Make You a Star' and 'Hold Me Close'.

Early in his career (in addition to *Carry On Henry*), David appeared in *Octaman* (1971), *Assault* (1971) and *All Coppers Are…* (1972). In 1980 he starred in, and recorded the lyrics for, *Silver Dream Racer* (with Harry H. Corbett, q.v.), and he played Don Pedro in *Shogun Warrior* (1992).

Over the past thirty years David Essex has proved himself to be an enduring performer. In addition to over twenty top 30 hits, he has worked for Lord Webber in *Evita* (as Che), written his own musical - *Mutiny* – and, in 1993, worked for Sir Peter Hall in a tour of *She Stoops to Conquer,* with Sir Donald Sinden and Miriam Margolyes OBE.

As well as continuing to tour the world as a singer, David Essex still appears on television, both as an actor and personality. He was the subject of *This Is Your Life* in 1995, played Johnny Lee in an episode of *Heartbeat* (2000) and joined the cast of *EastEnders* (as Eddie Moon) in 2011.

David, who is married with two children, was awarded the OBE in 1999 for services to charity.

Carry On … ***Quotes***

I did one day's filming for Carry On Henry *and had to deliver the immortal line "Wot about the workers!" Thankfully it finished up on the cutting room floor!*
David Essex OBE, 2000

Barbara Evans ARAD

Barbara played one of the Khasi's wives in *Carry On Up the Khyber* and went on to become a professional dance instructor.

Barbara, who was born in Birmingham and educated at the King Edward School, won a scholarship and trained at RADA for five years. She was also an Associate of The Royal Academy of Dance and was a fully registered dance teacher.

In addition to countless roles on stage, including revues such as *Share My Lettuce* (with Kenneth Williams and Dame Maggie Smith) and *One to Another* (with Beryl Reid and Sheila Hancock, both q.v.), Barbara had leading roles in musicals and pantomime. On television, as a singer, dancer and actress, Barbara Evans appeared in *The Avengers, Ghost Squad, Terry and June, Call My Bluff* and *Going for a Song*. Sadly, her career was cut short following a serious car accident, in which she broke her pelvis, right arm and left leg and dislocated her hip.

In later years Barbara was the founder of the Barbara Evans School of Dance (Worcester) and she trained in ballet, modern dance and tap. She was Chair of the Royal Academy of Dance for the Midland Region from 1985 to 1990.

Barbara, who enjoyed collecting antiques, swimming, cooking and travelling, lived in Worcester. Her first husband was musician Harry Roche and she subsequently married television producer/director Patrick Johns.

Following a long illness, Barbara died peacefully at her home in Martin Hussingtree on 4 July 2010. She was seventy-eight years old.

*Carry On ... **Quotes***

I played the Indian girl locked in the cupboard by Sid James in Carry On Up the Khyber. *I simply had a couple of days free and was called to play this small part.*
Strangely, I danced with Sid twice on TV: a trio with Sid and Tony Hancock on 'The Ladies Man', an episode of Hancock's Half Hour, *and another trio with Sid and Lionel Blair in 'Entente Cordial', an episode of* Bless This House. *I believe they were the only occasions Sid danced seriously – actually he was quite a good mover.*
Barbara Evans, 2000

Rupert Evans

Rupert was a stunt double for the hospital orderly in *Carry On Again Doctor* and played the Major in 'The Prisoner of Spenda', an episode of *Carry On Laughing* (TV, 1975).

EXTRAS: Although many 'uncredited' actors are included in this reference, it has not been possible to include individual entries for the vast number of 'extras' who also appeared in the series. The list below, although by no means comprehensive, serves as an acknowledgement to just some of the extras featured in the series.

Sergeant: Ivor Danvers, Norman Hartley, Benny Lee. *Nurse:* Raymond Glendenning. *Constable:* Ronald Adam, Tom Cubitt, Tex Fuller, Colin Gordon, Mary Jones (voice only), Alfred Pim, Bruce Seton, Frederick Treves (voice only), Margaret St. Barbe West. *Regardless:* Yvonne Ball, Sylvia Bidmead, John Cabot, Jane Cavendish, Carl Conway, Helen Frayling, Arthur Gomez, Tom Hankey, George Rigby, Sherry Ann Scott. *Cruising:* Jan Williams. *Cabby:* Geoffrey Colville, Alexandra Dore, Michael Graham, Joan Green, Frank Lawless, Penelope Lee, Anabella McCartney, Olive Milbourn, Sally Ann Shaw, Mavis Trent. *Spying:* Olive Gregg (voice only), John Jardine. *Again Doctor:* Jill Damas, Johnnie Wade. *Up the Khyber:* Nigel Kingsley. *Up the Jungle:* Willie Jonah, Shalini Waran. *Loving:* Betty Huntley-Wright. *Abroad:* Tony Allan, Gerald Paris, Mike Stevens. *Matron, Girls, Emmannuelle:* Shirley English. *Girls*: Ron Tarr, Cy Town. *Dick*: Mike Stevens, Michael Stainton. *Columbus*: Peter Pedrero. Special mention must also be given to Harry Fielder (1940-), who appeared as an extra in *Carry On Follow That Camel, Up the Khyber, Henry, Abroad* and *Dick*.

Mario Fabrizi

Mario Fabrizi was already a familiar face to television audiences when he played the 2nd Chef in *Carry On Cruising*.

By the time he made his screen debut in 1960 Mario had appeared on television in *Hancock's Half Hour* and *The Army Game* (1960-61). In addition to *Carry On Cruising*, his film appearances included *Two-Way Stretch* (1960), *The Rebel* (1961), *Operation Snatch* (1962), *On the Beat* (1962), *Mouse on the Moon* (1963) and *The Punch and Judy Man* (1963).

Mario's film credits were escalating when he died in London on 5 April 1963, aged just thirty-eight.

James Fagan

James had an uncredited role in *Carry On Emmannuelle*.

Sonny Farrar

Sonny, who also appeared in *Half a Sixpence* (1967), played the violinist in *Carry On Loving*.

James Faulkner

One of the most distinctive actors of his generation, James Faulkner was ideally cast to play Torquemada, of the Spanish Inquisition, in *Carry On Columbus*.

James Faulkner was born in Hampstead, North London, on 18 July 1948, and began his acting career in his early twenties.

Over the past forty years James has appeared in over thirty films, including *The Great Waltz* (1972), *The Abdication* (1974), *Zulu Dawn* (1979), *Priest of Love* (1981), *Real Life* (1983), *Eureka* (1983), *The Maid* (1990), *E=mc2* (1996), *Crimetime* (1996), *The Commissioner* (1998), *All the Little Animals* (1998) and *Vigo* (1998), and he played Uncle Geoffrey in *Bridget Jones's Diary* (2001) and its sequel *Bridget Jones: The Edge of Reason* (2004).

James has also featured in a wide variety of tele-movies and mini-series, such as *Great Expectations* (1974), *I, Claudius* (1976), *Lace II* (1985), *Deceptions* (co-starring Joan Sims, 1985), *Minder on the Orient Express* (1985), *Still Crazy Like a Fox* (1987), *The Hound of the Baskervilles* (1988), *Devices and Desires* (1991), *The Blackheath Poisonings* (1992), *Guinevere* (1994), *The Lost Empire* (2001), *Leonardo* (2003) and *Ben Hur* (2010).

James has made guest appearances in over sixty television series and has thus become a familiar face to small-screen audiences. He remains at his best in villainous roles and recently has turned up for guest roles in *Highlander, Wycliffe, A Touch of Frost, Pie in the Sky, Relic Hunter, Heartbeat, The Royal* and *Spooks*.

James is married and has two sons. He lives in North London.

Max Faulkner

Max, who played a highwayman in *Carry On Dick*, has appeared in a variety of film and television roles over the past thirty years.

On the small screen he made several appearances in *Doctor Who* in the 1970s and around the same time he also made guest appearances in *Robin's Nest, Space: 1999* and *Blake's 7*. His film credits range from *Bedazzled* (1967) to *GoldenEye* (1995).

Pat Feeney

Pat played the 4th Storeman in *Carry On Sergeant*.

Hilda Fenemore (b. Hilda Lilian Fenemore)

One of Britain's most prodigious film and television actresses, Hilda Fenemore's two *Carry On* roles typified a career spent in thoroughly working-class character roles.

Born in London on 22 April 1914, Hilda Fenemore trained on stage as an amateur and later took voice production lessons at the Central School of Speech and Drama (London). She made her film debut with Dirk Bogarde in *Esther Waters* in 1948 and her professional stage debut at St James's Theatre (Piccadilly) in *No Trees in the Street* in 1951.

Throughout the 1950s and 1960s Hilda was at her busiest in film roles, usually as wives, mothers or working women. She made over ninety film appearances, usually in cameo roles, including *Chance of a Lifetime* (1950), *The Titfield Thunderbolt* (1953), *The Tommy Steele Story* (as Tommy's mother, 1957), *Doctor in Distress* (1963), *This Is My Street* (1964), *Casino Royale* (1967), *The Double Kill* (1974), *The Bawdy Adventures of Tom Jones* (1976), *The Stud* (1978), *South of the Border* (1986) and *Broke* (TV, 1991).

In *Carry On Nurse* Hilda played Rhoda Bray, the doting wife of Brian Oulton (q.v.), and in *Carry On Constable* she made a brief appearance as the 'agitated woman' who is helped by Kenneth Connor when she finds herself in need of a "copper"!

On television Hilda made countless appearances in comedy, drama and commercials. Her small-screen credits ranged from Jane Austen's *Emma* (1972) to *Goodnight Sweetheart* (1993). In the 1960s she was a familiar face in four series of *Dixon of Dock Green* and she also featured in *Dad's Army, Are You Being Served?, The Duchess of Duke Street, Minder, Roll Over Beethoven, Vanity Fair* (1987), *French and Saunders, Gone to Seed* (1992, as Miss Pringle) and *Harry Enfield and Chums*.

In 1997, fittingly for an actress who has spent a lifetime playing working-class characters, Hilda appeared in a promotional television film for the Labour Party – and was delighted when they won. In her final years she worked on television in commercials for Mr Sheen and Nescafe and remained thankful for fifty years of 'continuous' work.

Hilda Fenemore was married to the late film and television scriptwriter and author Rex Edwards. They had two sons, one a professional educational psychologist and the other an artist and lecturer. In private Hilda enjoyed collecting antiques and gardening. She lived in Hertfordshire until her death on 13 April 2004, shortly before her ninetieth birthday.

*Carry On ... **Quotes***

I was on location for Carry On Nurse *at Pinewood Studios and for* Carry On Constable *at Ealing Broadway, London. Very enjoyable. I was in the theatre (Albery) in* The Winslow Boy *and did a day's filming at Woking (for* Constable*). I had to hurry to catch the train to the theatre. Got on one moving off, and said to the man next to me, "This is the fast train to Waterloo," and he said, "No, it's the fast train to Portsmouth"! I was gobsmacked, but luckily it had one stop on the way and I changed there and managed to make the curtain in time!*
Hilda Fenemore, 1997

Fenella Fielding

An iconic British actress and one of cinema's best-known femme fatales, Fenella Fielding provided two unique *Carry On* performances. In *Carry On Regardless* she played the bosom-heaving Penny Panting (opposite Kenneth Connor), before taking on the unforgettable role of the seductive vamp – Valeria – in *Carry On Screaming*.

Born in London on 17 November 1934, Fenella Fielding began her career on stage in 1954. Her first major role was as Lady Parvula De Panzoust in Sandy Wilson's legendary Firbank musical *Valmouth*. She went on to gain critical acclaim in 1959 for her role in the revue *Pieces of Eight* (which ran for 429 performances) and quickly rose to fame.

On stage and in films and television Fenella's talents were obviously too exceptional to waste, and since those early days she has been kept busy with a variety of roles. After a screen debut in *Sapphire* in 1959 she went on to appear in films such as *Follow A Star* (1959), *Doctor in Love* (1960), *No Love for Johnnie* (1961), *The Old Dark House* (1962), *Doctor in Distress* (1963), *Doctor in Clover* (1966), *Drop Dead Darling* (1966) and *Lock Up Your Daughters* (1969). During the 1960s Fenella also made a variety of television appearances, including *The Ides of March* (as Cleopatra), *Saki* (as Mary Drakmanton), *The Importance of Being Earnest* (as Gwendolyn), *The Avengers,* the Feydeau farce series *Ooh La La, That Was The Week That Was, Dean Martin and the Gold Diggers* and three guest starring appearances in *Morecambe and Wise*.

Over the past forty years she has built up an incredible list of stage credits. Like Kenneth Williams (her co-star in *Pieces of Eight*) Fenella Fielding's voice has always been her greatest asset and her deep, alluring tones continue to attract theatre-goers. On stage her favourite role is that of Hedda in *Hedda Gabler* (1969). She made her American stage debut in the title role of *Lysistrata* in 1968 and went on to play the title role in *Colette* in New York, off-Broadway, in 1970. Still constantly in demand, more recently Fenella has been seen in one woman shows, including *Maria* (1996) and *A Dangerous Woman* (as the Duchess of Windsor, 1999), has toured in *Lady Windermere's Fan* in 2000 and starred in *The Vagina Monologues* (Irish tour, 2006), *An Ideal Husband* (2008) and *Dearest Nancy, Darling Evelyn* (2011, as Nancy Mitford).

Fenella's recent television appearances have included four series of *Uncle Jack* (1990-93, as The Vixen), a guest starring role in *The Legend of Dick and Dom* (2010, as Lotte Lawoo) and she has also taken part in a number of documentaries such as *Reputations – Kenneth Williams* (1998), *The 100 Greatest Scary Moments* (2003) and *Eric and Ernie: Behind the Scenes* (2011). On the big screen Fenella played Mrs Foxfur in *Guest House Paradiso* (1999) and since then has taken on roles in *Beginner's Luck* (2001) and *The All Together* (2005) and starred as Eve in *Wish Baby* (2008).

Since the mid-1990s Fenella Fielding has helped promote renewed interest in the *Carry On* series, hosting the BBC Radio 2 programme *Carry On Carrying On* in 1994 and attending the 40th Anniversary reunion in 1998. In 2000 Fenella returned to Pinewood Studios as a special guest at the *Carry On Screaming* celebrations and was present at the 50th Anniversary celebrations in 2008. She also provided commentary for the DVD release of *Carry On Screaming*. A delightfully captivating real-life personality, she has built up a cult fan base and is a frequent guest at film conventions. Of Russian/Romanian descent, in private Fenella enjoys reading and diarising. She lives in London.

Ann Firbank

A leading lady of stage, screen and television, Ann Firbank played Nurse Helen Lloyd in *Carry On Nurse*. It was her only appearance in the series.

Ann, who was born on 9 January 1933, made her professional debut over fifty years ago. She has since enjoyed a distinguished theatrical career, usually as refined characters, with countless appearances ranging from *Macbeth* to *A Handful of Dust*. Ann has also toured the world in *The Hollow Crown* and in 2000 she spent time with the RSC as the Lady Abbess in *The Comedy of Errors* and as Alice in *Henry V*.

Ann Firbank's film credits include *Behind the Mask* (1959), *Darling* (1965), *A Severed Head* (1970), *Sunday, Bloody Sunday* (1971), *Stories from a Flying Trunk* (1979), *A Passage to India* (1984), *Lionheart* (1987), *Strapless* (1988), and *Anna and the King* (2000, as Lady Bradley).

On television Ann has mainly been seen in dramatic productions, including *Persuasion* (1969), *The Lotus Eaters* (1973), *Lillie* (1978), *The Scarlet Pimpernel* (1982), *Poirot* (1989), *Boon, Growing Rich, Heartbeat*

(1994), *Animal Ark, Kavanagh QC* (1998), *The 10th Kingdom* (2000), *Elizabeth I* (2005, as Lady Anne) and *Midsomer Murders: The Black Book* (2009, as Felicity Law).

Ann Firbank lives in London.

*Carry On ... **Quotes***

... the Carry On *film was so long ago I can't remember a thing, except that we laughed a great deal and had a very good time!*
Ann Firbank, 2000

Charles Fleischer

American comedian Charles Fleischer is perhaps best known as the voice behind the successful cartoon character Roger Rabbit. He featured in *Carry On Columbus*, playing Pontiac.

Born in Washington D.C. on 27 August 1950, Charles moved to Los Angeles in the early 1970s and began his career performing in comedy clubs. In the mid-1970s he featured in several television sketch shows, including *Keep Trucking* (1975), *Welcome Back, Kotter* (1975), *The Richard Pryor Show* (1977) and *Wacko* (1977).

Charles made his film debut in *Die Laughing* in 1980 and has since appeared in *The Hand* (1981), *A Nightmare on Elm Street* (1984, as Dr King), *Back to the Future II* (1989), *Dick Tracy* (1990), *Big Monster on Campus* (1998), *Bel Air* (2000) and *The Polar Express* (2004). He secured success when he provided voices (including that of the lead role) for *Who Framed Roger Rabbit* in 1988 and has gone on to become one of America's best-known voice artistes, working on a range of cartoons and numerous Roger Rabbit video specials.

Helen Ford

Helen played a nurse in *Carry On Doctor*.

Joanna Ford

Joanna had an uncredited role as a Vestal Virgin in *Carry On Cleo*. She is also sometimes credited with the role of a GlamCab driver in *Carry On Cabby*.

Frank Forsyth

Cameo player Frank Forsyth featured in a total of seven *Carry On* films and also appeared in Gerald Thomas's *Raising the Wind* (1961) and *The Big Job* (1965).

Born in London on 12 December 1905, Frank made his London stage debut in *Wonder Bar* in 1930 at the Savoy Theatre. He went on to appear as the solicitor in *Once a Crook* (1940, Aldwych), *Strange As It May Seem* (1946, tour), *Noose* (1947, as Basher Marx), *Lute Song* (1948), *Gay's the Word* (1952, with Dame Cicely Courtneidge), *Malice Domestic* (1956, as Dr Royes Bell) and *Something About a Sailor* (1957).

Frank made his screen debut in an uncredited role in *The Lavender Hill Mob*. He acted in more than a hundred films, including *The Embezzler* (1954), *Tiger by the Tail* (1955), *No Smoking* (1955), *The Man Without a Body* (1957), *Innocent Meeting* (1958), *Devils of Darkness* (1965), *The Deadly Bees* (1966), *The Terrornauts* (1967), *Oh! What a Lovely War* (1969), *Tales from the Crypt* (1972), *Asylum* (1972) and *The Screaming Starts!* (1973).

In the *Carry On* films Frank became a semi-regular for the first half of the series. He played the 2nd Specialist examining Kenneth Connor in *Carry On Sergeant*, John Gray in *Carry On Nurse* and the 4th Citizen in *Carry On Constable*. Gradually, his contribution to the series increased and he went on to play the chauffeur in *Carry On Cabby*, the unfortunate Professor Stark in *Carry On Spying* and the 2nd Sea Lord in *Carry On Jack*. Frank's final *Carry On* role was as the Desk Sergeant in *Carry On Screaming*.

One of Frank Forsyth's final appearances was among the all-star cast of the TV-movie *Love Among the Ruins* (1975) and in the late 1970s he played Mr Brownlow on stage in *Oliver!*. His last television role was as Briggs in an episode of *Dick Turpin* in 1980.

Frank Forsyth died suddenly in Poole on 2 May 1984, aged seventy-eight.

Derek Francis

A wide-ranging actor, Derek Francis appeared in superb character roles in six *Carry On* films, thus securing a notable place in *Carry On* history.

Derek Francis was born on 7 November 1923 in Brighton. Against the wishes of his parents, he wanted to pursue an acting career and he made his stage debut in repertory at the age of seventeen. After training as an art teacher Derek joined the army, returning to repertory at the end of the Second World War and eventually working at Oxford Playhouse, where he spent two years.

By the mid-1950s Derek was an established character actor. For four years (from 1955) he worked with the Old Vic Company, appearing in an assortment of stage plays that included *Julius Caesar, The Merry Wives of Windsor, Macbeth* (as Lennox), *Richard II* (as the Duke of York), *Hamlet* (as Polonius) and *King Lear* (as the Duke of Gloucester). His later stage credits included *Charley's Aunt* (1979), *The Merchant of Venice* (1982, as Shylock) and *Gas and Candles* (1983, as Frank Martin).

Derek appeared regularly in films from the early 1960s. The portly actor was often called upon to play religious figures or men of authority. His screen credits included appearances in *The Criminal* (1960), *No Love for Johnnie* (1961), *Bitter Harvest* (1963), *The Comedy Man* (1963), *Rasputin: The Mad Monk* (1966), *Scrooge* (1970), *Up the Creek* (1971), *To the Devil ... A Daughter* (1975), *Jabberwocky* (1977) and *The Wicked Lady* (1983).

Derek made his *Carry On* debut as Sir Edmund Burke, the north country official interrogating Jim Dale, in *Carry On Doctor*. In the same year he played Patricia Franklin's protective father in *Carry On Camping*, giving perhaps his finest *Carry On* performance. After 'shooting' Terry Scott in *Camping*, the two were again seen together when Derek had a cameo role as the Bishop on the train in *Carry On Loving* and he played the farmer in *Carry On Henry*. In 1972 Derek made his final *Carry On* appearances, in two very different character roles: as Arthur, the hospital porter, in *Carry On Matron*; and as the serious Brother Martin, with Bernard Bresslaw, in *Carry On Abroad*.

On television Derek Francis was one of the country's busiest actors. Among his many credits were programmes such as *Oh, Brother!* (2 series, 1969-70, as Sub-Prior Father Matthew), *Whoops Baghdad* (series, 1973, as The Wazir, with Frankie Howerd), *The Beryl Reid Show* (1977), *Nicholas Nickleby* (1977) and *Bless Me, Father* (series, 1978, as Bishop O'Reilly). Busy until the very end of his life, his final TV appearances included *Partners* (series, 1981, as George Gilkes), *Shelley* (1982, as a Lawyer), *Pinkerton's Progress* (series, 1983, as Mr Beech), *Pope John Paul II* (1984) and *Winter Sunlight* (1984). He also made guest appearances in programmes ranging from *Doctor Who* to *The Sweeney*.

Derek and his wife Penelope (whom he married in 1954) had two daughters, Tessa and Julia. Away from acting he enjoyed art and making puppets.

Derek Francis died suddenly from a heart attack on 28 March 1984. He was sixty years old

Patricia Franklin

RADA-trained actress Patricia Franklin carved a niche for herself in five *Carry On* films, invariably as dour characters not taken to suffering fools!

Born in London in 1942, Patricia made her *Carry On* debut as the heavily pregnant farmer's daughter in *Carry On Camping*, opposite Charles Hawtrey and Derek Francis (both q.v.). She was perfectly cast as the aptly named Mrs Dreery in *Carry On Loving* (providing a memorable cameo scene with Kenneth Williams and Bill Maynard, both q.v.), and in *Carry On Girls* she played Rosemary, June Whitfield's (q.v.) masculine feminist ally. In *Carry On Behind* Patricia played Jack Douglas's concerned wife, Vera Bragg, and in 1976 she made her final *Carry On* appearance (playing a typically no-nonsense character), as the Corporal Cook in *Carry On England*.

In addition to the *Carry On*'s, Patricia adopted a Scottish accent to play Molly Weir's (q.v.) daughter in the film version of *Bless This House*, and also featured in a couple of 1970s tele-movies, notably *Brief Encounter (1974)*.

Patricia took time out of acting (1984-94) to concentrate on family life, but in recent years she has returned to the profession, notably as the Spinster in *Shaun of the Dead* (2004) and as Annette Roper in *Hot Fuzz* (2007). She has also appeared on television in episodes of *The Bill, Silent Witness* (1995) and *Black Books* (2004) and the stage play *Under the Sink* (1996).

Patricia attended the gala screening of *Carry On Up the Khyber* in 1995 and has made several appearances at autograph conventions in recent years.

Liz Fraser (b. Elizabeth J. Winch)

Liz Fraser appeared in three early *Carry On* films playing characters that were, in fact, a forerunner to those taken on by Barbara Windsor in most of the later films. Ironically, when Barbara left the *Carry On*'s, Liz returned to the series for a fourth and final appearance.

Liz Fraser was born in London on 14 August 1930 (some sources say 11 August 1933 or 1935). She trained at the London School of Dramatic Art and originally acted under the name of Elizabeth Fraser.

Liz made her screen debut in *Touch and Go* in 1955. Usually cast in comic roles, she has since appeared in more than fifty films, including *Alive and Kicking* (1958), *I'm All Right Jack* (1959), *Follow a Star* (1959), *Doctor in Love* (1960), *The Bulldog Breed* (1960), *The Americanization of Emily* (1964), *The Family Way* (1966), *Dad's Army* (1971), *Three for All* (1974) and *Chicago Joe and the Showgirl* (1988).

Liz joined the series as the shapely Delia King ('Miss') in *Carry On Regardless*, replacing Shirley Eaton as the classic blonde leading lady so prevalent throughout the series. The following year she played Glad Trimble, opposite Dilys Laye (q.v.) in *Carry On Cruising*, and in *Carry On Cabby* she was Hattie Jacques's stalwart friend, Sally. Interestingly, shortly before *Carry On Cabby* Liz had worked opposite Sid James on television in three series of *Citizen James* (1960-62).

After Liz was dropped from the *Carry On* series in 1963 her shoes were quickly filled by Barbara Windsor. However, after an absence of twelve years, Liz returned to play Sylvia Ramsden in *Carry On Behind*. She then went on to appear on stage in *Carry On Laughing at the Slimming Factory* in 1976, before becoming a key actor in the *Confessions* films during the late 1970s.

One of the country's busiest actors, Liz has made over 600 appearances on the small screen. They include *Sixpenny Corner* (1955), *Hancock's Half Hour, The Benny Hill Show, Turnbull's Finest Hour* (1972, as Faye Bush), *Robin's Nest, Rumpole of the Bailey, Fairly Secret Army* (1984-86, 2 series, as Doris), *Miss Marple – Nemesis* (1987, as Mrs Brent), *Rude Health* (1988), *Birds of a Feather* (1992, as Olive Stubbs), *Minder, Demob* (1994), *Drover's Gold* (1997, as Ma Whistler), *Last of the Summer Wine* (2000, as Reggie Unsworth) and *Unforgettable Sid James* (doc., 2000). The popular actress was remarkably unchanged in 2006 when she played Ada in the telemovie *Pickles: The Dog Who Won the World Cup*.

Although best known for her work in film and television, Liz also has numerous stage appearances to her credit, including national tours of *Oliver!, Sweeney Todd, Donkey's Years* and *Alfie*. She has also worked consistently on radio, notably in two series of *Truly, Madly, Bletchley* and in the late 1990s with Joan Sims in *Bristow*.

During her fifty-year career Liz Fraser has worked with most of Britain's legendary comedians (particularly Peter Sellers) and is now recognised as a leading veteran comedienne. In addition to her acting credits she is also a prodigious charity worker.

Liz Fraser, who was married to the late Bill Hitchcock, was a guest at the *Carry On* 40th Anniversary reunion in 1998 and returned to Pinewood Studios two years later as a special guest at the *Carry On Screaming* celebrations. In 2002 she was present at the unveiling of a Comedy Heritage plaque in memory of Joan Sims, and she has provided commentary for DVD releases of the *Carry On* series.

Her autobiography, *Adventures of a Carry On Girl* (with Robert Ross), was published in 2011.

Judith Furse

One of the most memorable character actors to grace the *Carry On* series, Judith Furse brought her considerable talents to three *Carry On* films, most notably as Dr Crow, the bizarre head of STENCH, in *Carry On Spying*.

Judith Furse was born in Deepcut Camp, Camberley, Surrey, on 4

March 1912. Her family was particularly well known, her father being Lieutenant-General Sir William Furse, her brother costume designer Roger K. Furse (1903-72) and her sister-in-law costume designer Margaret Furse (1911-74).

Judith made her stage debut in 1924 at Wembley Stadium in *The Pageant of Empire*. After training at the Old Vic (1931-32) she made her professional stage debut in *King John* at Sadler's Wells Theatre in 1931. She then went on to pursue a busy stage career, both as an actress and a director, until the late 1950s, with credits including *Distant Point, First Stop North, Lady Audley's Secret, Intimate Relations, Spider's Web* (1954, with Margaret Lockwood) and *The Rape of the Belt* (1957).

Judith Furse made her film debut in *Goodbye, Mr. Chips* in 1938. She went on to appear in over forty feature films, including *English Without Tears* (1944), *Quiet Weekend* (1946), *Marry Me* (1949), *Mother Riley Meets the Vampire* (1952), *Doctor at Large* (1957), *Blue Murder at St Trinian's* (1958), *In the Doghouse* (1961), *The Iron Maiden* (1962), *The Amorous Adventures of Moll Flanders* (1965), *Sinful Davey* (1969), *Twinky* (1970) and *Man in the Wilderness* (1971).

After several serious film roles in her early career, most notably as Sister Briony in *Black Narcissus*, Judith (like Hattie Jacques) tended to be typecast as bossy figures of authority due to her size and deep masculine tones. In the mid-1950s she moved into comic roles and made her *Carry On* debut as the formidable schoolteacher who rebuked Kenneth Williams in *Carry On Regardless*. In *Carry On Cabby* (as the 'battle axe woman') she played a passenger startled by Sid James, and she made her mark on the series as the evil Dr Crow in *Carry On Spying*. Although Judith's voice was dubbed over for this sinister role, it was one of her most memorable film appearances.

In addition to her work on stage and screen, Judith also featured in television programmes, including *The Three Fat Women of Antibes* (1960), *Dial RIX – Rolling Home* (1963), *Pardon the Expression* (1965, series, as Miss Buxton), *Haven of Rest* (series, 1970, as Muriel Crump) and *Doomwatch* (1971, as Mary Lincoln).

Judith continued to work in films, television and radio into the 1970s. Her final screen role came in *The Adventures of Barry McKenzie* (1972), in which she played a minder. In 1973 she worked on the radio series of *Dad's Army* for the BBC.

Very little is known about Judith's private life. She never married and spent many years living at Provident Cottage, Shottenden, in Kent.

Judith Furse was suffering from cirrhosis of the liver when she died from a heart attack at Kent & Canterbury Hospital on 29 August 1974, aged sixty-two.

Carry On ... ***Quotes***

Judith was a lovely person to work with and such a great talent. When not acting we used to sit on the set – all the nuns – to do Times *crossword puzzles. Judith was brilliant at them. I had lots of rows with Michael Powell, which she found very amusing. One felt that she could cope with anything and yet she was very thoughtful and caring for others. I think of her always with great affection.*
Kathleen Byron,
co-star in Black Narcissus, *1998*

Hugh Futcher

A veteran actor of stage, screen and television, Hugh Futcher became a familiar *Carry On* cameo player, with roles in seven films in the latter half of the series.

Hugh, who trained at RADA, has a long list of stage credits, ranging from Dogberry in *Much Ado About Nothing* and Feste in *Twelfth Night* to Bert Barry in *42nd Street* and Dame in *Emu in Pantoland.*

Hugh made his *Carry On* debut as the Native on the bed of nails in *Carry On Spying*. He then went on to play a guard in *Carry On Don't Lose Your Head* and the taxi driver in *Carry On Again Doctor*, with Sid James. His greatest role in the series was as Ernie, one of the factory workers in *Carry On At Your Convenience*, opposite Geoffrey Hughes (q.v.). In *Carry On Abroad* Hugh featured in a cameo role as one of the Spanish guards and he played an irate citizen at the beauty contest in *Carry On Girls*. His final *Carry On* appearance was as the painter in the final stages of *Carry On Behind*, another effective cameo role, opposite Kenneth Connor.

In addition to the *Carry On* films, Hugh's screen credits include *Rattle of a Simple Man* (1965), *Repulsion* (1965), *Quatermass and the Pit* (1967), *Mrs Brown, You've Got a Lovely Daughter* (1968), *Before Winter Comes* (1969), *Johann Strauss: The King Without a Crown* (1987) and *102 Dalmatians* (2000)

On the small screen Hugh has featured in a variety of programmes, including *Camino Real, Beyond Belief, Doctor Who, Whistling Wally (Play for Today), The Sweeney, Just Liz* (1980), *Secret Army, Selling Hitler* (1991) and *The Apocalypse Watch* (1997). Hugh has also directed on stage and is on the panel of script readers for Teddington Arts Performance Showcase.

A popular addition to the *Carry On* series, Hugh Futcher returned to Pinewood Studios in November 1999 for the *Carry On Stuffing* celebrations and has since attended several other events at the Studios including the 50th Anniversary celebrations in 2008.

*Carry On ... **Quotes***

... it was all rather joyous, seven times around.
Hugh Futcher, 2000

Mavis Fyson

Mavis played beauty contestant Miss Frances Cake in *Carry On Girls*.

Hal Galili

In addition to playing a young cowhand in *Carry On Cowboy*, Hal Galili appeared in a variety of films over a twenty-year period, including *The Girl Hunters* (1963), *Goldfinger* (1964), *The Adding Machine* (1969), *The Pink Panther Strikes Again* (1976), *The Ritz* (1976), *The Warlords of Atlantis* (1978), *An Arabian Adventure* (1979) and *Superman II* (1980). He appears to have died in 1984.

Stephen Garlick

Best known on television as Ned Lewis in the series *Black Beauty* (1972), Stephen played the mischievous grandson (opposite *Carry On* regular Marianne Stone) in *Carry On Doctor*.

Born in Swansea, Wales, on 7 July 1959, Stephen also appeared in *Headline Hunters* (1967) and *Scrooge* (1970), and he provided the voice of Jen in *The Dark Crystal* (1982). He left the acting profession in the 1980s.

John/(Jack) Gatrell

John played the 4th Specialist examining Kenneth Connor in *Carry On Sergeant*. His additional film appearances included *The Private Life of Sherlock Holmes* (1970) and *Games That Lovers Play* (1970). He also made appearances on television in *Death in Deep Water* (1975) and *Lillie* (1978). John Gatrell died on 3 January 1981, aged seventy-four.

Judy Geeson (b. Judith Amanda Geeson)

A leading lady and sex symbol of the 1970s, Judy Geeson made a guest appearance as Sergeant Tilly Willing in *Carry On England*. Along with her co-star Patrick Mower (q.v.), Judy was a fresh face to the series in the second last of the 'true' *Carry On*'s.

Born in Arundel, Sussex, on 10 September 1948, Judy began her acting career as a teenager. Although she originally trained as a dancer, Judy turned to acting while attending the Corona Stage School.

Judy made her film debut in *Wings of Mystery* in 1963 and gradually moved from teenage roles, notably featuring in *To Sir, with Love* (1967) and *Here We Go Round the Mulberry Bush* (1968), to less worthy material that required the removal of most of her clothing. During the 1970s the attractive, blonde-haired actress was seen in a range of leading film roles in comedies, horror and drama, including *The Executioner* (1970), *Doomwatch* (1972), *Percy's Progress* (1974), *Adventures of a Taxi Driver* (1976), *The Eagle Has Landed* (1976) and *Inseminoid* (1980).

On television Judy began her career with appearances in *Emergency Ward 10* and *Dixon of Dock Green* and became well known as Maria Cooper in *The Newcomers* (1965). Since moving to America in the early 1980s she has gone on to find a greater range of acting parts on television, with appearances in *Murder, She Wrote* (several episodes), *The A-Team* (1986), *MacGyver* (1988), *Star Trek: Voyager* (1995, as Sandrine), *Mad About You* (as Maggie Conway), *Touched by an Angel* (2000) and *Charmed* (2000). In 1996 Judy resurrected her role as Pamela Dare in the tele-movie *To Sir, with Love II* and she played Lady Fautsblossom in the 1998 tele-movie, *Houdini*.

Judy's stage credits include time with the Royal Shakespeare Company and she played Desdemona in *Othello*. She has also toured in *An Ideal Husband* and *The Sleeping Prince*.

The elder sister of Sally Geeson (q.v.), Judy married actor Kristoffer Tabori in 1984. The couple divorced five years later.

Sally Geeson

Sally Geeson made guest appearances in two *Carry On*'s – as eager tourist Lily in *Carry On Abroad* and as Debra (Cecil Gaybody's assistant) in *Carry On Girls*. By the time she joined the series Sally was already familiar to the general public as Sid James's teenage daughter in the popular sitcom *Bless This House*.

The pretty, dark-haired, younger sister of Judy Geeson, Sally was born in Cuckfield, Sussex, on 23 June 1950. Like her elder sibling, Sally began her career as a teenager, appearing in films such as *What's Good for the Goose* (1969), *The Oblong Box* (1969) and *Cry of the Banshee* (1970).

Sally found lasting success as Sid James's daughter, Sally Abbot, in four series of the popular television sitcom *Bless This House*. Thanks to regular repeats of the series, it is a role for which Sally is still well remembered. She also appeared in the 1972 film version of the series, produced and directed by Peter Rogers and Gerald Thomas.

In the 1970s Sally was romantically linked to actor Robin Askwith (q.v.)

and *Bless This House* director (and *Fifteen to One* presenter) William G. Stewart. The latter relationship lasted ten years and the couple had two children.

When *Bless This House* ended with the death of Sid James in 1976, Sally Geeson's appearances dwindled and after a final appearance on television in *Spooner's Patch* (with Norman Rossington, q.v.) in 1979 she left the world of acting to concentrate on family life. In the 1990s she became a special needs primary school teacher.

After almost three decades out of the public eye Sally provided commentary on the 2003 DVD release of *Carry On Abroad* and since then has proved to be a popular guest at film conventions. Now a grandmother, Sally, who lives in Surrey, is remarkably unchanged since her *Carry On* days.

Carry On ... ***Quotes***

I am so pleased you enjoyed my work in the Carry On *films and* Bless This House. *Working on* Bless This House *was a particularly happy time in my life.*

Sally Geeson, 2005

Gina Gianelli

Gina played a Harem Girl in *Carry On Follow That Camel*. Her other film appearances were as Gina in *The Psychopath* (1966) and playing the secretary in *The Deadly Bees* (1966).

Alan Gifford (b. John Lennox)

American character actor Alan Gifford appeared in just one *Carry On* film, appropriately playing Fiddler in *Carry On Cowboy*.

Alan Gifford was born in Taunton, Massachusetts, on 11 March 1911 (some sources say 1905). He appeared in well over forty films, including *The Kangaroo Kid* (1950), *No Smoking* (1955), *The Iron Petticoat* (1956), *A King in New York* (1957), *The Flying Scot* (1957), *Too Young to Love* (1960), *The Road to Hong Kong* (1962), *Drop Dead Darling* (1966), *The Legend of Nigger Charley* (1972) and *Ragtime* (1981).

On television Alan was best known as Lloyd Munroe in *Crossroads* (1964-66) and he played Senator Gordon Whitney in *The Edge of the Night* (1970-71). Alan also turned up for guest roles in series such as *Perry Mason, Danger Man* and *Randall and Hopkirk (Deceased)*. One of his final roles was playing William Waldorf Astor in the 1984 mini-series *Nancy Astor.*

Alan Gifford had been ill for some time and had just turned seventy-eight when he died in Blairgowrie, Perthshire, Scotland, on 20 March 1989.

Tom Gill

In a screen career spanning over thirty years Tom Gill made more than forty film appearances. He can be spotted as the First Citizen in *Carry On Constable* and later worked for Gerald Thomas in *The Iron Maiden* (1962).

Tom was born in Newcastle upon Tyne on 26 July 1916. He made his film debut in *Midshipman Easy* in 1935. His screen career consisted mainly of cameo roles, including appearances in *Lady Godiva Rides Again* (1951), *Hotel Sahara* (1951), *The Black Orchid* (1953), *Simon and Laura* (1955), *Jumping For Joy* (1955), *Carry On Admiral* (1957), *Up the Creek* (1958), *Further Up the Creek* (1958), *The Navy Lark* (1959), *Smashing Time* (1967) and *For Men Only* (1968).

Tom died on 22 July 1971, shortly before his fifty-fifth birthday.

Peter Gilmore

With eleven *Carry On* films to his credit, Peter Gilmore was one of the most prolific supporting actors to grace the series. From *Carry On Cabby* in 1963 to *Carry On Columbus* almost thirty years later, he turned up in a variety of roles, ranging from the villainous Patch in *Carry On Jack* to the cheeky ambulance driver in *Carry On Doctor*.

Peter Gilmore was born in Leipzig, Germany, on 25 August 1931. He came to Britain when he was six and was raised in Yorkshire. He trained for acting at RADA, although his time there was brief, and went on to complete his National Service. Peter later joined the George Mitchell Singers before making his first professional stage appearance as a stooge in variety in 1952. Over the past five decades Peter has made numerous stage appearances, utilising his talents as both an actor and a singer. He made his West End debut as David Tooke in *Valmouth* in 1959 and subsequently went on to appear in plays such as *Follow That Girl* (1960, as Tom), *Lock Up Your Daughters* (1962, as Ramble), *Cinderella* (1966, as Prince Charming), *A Midsummer Night's Dream* (1967, as Lysander), *The Beggar's Opera* (1968, as Captain Macheath) and *The Rainmaker* (1975, tour, as Starbuck).

Peter made his film debut in *Bomb in the High Street* in 1961. In 1963 he joined the *Carry On* series as Dancy in *Carry On Cabby* and a year later was seen in an even meatier supporting role as the villainous Patch in *Carry*

On Jack. In *Carry On Cleo* (as the Galley Master) and *Carry On Cowboy* (as Short) he made cameo appearances, before taking on the role of Bagshaw in *Carry On Follow That Camel*. In *Carry On Don't Lose Your Head* Peter stood out as Citizen Robespierre and in *Carry On Up the Khyber*, opposite Charles Hawtrey, he gave one of the finest cameo performances of the entire series, as Private 'Ginger' Hale. Another memorable cameo role for Peter came as Henry – the ambulance driver who comments on Barbara Windsor's lovely looking pear – in *Carry On Doctor*. In *Carry On Again Doctor* Peter can be glimpsed opposite Jim Dale doing some 'spot diagnosis', and in *Carry On Henry* he played the devilish King Francis of France, again opposite Barbara Windsor. In 1992, more than twenty years after his final appearance in the series, Peter Gilmore returned to Pinewood Studios to play the Governor of the Canaries in *Carry On Columbus*. Although a welcome familiar face, Peter's talents were overlooked as he was relegated to a shamefully small cameo.

In addition to the *Carry On* series, Peter's film credits include *I Gotta Horse* (1965), *Doctor in Clover* (1966), *The Great St Trinian's Train Robbery* (1966), *Oh! What a Lovely War* (1969), *The Abominable Dr. Phibes* (1971), *Warlords of Atlantis* (1978) and *The Lonely Passion of Judith Hearne* (1987).

Peter's small-screen appearances over the past forty years have ranged from *Ivanhoe* (1958) to singing and dancing in the Ron Moody show, *Moody In ...* (1961). In the 1970s he gained national fame as sea captain James Onedin in the popular series *The Onedin Line*, which ran for nine series until 1980. During this time, at the peak of his professional success, Peter released an album, *Peter Gilmore Sings Gently* (1978). Sadly, following *The Onedin Line* Peter made only sporadic appearances on the small screen, including two series of *One by One* (1984-86, as safari park keeper Ben Bishop), Ruth Rendell's *Master of the Moor* (1994) and *On Dangerous Ground* (1996). Peter's guest appearances on the small screen include *Doctor Who* (1984), *Casualty* (1992) and *Heartbeat* (1993, as Raymond Walker). Ill health in the late 1990s forced Peter's retirement from the profession.

Peter Gilmore was married to actress Una Stubbs (1937-) and they have one adopted son, Jason. Following his divorce from Una, Peter married actress Jan Waters (1937-) and when this marriage too ended in divorce he married his *Onedin Line* co-star Anne Stallybrass (1940-).

In 1998 Peter returned to Pinewood Studios for the *Carry On* 40th Anniversary reunion and three years later was back again for the Kenneth Williams Weekend.

David Glover

David Glover, who played the hotel manager in *Carry On Follow That*

Camel, is still a busy television actor into his eighties.

Born in London on 24 September 1927, David has been acting on screen and television since the late 1950s. He began his film career with appearances in the popular comedies *Dentist in the Chair* (1960) and *Dentist on the Job* (1961). His film appearances since have included *The Ipcress File* (1965), *Kes* (1969), *Priest of Love* (1981), *Princess Caraboo* (1994), *Blue Juice* (1995) and *Shooting Fish* (1997).

Among David's most recent television appearances are *Lady Audley's Secret* (2000, as the mariner) and episodes of *Recap* (2003), *Casualty* (2005), *The Amazing Mrs Pritchard* (2006) and *Lewis* (2007). Previously he has appeared in programmes ranging from *The Avengers* to *Kavanagh QC*.

Willoughby Goddard

A rotund character actor of stage, screen and television, Willoughby Goddard's ample proportions stood out when he played a bit-part role as a passenger in *Carry On Cruising*.

Born in Bicester, Oxfordshire, on 4 July 1926, Willoughby entertained audiences for almost forty years. He made his film debut in *Bait* in 1950 and over the next three decades made sporadic screen appearances, including *Inn for Trouble* (1960), *The Wrong Box* (1966), *Charge of the Light Brigade* (1968) and *Young Sherlock Holmes* (1985).

Willoughby was most familiar for his numerous roles on television, from Gessler in *William Tell* in 1958 to Professor Siblington in the David Jason tele-movie *Porterhouse Blue* in 1987. In addition, he played Lord Charley in the 1970 sitcom *Charley's Grants* (with Hattie Jacques), appeared opposite Charlie Drake in *Drake's Progress* (1957) and *The Charlie Drake Comedy Hour* (1972) and played the Archbishop in *The Black Adder* (1983). Willoughby's frequent guest roles on the small screen included appearances in *The Avengers, Nearest and Dearest* and *The Sweeney*. On stage from 1943 his numerous credits included Mr Bumble in *Oliver!* (on Broadway) and the Duke of Venice in *Othello* (1980, with the RSC), and in 1988 he appeared at the Old Vic in *Serjeant Musgrave's Dance*.

Willoughby Goddard married actress Ann Phillips in 1950 and they had one son. He retired from acting in the late 1980s. After suffering from arthritis in his later years Willoughby died in London on 11 April 2008, aged eighty-one.

Liz Gold

Liz played one of the Khasi's wives in *Carry On Up the Khyber*.

Peter Gordeno/(Godenho)

Born in Rangoon, Burma, on 20 June 1939, Peter played the Shaman in *Carry On Columbus*. A West End theatre star, Peter's most notable acting role was as Captain Peter Carlin the popular TV series *UFO* (1970). As an actor and singer, Peter's career began in 1959 in *Blue Magic*, a revue starring Dame Shirley Bassey. He subsequently appeared in a string of variety shows on stage and television, including *West Side Story* (1959-61), *The Kathy Kirby Show* (1964-65), *Boxing Night Out* (1964) and *Cilla at the Savoy* (1966).

In addition to *Carry On Columbus*, Peter had minor film roles in *Secrets of a Windmill Girl* (1965), *The Touchables* (1968) and *Urge to Kill* (1988). On television he also featured in the Jimmy Tarbuck show, *It's Tarbuck* (1970).

Peter was married to Angie Wallace and had two sons and one daughter. He died on 18 October 2008, aged sixty-nine.

Norah/(Nora) Gordon

Homely looking character actress Norah Gordon is credited with the role of 'old lady' in *Carry On Spying*. Some filmographies also credit her with a role in *Carry On Regardless*, although she does not seem to appear in the final release.

Norah Gordon was born in West Hartlepool on 29 November 1893. After making her film debut in *Danny Boy* in 1941 Norah appeared in over fifty films, usually in tiny bit-part roles. She remained busy on screen until 1965.

Norah Gordon was married to character actor Leonard Sharp (1890-1958) and their daughter is actress Dorothy Gordon (1924-), who has acted in Britain and latterly Canada and America.

Norah Gordon died in London on 11 May 1970, aged seventy-six.

Barrie Gosney

Barrie Gosney's long professional career as a character actor on stage, screen and television spanned fifty years – from repertory around the country to pantomime in South Africa.

Born in Surrey in 1925, Barrie Gosney began his acting career in the 1940s, so he was already an established performer when he played the coach driver in *Carry On Jack*. On stage Barrie's countless credits included *A Bedfull of Foreigners* (with Terry Scott), *There Goes the Bride, Anybody for Murder* and *My Cousin Rachel*. One of his most successful roles was as Dr Fiuk in *Come Spy with Me* at the Whitehall Theatre and he appeared in almost thirty pantomimes.

On the small screen Barrie was latterly seen in three series of *The Harry Hill Show, Time Gentlemen Please* (2000, as Uncle Barrie) and *Last of the Summer Wine* (2004). Among his other TV credits were guest appearances in *The Beryl Reid Show, According to Dora* (with Dora Bryan, q.v.), *Please Sir!, Dixon of Dock Green, The Two Ronnies, Happy Ever After, Don't Wait Up, After Henry, Casualty, The Bill* and *Keeping Up Appearances* (1993, as a country yokel).

In addition to *Carry On Jack*, Barrie's film appearances included *The Life and Death of Colonel Blimp* (1943), *A Home of Your Own* (1964), *Up Pompeii* (1971), *Up the Front* (1972), *Don't Just Lie There, Say Something!* (1973) and *The Big Sleep* (1978).

Barrie and his wife, actress Jacqueline Clark (1942-), lived in Peterborough. He died in London, from complications following a fall, on 24 January 2008, aged eighty-two.

Carry On ... ***Quotes***

I'm sorry I wasn't more connected with the Carry On *series ... but that's show business!!!*
Barrie Gosney, 2000

Helen Goss

A cheerful-looking character actress of stage and screen, Helen Goss is credited with the bit-part role of Shirley Eaton's mother in *Carry On Sergeant*.

Born in London on 15 October 1903, Helen was on stage - with contemporaries such as Sir John Mills - from the 1920s. Her film credits, spanning almost forty years, included *Bachelor's Baby* (1932), *A Place of One's Own* (1944), *Fanny by Gaslight* (1944), *The Wicked Lady* (as Mistress Betsy, 1945), *The Mark of Cain* (1947), *The Weaker Sex* (1948), *The Pickwick Papers* (1952), *The Hound of the Baskervilles* (1959) and *Half a Sixpence* (1967).

Helen was also well known as a drama coach and following the end of the Second World War she was kept busy 'grooming' starlets for the Rank 'Charm' School. Helen's last acting role was as Lady Lynn in the 1970 television adaptation of *Jane Eyre*.

Helen Goss died in 1985.

Graydon Gould

Character actor Graydon Gould has acted on both sides of the Atlantic. He played the 9th Recruit, a bit-part role, in *Carry On Sergeant*.

Graydon's additional film credits include *Floods of Fear* (1959), *During One Night* (1961), *The Visitors* (1963), *Executive Action* (1973) and more recently *Mission: Impossible* (1996) and *Déjà Vu* (1997).

Graydon Gould's most notable television role was as George Keeley in 102 episodes of the Canadian series *The Forest Ranger* (1963-65). His additional small-screen credits, in Britain and America, range from *The Big Valley* (1965) to *Emmerdale* (1999, as Herb Kastner).

Mike Grady

Best known as the long-suffering Barry in *Last of the Summer Wine*, Mike Grady played the boy lover perennially snogging with Valerie Shute in *Carry On Loving*.

Mike was just beginning his career when he was cast for *Carry On Loving*. He went on to appear in two other classic comedies of the 1970s, playing the newsboy in Frankie Howerd's *Up the Front* (1972) and the bellboy in *The Return of the Pink Panther* (1975). Mike's additional screen credits include *I'm Not Feeling Myself Tonight* (1976), *Britannia Hospital* (1982), *The Pirates of Penzance* (1983) and *Bert Rigby, You're a Fool* (1989). A well-known face on television since the late 1970s, Mike has appeared in a succession of popular sitcoms. He is still well remembered as Ken in four series of *Citizen Smith* (1977-80), with Robert Lindsay and Cheryl Hall, and he later went on to play Dr Ballantine in *Sweet Sixteen* (series, 1983), with Penelope Keith.

Following his appearance in *Uncle of the Bride* – a *Last of the Summer Wine* tele-movie – Mike joined the regular cast of the series in 1987 as Dame Thora Hird's hen-pecked son-in-law. The role kept him busy until the series ended in 2010. Mike's additional television credits include the 1986 series of *Troubles & Strife* (as Christopher) and *Colin's Sandwich* (2 series, 1988-90, as Des) and he played Dick Barnes in *Up the Garden Path* (3 series, 1990-93). His guest appearances on the small screen have ranged from *Minder* to *As Time Goes By* and he also featured in the children's series *Tales from the Poop Deck* (1992), as Honeywell.

Carry On ... **Quotes**

I made a very brief appearance in the 21st Carry On *film ... My main memory is of Kenneth Williams and Charles Hawtrey working very hard and*

in great detail, and the smell of congealed cream going rancid in the last scene. The stench!
Valerie Shute was very nice to work with and Sidney James seemed a very kind person.
Mike Grady, 2001

Gail Grainger

Gail made a notable impact on the *Carry On* series when she played Moira, Kenneth Williams's assistant/love interest in *Carry On Abroad*. Surprisingly, it was her only appearance in the series.

Having worked with Leslie Phillips (q.v.) on stage, Gail went on to appear in his television series *Casanova '73* (1973), playing the secretary. She later turned up for guest appearances in *The Sweeney* and *Rings On Their Fingers* before making her second (and final) film appearance in *Jaguar Lives* (1979).

Well remembered by *Carry On* fans, Gail Grainger appears to have completely left the acting profession in 1980, and attempts to trace her whereabouts have been unsuccessful.

Angela/(Angie) Grant

Angela Grant appeared as a glamour girl in three *Carry On*'s: playing a Harem Girl in *Carry On Follow That Camel*, a Hospitality Girl in *Carry On Up the Khyber* and beauty contestant Miss Bangor in *Carry On Girls*.

In addition to the *Carry On* series, Angela Grant 'decorated' several other films, including *Zeta One* (1969), *A Promise of Bed* (1969, as the flower girl) and *Tales from the Crypt* (1972, as Susan Blake in *Reflection of Death*). Angela's best-known screen appearances to date were in the 1970s sex comedies, *What's Up Nurse!* (1977, as Helen) and *What's Up Superdoc!* (1978, as Kim). The latter two films also included a range of other *Carry On* actors, including Peter Butterworth, Harry H. Corbett, Bill Pertwee and Marianne Stone (all q.v.).

Born in Scarborough and raised in Leeds, Angela began her career as a model. After the 1970s Angela largely disappeared from the acting profession, but she still remains a working actress, one of her most recent appearances being an episode of the Sean Pertwee series *Bodyguards* in 1996.

Angela Grant was a guest at the *Carry On* 40th Anniversary reunion in 1998. In more recent years the glamorous actress has returned to Pinewood for the *Carry On Screaming* celebrations (2000), the Kenneth Williams celebrations (2001) and the 2004 tribute to Joan Sims. She remains a popular drawcard for *Carry On* fans.

Gilly Grant

Gilly Grant was immortalised in the *Carry On* series as Sally G-String, the topless holidaymaker who featured in the nudist film of *Carry On Camping*. She was later seen – again semi-naked - as the nurse in the bath taken by surprise by Sid James in *Carry On Matron*.

In addition to the *Carry On*'s, Gilly's short film career included appearances in *School for Sex* (1968), *Zeta One* (1969), *Clegg* (1969, as Suzy the Slag) and *The Big Switch* (1970).

Peter Grant

Peter Grant, who played the Cardinal in *Carry On Columbus*, made his name and fortune as the manager of Led Zeppelin.

Peter's colourful life included time as a wrestler, a bouncer and an extra at Pinewood Studios. Before managing Led Zeppelin he had worked with a variety of bands, from The Yardbirds to the New York Vaudeville Band. When Led Zeppelin disbanded in 1980 Peter retired from the music business.

Born in South London in 1935, Peter Grant died of a heart attack in 1995, aged sixty. His son Warren and daughter Helen survived him.

Leon Greene

One of Britain's best-known pantomime villains, Leon Greene was also a memorable supporting actor in three *Carry On* films. He played Malabonce the executioner in *Carry On Don't Lose Your Head* and Charles Hawtrey's torturer in *Carry On Henry* and he made a final appearance in *Carry On At Your Convenience* as the massive chef with Bernard Bresslaw and Kenneth Cope (both q.v.).

Born in 1933, Leon Greene began his professional career with the D'Oyly Carte Opera Company and has appeared in many stage musicals, including *Carousel, Annie Get Your Gun* (as Buffalo Bill) and *Calamity Jane* (as Bill Hickok). He has also played the title role in *Sweeney Todd*.

One of Leon's most notable stage appearances was as Miles Glorious in *A Funny Thing Happened on the Way to the Forum*, with fellow *Carry On* actors Frankie Howerd and Kenneth Connor, and he also appeared in the 1966 film version. He has also worked with the RSC and is perhaps most familiar as one of panto's most prodigious villains, both in the UK and Canada.

In addition to the *Carry On*'s, Leon Greene's screen credits include *The Devil Rides Out* (1968), *Assignment to Kill* (1968), *The Four Musketeers*

(1974), *The Ritz* (1976), *Adventures of a Plumber's Mate* (1978), *Flash Gordon* (1980) and *The Return of the Musketeers* (1989).

On television Leon's appearances have included *Matlock, The Persuaders, The Ravelled Thread, Massada, Terry and June, Lorna Doone* and *Ever Decreasing Circles*. Most recently he played Harry the Doorman in *Cold Lazarus* (1996).

Carry On ... ***Quotes***

The anecdotes about the Carry On *team are legion and have been repeated again and again, so there is very little to add. I can, however, tell you that no matter how big or small your role in the film you were made to feel very welcome by the main cast. From being invited to join their table at lunch, to being included in their conversations and joke sessions (and there were many) on set, you felt you were part of a large and very happy family.*
Leon Greene, 1999

Fred Griffiths

A prodigious character actor, Fred Griffiths had the unique distinction of playing a taxi driver in no less than twenty of his screen appearances. Fittingly, he played the 2nd Ambulance Driver in *Carry On Nurse* and the Taxi Driver in both *Carry On Regardless* and *Carry On Loving*. He also played the dustbin man in the Peter Rogers/Gerald Thomas comedy, *The Big Job* (1965).

Born in Ludlow on 8 March 1912, Fred Griffiths was over thirty when he made his film debut, having previously worked as a fireman. For over thirty years he was a stalwart bit-part player in more than sixty films, ranging from *Nice Men* (1943) to *Confessions of a Window Cleaner* (1974).

Often Fred's roles lasted no more than a few seconds, but he can be spotted in *Meet Mr. Lucifer* (1953, as a removal man), *Genevieve* (1953, as the ice cream seller), *Doctor in the House* (1954, as a taxi driver), *The Ladykillers* (1955, as a removal man), *Reach for the Sky* (1956, as a lorry driver), *I'm All Right Jack* (1959, as Charlie), *Steptoe and Son* (1972, as the barman) and *No Sex Please, We're British* (1973, as the delivery man).

Fred Griffiths was eighty-two years old when he died in London on 27 August 1994.

Lucy Griffiths

A distinctive character actress who specialised in comic cameo roles, Lucy

Griffiths became a familiar member of the *Carry On* team, appearing in seven films from *Carry On Nurse* in 1959 to *Carry On Behind* sixteen years later.

Lucy Griffiths was born in Birley, Herefordshire, in 1915 (some sources say 1919). At the age of fourteen she entered the Civil Service ("unwillingly"), and whilst there she won gold and silver medals for elocution. She began her stage career with walk-on parts and stage-managing, gradually working her way up to lead roles in repertory. By the late 1930s she was working consistently at the Alexandra Theatre, Birmingham. During the Second World War Lucy was a member of a fighter control unit of the WAAF (Women's Auxiliary Air Force) and also flew with an RAF Reserve Flying School.

In 1944 Lucy returned to the theatre as Mrs Gerton in *The Rest Is Silence*, at the Prince of Wales Theatre. Over the next thirty years she would make occasional appearances on stage, including time with the Birmingham Repertory Company and seasons in rep. at Leicester, Stratford-upon-Avon and Bournemouth. Her final stage role was in *The Millionaires* in 1978.

Lucy Griffiths made her screen debut in *Will Any Gentleman...?* in 1953. Over the next twenty-five years she appeared in more than forty films, often in cameo roles as little old ladies.

In the *Carry On*'s Lucy played the trolley lady who offers Kenneth Connor a sliced nut in *Carry On Nurse*, Miss Horton, the "10/4" neighbour in *Carry On Constable*, and Auntie in *Carry On Regardless*. Her appearances in *Carry On Doctor* and *Carry On Again Doctor* were her most memorable in the series, particularly as the toothless old lady mistakenly attracted to Bernard Bresslaw in *Doctor*. Lucy went on to appear in *Carry On Loving* (her scenes sadly hit the cutting room floor) and she was the 'lady with the hat' (a member of the audience of Kenneth Williams's lecture) in *Carry On Behind*.

Among Lucy's other film credits were *Children Galore* (1954), *The Ladykillers* (1955), *The Green Man* (1956), *Please Turn Over* (1960), *Murder, She Said* (1961), *She Knows Y'Know* (1962), *Mouse on the Moon* (1963), *Murder Ahoy!* (1964), *Under Milk Wood* (1973), *No Sex Please, We're British* (1973), *Frankenstein and the Monster from Hell* (1974), *One of Our Dinosaurs Is Missing* (1975) and *The Hound of the Baskervilles* (1978)

On television, from the early 1950s, Lucy made appearances in *Emergency Ward 10, On the Buses* and *All Creatures Great and Small*. Her final television role was in *Dangerous Davies – The Last Detective* in 1981.

Lucy Griffiths died in London on 29 September 1982, aged sixty-seven.

Deryck Guyler

Forever remembered for his roles in two long-running sitcoms, Deryck Guyler played a memorable cameo role as Hardcastle, the doddery surgeon, opposite Kenneth Williams, in *Carry On Doctor*.

Deryck Guyler was born in Wallasey, Cheshire, on 29 April 1914. His early years included time spent working in the family's jewellery shop, farming and studying for a year at a Church of England theological college. Eventually deciding upon a theatrical career, he joined Liverpool rep., following elocution lessons, in 1935. From 1939 Deryck spent three years serving with the RAF police, until he invalided out in 1942.

Deryck's initial success came on radio, where he made his debut in 1935. From 1946 he was a familiar voice with Tommy Handley in *ITMA* and over the next five decades made more than 6,000 broadcasts, including *Just Fancy* (nine years, with Eric Barker, q.v.), *The Men from the Ministry* (eleven years) and *Inspector Scott Investigates* (six years).

Although mainly a radio and television actor, Deryck also managed to make over a dozen screen appearances, usually as minor officials, including *Mad About Men* (1954), *Ramsbottom Rides Again* (1956), *The Fast Lady* (1962), *A Hard Day's Night* (1964), *Ferry Cross the Mersey* (1964), *No Sex Please, We're British* (1973) and *Barry McKenzie Holds His Own* (1974), and he featured among the all-star cast of *One of Our Dinosaurs Is Missing* (1975). In addition to *Carry On Doctor*, Deryck also worked for Peter Rogers and Gerald Thomas in *Nurse on Wheels* (1963, as the examiner) and *The Big Job* (1965, as the Police Sergeant).

Deryck gained national recognition as school caretaker, Norman Potter, in *Please Sir!* (1968-72) and continued his television success as PC Wilfred 'Corky' Turnbull in *Sykes* (1972-79), with Eric Sykes and *Carry On* legend Hattie Jacques (q.v.).

After 1980 Deryck was largely retired from show business, although he was occasionally heard on radio until the late 1980s.

Deryck spent the last seven years of his life living in Brisbane, Australia, with his wife Paddy. His time there was spent indulging his varied hobbies: listening to jazz records, playing the washboard and collecting toy soldiers.

Deryck Guyler died peacefully on 8 October 1999, aged eighty-five.

John Hallam

A distinctive film and television actor, John Hallam can be glimpsed as the Burpa on the roof in the latter scenes of *Carry On Up the Khyber*. It was his only appearance in the series, at the very beginning of his long acting career.

John was born in Lisburn, Northern Ireland, on 28 October 1941. After training at RADA he made his first professional acting appearances from the mid-1960s. Throughout his forty-year career John was frequently called upon to play villainous characters. Tall and dark-haired with well-defined, craggy features, he was a familiar face from over thirty film appearances, including *Charge of The Light Brigade* (1968), *Villain* (1971), *Nicholas and Alexandra* (1971), *Hitler: The Last Ten Days* (1972), *Trial by Combat* (1976), *Flash Gordon* (1980), *Dragonslayer* (1981), *King David* (1985), *Santa Claus* (1985), *Robin Hood: Prince of Thieves* (1991), *Kull the Conqueror* (1997) and *Arabian Nights* (TV, 2000).

On the small screen John is probably best remembered as Thomas Mallen, Lord of High Banks Hall, in *The Mallens*. At his best in brooding roles, he was also familiar in the 1980s as the father in *White Peak Farm* and played Barnsey (Dirty Den's jail mate) in *EastEnders*. Among John's other TV credits were *The Pallisers* (1974), *Dick Turpin* (1979), *Miss Marple: The 4.50 from Paddington* (1987), *Doctor Who* (1989), *She-Wolf of London* (1990), *Wycliffe* (1993), *Lovejoy* (1993) and *The Memoirs of Sherlock Holmes* (1994), and he was reunited with Leslie Grantham in 1994 for the series *99-1*.

John's final work included the 2000 mini-series *The 10th Kingdom* and the Australian tele-movie *Capricorn* (2000). He lived in Oxford until his death on 14 November 2006, aged sixty-five.

John Hallet

John played the substitute footballer in *Carry On Emmannuelle*. It was his only appearance in the *Carry On* series.

Jean Hamilton

Jean played one of the girls at Dirty Dick's Tavern in *Carry On Jack*.

John Hamilton

John played a native in *Carry On Up the Jungle*.

Barbara Hampshire

Barbara played Private Carter in *Carry On England*.

Sheila Hancock CBE

One of Britain's best-known leading ladies, Sheila Hancock appeared in a guest role as the awfully named Senna Pod – Kenneth Connor's nagging wife – in *Carry On Cleo*. It was her only appearance in the series.

Sheila Hancock was born in Blackgang, on the Isle of Wight, on 22 February 1933. She trained for acting at RADA, and following her stage debut at the age of seventeen she spent several years touring the country in repertory.

Tall and fair-haired with distinctive features, Sheila made her screen debut in *Light Up the Sky* in 1958. Her sporadic screen appearances over the past fifty years have included *Doctor in Love* (1960), *The Bulldog Breed* (1961), *Twice Round the Daffodils* (1962), *The Anniversary* (1968), *Take a Girl Like You* (1970), *The Wildcats of St Trinian's* (1980), *Buster* (1988), *Hawks* (1989), *Three Men and a Little Lady* (1990), *Love and Death on Long Island* (1997), *Alice in Wonderland* (TV, 1999), *Hold Back the Night* (1999), *After Thomas* (TV, 2006) and *The Boy in the Striped Pyjamas* (2008).

On television Sheila received acclaim in the 1960s for her roles in *The Rag Trade* (1961-63, as Carol) and *The Bed-Sit Girl* (1965-66, as Sheila Ross, with Dilys Laye, q.v.). Her other small-screen credits have included *Mr Digby, Darling* (1969, with Peter Jones), her own show *Now Seriously – It's Sheila Hancock, Doctor Who* (1988, as Helen A.), *Jumping the Queue* (1989, as Helen), *Gone to Seed* (1992) and *Brighton Belles* (1993). The versatile actress has played the Dowager Duchess in *The Buccaneers* (1995), Dorothy Hammond in *Close Relations* (1998), Pat in *The Thing About Vince* (1999) and Barbara Owen in *EastEnders* (2001). In 2002 she received a BAFTA Award nomination (Best Actress) for her role as Dora in *The Russian Bride,* and in recent years she has starred in *Fortysomething* (series, 2003), *Feather Boy* (series, 2004), *Bleak House* (2005, as Mrs Guppy) and *Fallen Angel* (2007). In 2010 she was a judge on *Over the Rainbow* as well as starring in the West End as Mother Superior in the musical *Sister Act.*

Essentially Sheila has been most at home on stage where she has built up a formidable list of credits ranging from *Little Women* in 1950 to *Then Again* ... fifty years later. Three years prior to her solo *Carry On* appearance Sheila had appeared on stage in the revue *Pieces of Eight* with Kenneth Williams. As one of the few actresses able to stand up to the notoriously acerbic Williams, she ultimately earned his friendship and respect.

In addition to her numerous stage credits as an actress, Sheila Hancock has also directed several plays and was Associate Director of the Cambridge Theatre Company (1980-82), Artistic Director of the RSC Regional Tour (1983-84) and, since 1978, has been a Director of the Actors Centre.

Sheila Hancock married actor Alexander Ross (1923-71) in 1955 and they had one daughter (actress Melanie Thaw). Following Alexander's death from cancer, Sheila married actor John Thaw (best known as television's Inspector Morse) and they had one daughter Joanna, born in 1975. Sheila was again widowed when Thaw succumbed to cancer in 2002.

Sheila, who successfully battled breast cancer in the late 1980s and who is now President of ABC (Action Against Breast Cancer), published her autobiography, *Ramblings of an Actress*, in 1987. This was followed by the best-sellers, *The Two of Us: My Life with John Thaw* (2004) and *Just Me* (2008). She was awarded the OBE in 1974 and CBE in 2011.

Irene Handl

The most popular character comedienne of her generation, Irene Handl appeared in cameo roles in two *Carry On* films: as the timid Madge Hickson, opposite Bill Owen, in *Carry On Nurse*, and as the short - tempered 'distraught woman' who gives Kenneth Connor short thrift in *Carry On Constable*.

Irene Handl was born in Maida Vale, London, on 27 December 1901. At the age of thirty-six, she was a late arrival to the acting profession, having studied for twelve months at the Embassy School of Acting. She made her stage debut as the Stout Woman in *Night Alone* in 1937 and shortly afterwards became an immediate success as the maid in *George and Margaret,* which ran for nearly two years. For the next five decades Irene continued her busy theatrical career, with numerous stage appearances in England, Australia and New Zealand. One of her most acclaimed roles was as Amelia Puffin in *Goodnight Mrs Puffin,* another success that kept her busy for almost two years.

Irene made her screen debut in *Missing – Believed Married* in 1937. She went on to make well over a hundred film appearances and was at her busiest throughout the 1950s and 1960s with cameo roles in a variety of comedies, including *The Belles of St Trinian's* (1954), *I'm All Right Jack* (1959), *Make Mine Mink* (1960), *Doctor in Love* (1960), *The Pure Hell of St Trinian's* (1961) and *Watch It, Sailor!* (1962).

Irene later appeared in sex comedies of the 1970s, including *Confessions of a Driving Instructor* (1976), *Come Play with Me* (1977) and *Stand Up, Virgin Soldiers* (1977), and among her final screen appearances were *The Hound of the Baskervilles* (1978), *Riding High* (1980) and *Absolute Beginners* (1986).

On the small screen Irene became a household name through her role in the popular sitcom *For the Love of Ada* (4 series, 1970-71, as Ada Cresswell/Bingley), co-starring Wilfred Pickles. She appeared in countless other series, including *Drake's Progress* (1957), *Barney Is My Darling* (series, 1965, as Ramona Pank, with Bill Fraser and Pat Coombs, q.v.), *Mum's Boy* (1968, series, as Crystal Pallise, with Bernard Bresslaw) and *Maggie and Me* (2 series, 1978-79, as Mrs Perry).

By the 1980s Irene was the grand old lady of British entertainment. Indomitably, she continued to work on stage and in films and television until the very end of her long life, and to a generation of television viewers she became familiar as Gran in *Metal Mickey* (series 1, 2 & 4, 1980-83). Irene's final television credits included *Emery Presents* (1982, as Cousin Looby), *It's Your Move* (1982), *Super Gran* (1985, as Clinging Ivey), *The Kenny Everett Show* (1986), *Mapp and Lucia* (1986, as Poppy, Duchess of Sheffield), *Hotel du Lac* (1986), *In Sickness and in Health* (1987, with Patricia Hayes, q.v.) and *Never Say Die* (1987 series, as Dorothy), which was transmitted around the time of her death.

In addition to her acting success (which also included frequent radio broadcasts, particularly in *Hancock's Half Hour*), Irene was a best-selling novelist. Her first critically acclaimed novel, *Sioux*, was published in 1965 and was followed eight years later by *The Gold Tip Pfitzer.*

Irene Handl, who never married, made her final television appearance (in a wheelchair) on *Wogan* in November 1987. Just over a week later, on 29 November, the lovable actress died peacefully in her sleep at the age of eighty-five.

Carry On ... **Quotes**

*I can say how terrific were the many, many times I worked with Irene Handl. She was an absolute joy and became a number one friend. I will never forget our radio series together (*Hello Playmates, *5 series) with Arthur Askey, written by Bob Monkhouse and Denis Goodwin. Irene insisted we dress up as Mrs Purvis – the studio cleaner - and her lank, unmarriageable daughter Nola (ME!!)!! But we did perform in front of an audience and it made it so real somehow!*

I also recall panto in London in '77/'78 with Emu called Emu in Pantoland *– almost a first for both of us.*

One of her classic remarks ... we were called to see Emu's dad for notes in the panto. Rod was with his wife but was stark NAKED doing up his shoes!! We collapsed when we came out and Irene said, "Pat dear, did you see it? It was the size of a walnut!!!"

It was a great loss for me and millions when she died peacefully in 1987 at the age of 85.

Pat Coombs, 1999

Sam Harding

Sam played the pianist in 'The Nine Old Cobblers' – an episode of *Carry On Laughing* on television in 1975.

Mark Hardy

Mark had an uncredited role in *Carry On Cleo*, playing a guard at Caesar's palace.

Juliet Harmer

Juliet Harmer made her final screen appearance, in an uncredited role (which was cut from the final film release), as Mrs Bentley in *Carry On Matron*. Previously Juliet had been seen in a handful of films, including *Just Like a Woman* (1968), *The Engagement* (1970) and *Quest for Love* (1971) but was best known on television in the 1966 series *Adam Adamant Lives!* Juliet's additional television credits included guest roles in *The Avengers, The Persuaders* and *Bless This House*.

Joy Harrington

In a rare film appearance Joy Harrington played the 'Lady' in *Carry On Dick*.

Joy Harrington was born on 22 February 1914 and after drama school began her career in repertory. She made her professional stage debut in 1933 before moving to America to work at Paramount Studios, where she edited scripts, made thirteen films and directed dialogue for nine others, including *National Velvet*. Upon her return to Britain Joy worked for the BBC (1951-61), producing children's series such as *Heidi, Billy Bunter* and *Jesus of Nazareth*, for which she won a BAFTA Award.

From 1970 Joy again worked as an actress and television producer. Her best-known role was as Miss Rumbelow in the final three series of *Sykes* (1976-79), with Eric Sykes and Hattie Jacques, and she played Mrs Brook in the 1978 series, *The Moon Stallion*.

Joy Harrington died in Bristol on 22 October 1991, aged seventy-seven.

Alexander Harris

Alexander played the 3rd Storeman in *Carry On Sergeant*.

Anita Harris

Beloved entertainer Anita Harris is best known for her four hit singles in the 1960s. At the same time she joined the *Carry On* series for two stunning appearances, as Corktip in *Carry On Follow That Camel* and

Nurse Clarke in *Carry On Doctor*.

Anita Harris was born in Midsomer Norton, Somerset, on 3 June 1942. After winning a talent contest, at the age of just three, Anita learned to play the piano and attended the Hampshire School of Drama. After training as a dancer she toured Europe and was in the chorus at the El Rancho in Las Vegas while still in her teens.

In 1961, while working with the Cliff Adams Singers, Anita was noticed by bandleader and composer John Barry and was offered a contract. Her first record was Lionel Bart's song 'I Haven't Got You', and in 1967 she won the Gold Medal for Britain at the San Remo Song Festival before having a top ten hit with 'Just Loving You'. Anita's other singles of the 1960s included 'Playground', 'Anniversary Waltz' and 'Dream a Little Dream of Me'. Her album releases include *Just Loving You* (1967), *Cuddly Toy* (1968), *Anita Is Peter* (1975), *I Love to Sing* (1976) and *The Best of Anita Harris* (1977).

Anita extended her output at the peak of her fame by appearing in leading roles in the *Carry On* series. Cast as Corktip in *Follow That Camel* she made an immediate impression as the seductive belly dancer. She was more demure as the love-struck Nurse Clarke in *Carry On Doctor* but proved her worth opposite *Carry On* legends Jim Dale, Hattie Jacques and Frankie Howerd. Anita did not return for further roles but remains well remembered as a leading lady of the series, and she returned to Pinewood Studios in 1998 and 2008 for the *Carry On* 40th and 50th Anniversary celebrations. In addition to the *Carry On*'s, Anita appeared in the 1966 film *Death Is a Woman*, and she was the singer in *Danger Route* (1968).

On stage and television Anita has proved to be a popular and versatile entertainer. In the 1970s she established herself as one of pantomime's leading principal boys and in the early 1980s she played Grizabella in *Cats*. On stage Anita remains as busy as ever, both in her cabaret act and in occasional dramatic roles, and her credits in the last decade include *Double, Double* at the Alexandra Theatre, Birmingham (2001), *Strangers on a Train* (national tour, 2006), *Come On, Jeeves* (tour, 2008) and *Fatal Encounter* (tour, 2010).

On television Anita has appeared in *Saturday Crowd* (with Leslie Crowther), *Magic Box* (with David Niven), *Morecambe and Wise*, *The Tommy Cooper Show* and the children's series *Jumbleland*. Most recently she has featured in *French and Saunders* (Christmas Special, 1994), *Give Us a Clue* (1998) and documentaries such as *What's a Carry On?* (1998), *Unforgettable Hattie Jacques* (2000) and *Heroes of Comedy: Hattie Jacques* (2002).

Anita, who remains stunning in her sixties, is married to

writer/director Mike Margolis. A vibrant and charming real-life personality, she describes her *Carry On* days as "wonderful memories" (2008).

David Hart

David played the customs officer in *Carry On Emmannuelle*.

William Hartnell (b. W. Henry Hartnell)

Immortalised in television history as the first *Doctor Who*, William Hartnell played Sergeant Grimshaw in *Carry On Sergeant*. Although it was his only appearance in the *Carry On* series, William's formidable leading role helped secure the success of Britain's favourite film series.

William Hartnell was born in Devon (or possibly St Pancras, London) on 8 January 1908. Until recently, William's early years were shrouded in mystery. As a teenager he worked as a jockey and in the mid-1920s he broke with family tradition by taking to the stage. From 1926 he worked in repertory for Sir Frank Benson's company. His subsequent stage appearances included Shakespeare and the classics, and although he made his film debut in *Say It with Music* in 1932 he continued to work on stage throughout the 1930s, mainly in repertory and often billed as Billy Hartnell.

During the 1940s William was often seen on screen as crooks and villains before earning the rare distinction of 'star' character actor in the 1950s. He later became well known as military types, and his role as the barking sergeant in his solo *Carry On* appearance was typical of his work at the time. Among William's seventy film appearances were roles in *Follow the Lady* (1933), *Seeing Is Believing* (1934), *Swinging the Lead* (1935), *Crimson Circle* (1936), *Farewell Again* (1937), *They Drive by Night* (1938), *Murder Will Out* (1939), *Flying Fortress* (1942), *The Goose Steps Out* (1942), *The Dark Tower* (1943), *The Way Ahead* (1944), *Strawberry Roan* (1945) and *Brighton Rock* (1947).

Throughout the 1950s and into the early 1960s William remained equally busy, with film appearances in *The Pickwick Papers* (1952), *Will Any Gentleman…?* (1953), *Private's Progress* (1955), *Hell Drivers* (1957), *The Night We Dropped a Clanger* (1959), *Tomorrow at Ten* (1962) and *This Sporting Life* (1963).

In 1957 William became well known to television viewers as Sergeant Major Percy Bullimore in the popular sitcom *The Army Game*. After appearing in the first two series (1957-58) William returned to the role in 1961, co-starring with Bernard Bresslaw, Charles Hawtrey and Norman Rossington (all q.v.).

In 1963 William was cast in the lead role of the BBC television series *Doctor Who.* The role as the time-travelling eccentric brought him a legion of fans around the world and helped create one of the most popular series in television history. William Hartnell quit his role in *Doctor Who* in 1966. His health was already beginning to suffer from the irreversible effects of arteriosclerosis. Although he continued to act for another couple of years, notably on stage with Sonia Dresdel (1909-76) in *The Brothers* (1967), by 1970 he was in very poor health. He made a final television appearance in *The Three Doctors,* filmed at the end of 1972.

William was married to actress/writer Heather McIntyre (d.1984) from 1928 and they had one daughter, Anne. William Hartnell's granddaughter is actress and writer Jessica Carney, who wrote an excellent biography of William – *Who's There?* - in 1996. Away from acting William enjoyed country life, fishing and horses.

In his final years, as the effects of his illness made him vague and withdrawn, he was cared for devotedly by his wife. William Hartnell spent the last five months of his life in a Kent hospital, where he died peacefully on 23 April 1975, aged sixty-seven.

Imogen Hassall

A glamorous leading lady of stage, screen and television, Imogen Hassall joined the *Carry On* series for a memorable guest appearance as Jenny Grubb in *Carry On Loving*.

Imogen Hassall was born in Woking, Surrey, on 25 August 1942. Her father, Christopher Hassall, was an actor, author and poet and her grandfather, John Hassall, was the famous poster artist. Imogen was educated at Elmhurst (with future *Carry On* leading lady Juliet Mills, q.v.) and trained at the Royal Ballet School. She subsequently trained for acting at LAMDA, and at the age of twenty she spent six months with the Royal Shakespeare Company. Despite an eighteen-year career on stage, she is best remembered as a buxom, stunningly attractive glamour girl in films such as *The Early Bird* (1965), *The Long Duel* (1967), *When Dinosaurs Ruled the Earth* (1969) and *The Virgin and the Gypsy* (1970). Indeed, Imogen once remarked that she had two careers – "as actress and as glamour girl".

In *Carry On Loving* Imogen's incredible metamorphosis from 'plain Jane' to sex goddess helped illustrate not only her more obvious assets but also an acting skill previously underused in her screen appearances.

From the mid-1970s Imogen chose to concentrate on stage work in an attempt to avoid her now famous title of 'The Countess of Cleavage'. She toured in plays such as *The Jockey Club Stakes* (1971), *Barefoot in the Park* (1973), *The Mating Game* (1973), *A Bit Between the Teeth* (1975) and *Say*

Who You Are (1978). Her final screen appearance was in *Licence to Love and Kill* in 1979, and she made her last stage appearances in the summer of 1980 in a tour of *Outside Edge,* with Liz Fraser (q.v.).

On the small screen Imogen appeared in episodes of *The Avengers, The Saint* and *The Persuaders* and also featured as a guest in quiz shows such as *Call My Bluff.*

In private Imogen Hassall was an insecure, deeply troubled lady. During her short life she attempted suicide on a number of occasions - obvious cries for help that were magnified by her eventual addiction to barbiturates. Ironically, her eventual death was arguably another cry for help, which went tragically wrong. It is now believed that Imogen's emotional problems stemmed from a chemical imbalance, sadly misdiagnosed at the time.

Imogen was briefly married to director Kenneth Ives and secondly to actor Andrew Knox, although they separated within a couple of months.

Imogen Hassall's life ended tragically, but perhaps not surprisingly, from a drug overdose at her home in Wimbledon on 16 November 1980, at the age of thirty-eight. Her biography, *Tuesday's Child – The Life & Death of Imogen Hassall*, by Dan Leissner, was published in 2002.

Carry On ... ***Quotes***

... for all the storms and demands that she made upon their time and patience, Imogen's friends remember her fondly. Her story is the tragedy of a warm and caring, loving individual, who was broken inside and lost.
Dan Leissner
(Imogen's biographer), 1999

Carol Hawkins (b. Carol Ann Hawkins)

Leading lady Carol Hawkins joined the *Carry On* team in 1970 and went on to make eye-catching appearances in *Carry On Abroad*, *Carry On Behind* and two episodes of *Carry On Laughing*.

Carol was born in Barnet, Hertfordshire, on 31 January 1949. After training at the Corona Stage Academy she made her first major television appearances in the popular series *Please Sir!* and its sequel *The Fenn Street Gang* (1971-74, as Sharon Eversleigh). It is a role for which she is still well remembered.

Carol Hawkins made her *Carry On* debut on television (in an uncredited role) as one of the girls with Sid James in the 1970 Christmas special, *Carry On Again Christmas*. Two years later she played Marge, who finds an unlikely romance in the form of Bernard Bresslaw, in *Carry On Abroad*. A refreshing addition to the cast, Carol returned to the team for episodes of *Carry On Laughing*, playing Lilly the housemaid in 'In My Lady's Chamber' and 'Who Needs Kitchener?' In the same year she played the shapely Sandra in *Carry On Behind*, but she sensibly turned down a role in *Carry On England* the following year because it required her to appear topless (the role eventually went to Trisha Newby, q.v.). An effective supporting actress in the series, it is a pity that Carol's appearances were limited to two films.

In addition to the *Carry On* films, Carol appeared in *Zeta One* (1969), *When Dinosaurs Ruled the Earth* (1970), *Please Sir!* (1971), the screen version of *Bless This House* (1972), *Percy's Progress* (1974) and *Not Now, Comrade* (1976).

On the small screen Carol's numerous credits include *Mr Big* (1977, as Norma), *Together* (1981), *C.A.T.S. Eyes, All at No. 20* (1987, as Candy), *My Husband and I* (1987-88, as Tracy), *Leaves on the Line* (1992), *Rides* (1993, as Charmain), *All Night Long* (1994, as Mrs Sleepwalker), *Hollyoaks* (1996-97, as Mrs Matthew) and *Trial & Retribution* (1998, as Monica Fuller). Carol has also made guest appearances in programmes such as *The Dick Emery Show, The Two Ronnies, Hale and Pace* and several episodes of *The Bill*.

On stage Carol was directed by Kenneth Williams in *The Undertaking* in 1980 and has since worked extensively in the plays of Ray Cooney, including tours of *See How They Run, Run for Your Wife, Wife Begins at Forty, Funny Money* and *Caught in the Net* (2001-02).

Carol, whose first marriage was dissolved, is married to Martyn Padbury and in private enjoys painting, reading and writing. She ran a string of shops for a number of years and now divides her time between homes in West Sussex and Spain.

Charles Hawtrey

(See MAIN TEAM).

Melvyn Hayes

Comic actor Melvyn Hayes is best known as Bombardier 'Gloria' Beaumont in eight series of *It Ain't Half Hot Mum*. In 1976 he made a memorable *Carry On* appearance as Gunner Shorthouse in *Carry On England*, having previously played Char Wallah Charlie in 'The Case of the Screaming Winkles', an episode of *Carry On Laughing*

Born in London on 11 January 1935, Melvyn began his career at the

Comedy Theatre, London, doing the Indian rope trick. As a teenager he appeared on television as one of the boys in *Billy Bunter of Greyfriars School,* with Gerald Campion (q.v.), and his diminutive stature allowed him to continue in juvenile roles well into his twenties, including playing the Artful Dodger in *Oliver Twist* for the BBC in 1962.

On stage, in addition to frequent appearances in panto, Melvyn has appeared in seasons of *Spring and Port Wine, Run for Your Wife, The Wind in the Willows, The Dresser* and *Cash On Delivery* (UK tour, 2007).

Melvyn made his film debut at the age of nineteen in *Face the Music* (1954) and went on to appear in minor roles in films such as *Adventures in the Hopfields* (1954), *The Good Companions* (1957), *The Curse of Frankenstein* (1957), *No Trees in the Street* (1958) and *Bottoms Up* (1960). His film career took off when he appeared in a string of hits with Sir Cliff Richard, including *The Young Ones* (1961, as Jimmy), *Summer Holiday* (1963) and *Wonderful Life* (1964, as Jerry). His additional film credits include *Crooks in Cloisters* (1964), *The Magnificent Seven Deadly Sins* (1971), *Love Thy Neighbour* (1973), *Man About the House* (1974), *What's Up Superdoc!* (1978), *Santa Claus* (1985) and *King of the Wind* (1989).

On television Melvyn Hayes is still best remembered for his role as drag artist Gunner/Bombardier 'Gloria' Beaumont in eight series of *It Ain't Half Hot Mum* (1974-81). His additional small-screen credits include *Here Come the Double Deckers* (series, 1972, as Albert), *Sir Yellow* (series, 1973, as Gregory) and *Potter's Picture Palace* (2 series, 1976-78, as Melvyn Didsbury). In the 1980s he was familiar as the voice of Skeleton in the popular cartoon series *SuperTed* and in the 1990s he voiced characters for cartoons such as *The Dreamstone* and *Little Dracula.* Most recently Melvyn has appeared in guest roles in *The Thin Blue Line, Drop the Dead Donkey, EastEnders* (2005, as Mr Rawlings) and *Benidorm* (2011).

Melvyn Hayes, who has been married twice (firstly to *Doctor Who* star Wendy Padbury) has four daughters and one son. Away from acting Melvyn also runs a pub in Gloucestershire.

Patricia Hayes OBE

Esteemed character actress Patricia Hayes played one of the most memorable cameo roles in the entire *Carry On* series, appearing as Mrs Beasley, Jim Dale's hypochondriac patient, in *Carry On Again Doctor.* It was her only appearance in the series.

Born in Camberwell, South London, on 22 December 1909, Patricia was encouraged to take up acting by her father, and after making her stage debut at the age of twelve she joined RADA in 1927. She spent the first ten years of her career touring the country in repertory, making her name as Ruby (the clumsy maid) in *When We Are Married*, and she became a founding member of the Players' Theatre. Over the next sixty years she continued to make regular stage appearances and she was still working in the theatre into the 1990s.

To the public at large Patricia was most familiar for her work on radio and television. In the 1950s and 1960s her shrill tones were heard in *Children's Hour* (ironically playing schoolboy Henry Bones) and *Ray's a Laugh*.

On the small screen Patricia is believed to have starred with more of Britain's top comedians than any other actress. She made hundreds of television appearances, including *Hancock's Half Hour, Educated Evans* (2 series, 1957-58, as Emma Toggs), *The Arthur Askey Show* (1961, as Mrs Rossiter), *Hugh and I* (4 series, 1962-66, as Mrs Wormold), *Benny Hill* (1962-63), *The Arthur Haynes Show* (2 series, 1964-66), *The Very Merry Widow* (1969, as Katie), *The Last of the Baskets* (2 series, 1971-72, as Mrs Basket), *Spooner's Patch* (2 series, 1980-82, as Mrs Cantaford), *The Lady Is a Tramp* (2 series, 1983-84, as Old Pat, with Pat Coombs, q.v.) and *Marjorie and Men* (series, 1985, as Alice Tripp).

Patricia was also familiar as Min in the long-running Warren Mitchell/Dandy Nichols (both q.v.) series *Till Death Us Do Part* and its sequels *Till Death ...* (series, 1981) and *In Sickness and in Health* (guest appearances from the mid-1980s). Patricia also teamed up with Dandy Nichols in the 1971 series *The Trouble with Lilian* (as Lilian).

Perhaps Patricia Hayes's most memorable television role was as Edna in *Edna the Inebriate Woman*, for which she received critical acclaim (and a BAFTA Award) in 1971. She was the subject of *This Is Your Life* in 1972.

Patricia made her film debut in *Broken Blossoms* in 1936 and went on to appear in over forty films, including *When We Are Married* (1943), *Nicholas Nickleby* (1947), *Reach for Glory* (1962), *A Hard Day's Night* (1964), *Help!* (1965), *Goodbye, Mr Chips* (1969), *Fragment of Fear* (1971), *Love Thy Neighbour* (1973), *The Neverending Story* (1984), *Little Dorrit* (1988), *Willow* (1988), *A Fish Called Wanda* (1988), *The Fool* (1990), *Blue Ice* (1993) and *The Steal* (1995).

Sprightly well into old age, Patricia continued to appear on television into the 1990s, notably as Mrs Templecombe in *Murder Most Horrid* (1994, with Dawn French) and as Colin Firth's grandmother in *Master of the Moor* (1994). One of her final roles was as an aged gypsy in a touching episode of *Heartbeat*, shortly after which she was forced to retire after breaking her hip in a fall.

Patricia Hayes married actor Valentine Rooke (Valentine Cozens-Brooke) in 1939 and they had one son, actor Richard O'Callaghan (q.v.) and two daughters, Teresa and Gemma, before they divorced in 1946. Patricia was awarded the OBE in 1987, and away from the screen she enjoyed homely pursuits. Her biography, *A Funny Old Life*, to which she contributed, was written by her daughter Teresa in 1990.

Patricia Hayes died peacefully (following a long illness) in a London nursing home, surrounded by her family, on 19 September 1998, aged eighty-eight.

Don Henderson

Prodigious character actor Don Henderson brought his considerable acting skills to *Carry On Columbus*, as the Bosun exchanging banter with Jim Dale.

Don Henderson was born in Leytonstone, London, on 10 November 1931 (some sources say 1932). As an amateur actor he accepted a dare from a colleague to audition for the Royal Shakespeare Company. He was accepted on the spot and stayed with the RSC for six years (1966-72). His numerous stage credits included *The Merry Wives of Windsor, Henry IV, Henry V, The Merchant of Venice* and *When Thou Art King* (Stratford, West End & world tour).

Don also appeared in more than twenty feature films, including *Callan* (1974), *The Ghoul* (1975), *Star Wars* (1977, as General Tagge), *The Big Sleep* (1978), *Crossed Swords* (1978), *The Island* (1980), *Brazil* (1985), *The Fool* (1990), *The Trial* (1993), *White Angel* (1993), *The Wind in the Willows* (1996) and *Fairy Tale: A True Story* (1997).

On television Don was one of the country's busiest character actors, turning up for a variety of roles in tele-films, mini-series and series. He received a BAFTA nomination for his role as a cancer patient in *Jumping the Queue* (1989, with Sheila Hancock, q.v.) and ironically, like Hancock, he had also suffered from cancer in real life, successfully battling the disease in the early 1980s. He received another BAFTA nomination for his role as ex-priest Frank Lane in *The Paradise Club* (1989-90, with Leslie Grantham).

On the small screen he was perhaps best known as Sergeant George Bulman in three separate series: *The XYY Man* (1976-77), *Strangers* (1978-92) and *Bulman* (1985-87). His additional series included *Warship* (1973-76, as Master-at-Arms, Heron), *Poldark* (1975, as Tom Carne) and *Knight and Gods* (1987, as Colley). His guest roles ranged from *Ripping Yarns* (1977) to *2point4 Children* (1992), and he made final appearances on the small screen in *Ruth Rendell: A Case of Coincidence* (1996), *The Famous Five* (1996, as Block) and *Red Dwarf* (1997, as Rogue Simulant).

Don's first wife Hilary died in 1977 and he married secondly actress Shirley Stelfox (q.v.) two years later. The couple later appeared together on television in *Making Out* (1989) and *Pat and Margaret* (1994). Don had a daughter and son, Louise and Ian, from his first marriage and a stepdaughter, Helena, from his second marriage.

Don Henderson died peacefully in his sleep, after a short battle with cancer, on 22 June 1997, aged sixty-five.

Percy Herbert

A character actor with over sixty film appearances to his credit, Percy Herbert appeared in two *Carry On* films: as Mr Angel in *Carry On Jack* and as Charlie, the likeable but unfortunate barman, in *Carry On Cowboy*.

Percy was born in London's East End on 31 July 1920 (some sources say 1925). He began acting under the guidance – and good nature – of Dame Sybil Thorndike and made his film debut in *They Were Not Divided* in 1950.

Over the next twenty-five years the solidly built actor was frequently seen on screen as soldiers, sailors and labourers. Among his numerous film appearances were *The Young Lovers* (1954), *Doctor at Sea* (1955), *Lost* (1956), *Cockleshell Heroes* (1956), *Dunkirk* (1958), *Idle on Parade* (1959), *There Was a Crooked Man* (1960), *Bunny Lake Is Missing* (1965), *One Million Years B.C.* (1966), *The Viking Queen* (1967), *Man in the Wilderness* (1971) and *Up the Front* (1972). Percy also had the distinction of appearing in classics such as *The Bridge on the River Kwai* (1957), *The Guns of Navarone* (1961) and *Mutiny on the Bounty* (1962). One of Percy's final screen appearances was among the all-star cast of Disney's *One of Our Dinosaurs Is Missing* (1975, with Joan Sims and Bernard Bresslaw) and he played Keith in *The Wild Geese* (1978) and Dennison in *The Sea Wolves* (1980).

Percy's television appearances included *Police Surgeon, Danger Man*, Charlie Drake's series *The Worker* (1965, as Mr Whittaker) and the American series *Cimarron Strip* (1967, as MacGregor). He also played Mr Preston in the 1975 series *Down the 'Gate*, with Reg Varney and Dilys Laye (q.v.).

By the 1980s Percy was semi-retired from acting. He made a final screen appearance in the 1987 film *The Love Child*.

Percy Herbert died from a heart attack on 6 December 1992, aged seventy-two.

Philip Herbert

Actor, comedian and fire-eater, Philip Herbert is best known for his work on television with Julian Clary (q.v.). Along with Clary, he was one of the newcomers cast to appear in *Carry On Columbus*, playing Ginger.

Born in London on 28 January 1957, Philip trained at East 15 Acting School and spent two years with the Royal Court Youth Theatre (1975-77).

On stage Philip's early work included *Waiting for Godot, Oh, What a Lovely War!* and *Charley's Aunt* (as Brassett). More recently he has played Mr Bumble in *Oliver!*, Toad in *The Wind in the Willows* and Fatty Arbuckle in several seasons of *Mack & Mabel*.

Philip's screen credits have mainly been cameo appearances and include *Victor/Victoria* (1982), *Fanny Hill* (1983), *Return of the Jedi* (1983, as Hermi Odle, one of the creatures in Jabba's palace), *Christmas Present* (1985), *Little Shop of Horrors* (1986), *Sabotage!* (2000), *City Rats* (2009) and *Tortoise in Love* (2010).

On television Philip has appeared in over fifty programmes, including *Comic Relief* (1991), *I Love Keith Allen, Bodger and Badger* (as Eamon Trout), *Mr. Majeika* (1991, as Billy Bloodcup), *The Bill, Carrott Confidential, The Pickwick Papers, Cadfael, Brookside and Trial & Retribution: Mirror Image* (2007). He is perhaps most familiar for his work with Julian Clary in two series of *Sticky Moments* (as Hugh Jelly) and the 1992 series *Terry and Julian*. Philip Herbert has also toured the world on stage with Julian as the madcap Hugh Jelly, a character he has also recreated in *The Good Sex Guide, The Jonathan Ross Show* and *The Steve Vizard Show*.

Philip also performs in cabaret as Randolph the Remarkable, performing "feats of skill involving fire and a blue bowl of lukewarm water". With this act, which he has performed for over a decade, he has established himself as a 'new variety' artist in Britain and Europe.

Philip is single and lives in London.

Donald Hewlett

Best known on television as Colonel Reynolds in *It Ain't Half Hot Mum*, Donald Hewlett played the university Dean, opposite Kenneth Williams, in the opening stages of *Carry On Behind*.

Donald was born in Manchester on 30 August 1920 and educated at Clifton and Cambridge. During the Second World War he joined the Navy as an ordinary seaman and eventually formed an 'Arts Club', whose numerous visitors included luminaries such as Sir John Mills, Sir John Gielgud (President) and Dame Sybil Thorndike. Donald was later drafted to Singapore, where he subsequently formed the Singapore Stage Club. After being demobbed Donald trained at RADA, where he won the Athene Seyler Prize for Comedy. He then joined the Oxford Playhouse Theatre, with Ronnie Barker. A member of the famous Cambridge Footlights, Donald Hewlett's numerous West End stage appearances included *And Another Thing, Look Who's Here, The Housemaster* and *The Pilgrim's Progress*, and he played Badger in *The Wind in the Willows* musical.

On television Donald was best known for his work in sitcoms, notably

It Ain't Half Hot Mum (1973-76, as Colonel Reynolds) and *You Rang, M'Lord?* (1991-93, as Lord Meldrum). He made his small-screen debut as the co-host of the children's series *Jigsaw* (with Rolf Harris) and went on to appear in episodes of *The Avengers, The Saint,* the 1978 series *Come Back Mrs. Noah* (with Mollie Sugden), *Callan, Lovejoy* and *Morris Minor and the Majors*. Additional credits included *The Very Merry Widow* (with Moira Lister), *That's Me Over Here* (with Ronnie Corbett) and the 1987 series *Pulaski* (as Charles Parker-Smith).

Donald's occasional film appearances include *Orders Are Orders* (1954), *Bottoms Up* (1959), *A Touch of Class* (1973), *The Great Train Robbery* (1979) and *Saving Grace* (1986).

Donald's first two marriages ended in divorce and he married thirdly former actress Therese McMurray in 1979. He had five children including actress Siobhan Hewlett (1983-). His final acting role came in a 1995 episode of *The Upper Hand* after which poor health forced him to retire from the profession. In his later life he featured in documentaries such as *Comedy Connections*; *It Ain't Half Hot Mum* (2007) and was a guest at the *Dad's Army* 40th Anniversary reunion in 2008.

Donald Hewlett developed Alzheimer's disease towards the end of his life and died at London's Chelsea and Westminster hospital on 4th June 2011 following a lengthy illness. He was 90 years old.

Carry On ... ***Quotes***

I'm afraid my work on Carry On Behind *was so brief that I have no anecdotes. I only wish I had!*
Donald Hewlett, 2000

Sherrie Hewson (b. Sherrie Lynn Hutchinson)

Best known for her roles in television soap operas *Coronation Street, Crossroads* and *Emmerdale*, popular actress Sherrie Hewson joined the *Carry On* series in 1975, playing Carol in *Carry On Behind*. She also appeared in four episodes of *Carry On Laughing*.

Sherrie was born in Burton Joyce, Nottinghamshire, on 17 September 1950. By the age of seven she was already singing and dancing in revues around the country, and at the age of seventeen she was accepted to train at RADA.

Sherrie's first success on the small screen was with Russ Abbot in his shows *Russ Abbot's Madhouse, The Russ Abbot Show* and *Russ Abbot*.

Sherrie was among several new faces cast in the *Carry On* series in the mid-1970s. Along with Carol Hawkins (q.v.), she played a 'love interest' (Carol) in *Carry On Behind*. In the same year Sherrie was able to display further comic range when she appeared in four episodes of *Carry On Laughing*, playing nurse Millie Teazel in 'The Case of the Screaming Winkles', Irma Klein in 'The Case of the Coughing Parrot' and the aristocratic Virginia in 'And in My Lady's Chamber' and 'Who Needs Kitchener?'.

Since her *Carry On* days, roles in a string of high-profile series have ensured that Sherrie remains a familiar face to television audiences. In the 1980s she played May in Thora Hird's series *In Loving Memory* (1984-86) and she was later seen as Paula, opposite Jim Davidson, in the popular sitcom *Home James!* (1987-90). In 1993 Sherrie joined the cast of *Coronation Street* as Maureen Naylor, who later married two of television's most memorable characters, Reg Holdsworth and Fred Elliott. Since leaving 'the Street' in 1997, Sherrie has played Jean in Gwen Taylor's series *Barbara* (1999-2003) and receptionist Virginia Raven in *Crossroads* (2001), and she joined the cast of *Emmerdale* in 2004 as Lesley Meredith (a semi-regular character for two years). In addition to her credits as an actress, Sherrie has also proved to be a popular television personality, especially as a frequent guest on *Loose Women* (since 2003). She also featured (undergoing a facelift) in a one-off special of *Ten Years Younger* in 2005.

Sherrie's additional television appearances have included *Z-Cars, My Son, My Son* (1979), *Minder, Juliet Bravo, Flickers* (1981), *Lovejoy* (1991) and *The Bill*. Her film roles, aside from *Carry On Behind*, have been as Palatine in *The Slipper and the Rose* (1976, with Margaret Lockwood) and as Phyllis in *Hanover Street* (1979).

Sherrie married Ken Boyd in 1983 and they had one daughter, Keely. The couple separated in 2004. Sherrie's autobiography, *Behind the Laughter*, was published in 2011.

Joan Hickson OBE

Now best remembered for her impeccable performance as Miss Marple on BBC television, Joan Hickson's appearances in five *Carry On* films were a small proportion of an enviable career spanning more than sixty years.

Joan Hickson was born in Kingsthorpe, Northamptonshire, on 5 August 1906. An only child, Joan decided upon a career as an actress after seeing a pantomime performance of *Cinderella* at the age of five. She trained at RADA from 1925 and made her first stage appearance in 1927 in a tour of *His Wife's Children*, as Lady Shoreham. Over the next six decades she would make frequent stage appearances, including three seasons with the Oxford Playhouse (1931-33). She made her New York stage debut in *A Day in the Death of Joe Egg* in 1968, and in 1979 she received a Tony Award for Best Supporting Actress for her role as Delia in *Bedroom Farce*.

Joan made her screen debut in *Trouble in Store* in 1933 and went on to make over a hundred film appearances, invariably in cameo roles. Graduating from maids to housekeepers, she was later seen to best effect as eccentric maiden aunts and ultimately became an indispensable part of British cinema.

Joan made her *Carry On* debut as the efficient Sister in *Carry On Nurse*, opposite Hattie Jacques. She gave a delightful cameo performance as the well-to-do but tipsy Mrs May in *Carry On Constable*, and in a role reversal with Hattie Jacques she played Matron in *Carry On Regardless*, opposite Sid James. Joan would return to the series, after an absence of almost a decade, to play elderly eccentrics. In 1970 she was seen as Mrs Grubb (Jenny's mother) in *Carry On Loving*, and she gave her finest *Carry On* appearance as Mrs Dukes, the hotel guest whose red, flannelette bloomers were the cause of much concern, in *Carry On Girls*.

In addition to her work on stage and in films, Joan was a popular radio actress from the late 1940s. Her numerous broadcasts included *The Bell Family* (1949, as Mrs Gage) and its subsequent follow-up series throughout the 1950s. She later featured in *Mister Morgan* (1962), *No Man's Land* (1964), *Mixed Feelings* (1969), *Open House* (1973) and *The Likely Lads* (1975).

From 1946 Joan appeared in countless television plays and series. Her formidable list of small-screen credits ranged from *Busman's Holiday* (1947) to *Great Expectations* (1981, as Miss Haversham). She also appeared in *David Copperfield* (1956, as Lavinia Spenlow), *The Royalty* (2 series, as Miss Plimm), *Our Man at St. Mark's* (4 series, 1963-66, as Mrs Peace, with Leslie Phillips, q.v.), *Bachelor Father* (1970, as Mrs Pugsley) and *Whatever Happened to the Likely Lads?* (appearances, as Mrs Chambers). Joan's guest roles included appearances in episodes of *Sykes, Father, Dear Father, Nanny, Poor Little Rich Girls* (1984, as Lady Harriet) and *Boon* (1989, as Delia).

Having appeared in so many character parts over fifty years, Joan took on the lead role of Miss Marple – Agatha Christie's spinster sleuth – in 1984. It was a role she would make her own. Described as the 'ultimate' Miss Marple, Joan appeared in adaptations of all twelve Miss Marple stories, filmed for BBC television over an eight-year period. The role also brought Joan two BAFTA nominations.

Joan's connection with Dame Agatha Christie was long-standing – she was a friend of the author who, ironically, hoped that Joan would one day play the role of Miss Marple. Further 'Christie' connections for Joan included the 1962 film *Murder, She Said*, with Dame Margaret Rutherford (who was godmother to Hickson's son) and also the 1980 television adaptation of *Why Didn't They Ask Evans?*

The final Miss Marple adaptation – *The Mirror Crack'd from Side to Side* – was filmed in 1992 and Joan Hickson retired from acting later that year, having spent three days working on the film *Century* (1993).

Joan Hickson was married to Doctor Eric N. Butler, who died in 1967, and they had one son and one daughter. Away from acting Joan was a keen supporter of students, turning a garage attached to her house into a studio flat for undergraduates at the University of Essex. She also renovated a property at Wivenhoe for the same purpose. She was awarded the OBE in 1987 and spent her final years living quietly in Essex. After suffering a series of minor strokes she withdrew from the public eye and enjoyed spending time in her garden, which she had substantially improved over many years.

Joan Hickson died peacefully in a Colchester hospital on 17 October 1998, at the age of ninety-two. One of the most prolific actors of her generation, she will always be fondly remembered for her delightful performances on stage, screen and television.

Note: The author would once again like to acknowledge the help of Joan Hickson's son - N.A.M. Butler - for sharing his research on Miss Hickson's early television credits and work on radio.

Carry On ... Quotes

My mother used to tell me that she admired the speed and skill with which the Carry On *films were made but other than that has no particular memories of them.*
Nicholas A.M Butler (Joan Hickson's son), 1997

*The Agatha Christie I did with Joan Hickson (*A Murder Is Announced, *1985) was filmed in a beautiful location in Dorset and I thought both Joan Hickson and Joan Sims were marvellous.*
Renée Asherson, 1998

Jennifer Hill

Jennifer Hill appeared briefly in one *Carry On* film at the beginning of

Left: Sid James in *Once a Jolly Swagman*, 1949
(Rex Features)

Below: *Carry On* Grande Dame, Hattie Jacques, 1967
(Rex Features)

Above: Peter Butterworth, the star of sixteen *Carry On* films, in character for an episode of *Catweazle*, 1971
(Rex Features)

Right: Jack Douglas in 1982 *(Rex Features)*

Sid James in 1961 *(Rex Features)*

Above: Shapely beauties: Joan Sims and her *Carry On Regardless* co-star Liz Fraser in *Doctor in Love* (1960) *(Rex Features)*

Left: Charles Hawtrey, the star of twenty-three *Carry On* films, 1973 *(Rex Features)*

Carry On femme fatale Fenella Fielding, 1964 *(Rex Features)*

Above: Terry Scott with his frequent co-star and fellow *Carry On* favourite, June Whitfield CBE, 1978 *(Rex Features)*

Left: Charles Hawtrey photographed during the filming of *The Plank* in 1979. It was one of his final television appearances *(Rex Features)*

Above: Kenneth Connor during a guest appearance on *Celebrity Squares*, 1976 *(Rex Features)*

Right: Hattie Jacques during the filming of *Rhubarb Rhubarb* in April 1980, just six months before her sudden death *(Rex Features)*

Kenneth Williams, the star of twenty-six *Carry On* films, photographed in September 1985
(Rex Features)

A *Carry On* reunion – Barbara Windsor, Terry Scott, Anita Harris, Jack Douglas and Bernard Bresslaw in 1987
(Rex Features)

The gentle giant of the *Carry On* series, Bernard Bresslaw in 1990
(Rex Features)

Kenneth Connor receiving his MBE at Buckingham Palace in 1991
(Rex Features)

Patsy Rowlands, with her son Alan, in 1998 *(Rex Features)*

The Queen of the *Carry On* series, Joan Sims in December 1998 *(Rex Features)*

Carry On leading man, Jim Dale MBE, in April 2009 *(Rex Features)*

The most visible figure-head of the *Carry On* series, a stunning Barbara Windsor MBE, photographed in April 2009 *(Rex Features)*

Rosalind Knight (*Nurse* and *Teacher*) in 2010

Television icon Amanda Barrie (*Cabby* and *Cleo*) in 2009

Beloved *Carry On* actress, Angela Douglas, (*Cowboy, Screaming, Follow That Camel* and *Up the Khyber*) in 2010

The ever-glamorous Valerie Leon in 2010

Peter Byrne, *Carry On Cabby* actor and star of *Dixon of Dock Green*, in 2010

The star of *Randall and Hopkirk (Deceased)* and *Coronation Street*, Kenneth Cope (*At Your Convenience* and *Matron*) in 2010

Alan Curtis (*Henry* and *Abroad*) in 2009

Robin Askwith, star of the *Confessions* films and *Carry On Girls*, in 2010

Carry On favourite, Jacki Piper (*Up the Jungle*, *Loving*, *At Your Convenience* and *Matron*) in 2009

Bless This House star Sally Geeson (*Abroad* and *Girls*) in 2009

Linda Regan, actress and author, in 2010

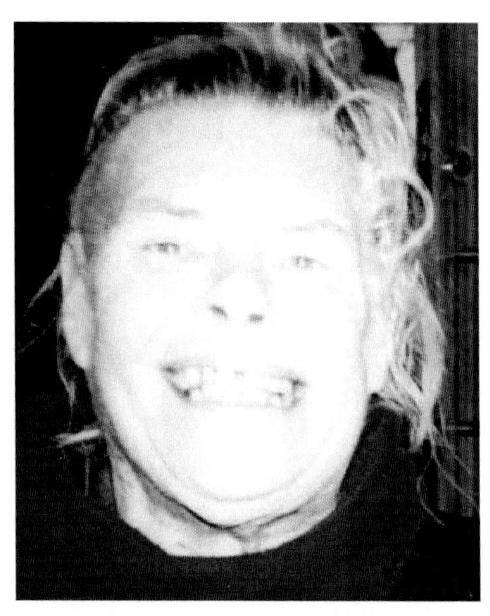

One of the last photographs of character actress Claire Davenport (*Emmannuelle*) taken in February 2001

her career. She played one of the girls at Dirty Dick's Tavern in *Carry On Jack*.

Jennifer spent two years training at LAMDA before beginning her career in repertory, touring the country. Her subsequent stage work has included over three years (and ten productions) with the Royal National Opera, appearances in pantomime and most recently Ray Cooney's *It Runs in the Family* and *Q.O.H.*, by Christine Watkins.

From the 1960s Jennifer's television credits have included *Softly, Softly, Z-Cars, The Basil Brush Show, The Kenny Everett Show, Crossroads* (over 3 years), *Grange Hill, Tenko* (1981), *In Sickness and in Health, The Bill, Bedside Manner* (1996), *Washed Up* (1997) and *Doctor Who* (2005, as Mrs Peace).

Jennifer has also broadcast frequently on radio, most recently in *A Child of Consequence* and *A Clockwork Orange*. Her film credits, aside from *Carry On Jack*, have been *Giro City* (1982), *Dreaming of Joseph Lees* (1998) and *Human Traffic* (1998).

Roy Hines

Roy played school student Harry Bird in *Carry On Teacher*.

Michael Hobbs

Stage, screen and television actor Michael Hobbs played one of the hooded Inquisitors in *Carry On Columbus*.

Michael, who trained at the Webber Douglas Academy, has appeared in a range of television programmes over the past two decades, including *Bergerac, Birds of a Feather, The Upper Hand, Surgical Spirit, Men Behaving Badly, Little Lord Fauntleroy* (as Bill Baker), *The Peter Principle, No Sweat* (as Colin Crabbe), *Spark, EastEnders* and *Lucy Sullivan Is Getting Married*.

On stage Michael's credits include the roles of Launcelot Gobbo in *The Merchant of Venice* and Mellefont in *The Double Dealer*. In addition to *Carry On Columbus*, Michael has appeared in *Neil Simon's London Suite* (TV, 1995) and *Remember Me* (2010).

Michael Hobbs lives in West London.

Carry On … ***Quotes***

I actually only spent one day filming Carry On Columbus *– it was at Pinewood Studios and we all sat around after being in make-up and costume. We were called to the set, shot the scene very quickly and were then sent away. I was probably there for no longer than six hours!*
Michael Hobbs, 1999

Nick Hobbs
Nick was a stunt double in *Carry On Girls*.

McDonald Hobley (b. Dennys Jack Valentine McDonald-Hobley)
A BBC radio personality for over thirty years and one of television's first announcers, McDonald Hobley played the Quaker reporter in 'Orgy and Bess', an episode of *Carry On Laughing*.

McDonald was born in Port Stanley, on the Falkland Islands, on 9 June 1917. His father was a naval chaplain in Port Stanley and his early education was in the Falklands before moving to South America and later attending Brighton College.

McDonald's early work was as an actor in repertory. During the Second World War he served with the Royal Artillery and worked in radio in Ceylon. In 1946 he became BBC television's only male continuity announcer (a role that required him to wear a dinner jacket), and in 1954 he was voted TV Personality of the Year. McDonald was especially well known for presenting the popular series *Kaleidoscope*. He continued to work at the BBC until 1956 and then went on to join Associated British Cinemas, where he worked as a commentator until 1959.

In addition to his credits as an announcer and broadcaster, McDonald appeared in a handful of films, including *No Place for Jennifer* (1950), *Meet Mr Lucifer* (1953, as himself), *Man of the Moment* (1955), *The Entertainer* (1960) and *Primitive London* (1965).

From 1960 he enjoyed success in a string of pantomimes and stage plays, including *No Sex Please, We're British*. In 1986 McDonald returned to the Falklands for a Channel 4 programme about the British South Atlantic dependencies.

McDonald Hobley was three times married and divorced. He died on 30 July 1987, aged seventy.

Katherina Holden
Katherina played one of the Khasi's wives in *Carry On Up the Khyber*.

Terence Holland
After working for Gerald Thomas in *Raising the Wind* (as the 1st Trombone Player) Terence Holland played the young passer-by in *Carry On Cruising*.

Bernard Holley

A busy stage and television actor, Bernard Holley played the Captain in 'The Sobbing Cavalier', an episode of the television series *Carry On Laughing*, in 1975.

Born in Eastcote, Middlesex, on 9 August 1940, Bernard began his career as Charlie Wingate in *Chips With Everything* at the Theatre Royal, Lincoln. He went on to work in repertory around the country before appearing on stage in London in plays such as *A Midsummer Night's Dream* (as Snug the Joiner), *My Fat Friend* (as Tom, with Kenneth Williams), *Noises Off* (as Gary) and *Wife Begins at Forty* (as Roger).

One of the country's busiest television actors over the past forty years, Bernard has made countless appearances on the small screen. In more recent times he has been familiar in two series of *Birds of a Feather* (1997-99, as Richard) and he played Reverend Green in *Hollyoaks*.

His additional television credits include drama and comedy, such as *Doctor Who, Elizabeth R* (1971, as Gifford), *Now and Then* (series, 1983, as Peter Elston), *Eureka, The Gentle Touch, The Bill, Keeping Up Appearances, Thatcher – The Final Days* (as Paddy Ashdown), *Taggart* and *A Touch of Frost*. Recent guest appearances have been in the comedy series *Barbara* and episodes of *EastEnders* and *Doctors*.

Carry On ... ***Quotes***

All I do remember about the Carry On's *is that it was the usual joyous chaos that you encounter whenever you are working with comedians of that calibre. I also worked with Kenneth Williams in a hugely successful stage play,* My Fat Friend, *which ran for 8 months in the West End. Once more joyful chaos!*
Bernard Holley, 2001

Julian Holloway (J. Robert Stanley Holloway)

Julian Holloway made his *Carry On* debut halfway through the series, in *Carry On Follow That Camel*. He subsequently went on to become a familiar member of the team, with eight *Carry On* films to his credit.

Julian, the son of actor Stanley Holloway (1890-1982) and his second wife, actress Violet Marion Lane (1916-96), was born in Watlington, Oxford, on 24 June 1944. He trained at RADA and made his first acting appearances in the early 1960s.

On stage Julian has starred in numerous plays since his debut in

Spitting Image in 1963. In recent years he has followed in his father's footsteps by playing Doolittle in *My Fair Lady* on Broadway and on tour. It was a role that earned him critical acclaim.

Julian made his film debut, aged seventeen, in *Dentist on the Job* and has since made over forty screen appearances, including *A Hard Day's Night* (1964), *The Knack ... and How to Get It* (1965), *The Jokers* (1967), *The Last Shot You Hear* (1969), *Young Winston* (1972), *The Stud* (1978), *Porridge* (1979), *Rough Cut* (1980) and *The Rum Diary* (2011). In addition, he was the co-writer and co-producer of two short films - *The Spy's Wife* (1971) and *The Chairman's Wife* (1981) - and also co-produced *Loophole* in 1981.

Julian Holloway made his *Carry On* debut as the well-spoken, obliging ticket collector, with Angela Douglas, in *Carry On Follow That Camel*. The role would set the tone for his further appearances, as he went on to play amiable light leading characters, often tackling 'Jim Dale' roles but in a minor capacity. Several of his *Carry On* appearances were cameos, playing the chirpy X-ray operator with Frankie Howerd in *Carry On Doctor* and Richard O'Callaghan's friend in *Carry On At Your Convenience*. His finest *Carry On* performance was as Sid James's weary administrator, Major Shorthouse, in *Carry On Up the Khyber*. He also played Jim – the driver who goes all the way – in *Carry On Camping* and had supporting roles in *Carry On Henry* and *Carry On Loving*. After an absence of five years Julian returned for a final *Carry On* appearance, as the serious medical officer in *Carry On England*.

On television Julian Holloway has been seen in a variety of series and mini-series, both in England and America. His first small-screen appearance was in the Leslie Phillips series *Our Man at St. Mark's* in 1963, and he has since appeared in *Elizabeth R* (1971), *Carry On Christmas* (1972), *A Policeman's Lot* (1974), *The New Avengers, Rebecca* (1978), *Nancy Astor* (1982), *The Scarlet and the Black* (1983), *Ellis Island* (1984), *If Tomorrow Comes* (1986), *Doctor Who* (1989), *Rumpole of the Bailey* (1991) *Conjugal Rights* (1993), *Remember WENN* (1996) and *My Uncle Silas* (2001, 2003). His most recent work has mainly been on stage and in voice-overs.

Julian Holloway was married to actress Zena Walker (1934-2003) but the marriage ended in divorce. He subsequently married actress Debbie Wheeler (in 1991) and from this marriage he has a stepson and stepdaughter. Julian is also the father of model and writer Sophie Dahl (1977-).

Julian now divides his time between London and Los Angeles.

Linda Hooks

Former Miss Great Britain (1972) and Miss International (1972), Linda

Hooks appeared in three *Carry On* films: as a Bird of Paradise in *Carry On Dick*, as the hospital Nurse with George Layton in *Carry On Behind* and as the Army Nurse with Julian Holloway in *Carry On England*. She also turned up for two episodes of *Carry On Laughing* on television in 1975, playing the serving wench in 'One in the Eye for Harold' and 'The Baron Outlook', and she was with the gang on stage in 1976 for *Carry On Laughing at the Slimming Factory*.

Linda Hooks was born in Liverpool in 1952. After training as a chiropodist she became a Model and won various national and international awards.

In addition to her appearances in the *Carry On* series, Linda also appeared on television, as a glamour girl and actress, in *The Jimmy Tarbuck Show, The Rough with the Smooth, Space 1999, The Little and Large Show, Sale of the Century, Celebrity Squares* (hostess, 1975-77) and *The Sweeney*. She left the world of show business around 1980.

John Horsley

A familiar face through countless roles on screen and television, John Horsley is credited with playing the anaesthetist in *Carry On Nurse*, although his scene was edited from the final release. It was one of over sixty film appearances.

Born in 1920, John made his acting debut at the Theatre Royal, Bournemouth. During the Second World War he served in Italy and Sicily, before becoming a member of the Army Bureau for Current Affairs - Play Unit, touring England, France and Germany.

John made his film debut in *Blackmailed* in 1950. For the next decade he had a busy screen career, with film appearances (to name a few) including *The Quiet Woman* (1950), *Time Bomb* (1952), *Forbidden Cargo* (1954), *Father Brown* (1954), *Impulse* (1955), *Dunkirk* (1958), *Ben-Hur* (1959), *Sink the Bismarck!* (1959) and *The Comedy Man* (1963).

From the 1950s he was also one of the country's busiest television actors, and from the early 1960s he devoted much of his energy to the small screen. Among his early television appearances were guest roles in *Out of This World, The Avengers, Counterstrike, The Champions, Doomwatch* and *The Professionals*. He was familiar in the 1970s as 'Doc' Morrisey in *The Fall and Rise of Reginald Perrin* (1976-79) and his additional series have included *Leave It to Charlie* (1978-80, as Folliott), *Oh Happy Band!* (1980, as Mr Braithwaite), *Don't Rock the Boat* (1982-83, as Wally), *Hot Meta*l (1986, as Father Teasdale) and Mollie Sugden's series *My Husband and I* (1987-88, as Mr Mundy), and he played Sir Ralph Shawcross in four series of *You Rang, M'Lord?* (1990-93).

In the 1980s John was also kept busy with a host of mini-series and tele-movies, including *Why Didn't They Ask Evans?* (1980), *Edward & Mrs. Simpson* (1980), *The Jewel in the Crown* (1984), *Deceptions* (1985, co-starring Stefanie Powers and Joan Sims, q.v.) and *The Woman He Loved* (1988). He also returned to the big screen after a fifteen-year absence, with roles in *Secrets* (1983), *The Doctor and the Devils* (1985) and *The Fourth Protocol* (1987).

Among John Horsley's most recent television appearances are *Hercule Poirot's Christmas* (1994) and the 1997 adaptation of *Rebecca* (as Frith).

Marion Horton

Marion had an uncredited role in *Carry On Cabby* as a GlamCab driver.

Donald Houston

Welsh leading man Donald Houston made a guest appearance in the *Carry On* series, playing First Officer Jonathan Howett in *Carry On Jack*. He also worked for Gerald Thomas in *Twice Round the Daffodils* (1962), playing John Rhodes.

Donald Houston was born in Tonypandy, Wales, on 6 November 1923. The handsome blond-haired actor shot to stardom in his first film, *The Blue Lagoon* (1949). Ironically, Vincent Ball (q.v.) played his stunt double.

Donald went on to make over thirty film appearances, mixing dramatic roles with comic performances, notably in *Doctor in the House* (1954) and *Doctor in Distress* (1963). Among his numerous other screen credits were *Dance Hall* (1950), *The Red Beret* (1953), *Find the Lady* (1956), *Yangtse Incident* (1957), *The Man Upstairs* (1958), *Room at the Top* (1958), *The Prince and the Pauper* (1962), *A Study in Terror* (1965), *The Viking Queen* (1967) and *Where Eagles Dare* (1968).

In the 1960s and 1970s Donald also made a variety of guest appearances on television, including episodes of *The Champions*, *The Adventurers* and *Jason King*. He also played Harry Love in the 1971 series *Now, Take My Wife* and was David Caulder in *Moonbase 3* (series, 1973).

Among Donald's final film appearances were *Voyage of the Damned* (1976), *Sea Wolves* (1981) and *Clash of the Titans* (1981, as Acrisius), after which he drifted away from the profession.

Donald, who was the elder brother of actor Glyn Houston (1926-), was married to actress Brenda Hogan (1928-). He died in Coimbra, Portugal, on 13 October 1991, aged sixty-seven.

Renée Houston (b. Katherina Houston Gribbon)

Leading character actress Renée Houston appeared on stage, film and television for sixty years. She made her mark on the *Carry On* series as the dragon-like Agatha Spanner in *Carry On At Your Convenience*, having previously been seen as Molly, the café owner, in *Carry On Cabby* and as the middle-aged brothel keeper in *Carry On Spying*.

Born in Johnstone, Renfrewshire, Scotland on 26 July 1902, Renée was the daughter of variety artistes James Gribbon (1874-1939) and Elizabeth Houston (d.1944). Renée made her first stage appearance while still a teenager in 1916. However, it was in partnership with her younger sister Billie (1906-1972) that she became best known. The pair toured Britain and South Africa between the wars, gaining phenomenal success. The partnership eventually ended due to Billie's poor health, and Renée embarked on a successful solo career on stage, later teaming up with her third husband, again in variety. Renée's glittering stage career included Royal Variety Performances, pantomimes and tours of *Sailor Beware* and *Roar Like a Dove*.

Fair-haired, blue-eyed, pretty and petite, Renée made her film debut in *Come Into My Parlour* in 1932, although the Houston sisters' double act had been filmed as early as 1926. She went on to appear in over forty films, first as a leading lady and latterly as a dominant character actress. Among her most notable credits were *A Girl Must Live* (1939), *2,000 Women* (1944), *The Belles of St Trinian's* (1954), *A Town Like Alice* (1956), *The Horse's Mouth* (1958), *Watch It, Sailor!* (1961), *Out of the Fog* (1962), *Repulsion* (1964), *Cul-de-Sac* (1966), *Secrets of a Windmill Girl* (1966), *The Spy with a Cold Nose* (1966) and *Legend of the Werewolf* (1975).

Along with the likes of Irene Handl, Joan Hickson and Judith Furse, Renée was one of the most experienced *Carry On* character players. A formidable real-life personality, she clearly did not suffer fools and clashed with Kenneth Williams on the set of *At Your Convenience*, as recalled in his published diaries. In addition to the *Carry On* films, Renée also worked for Gerald Thomas in *Twice Round the Daffodils* (1962, as Matron) and *Nurse on Wheels* (1963, as Mrs Beacon).

On the small screen Renée appeared in guest roles in *Charivari* (1951), *The Adventures of Robin Hood, Maigret, Dr. Finlay's Casebook* and *Doctor Knock* (1961). From the 1960s she also enjoyed success as a popular panellist on radio's *Petticoat Line*. Indomitably, Renée continued to work into her mid-seventies, making her final stage appearances in a tour of *Little Women* in 1976.

Renée Houston's first marriage (which was never consummated) ended in an amicable divorce and she married secondly actor Patrick Aherne (1901-70), although this marriage also ended in an amicable divorce. She found lasting happiness with actor Donald Stewart (1910-65) from 1948. Renée Houston had four children: two adopted sons from her first marriage and a son and daughter from her marriage to

Aherne. Her autobiography, *Don't Fence Me In*, was published in 1974. She spent her final years living in Weybridge.

Renée Houston died from bronchopneumonia (following a stroke) at St Peter's Hospital, Chertsey, on 9 February 1980, aged seventy-seven.

Carry On ... ***Quotes***

Regarding Renée Houston and A Town Like Alice. *It was the first time she had to make herself unglamorous – dressed in rags, bad skin problems, etc., and she hated it. I remember talking to her as we became friends and trying to convince her that she could have a great future as the Scottish equivalent of the two great Irish actresses Sara Allgood and Marie O'Neill. Don't think I convinced her! I hope you have a wonderful 'still' of her death in the mud, with Marie Lohr and myself – a very moving picture – we all look as dreadful as we should!*
She needed (and had) great support from her husband, Donald. He was often at the studios with us. I liked her – when not worried about her profession she was great fun. I also happened to give Hattie Jacques (and James Robertson Justice) their first professional jobs! During the war when I was saving the Players' Theatre Club.
Jean Anderson, 1998

A Town Like Alice *was many, many years ago and my memory isn't that wonderful! However, I do remember plodding through a dark and dismal pond with Renée Houston and other splendid actors and actresses pretending to be sweating in the heat of the Malaysian jungle. We were laughing or tripping over bottles and cans in the depths of the pond, or standing shivering wrapped in blankets on the bank, being given little sips of brandy to keep us warm! I think quite a few jokes were told.*
Virginia McKenna CBE, 1998

George Howell

Born in 1943, George Howell was just sixteen when he played the role of Billy Haig in *Carry On Teacher*. Having trained at the Corona Academy he made his screen debut in Gerald Thomas's *Please Turn Over* in 1959. He went on to enjoy a busy career on stage and television, with roles in *Crossroads* and *Take the High Road* (1980, as Colin Young) before retiring from the profession in 1996.

Frankie Howerd OBE (b. Francis Alick Howerd)

Like Sid James and Kenneth Williams, so much has been written about Frankie Howerd that it is difficult to know where to begin. A comic legend in his own lifetime, Frankie appeared in guest-starring roles in two *Carry On* films, and through his scene-stealing performances he secured a lasting place in *Carry On* history.

Frankie Howerd was born in York on 6 March 1917. He made his stage debut at the age of thirteen in a church dramatic society production of *Tilly Bloomsbury*, in which he stole the show as Tilly's father. He went on to enter talent contests and perform at concert parties, but he failed to get into RADA and was turned down by talent scout Carroll Levis four times because he stammered and stuttered.

After working as an insurance clerk Frankie served as a gunner in the Royal Artillery during the war, producing and starring in numerous shows for the troops, although he failed to get into Stars in Battledress.

Despite his setbacks, Frankie's heart was always in the theatre and he made his professional stage debut in *For the Fun of It* at the Empire Theatre, Sheffield, in July 1946. He went on to appear in a variety of stage plays before becoming a household name on radio in the mid-1950s.

Throughout his long career Frankie was perhaps most at home on stage, with countless appearances that included *The Orchid Room* (1949), *Dick Whittington* (106 performances at the Palladium, 1952), *Charley's Aunt* (102 performances, 1956), *Hotel Paradiso* (tour, 1957), *A Midsummer Night's Dream* (as Bottom, 1957) and *Alice in Wonderland* (1959, various roles).

In the early 1960s he suffered a nervous breakdown, but he made one of many comebacks when he returned to the profession with a hugely successful run in *A Funny Thing Happened on the Way to the Forum* in 1963. The play also co-starred Kenneth Connor and Charles Hawtrey (both q .v.). During the 1970s television success ensured that Frankie became one of the country's busiest pantomime actors, and he received acclaim for his performances in *Jack and the Beanstalk*, *Cinderella* and *Goldilocks and the Three Bears*. In 1986 Frankie returned to the stage in *A Funny Thing Happened on the Way to the Forum* at the Chichester Festival, and in 1990 he performed his one-man show – *Quite Frankly: Frankie Howerd at His Most Outrageous* - at the Lyric Hammersmith and Garrick Theatre.

Frankie Howerd made his film debut in *The Runaway Bus* in 1954 and went on to appear in *The Ladykillers* (1955), *Jumping for Joy* (1955), *An Alligator Named Daisy* (1955), *A Touch of the Sun* (1956) and *Further Up the Creek* (1958). He later went on to feature in *Watch It, Sailor!* (1961), *The Fast Lady* (1962), *The Cool Mikado* (1962), *The Great St Trinian's Train*

Robbery (1966), *The House in Nightmare Park* (1973) and *Sgt. Pepper's Lonely Hearts Club Band* (1978).

Frankie, who always considered himself a comedian rather than an actor, made his *Carry On* debut as Francis Bigger in *Carry On Doctor*. His guest-starring role, featuring many trademark Howerd "oohs" and "eeers", was outstanding and he was later called upon to play Professor Indigo Tinkle in *Carry On Up the Jungle*. Once again he proved superb in a leading role, playing perfectly against Sid James, Joan Sims and Kenneth Connor.

To the public at large Frankie was best known on television through a succession of popular series, most notably as Lurcio the slave in *Up Pompeii!* (2 series, 1969-70). The phenomenally successful cult series (written by Talbot Rothwell and guest-starring numerous *Carry On* actors) led to starring film roles for Frankie in *Up Pompeii* (1971), *Up the Chastity Belt* (1971) and *Up the Front* (1972). Frankie's additional television series included *The Howerd Crowd* (debut, 1952), *The Frankie Howerd Show* (1969), *Whoops Baghdad* (1973), *The Howerd Confessions* (1976), *Frankie Howerd Strikes Again* (1981) and *All Change* (2 series, 1989-91, as Uncle Bob). In 1991 he resurrected the character of Lurcio for a one-off television special, *Further Up Pompeii*, and in 1992 he filmed four episodes of *Frankie's On ....*

A lifelong bachelor, one of Frankie's closest friends was Cilla Black OBE. The two appeared together frequently in pantomime and on television from the mid-1960s. Equally close to Cilla's husband, the late Bobby Willis, Frankie was also acknowledged as an "honorary grandfather" to the Willis's three sons. A private person, well known as a very serious real-life personality, Frankie was awarded the OBE in 1977 and in the same year released his autobiography, *On the Way I Lost It*. Away from the stage he enjoyed tennis, swimming, reading and music.

In 1992 Frankie was rumoured to be among those veteran actors cast to appear in *Carry On Columbus*. He allegedly accepted the role of King Ferdinand, opposite Joan Sims as Queen Isabella. Sadly, such rumours did not come to fruition – Joan was already busy working on television and, like the majority of her contemporaries, had no desire to appear in the film. Meanwhile, Frankie's health took a downward slide and he was hospitalised in early 1992, having contracted a mysterious virus after returning from a trip to South America. Weeks later he was again admitted to intensive care with severe breathing difficulties.

Not long after his release from hospital Frankie Howerd died at his home, on Easter Sunday, 19 April 1992, after suffering a heart attack. He was seventy-five years old.

A distraught Cilla Black and his frequent co-star through the years,

June Whitfield (q.v.), attended Frankie Howerd's funeral. In the years since Frankie's death numerous biographies have been written on his life and work and he has been honoured with a British Comedy Society plaque.

Geoffrey Hughes

Geoffrey Hughes appeared in a supporting role in *Carry On At Your Convenience* before going on to create two of television's most memorable characters: Eddie Yeats in *Coronation Street* and Onslow in *Keeping Up Appearances*.

Geoffrey Hughes was born in Liverpool on 2 February 1944. He made his first stage appearances at Newcastle University and the Merseyside Unity Theatre before working in repertory in Stoke-on-Trent. Geoffrey's subsequent stage appearances in the past forty years have included several seasons of *Run for Your Wife*, Pistol in *Henry V* (at Barnwell Manor) and an Australian tour of *A Passionate Woman* (1999, with Linda Robson).

Geoff began his film career as the voice of Paul McCartney in *Yellow Submarine* in 1964. He has since made a dozen screen appearances, including *Smashing Time* (1967), *Till Death Us Do Part* (1968), *The Bofors Gun* (1968), *The Man Who Had Power Over Women* (1970), *Adolf Hitler: My Part in His Downfall* (1972), *Confessions of a Driving Instructor* (1976), *Nijinsky* (1980) and *Flick* (2008). In *Carry On At Your Convenience* Geoffrey played Willie, the genial factory worker, opposite Hugh Futcher. It was to be his only appearance in the series, but almost thirty years later he would still recall his three weeks working on the film with happy memories. While admitting that his solo role in the *Carry On* series was just another "one-off job", Geoff remembered the main team, "divided into the Sid James clique and the Kenneth Williams clique", with affection.

Geoff made his first television appearances in the late 1960s with roles in *Curry and Chips* (1969), *Randall and Hopkirk (Deceased), Up Pompeii!, The Saint* and *Z-Cars*. In 1974 he joined the cast of *Coronation Street* as the roguish but lovable dustbin man Eddie Yeats. As Hilda Ogden's lodger, Eddie became a popular member of 'the Street' until his departure in 1983. Following *Coronation Street* Geoff proved his versatility as an actor by accepting roles in *The Bright Side* (1985 series, as Mr Lithgow), *Doctor Who* (1986, as Popplewick) and *Making Out* (1991, as Dilk). In 1990 he went on to create another long-running and popular television character as Hyacinth Bucket's "less than salubrious brother-in-law" in five series of *Keeping Up Appearances* (1990-95). Most recently Geoff played Twiggy in *The Royle Family* (1998-2008) and Vernon Scripps in *Heartbeat* (2000-07). Geoff was the subject of *This Is Your Life* in 2001.

Away from acting Geoff, who successfully overcame prostate cancer in the late 1990s, enjoys country life and lists his hobbies as sailing, golf, cricket, music, tress and beer! He and his wife Susan live in Northamptonshire.

Laraine Humphrys

Laraine Humphrys came to films from modelling and made her *Carry On* debut as Miss Eileen Denby, a beauty contestant, in *Carry On Girls*. In the same year she played a serving wench in *Carry On Christmas* on television before turning up (appropriately) as one of Joan Sims's Birds of Paradise in *Carry On Dick*.

Laraine's additional film appearances were *Say Hello to Yesterday* (1971), the screen version of *Up Pompeii* (1971, as Flavia) and *The Great Riviera Bank Robbery* (1979). She also appeared in *The Benny Hill Show* in the mid-1970s.

In recent years Laraine, now a "busy mum", has returned to the modelling profession and also appears in television commercials.

Michael Hunt

Michael played the 14th Recruit in *Carry On Sergeant*.

Bernard Hunter

Bernard Hunter, who played the wine waiter in *Carry On Regardless*, appeared in several film and television series of the late 1950s and '60s. He made his screen debut in *The Tommy Steele Story* (1957) and went on to appear in minor roles in *The Hellfire Club* (1960), *Raising the Wind* (1961) and *Operation Snatch* (1962). He also joined several other *Carry On* actors on television when he played Captain Pilsworth in *The Army Game* (1958).

Robin Hunter

The son of actor Ian Hunter (1900-75), Robin played Mr Darling, Valerie Leon's over-sexed husband, in *Carry On Matron*. His additional acting career, spanning over thirty years, included films such as *Three Spare Wives* (1961), *Doctor in Clover* (1966, as Sydney), *All the Way Up* (1970) and *Vampire Circus* (1972). On television he played Sir Gilbert in *Richard the Lionheart* (series, 1962) and Lt. Pouter in *HMS Paradise* (1964).

Born in London on 4 September 1929, Robin trained at the Webber Douglas Academy. His later credits included *The Phantom of the Opera* (1989) and television appearances in *Sherlock Holmes: Sign of Four* (1987) and *Poirot*. He married *Carry On* leading lady Amanda Barrie (q.v.) in

1967, and although they separated in 1980 the couple never divorced and remained good friends.

Robin Hunter died in London from emphysema on 8 March 2004.

William Hurndell

William played Raff in *Carry On Follow That Camel*.

Bill Hutchinson

Bill Hutchinson featured in an uncredited role in *Carry On Emmannuelle*. His sporadic acting career has included bit parts in a couple of films, including *Battle Beneath the Earth* (1967), *The Adding Machine* (1969) and *Diamonds Are Forever* (1971), and in television mini-series such as *Ellis Island* (1984) and *Lace* (1984).

Wilfrid Hyde-White

Wilfrid Hyde-White played dapper old gents in British and American films for well over thirty years. Perhaps best known as Colonel Pickering in the 1964 film version of *My Fair Lady*, he played the roughish Colonel in *Carry On Nurse*, with Joan Sims, Susan Beaumont – and a daffodil!

Wilfrid Hyde-White was born in Bourton-on-the-Water, Gloucestershire, on 12 May 1903. He studied acting at RADA and made his stage debut in 1922 as Maitland in *Tons of Money*. Three years later he made his London stage debut in *Beggar on Horseback* and over the next six decades made regular stage appearances. He was especially busy with theatre work in the mid-1970s, when he toured Britain in plays such as *An Ideal Husband, A Perfect Gentleman* and *Lady Windermere's Fan*.

Wilfrid made his film debut in *Night Mail* in 1934. He subsequently went on to appear in more than a hundred films, gradually working his way up to starring character roles. Sometimes billed simply as Hyde White, his numerous screen credits included *Meet Mr. Penny* (1938), *I've Got a Horse* (1938), *The Lambeth Walk* (1940), *While the Sun Shines* (1947), *The Ghosts of Berkeley Square* (1947), *The Winslow Boy* (1958), *Adam and Evelyn* (1949), *Helter Skelter* (1949), *Highly Dangerous* (1950), *The Gilbert and Sullivan Story* (1953), *The Million Pound Note* (1954), *To Dorothy a Son* (1954), *John and Julie* (1955), *The Silken Affair* (1957), *His and Hers* (1961), *On the Fiddle* (1961), *You Must Be Joking!* (1965), *Ten Little Indians* (1966), *The Sandwich Man* (1966), *Fragment of Fear* (1970), *The Cherry Picker* (1972) and *No Longer Alone* (1978).

From the 1950s until the early 1980s he made guest appearances in a diverse range of television programmes, including *The Twilight Zone* (1963), *Mission: Impossible* (1967), *Columbo* (1972), *The Associates* (series,

1979), *Laverne and Shirley* (1980), *Dick Turpin* (1981) and *Father Murphy* (1982). Wilfrid also featured among the all-star cast of Eric Sykes's 'silent' comedy *The Plank* in 1979.

A working actor until his eightieth year, Wilfrid gained a new legion of fans through his role as Doctor Goodfellow in *Buck Rogers in the 25th Century* (1979-81). His final film appearances were *Tarzan, the Ape Man* (1981), *The Toy* (1982) and *Fanny Hill* (1983).

For the last twenty years of his life Wilfrid divided his time between America and Britain and had homes in London and California. He married firstly actress Blanche Glynne and, following her death, Ethel Drew. He had three children, including Alex Hyde-White, now a busy television actor in America.

Wilfrid Hyde-White spent the final years of his life in poor health and confined mainly to bed. He died from congestive heart failure in a Los Angeles hospital on 6 May 1991. The grand old man of cinema was six days short of his eighty-eighth birthday.

Joan Ingram

Joan Ingram had a wordless – but memorable – bit-part role in *Carry On Don't Lose Your Head*. She played the bald-headed Dowager whose wig is blown off by Kenneth Williams during Sir Rodney Ffing's ball.

Joan Ingram featured in minor roles in films for thirty years. Her screen career began among the all-star cast of *2,000 Women* (1944) and she was later seen in *Trouble in Store* (1953), *The Man Inside* (1958), *The Blood Beast Terror* (1967, as the cook), *Ooh … You Are Awful* (1972) and *Steptoe and Son Ride Again* (1973).

Jill Ireland (b. Jill Dorothy Ireland)

A well-remembered leading lady, and wife of Hollywood actor Charles Bronson, Jill Ireland played Jill Thompson in *Carry On Nurse*. It was her only appearance in the series.

Jill Ireland was born in London on 24 April 1936. She began her career on stage as a dancer before signing a contract with Rank Studios in 1955 and making her film debut in *Oh, Rosalinda!!*

The attractive, slender, blonde-haired actress subsequently went on to appear in more than thirty films, including *Simon and Laura* (1955), *Three Men in a Boat* (1956), *Hell Drivers* (1957) and *So Evil, So Young* (1961). Following *Carry On Nurse* Jill was called upon by Gerald Thomas to play Jill in *Raising the Wind* (1961) and also featured in *Twice Round the Daffodils* (1962).

Jill Ireland married actor David McCallum (1933-) in 1957 and they had three sons (one adopted) before their divorce in 1967. Jill married secondly legendary American actor Charles Bronson (1922-2003) and they had one daughter.

Following her second marriage Jill spent the rest of her life living in America. From 1970 she made only sporadic film appearances, usually in partnership with Bronson, including *The Valachi Papers* (1972), *The Mechanic* (1972), *Hard Times* (1975), *Love and Bullets* (1979) and *Death Wish II* (1982). She made her final screen appearances in *Caught* (1987) and *Assassination* (1987).

Jill was diagnosed with breast cancer at the age of forty-eight and subsequently underwent a double mastectomy. In 1989 she suffered the tragic death of her adopted son following a drug overdose. Her tribulations were recalled in a series of best-selling autobiographies: *Life Wish* (1987), *Life Lines* (1989) and *Life Time* (1990).

Jill Ireland died from cancer in Malibu, California, on 18 May 1990, aged fifty-four.

Penny Irving

A glamour girl of the 1970s, Penny Irving played one of Madame Desirée's 'Birds of Paradise' in *Carry On Dick*.

Born in 1955, Penny was probably best known for her work in over twenty episodes of *Are You Being Served?* (1976-79), playing Miss Bakewell (Mr Grace's secretary). She also featured in the 1977 film version of the popular sitcom, playing Miss Nicholson. Her additional television credits included *Dad's Army* and early episodes of *Hi-De-Hi!*, as Mary.

In addition to *Carry On Dick*, Penny appeared in a handful of other films, including *Vampira* (1974), *Percy's Progress* (1974), *The House of Whipcord* (1974), *Aces High* (1976), *The Likely Lads* (1976), *The Bawdy Adventures of Tom Jones* (1976) and *The Comeback* (1978).

Penny Irving left the acting world in the early 1980s. Since then, several writers have attempted to make contact with her, without success.

Douglas Ives

Douglas Ives played the 'fanatic patient' in *Carry On Regardless* and also worked for Gerald Thomas in *Raising the Wind* (1961, as the street musician) and *The Iron Maiden* (1962).

Douglas, who was born in Sheffield, Yorkshire, on 16 August 1898, made bit-part film appearances from the early 1950s, including *Doctor in the House* (1954), *Life in Emergency Ward 10* (1959), *Live It Up* (1963) and *Be My Guest* (1965).

Douglas Ives died in London on 6 March 1969, aged seventy.

Brian Jackson

Brian Jackson is best known in television commercials as 'The Man from Del Monte' who famously said 'yes' for six years during the 1980s. He played the 2nd Recruit in *Carry On Sergeant*.

Born in 1931, Brian has appeared in well over a hundred plays, with highlights including seasons with the Old Vic and the Royal Shakespeare Company.

His sporadic screen appearances, aside from *Carry On Sergeant*, include *Some Like It Cool* (1961) and *Revenge of the Pink Panther* (1978), and he played the American President in *Shadowchaser* (1992).

Apart from his famous role as the man from Del Monte (which was broadcast in 32 countries and in 28 languages!), Brian's television credits date back fifty years. He received rave reviews for his small-screen debut as George Lovelace in the BBC epic *Six Men of Dorset* and has since appeared in a wide selection of programmes, from *The Avengers* to *EastEnders*.

Brian, who is still in the business, has also worked extensively in voice-overs and corporate videos. He lives in West London.

Helli/(Heli) Louise Jacobson

Amply proportioned Danish-born glamour girl, Helli Louise (as she was often billed) played the nude girl in the shower in *Carry On Behind*.

Born in 1949, Helli Louise began her career as a teenager in low-budget sex films such as *Daddy, Darling* (1970) and *Dagmar's Hot Pants* (1972). In Britain she went on to feature in *Soft Beds, Hard Battles* (1973), *Confessions of a Pop Performer* (1975), *The Ups and Downs of a Handyman* (1975) and *Hardcore* (1977).

Her film career came to an end with the decline of comedy sex films, and she made her final screen appearance in *The World Is Full of Married Men* in 1979.

Hattie Jacques

(See MAIN TEAM).

June Jago

Leading Australian stage actress June Jago appeared in supporting roles in the *Carry On* series: as a Nurse in *Carry On Regardless* and a Sister in *Carry On Doctor*.

June Jago was born in Melbourne and was trained for acting by W.P. Carr of the National Theatre Company. She joined the Union Theatre

Repertory Company in 1955, gaining fame as Olive in *Summer of the Seventeenth Doll,* a role she would eventually play all over the world. June moved to England in 1957 to act with the Bristol Old Vic and the Royal Shakespeare Company. While in Britain, June also worked on television, notably as Mary in *All Aboard* (1959) and as a guest actor in an episode of *The Good Life*.

June made her screen debut in *The Captain's Table* in 1959 and went on to appear in *Please Turn Over* (1960, produced by Peter Rogers), *No Kidding* (1961), *The Games* (1970), *Melody* (1971), *Double Deal* (1980), *The Man from Snowy River* (1982) and *The Departure* (1986).

June Jago returned to Australia with the Chichester Festival Company in 1978 and worked with the Melbourne Theatre Company (1979-80). She retired from acting in the mid-1980s and for some years lectured at the Victorian College of the Arts (Melbourne).

A popular addition to the *Carry On* films, June told the author in September 1998 that she had been contacted on a number of occasions in connection with the series, but having been happily retired for some years she no longer gave interviews and therefore regretfully declined the request for information on her life and work, stating that she was now blissfully happy to have disappeared from public view! June Jago lives in Melbourne, Australia.

Carry On ... ***Quotes***

June Jago was always a favourite of mine. I have a soft spot for Aussies. I have quite a few relations living in Australia. My uncle, Sam Webb, was mayor of Bustleton (Perth).
Peter Rogers, 1998

Oscar James

Best known as Tony Carpenter in *EastEnders* and also familiar in *London's Burning*, Oscar James appeared in two episodes of *Carry On Laughing* on television in 1975. He played the Black Knight in 'Under the Round Table' and the Witch Doctor in 'Lamp-Posts of the Empire'. He also had an uncredited role in *Carry On Up the Jungle*, as a Nosha Warrior.

Oscar, who was born in Trinidad on 25 July 1942, travelled the world from his late teens before settling in London. He began his acting career in the late 1960s and has appeared in countless series, including *UFO, Minder, The Gentle Touch* and *The Bottle Boys* (1984, as Joe, with Robin

Askwith, q.v.). A member of the original cast of *EastEnders,* he gained public recognition as Tony Carpenter, a role that kept him busy for two years, until 1987.

More recently Oscar James has appeared in guest roles in *Casualty, Loved by You* and *Doctors,* and he played Dexter Ross in *London's Burning*. His film appearances include *Gumshoe* (1972), *Pressure* (1976), *Black Joy* (1977), *Jaguar Lives!* (1979), *Three Kinds of Heat* (1987) and *Charlie and the Chocolate Factory* (2005).

Oscar, who lives in London, has two daughters.

Sidney James

(See MAIN TEAM).

Paul Jesson

Paul, who played the Messenger in 'One in the Eye for Harold' (an episode of *Carry On Laughing*), is an award-winning actor who has enjoyed a busy career on stage, screen and television.

Born in 1946, among his most recent work has been the stage play *Awake and Sing* in 2007, with Stockard Channing, and a supporting role in the all-star feature film *Coriolanus* in 2010.

Peter Jesson

Peter Jesson was a semi-regular *Carry On* performer during the 1960s, with bit-part roles in *Carry On Cabby* (as the car salesman with Hattie Jacques), *Carry On Cleo* (as Seth, Horsa's companion) and *Carry On Follow That Camel* (as Lawrence – scenes deleted from the final film release). He also featured in *The Big Job* (1965), again for Peter Rogers and Gerald Thomas.

After returning to the *Carry On* team in an episode of *Carry On Laughing* ('One in the Eye for Harold') on television in 1975, Peter appears to have left the acting profession.

Malcolm Johns

Malcolm played the winking Sentry in *Carry On Emmannuelle*. His brief acting career included episodes of *Bless This House* and the 1970 film *Perfect Friday*.

Gloria Johnson

Gloria had an uncredited role as a vestal virgin in *Carry On Cleo*.

Judi Johnson

Judi had an uncredited role in *Carry On Spying* as a funhouse girl and played Gloria's bridesmaid in *Carry On Cleo*.

Sidney Johnson

Sidney Johnson played the 'man in glasses' (an uncredited bit-part role) in *Carry On Behind*. He began his acting career in later life, having previously run his own publicity firm. He made numerous stage appearances and popped up on television in programmes ranging from *Z-Cars* to *Doctor Who*. He died suddenly in 1990, aged eighty-six.

Vivienne Johnson

Vivienne Johnson made her *Carry On* debut in episodes of *Carry On Laughing* on television in 1975, playing Freda Filey in *The Case of the Coughing Parrot*t and Teeny in *And In My Lady's Chamber* and *Who Needs Kitchener?* She later played Freda in *Carry On England*, although most of her scenes hit the cutting room floor.

Vivienne Johnson was born in Sheffield, Yorkshire. She studied art and qualified as an art teacher in Liverpool, after attending a very academic school that was "not favourably inclined to acting as a profession". Vivienne began her acting career in repertory theatre in Chesterfield as acting ASM. She made her stage debut as the Scottish Union representative in *Scotch on the Rocks,* following which she toured the country in various productions.

On television Vivienne is best known as Mr Grace's nurse in three series of *Are You Being Served?* (1978-81). During the 1970s she also appeared in *Whodunnit?, Open All Hours, The Dick Emery Show, Odd Man Out* (1977, as Marilyn), *The Sweeney* and *Potter* (1979). In addition to *Carry On England*, Vivienne also appeared in *Savage Messiah* (1972) and *Yesterday's Hero* (1979).

Since *Are You Being Served?* Vivienne has concentrated on family life, with occasional stage appearances to add to her credits. She is married to a lawyer and has one son (b.1983). In private Vivienne enjoys theatre, film, dance and tennis and has a deep interest in ancient history, which has been a great influence on her extensive foreign travels.

In recent years Vivienne has attempted to relaunch her acting career. She returned to Pinewood Studios for the *Carry On* 50th Anniversary celebrations in April 2008.

Carry On ... ***Quotes***

Apart from being involved with the Carry On *series on television and* Carry On England *I was also involved in three series of* Are You Being Served? *at the end of its ten-year run.*
It's very difficult to remember any specific anecdotes when you're involved in a programme. Many things are amusing at the time but you don't realise anyone will be interested in them in the future.
The casts of Carry On *and* Are You Being Served? *were great fun to work with and very professional, and consequently they were very happy, which I think contributes to their success.*
As you may know, Barbara Windsor and Wendy Richard have gone on to do EastEnders, *probably Britain's top 'soap' and very good. I have been bringing up my family, with a few forays into the theatre. On perhaps a more serious note, however, I'm trying to get back into television. It's not easy because everything changes all the time.*
Vivienne Johnson, 1998

Helga Jones

Helga played a Harem Girl in *Carry On Follow That Camel*.

Peter Jones

An indispensable character actor throughout the 1950s and 1960s, Peter Jones appeared in guest roles in two *Carry On* films: as the deaf Chaplain conducting Joan Sims's and Frankie Howerd's marriage ceremony in *Carry On Doctor*, and as the wise-cracking but tedious Brigadier in *Carry On England*. His roles in the series typified a career spent as incompetent minor officials.

Peter Jones was born in Wem, Shropshire, on 12 June 1920. He began his career as a teenager in the theatre before being accepted into the London School of Dramatic Art, with fellow pupils including Frank Thornton (q.v.).

By the age of eighteen Peter had made his radio debut, and in his early twenties he toured in the stage play *The Doctor's Dilemma* (1942), with Vivien Leigh. He went on to appear in more than thirty plays, from Shakespeare to comedy, including *Morning's at Seven* (1955-56), *Scenes from a Marriage* (1986, with Miriam Karlin) and *Bedroom Farce* (Middle East tour, 1988, with Joan Sims). His favourite engagement, as recalled in 1998, was *Boeing-Boeing*, which toured Australia and New Zealand in the mid-1960s.

Peter Jones made his screen debut in *Fanny by Gaslight* in 1944 and went on to appear in more than fifty films. He was at his busiest on screen during the fifties and sixties, with appearances in *Time Gentlemen, Please!* (1952), *For Better, for Worse* (1954), *John and Julie* (1955), *Private's Progress* (1956), *Blue Murder At St Trinian's* (1957), *Operation Bullshine* (1959), *The Bulldog Breed* (1960), *Nearly a Nasty Accident* (1961), *Press for Time* (1966) and *The Sandwich Man* (1967). His later film appearances included *Confessions of a Pop Performer* (1975), *The Return of the Pink Panther* (1975), *Whoops Apocalypse* (1986), *In Too Deep* (1990) and *Milk* (1999).

On the small screen Peter achieved fame as Mr Fenner in *The Rag Trade* (4 series, 1961-63 & 1977). He also played Gerald Garvey in *Beggar My Neighbour* (1967, with June Whitfield and Pat Coombs, both q.v.) and was seen opposite Sheila Hancock (q.v.) in *Mr Digby, Darling* (series, 1969). He also starred in and co-wrote two series of *Mr Big* (1977), was the voice of The Book in the cult series *The Hitch Hikers Guide to the Galaxy* (1981) and appeared with Rosalind Knight (q.v.) in the 1984 series *I Thought You'd Gone Away*, which he also co-wrote. His numerous guest appearances included episodes of *The Goodies, Love Thy Neighbour, Randall and Hopkirk (Deceased), Rumpole of the Bailey, C.A.T.S. Eyes* and *The Upper Hand.*

Peter continued to appear on television until the end of his life. His later appearances included *Tender Loving Care* (1993, co-starring Dawn French and Joan Sims) and he was especially memorable opposite Eleanor Summerfield (q.v.) in *Midsomer Murders – Faithful Unto Death* (1997, as Bunny Dawlish). He also played Greg Monteith in the 1998 Christmas special of *The Bill* and in 1999 featured in *Holby City* and the television series of *Just a Minute*.

In addition to the above-mentioned writing credits, Peter also wrote the stage thriller *Marion* (which was adapted into the 1953 film *Marilyn*) and wrote and starred in the 1954 film *Always the Bride*.

A familiar voice on radio, Peter performed with Sir Peter Ustinov in *In All Directions* (1952-53 and 1955) and was a regular guest on *Just a Minute* from 1961 until his death. He also wrote the radio and television series *J. Kingston Platt.*

Peter Jones was married for many years to American actress and writer Jeri Sauvinet (who died in 1999) and they had one daughter and two sons, one of whom is producer Bill Dare (William Dare Jones).

Peter Jones died on 10 April 2000, aged seventy-nine, following a short illness.

Carry On ... Quotes

I'm pleased you have enjoyed the Carry On *movies, though I must add straight away that they have never appealed to me very much. But, being a jobbing actor, I have accepted all engagements offered whenever I have been free to do so. I remember the second* Carry On *I did was filmed during the day and I rehearsed Polonious in a Hamlet production during the evenings. Although I didn't like the* Carry On *scripts, I enjoyed being with the other actors and we had lots of fun - many of them old friends who have sadly left us.*
Peter Jones, 1998

Edward Judd

Leading character actor Edward Judd was just a few short years away from screen fame when he appeared as a glorified extra in *Carry On Sergeant*. His role as the 5th Storeman in the first ever *Carry On* was his only appearance in the series.

Edward Judd was born in Shanghai, China, on 4 October 1932. After making his screen debut at the age of sixteen in *Guinea Pig* (1948) he appeared in bit-part roles in films such as *The Large Rope* (1953), *The Good Die Young* (1954), *I Was Monty's Double* (1958) and *Sink the Bismarck!* (1960), until his role as Peter Stenning in *The Day the Earth Caught Fire* (1961) rocketed him to film stardom.

During the 1960s he starred in films such as *Mystery Submarine* (1963), *Island of Terror* (1966) and *Invasion* (1966), but by the end of the decade he had slipped into character roles and his appearances became less frequent.

Among Edward's later screen credits were *Universal Soldier* (1971), *O Lucky Man!* (1973), *Vault of Horror* (1973) and *The House on Garibaldi Street* (1979), and he continued to act sporadically into the 1980s, with appearances in *Boys in Blue* (1983), *The Kitchen Toto* (1987) and *Jack the Ripper* (TV, 1988).

Edward was married to actress Gene Anderson (1931-65) and secondly to actress Norma Ronald (d.1993) and had two daughters. His final acting roles were on the small screen in the early 1990s in *Van der Valk* and *The Alleyn Mysteries*.

Edward Judd died in Mitcham, Surrey, from bronchial pneumonia on 24 February 2009, aged seventy-six.

Charles Julian

Charles had an uncredited role as the Old Man in the Ruby Room with Kenneth Connor in *Carry On Regardless*.

Anna Karen

Well remembered for her role as Olive in the long-running series *On the Buses*, bespectacled character actress Anna Karen made cameo appearances in two *Carry On* films.

Anna Karen was born in South Africa on 19 September 1936. After training at the South African National Theatre she moved to England in 1953 to join LAMDA. After spending four years in Italy with her first husband, Anna returned to England and resumed her career touring in repertory and gaining small parts on television.

Anna made her screen debut in *The Wrong Man* in 1957 and went on to appear in *Poor Cow* (1967), *The Ski Bum* (1971), *On the Buses* (1971), *Mutiny on the Buses* (1972), *Holiday on the Buses* (1974), *What's Up Nurse?* (1977), *Beautiful Thing* (1996) and *Flick* (2008). Anna made her *Carry On* debut as the 'hefty girl' seen fighting with Barbara Windsor at Chaste Place School in *Carry On Camping*. Ironically, Anna and Barbara were already close friends and remain so to this day. Over twenty years after their catfight in *Camping* they were reunited on television in *EastEnders*, in which Anna has made guest appearances (as Aunt Sal) since 1996. Anna returned to the *Carry On* series for a bit-part role as the wife in the audience of Kenneth Williams's lecture in *Carry On Behind*.

In 1969 Anna created the character of Olive in the television sitcom *On the Buses*. It was a role that would immortalise her to the viewing public, and the success of the series, which ran for four years and seven series, led to feature films and several stage productions. Among Anna's other television appearances are *Wild, Wild Women* (series, 1969, as Maude), *Milk-O* (1975, as Rita Wilkins), *The Kenneth Williams Show* (1976), *The Rag Trade* (1977-78, in which she resurrected the character of Olive), *Troubles and Strife* (2 series, 1985-86, as Rosita Pearman) and *Roland Rat – The Series* (1986). Anna has also made guest appearances in *Celebrity Squares, Boyz Unlimited, Birds of a Feather* and *Goodnight Sweetheart*.

Anna Karen's first marriage ended in divorce and she married secondly comedian Terry Duggan. Anna has one daughter, Gloria.

Harold Kasket/(Kaskett)

Stage and screen actor Harold Kasket appeared in an uncredited role in *Carry On Follow That Camel*, playing the gentleman in the hotel. It was his only appearance in the *Carry On* series.

Born in London on 26 July 1926, Harold was the son of dance bandleader Maurice Kasket. He was educated in Boston, Massachusetts, and returned to England to study art in Bournemouth and London. He joined ENSA in 1945 as a stand-up comedian and then spent three years with the Colchester Repertory Company.

Harold's long stage career included time with the Oliviers, Sir John Gielgud and Dame Peggy Ashcroft. He played Uncle Max in the original London stage production of *The Sound of Music* (1961-64, 1,664 performances) and was later seen in *The Mousetrap, The Doctor's Dilemma, Death of a Salesman* (1981) and *The Follies* (1988).

Dark-haired and often moustachioed, Harold made his screen debut in *No Orchids for Miss Blandish* in 1948. He went on to make just over fifty film appearances and was often called upon to play greasy foreigners. Among his film credits were *Hotel Sahara* (1951), *Moulin Rouge* (1952), *Doctor at Sea* (1955), *Bhowani Junction* (1956), *The Lady Is a Square* (1958), *The Voyage of Sinbad* (1958), *Tommy the Toreador* (1959), *The Navy Lark* (1959), *A Weekend with Lulu* (1961) and *The Roman Spring of Mrs. Stone* (1961). After 1961 he largely abandoned film work for the theatre and television, and during the 1960s he was a member of the BBC Radio Drama Company. His later film appearances included *Doctor in Clover* (1966), *Where's Jack?* (1969), *Trail of the Pink Panther* (1982) and *Curse of the Pink Panther* (1983).

A working actor until the late 1980s, Harold's final appearances included the 1985 mini-series *A.D.* and *War and Remembrance* (1989).

Harold Kasket was married to Esther Larendo from 1958 and they had one son and one daughter. In later years, when his health began to fail, Harold withdrew from the acting profession but delighted friends with his culinary skills. Harry Towb (q.v.), in an obituary for Harold, wrote, "He could spot a rotten apple at twenty paces. This applied to the human variety as well."

Harold Kasket died in London on 20 January 2002, aged seventy-five.

Darryl Kavann

Darryl played Punchy in *Carry On Cabby*.

Bernard Kay

Stage, film and television actor Bernard Kay appeared as the 13th Recruit (and injured Recruit) in *Carry On Sergeant*. It marked his film debut, although forty years later he had quite forgotten about his role as a glorified extra in the series!

Born in Bolton, Lancashire, on 23 February 1928, Bernard trained at the Old Vic and spent six years heavily involved in theatre work (including two seasons at Stratford-upon-Avon and thirty-seven plays at the old Nottingham Playhouse). In 1957 he toured in *Titus Andronicus* with Laurence Olivier and Vivien Leigh and has since appeared in countless plays, including *An Inspector Calls* (2000-01), with Rula Lenska.

In addition to *Carry On Sergeant*, Bernard's film credits include *Doctor Zhivago* (1965), *Darling Lili* (1970), Joan Crawford's last film, *Trog* (1970), *Lady Caroline Lamb* (1972), *Sinbad and the Eye of the Tiger* (1977), *A Ghost in Monte Carlo* (TV, 1990), *Pierrepoint* (2005) and *Psychosis* (2010).

On television Bernard has appeared in four series of *Doctor Who*, was the man who killed Ida Barlow (Noel Dyson, q.v.) in *Coronation Street* and was known as the 'J.R.' of *Crossroads* with his role as Harry Maguire. He has made countless other television appearances and his credits read like an A-Z of British television. Most recently he has been seen in guest appearances in *Jonathan Creek, Casualty* and *Doctors*.

Davy Kaye MBE (b. David Kodeish)

A diminutive, dark-haired, wise-cracking entertainer, Davy Kaye made guest appearances in two *Carry On* films: as Josh, the eager undertaker in *Carry On Cowboy*, and as Benny, the bookie, in *Carry On At Your Convenience*.

Davy Kaye was born in London on 25 April 1916. Davy began his career in variety in the 1930s as part of a double act with Ivor Morton. When the act spilt up Davy went on to enjoy a successful solo career and was well known for his one-man-band routine.

In addition to the *Carry On* series, Davy appeared in a handful of other films, including *Everything in Rhythm* (1936), *Fun at St Fanny's* (1956) and *The Wrong Arm of the Law* (1962). He also featured in *Crooks in Cloisters* (1964), co-starring Barbara Windsor and Bernard Cribbins, *Those Magnificent Men in Their Flying Machines* (1965), *The Magnificent Seven Deadly Sins* (1971) and *A Nightingale Sang in Berkeley Square* (1979). He was especially memorable as the Admiral in *Chitty Chitty Bang Bang* (1968) and the mouse in *Alice's Adventures in Wonderland* (1972).

Davy remained active well into old age and in 1992 turned up for a guest appearance as King Boris in an episode of *You Rang, M'Lord?* One of his last professional appearances was at the request of John Major at a Water Rats social event.

A member of the Grand Order of Water Rats, whose additional members have included Bernard Bresslaw, Ted Ray and David Lodge (all q.v.), Davy Kaye was King Rat in 1984 and was awarded the MBE for services to charity in 1995. His only marriage ended in divorce and he had one son.

Davy Kaye died while on holiday in the Bahamas on 3 February 1998. He was eighty-one years old.

Penny Keen

Penny had an uncredited role in *Carry On Don't Lose Your Head*.

Penelope Keith CBE (P. Anne Constance Hatfield)

A leading lady of stage, screen and television, Penelope Keith is best known for her work in a succession of television series, including *The Good Life, To the Manor Born* and *Next of Kin*. Now regarded as one of Britain's finest comediennes, she is credited with the role of a plain-clothes nurse in *Carry On Doctor*. Alas, her scenes with Peter Gilmore (q.v.) were edited from the final film release.

Penelope Keith was born on 2 April 1940 in Sutton, Surrey. She trained at the Webber Douglas Academy and made her first stage appearances in 1959 before three years in repertory and a further two years with the Royal Shakespeare Company. Despite a stage career spanning fifty years, Penelope is perhaps best known for her work in situation comedies.

Tall (5ft 10in) and naturally poised, Penelope made her first major television appearances opposite Phyllis Calvert in the series *Kate* (1970-72, as Wenda Padbury). Penelope's grace and cut-glass elocution have tended to typecast her as haughty, aristocratic characters, and in such roles she has given some of her finest performances.

On television Penelope gained national recognition as Margo Ledbetter in three series of the television classic, *The Good Life* (1975-77, with Richard Briers, Felicity Kendal and the late Paul Eddington). Penelope's small-screen success continued with three series of *To the Manor Born* (1979-81, as Audrey Fforbes-Hamilton, with Peter Bowles), and throughout the 1980s and into the 1990s she was kept busy with a string of hit series, including *Executive Stress* (1986-88, as Caroline Fairchild/ Fielding), *No Job for a Lady* (1990-92, as Jean Price), *Law and Disorder* (1994, as Philippa Troy) and *Next of Kin* (1995-97, as Maggie Prentice). She resurrected the role of Audrey Fforbes-Hamilton in 2007 for a one-off Christmas special of *To the Manor Born.*

Penelope's additional television credits include *The Avengers* (1969), *Morecambe and Wise* (1969), *The Pallisers* (1974, as Mrs Hittaway), *The Norman Conquests* (1977), *The Spider's Web* (1982), *Sweet Sixteen* (series, 1983) and *Moving* (1985, series, as Sarah Gladwyn), and she hosted *What's My Line?* in 1988.

Although mainly seen on stage and television, Penelope has also appeared in a handful of films, including *Every Home Should Have One* (1970), *Take a Girl Like You* (1970), *Think Dirty* (1970), *Rentadick* (1972), *Penny Gold* (1972), *Ghost Story* (1974), *The Hound of the Baskervilles* (1978) and *Priest of Love* (1981).

More recently Penelope starred in the 1998 mini-series *Coming Home* (as Aunt Louise) and *Margery and Gladys*, with June Brown, in 2003. She has also featured in numerous documentaries, such as *Laughter in the House* (1999), *Paul Eddington: A Life Well Lived* (2001) and *Comedy Connections*.

Penelope has been married to Rodney Timson since 1977 and they have one (adopted) son. As well as her busy acting career, Penelope is associated with a number of charitable organisations. She has been President of the Actors' Benevolent Fund since 1990 and Governor of the Queen Elizabeth's Foundation for the Disabled since 1990. She is also Governor of the Guildford School of Acting, a Trustee of the Yvonne Arnaud Theatre and High Sheriff of Surrey. Penelope Keith was awarded the OBE in 1989 and CBE in 2007.

Sam Kelly

A popular television actor, familiar from roles in various long-running series, Sam Kelly appeared in two *Carry On*'s at the beginning of his career. He can be spotted as a Sir Roger's coach driver in *Carry On Dick* and in the following year he featured as the projectionist at Kenneth Williams's lecture in *Carry On Behind*.

Sam Kelly was born in Manchester on 19 December 1943. He trained at LAMDA (1964-67) and made his television debut in *Emergency Ward 10* in 1967.

Sam came to prominence in the late 1970s as Warren in the popular sitcom *Porridge* (1974-77), opposite Ronnie Barker and Richard Beckinsale. Since then he has appeared in a string of comedy series, including *'Allo 'Allo* (2 series, 1984-85, as Hans Geering, with Kenneth Connor), *On the Up* (3 series, 1990-92, as Sam, with Joan Sims and Dennis Waterman) and *Barbara* (1999-2003, with Gwen Taylor). His additional credits include *The Liver Birds, The World of Cilla, Now and Then* (1983-84, as Norman Elston), *We'll Think of Something* (series, 1986, as Les Brooks), *Haggard* (1991-92, as Grunge) and *Micawber* (2001, as Mr Cudipp).

Sam has also featured in dramatic roles, notably as Mr Mould in *Martin Chuzzlewit* (1994) and as Giles in *Oliver Twist* (1999). His additional dramatic appearances include *Boys from the Blackstuff* (1982), *Inspector Morse, A Touch of Frost, The Bill, Where There's Smoke* (2001) and *Midsomer Murders: Down Among the Dead Men* (2006).

In addition to the *Carry On* series, Sam's film credits include *A Day at the Beach* (1970), *Tiffany Jones* (1973), *Porridge* (1979), *Arthur's Hallowed Ground* (1986), *Blue Ice* (1992), *Topsy Turvy* (1999), *Honest* (2000), *All or Nothing* (2002) and *Nanny McPhee* and *the Big Bang* (2010).

Sam Kelly, who is single, lives in London.

Sally Kemp

Sally played the girl with the cow, opposite Charles Hawtrey, in *Carry On Camping*. She is not to be confused with the American actress (b.1933) with the same name.

Faith Kent

Character actress Faith Kent appeared in a minor role in *Carry On Again Doctor*, playing the matron at Berkeley, opposite Kenneth Williams.

Faith Kent was born in New York, America, where her father was a journalist for the Republican newspaper. Her acting career spans four decades and she made the first of several film appearances as Nanny in *The Pumpkin Eater* (1964). She went on to appear in *Our Mother's House* (1967), *The Darwin Adventure* (1972), *Home Before Midnight* (1979), *Half Moon Street* (1986) and *Beyond Bedlam* (1993).

On stage Faith has appeared in more than a dozen plays, ranging from *The Glass Menagerie* to *Aladdin*. She has also toured in her one-woman show, *Just Like a Woman*, which she also devised.

On the small screen Faith has been seen in a wide variety of roles. She is perhaps best known as Olive in the ill-fated series *Eldorado* (1992), but she has also appeared in *Cathy Come Home* (1965, with Carol White, q.v.), *Weavers Green* (series, 1966), *Dr. Finlay's Casebook, Emmerdale, Longitude* (2000, as the Lady Curator), *Finding Tracy Beaker* (series, 2004), *Casualty* and *Little Britain* (2004).

Faith Kent was married to the late classical actor Anthony Nicholls (1902-77) and they had two daughters, former actress Kate Nicholls and actress Phoebe Nicholls. Faith, who is now a grandmother, lives in Herefordshire.

Carry On ... **Quotes**

All I remember about my Carry On *experience was talking about books for one brief moment with Kenneth Williams. He was a very serious minded man off the set!*

Faith Kent, 2004

Bill Kenwright CBE

Now a hugely successful theatre impresario and well known as the owner of Everton Football Club, Bill Kenwright played the reporter lurking in the hospital foyer in *Carry On Matron*.

Without any formal training as an actor, Bill gained his first television role in Granada's *Villains*. He later signed with *Coronation Street* for a year (1968-69), playing Gordon Clegg, Betty Turpin's illegitimate son. It is a role to which he has returned occasionally over the years (most recently in 1995 for Betty's marriage to Billy Williams).

Following *Coronation Street*, finding himself typecast and unable to secure television work, Bill began to produce and star in his own shows on stage. He eventually acquired the rights to *Joseph and the Amazing Technicolor Dreamcoat* (which he later sold to Lord Webber for over £1 million) and went on to produce a string of hit stage shows, including *Blood Brothers, Shirley Valentine* and *An Ideal Husband*. Now the Director of BKL (Bill Kenwright Ltd), he remains one of the most powerful figures in British theatre.

More recently Bill has ventured into producing films, including *Us Begins With You* (1998), *Zoe* (2000) and *Chéri* (2009).

Bill, who was born in Liverpool on 4 September 1945, was awarded the CBE in the New Year's Honour's List 2001.

David Kernan

In his solo appearance in the *Carry On* series actor and singer David Kernan played Nicholas in *Carry On Abroad*.

Born in London on 23 June 1938, David is best known for his work in stage musicals. He began his stage career as a child walk-on in *Quality Street* in 1945, and after working as a trainee catering manager he returned to the stage in 1958 in *Where's Charley?* He subsequently went on to appear in *On the Brighter Side* (revue, 1961), *Our Man Crichton* (1970), created the role of Count Malcolm in *A Little Night Music* (1976, with Jean Simmons OBE) and received an Olivier Award nomination for *The Ratepayers' Iolanthe*.

His success has spread across both sides of the Atlantic and he received a Tony Award nomination for Side By Side By Sondheim (1976-77), the musical revue that he created and starred in, in both London and New York.

In addition to *Carry On Abroad*, David's film credits include *Mix Me a Person* (1962), *Jailbreak* (1962), *Farewell Performance* (1962), *Zulu* (1964), *For Men Only* (1968), *Otley* (1968), *Up the Chastity Belt* (1971) and *The Day of the Jackal* (1973).

In 1983 David began producing and directing stage shows, and his company, Showpeople, presented a series of one-man performances at the Playhouse Theatre, London, which included Dame Judi Dench, Sir Derek Jacobi and Alan Bates. David's subsequent company – Showpeople '90 - has specialised in small-scale musical shows and fund-raising galas.

Since 1959 David has made over 300 television appearances, notably in *Song by Song, That Was The Week That Was* and *Upstairs, Downstairs.* Most recently he starred with Martin Shaw in an episode of *The Chief* and he also featured among the all-star cast of *Hey, Mr. Producer!* (1998).

When not performing or directing, David teaches song interpretation and writes for television. He has also run musical theatre workshops at London's Theatre Museum. In 2003 he provided commentary for the DVD release of *Carry On Abroad.*

Fraser Kerr

Stage actor Fraser Kerr appeared in just one *Carry On* film, as the hospital Houseman examining the nurses in *Carry On Regardless.* It was a rare screen appearance for the amiable Scottish-born actor.

Fraser Kerr was born in Glasgow on 25 February 1931. Following National Service in the 17/21st Lancers (Death or Glory Boys) he began his theatrical career in repertory in Glasgow, Edinburgh, Leicester and Nottingham. Much of his subsequent career was spent on the stage, and he joined the Old Vic for a time before touring America and Canada, including seasons on Broadway in *Romeo and Juliet, Troilus and Cressida, Richard II* and *Macbeth.* In the West End he appeared with Esma Cannon (q.v.) and later Kathleen Harrison in *Watch It, Sailor!* (as Carnoustie Bligh), which ran for over two years. His later stage credits included *The Hard Man* and *Brigadoon* (1989, as Andrew MacKeith).

On the small screen Fraser made appearances in *Doctor in the House, The Rag Trade, Mind Your Language, Metal Mickey, Yes Minster* and *Howards' Way.* A gymnast of Olympic standard, one of his most memorable television roles was as a keep-fit freak murderer in *Bloomfield.*

Fraser's voice was well known to radio listeners, having made thousands of broadcasts. In addition to several episodes of *Hancock's Half Hour* on radio, he was notable as Gillie in *Mary Rose* and as Hubert in *Night Must Fall*, with Dame Sybil Thorndike and Sir Lewis Casson. As well as *Carry On Regardless,* Fraser appeared in a handful of other films, including *What a Whopper* (1961), *Thomasina, Way of the Eagle* and *Theatre of Dea*th (1966), and he provided voices for the cartoon version of *Lord of the Rings* (1978).

Away from acting, Fraser Kerr enjoyed gardening, weight training and music. In his final years he lived in West London.

Fraser Kerr died from cancer at Middlesex Hospital on 19 March 2000, just three months after contributing to this book. He was sixty-nine years old.

Carry On ... **Quotes**

When I was in Carry On Regardless *I was also in* Watch It, Sailor!, *starring Kathleen Harrison at the Aldwych, then the Apollo with Esma Cannon. Betty White, the casting director for the* Carry On *films, was always ringing to book me for some film, but as I was in the West End it wasn't easy. She originally wanted me to play a gambler in a sequence but it was changed to a young doctor, with Sid as the fraudulent one. When we came to film the young nurses being examined by me, word must have got round Pinewood, for suddenly about 100 stagehands from every studio turned up to stand and watch us. The girls were very embarrassed, but we got on with it. Recently a still from that scene of me examining a nurse turned up in a Scottish newspaper, castigating the NHS for overwork done by junior doctors - 37 years after the photograph was taken, and in a* Carry On *film!*
I loved Esma Cannon, now no longer with us, and Sid James, also gone alas. During the shooting of Regardless *he had just bought some land nearby and was going to build a house there. He was very excited.*
I did a lot of radio work with Sid: Hancock's Half Hour *and* It's a Deal, *a series with Dennis Price. This was supposed to take the place of* Hancock *but it wasn't a great success ...*
Betty White rang me and said there was nothing for me in Carry On Cabby, *but she phoned to ask if I would do a very important reaction shot, as Peter Rogers had asked for me and they did pay the equivalent of my week's West End pay for a day's work in the studio!*
Esma Cannon was one of my closest friends. We worked together for two years on Watch It, Sailor! *and remained close till she died in France. She was Australian, you know. She did a dancing act called 'Master Bobby Helpmann and Miss Esma Cannon, the pocket ballerina'. During a long run of a play everyone goes through a period of stage fright and they 'dry up'. This usually happens after six months, but it happened to me after 18 months in* Watch It, Sailor!, *and I dried up on two separate nights in the middle of a sentence. Someone finished my line but I became a bag of nerves that week and was only able to go on with a tranquilizer. On the day of filming* Regardless, *a Monday, it was declared a 'late night' finishing at 6 p.m. I was in such a state to get to the theatre by 7 p.m. that I was halfway through the play before*

realising I had got over my temporary stage fright!!!
Fraser Kerr, 1999

Gertan Klauber

Czechoslovakian-born character actor Gertan Klauber became a familiar member of the *Carry On* team, with cameo roles in seven of the films, from *Carry On Spying* to *Carry On Emmannuelle*.

A long-time resident in Britain, Gertan, was born on 5 March 1932. After training at the Birmingham Theatre School he was on stage from 1957, working with the Royal Shakespeare Company in the early 1960s and continuing in the theatre until 1991. After making his screen debut in *Don't Panic Chaps!* in 1959 he went on to appear in more than thirty films, usually in comic roles though he was equally adept as jovial types or dubious, sweaty foreigners. He made his *Carry On* debut as the foreign Code Clerk in *Carry On Spying* and in the same year was seen as the auctioneer, Marcus, in *Carry On Cleo*. *Carry On Follow That Camel* saw Gertan as the Algerian Spiv, while in *Carry On Doctor* he turned up as the wash orderly scrubbing Frankie Howerd. Two years later he was cast as Bidet in *Carry On Henry*. His final roles in the series again saw Gertan as foreign characters: as the seedy postcard seller outraging Kenneth Williams in *Carry On Abroad* and as the German Soldier in Peter Butterworth's flashback scene in *Carry On Emmannuelle*. In addition to his cameo appearances in the *Carry On* series, Gertan also worked for Rogers and Thomas in their 1965 film comedy *The Big Job*.

Gertan's additional film appearances included *The Kitchen* (1961), *Dateline Diamonds* (1965), *Cry of the Banshee* (1970), *Wuthering Heights* (1970), *Escape from Colditz* (1972), *Soft Beds, Hard Battles* (1973), *Percy's Progress* (1974), *Octopussy* (1983), *The Living Daylights* (1987) and *Backbeat* (1994).

On television Gertan's frequent appearances included *Thomas and Sarah* (1980), *Charles & Diana: A Royal Love Story* (1982), *The Pirates of Penzance* (1983) and *The First Olympics: Athens 1896* (1984). He was also memorable as King George III in *Blackadder the Third* (1987) and made countless guest appearances in series ranging from *Doctor Who* to *The Goodies*. He remained a working actor on television well into the 1990s and beyond, and his final credits included *Young Indiana Jones and the Attack of the Hawkmen* (1995), *The Famous Five* (1997), *Fugee Girl* (2001) and *Red Cap* (2003).

Gertan Klauber married actress Gwendolyn Watts (q.v.) in 1959 and they had two children, David and Holly. Having outlived both his wife and son, Gertan died on 1 August 2008, aged seventy-six.

Elizabeth Knight

Light leading lady Elizabeth Knight appeared in two *Carry On* films: as Jane, Terry Scott's schoolgirl love interest in *Carry On Camping*, and as Nurse Willing in *Carry On Again Doctor.*

Elizabeth began her career on television at the end of the 1960s in the series *Sorry I'm Single* (as Karen, with Derek Nimmo and Gwendolyn Watts, q.v.). She went on to appear in films such as *Oliver!* (1968), *Villain* (1971), *McCabe & Mrs. Miller* (1971) and the screen version of *Porridge* (1979). Elizabeth also played Clover Mason on television in *It's Awfully Bad for Your Eyes, Darling* (1971) and was the first lady guest in the 1979 version of *Pride and Prejudice*.

Elizabeth Knight retired from acting in 1990.

Rosalind Knight

One of the country's busiest performers, Rosalind Knight made two appearances in the *Carry On* series: as the eagle-eyed trainee Nurse Nightingale in *Carry On Nurse* and as Miss Felicity Wheeler, the dragon-like school governor whose heart is warmed by Kenneth Connor, in *Carry On Teacher*.

The daughter of leading actor Esmond Knight (1906-87) and his first wife Frances Clare (1904-94) and the stepdaughter of actress Nora Swinburne (1902-2000), Rosalind was born in London on 3 December 1933. During the Second World War she was evacuated to Hampshire, where she lived with the village baker and attended dance school. Her father, on active duty, was temporarily blinded during the war and at the same time Rosalind was sent to Cheltenham Ladies' College while her parents tried to find a permanent home in London.

Following in her father's footsteps, Rosalind made the first of many stage appearances with the Royal Shakespeare Company before appearing in many productions at the Royal Exchange Theatre. She has since appeared in well over forty stage plays, including *The Merchant of Venice* (as Nerissa, Old Vic), *She Stoops to Conqueror* (as Mrs Hardcastle), *Love on the Dole* (as Mrs Jike) and *The Cherry Orchard* (as Charlotta, Crucible, Sheffield). Among Rosalind's more recent stage credits are *The Importance of Being Earnest* (1995, as Miss Prism), *Lady Windermere's Fan* (1997, as the Duchess of Berwick) and *Calender Girls* (2009-10, Noel Coward Theatre, London).

Rosalind made her film debut in *Fortune Is a Woman* in 1957. The striking, dark haired actress has since stood out in more than twenty films, including *Blue Murder at St Trinian's* (1957), *The Horse's Mouth* (1958), *Doctor in Love* (1960), *Tom Jones* (1963), *Start the Revolution Without*

Me (1967), *Mister Quilp* (1975), *The Lady Vanishes* (1979), *The Wildcats of St Trinian's* (1980), *Prick Up Your Ears* (1987), *Till We Meet Again* (1989), *Solitaire for Two* (1994), *My West* (1998), *About a Boy* (2002), *Cheeky* (2003) and *The Shell Seekers* (TV, 2006).

On television over the past fifty years Rosalind Knight has been equally busy. Her countless credits began with appearances in *Nicholas Nickleby* (as Fanny Squeers) and *Martin Chuzzlewit* (as Charity Pecksniff), and in the past twenty years alone she has appeared in well over fifty programmes. Among her later credits are *The Pallisers* (1974, as Aspasia Fitzgibbon), *Coronation Street* (as a probation officer), *Tropic* (1981), *Nancy Astor* (1982, as Margot Asquith), *I Thought You'd Gone Away* (series, 1984, as Ruby Pugh, with Peter Jones, q.v.), *Mapp and Lucia* (1985), *Up the Elephant and Round the Castle* (guest appearances, as Jim Davidson's mother), *Only Fools and Horses* (as Mrs Cresswell), *Very Big Very Soon* (series, 1991, as Miss Burchall), *May to December* and *The Upper Hand*.

Additional television appearances have been *A Royal Scandal* (1996), *My Good Friend* (1996, as Nora), *Ivanhoe* (1997, as Edith), *Berkeley Square* (1997, as Great Aunt Effie) and *Tess of the D'Urbervilles* (1998, as Mrs D'Urberville). She also played Beryl in *Gimme, Gimme, Gimme* (3 series, 1998-2000) and has made guest appearances in *Dalziel and Pascoe* (1999), *Jack and the Beanstalk* (2001, as the cook), *Midsomer Murders: Birds of Prey* (2003), *Marple: The Moving Finger* (2006, as Partridge) and most recently *Holby City* and *Doctors*.

Rosalind Knight was married to the late stage and television director Michael Elliott, who started the Royal Exchange Theatre (Manchester) and also managed the London Old Vic. Sadly, Rosalind was widowed when her husband died from a heart attack at the age of fifty-two after undergoing a third kidney transplant. The couple had two daughters, actress Susannah Elliott-Knight and Marianne Elliott, who is now Associate Director of the National Theatre (London). Apart from 'living', Rosalind lists her hobbies as gardening, visiting art exhibitions, cinema and travel. She lives in London.

Carry On ... ***Quotes***

I don't have many recollections about the Carry On's – *except that they were made very, very fast and for little money. On the first day of* Carry On Teacher, *they had finished the scheduled work by 4 p.m. in the afternoon, and as they hurriedly built the science laboratory set, Kenneth Connor and I had to play our love scene, and we hadn't even met before that day. It was very*

difficult and we had to concentrate very hard on the situation and learn the words in ten minutes.
Rosalind Knight, 1997

Chris Konyils

Chris played a Native in *Carry On Up the Jungle*.

Maya Koumani

In addition to playing an Amazon Guard in *Carry On Spying* (her last screen appearance to date), Maya Koumani appeared in minor roles in over a dozen films, including *Fire Maidens from Outer Space* (1956), *Undercover Girl* (1957) and *The Son of Robin Hood* (1959).

Burt Kwouk OBE

Best known as Cato, the crazy man servant in the *Pink Panther* films, Burt Kwouk turned up for a cameo role as Wang in *Carry On Columbus*. It was his only *Carry On* appearance.

Burt Kwouk was born in Manchester on 18 July 1930. At the age of ten months he returned with his family to Shanghai, where he lived until 1947. Burt then travelled to America, where he attended Riverdale School (New York) and gained a Bachelor of Arts Degree at Bowdoin College (Maine). At the age of twenty-three he returned to Britain and began working as a professional actor, making his first professional break in *The Charlie Drake Show*.

Since 1957 Burt has occupied a unique position as Britain's busiest 'Oriental' actor, with over forty film appearances to his credit. By the time Burt began working on the *Pink Panther* films (with comic legend Peter Sellers) he had already made more than twenty film appearances, including *Windom's Way* (1957), *Upstairs and Downstairs* (1959), *Expresso Bongo* (1959), *Satan Never Sleeps* (1962), *Goldfinger* (1964), *The Sandwich Man* (1966) and *The Vengeance of Fu Manchu* (1966).

Between 1974 and 1993 Burt appeared in six *Pink Panther* films and is now immortalised to audiences as Cato. Among his most recent film credits are *Leon the Pig Farmer* (1992), *Bullet to Beijing* (1995), *Kiss of the Dragon* (2001) and *Wake of Death* (2004).

On television Burt's best-known role was as Captain Yamauchi in three series of *Tenko* (1981-84). In a fifty-year career on the small screen he has also made guest appearances in a wide variety of programmes, ranging from *Hart to Hart* to *Super Gran*. Still busy in his eighties, Burt has worked on three series of *The Harry Hill Show* and appeared in the 1999 stage play *Plenty,* with Cate Blanchett. He joined the cast of *Last of the Summer Wine* in 2003 as Entwistle and stayed with the series until it ended in 2010.

In 1995 Burt returned to Pinewood Studios for the unveiling of the British Comedy Society plaque in memory of Gerald Thomas and three years later was a guest at the *Carry On* 40th Anniversary celebrations. He was awarded the OBE in 2011.

Rebecca Lacey

Rebecca Lacey was one of the most versatile actors to join the series when it was unsuccessfully revived in 1992. She played Chiquita in *Carry On Columbus*, a supporting role that left fans wanting more.

Rebecca Lacey was born in Watford on 20 April 1969, the daughter of Ronald Lacey (the late character actor who was well known for a variety of film roles, including appearances in *Raiders of the Lost Ark* and *Red Sonja*) and actress Mela White.

Rebecca made her first television appearances as a child, achieving stardom in *Black Beauty*. In her late teens the petite actress built up her range with guest appearances in programmes such as *Fresh Fields* and *Home to Roost* before becoming a familiar face to viewers as the dizzy secretary Hilary in three series of *May to December* (1989-93). Her superb comic timing made the character of Hilary an unforgettable part of the series and she was a natural choice for a role in *Carry On Columbus*.

After guest appearances in *The Darling Buds of May* (appropriately as '*Carry On*' Marion) and *The Bill* Rebecca took on the role of Doctor Georgina Woodman in *Casualty* (1997-99). In an effort to avoid typecasting, Rebecca left the popular series to play Claire Armitage in two series of *Badger* (1999-2000). More recently she has appeared in guest roles in series such as *Heartbeat, Monarch of the Glen* and *The Bill* (2007).

Janetta Lake

Janetta played the girl with the dog in *Carry On Constable*.

Ann Lancaster (b. Lilian May Lancaster, aka: Lilian May Hopper)

Versatile actress Ann Lancaster played Miss Armitage in *Carry On Again Doctor*. It was a role notable as her only appearance in the series and one of her final screen credits.

Ann Lancaster was born in Middlesex on 4 May 1920. She trained at RADA and worked under Sir Robert Watson Watt during the war. She began her stage career in repertory and made regular appearances in the theatre over a twenty-year period, including *Table for Two* (1949, as Nelly), *Between Ourselves* (1955), *Watch It, Sailor!* (1959-60, 604 performances, with Kathleen Harrison and Marjorie Rhodes) and *Fallen Angels* (1967, as Saunders, with Joan Greenwood).

On television Ann became well known in the 1950s and '60s as a 'foil' for top comedians such as Tony Hancock, Dick Emery and Benny Hill. Her small-screen credits included *Z-Cars, Meet the Wife, The Chars* (1963, as Amanda), *Tea at the Ritz* (1963), *Hughie* (1967), *Dear Sir* and *The World of Beachcomber* (1969).

Ann made her film debut in *Judgement Deferred* in 1951 and over the next two decades made over a dozen film appearances, including *I've Gotta Horse* (1965), *Till Death Us Do Part* (1968, as Alf's sister-in-law), *Hot Millions* (1968), *A Nice Girl Like Me* (1969) and *The Railway Children* (1970). In *Carry On Again Doctor*, opposite Charles Hawtrey, Jim Dale and Hattie Jacques, Ann had a memorable cameo role as the patient whose toilette is interrupted by the antics of a semi-clad Jim Dale!

In private Ann enjoyed collecting antiques (and had a large collection of 16th and 18th century bottles), riding and tennis. In later life she lived in Colville Mews, Kensington.

Ann Lancaster underwent surgery for lung cancer in July 1970 and died from brain cancer at St. Mary's Hospital, Paddington, on 31 October 1970. She was fifty years old.

Chris/(Christopher) Langham

An award-winning actor, Chris Langham was among the many alternative comedians recruited for *Carry On Columbus*, in which he played Hubba.

Born in London on 14 April 1949, Chris is best known for his work on television, which since the late 1970s has included *The Gaffer* (1981), *The Comic Strip Presents…*, *Happy Families* (1985), *Alas Smith and Jones*, *Bottom* and *Murder Most Horrid*. Chris won an Emmy Award for writing on *The Muppet Show* and gained a cult following through his work in *Kiss Me Kate* (1998, as Douglas Fielding) and *People Like Us* (1999-2001, as Roy Mallard). More recently he won a BAFTA Award for his role as MP Hugh Abbot in *The Thick of It* (2006).

His screen appearances have included small roles in *The Return of the Pink Panther* (1975), *Life of Brian* (1979), *The Big Tease* (1999), *Room to Rent* (2001) and *The Emperor's New Clothes* (2001).

Twice married with three children, Chris's career was halted when he was sentenced to ten months in prison in 2007.

Diane Langton

A beaming leading lady on stage and television, Diane Langton made her *Carry On* debut in three episodes of *Carry On Laughing* on television in 1975 and followed in the footsteps of Barbara Windsor when she played the busty Private Alice Easy in *Carry On England*.

Born in Somerset on 31 May 1947, Diane trained at the Corona Academy and began her career as a dancer. Her early work was in ballet, touring Europe. Diane's theatre credits include straight plays and countless musicals, such as *Hair, Jesus Christ Superstar, A Little Night Music* and *Steppin' Out*. Recently she has performed in her own one-woman show and received critical acclaim for her role as Mama Morton in *Chicago*.

Although best known on stage for her roles as a singer and actress, Diane has also made several film appearances since her screen debut in *Don't Just Lie There, Say Something!* in 1973, including *Percy's Progress* (1974), *Eskimo Nell* (1975), *Confessions of a Pop Performer* (1975), *Trial by Combat* (1976) and *The Cook, The Thief, His Wife and Her Lover* (1989).

A member of the pop group The Rock Bottom Group in the 1970s, Diane played Kathy in the 1977 television series of *The Rag Trade* and more recently has been seen as Ruby Rowan (Nick Berry's mother) in two series of *Heartbeat* (1995), as Cindy's mother in *EastEnders* (1998-99) and as Nana McQueen in *Hollyoaks* (2007-09). She has also made numerous guest appearances in programmes ranging from episodes of *Only Fools and Horses* (1983 & '86, as June) and *Boon* to *Give Us a Clue* and *The Bill*.

Lauri Lupino Lane

A variety entertainer from a distinguished theatrical family, Lauri Lupino Lane played the Husband in *Carry On Loving*. It was one of his rare film appearances and his only role in the *Carry On* series.

Born in London on 26 July 1921, Lauri was the only child of legendary actor Lupino Lane (1892-1959). Lauri made his first stage appearances at the age of eight with his cousin Ida Lupino (1916-95), the future Hollywood star.

On stage Lauri was best known for his slapstick act in partnership with George Truzzi (d.1995). He also made very occasional film appearances, including *A King in New York* (1957), *The Great Waltz* (1972) and *Confessions from a Holiday Camp* (1977).

Lauri Lupino Lane died on 4 June 1986, aged sixty-four.

Ian Lavender (b. Arthur Ian Lavender)

Through his role as 'silly boy' Private Pike in ten series of *Dad's Army* Ian Lavender secured his place in television history. Midway through appearing in *Dad's Army* he played Joe Baxter in *Carry On Behind*.

Ian Lavender was born in Birmingham on 16 February 1946, and after leaving school he joined the Bristol Old Vic Drama School. He had only been acting for two months when he joined the cast of *Dad's Army* in 1968, playing seventeen-year-old Private Frank Pike. The overwhelming success of the series made Ian a household name and he also appeared in the 1971 feature film, numerous stage shows and the radio series.

In the 1970s, in addition to *Carry On Behind*, Ian appeared in a handful of other films, including *Three for All* (1974), *Not Now, Comrade* (1976), *Adventures of a Taxi Driver* (1976) and *Adventures of a Private Eye* (1977).

Since *Dad's Army* ended in 1977 the majority of Ian's time has been spent working in pantomime, as both an actor and a director. His additional small-screen credits include *Mr. Big* (series, 1977, as Ginger), *Come Back Mrs. Noah* (series, 1978, as Clive Cunliffe, with Mollie Sugden), *The Glums* (series, 1979, as Ron), *The Hello Goodbye Man* (series, 1984, as Denis) and *Cluedo* (series, 1990, as Professor Plum). Ian has also made numerous television guest appearances in programmes ranging from *Yes Minster* to *Give Us a Clue*.

In recent years Ian has continued to work on television, turning up for roles in *Casualty* (1998), *Goodnight Sweetheart* (1998, as Michael Sparrow) and *Peak Practice*. In 2001 Ian was reunited with Wendy Richard MBE (q.v.), who appeared in several episodes of *Dad's Army,* when he played Derek in *EastEnders* for four years.

Twice married, Ian has two sons, Sam and Daniel (from his first marriage to actress Suzanne Kerchiss, which ended in divorce in 1976). He successfully recovered from cancer of the bladder in 1993 and is a popular guest at *Dad's Army* conventions.

Mary Law

In addition to playing the shop assistant in *Carry On Constable*, Mary Law appeared on television as Janet Campbell in *The Lost Planet* (1954) and as Peggy Simpson in *Deadline Midnight* (1960).

Marjie Lawrence

Perhaps best known as the mother of television presenter Sarah Greene, Marjie Lawrence played the serving maid (opposite Terry Scott) in *Carry On Henry* and also worked for Rogers and Thomas in the film version of *Bless This House*, playing a barmaid.

Marjie Lawrence was born in Birmingham on 21 January 1932. She trained at the Birmingham School of Dramatic Art and began her acting career on stage after being chosen by the formidable Joan Littlewood to play fortnightly rep. at the Theatre Royal, Stratford, in the early 1950s. Her contemporaries at the Joan Littlewood Theatre Workshop would later include actors such as Brian Murphy, Yootha Joyce, Richard Harris, Victor Spinetti and *Carry On* actors Barbara Windsor, Peggy Ann Clifford and Valerie Walsh (all q.v.). Marjie's subsequent stage work included an appearance at the Paris International Festival, leading roles in seven West End plays and two seasons with the Royal Shakespeare Company. She worked with Spike Milligan in 1963 and 1964 in the stage productions of *The Bed Sitting Room* and *Son of Oblomov,* played Natasha in *Three Sisters* at the Royal Court in 1967, with Glenda Jackson and Marianne Faithfull, and starred in the West End in 1979, with Richard Briers and Paul Eddington, in *Middle Age Spread.*

Following her screen debut in *The Counterfeit Plan* in 1957 Marjie went on to appear in over thirty films, including *Sparrows Can't Sing* (1962), *The Early Bird* (1965), *Inspector Clouseau* (1968), *Hands of the Ripper* (1971), *Remembrance* (1982) and *Large* (2001).

Marjie's television appearances began in the mid 1950s and she went on to have a leading role in the Pebble Mill play, *All Who Sail in Her* (with Bob Hoskins), in 1973. Among her numerous other small screen credits were *Moment of Decision, Steptoe and Son, Nearest and Dearest, Coronation Street, Cheap at Half the Price* (1972), *Out of the Trees* (1976), *George and Mildred, What a Performance* (1977, as Brenda), *The Marshal and the Mad Woman, Happy Feet, Unnatural Causes* and *The Bill.* Despite being diagnosed with rheumatoid arthritis in 2004 she continued to work, making her final television appearance as a bedridden patient in an episode of *Doctors* in 2007.

Marjie Lawrence married actor/presenter Harry Greene in 1955. The couple met while working for Joan Littlewood and had two daughters, television presenters Sarah and Laura Greene, and one son, producer Robin Greene. Away from acting Marjie enjoyed walks in the country, gardening, cinema, theatre, foreign travel and going to the gym.

Marjie died on 16 June 2010, aged seventy-eight.

Carry On ... **Quotes**

My work in Carry On Henry *was a very long time ago so I don't remember details but I know I had great fun on those days I worked on it. I enjoyed the never-ending flow of wit and sarcasm from Kenneth Williams, and the more*

earthy, throwaway humour from Sid James. It was a great contrast to my other work at that time, in more serious drama with the Royal Shakespeare Company and in Chekhov at the Royal Court Theatre.
Marjie Lawrence, 2000

Dilys Laye/(Lay)

Dilys Laye was an ideal choice for supporting roles in the *Carry On* series and her impish grin and natural mischievousness were used to full advantage in her four *Carry On* appearances.

Dilys Laye was born in London on 11 March 1934 and trained for acting as a child at the Aida Foster School (whose later pupils would include Shirley Eaton and Barbara Windsor). As a child player Dilys made her stage debut in *The Burning Bush* in 1948 before making her London stage debut, three years later, in *And So to Bed*. Dilys made her New York stage debut with Dame Julie Andrews in *The Boy Friend* in 1954.

After making her screen debut as the young Trottie in *Trottie True*, in 1949, Dilys appeared in a variety of film comedies, including *Blue Murder at St Trinian's* (1957), *Doctor at Large* (1957), *Upstairs and Downstairs* (1959), *Idol on Parade* (1959), *Please Turn Over* (1960) and *A Countess from Hong Kong* (1967). She made her *Carry On* debut as the love-struck Flo Castle in *Carry On Cruising*, and then two years later played the seductive nightclub singer Lila, who turns out to be a cunning secret agent, in *Carry On Spying*. From purring her way through 'The Magic of Love' to paying mock-tribute to Kenneth Williams's catchphrase "Stop messin' about", in *Spying* she gave her finest *Carry On* performance. In *Carry On Camping* Dilys played the carsick Anthea, and she was again seen opposite Bernard Bresslaw when she played feisty hospital patient Mavis Winkle in *Carry On Doctor*.

A popular addition to the series, Dilys was already good friends with most of the main stars prior to joining the team. She had known Joan Sims, for example, from her teenage years (the pair worked together in the revue *High Spirits*), and over thirty years after they worked together in the *Carry On's* Dilys visited Joan in hospital in her final days and read a poem at her funeral. She had also worked with Kenneth Williams in the 1958 TV series *Peter Patter* and in 1994 was briefly reunited with Barbara Windsor in *EastEnders*.

On the small screen, from the mid-1950s, Dilys appeared in a variety of series and specials, including *The Bed-Sit Girl* (series, 1965, with Sheila Hancock, q.v.), *Down the 'Gate* (1975-76, with Reg Varney), *Chintz* (series and co-adapted), *Waters of the Moon* (1986), *Hard Times* (1994, as Mrs

Sparsit) and *EastEnders* (1994-95, as Maxine).

At the end of the 1960s Dilys Laye returned to work on stage, where she remained busy until 2007. As one of Britain's most prolific theatre actors her countless credits ranged from musicals such as *The Pirates of Penzance* and *Sweeney Todd* to four years with the Royal Shakespeare Company (1986-90). Her later stage plays included *Dreaming* (1999, as Bess), *Single Spies* (as the Queen, 2000), *The Secret Garden* (2001) and *The Witches* (2005). In 2002 Dilys took over from Patsy Rowlands (q.v.) in the stage musical *My Fair Lady* (as Mrs Pearce) and returned to the role in 2007. In addition, Dilys was associated with the work of writer Peter Barnes on stage and television and was also godmother to his daughter.

Busy acting until the end of her life, Dilys, who had a cameo role in the 1995 film *Voices from a Locked Room*, latterly appeared in *Alice in Wonderland* (TV, 1999), *Lucy Sullivan Is Getting Married* (series, 1999), *Coronation Street* (2000-01, as Isabel Stephens), *Mr. Charity* (2002, as Margaret), *Midsomer Murders: Market for Murder* (2002), *The Amazing Mrs Pritchard* (2006, as the Queen), *Frankie Howerd: Rather You Than Me* (2008) and finally *The Commander: Abduction* (2008).

Dilys Laye was married firstly to stuntman Frank Maher (1929-2007) and secondly to actor Garfield Morgan (1931-2009), but both marriages ended in divorce. She found more lasting happiness with her third husband, actor and writer Alan Downer (1930-95), whom she married in 1972 and they had one son, theatrical agent Andrew Downer.

In August 1995 Dilys attended the gala screening of *Carry On Up the Khyber*. She went on to attend various *Carry On* events (including the 1998 40th Anniversary reunion and the 2004 Pinewood Tribute to Joan Sims), as well as recording commentaries for DVD releases of three of her four *Carry On* appearances. She looked back on her *Carry On* days with happy memories, describing the films as "such fun to do". The fun continues to be appreciated.

Dilys Laye, who overcame bowel cancer in the 1990s, died of lung cancer in London on 13 February 2009, aged seventy-four.

Carry On ... ***Quotes***

Q. Most sources say you were called upon to replace a sick Joan Sims in Carry On Cruising. *Do you recall anything about being cast for the film?*
A. Only that it was at 3 or 4 days' notice – a whirlwind of costume buying and learning lines!

Q. I loved your role in Carry On Spying *and especially your imitation of Kenneth Williams's catchphrase "Stop Messin' About" in the final scenes of the film. Was this an ad-lib or part of the script?*
A. It was an ad-lib – which originally amused Ken – and indeed the director, who kept it in!

Q. You seemed to fit in perfectly with the main team of the Carry On *series. What was the camaraderie like on set?*
A. Great friendships – no time on set for any prima donnas.

Q. In Cruising *and* Spying *you starred opposite two prolific character actresses, Esma Cannon and Judith Furse. What are your memories of these two ladies?*
A. Esma was enchanting – very professional. Judith was also charming, but I didn't have too many scenes with her.

Q. You went on to appear in two Carry On's *with Bernard Bresslaw. What are your memories of the actor described by many as a 'gentle giant'?*
A. He was exactly that – highly intelligent – a wonderful family man and a pleasure to work with.

Q. Do any amusing incidents stand out from your time on the set of the films?
A. I think filming Camping *in the rain was something to remember, especially as one scene was meant to be raining and they had to use fire hoses – the car was inches deep in water!*

Q. What are your thoughts on the renewed popularity of the Carry On *series?*
A. Good clean fun will always be popular!

Dilys Laye, 2001

George Layton (b. George Michael William Layton)

Well-known actor and writer George Layton appeared in a guest role as the perky doctor treating Kenneth Williams's foot in *Carry On Behind*. It was his only appearance in the *Carry On* series.

George Layton was born in Bradford on 2 March 1943. He trained at RADA and won the Emile Littler Award for Most Promising Actor. His early work was on stage, initially at the Belgrade Theatre (Coventry) and Nottingham. He subsequently went on to appear in *Chips with Everything* at the Royal Court and featured in lead roles in *Funny Peculiar* and *Chapter Two*, with Maureen Lipman (q.v.). More recently on stage George has played Fagin in *Oliver!* and Amos Hart in *Chicago*.

On television George has combined his acting work with a successful career as a writer. He is perhaps best known as the writer of the long–running Nigel Havers sitcom *Don't Wait Up* (1983-90) and he created and wrote *Executive Stress* (1986-87, starring Penelope Keith, q.v.). He also starred in (and wrote) *Doctor in the House* (1969, as Paul Collier) and wrote the last two series of *Robin's Nest* (1977-79, with Richard O'Sullivan, q.v.). George's additional small-screen credits include *The Liver Birds* (1969-71, as Joe), *It Ain't Half Hot Mum* (1974-75, as Bombardier Solomons), *That's Life* (presenter, 1976) and *Minder* (guest appearances, 1979-84, as Des).

In addition to *Carry On Behind*, George has appeared in a handful of other films, including *Here We Go Round the Mulberry Bush* (1968), *Mosquito Squadron* (1969), *Stand Up, Virgin Soldiers* (1977) and *Don't Go Breaking My Heart* (1998).

In more recent years George has again been familiar to television viewers through his role as Alan Brookes in *Sunburn* (1999-2000) and he joined the cast of *EastEnders* (as Norman Simmonds) in 2011. He was the subject of *This Is Your Life* in 1999.

The best-selling author of *The Fib* and *The Swap*, George received an Honorary Doctorate of Letters from the University of Bradford in 2000 in recognition of his work as an actor and writer.

George Layton has been married twice and has two sons and five daughters.

Valerie Leon

A stunning leading lady, Valerie Leon appeared in six *Carry On* films and is now one of the best-loved members of the *Carry On* team.

Valerie Leon was born in London on 12 November 1945 and began her career as a chorus girl in *The Belle of New York*. She went on to appear in the stage production of *Funny Girl* with Barbra Streisand.

Valerie made her film debut in *Smashing Time* in 1967 and in the following year made her first *Carry On* appearance, as one of the hospitality girls in *Carry On Up the Khyber*. By the following year Valerie had graduated to a speaking role as Miss Dobbin, the shop assistant who shows Charles Hawtrey how to get his pole up in *Carry On Camping*. In *Carry On Again Doctor* Valerie played Jim Dale's seductive secretary Deirdre, before tackling her finest *Carry On* role as the leader of the Lubi-Dubis in *Carry On Up the Jungle*. In *Carry On Matron* Valerie had a cameo role as actress Jane Darling (delivering triplets with the help of Kenneth Cope, q.v.), and in *Carry On Girls* she was transformed into the glamorous beauty queen Paula Perkins.

As well as the *Carry On* series, Valerie is well remembered for her roles in two James Bond films: as the receptionist in *The Spy Who Loved Me* (1977) and the glamour-puss in *Never Say Never Again* (1983). Her additional film appearances include *Zeta One* (1969), *The Italian Job* (1969), *The Rise and Rise of Michael Rimmer* (1970), *Blood from the Mummy's Tomb* (1972), *The Ups and Downs of a Handyman* (1975), *Wild Geese* (1978) and *Revenge of the Pink Panther* (1978).

On the small screen Valerie was at her busiest during the 1970s, in programmes such as *The Saint, Up Pompeii, The Avengers, Randall and Hopkirk (Deceased), The Goodies, Carry On Stuffing* (1972, as the maid), *Morecambe and Wise* and *The Des O'Connor Show*. She was also well known around the same as the girl in the famous 'High Karate' adverts.

In recent years, in addition to running her own successful PR Company, Valerie's acting credits have mainly been on stage, notably as the Wicked Queen in *Snow White* (1996-97) and as the Fairy Godmother in *Cinderella* (1998-99). She featured in the 2006 short films *Gas* and *A Neutral Corner* and in the same year made a guest appearance in the TV series *Last of the Summer Wine*.

Since 1994 Valerie Leon has been present at numerous *Carry On* celebrations, including the 40th Anniversary reunion (1998), the *Carry On* Weekend (1999 & 2001) and the 50th Anniversary celebrations (2008). She also took part in the 1998 documentary *What's a Carry On?* (1998). Valerie happily admits that the *Carry On*'s have brought her "a whole new generation of fans", saying in 2001, "Children whose parents watched the *Carry On* films are now writing to me!" Through her roles in the *Carry On* series and the Bond and Hammer Horror films she now enjoys 'cult' status and is a popular guest at film conventions and signing sessions.

Valerie Leon was married to the late BBC producer Michael Mills (d.1988), the creator of countless hit shows, including *Some Mothers Do Have 'Em*. She has two grown-up children and lives in London.

Carry On ... ***Quotes***

I'm afraid I'm not very good on anecdotes so can't add to the many I'm sure you will have received. I can only say that I loved working on the Carry On *films and am thrilled that a series I was involved in is still loved so much and by so many.*
Valerie Leon, 2000

John Levene (b. John Anthony Woods; aka: John Anthony Blake)

A cult television figure through his work in *Doctor Who*, John Levene played a soldier in 'The Baron Outlook', an episode of *Carry On Laughing*.

John Levene was born in Salisbury on 24 December 1941. Without any formal training, he made his way into television and made numerous appearances, including *Z-Cars, UFO* and *Space: 1999*. He is best known to the viewing public as Sergeant John Benton in *Doctor Who* (1968-75), having previously appeared in several episodes of the popular sci-fi series as a cyberman and yeti!

John has also made a handful of film appearances, including *When Dinosaurs Ruled the Earth* (1969), *Psychomania* (1971), *Go for a Take* (1972), *Dark Places* (1974), *Permission to Kill* (1975) and *Satan Hates You* (2009).

For some years John, who moved to America in the mid-1980s, ran his own audio-visual company – Genesis Communications. In recent years he has returned to acting and has also been kept busy with *Doctor Who* conventions in Britain and America.

John Levene is married with two children.

Jacqueline Lewis

Jacqueline played Pat Gordon, one of the pupils in *Carry On Teacher*.

Maureen Lipman CBE

One of the finest character comediennes of her generation, Maureen Lipman's forty-year career on stage and television has ranged from hit one-woman shows to television commercials. She joined the *Carry On* team in 1992 for a one-off appearance as Countess Esmerelda in *Carry On Columbus*.

Maureen Lipman was born in Hull, Yorkshire, on 10 May 1946. She trained at LAMDA and spent three years with Olivier's Old Vic Company, appearing in plays such as *The Front Page* and *Long Day's Journey Into Night*.

Most at home on stage, in the 1990s Maureen received critical acclaim for her one-woman show, *Re:Joyce*, a tribute to actress Joyce Grenfell (1910-79). The show included four West End runs and tours of the UK and USA (1988-89, '91, '93-'94). Since then she has gone on to receive equal applause as Aunt Eller in successive runs of the smash hit musical *Oklahoma!*. In 1984 Maureen received the Olivier Award for her role in *See How They Run* and in the same year won the Variety Club Award for Best Stage Actress.

On the small screen Maureen became well known to the public at the end of the 1970s as Jane Lucas in *Agony* (3 series, 1979-81). The role earned her a BAFTA Award nomination and also inspired the follow-up series, *Agony Again* in 1995. In the mid-1980s she starred in three series of *All at No. 20* (1986-87), for which she received the TV Times Award for Favourite Female Comedy Performance. In the early 1990s Maureen appeared as Beattie, the neurotic Jewish housewife, in more than thirty television adverts for BT, which earned her a BAFTA Award. In recent years Maureen has been familiar on television as Irene Spencer in two series of *Ladies of Letters* (2009-10).

In addition to *Carry On Columbus*, Maureen's film credits include *Up the Junction* (1967), *The Smashing Bird I Used to Know* (1968), *Gumshoe* (1971), *The Wildcats of St Trinian's* (1980), *Water* (1985), *Solomon and Gaenor* (1998), *Captain Jack* (1999), *The Pianist* (2002), *A Flight of Fancy* (2002), *Lighthouse Hill* (2004) and *Caught in the Act* (2008). Maureen received a BAFTA nomination (for Best Supporting Actress) for her role in *Educating Rita* (1983), with Julie Walters.

Maureen's celebrated acting career has also been combined with success as a writer, and her volumes of memoirs, including *How Was It for You?* (1985), *Something to Fall Back On* (1987), *Thank You for Having Me* (1990), *When's It Coming Out?* (1992), *You Can Read Me Like a Book* (1995), *Lip Reading* (1999), *Past-It Notes* (2008) and *I Must Collect Myself: Choice Cuts for a Long Shelf Life* (2010), have all proved highly popular. She also contributes regularly to newspapers and magazines.

Maureen Lipman was married to writer Jack Rosenthal, CBE, (1931-2004) from 1973 and they had two children, Adam and Amy. Maureen, who successfully overcame operations to remove spinal tumours in the 1990s, has received several honours, including an Honorary Doctor of Letters from the University of Hull (1994) and an Honorary MA from the University of Salford (1995). She was awarded the CBE in 1999.

*Carry On ... **Quotes***

When I first read the script I assumed I would be playing Esmerelda as a Spaniard ... One phone call dashed my hopes.
"No," said the producers. "If you play it Spanish, then everyone will have to play it Spanish. This is not the Carry On way of carrying on." I stared at the part for a few days hoping for inspiration and finally had a chat with the author, the amicable Dave Freeman.
"Dave, er – I'm not sure I've quite got the handle on Esmerelda yet ... er, the character, I mean, er I just wondered whether you see her as pretentious nouveau riche, or very upper crust or ..."

"Well she'd determined to marry off her daughter to this rich old man," he told me helpfully, "and she's got this wedding to ..."
"Yes, I realize that's the story ... but I usually have a physical grasp of ... you know ...
"Yes, yes, I do see your problem," he mused. Then, "Tell you what, love, have you thought of having a fan?"
I got my motivation. In one. Turn up. Know your lines. Don't bend them. Then go for it.
The first day of filming, a polite early morning call at the studio. I stand in three layers of black wool and meet my daughter, Holly Aird, her maidservant, Rebecca Lacey in the Barbara Windsor neckline, Su Douglas and Jon Pertwee, who's got his vocal tic all ready and worked out. I decided to go for the facial tic, an upper lip twitch reminiscent of my last close encounter with the cat litter. Just in case it's a total failure, I'm carrying a fan.
The director, Gerald Thomas, is a gentle man in the truest sense of both words. Kindly, avuncular and charming, he is the veteran of thirty-one Carry Ons, and is still amusing and amused by the whole charabanc.
Filmically the mix is the danger. In the right-hand corner you've got yer diehards and yer stalwarts led by the ever youthful Jim Dale ... he jumped at the chance to Carry On carrying on, in the company of past revellers Bernard Cribbins, Jack Douglas, Jon Pertwee, Leslie Phillips and June Whitfield. There were several rumours buzzing around as to the reason for the marked absence of Barbara Windsor, Bernard Bresslaw and Kenneth Connor – but the sensible if not the most gossip-worthy one is that they were doing a Carry On summer season at Blackpool.
Meanwhile, in the far left-hand corner were what are often referred to as the Alternative Comedians.
Well there was Rik Mayall and Nigel Planer who I only really encountered at the initial get-together, where Gerald Thomas and my mother discovered they were practically from the same street. Mayall is, I don't know if you know, ridiculously handsome.
I did encounter Alexei Sayle ... he seemed to be a rather benign, friendly sort of chap, if somewhat bemused by what he was doing there, saying the lines as written. Julian Clary is a real beauty and rather shy. Rather normal actually. The sort of boy your mother would be pleased if you brought home. At first. He fractured his foot during the filming. "I wasn't doing anything. I just sort of walked on it and heard it snap ...". So there was a frailty about him which added to the charm.
The Comic Strip was represented by Peter Richardson and Keith Allen who were not entirely happy with the fairly rigid format. Keith is a comic with an air of barely suppressed danger about him and a tendency to rip off his clothing at the least possible provocation. Then somewhere in the middle are

the American actors Charles Fleischer, voice of Roger Rabbit, and Larry Miller, and the English actors ... and, I suppose, me, doing the Hattie Jacques role – flyweight version.
On the last day of shooting we had a 'wrap' party in the Pinewood Green Room ... Keith Allen appeared bearing a tray of drinks and calling, "Your drinks, Miss Lipman." It goes without saying he was stark naked. It was a surprise. Not a big one, but a surprise. It was a good evening. I'd worked for only seven days, but I said goodbye to a family.
Maureen Lipman, CBE
* *Quotes from* When's It Coming Out? *(1992) by kind permission of Maureen Lipman CBE.*

Henry Livings

Henry played the 12th Recruit in *Carry On Sergeant*. Born in Prestwich, Lancashire, on 20 September 1929, as well as being an occasional actor, he went on to have considerable success as a playwright and screenwriter for both stage and television. Henry died on 20 February 1998, aged 68.

Vivien Lloyd

Vivien played Verna, one of the pupils, in *Carry On Camping*. Her only other film appearance was as the bride in the film version of *Steptoe and Son* (1972).

Harry Locke

Often seen on screen as cheeky cockneys, Harry Locke enlivened three *Carry On* films. For the stocky, dark-haired actor the *Carry On* series represented a small portion of a long career invariably spent as working-class characters.

Harry Locke was born in London on 10 December 1912 (some sources say 1913). He was on stage in repertory at the age of sixteen and made his professional stage debut in 1931. During the Second World War Harry served for five years with the Intelligence Corps, appearing in many different plays on current affairs for the ABCA Play Unit.

In April 1945 Harry joined the Birmingham Repertory Company and later worked with the Old Vic Company in Liverpool. His subsequent stage appearances over the next twenty-five years included an original act at the Windmill Theatre, *Touch It Light* (1958), *Lock Up Your Daughters* (1959-60, as Justice Squeezum) and *The Boy in the Gallery* (1969).

Soon after the war Harry made his film debut, and for almost thirty years he was a familiar cameo player in over seventy films. Often seen as cab drivers and workmen, his screen appearances included *Piccadilly Incident* (1946), *Passport to Pimlico* (1948), *Treasure Island* (1950), *Doctor in the House* (1954), *Reach for the Sky* (1956), *Doctor at Large* (1957) and *I'm All Right, Jack* (1959). He was especially busy throughout the first half of the 1960s, with appearances in *Light Up the Sky!* (1960), *In the Doghouse* (1961), *She'll Have to Go* (1962), *The Small World of Sammy Lee* (1963), *The Early Bird* (1965) and *The Family Way* (1966). Harry's final film appearances were *Oh! What a Lovely War* (1969), *Tales from the Crypt* (1972) and *The Creeping Flesh* (1973).

Harry made his *Carry On* debut as Mick, the lovable hospital orderly, in *Carry On Nurse*. After an absence of almost a decade he returned to the series to play Sam, the ambulance driver, in *Carry On Doctor* and the hospital porter in *Carry On Again Doctor.*

From 1945 Harry appeared on radio in *The Will Hay Show* and over sixty broadcasts of *Just William* (1946-47). On the small screen he was the star of the children's series *Comedy Corner* (1952) and he also appeared in sitcoms and television plays, including *Early to Braden, Impasse* (1963, with Leslie Phillips and Bernard Cribbins, both q.v.), *Man with a Mission* (1965) and *Behind the Line*.

Away from acting Harry, who was married and had one son, enjoyed writing, oil painting and spending time on his boat at Hammersmith - "not sailing, but trying to make it float!"

Harry Locke retired from acting due to ill health in the late 1970s, having made a final television appearance in *Just William* in 1977. He died in London on 7 September 1987.

David Lodge (b. David William Frederick Lodge)

Character actor David Lodge appeared in well over a hundred films, including five *Carry On* films. With Marianne Stone (q.v.), he was one of the most prodigious actors to have graced the *Carry On* series.

David Lodge was born in Strood, near Rochester, Kent, on 19 August 1921. He was educated at St Nicholas Church School (London) and attained a Civil Service Certificate of Education in 1937.

During the Second World War David served in the RAF, first in Bomber Command and later in the RAF Entertainment Unit. After a long apprenticeship in variety, circus and music hall, David made his film debut at the age of thirty-three in *Orders Are Orders*. Amazingly, it was an auspicious start to a long screen career, since his scenes were cut from the film release.

From 1955 David appeared in almost every British film produced, with a string of screen credits including *Cockleshell Heroes* (1955), *The Naked Truth* (1957), *Up the Creek* (1958), *I'm All Right, Jack* (1959) and *The League of Gentlemen* (1960). Often cast in 'tough' character roles the moustachioed actor proved adept as a character comedian in a variety of films throughout the 1950s, '60s and '70s.

David made his *Carry On* debut as the wine connoisseur, among the all-star cast of *Carry On Regardless*. After an absence from the series of well over a decade he returned to play the Police Inspector overseeing the gender-swapping antics in *Carry On Girls* and Bullock in *Carry On Dick*. In *Carry On Behind* David featured in a cameo role as the overbearing publican and also made a brief appearance in *Carry On England* as the inebriate Captain Bull. In addition to his appearances in five *Carry On* films, David featured in the 1975 television series *Carry On Laughing*, playing Duke Boris in 'The Prisoner of Spenda', Sir Simon de Monfort in 'The Baron Outlook', the Colonel in 'The Sobbing Cavalier' and William the Conqueror in 'One in the Eye for Harold'. He also played the leading role of Inspector Bungler in 'The Nine Old Cobblers', 'The Case of the Screaming Winkles' and 'The Case of the Coughing Parrot'.

In addition to the *Carry On* series, David also worked for Gerald Thomas and Peter Rogers in *Watch Your Stern* (1960) and *Raising the Wind* (1961). He was also memorable in several Peter Sellers films, including *The Return of the Pink Panther* (1975), *Revenge of the Pink Panther* (1978) and *The Fiendish Plot of Dr Fu Manchu* (1979). He first met Sellers during their RAF days and the pair also worked together in variety.

On the small screen David featured in dozens of guest roles, including episodes of *The Avengers, Bless This House, Father Brown, Robin's Nest, The Beryl Reid Show, Worzel Gummidge* and *International Superstars*. He also played Frank Baker in the Norman Wisdom series *Norman* (1970), PC Potter in *Tottering Towers* (series, 1971-72, with William Mervyn and Patsy Rowlands, both q.v.), Sam in *Alexander the Greatest* (series, 1972), Reggie Turpin in *Potter's Picture Palace* (series, 1976) and Hector Dent in *Lovely Couple* (series, 1979) and featured in Spike Milligan's *Q* ... series (1975-82).

David's film career came to an end in the 1980s, his final screen appearances including *Sahara* (1983), *Bloodbath at the House of Death* (1983) and *Edge of Sanity* (1989).

He continued to act on television until the early 1990s, his later appearances including roles in *Minder, Hot Metal* and *Lovejoy* (1993). A proud member of the Grand Order of Water Rats (he was King Rat 1989-90), David's charity work kept him busy into his eighties. He received several awards for his work with the Children's Film Foundation and was a Barker of the Variety Club.

David Lodge, who was made a Freeman of the City of London in 1982, released his autobiography, *Up the Ladder to Obscurity*, in 1986. David and his wife, Lyn (who predeceased him), lived for many years in Richmond. He died from cancer on 18 October 2003, aged eighty-two.

Carry On ... ***Quotes***

I have never considered Carry On *films terribly important in my film career of 115 films. Just fun and badly paid!*
David Lodge, 2001

Jimmy Logan OBE (b. James Allan Short)

A national icon, well known for his countless appearances on stage, screen and television, actor, producer and director Jimmy Logan brought his talents as a guest actor to two *Carry On*'s.

Jimmy Logan was born on 4 April 1928 in Dennistoun, Glasgow, the third son of Scottish music hall entertainers Jack Short and May Dalziel. His younger sister is the singer/actress Annie Ross (1930-), and his aunt, Ella Logan (1913-69), was the original star of the Broadway musical *Finian's Rainbow*.

As a child Jimmy toured with his parents in Summer Shows, and after leaving school at the age of fourteen he became an ASM at the Victory Theatre in Paisley. Five years later he was a top comedian at the Old Metropole Theatre, Glasgow, and he starred for years in the *Five Past Eight Revues* at Glasgow's Alhambra Theatre.

Jimmy made his film debut in 1948 and went on to appear in *Floodtide* (1949, alongside Peter Butterworth and Janet Brown). Further screen credits included *The Accidental Golfer* (1991), *Hey, Mr. Producer!* (video, 1998), *Captain Jack* (1998), *The Debt Collector* (1998) and *My Life So Far* (1999). Jimmy made a special guest appearance in *Carry On Abroad* as the raucous Bert Conway and later had an uncharacteristic – and unforgettable - cameo role as Cecil Gaybody in *Carry On Girls*. A popular addition to the team, Jimmy contributed to Barbara Windsor's *This Is Your Life* tribute in 1973, the same year he was also honoured with the famous 'red book'.

In his sixty-five year career Jimmy Logan starred in countless stage productions, from his one-man musical based on the life of his hero Harry Lauder to over thirty-five appearances in pantomime. In addition, he appeared in nine Royal Variety Performances and made tours of America, Canada, South Africa, Australia and New Zealand. On television Jimmy was perhaps best remembered for his own series in the

1950s and 1960s. Latterly he appeared in the critically acclaimed *The Nuclear Family* and played a retired major in *Take the High Road*.

Three times married, Jimmy successfully recovered from open-heart surgery in his mid-sixties to continue a hectic work schedule on stage and screen. His numerous honours included an Honorary Doctor of Letters from Glasgow's Caledonian University (1994), a fellowship of the Royal Scottish Academy of Music and Drama and the OBE (1996). He was patron of numerous charities and a member of the Grand Order of Water Rats. Jimmy's detailed autobiography, *It's a Funny Life*, was published in 1998.

Jimmy Logan died from cancer of the oesophagus at Clydebank's HCI Centre on 13 April 2001, aged seventy-three.

Carry On ... ***Quotes***

Like yourself, I have often wondered what it is about Carry On *films that fascinates people after so many years.*

I think it is family humour that is 'near the edge' but never goes into the actual deed, for instance Kenneth Williams had many girls chasing him but you knew he would never get into bed with them; he would always react as if he would, and it would be a lark, but if caught in a sexy situation he would be as shocked as anybody else. An innocent wickedness.

Barbara Windsor was always going to be the 'girl on the side' that all men saw and said 'OOH' and they all fancied like mad, but although she was in compromising positions she was never caught 'at it' as they say. She was the 'warning beacon' to every wife, the reason why an eye had to be kept on Dad. What a pleasure it is to see her on television proving she is an excellent actress of great quality and the public realising how special she is, so the love they have had for her over the years is something she can now enjoy. All the stars brought something to the films they were in but the cornerstone of the performances was always Sid James and his long-suffering wife, his attempts to 'get away with it' and his failure to do so. Another puzzlement was the number of references to the female 'bust' and the many variations often made me wonder how they could find another way of saying the same thing, but they did!

In my opinion the real secret of the success was the work of the director Gerald Thomas, who understood comedy and comedians, the rare gift of dealing with the personalities and getting the best out of them no matter what part they played.

They were like a number of top racehorses - each one with a different temperament and if you arrived as a newcomer they welcomed you but they guarded their own area. Some, like Peter Butterworth, were just lovely people. All could make you laugh when they told stories of what happened as they went through life.

I have seen Jack Douglas over the years and he is well, but sadly so many of the team have gone and an attempt to get another team together did not go so well. Every now and again I catch a glimpse of the lovely Joan Sims on television.

I am still busy in the theatre but still get letters from all over the world about the Carry On *films, which are regarded as family entertainment and humour for all.*

Jimmy Logan OBE, 1999

Terence Longdon

As a good-looking leading man of the *Carry On* series Terence Longdon was certainly partly responsible the success of the early *Carry On* films. He was there from the start, as Miles Heywood in *Carry On Sergeant*, and he was equally successful as the romantic lead (Ted York) in *Carry On Nurse*. In *Carry On Constable* he appeared in a cameo role as con artist Herbert Hall, and in his final role in the series he featured as 'helping hand' Montgomery Infield-Hopping in *Carry On Regardless*.

Born in Newark-on-Trent in Nottingham on 14 May 1922, Terence Longdon trained at RADA (1946-48). He made his stage debut as Robin in *The French for Love* in 1948 and subsequently made numerous stage appearances, including three years at Stratford (1951-54). From the mid-1960s he was particularly busy in the theatre, notably playing John Brownlow in over a thousand performances of *The Secretary Bird* (1968-70). Active on stage into his late seventies, his later theatre credits included *Othello* (1984, as the Duke of Venice), *Paris Match* (1989, as Mr Vallere) and *Augustine* (1999).

Although most at home on stage, as a leading man from the 1950s Terence managed to make over thirty film appearances, including *Angels One Five* (1951), *Never Look Back* (1952), *Appointment in London* (1953), *Simon and Laura* (1955), *Jumping for Joy* (1955), *Doctor at Large* (1957), *Dangerous Exile* (1957), *Ben-Hur* (1959), *What a Whopper* (1961), *On the Fiddle* (1961), *Clash by Night* (1964), *The Wild Geese* (1978), *Sea Wolves* (1980) and *Letters from the East* (1995).

On the small screen Terence's credits from 1947 included the lead role in *Garry Halliday* (1959-62), *Ivanhoe* (1958), *Redcap* (1966), *The New Avengers, The Cedar Trees, The Sandbaggers, The Martian Chronicles* (1980), *The Man with the Twisted Lip* (1986) and *The Return of Sherlock Holmes*

(1986).

Terence Longdon featured in the 1998 documentary *What's a Carry On?* and subsequently attended numerous events at Pinewood Studios, including the 50th Anniversary celebrations in 2008, as well as providing commentary on DVD releases of the films.

Terence, who was the first husband of leading actress Barbara Jefford OBE (1930-), died on 23 April 2011, following a short illness. He was remembered in one obituary as "a great actor, a true gent and, above all, a loving husband and father - one of a kind".

Arthur Lovegrove

Character actor Arthur Lovegrove played the Old Farmhand in *Carry On Cowboy*. Surprisingly, it was to be his only appearance in the *Carry On* series.

Arthur Lovegrove was born Fulham, London, on 15 July 1913. He appeared on screen from 1950, mainly in cameo roles, including *The Galloping Major* (1951), *The Runaway Bus* (1954), *The Quatermass Experiment* (1955), *Lost* (1956), *Carry On Admiral* (1957), *The Night We Dropped a Clanger* (1959), *Smashing Time* (1967) and *The Rise and Rise of Michael Rimmer* (1970).

On television from the 1950s Arthur's numerous credits included *Glencannon* (1959, series, as Alf), *Biggles* (1960, as Pybus), *The Chars* (1963, with Doris and Elsie Waters), *The Avengers* (1964, as Michael Lynden), *The Dick Emery Show* (1971), *Please Sir* (1971), *Bless This House* (1976) and *Now and Then* (series 1, as Grandad) which was screened after his death. He also wrote a number of stage plays, most notably *Goodnight Mrs Puffin*.

Arthur also continued to work on the big screen until the end of his life, making his final film appearances in *Eye of the Needle* (1981) and *Memoirs of a Survivor* (1981). He died in Surrey on 7 November 1981, aged sixty-eight.

Michael Low

Michael, along with Michael Lucas (q.v.), was one of the 'lusty youths' in *Carry On Camping*.

Len Lowe

Len, who played the Maitre d' in *Carry On Loving*, was an actor, singer and musician best known for his work in variety with his brother Bill.

Born in Fulham, London, on 17 December 1915, Len also acted on television in a range of comedy series, including *Bless This House*, *One Foot in the Grave*, *Grace and Favour*, *Keeping Up Appearances* and *Last of the Summer Wine*. He died in London on 21 August 1999, aged eighty-three.

Olga Lowe

Olga Lowe played Madame Fifi, the fiery brothel owner, in *Carry On Abroad*. Her link to the *Carry On* series was more notable, however, through her long professional association with Sid James, from 1940 until his death in 1976.

Olga Lowe was born in South Africa in 1925 and began her career as a teenager. She first appeared with Sid James on stage when she was just fifteen, in a performance of *Hoop-la*. Like Sid, Olga moved from South Africa (with her actor husband, John Tore) following the Second World War. During the final years of the war she had entertained the troops, again with Sid.

Olga Lowe's first stage appearances in Britain were at The Palladium as a comedy feed to Harpo Marx, and for fifty years she worked consistently in English theatre, where she made her final appearances in repertory at the Old Vic in 1997.

Tall and striking, Olga made an impressive film debut in *Trottie True* in 1949. Her occasional film appearances since then have been *State Secret* (1950), *Hotel Sahara* (1951), *So Little Time* (1953), *Oh, Rosalinda!!* (1955), *Where Eagles Dare* (1969), *The Riddle of the Sands* (1978) and *Nijinsky* (1980).

On television Olga has appeared in a wide variety of productions, most recently *Perfect Scoundrels* (as Mrs Illingsworth), *Hercule Poirot's Christmas* (1994, as Stella) and *EastEnders* (1994, as Doreen Ellis). Olga also featured in the television documentaries *Unforgettable Sid James* (2000) and *Heroes of Comedy – Sid James* (2001).

In 1976 Olga, with fellow *Carry On* actor Terry Scott, appeared with Sid James in the stage production of *The Mating Season* in Sunderland. She was on stage with Sid when he suffered a fatal heart attack on the evening of 14 April 1976.

Carry On ... **Quotes**

I had known Sid for years. We came to England from South Africa together, he with his wife and me with my husband, to start our careers here. We were both in the South African army entertainment unit during the latter part of the war, playing to the troops in Cairo, Alexandria and the desert.
Olga Lowe, 1997

Mike Lucas

Mike played one of the 'lusty youths' seen with Barbara Windsor and Sandra Caron in *Carry On Camping*. He also appeared on television as Albert Pike in *Thicker Than Water* (1969) and as Jerry in *The Liver Birds* (1971).

Jane Lumb

Jane had uncredited roles in two *Carry On*'s: as an Amazon guard in *Carry On Spying* and as a vestal virgin in *Carry On Cleo*.

Kenny Lynch OBE

A singer-songwriter and actor, Kenny Lynch played the cheerful bus conductor amused by the antics of his passengers in *Carry On Loving*. It was his only appearance in the series.

Born in Stepney, East London, on 18 March 1938, Kenny Lynch was the youngest of thirteen children. He made his first stage appearance at the age of twelve with his sister Maxine Daniels, and in the early 1960s he had a couple of top ten hit records, including 'You Can Never Stop Me Loving You' and 'Up on the Roof'. His 1963 single 'Misery' was the first cover song released by the Beatles – ironically, it had flopped for Kenny! Ultimately Kenny would have greater success as a songwriter, his own compositions being sung by The Drifters, Cilla Black and Dusty Springfield.

In addition to his singing and writing, Kenny also acted from the early 1960s, appearing in films such as *Just for Fun* (1963), *Dr. Terror's House of Horror* (1965), *The Plank* (1967), *The Alf Garnet Saga* (1972, as himself), *The Playbirds* (1978) and *Confessions from the David Galaxy Affair* (1979).

Kenny has also acted on television, usually in comic roles, including *Room at the Bottom* (series, 1966, as Horace Robinson), *Curry and Chips* (series, 1969, as Kenny), *Psst!* (1969), *The Les Dawson Show, Tell Tarby* (1973), *Francis Howerd in Concert* (1974), *The Sweeney and Mike Reid's Mates & Music* (1984). He also featured among the all-star cast of *Eric Sykes's The Plank* (1979) and *Mr. H Is Late* (1987).

Kenny still tours the UK on stage and also works for several charities.

Jack Lynn

Jack, who played the Admiral of the Fleet in *Carry On Emmannuelle*, was born in London on 30 January 1923. His additional film credits included *Never Take Sweets from a Stranger* (1960), *Witchfinder General* (1968) and *Yentl* (1983).

Tamsin MacDonald

Tamsin played one of the Khasi's wives in *Carry On Up the Khyber*.

Verna Lucille MacKenzie

Verna played the Lubi striking the gong in *Carry On Up the Jungle*.

Don MacLean

Don played the Inquisitor with the ham sandwiches in *Carry On Columbus*. Born in Birmingham on 11 March 1944, Don was a regular on *Crackerjack* in the 1970s and presented the 1993 TV series *First Letter First*.

Diana MacNamara

Diana had an uncredited role in *Carry On Don't Lose Your Head*, playing Princess Stephanie.

Victor Maddern

Victor Maddern was already a film veteran – with over forty films to his credit – when he joined the *Carry On* series as Detective Sergeant Liddell in *Carry On Constable*. He went on to become a familiar supporting actor in the series, playing the 1st sinister passenger in *Carry On Regardless*, the unfortunate Milchmann in *Carry On Spying*, the Sergeant Major in *Carry On Cleo* and the man in the launderette (opposite Joan Sims) in *Carry On Emmannuelle*.

Victor Maddern was born in Seven Kings, Ilford, on 16 March 1926. At the age of just fifteen he went to sea, but after three years he decided he wanted to be an actor. He subsequently gained a scholarship and trained at RADA (1947-49). Shortly after completing his professional training he made his film debut in *Seven Days to Noon* in 1950.

Over the next forty years Victor proved to one of Britain's most prodigious actors. He built up his acting experience with repertory seasons throughout the country, and his regular stage appearances included *The Trial of Mr. Pickwick* (1952, as Sam Weller), *The Touch of Fear* (1956, as Tommo), *Hamlet* (1961, as the first gravedigger), *My Darling Daisy* (1970, as Frank), *Treasure Island* (1979, as Long John Silver) and *Fighting Chance* (1985, as Len).

Victor's screen credits often saw him in cameo roles as menacing types. With over seventy film appearances, he became one of the country's best-known character actors. His screen credits included *The Cockleshell Heroes* (1955), *Private's Progress* (1956), *Happy Is the Bride* (1958), *Blood of the Vampire* (1958), *I Was Monty's Double* (1958), *I'm All Right, Jack* (1959),

H.M.S. Defiant (1962), *Circus of Fear* (1966), *Chitty Chitty Bang Bang* (1968), *Steptoe and Son* (1973), *Digby, the Biggest Dog in the World* (1973), *Sweet Nothing* (1990) and *Freddie as F.R.O.7* (voice as Old Gentleman Raven, 1992).

In addition to the *Carry On* series he worked in several other Rogers/Thomas productions, including *Please Turn Over* (1959), *Watch Your Stern* (1960) and *Raising the Wind* (1961). In 1975 he appeared in episodes of *Carry On Laughing*, playing a sailor in 'Orgy and Bess', Charlie in 'The Nine Old Cobblers' and Sir Osis in 'Under the Round Table'.

On the small screen Victor appeared in an array of roles from the mid-1950s. He played Tug Nelson in the 1960 series *Mess Mates* and was later seen in *Fair Exchange* (series, 1963) as Tommy Finch. His guest appearances ranged from episodes of *The Avengers* and *The Saint* to *Doctor Who* and *Randall and Hopkirk (Deceased)*. In 1985 Victor played PC Johnson in *Miss Marple: The Moving Finger* (with Joan Hickson, q.v.) and his final television appearance was opposite David Jason in an episode of *The Darling Buds of May* in 1992.

Victor was married for over forty years and had four daughters: Emma, Jamie, Kim and Eva. In later years he lived in a rambling farmhouse in Essex. An active supporter of religious associated charities, he was also a proud grandfather.

Victor Maddern died in London (from a brain tumour) on 22 June 1993, aged sixty-seven.

Leigh Madison (Pamela Williams)

A light leading lady of the late 1950s, Leigh Madison played Sheila in *Carry On Sergeant* and Miss Winn in *Carry On Nurse*. She also worked for Gerald Thomas in *Please Turn Over* (1959).

In addition to the *Carry On* series, Leigh, who was born in Aldershot, Hampshire, on 11 March 1934, appeared in a handful of other films during her brief acting career, including *6.5 Special* (1958), *High Jump* (1958), *Serious Charge* (1959) and *Naked Fury* (1959).

One of her final acting roles was in the television series *Our House* (1960, as Marcia Hatton), alongside many members of the *Carry On* team including Charles Hawtrey, Joan Sims and Hattie Jacques.

Leigh quit acting following her marriage in 1960 to producer Ernest Maxim (1923-) and the couple had one son, Paul. In the late 1970s she made a brief return to the profession with television appearances in *Tycoon* (1978) and *A Family Affair* (1979).

Leigh Madison died on 8 January 2009, three years after being diagnosed with Progressive Supranuclear Palsy (PSP), a rare and degenerative neurological condition, aged seventy-four.

Janet Mahoney

Janet Mahoney made a notable appearance in the *Carry On* series, playing Gay, Jacki Piper's flat (in more ways than one!) mate in *Carry On Loving*. Surprisingly, it was her only appearance in the series.

Janet's additional acting credits included the films *Doctor in Trouble* (1972) and *Mutiny on the Buses* (1972), as well as television programmes such as *Howerd's Hour, Up Pompeii* and *Dad's Army* (1975).

Janet Mahoney has been married to renowned theatre director Duncan C. Weldon since 1974 and now lives in Halifax, West Yorkshire.

Melita Manger

Melita Manger, who played the lady with the salad in *Carry On Behind*, has been acting since the late 1960s.

She made her film debut as the squirrel in *Alice's Adventures in Wonderland* (1971) and also played a dancer in *Adolf Hitler – My Part in His Downfall* (1972). On television Melita's credits include appearances in *Dad's Army, Are You Being Served?* and *Waiting for God*.

Recently Melita, who is a busy wife and mother, has been helping to run her family business in Wales, but she is still a working actress.

Rosemary Manley

Rosemary had an uncredited role in *Carry On Jack* as one of the girls at Dirty Dick's Tavern.

Elspeth March (b. Jean Elspeth Mackenzie)

A 'grande dame' of British theatre and the first wife of actor Stewart Granger, Elspeth March appeared in cameo roles in two *Carry On* films. She was unforgettable as Lady Binder in *Carry On Don't Lose Your Head*, congratulating Sid James on his "magnificent balls", and was later seen as a member of the hospital board in *Carry On Again Doctor*.

The daughter of Colonel Henry Malcolm Mackenzie and his wife Elfreda, Elspeth March was born in London on 5 March 1911. She studied at the Central School of Speech Training and Dramatic Art and made her stage debut in *Jonah and the Whale* in 1932. Elspeth then went on to spend several years in repertory at Birmingham (1934-37) and appeared in the title role in Bernard Shaw's *The Millionairess* (1937). During the Second World War she left the stage to work as a driver for the American Red Cross (1940-44). Upon her return to the theatre Elspeth became one of the country's busiest character actresses, with roles such as Widow Quin in *The Playboy of the Western World* (1948), Ftatateeta in *Caesar and Cleopatra* (1951) and Ma Larkin in *The Darling Buds of May* (1959). Her later stage appearances included *A Public Mischief* (1966, as Mrs Potter), *The Dark River* (1972), *Snap* (1974, as Maude) and *Anastasia* (1976, as Dowager Empress). Her final stage appearance was in *Underground* (1983, with Raymond Burr).

Elspeth made her screen debut in *Mr Emmanuel* in 1944. Over the next fifty years she would make sporadic screen appearances, including *Quo Vadis* (1951), *His Excellency* (1952), *Midnight Lace* (1960), *The Roman Spring of Mrs. Stone* (1961), *Dr. Crippen* (1962), *Goodbye, Mr. Chips* (1969), *The Rise and Rise of Michael Rimmer* (1970), *Lola* (1971), *Charlie Muffin* (TV, 1979) and *The Casebook of Sherlock Holmes: The Eligible Bachelor* (TV, 1993, as Lady Blanche).

On television Elspeth appeared in guest roles in a range of series, including *Alfred Hitchcock Presents, Three Fat Ladies* (1960), *Rebecca* (1979, as Mrs van Hopper) and *Cribb* (1980). She also played Mother in two series of *Let There Be Love* (1982-83, with Paul Eddington & Nanette Newman) and Penelope Keith's mother-in-law in an episode of *Executive Stress* in 1987. Elegant into her eighties, in her final years she made occasional appearances as an interviewee in television documentaries.

Elspeth March married actor Stewart Granger (1913-93) in 1938 and they had two children, Jamie and Lindsey. The couple divorced in 1949 and Granger went on to marry actress Jean Simmons OBE (1929-2010).

A survivor from a bygone age, with contemporaries including Laurence Olivier and Vivien Leigh, Elspeth March spent her final years living in Denville Hall, where she reigned supreme as the 'Queen' of the actors' retirement home. She died on 29 April 1999, aged eighty-eight.

Betty Marsden

Betty Marsden, a veteran actress of stage, screen, television and radio, appeared in two *Carry On* films: as the Mata Hari character with Kenneth Connor in *Carry On Regardless* and as the unforgettable Harriet Potter in *Carry On Camping*.

Born in Liverpool on 24 February 1919, Betty's first stage appearance, at the age of seven, was as the First Fairy in *A Midsummer Night's Dream*. Shortly afterwards, she gained a scholarship and spent six years training at the Italia Conti Stage School. Her subsequent stage appearances over the next sixty years ranged from the musical *Keep Your Hair On* to *The Importance of Being Earnest* (as Lady Bracknell).

Despite her numerous theatre credits, Betty Marsden is best remembered for her work on radio, notably in *Beyond Our Ken* and *Round the Horne* (both with Kenneth Williams), in which she broadcast for eleven years. Her distinctive husky tones continued to be heard on radio until the very end of her life; indeed, she recorded an episode of the *Narnia Chronicles* for BBC radio just ten days before her death.

An animated character actress, Betty Marsden made her screen debut in *Ships with Wings* in 1942 and went on to appear in *Chance Meeting* (1956), *Ramsbottom Rides Again* (1956), *The Leather Boys* (1965), *The Wild Affair* (1966), *Sudden Terror* (1970), *The Lovers* (1972), *Britannia Hospital* (1982), *The Dresser* (1983) and *Little Dorrit* (1988).

On television Betty appeared in both comedy and drama, including *On the Bright Side* (1959), *The More We Are Together* (1971, as Norma Dunk), *The Cabbage Patch* (1983, as Julia Foster's mother), *Anastasia – The Mystery of Anna* (1986), *Inspector Morse* (1989) and *The Darling Buds of May* (1992), and she was touchingly reunited with Kenneth Connor at the very end of his life in *The Memoirs of Sherlock Holmes* (1994).

In 1998 Betty was a guest at the *Carry On* 40th Anniversary reunion and in the same year contributed to the Kenneth Williams *Reputations* documentary. She was married for over thirty years to Doctor James Wilson Muggoch and had two children.

Betty Marsden was suffering from heart problems and slight pneumonia when she collapsed and died suddenly in the bar of Denville Hall (the actors' retirement home) on 19 July 1998, aged seventy-nine.

Cathi Marsh

Cathi played the Lubi Lieutenant standing in several scenes with Valerie Leon in *Carry On Up the Jungle*.

Lindsay Marsh

Lindsay played the 'shapely nurse' in *Carry On Matron* and in the same year worked for Rogers and Thomas in the film version of *Bless This House*, playing Myra.

Reed Martin

Reed played Poca Hontas in *Carry On Columbus*.

Reuben Martin

Reuben was the man inside the gorilla suit in *Carry On Up the Jungle*. He was later called upon for the same task in 'Lamp-Posts of the Empire', an episode of *Carry On Laughing*, on television in 1975.

Derek Martinus

Derek had an uncredited role in *Carry On Sergeant*.

Larry Martyn

Larry Martyn, who played the irate shooting gallery manager in *Carry On At Your Convenience* and the electrician in *Carry On Behind*, was a television actor best known as Mr Mash in *Are You Being Served?*.

Larry, who was born in London's East End on 22 March 1934, began his career in variety as a singer and comedian, following National Service with the Parachute Regiment. During the 1970s he became well known on television, with a range of guest appearances in series such as *Dad's Army, Up Pompeii, Doctor at Large, Upstairs, Downstairs, On the Buses, Rising Damp, For the Love of Ada* and episodes of the *Mike Yarwood Show.*

In addition to three series of *Are You Being Served?* (1973-75), Larry also appeared in the 1973 series *Whoops Baghdad!* (as Derti Dhoti), four series of *Spring and Autumn* (1973-76, as Brian Reid) and *West End Tales* (1981, as Checkie). He continued acting until the end of his life, his later appearances including episodes of *The Bill* and *Don't Wait Up*.

As well as the *Carry On* series, Larry appeared in a handful of other films, including *And the Same to You* (1960), *Breath of Life* (1962), *Up the Junction* (1967) and *Omen III: The Final Conflict* (1981).

Larry Martyn died in Kent on 7 August 1994, aged sixty.

Marianne Maskell (aka: M. Friend)

Marianne played a maternity nurse in *Carry On Emmannuelle*. She was still in the acting profession in the 1990s.

John Matthews

John played Sergeant Matthews in *Carry On Sergeant* and Tom Mayhew in *Carry On Nurse*.

Margot Maxine

Margot played a harem girl in *Carry On Follow That Camel*.

Rik Mayall (b. Richard Michael Mayall)

For the past thirty years Rik Mayall has been one of Britain's best-known comedians. In 1992 he gave a unique characterisation - reminiscent of nostril-flaring *Carry On* legend, Kenneth Williams - when he was cast as the Sultan in *Carry On Columbus*.

Rik Mayall was born in Harlow, Essex, on 7 March 1958. In the late 1970s he teamed with Adrian Edmondson while studying in Manchester and the pair formed a comedy group called 20th Century Coyote. They went on to perform at the famous comedy club, The Comedy Store, along with future famous faces such as Dawn French and Jennifer

Saunders.

Rik's rise to fame predominantly came via the character of Kevin Turvey in *A Kick Up the Eighties*. He went on to reprise the character in his own television series, *Kevin Turvey Investigates* (1981-82), before gaining cult status as Rik in *The Young Ones* (1982-84).

The overwhelming success of *The Young Ones*, which was co-written by Rik and starred Adrian Edmondson, Nigel Planer (q.v.), Christopher Ryan and Alexei Sayle (q.v.), made Rik a household name and inspired a series of similarly anarchic sitcoms. Rik subsequently went on to enjoy stardom playing sweaty, sneering and highly unlikeable characters!

In addition to *The Young Ones*, Rik was also hugely popular in *The New Statesman* (1987-92, as Alan B'Stard) and *Filthy, Rich & Catflap* (1987, as Richie Rich). In the 1990s he again teamed up with Adrian Edmondson in *Bottom* (1991-93, as Richie Richard), another cult hit written by the pair that inspired video releases and a succession of stage tours around the country.

Rik Mayall's additional television credits are many and varied and include guest appearances in *The Comic Strip Presents ...*, *Blackadder* and French and Saunders. He has also proved himself to be an insightful serious actor, with surprisingly chilling guest appearances in dramas such as *Jonathan Creek, The Bill, Marple: Why Didn't They Ask Evans?* (2009) and *Midsomer Murders: The Creeper* (2009).

On stage Rik has appeared in *Cell Mates, Waiting for Godot* and *The Government Inspector*. His live stand-up shows have seen him combine talents with Ben Elton and Adrian Edmondson for sell-out tours of the UK and Australia since the early 1980s. Most recently he has been familiar on stage in live versions of *Bottom*.

Although best known as a television actor, Rik has also appeared in a variety of films and TV-movies over the past two decades. He began his screen career in *Eye of the Needle* (1981) and can also be spotted as the 2nd Chess Player in *An American Werewolf in London* (1981). He went on to feature in *Whoops Apocalypse* (1982) and *Eat the Rich* (1987) and starred in *Drop Dead Fred* (1992). More recently he played Reverend Augustus Dampier in *The Canterville Ghost* (TV, 1996) and Merlin in *Merlin: The Return* (1998), starred with Adrian Edmondson (and *Carry On* favourite Fenella Fielding, q.v.) in *Guest House Paradiso* (1999), played Baxter in *Churchill: The Hollywood Years* (2004) and featured in the all-star cast of *Eldorado* (2010).

An Emmy Award-winning voice-over artist, Rik's unique tones have provided voices for a range of animated films and series, including *The Wind in the Willows, The World of Peter Rabbit and Friends, The Princess and the Goblin, Tom and Vicky* and *Jellabies*.

Away from acting Rik enjoys relaxing in the countryside. In 1998 he suffered serious head injuries after being involved in a quad bike accident on his farm. To the relief of his many fans he made a full recovery and returned to acting within months of the accident.

Rik has been married to Barbara, a make-up artist, since 1985 and they have three children, Rosie, Sydney and Bonnie.

Bill Maynard (b. Walter Frederick George Williams)

Now probably best known for his role as Claude Greengrass in *Heartbeat*, Bill Maynard joined the *Carry On* series in 1970. Over a period of four years he gave memorable cameo performances in five *Carry On* films.

Bill, who was born in Farnham, Surrey, on 8 October 1928, began entertaining as a child. He became a professional football player at the age of fifteen before becoming a band singer at Butlins. By the age of twenty-four he was the highest paid artist at the Windmill Theatre, and after several years of theatre and variety work he made his television debut in the hugely successful *Great Scott, It's Maynard!* (1956, with Terry Scott).

Bill's early years in show business were something of a roller-coaster ride, and after his initial success he hit hard times at the end of the 1950s. After working on stage for John Neville at the Nottingham Playhouse Bill's career again took off and he made the first of over thirty film appearances in the screen version of *Till Death Us Do Part* in 1968. He subsequently appeared in *Bless This House* (1972), *Adolf Hitler – My Part in His Downfall* (1972), *Steptoe and Son Ride Again* (1973), *Confessions of a Window Cleaner* (1975), *All Things Bright and Beautiful* (1976), *Dangerous Davies – The Last Detective* (TV, 1981), *Screen One: Filipina Dreamgirls* (1991, TV) and *Hear My Song* (1991).

Bill Maynard made his *Carry On* debut as Mr Dreery, one of Kenneth Williams's clients, in *Carry On Loving*. He later turned up as the tedious Guy Fawkes in *Carry On Henry* and in the same year played Joan Sims's uptight husband who enjoys a 'regular' life in *Carry On At Your Convenience*. Bill's most memorable role in the series was as Freddy, Sid James's crony, in *Carry On Matron*, and he made a final appearance as Bodkin, the innkeeper, in *Carry On Dick*.

On television, in addition to *Mostly Maynard* (his own show) and guest appearances in programmes such as *Up Pompeii* and *Till Death Us Do Part*, Bill was well known in the seventies as Selwyn Froggitt in *Oh No, It's Selwyn Froggitt* (1976-77) and its successor *Selwyn* (1978). In the 1980s he made guest appearances in *Worzel Gummidge, Minder* and *Tales of the Unexpected* and played Fred Moffatt in three series of *The Gaffer* (1983) and Seth Raven in *Langley Bottom* (1986).

Bill Maynard was semi-retired from acting when he was offered the role of Claude Jeremiah Greengrass in *Heartbeat* in 1992. It is a role he made his own and his brilliant characterisation of the lovable rogue brought him a legion of new fans and kept him busy into his early seventies. Bill suffered a series of strokes in July 2000 while filming the tenth series of *Heartbeat* but happily has returned to the small screen in the *Heartbeat* spin-off *The Royal* (7 episodes, 2003) and played Councillor Cyril Steel in an episode of *Dalziel and Pascoe* in 2002. More recently he has worked for BBC Radio Leicester (2003-08).

Bill Maynard's first wife, Muriel, died from cancer in 1983. They had two children, Jane and Martin (singer Maynard Williams). In 1989 Bill married Tonia, widow of racing car driver Donald Campbell. Bill Maynard has written two autobiographical volumes: *The Yo-Yo Man* (1973) and *Stand Up and Be Counted* (1996).

Cal McCord

Cal played a young farmhand in *Carry On Cowboy*. It was one of several minor appearances in films of the 1960s, which included *Too Young to Love* (1960), *I've Gotta Horse* (1965) and *The Adding Machine* (1969).

Don McCorkindale

Don McCorkindale played one of the recruits in *Carry On Sergeant* and five years later turned up as Tubby in *Carry On Cabby*.

Born in London on 27 January 1940, the son of "Big" Don McCorkindale, the South African heavyweight boxing champion, Don trained for acting at the Italia Conti Stage School and PARADA.

Don made his film debut in *The Blue Peter* in 1954 and during the "heady days of a flourishing British film industry" in the 1950s and 1960s he was involved in numerous productions. Although Don's roles in the *Carry On* series were minor, he also has a curious link to another *Carry On* cameo player, Freddie Mills (q.v.), who was his beloved stepfather.

Over the past fifty years he has built a career on small part roles on stage, film, television and radio. His countless stage appearances have recently included *The Tempest* (as Prospero) and *The Mousetrap* (as Major Metcalf). He was nominated for Best Actor by the Jo'Burg Critics Society in 1976 for his lead role in *The Marowitz "Shrew"*. On television Don has played Mike Baldwin's best man in *Coronation Street*, Mr. Windigate in *Sherlock Holmes* and most recently has been familiar as the evil Mr Forbes in two series of *Grange Hill*. In 2008 he starred in his first ever horror film, *Call of the Hunter*, which has now been released on DVD. His recent small-screen guest appearances include roles in *Doctors, Heartbeat* and *Bad Girls* and he remains active in the business with television roles and voice-over work.

Don McCorkindale has been married to Kate Sanders since 1965 and they have two children, Danny and Sara. He lives in London.

Carry On ... ***Quotes***

After all these years it's quite difficult to believe that I was actually a small part of the Carry On *legend. The reply to which, in showbiz terms is, "There is no such thing as a small part, only small actors!"*

I was just eighteen when I was lucky enough to get a glorified extra job on the first Carry On *film.* Sergeant *was the title. On set I was in the company of another supernumery by the name of James Villiers, who confided in me that he was 74th in line to the British throne. He went on to have a wonderful film career, locally and internationally. I suppose I held the attraction that the aristocracy in this country has always had for the working class. I never pull punches, say what I feel and bugger the consequences.*

Kenneth Williams was very kind to me during the Sergeant *filming. He sort of took me under his wing and even arranged for free tickets for a revue he was in at the time called* Share My Lettuce. *Bob Monkhouse was another very important part of that time. He was really very kind and helpful to us 'just out of drama school' kids, giving a favoured few lifts back to London from the studio in his gold lame upholstered Cadillac.*

As Sergeant *was the last movie I did, literally days before being conscripted into National Service (RASC British Army on the Rhine) it was a kind of foretaste of the military. Not really. With Charles Hawtrey, Kenneth Connor, Dora Bryan and Peter Rogers making things so easy, what awaited me at Aldershot army barracks was nothing like the film set!*

The thing about Cabby *I remember most is that I'd come back after two years' army service and everything was exactly the same, with the exception of the addition of Sid James, the legend in his own wassername. He was a fellow South African. My father 'Big Don' had been a world-class Cruiser and Heavyweight boxer for that country both in the '36 Olympics and later contender for the world heavyweight title against Kingfish Lewisky. He later divorced my mother, who then married the late, great Freddie Mills - my stepfather, mentor and a man I worshipped.*

Sid and I had many chats about S.A. He remembered dad well, having been in the ring himself. He was a gentleman, flawed like us all, but never did he raise anyone's expectations of what they could get from him. When he was

there he was yours. Otherwise, forget it. I don't think there was a mean bone in that man's body. He was forever giving and forgiving.
The time I spent on set with 'the team' and later watching Carry On's were some of the happiest in British cinema.
Don McCorkindale, 2000

Stanley McGeagh

Stanley played the short-sighted man in *Carry On Behind* and later turned up as a reporter in *Carry On Emmannuelle*. He is still acting, latterly on television in Australia.

Henry McGee

Best known around the world for his appearances with comic icon Benny Hill, Henry McGee played Harold Hump in *Carry On Emmannuelle*. It was his only appearance in the series.

Henry McGee was born in Kensington, London, on 14 May 1929. He trained at the Italia Conti Stage School and built up his experience with years of repertory work, in both England and Australia. Henry's stage appearances, which kept him busy well into the 1990s, included *Uproar in the House*, *The Cat and the Canary* and *Run for Your Wife*.

On television Henry will be forever remembered for his work with Benny Hill. Their successful association spanned twenty years, until Benny's death in 1992. Henry was also well known as a comic 'stooge' to many of Britain's other top comedians, including Tommy Cooper, Dick Emery and Charlie Drake.

Henry's small-screen credits, dating back to the 1950s, included *Let's Stay Home* (series, 1956), *Tell It to the Marines* (1959-60, as Lt. Raleigh) and *The Benny Hill Show* (from the late 1960s until 1989). By the 1960s he was a well-established television comedian, appearing in series such as *It's Tarbuck* (1964-65), *The Worker* (2 series, 1965 & '78, as Mr Pugh, with Charlie Drake), *No – That's Me Over Here!* (3 series, 1967-70, as Henry) and *Up the Workers* (2 series, 1974-76, as Dicky Bligh). His additional television credits included *The Goodies, Rising Damp, Cilla's Comedy Six – Every Husband Has One!* (1975), *Frankie Howerd Strikes Again* (series, 1981), *Mr. H. Is Late* (1987) and *Benny Hill – Unseen* (1994). His final television appearance was in 2003, playing Goff Helliwell in an episode of *Last of the Summer Wine*.

Although mainly a television and stage actor, Henry also made occasional film appearances, including *Sailor Beware!* (1956), *The Cherry Picker* (1972), *Holiday on the Buses* (1973), *Digby, the Biggest Dog in the World*

(1973), *Adventures of a Taxi Driver* (1976) and *Revenge of the Pink Panther* (1978), and he provided voices for the 1994 cartoon *Asterix in America*.

Henry McGee died at the actors' retirement home in Twickenham on 28 January 2006 after suffering from Alzheimer's disease during his final years.

William McGuirk

William played the flunkey in *Carry On Henry*. He also appeared on television (sometimes credited as Bill McGuirk) in programmes such as *Doctor Who*, *The Professionals* and *Juliet Bravo*. He died in 2001, in his 71st year.

T.P. McKenna (b. Thomas Patrick McKenna)

Irish character actor T.P. McKenna played an Archbishop in *Carry On Columbus*, but his scenes were edited from the final film release – much to the relief of the actor himself!

T.P. was born in Mullagh, County Cavan, on 7 September 1929. After initially working in a bank he trained at the Abbey Theatre of Acting and made his first stage appearances in 1953. He joined the Abbey Theatre Company in 1955 and remained with them for eight years. He was made an Honorary Life Member of the Company in 1966 and was one of only ten performers to receive this honour.

T.P.'s work in the theatre spanned over fifty years and his countless credits were testament to a truly distinguished theatrical career. In addition to numerous credits in Ireland, he also spent time with the Royal Shakespeare Company at Aldwych and in later years played at the Gate Theatre in Dublin in *Uncle Vanya*.

T.P. McKenna made his screen debut in 1959 and made over thirty film appearances, including *A Terrible Beauty* (1960), *Ferry Cross the Mersey* (1964), *Anne of a Thousand Days* (1969), *The Beast in the Cellar* (1971), *Percy* (1971), *Silver Dream Racer* (1980), *Britannia Hospital* (1982), *The Doctor and the Devils* (1985), *Valmont* (1989), *Monarch* (2000), *The American* (TV, 2001) and *The Libertine* (2004).

On the small screen T.P. was mainly seen in guest starring roles. Following his television debut in 1963 he made countless appearances, latterly in *Jack the Ripper* (1988), *Agatha Christie's A Caribbean Mystery* (1989), *Parnell & the Englishwoman* (1991), *Heartbeat, Monarch* (1996), *The Ambassador* (1997), *Kings in Grass Castles* (1998), *Making the Cut* (1999), *Longitude* (2000) and *Fair City* (2004).

T.P. McKenna was married to May White from 1956 until her death in 2006 and they had four sons and one daughter. Following a long illness,

T.P died 'quietly in his sleep' at the Royal Free Hospital, London, on 13 February 2011. He was eighty-one years old.

*Carry On ... **Quotes***

The best thing to happen to me was to have been cut out of that piece of rubbish Carry On Columbus*!*
T.P. McKenna, 1998

Desmond McNamara

A familiar face to audiences through his countless stage and television appearances, Desmond McNamara joined the *Carry On* team in 1975 for two episodes of *Carry On Laughing*. He can be spotted as the minstrel in 'Under the Round Table' and 'Short Knight, Long Daze'.

Desmond was born in St Bartholomew's Hospital, London, in 1938. After leaving school at the age of fifteen he started work as soon as possible to help out his widowed mother. His first job was 'in the print' in Fleet Street. After two years' National Service (1956-58) in Gütersloh, Germany, in Air Traffic Control he worked as a manager of a large London printing company.

Desmond began his acting career as an amateur at the Islington Players and after eighteen months auditioned for RADA. At the age of twenty-eight he gave up his job and trained for two years at the Royal Academy, where he later won the Bancroft Gold Medal.

Desmond began his professional acting career with two years in repertory at Birmingham (1968-70) in plays such as *Henry IV, Part 1*, *Volpone*, *Hamlet* and *The Italian Straw Hat*. This was followed by a further two years with the Young Vic Company, where he worked opposite Jim Dale (q.v.) in *Scapino*.

Since those early days Desmond has become one of the country's busiest stage actors, especially in Shakespearian productions. He worked for two years at the National Theatre (1972-74) and returned to the Young Vic for a further three years (1980-83). More recently he worked with the Cambridge Theatre Company (1986-89) and in the early 1990s he toured the USA in *Macbeth*, *Measure for Measure* and *The Blue Angel* (for the RSC). His additional stage credits include *Front Page* (Australian tour, 1974), *The Rocky Horror Show* (Japanese tour, 1975-76, as Riff Raff), *Camelot* (Covent Garden Festival, 1996) and *Deadwood* (1997, as Uncle Willy).

Desmond made his television debut playing a waiter in *Nearest and Dearest* in 1969. His innumerable appearances on the small screen have since included comic roles in *All at No. 20, Roll Over Beethoven, Only Fools and Horses, Streets Apart* (2 series, 1987-88, as Cliff) and *Birds of a Feather*. His dramatic appearances on TV include ten episodes of *The Bill, Wycliffe, Pie in the Sky, Maisie Raine* and *Doctors* (2005).

In addition to his prodigious list of stage and television credits, Desmond has appeared in minor roles in a handful of films, including *Adventures of a Taxi Driver* (1976), *Superman* (1978), *Staggered* (1994) and *Shakespeare in Love* (1999).

Desmond and his wife Pamela have been married since 1961 and have two sons, Robin and David. Desmond McNamara lives in Islington, North London.

Carry On ... ***Quotes***

Regarding doing the Carry On Laughing *series, it was so long ago that my memory is a bit hazy. I do remember that I was not very experienced in TV technique then, and I had to play the guitar and make up my own tune and generally get on with it! I briefly met Bernard Bresslaw – I may be wrong but I feel he was directing! Of course it rained. It had been planned that I literally 'stroll around' while singing the linking verses. Not much chance of that. I ended up doing odd snatches in doorways and under trees. I was just pleased to be able to get through it without making a complete hash of it. Even more surprising, I have never seen it!*
Working with the Young Vic at the beginning of the '70s I became friendly with Jim Dale. We had a lot of fun during those early shows and he is a very talented actor, in comedy or classics. He was superb in Scapino *(the opening show of the Young Vic) - lots of marvellous slapstick, some of it quite dangerous. In fact Jim broke an ankle leaping across a gap 10 feet above the stage! I do see him from time to time. He lives in New York and is doing very well. He came to London a while back doing Fagan in* Oliver!
Desmond McNamara, 1999

Michael Medwin OBE

An effervescent character actor and producer, Michael Medwin joined the *Carry On* team in a special guest appearance as Ginger, Kenneth Connor's boxing manager, in *Carry On Nurse*. Surprisingly, it was his only appearance in the series.

Born in London on 18 July 1923, Michael Medwin began his career in repertory theatre in 1940. He has since made countless stage appearances, perhaps most notably in the title role of *Alfie*.

Michael made his screen debut in *The Root of All Evil* in 1946. During the 1950s he was one of the country's most popular young character actors, often cast as cheeky cockneys, in films such as *An Ideal Husband* (1947), *Trottie True* (1949), *Hindle Wakes* (1952), *Genevieve* (1953), *Malta Story* (1953), *Doctor at Sea* (1955), *Doctor at Large* (1957) and *I Only Arsked* (1958). By the time he appeared in *Carry On Nurse* Michael had already appeared in fifty films.

After a decade as a jobbing film actor Michael gained overwhelming popularity on television as Corporal Springer in three series of *The Army Game* (1957-59). A forerunner to *Carry On Sergeant* (with *Carry On* actors William Hartnell, Charles Hawtrey, Norman Rossington and Bernard Bresslaw among the cast), the series was so successful that the cast even featured in The Royal Variety Performance of 1959.

The blond-haired, good-looking actor then went on to star in his own television series, *For the Love of Mike* (1959, which ran for thirty episodes) and *Three Live Wires* (1961, as Mike) before returning to film roles in 1962.

From the late 1960s Michael was rarely seen on screen or television as he chose to pursue his career as a producer, in partnership with Albert Finney. Among his credits as producer are *Charlie Bubbles* (1968), *If* (1968), *Spring and Port Wine* (1969), *Gumshoe* (1971), *Alpha Beta* (1973), *O Lucky Man!* (1973) and *Law and Disorder* (1974).

In the late 1970s he returned to the acting profession, notably on television in *Shoestring* (1979), as Don Satchley. He also resumed his film career, with roles in *The Sea Wolves* (1980), *Britannia Hospital* (1982) and *Never Say Never Again* (1983). In the 1990s he appeared in *Lovejoy* and *The Endless Game* and featured among the all-star cast of the 1994 film *Staggered*.

Still active in his eighties, most recently Michael has appeared in *Alice Through the Looking Glass* (TV, 1998) and a succession of films that included *Fanny and Elvis* (1999), *Invasion* (2005), *Framed* (2006) and *The Duchess* (2008). In 2002 he featured as Will Sanderson in an episode of *Holby City* and in the same year played Baron Hardup on stage in *Cinderella*, with Lynda Baron (q.v.). At the age of eighty-seven he was still treading the boards, playing an ageing Paris in a new version of *Romeo and Juliet* at the Bristol Old Vic. He was awarded the OBE in 2005.

Michael Mellinger

In his only *Carry On* appearance Michael Mellinger played Shindi, the faithful butler who continues to serve until the bitter end, in *Carry On Up the Khyber*.

Michael, who was born in Bavaria, Germany, on 30 May 1929, made his film debut in *South of Algiers* in 1953. He went on to make twenty screen appearances, usually in minor supporting roles, including *Stars in Your Eyes* (1956), *Three Crooked Men* (1958), *It Happened Here* (1961), *Goldfinger* (1964), *The Awakening* (1980), *Three Kinds of Heat* (1987), *Gladiator* (uncredited, 2000), *Charlotte Gray* (2001) and *Dirty Pretty Things* (2002).

On the small screen his later work included *The Ebb-Tide* (1996), *Next of Kin* (1996, as a shop owner), *Jonathan Creek* (1996) and two series of *Roger Roger* (1997-98, as Mr Mahmood).

Michael's stage credits included seasons with the RSC and Bristol Old Vic and two years with the Berliner Ensemble. He died in London on 17 March 2004.

Carry On ... **Quotes**

Carry On Up the Khyber *was rather a long time ago and my contribution very modest. The only thing I can remember about it is my attempt to keep a straight face while I was serving at the table when everything around us was collapsed and the diners continued eating as though nothing was happening.*
Michael Mellinger, 1999

Jill Mai Meredith

Jill Mai Meredith appeared in minor roles in two *Carry On* films: as the 'shapely miss' in *Carry On Cruising* and as the cigarette girl, opposite Kenneth Williams, in *Carry On Spying*.

Jill, who was born in Colchester, also appeared in *The Cool Mikado* (1962), *The Leather Boys* (1963) and *Billion Dollar Brain* (1967). She ended her brief acting career playing the secretary in three series of Ronnie Corbett's television sitcom, *No – That's Me Over Here!* (1967-70) and as Jill in *Now Look Here* (1973).

William Mervyn (b. W.M. Pickwood)

A portly, plummy-voiced character actor, well known and respected in all media, William Mervyn brought his talents to three *Carry On* films. He played Lord Paragon in *Carry On Again Doctor*, the slightly dotty physician in *Carry On Henry* and Ponsonby in *Carry On Follow That Camel*.

William Mervyn was born in Nairobi, Kenya, on 3 January 1912, and was educated in Britain. He spent the first five years of his career in repertory before making his London stage debut in *The Guinea Pig* in 1946. Over the next thirty years he built up a formidable list of stage credits, including *Ring Round the Moon, A Woman of No Importance, Charley's Aunt, The Rivals* and *The Doctor's Dilemma.*

William also found time to appear in forty films, ranging from *The Mark of Cain* (1947) to Frankie Howerd's *Up the Front* (1972). He was especially busy with screen roles from the late 1950s, with appearances in *Upstairs and Downstairs* (1959), *No Love for Johnnie* (1961), *Watch It, Sailor!* (1961), *Murder Ahoy* (1964), *The Jokers* (1967), *Hot Millions* (1968), *The Best House in London* (1969) and *The Railway Children* (1970).

On television William was perfectly cast as the Bishop in the Derek Nimmo sitcom *All Gas and Gaiters* (1967-71). By that time he was already a familiar figure to television viewers through his role as Chief Inspector Rose in *The Odd Man* (1962-63) and its subsequent spin-offs, *It's Dark Outside* (series, 1964) and *Mr. Rose* (series, 1967).

William's additional small-screen credits included *Parent-Craft* (series, 1951, as Mr Pebble), *The Skylarks* (1958), *The Young Lady from London* (series, 1959), *Saki* (1962), *Doctor Who* (1966), *The Beryl Reid Show* (1967), *Tottering Towers* (1971-72, as the 43rd Duke of Tottering) and *Mr. Wodehouse Speaking* (1972, as P.G. Wodehouse).

William continued to work until the very end of his life. His final acting roles included playing Alworthy in the 1976 film *The Bawdy Adventures of Tom Jones* and Osborne in the television series *Raffles*, which was screened after his death.

William Mervyn was married to Anne Margaret Payne Cooke and they had two sons. He died in London on 6 August 1976, aged sixty-four.

Larry Miller (b. Lawrence J. Miller)

In one of his earliest screen appearances American comedian and actor Larry Miller played the Chief in *Carry On Columbus*. He has since gone on to become one of the busiest actors of his generation.

Larry Miller was born on 15 October 1953 in Valley Stream, Long Island, New York. He had already made his mark on Hollywood playing the manager in *Pretty Woman* (1990) when he was cast to appear in *Carry On Columbus*. Almost two decades later Larry now has over fifty film appearances to his credit, including *Radioland Murders* (1994), *Corrina, Corrina* (1994), *The Nutty Professor* (1996), *For Richer or Poorer* (1997), *Nutty Professor II: The Klumps* (2000), *The Princess Diaries* (2001), *Kiss Kiss Bang Bang* (2005), *Get Smart* (2008) and *Valentine's Day* (2010).

He has also appeared just as frequently on television, notably in *The*

Pursuit of Happiness (series, 1995, as Larry), *Life's Work* (series, 1996, as Jerome Nash), *Mad About You*, *Law & Order*, *Seinfeld* and *3rd Rock from the Sun*. Larry is the author of the best-selling book, *Spoiled Rotten in America* (2005).

Freddie Mills

Former world light heavyweight boxing champion Freddie Mills appeared in two *Carry On* films: as the jewellery shop thief in *Carry On Constable* and as Lefty in *Carry On Regardless*.

Freddie Mills was born in Parkstone, Poole, on 26 June 1919. A professional boxer from the age of seventeen, he quit the profession after losing his title to Joey Maxim in 1950.

Aside from the *Carry On* series, Freddie appeared in more than a dozen films, including *Emergency Call* (1952), *One Jump Ahead* (1954), *Breakaway* (1955), *Chain of Events* (1957), *6.5 Special* (1958), *The Comedy Man* (1963) and *Joey Boy* (1965).

In an apparent suicide (though the exact circumstances remain a mystery to this day) Freddie Mills was found shot dead outside his London nightclub on 22 July 1965. He was forty-six years old.

Freddie's autobiography, *Twenty Years*, was published in 1950 and several subsequent books on his life have been released, including *Freddie Mills: His Life & Death* (by Jack Birtley, 1978) and *Who Killed Freddie Mills?* (by Tony Van Den Bergh, 1991).

Actor Don McCorkindale (q.v.) is Freddie Mills's stepson.

Juliet Mills

As the daughter of Sir John Mills and the god-daughter of Noel Coward and Vivien Leigh, Juliet Mills arguably has the finest 'pedigree' of any *Carry On* actor. Her talents were brought to just one *Carry On* film, when she bridged the gap between Shirley Eaton and Angela Douglas, to play Sally in *Carry On Jack*.

Juliet Mills was born in London on 21 November 1941, the eldest child of Sir John Mills (1908-2005) and playwright Mary Hayley Bell (1911-2005). Her younger sister is actress Hayley Mills (1946-). Educated at Elmhurst, with Imogen Hassall (q.v.), Juliet made her stage debut in 1955 playing Alice in *Alice Through the Looking Glass*. She then went on to play Pamela Harrington in *Five Finger Exercise* in London and New York and has since toured the world in plays ranging from *The Elephant Man* to *Fallen Angels*.

Juliet made her film debut at the age of eleven weeks, playing Freda's baby in *In Which We Serve* (1942). As a child she appeared in *So Well*

Remembered (1947), *The October Man* (1947) and *The History of Mr. Polly* (1949), as Little Polly.

By the age of twenty Juliet had proven herself as a capable comedy actress with her appearance in Ralph Thomas's *No, My Darling Daughter* (1961) and she subsequently worked for Peter Rogers and Gerald Thomas in *Twice Round the Daffodils* (1962) and *Nurse on Wheels* (1963). Both films were *Carry On*'s in all but name, and so it is not surprising that Juliet went on to have a lead role in the series.

Juliet's additional film credits include *The Rare Breed* (1966), *Oh! What a Lovely War* (1969), *Avanti!* (1972), *QB VII* (TV, 1974), *Waxwork II: Lost in Time* (1992) and *The Other Sister* (1999).

Since the mid-1960s Juliet has spent most of her time in America, where she made her television debut in 1960. She is still well remembered in the USA for her role in *The Nanny and the Professor* (1970), and she has made appearances in a variety of series, including *The Man from U.N.C.L.E., Hart to Hart, Columbo, Dynasty, Wonder Woman* and *Murder, She Wrote*. More recently Juliet has been familiar on US television as Tabitha Lenox in the soap *Passions* (1999-2008). In 2009 she returned to the UK and played Georgina in *Wild at Heart*, before touring on stage the following year with her husband in *Bedroom Farce*.

Juliet Mills has a son, Sean (1964-), and a daughter, actress Melissa Caulfield (1978-). Juliet married (secondly) British-born actor Maxwell Caulfield, eighteen years her junior, in 1981. The couple divide their time between California, New York and the UK.

Billy J. Mitchell

American-born actor Billy J. Mitchell played Gunner Childs in *Carry On England*.

Born in 1942, Billy came to England in the late 1960s and began his career in repertory. He quickly established himself as a versatile character actor, and over the next thirty years he made frequent appearances on stage. Among his latter appearances were *Driving Miss Daisy* and *The Dining Room* (Vienna, 1989), *On Golden Pond* (1992, as Charlie), *Porgy and Bess* (Royal Opera House, 1992, as the Coroner), *City of Angels* (Prince of Wales, 1993), *The Rainmaker* (1996, as H.C. Curry), *Born Yesterday* (1997, as Senator Hedges) and *They Offered Bob & Wilma Cash* (1998, as Lunk).

Billy also made cameo appearances in more than a dozen films. His screen roles ranged from the 1st Editor in *Superman* (1978) to Admiral Chuck Farrell in *GoldenEye* (1995). He also played Captain Pederson in *Never Say Never Again* (1983), a lawyer in *Death Wish 3* (1986), a forensic scientist in *Who Framed Roger Rabbit* (1988) and Dr Mulbray in *Indian*

Jones and the Last Crusade (1989).

On television Billy was frequently called upon for guest roles. His credits included *Space: 1999, Bergerac* (1989), *Jeeves and Wooster* (1989 & '91), *Runaway Bay* (1992), *Full Stretch* (1992), *The Famous Five* (1995) and *Kavanagh QC* (1996). One of his final roles was as an American customer at Freshco in a 1998 episode of *Coronation Street*.

Billy J. Mitchell died from cancer on 1 February 1999, aged fifty-six.

Norman Mitchell (b. Norman Mitchell Driver)

A true stalwart of British entertainment, character actor Norman Mitchell appeared in over 170 films, so it is perhaps not surprising that he found time to appear in five *Carry On* films. Norman's cameo appearances in the series represented a small proportion of a long and remarkable career.

Born in Sheffield, Yorkshire, on 27 August 1918, Norman trained as a medical student for three years before 'running away' to London to become an actor. Sixty years later Norman would admit that with his thick Yorkshire accent he found acting work difficult to find, and for some time he earned a living as a labourer and scene-shifter in Covent Garden. His acting career began in 1937 when he made his stage debut as the dwarf in *The Idiot of the Grange* after he responded to an advert in *The Stage*.

Norman was called up for active war service on 6 June 1939 and served with the Medical Corps. He was sent to the Middle East in August 1940, before spending three months with the 50th Black Cat City of London Division at Cassino and Anzio. In 1999 he would describe this experience as "... real hell – we all became bomb happy – twitchy. If anyone farted you hit the deck!". During his six years' war service Norman was also part of the Army Bureau of Current Affairs, helping to supply propaganda plays for the army, navy and air force.

Following the war Norman worked for three years on stage and he travelled to Australia in 1949 with the Stratford-upon-Avon Shakespeare Company, playing Dogberry in *Much Ado About Nothing*. He continued to make stage appearances into his eighties, his later credits including *View from the Bridge, Sir Arthur Conan Doyle* (as Sir Arthur), *Hobson's Choice* (as Hobson), *Worzel Gummidge* (1981, with Jon Pertwee, q.v.) and *J'Accuse* (1998, as Emile Zola at the French Institute).

A tall, solidly built actor, Norman Mitchell made his film debut in *The Seekers* (1954) and went on to make countless screen appearances, invariably in cameo roles. In the *Carry On*'s he can be seen as the bespectacled businessman in *Carry On Cabby*, the native policeman with Kenneth Williams in *Carry On Spying*, the heckler in *Carry On Cleo* and

Joan Sims's cab driver in *Carry On Screaming*. After an absence of over a decade Norman returned for a final role in the series as the 'Drunken Sailor' husband in Kenneth Connor's flashback scene in *Carry On Emmannuelle*.

Norman's other film appearances included *The Great St Trinian's Train Robbery* (1966), *Oliver!* (1968, as the policeman), *Bless This House* (1972, as the policeman), *Man About the House* (1974), *Legend of the Werewolf* (1975), *The Pink Panther Strikes Again* (1976), *The Revenge of the Pink Panther* (1978), *The Return of the Soldier* (1982), *The Wicked Lady* (1983), *Morons from Outer Space* (1985), *Dirty Weekend* (1987), *Revenge of Billy the Kid* (1992) and *The Lighthouse* (1999). His appearances in *Fate and Fortune* (2002) and *Meanwhile* (2003) were not seen until after his death.

Norman made his television debut in *The Way of the World* in 1951 and went on to make more than 2,000 appearances on the small screen. Indeed, his television credits read like an A-Z of British television and included appearances in *The Adventures of Sir Lancelot* (1956), *Crossroads* (as Sgt Tidmarsh), *Doctor Who, Dad's Army, The Goodies* (1970), *The Train Now Standing* (1972-73), *Some Mothers Do Have 'Em, Whatever Happened to the Likely Lads?, George and Mildred* (2 episodes), *Come Back Mrs. Noah* (1978), *Are You Being Served?, All Creatures Great and Small, Why Didn't They Ask Evans?* (1980), *Never the Twain, The Secret Diary of Adrian Mole* (1985), *Vanity Fair* (1987), *You Rang, M'Lord?* (1992), *Last of the Summer Wine* (1998, as Duckworth) and *The Lily Savage Show* (1998, as the doorman).

By the late 1990s Norman's career (which also included 500 radio broadcasts and 350 revoicing credits) spanned sixty years, and he toured the country with his lecture '60 Years in the Business'. In 1998 Norman was a welcome guest at the *Carry On* 40th Anniversary celebrations and in 1999 he played Father Christmas at the *Carry On Stuffing* celebrations. A popular and generous actor, with a fund of stories to tell, he was admired and respected by colleagues and fans alike.

Norman and his wife Pauline (who died in 1992) had one son - actor Christopher Mitchell (1947-2001) - and a daughter Jackie Mitchell, who is a writer. In his final years Norman lived in Downham Market, Norfolk, where any spare time was spent working on his autobiography, *An Actor's Life for Me*, which was published posthumously in 2003.

Although active into his eighties, the death of Norman's son from cancer on 22 February 2001 was a crushing blow from which he never recovered.

Norman Mitchell died on 19 March 2001, aged eighty-two.

Carry On ... **Quotes**

I did weekly rep. in Birmingham, Ipswich, Croydon, Sheffield ... at Eastbourne I met Kenneth Williams, who introduced me to Gerald Thomas and Peter Rogers – the Carry On *team. I was with Leo McKern (Toad) playing the fat-faced policeman in* Toad of Toad Hall *and Ken came to the stage door (the Princess Theatre) just behind Russell Square, and he said, "I live here, my father has a barbers shop and we live above it – bring Susie Maryott (John Schlesinger's sister) with you for tea between shows. I took a taxi, cost me 2/6 (half a crown). Charlie (Ken's father) was a real cockney with a moustache quiff in his waistcoat pocket. He shook my hand and said, "Hello Norman, lovely to see you – come along up." So up the stairs I went and there was Ken's mum, looking just like Ken, pouring out the tea and saying to the lady next to her, "She told me she had a 17 inch console and I said 17 inches should be enough to console anyone. Two lumps?" He (Ken) was very eccentric. When he got a flat of his own he had no furniture and you had to sit on cushions on the floor. If you wanted to use the loo he would give you a penny to go to the public lavatory across the road! I won't expand on that. I was 10 years on the council of British Actors' Equity at the same time as Ken. He was very intelligent, very astute and very well read – and of course a character.*

Norman Mitchell, 1998

Warren Mitchell (b. Warren Misell)

Warren Mitchell will be forever remembered as the bigoted Alf Garnett in the long-running sitcom *Till Death Us Do Part*. In 1964 he turned up in a memorable cameo role as auctioneer Marcius in *Carry On Cleo*.

Born in London, on 14 January 1926, Warren Mitchell trained at RADA. From a Russian-Jewish background, he has spent a lifetime in a variety of foreign character roles, specialising as Jewish cockneys.

Warren made his stage debut in 1950 at the Finsbury Park Open Air Theatre. His subsequent stage work included time with the Royal Shakespeare Company and he won the SWET Award for Best Actor for his role as Willy Loman in *Death of a Salesman*. Warren has also toured Britain and Australia in his one-man show, *The Thoughts of Chairman Alf*, and he has played the title role in *King Lear* on numerous occasions. In 1992 he was nominated for the 16th Annual Sydney Outer Critics Award for Best Male Performance and he received the Laurence Olivier Theatre Award for his role in *The Prince* in 2004.

Warren Mitchell made his film debut in *The Passing Stranger* in 1954.

He has since made over fifty screen appearances, including *Tommy the Toreador* (1959), *The Pure Hell of St Trinian's* (1960), *Doctor in Love* (1960), *The Curse of the Werewolf* (1961), *The Roman Spring of Mrs. Stone* (1962), *The Small World of Sammy Lee* (1963), *The Intelligence Men* (1965), *San Ferry Ann* (1965), *The Sandwich Man* (1966), *Drop Dead Darling* (1969), *The Assassination Bureau* (1969) and *All the Way Up* (1972). In *Carry On Cleo* he can be seen opposite Jim Dale and Kenneth Connor. His appearance was one of the most memorable cameo roles in the entire series, although in 1999 he recalled with characteristic honesty, "I can't remember a thing about *Cleo*." Later in his film career Warren starred in *Till Death Us Do Part* (1968) and *The Alf Garnett Saga* (1972), and he also featured in *Jabberwocky* (1977), *Stand Up, Virgin Soldiers* (1978), *Knights and Emeralds* (1986), *Kokoda Crescent* (1988), *Crackers* (1998) and *The 10th Man* (2006).

From the mid-1950s Warren's career took off. He played Cromwell in *The Children of the New Forest* and featured in thirteen episodes of *Hancock's Half Hour*. He went on to play Pan Malcov in *Colonel Trumper's Private War* (series, 1961) and made appearances in *Man of the World* (1962), *Out of the Unknown* (1965) and *The Avengers* (1965). In 1966 he became an overnight success as Alf Garnett in *Till Death Us Do Part*, opposite Dandy Nichols (q.v.), Una Stubbs and Tony Booth. The role of Alf, which kept Warren busy for eight years and seven series, led to a string of spin-off television series playing the same character, in *Till Death ...* (1981), *In Sickness and in Health* (1985-92) and *The Thoughts of Chairman Alf* (1998). One of the busiest actors of his generation, his many additional small-screen credits included *The Merchant of Venice* (1980), *Waterfront* (1983), *The Last Bastion* (1984), *The Dunera Boys* (1985), *Jackaroo* (1990) and *So You Think You've Got Troubles* (series, 1991, as Ivan Fox).

Since the early 1980s Warren has also worked consistently on stage and television in Australia and he became an Australian citizen in 1992. Still busy acting, his most recent television appearances include *Gormenghast* (2000), *A Christmas Carol* (2000), *Waking the Dead* (2002) and *The Shark Net* (2003). He has also toured the UK in his eighties in the stage play *Visiting Mr. Green*.

Warren has been married to former actress Constance Wake for fifty years and they have two daughters, Rebecca and Anna, and one son, actor Daniel Mitchell (who has appeared frequently on stage with his father).

Warren Mitchell divides his time between Sydney and London.

Carry On ... ***Quotes***

We worked on Till Death Us Do Part *for a period of 21 years! During which time a lot happened to all our lives, and when any of us now meet we sense that there is a curious family link having spent so many years together.*
Una Stubbs, 1999

Cheryl Molineaux

Cheryl had an uncredited role as the Women's Ward Nurse in *Carry On Doctor*.

Bob Monkhouse OBE (b. Robert Alan Monkhouse)

An effervescent national institution, Bob Monkhouse featured in a leading guest role as Charlie Sage in *Carry On Sergeant*. It was his only *Carry On* appearance.

Born on 1 June 1928 in Beckenham, Kent, Bob Monkhouse teamed up with Denis Goodwin to write scripts and short stories while they were still students; indeed, they even sold several scripts while still at school! After leaving school he trained as a cartoon animator with Gaumont British and worked as a stand-up comedian.

During his National Service with the RAF (1947-49) Bob continued to develop his comic talents by writing and performing for British forces radio. He subsequently teamed up again with Denis Goodwin and the pair became one of radio's most sought-after writing duos. In 1949 Bob became the first comedian to be put under exclusive contract by the BBC, and by the mid-1950s he was at the peak of his radio success, particularly as the writer of *Hello Playmates* (in which he also played minor characters).

Bob went on to work in stand-up, film and television comedy and drama, as a chat show guest and host and as a quiz show host. Although often attacked by critics for lack of sincerity and wasting his undoubted talents, Bob's public popularity during his fifty-year career has never faded.

By the time he appeared in *Carry On Sergeant* Bob was already a household name. Following his solo appearance in the series he went on to star in *Dentist in the Chair* (1960), *Dentist on the Job* (1961), *A Weekend with Lulu* (1961) and *She'll Have to Go* (1962), alongside many *Carry On* regulars. His additional screen credits included *Secret People* (1951, debut), *All in Good Fun* (1956) and *The Bliss of Mrs. Blossom* (1968).

In later years he made only occasional appearances as an actor, including *All or Nothing at All* (TV, 1993) and episodes of *The Upper Hand* and *Big Bad World* (2001). In 1998 he made a guest appearance in an episode of *Jonathan Creek*, playing Sylvester Le Fley, a performance that showed he was equally at home in dramatic roles.

From the late 1960s Bob Monkhouse was best known as the host of a succession of television quiz shows, including *Celebrity Squares, Family Fortunes* (1978-83), *The Bob Monkhouse Show* (1983), *Opportunity Knocks* (1987-90), *Bob's Your Uncle* (1991) and *Gagtag* (1994). In the 1990s and beyond he remained one of television's best-known faces, hosting the *National Lottery* and *Wipeout*. He was the subject of *This Is Your Life* in 1983.

Bob's first marriage, to Elizabeth, ended in divorce after twenty-three years, in 1972. The couple had one daughter, Abigail, and two sons, Gary (who died from cerebral palsy in 1992) and Simon (who died in mysterious circumstances in Thailand in 2001). Bob married his second wife, Jacqueline, in 1973.

Bob Monkhouse wrote several books, including autobiographical volumes: *Crying With Laughter* (1993) and *Over the Limit: My Secret Diaries, 1993-98* (1998). He was awarded the OBE in 1993. Indomitably, despite suffering from prostate and bone cancer, Bob continued to work until the very end of his life, taking part in numerous documentaries (including *The Unforgettable Hattie Jacques*, 2000, and *Bob Hope at 100*, 2003) as well as featuring in the 2002 Royal Variety Performance. In March 2003 he was awarded a Lifetime Achievement Award from the Television and Radio Industries Club.

Bob Monkhouse died peacefully in his sleep at his home in Eggington, Bedfordshire, on 29 December 2003, aged seventy-five.

Richard Montez

Richard played the Riff at Abdul's first tent in *Carry On Follow That Camel*.

George Moon

Character actor George Moon is credited with appearances in two *Carry On* films: as the 'scrawny man' in *Carry On Camping* and as Mr Giles (Patsy Rowlands's husband) in *Carry On Dick*.

George Moon was born in London on 19 March 1909. His screen career began with *Diggers* in 1931 and over the next forty years he appeared in over twenty films, including *An Alligator Named Daisy* (1955), *Davy* (1957), *Carry On Admiral* (1957), *Die Monster, Die!* (1965), *Promise Her Anything* (1966) and *Eskimo Nell* (1975).

On television George appeared in a range of comedy series and specials, such as *Kaleidoscope* (1953), *Shadow Squad* (1957), *Skyport* (1959), *Deep, Crisp and Stolen* (1964), *Bright's Boffins* (1970-72, as Berk), *Coppers End* (1971, as Chipper Collins), *The Fosters* (1977) and the 1977 series *Lord Tramp* (as Tipping, with Joan Sims).

George Moon died in London on 17 December 1981, aged seventy-two.

Georgina Moon

Light leading lady Georgina Moon is best remembered for her role as Erotica in Frankie Howerd's TV series *Up Pompeii* (1969-70). In the *Carry On*'s she played Joy, one of the schoolgirls, in *Carry On Camping* and Sally (opposite Diana Darvey, q.v.) in *Carry On Behind*.

Georgina began her career on stage and has since made many appearances in the theatre, both in West End productions and pantomime. She has toured the Middle and Far East (for Derek Nimmo) in *No Sex Please, We're British* and toured Norway and Sweden as Mrs Bradman in *Blithe Spirit*. In panto, Georgina has appeared in *Aladdin, Emu in Pantoland* (1978) and *Dick Whittington*.

Georgina made her film debut in *Mind Benders* (1963), and in addition to the *Carry On* series she also worked for Rogers and Thomas in the film version of *Bless This House* (1972), playing Sally Geeson's (q.v.) friend. Georgina also appeared in *Assassination Bureau* (1968) and played a schoolgirl in *Fragment of Fear* (1970).

In addition to her television role in *Up Pompeii*, Georgina played Christine in two series of *How's Your Father?* (1974-75) and Miss Finch in *You're Only Young Twice* (1977-79 & '81), with Pat Coombs (q.v.) and Peggy Mount. Georgina's guest appearances on the small screen include episodes of *Bless This House, The Dick Emery Show, Clochemerle, Doctor's Daughters* (1981), *Jim'll Fix It* (as a maiden in distress) and *Two World Wars and a Gold Clock* (as Jo). More recently she worked on stage with the late John Inman and Robin Askwith (q.v.) in *Bedside Manners* (2004).

The daughter of actor George Moon (q.v.), Georgina, who is still a working actress, lives in West London.

Maureen Moore

Maureen is credited with the role of the Pretty Probationer in *Carry On Regardless*. It was her only appearance in the series.

Valerie Moore

Valerie played a Lubi Lieutenant in *Carry On Up the Jungle*.

Albert Moses

In his only appearance in the *Carry On* series Albert Moses had the dubious task of examining Kenneth Williams when he played the Doctor in *Carry On Emmannuelle*.

Albert, who was born in 1937, has worked in films and television for the past forty years. His most recent screen appearances include *East Is East* (1999) and *The Second Jungle Book* (1997). Previously he was seen in a variety of films, including *The Spy Who Loved Me* (1977, as the barman), *What's Up Nurse?* (1977), *An American Werewolf in London* (1981, as the hospital porter) and *Octopussy* (1983, as Sadruddin).

On television Albert played Doctor Singh in *Tenko* (1981) and Suleiman in *The Jewel in the Crown* (1984). His guest appearances include episodes of *On the Buses, Robin's Nest, Minder, The Benny Hill Show* and *Boon*. He is still a working actor.

George Mossman

George played the stagecoach driver, with Brian Rawlinson (q.v.), in *Carry On Cowboy*. He is also credited as the horse master for *Barry Lyndon* (1975) and horse supplier in *Jabberwocky* (1977).

Patrick Mower (b. Patrick Archibald Shaw)

A television heart-throb of the 1970s, Patrick Mower was at the peak of his professional career when he joined the *Carry On* series for a guest appearance as Sergeant Len Able in *Carry On England*.

Born in Oxford on 12 September 1940, Patrick won a scholarship and trained at RADA. He made his stage debut starring in the musical *House of Cards* at the Phoenix Theatre. He has since appeared in numerous West End plays, including *Caesar and Cleopatra, John Gabriel Borkman* (with Sir Donald Wolfit and Dame Flora Robson), *Twelfth Night* (Royal Court), *Saint Joan* (with Dame Eileen Atkins) and *Seven Year Itch* (Albery). Patrick also ran his own theatre, the Act Inn, in Soho, where as a member of the Theatre Company he produced, directed and starred in a variety of plays, including *Wife Begins at Forty* and *Run for Your Wife*. Patrick's stage tours have included *Don Juan* and *Bing Bong* (1999, with Dennis Waterman).

Patrick Mower made his film debut in *The Devil Rides Out* in 1968. He has subsequently appeared in *Cry of the Banshee* (1970), *Percy* (1971), *Black Beauty* (1971), *Incense for the Damned* (1972), *Peer Gynt* (1976, starring role), *Manella/Frivolous Lola* (1998) and *The Asylum* (2000). In *Carry On England* Patrick was effectively cast opposite Judy Geeson (q.v.). Still well remembered for his solo appearance in the series, Patrick contributed to the 1998 documentary *What's a Carry On?*.

To the public at large Patrick is best known for his starring roles in a succession of television series, including *Callan* (1970-72, as agent James Cross), *Special Branch* (1973-74, as Detective Chief Inspector Tom Haggerty) and *Target* (1977, as Detective Superintendent Steve Hackett).

Among Patrick's additional small-screen credits are *The Avengers* (1966), *Dixon of Dock Green, Haunted* (series, 1967, as Michael West), *UFO, The Sweeney, Minder, Bergerac* and *Tales of the Unexpected*, and he has been a panellist on games shows such as *Whodunnit?* and *What's My Line?*.

Patrick has also been seen in television mini-series, including *Marco Polo* and *Samurai Wind* and he has played Rodney Blackstock in *Emmerdale* since 2000.

Patrick and his wife Anya have one son, Maxim, born in April 1999. His autobiography, *My Story*, was published in 2007.

Peter Munt

Peter is credited with the role of one of King Henry's courtiers in *Carry On Henry*.

Vicki Murden

Vicki played one of the hospitality girls in *Carry On Up the Khyber*.

Jane Murdoch

Jane Murdoch played an uncredited role as a nurse in *Carry On Doctor*.

Lionel Murton

Character actor Lionel Murton appeared in one *Carry On* film, playing the bank clerk in *Carry On Cowboy*.

Lionel Murton was born in London on 2 June 1915 and spent his early years in Canada and America.

Lionel came to prominence in the Canadian navy show, *Meet the Navy*, during the Second World War. He subsequently went on to make over forty film appearances, often in comic roles, including *The Girl Is Mine* (1950), *The Pickwick Papers* (1952), *Our Girl Friday* (1953), *Carry On Admiral* (1957), *Up the Creek* (1958), *The Captain's Table* (1959), *Make Mine a Million* (1959), *Petticoat Pirates* (1961), *On the Beat* (1962), *Summer Holiday* (1962), *Doctor in Clover* (1966), *The Dirty Dozen* (1967), *Zeta One* (1970), *Confessions of a Window Cleaner* (1974) and *The London Connection* (1979).

On television Lionel had guest roles in *The Invisible Man, Danger Man* and *The Persuaders*, and he played Colonel Irving in the 1977 series of

Yanks Go Home. His final acting role was in a 1978 episode of *George and Mildred*.

Lionel Murton, known to his friends as 'Murt', died peacefully in Basingstoke on 26 September 2006, aged ninety-one.

Jan Muzurus

Jan played the Captain of the Spanish Guard in *Carry On Jack*.

Howard Nelson (H. Vanderhorn Nelson)

Ex-bodybuilder Howard Nelson played Harry Hernia in *Carry On Emmannuelle*. He also appeared in several low-budget sex films of the 1970s and early 1980s. Howard died in London on 7 December 2007, aged seventy-three. In 2009 a police report was issued in an attempt to trace his surviving relatives.

Tricia Newby

Tricia played the topless Private Murray in *Carry On England* and two years later was seen as the nurse in the surgery in *Carry On Emmannuelle*.

Dandy Nichols (b. Daisy Sander)

Famous as the long-suffering Else Garnett in *Till Death Us Do Part*, Dandy Nichols appeared as Sid James's down-to-earth wife, Mrs Roper, in *Carry On Doctor*. It was a memorable cameo role for the talented comedienne.

One of five children, Dandy was born in Hammersmith, London, on 21 May 1907. 'Dandy' was her childhood nickname and a welcome relief to the actress who once said, "Only cows and barges are named Daisy!" Stage-struck from an early age, Dandy began her professional life as a secretary in a London boot polish factory, where she worked for twelve years. In her spare time she acted with a local dramatic society, and she was spotted by a producer who offered her work in repertory theatre in Cambridge.

During the Second World War Dandy returned to office work for two years and spent six weeks touring with the services entertainment unit, ENSA. In 1945 she returned to the acting profession and would remain busy on stage, screen and television for the next forty years.

Dandy made her film debut in *Hue and Cry* in 1947 and went on to appear in over sixty films, including *Nicholas Nickleby* (1947), *The Winslow Boy* (1948), *Here Come the Huggetts* (1948), *The History of Mr. Polly* (1949), *Dance Hall* (1950), *Mother Riley Meets the Vampire* (1952), *Meet Mr. Lucifer* (1953), *Lost* (1956), *Doctor at Large* (1957), *Ladies Who Do* (1963), *The Leather Boys* (1965), *Help!* (1965), *The Amorous Adventures of Moll Flanders*

(1965), *Doctor in Clover* (1966), *Confessions of a Window Cleaner* (1974), *Three for All* (1974) and *Britannia Hospital* (1982). Dandy is sometimes credited with a role in *Carry On Sergeant*, although she does not appear in the final film release.

From the 1950s Dandy appeared on television in *Emergency Ward 10, Dixon of Dock Green* and *Ask Mr. Pastry* (1961, series, as Mrs Spindle). From 1966 she gained worldwide recognition as Else Garnett, Warren Mitchell's "silly old moo" wife in the hugely successful sitcom *Till Death Us Do Part*. The series ran for eight years and included two feature film spin-offs (in 1968 and 1972) and an appearance in the Royal Variety Performance (1972).

After leaving *Till Death Us Do Part* Dandy gained critical acclaim for her appearances on stage, notably in *The Birthday Party, The Clandestine Marriage* and *Home* (in London and New York). She also continued her television work, notably in *The Trouble with Lilian* (1971, as Madge, with Patricia Hayes, q.v.) and *Tea Ladies* (1979, with Patricia Hayes and Mollie Sugden).

Dandy Nichols made her final television appearances in the 1985 series (and special) of *In Sickness and in Health*, by which time she was mainly confined to a wheelchair due to the effects of rheumatoid arthritis and a serious fall.

Dandy Nichols, whose only marriage was dissolved, died in a London hospital on 6 February 1986 following a long illness, aged seventy-eight.

Michael Nightingale (b. Alfred George C. Michael Nightingale)

With cameo appearances in thirteen *Carry On* films, Michael Nightingale became a familiar face to fans of the series. A reliable player in several Rogers/Thomas productions, he also appeared in two episodes of *Carry On Laughing* on television in 1975.

Michael Nightingale was born in Brighton, Sussex, on 6 October 1922. Three generations of his family worked in the entertainment industry, his father Alfred Nightingale being a stage manager and his grandfather having worked in musical comedy.

Michael joined the Royal Navy in June 1940, at the age of seventeen. He travelled to Canada to help bring over the first batch of US Destroyers and while there formed the Flotilla Concert Party, which collected $30,000 for the Spitfire Fund. In the later years of the war he was a liaison officer in France, where he broadcast in French and Italian.

In 1946 Michael joined the William Barrett Company in repertory in Scotland. His subsequent stage appearances over the next twenty years included *Twelfth Night* (1948, Open Air Theatre, Regent's Park), *Royal Highness* (1949, as Major Warchinsky), *The Winter's Tale* (1951-52, 212 performances), *The White Carnation* (1953, as Major Howard, with Ralph Richardson), *Mrs. Willie* (1955, 141 performances, with Yvonne Arnaud), *Towards Zero* (1957, 194 performances), *Not in the Book* (1958-59, 507 performances, with Wilfrid Hyde-White, q.v.) and *Two Accounts Rendered* (1964).

Michael Nightingale made his film debut in 1946 and aside from the *Carry On* series he appeared in more than thirty films. They included *Paris Express* (1953), *The Young Jacobites* (1960), *The Curse of Simba* (1963), *Sky West and Crooked* (1965), *Mutiny on the Buses* (1973), *The Return of the Pink Panther* (1975), *Dominique* (1978) and *Priest of Love* (1981). He also worked for Rogers and Thomas in *Raising the Wind* (1961) and *Bless This House* (1972).

In the *Carry On* series Michael turned up for a wonderful array of cameo roles, often as 'professional' types. He made his series debut as a bystander at Joan Sims's wine-tasting session in *Carry On Regardless*. He then played a businessman in *Carry On Cabby* and the Town Crier in *Carry On Jack*, followed by an uncharacteristic role as a caveman in *Carry On Cleo*, and played the unfortunate bank manger in *Carry On Cowboy*. In *Carry On Don't Lose Your Head* he was the "what locket?" man dancing with Joan Sims, and in *Follow That Camel* he played Nightingale, the butler. In *Carry On Camping* – again opposite Joan Sims – he was the annoying man in the cinema, and after a brief absence from the series he returned as Pearson in *Carry On Matron*. In *Carry On Girls* – in typical business-like fashion – Michael was the man on the tube with Valerie Leon, and in *Carry On Dick* he had his largest role in the series as Squire Trelawney. As a stalwart supporting actor of the series, Michael continued to appear in the *Carry On's* until the bitter end. His final two appearances, in *Carry On England* and *Carry On Emmannuelle*, saw him as an Officer and a Police Commissioner. Michael also turned up for two appearances in television's *Carry On Laughing*, playing Colonel Postwick in 'The Case of the Screaming Winkles' and as the neighbouring man at the club in 'Lamp-Posts of the Empire'.

By the 1980s Michael was semi-retired from acting. His final roles included the clerk of the court in *Witness for the Prosecution* (1982) and guest appearances in *Victoria Wood – As Seen on TV* (1986) and *Cadfael* (1994), playing Ailwin Corde.

Michael, who devoted much of his time to the Talking Newspaper for the Blind in Farnham (which he helped set up), was married and had one son, Simon.

Michael Nightingale died on 11 May 1999, aged seventy-six.

Lisa Noble

Lisa is credited as one of the Khasi's wives in *Carry On Up the Khyber*.

Trisha Noble (Patricia Ann Ruth Noble)

Leading Australian singer and actress Trisha Noble played Sally - the stunning schoolgirl who "doesn't have a pair" - in *Carry On Camping*. It was her only appearance in the series.

Trisha Noble, born in Sydney on 3 February 1944, is the daughter of Australian actor Clarence 'Buster' Noble (1913-90) and choreographer and producer Helen de Paul (1921-2007). She began her career (as Patsy Ann Noble) singing on Australian radio from the age of six. Trisha quickly became a household name, signed a contract to appear on the television programme *Bandstand* and won the first Australian Logie Award for Female Singer in 1962.

In the mid-1960s Trisha moved to England to perform as a singer and actress. One of her most memorable appearances was in the television series *Up Pompeii*, with Frankie Howerd (q.v.).

Having made her film debut in *Live It Up* in 1963, she went on to appear in a handful of films and tele-films up until the early 1980s, including *Death Is a Woman* (1966), *Fall of a Goddess* (TV, 1969), *The Private Eyes* (1980) and *Deadline* (TV, 1982).

In America, for most of the 1970s, Trisha appeared in television series such as *The Mary Tyler Moore Show*, *Police Woman*, *The Love Boat*, *Fantasy Island*, *How the West Was Won*, *Buck Rogers in the 25th Century*, *Hart to Hart* and *T.J. Hooker*. Returning to Australia in 1983 after her father suffered a heart attack, she briefly resumed her career on Australian television, notably in *Body Business* (TV, 1986). She then quit show business for almost fifteen years to concentrate on family life and private business interests.

Trisha Noble revived her career in 2000, appearing in a cameo role in *Star Wars: Episode II – Attack of the Clones* (released 2002, scenes deleted from theatrical release) and she was seen briefly in *Star Wars: Episode III – Revenge of the Sith* (2005). Since then Trisha - still stunning in her sixties - has made guest appearances on Australian TV in *Water Rats* and *All Saints* and she featured in the 2001 mini-series *Blonde*. In 2000 and 2001 she received critical acclaim touring Australia in the stage musical *Shout* and her most recent work on stage has been *Dusty – The Musical* (2006) and *Pippin* (2007). Although very much a private person who shuns publicity, Trisha was the subject of *This Is Your Life* in 2001.

Trisha's three marriages, to Alan Sharpe, Scott MacKenzie and Peter Field, all ended in divorce. From her second marriage she has one son,

Patrick (1977-), and she is now a grandmother.

*Carry On ... **Quotes***

Regarding the one Carry On *film in which I appeared – it was a very long time ago and I really have no memories of any consequence – other than it was a very enjoyable experience to work with Julian Holloway, though very few of our cute scenes together made it to the screen.*
Trisha Noble, 2001

Margaret Nolan (aka: Vicki Kennedy)

Leading lady Margaret Nolan appeared in supporting roles in the *Carry On*'s for almost a decade. Her six *Carry On* credits, which invariably saw her as a buxom beauty, secured her a memorable place in the series.

Margaret Nolan was born in Hampstead, London, on 29 October 1943. She began her career as a model under the name of Vicki Kennedy in the early 1960s before making an impressive (albeit uncredited) film debut as Dink in *Goldfinger* in 1964.

Margaret then went on to pursue a busy screen career, making over a dozen film appearances, including *Ferry Cross the Mersey* (1964), *Hard Day's Night* (1964), *The Beauty Jungle* (1965), *The Great St Trinian's Train Robbery* (1966), *Tomorrow* (1970) and *No Sex Please, We're British* (1973).

Margaret Nolan made her *Carry On* debut as Miss Jones in the opening scenes of *Carry On Cowboy*. She returned to the series in 1970 as the 'buxom lass' chased (and caught!) by Sid James in *Carry On Henry*. In *Carry On At Your Convenience* she played Popsy, Bernard Bresslaw's girlfriend, and she also turned up for a memorable cameo role as Mrs Tucker, the newly expectant mother, with Terry Scott, in *Carry On Matron*. Margaret's finest *Carry On* role was as Dawn Brakes (Miss Dairy Queen) in *Carry On Girls*, and her catfight with Barbara Windsor has gone down in *Carry On* history as a 'classic' scene. Margaret was more subdued in her final *Carry On* - *Carry On Dick* – in which she played the prim Lady Daley.

Following the *Carry On*'s Margaret continued to act for over a decade. On the small screen she appeared in episodes of *Last of the Summer Wine, The Likely Lads, The Persuaders, Q9* and *The Sweeney*. In the 1980s, slimmer than in her twenties, she was seen in *Fox* (1980) and *Crossroads* (1983, as Denise Paget), and she played a waitress in the 1986 film *Sky Bandits*. Margaret, who has been married twice and has two sons, moved to Spain in 1990.

With the revived interest in the *Carry On* series in the 1990s, Margaret Nolan became a popular figure among fans but for many years remained shy of public attention, admitting in 1999, "In light of the enormous interest in the *Carry On* films I receive constant requests for photos. My life is much too busy to answer any of them." Since her return to the UK in 2007 Margaret has become a key attraction at autograph conventions and remains outspoken in her views on the *Carry On* films. In addition to becoming well known for her artwork, Margaret Nolan has also returned to acting, and recently played Dame Margaret in the feature film *Power of Three* (2010).

Carry On ... ***Quotes***

The Carry On's *were low budget and consequently we were paid very low wages. Comedy actors, like myself, did them for the fun and the slight kudos – all the best comedians were in them. The most ever paid to an actor was £5,000 (Sid James) ... we have received nothing [since] in royalties for the constant re-runs on TV and video compilations, etc., that have sold millions worldwide ... So I have no fond memories – the fun of the work itself (if you like schoolboy humour) has been quite outweighed by the feeling of extreme exploitation.*
Margaret Nolan, 1999

Jane Norman

Jane featured in an uncredited role in *Carry On Emmannuelle*.

Richard O'Brien (b. Richard Timothy Smith)

Richard O'Brien's career was just beginning when he played an extra in *Carry On Cowboy*. He subsequently went on to work as an actor, musician, dramatist and screenwriter,

Born in Cheltenam, Gloucestershire, on 25 March 1942, Richard spent much of his early life in New Zealand. He had no formal training as an actor, although this did not prevent him beginning a film career in the early 1960s. In *Carry On Cowboy* he played an Indian on horseback. It was his second film appearance and one he recalls with special memories.

Richard O'Brien's greatest claim to fame is as the creator of the hit musical *The Rocky Horror Show*, which has enjoyed phenomenal success for more than thirty years. The film version was produced in 1975 (as

The Rocky Horror Picture Show), with Richard in a lead role. His additional screen appearances have included *A Tiger Walks* (1963), *Chamber of Horrors* (1966), *The Andromeda Strain* (1970), *The Honkers* (1972), *Jubilee* (1978), *Flash Gordon* (1980), *Shock Treatment* (1981, and wrote), *The Wolves of Willoughby Chase* (1989), *Spice World* (1997), *Dark City* (1998), *Dungeons & Dragons* (2000), *Elvira's Haunted Hills* (2001), *The Ten Commandments* (TV, 2006) and *Manor Hunt Ball* (2011).

A popular and zany personality with an obvious flair for the unusual, Richard has been seen on television as Druid Gulnar in *Robin of Sherwood* (1984-86) and he achieved cult status through his role in the popular Channel 4 game show *The Crystal Maze* (1990-96). His additional small-screen credits have included *A Hymn for Jim* (1977, and scriptwriter), *The Ink Thief* (1994) and *A Perfect Carry On* (doc. 1998).

Richard O'Brien has been married twice and has two sons and a daughter. He lives in London.

Carry On ... ***Quotes***

My memories of Carry On Cowboy *include being thrown over a horse's head, being sneered at by the riding supervisor and then watching him go over the same horse's head seconds later (there is a God), meeting several of the cast, Jim Dale and so on, and listening to tall stories told by the stuntmen. I even wrote a theme song for the show, which was listened to by Mr Rogers but politely rejected. I hung around the shooting even on my days off, as I was hooked on the whole process of film-making. I know they wondered who the hell I was, but I was never asked to leave.*
Richard O'Brien, 1998

Richard O'Callaghan (b. R. Brooke)

Leading stage and television actor Richard O'Callaghan joined the *Carry On* series for two notable and well-remembered roles: as Bertram Muffet in *Carry On Loving* and as the avaricious Lewis Boggs in *Carry On At Your Convenience*.

Richard was born in London on 4 March 1940, the only son of actress Patricia Hayes (q.v.) and actor Valentine Rooke (real name Valentine Cozens-Brooke). He trained for acting at LAMDA and made his professional stage debut in 1965 at the Royal Court as Moritz in *Spring Awakening*.

Richard has since enjoyed a busy stage career, often appearing in

Shakespearian plays. In the mid-1970s he worked for the Young Vic in numerous productions, and throughout the 1980s he toured with the Royal Shakespeare Company. His more recent credits include *Richard III* and *King Lear* (world tour, 1990), *A Midsummer Night's Dream* (Open Air, Regent's Park, 1991, as Puck), *Love's Labour's Lost* (Barbican, 1995), *The Misanthrope* (Young Vic, 1997, as Alexander), *Flight* (Olivier, 1998), *God Only Knows* (2001), *Romeo and Juliet* (2002, as Friar Laurence), *King Lear* (2005, as Gloucester) and *The Story of Vascoe* (2008, as Caesar).

In addition to the *Carry On* series, Richard's other films appearances have been *The Bofors Gun* (1969), *Butley* (1973), *Galileo* (1974), *Watership Down* (1978, voice as Dandelion) and *Dangerous Beauty* (1998).

Richard's television appearances since the mid-1960s have included *The Ronnie Barker Playhouse* (1968), *Stealer of Darkness* (1969), *Seven of One* (1973), *Born and Bred* (1978 & '80, 2 series, as Stephen Benge, with Joan Sims), *The Little World of Don Camillo* (1980), *The Merry Wives of Windsor* (1982, as Slender), *Mr Pye* (1985), *Paying Guests* (1986), *Pastoral Care* (1988, as Tom), *McCallum* (1995 & '99, as Bobby Sykes), *Agatha Christie's The Pale Horse* (1996, as Donald), *Tom Jones* (1997, as Mr Fitzpatrick), *Midsomer Murders: Bantling Boy* (2005), *Heartbeat* (2005), *Dalziel and Pascoe* (2007, as Aiden Scarman) and *New Tricks* (2008).

Richard O'Callaghan attended the *Carry On* 40th Anniversary reunion in 1998 and since then has taken part in several reunions and acted as tour guide at the *Carry On* Weekend in 1999. Richard also took part in the 1998 documentary *What's a Carry On*?, returning to Brighton to recall his memories of *Carry On At Your Convenience*, and in 2008 he was a special guest at the 50th Anniversary celebrations at Pinewood Studios.

Richard is married to Juliet Elizabeth Alliston.

Carry On ... ***Quotes***

Although I only took part in two of the Carry On *films, it delights me that people are still interested in them and enjoy watching them as much as ever. I was very fond of Charles Hawtrey, who was just as extraordinary off the screen as on. When he was once asked by a young man when he had made his first film, he became rather coy and said, "I'm not going to tell you when I made my first movie, but I made my first talkie in 1932." At which point I fell under the table, laughing. I've since discovered it was absolutely true!*
As far as making them is concerned, I have very happy memories. I remember there was always a jolly atmosphere in the studios, which was not only down to the actors, but also to the very good-humoured director, Gerald Thomas, who

kept things going at quite a lick, but still managed to encourage a great deal of hilarity while we were waiting for the shots to be set up. All the other cast members that I worked with were funny and a delight to work with.
Richard O'Callaghan, 2002

Milo O'Shea

Guaranteed to stand out in any film, Irish character actor Milo O'Shea made a notable guest appearance in the *Carry On* series as Len in *Carry On Cabby*.

Born in Dublin on 2 June 1923 (some sources say 1926), the dark-haired, bushy-browed actor began his career on stage at the age of ten. He was 'discovered' by Sir John Gielgud and joined Dublin's Abbey Players at the age of nineteen.

A relatively late arrival to the screen, Milo made his film debut as a signwriter in *Talk of a Million* in 1951. He went on to appear in *Rooney* (1958), *This Other Eden* (1959) and *Mrs. Gibbons' Boys* (1962) before his solo appearance in the *Carry On* series.

Although he went on to make over forty film appearances, Milo has been seen in fewer films than one would like. Always distinctive, his additional screen credits include an acclaimed performance in *Ulysses* (1968), *Barbarella* (1968), *Romeo and Juliet* (1968), *Paddy* (1971), *The Love Ban* (1972), *Theatre of Blood* (1973), *Steptoe and Son Ride Again* (1973), *Digby, the Biggest Dog in the World* (1973), *Arabian Adventure* (1979) and *The Verdict* (1982).

Milo found fame on British television in three series of *Me Mammy* (1969-71, as Bunjy Kennefick), with Yootha Joyce and Anna Manahan. In 1970 he featured in a one-off Milo O'Shea television special in which he performed sketches, read and sang, and later he starred in *Tales from the Lazy Acre* (series, 1972).

Milo made his New York stage debut in *Staircase* in 1968 and since then has spent most of his time in America, where he has also made numerous television appearances in series such as *St. Elsewhere*, *The Golden Girls*, *Beauty and the Beast* and *Cheers* (as Uncle Roger).

Constantly busy on stage throughout his long career, Milo managed to find time to return to film roles in the 1990s, notably opposite Maureen O'Hara in *Only the Lonely* (1991), and he was nominated for a Grammy Award (for Best Comedy Actor) for his role in the TV series *Seinfeld* in 1996.

Still busy into his eighties, Milo's recent appearances have been in films such as *The Matchmaker* (1997), *Moonglow* (2000), *Puckoon* (2001) and *Happy As Larry* (2002), and his latest television roles have included Milo in *Madigan Men* and Chief Justice Roy Ashland in *The West Wing* (2003-04).

Milo continues to divide his time between America and the UK. He is married to actress Kitty O'Sullivan.

Richard O'Sullivan

Now best known for his roles in the long-running sitcoms *Man About the House* and *Robin's Nest*, Richard O'Sullivan was still a teenager when he played school pupil Robin Stevens in *Carry On Teacher*. It was his only role in the *Carry On* series.

Richard O'Sullivan was born in Chiswick, London, on 7 May 1944. He began his career as a child actor and trained at the Corona Stage Academy. After making his screen debut in *The Stranger's Hand* in 1952 Richard went on to appear in more than twenty films, including *Dance, Little Lady* (1954), *The Secret* (1955), *It's Great to be Young* (1956), *No Time for Tears* (1959), *The Nun's Story* (1959), *The Prince and the Pauper* (1962) and *Cleopatra* (1963). Richard also appeared with Sir Cliff Richard in the musicals *The Young Ones* (1961) and *Wonderful Life* (1964).

Richard began his rise to television stardom in *Doctor at Large* (series, 1971, as Lawrence Bingham) and opposite Beryl Reid (q.v.) in *Alcock and Gander* (series, 1972, as Richard Gander). He became an overnight star as Robin Tripp in the long-running sitcom *Man About the House* (6 series, 1973-76), with Paula Wilcox, Sally Thomsett, Yootha Joyce and Brian Murphy. The success of *Man About the House* made Richard one of the country's best-known comedy actors and also inspired a 1973 feature film and spin-off series for both Richard and Yootha Joyce and Brian Murphy.

Following *Man About the House* Robin resurrected the character of Robin Tripp in six series of *Robin's Nest* (1977-81). In the early 1980s he starred in the title role of *Dick Turpin* before returning to television sitcom in *Me and My Girl* (6 series, 1984-88, as Simon Harrap).

His additional small-screen appearances include *Foreign Affairs* (series, 1966, with Leslie Phillips), *Great Expectations* (1967, as Herbert Pocket), *Now Look Here ...* (series, 1971, as Keith), *Mr. H Is Late* (1987) and *Trouble in Mind* (series, 1991, as Adam Charlesworth).

In the early 1990s Richard battled alcohol addiction before returning to the profession on radio and doing voice-overs. In poor health for some time, he suffered a stroke in 2003 and has since lived at the actors' retirement home in Twickenham. His last acting role to date was as Henry in the 1996 short film *Holed*, although he did provide commentary for the DVD release of *Carry On Teacher*.

Richard's first marriage to model Diana Terry ended in divorce and he married secondly (in 1988) Christine Smart. He has one son, James, from a relationship with his *Robin's Nest* co-star, actress Tessa Wyatt (1948-).

Richard Olley

Richard played Gunner Parkes in *Carry On England*.

Julian Orchard

A popular supporting actor in more than thirty films, Julian Orchard appeared in four *Carry On* films and also worked for Peter Rogers and Gerald Thomas in the film version of *Bless This House* (1972), playing Sid James's neighbour.

Julian Orchard was born in Wheatley, Oxfordshire, on 3 March 1930. He was an art student at Oxford before joining the RAF, where his talent for acting and singing emerged. Following demobilisation he attended the Guildhall School of Music and Drama, and after a couple of terms he made his stage debut in *Penny Plain* (St Martins, 1951, with Joyce Grenfell).

Julian's subsequent stage appearances included *Wild Thyme* (1955, as Ernie Walker), *Pickwick* (1963, as Augustus Snodgrass), *Winnie the Pooh* (1970, as Eeyore), *Alice in Wonderland* (1973, as Caterpillar/Mouse), *The Tempest* (1974, as Trinculo) and *Cinderella* (1976, as an Ugly Sister).

In films from the 1950s, Julian's screen credits included *On the Beat* (1960), *Crooks Anonymous* (1962), *Hide and Seek* (1963), *The Spy with the Cold Nose* (1965), *Man About the House* (1974) and *The Adventure of Sherlock Holmes' Smarter Brother* (1975). Among his final film appearances were *The Slipper and the Rose* (1976), *Adventures of a Private Eye* (1977), *Revenge of the Pink Panther* (1978) and *The London Connection* (1979).

Tall and dark-haired, Julian made his *Carry On* debut as the doctor in *Carry On Follow That Camel*. He had an uncredited role as the 'Rake' in *Carry On Don't Lose Your Head* and in the following year he played Bernard Bresslaw's friend, Fred, in *Carry On Doctor*. His final role in the series was his most memorable, when he played the Duc de Poncenay in *Carry On Henry*.

On the small screen Julian worked opposite most of Britain's top comedians, including Benny Hill, Frankie Howerd and Roy Kinnear. He also featured in guest roles and numerous specials, including *Haven of Rest* (1970), *Cucumber Castle* (1970), *Grubstreet* (1973) and *Dawson and Friends* (1977) as well as two series of *Whack-O!* (1971-72, as Oliver Pettigrew).

Julian Orchard was married to former dancer Susan and they had one son, Christopher. Julian died in London, following a short illness, on 21 June 1979. He was just forty-nine years old.

Brian Osborne

A diverse character actor, whose credits range from bit-parts on television to seasons with the Royal Shakespeare Company on stage, Brian Osborne became a familiar supporting actor in the *Carry On* series in the 1970s. In addition to appearing in six *Carry On* films, Brian was a regular in *Carry On Laughing* on television in 1975.

Born in Bath in 1940 and from a Welsh background, Brian made his *Carry On* debut as the ambulance driver in *Carry On Matron*. He went on to play a stallholder (selling the love potion) in *Carry On Abroad*, the 'half quid' citizen in *Carry On Girls*, Browning in *Carry On Dick* and Bob in *Carry On Behind*. In the same year Brain secured his position in the history of the *Carry On's* with appearances in seven episodes of *Carry On Laughing*: 'The Baron Outlook' (as Gaston), 'The Sobbing Cavalier' (as Cavalier), 'Orgy and Bess' (as Second Crew Member), 'One in the Eye for Harold' (as Herald), 'The Case of the Coughing Parrot' (as Harry), 'Under the Round Table' (as Knight), 'Short Knight, Long Daze' (as Herald) and 'Who Needs Kitchener?' (as Newsboy). Brian made his final *Carry On* appearance as Gunner Owen in *Carry On England* in 1976.

Brian's numerous television appearances have ensured that he has become a familiar face to viewers. His cameo performances on the small screen include a range of series, such as *Coronation Street* (Harry Watt), *Upstairs, Downstairs* (1971-72, semi-regular role, as Pearce), *Some Mother Do Have 'Em, Shine On Harvey Moon* (as Freddie) and *Minder* (as Ed). More recently Brian has been seen in *All Creatures Great and Small* (1988-90, semi-regular in 2 series, as Bert Chapman), *The Vet* (as Gallagher), *Casualty* and *Strange But True* (1997).

In addition to the *Carry On* series, Brian has appeared in a handful of other films, notably *Lock Up Your Daughters* (1969), *Women in Love* (1969), *Under Milk Wood* (1973), the screen version of *Are You Being Served?* (1977) and *Nighthawks* (1981, starring Sylvester Stallone). Brian also worked for Peter Rogers and Gerald Thomas in the 'unofficial' *Carry On* of 1972, *Bless This House* (playing the removal van driver).

Away from acting, Brian, who is a trained engineer, enjoys rugby, swimming, motorcycles and tanks.

Zorenah Osborne

Zorenah played one of the Harem Girls in *Carry On Follow That Camel* and also had an uncredited appearance in the Beatles film *Help!*, playing a High Priestess.

Brian Oulton

A master of outrage and one of Britain's finest character actors, Brian Oulton appeared in four *Carry On* films and also worked in several other Peter Rogers/Gerald Thomas productions.

Brian Oulton was born in Liverpool on 11 February 1908. He trained for acting at RADA and made his theatrical debut as Stephani in *The Listeners* in 1928. Fifty years later he was still busy on stage.

During the Second World War Brian served in the Army (1941-46), before returning to the stage in leading parts at the Birmingham Repertory Theatre. He subsequently went on to appear in numerous productions and also directed, wrote and co-adapted several plays, including *The Thunderbolt* (1966), *Upstairs, Downstairs* (1976, in which he also played Mr Caudle) and *For Entertainment Only* (1977).

Brian made his screen debut in *Sally in Our Valley* in 1931, although his film career did not take off until the late 1940s. He made over fifty film appearances, usually in comic cameo roles as supercilious or outraged characters. Among Brian's numerous credits were roles in *The Huggetts Abroad* (1949), *Will Any Gentleman...?* (1953), *The Million Pound Note* (1954), *Doctor in the House* (1954), *Brothers in Law* (1956), *I'm All Right, Jack* (1959), *No Love for Johnnie* (1961), *On the Buses* (1971), *Ooh ... You Are Awful* (1972) and *Emily* (1976).

Brian Oulton made his *Carry On* debut in *Carry On Nurse* as the would-be snob Henry Bray, opposite Hilda Fenemore (q.v.). It set the tone for his further appearances as the store manager in *Carry On Constable*, the over-officious Brutus in *Carry On Cleo* and the superb store manager in *Carry On Camping*, opposite Charles Hawtrey and Valerie Leon (q.v.). Brian also featured in a cameo role in the 1972 Christmas special, *Carry On Stuffing*, and worked for Gerald Thomas in *No Kidding* (1960), *Raising the Wind* (1961) and *The Iron Maiden* (1962).

On television from 1937, Brian was seen in countless guest roles in a wide variety of series, including *Emergency Ward 10, The Avengers*, *Softly, Softly*, *George and the Dragon*, *Department S, Father, Dear Father*, *The Adventures of Black Beauty*, *Crown Court*, *The Squirrels*, *Happy Ever After* and *The Lenny Henry Show*. He also played Mr Hay in two series of *Hotel Imperial* (1958-60), featured in *Moody in ...* (1961) and was seen with Sheila Hancock (q.v.) in *Mr. Digby, Darling* (1969, as Mr Trumper) and *Scoop* (series, 1972, as Salter).

A scene-stealer well into his seventies, Brian's final appearances included *Gandhi* (1982, as the Clerk of the Court), *Young Sherlock Holmes* (1985, as Master Snelgrove) and *The Canterville Ghost* (TV, 1986, as Uncle

George). He also remained busy with guest roles on television and made his final acting appearance in the 1987 tele-movie *Suspicion*.

Brian Oulton was married to stage actress Peggy Thorpe-Bates (b.1914), perhaps best known to the public at large as Mrs Rumpole in the first five series of *Rumpole of the Bailey*. The couple appeared together on television as Mr and Mrs Pye in *The Young Ones* (1984), and when Peggy suffered a debilitating stroke in 1987 Brian devotedly cared for her until her death on Boxing Day 1989. Brian and Peggy had two children, Jennifer and Nicholas.

Brian Oulton died in London on 13 April 1992. He was eighty-four years old.

Bill Owen MBE (b. William John Owen Rowbotham)

Fondly remembered as one of Britain's most popular actors, Bill Owen was a regular member of the *Carry On* team during the formative years of the series. His four appearances in the series were a small part of an acting career that spanned sixty years.

Bill Owen was born in Acton Green, London, on 14 March 1914. As a teenager he performed as a singer in working men's clubs, and while employed at a clothes dying factory he became involved in amateur dramatics. By 1937 he was working as an entertainer in holiday camps, and in 1938 he began a long professional association with the Unity Theatre where between 1939 and 1952 he worked as an actor, producer, writer and eventually artistic director. In 1940 Bill was called up for war service and was enlisted in the Royal Pioneer Corps. During his leave he returned to the Unity Theatre and he was eventually discharged from the army on medical grounds.

Small, trim and dark-haired, Bill made his film debut in 1945 in *The Way to the Stars*, with Sir John Mills and Rosamund John. Subsequently he was placed under contract by the Rank Organisation and had his first starring role in *When the Bough Breaks* (1947). It was while under contract that he changed his surname. An early attempt to mould Bill into a leading man did not succeed and he would later admit, "No one knew what to do with me." He did, however, become a telling character actor in over forty films, including *Holiday Camp* (1947), *The Weaker Sex* (1948), *Trottie True* (1949), *Hotel Sahara* (1951), *Robin Hood and His Merry Men* (1952), *The Square Ring* (1953), *Davy* (1957), *On the Fiddle* (1961), *Georgy Girl* (1966), *O Lucky Man!* (1973), *In Celebration* (1974) and *Laughterhouse* (1984).

Bill made his *Carry On* debut as Corporal Bill Copping in *Carry On Sergeant* and went on to play hospital patient Percy Hickson in *Carry On Nurse*, the ever-cheerful Mike Weston in *Carry On Regardless* and Smiley

Sims in *Carry On Cabby*.

Bill Owen made his television debut in 1951 and found fame as the lovable Compo in *Last of the Summer Wine*, a role that kept him busy from 1972 until his death. As the scruffy layabout he became one of television's best-loved characters. At the same time Bill also managed occasional stage appearances, including *In Celebration* and *The March on Russia* (1989, with Patsy Rowlands, q.v.). He also played Billy Rice in a 1993 television adaptation of *The Entertainer*.

Bill married Edith Stevenson in 1946 and they had one son, Tom (1949-), who has followed in his father's footsteps with his role in *Last of the Summer Wine*. Bill's first marriage ended in divorce in 1964 and in 1977 he married former actress Kate O'Donoghue. Bill Owen was awarded the MBE in 1976 and published his autobiography, *Summer Wine and Vintage Years – A Cluttered Life*, in 1994. In private he enjoyed fishing and writing and he had a keen interest in politics.

Bill Owen, who continued to work until the end of his long life, died in London's King Edward VII Hospital on 12 July 1999, after suffering from pancreatic cancer. He was eighty-five years old.

Carry On ... **Quotes**

I am nearly 84 years old, still working after 61 years as a pro and I have few memories of the Carry On *films. I only appeared in four.*
Bill Owen MBE, 1997

I worked with Bill Owen when he was very young and called Bill Rowbotham. It was on the film Way to the Stars *where they offered him a contract but insisted he change his name. I thought it was cruel to call him Bill Owing! I last saw him at a Labour Party Conference with my late husband – by then a Cabinet Minister.*
Rosamund John (Silkin), 1998

I first met Bill Owen when I was asked to do the stage version of Summer Wine *in 1983. I had always been a fan of the programme and was thrilled to get the part of Marina, which as it turned out became the 'lucky break' that all actors dream of! It was when we did the second summer season that Roy Clark decided to put me in the series. Those two seasons were memorable in more ways than one as I got to know Bill very well. He would give parties for the company and I well remember helping him plan them, doing the shopping at Marks and Spencer, then spending the afternoon at his flat doing the preparation. The scenes we had together on stage were a joy, and often resulted in my not being able to contain my laughter when he 'improvised'. Needless to say, the audience loved it. He was always ready to listen if you wanted advice, which was invaluable.*

It may seem hard to believe, but I have no specific anecdotes. My main memory of Bill is that on many occasions I have been required to sit on his knee while bouncing around in the back of a van or sliding down a hillside and never once did he wince at my weight. Neither did he complain when we had to lie down for ages in a freezing river. He was a true gentleman. We did play a bit of a trick on him when I had jokingly said to the director I would put on a heavy disguise and play one of the small parts in an episode. He took me up on it, but decided not to inform Bill and the others. He called them for a rehearsal, I sat next to Bill, we read the scene and when I did the line I yelled it in his ear. He jumped a mile but still didn't realise it was me. After that he kept looking at me and gave me a wide berth. I was 'rumbled' though when he saw me sitting giggling with Frank (Thornton). I don't think I've ever seen him laugh so much.

It is strange on the set without him. He was so brave and never complained when it was obvious he was in terrible pain. He was a true 'pro', so determined to finish filming. When we began the other episodes, there were many occasions when I glanced across and thought I could see him sitting in his chair doing the crossword. His ghost has been there with us, and I know it always will be.

Jean Fergusson, 1999

Christine Ozanne

Stage and television actress and co-founder of the Original Shakespeare Company (OSC), Christine Ozanne made her screen debut as the 'fat maid' in *Carry On Nurse*. It was the beginning of a career that has spanned fifty years.

Christine Ozanne was born in Leicester on 28 July 1936. She left school at fourteen to train as a typist, and as a teenager she joined the local amateur dramatic society. At the age of twenty Christine was accepted for RADA, where she trained as an actress and singer and won three prizes for comedy.

Over the past five decades Christine Ozanne has worked extensively on stage in plays as diverse as *The Importance of Being Earnest* (as Lady Bracknell) to a West End version of *Grease*. In 1991 Christine and her partner, theatre director Patrick Tucker (whom she met in 1965), formed the OSC, designed to discover, develop and promote the original Shakespearian methods of producing and presenting plays. Christine now devotes most of her time to running (and acting for) the OSC, which has visited America and Australia.

In addition to *Carry On Nurse*, Christine's film appearances include minor roles in *David Copperfield* (1970), *Ooh … You Are Awful* (1972), *The Bawdy Adventures of Tom Jones* (1976), *Mr Selkie* (1978) and *Lassie* (2005).

Christine made her small-screen debut in a walk-on role in *Emergency Ward 10* in 1958 and has since appeared in bit-parts in a range of series, including *Nearest and Dearest* (1968), *The Flaxton Boys* (1969, as Queen Victoria), *It's Only Me – Whoever I Am* (1974), *Within These Walls* (1975), *General Hospital* (1978), *Angels* (1980-83), *Shine on Harvey Moon* (1984), *Foul Pest* (1984, with Joan Sims and Irene Handl, q.v.), *A Small Problem* (1986, series, as Lily Harris), *Uncle Jack* (1990) and *Stick with Me, Kid* (1995, as Vera). Christine also worked frequently with Ronnie Barker in several of his series and with the 'master of mirth', Dick Emery.

Away from theatre and cinema-going, Christine's interests include cricket and maps and she has a large collection of theatre programmes dating back to 1945. She is the author of *The Actor's Survival Handbook* (with Patrick Tucker, 2005). Christine, who was present at the *Carry On* Weekend in 1999, lives in Chiswick, West London.

Carry On … ***Quotes***

I have a very clear recollection of the four days I spent filming at Pinewood in the autumn of 1958. I had just left RADA and had been pursued by an agent who saw me in a final production there and managed to get me this small part of 'Fat Maid'. I was paid £15 a day - £60 in total guaranteed - a fortune. I was rehearsing Aladdin *in Northampton, some 70 miles north of London, when my filming days came up, and I found myself at Euston Station the night before my first day's shoot with nowhere to sit and 10 hours to kill before my 'call', so I walked down Tottenham Court Road and threw myself on the mercy of the desk sergeant at the Police Station who took pity on me and let me spend the night there. Sitting at a desk in an upright chair with a single light bulb suspended above my head in an 'interrogating' position was not my idea of the glamorous life I was fully expecting to lead as a potential film star about to launch myself into the studios at Pinewood - so, with stiff joints and empty stomach, I caught the central line train to Uxbridge at 7 a.m., took a bus to the Crooked Billet Public House, and walked one mile up a country road (a familiar journey for many actors without a car in those days), but there it was, the magical entrance to Pinewood Film Studios.*

I started to recognise many well-known faces in make-up and wardrobe, but kept quiet and listened. I was totally unprepared for screen work and camera technique (like - no training at all), but it all started to come together and slotted into place as the day went on. We were constantly fed and watered, which was wonderful. I stocked up for the week, and I felt very happy and comfortable with the set-up and found the regular actors very friendly and helpful, although I do recall Kenneth Williams couldn't resist a 'newcomer' with a quick 'put-down'. We were lining up for my close-up, which was just in front of his bed, when he looked down his nose at me and said, "Of course, you're very inhibited aren't you, dear?" I expect I blushed, but I had no idea what he meant. I did my one line "Do you mind?" on the first day, and I did it in one take! I remember thinking - this is Kenneth Connor's catchphrase, but no one mentioned it at the time. At the end of the day Joan Sims offered me a lift in her chauffeur-driven limousine. She was appearing in Breath of Spring *at the Duke of York's every evening, and as we arrived at the theatre she instructed the driver to "take this young lady wherever she wants to go". (I met up with Joan again about 30 years later on a TV show, and I reminded her of her kindness. She didn't remember it at all.) So I was dropped off at Euston Station and caught the train back to Northampton.*

My next three days working on Carry On Nurse *were terrific and I learnt so much about film-making and the fabulous actors whom I had admired for so long. I travelled on the tube with Joan Hickson one day who chatted to me about her career. She was very well known in those days for small cameo roles, but she said she always got terribly nervous before each 'take', so much so that she wondered why she did it! Susan Stephen, who was a real treat to be with, gave me a lift back to town at the end of one day. I said how paranoid I was about being 'on time', but her advice was that as long as you had a good reputation for time-keeping, you should never worry on the odd occasion when something happens to delay you. The calls were always early, long before you were actually needed, so it's unlikely anyone will notice anyway.*

I was involved in one sequence of the film that was never included in the final cut. When Joan Sims picks something up under the Colonel's bed (Wilfrid Hyde White), he sticks an 'L' plate on her back. There was a follow-up shot of her walking the full length of the ward during the tea trolley round (me serving), and all the patients and staff snigger and giggle as she passes them. I have no idea why it was cut because it seemed very funny at the time and was a 'pay-off' to the gag.

All the publicity for the film suggests it was based on a play by Patrick Cargill called Ring for Catty. *Although there is some truth in this - that the idea came from him - the play was the basis for the film* Twice Round the Daffodils *starring Juliet Mills and Ronald Lewis, but you probably knew this already.*

Watching the 'rushes' at lunchtime each day was a special treat. The first one

I saw was the scene between Irene Handl and Bill Owen, who were both brilliant, of course, and did the whole thing in two 'takes' – one on her and one on him.
My biggest thrill was taking my parents to the local cinema in Leicester, my hometown, to see ME up on the big screen. Such a tiny part, but a FIRST in so many ways.
Christine Ozanne, 1998

Edward Palmer

Stage character actor Edward Palmer made his final film appearance in *Carry On Girls* when he played the harassed elderly resident.

Edward Palmer began his career with five years in repertory at York. Among his numerous stage credits over twenty-five years were *Appointment with Death* (1955), *Any Other Business* (1958, 178 performances, as Sergeant Roberts), *Look Homeward, Angel* (1962, 45 performances as Mr Farrell), *Peter Pan* (1963-65, as Smee), *I Want to See Mustov* (1967, with Terry Scott, q.v.) and *Bingo* (1979, as the Gardener).

Edward, who specialised in regional dialects, was familiar as postmen, drivers and porters in films such as *The Small Voice* (1948), *Look Before You Love* (1948), *Room at the Top* (1959), *Three Spare Wives* (1962) and *Witchfinder General* (1968).

His numerous small-screen credits included *Ivanhoe*, *Great Expectations*, *The Newcomers*, *The Railway Children*, *Upstairs, Downstairs* and *Coronation Street*. He continued to work on television up until his death.

Edward Palmer died from a heart attack on 1 December 1982.

Cecil Parker (b. C. Schwabe)

Respected character actor Cecil Parker played the First Sea Lord in *Carry On Jack*. This was his only *Carry On* appearance, although had previously worked for Peter Rogers and Gerald Thomas in *The Iron Maiden* (1962), playing Sir Giles Thompson.

Cecil Parker was born in Hastings, East Sussex, on 3 September 1897. He made his stage debut in 1922 and the first of almost ninety film appearances six years later.

On screen the rotund actor was frequently called upon to play aristocratic or military types in a wide range of 'star' character roles. He is perhaps best remembered as the cowardly Mr Todhunter in *The Lady Vanishes* (1938) and as Major Courtney in *The Ladykillers* (1955). His additional film appearances included *Princess Charming* (1933), *Lady in Danger* (1934), *Jack of All Trades* (1936), *The Spider* (1939), *Ships with Wings*

(1941), *The Weaker Sex* (1948) and *The Magic Box* (1951).

From the 1950s Cecil was mainly seen in comic roles, with appearances in *The Court Jester* (1955), *The Night We Dropped a Clanger* (1959), *The Navy Lark* (1959), *The Pure Hell of St Trinian's* (1960), *On the Fiddle* (1961) and *Heavens Above!* (1963).

In addition to his numerous film appearances, Cecil worked on television, notably as Glover in 'The 50,000 Breakfast', an episode of *The Avengers* in 1967. His final screen appearances were *The Magnificent Two* (1967), with Morecambe and Wise, and as Sir John in *Oh! What a Lovely War* (1969).

Cecil Parker died in Brighton on 20 April 1971. He was seventy-three years old.

Nicholas Parsons OBE (b. Christopher Nicholas Parsons)

A popular light actor and entertainer, Nicholas Parsons appeared in a cameo role as the 'wolf' opposite Joan Sims in *Carry On Regardless*. It was his only appearance in the series.

Nicholas Parsons was born in Grantham, Lincolnshire, on 10 October 1928 (some sources say 1923). He began his professional career as a Carroll Levis 'discovery', doing impressions and working in repertory while studying engineering at Glasgow University (and serving his apprenticeship on Clydebank). He made his stage debut as an understudy in *Chicken Every Sunday* in 1945 and went on to appear in repertory tours before becoming a resident comedian at the Windmill Theatre in the 1950s. His subsequent stage appearances have included *Boeing-Boeing* (1963-66), *Uproar in the House* (1967, with Joan Sims), *Charley Girl* (1986-87) and *The Rocky Horror Picture Show* (narrator, 1994-95).

Nicholas made his film debut at the age of nineteen in *Master of the Bankdam*. He went on to appear sporadically in comedies such as *Doctor in the House* (1954), *Simon and Laura* (1955), *An Alligator Named Daisy* (1955), *Upstairs and Downstairs* (1959) and *Doctor in Love* (1960). His film appearances dwindled after the 1960s, with only a handful of further appearances that included *Don't Raise the Bridge, Lower the River* (1968), *Danger Point* (1971), *The Best of Benny Hill* (1974) and *Mr Jolly Lives Next Door* (1987). He has also directed a couple of short films.

His career took off in 1956 when he became the 'straight man' for Arthur Haynes (1915-66). The pair appeared together on television for a decade until Arthur's sudden death. Nicholas later worked with Benny Hill, before becoming the host of game shows such as *Sale of the Century* (1971-84) and *The All New Alphabet Game Show* (1987). He is also well known as the host of radio's *Just a Minute*, a position that has kept him occupied since 1968.

Nicholas also appeared on television in *The Eric Barker Half Hour, What's It All About* (host, 1955), *The Ed Sullivan Show* and *The Ugliest Girl in Town* (1967). His more recent small-screen credits include *The Comic Strip Presents…, The New Statesman, Doctor Who* (1989, as Rev. Wainwright), *Cluedo* (series, 1993, as Rev. Green), *Hospital* (1997, as the man in the wheelchair) and *Marple: The Pale Horse* (2010). He hosted *Just a Minute* on television in 1994 and 1999 and was the subject of *This Is Your Life* in 1977. In 1995 Nicholas appeared on *The Big City*, with Peter Rogers, Jack Douglas and Fenella Fielding (q.v.), to help promote the *Carry On's*.

Away from the entertainment industry, Nicholas Parsons, who is a member of The Grand Order of Water Rats, is deeply involved with a number of children's charities, including the NSPCC, the Lord's Taverners and the Variety Club. In 1988 he was elected as Rector of St Andrew's University (a position he held for three years), and he was later given an honorary degree (Doctor of Law) by the same university. Nicholas was married to actress Denise Bryer for thirty years and they had two children, Suzy (b.1958) and Justin (b.1961), before their amicable divorce in 1984. Nicholas married secondly Annie Reynolds in 1995. In private he enjoys gardening, photography and sports. His autobiography, *The Straight Man – My Life in Comedy*, was published in 1994 and was followed up by a further volume, *With Just a Touch of Hesitation, Repetition or Deviation*, in 2010.

Nicholas Parsons was awarded the OBE in the New Year's Honours List 2004.

Drina Pavlovic

Drina had an uncredited role as the courting girl in *Carry On Behind*.

She began her career on television playing Celia in *Please Sir!* (1970-71) and went on to make film appearances in *Vampire Circus* (1972), *Bunny Capers* (1974) and *The Prisoner of Zenda* (1979). She is still a working actress, latterly mainly on stage.

Daniel/(Danny) Peacock

Actor, writer and director Daniel Peacock was among the many contemporary actors cast to appear in *Carry On Columbus*. He played Tonto the Torch.

The son of actor Trevor Peacock (best known for his role in *The Vicar of Dibley*), Daniel Peacock was born in London on 2 October 1958. He began his career in his teens after training at the Central School of

Speech and Drama.

Dark-haired and dishevelled-looking, Daniel's career as an actor has been especially diverse. He made his screen debut in *Scrooge* (1970) and has since appeared in a dozen films, including *Quadrophenia* (1979), *Porridge* (1979), *Bloody Kids* (1980), *Riding High* (1980), *Trail of the Pink Panther* (1982), *Gandhi* (1982) and *The Jewel of the Nile* (1985). He found his niche in the mid-1980s with appearances in 'alternative comedies' such as *The Supergrass* (1985), *Whoops Apocalypse* (1986) and *Eat the Rich* (1987). He also played Bull in *Robin Hood: Prince of Thieves* (1991) and featured in *Small Time Obsession* (2000) and *The Nutcracker in 3D* (2010).

On television Daniel has appeared in more than fifty programmes, ranging from children's series such as *Super Gran* and *Mr. Majeika* to classic sitcoms like *Shine on Harvey Moon* and *One Foot in the Grave*. He has also featured in dramatic roles in *Doctor Who, Boon* and *C.A.T.S. Eyes*. Among his additional credits are roles in *Robin of Sherwood*, *Girls on Top*, *Valentine Park*, *Only Fools and Horses* (as Mental Mickey), *Cluedo* and numerous episodes of *The Comic Strip Presents*....

Among Daniel's writing credits are the 1991 sitcom *Very Big, Very Soon* and the 1999 series *Harry and Cosh,* which he also directed.

Daniel Peacock is married and has one daughter (from a previous relationship).

Jacqueline Pearce (aka: J.K. Pearce)

A striking leading lady of stage, screen and television, Jacqueline Pearce appeared in a cameo role in *Carry On Don't Lose Your Head*, playing the third lady with Charles Hawtrey at Sir Rodney Ffing's ball.

Born on 20 December 1943 (some sources say 1939), Jacqueline trained for acting at RADA and later at Lee Strasberg's Actors' Studio in Los Angeles.

Jacqueline's screen credits have been diverse and include Hammer Horrors - *The Plague of the Zombies* (1966) and *The Reptile People* (1966), *Sky West and Crooked* (1966), *Don't Raise the Bridge, Lower the River* (1968), *White Mischief* (1987), *How to Get Ahead in Advertising* (1989), *Princess Caraboo* (1994, as Lady Apthorpe), *Guru in Seven* (1998) and *Daniel Deronda* (TV, 2002).

On television Jacqueline is best known as Supreme Commander Servalan in the cult 1970s sci-fi series *Blake's Seven* (1978). Among her other small-screen appearances are guest roles in *Danger Man* (1964), *The Avengers* (1966), *Callan* (1969), *Special Branch* (1974), *Measure for Measure* (1979, as Mariana) and *Doctor Who* (1985, as Chessene). She excelled in villainous roles in children's series such as *Moondial* (1990, as Miss Vole) and *Dark Season* (1991, as Miss Pendragon), and in more recent years she has been seen in *The Young Indiana Jones Chronicles, Ustinov on the Orient Express* (as Wallis Simpson), *Mrs Pollifax* (1998, with Angela Lansbury) and episodes of *Doctors* (2005) and *Casualty* (2006).

On stage, where she has been most at home in recent years, Jacqueline has appeared in *The Judge*, *A Midsummer Night's Dream*, *Wait Until Dark*, *Private Lives*, *Let's Keep in Touch* (as Rita Hayworth), *Shirley Valentine* (1998) and *A Star Is Torn* (1999, Edinburgh Festival).

Pauline Peart

Pauline played Miss Gloria Winch, a beauty contestant in *Carry On Girls*. She also played a vampire in *The Satanic Rites of Dracula* the following year.

Edmund Pegge

Character actor Edmund Pegge played the bowler in the opening scenes of *Carry On Follow That Camel*. It was his only appearance in the series.

Edmund was born in London in 1939 and emigrated to Australia when he was fifteen. He later attended Adelaide University and was a member of their Dramatic Society and Footlights Club. After extensive experience in amateur theatre productions he won a scholarship to train at NIDA (National Institute of Dramatic Art) in 1960. He returned to England in 1965 and has since spent the past four decades commuting between Britain and Australia.

In his fifty-year career, Edmund Pegge has appeared in countless stage and television productions, toured in a one-man show and worked in corporate training sessions and television and radio commercials.

In Australia, Edmund's television credits include *Home Sweet Home* (1980, as Father Murphy, with John Bluthal, q.v.), *Robbery Under Arms* (1984), *The Anzacs* (1985), *Heartbreak High* (1996), *Murder Call* (1998) and *The Potato Factory* (mini-series, 1999). In Britain he has appeared in *Take Three Girls* (1970), *It Ain't Half Hot Mum*, *Doctor Who*, *The Day of the Triffids* (1981, as Walter), *Tenko* (1984), *Chance in a Million* (1985), *Big Deal* (1986), *Howards' Way*, *Boon*, *The Bill* and *Rosemary & Thyme* (2006).

Edmund's film appearances, in addition to *Follow That Camel*, include *Scream ... and Die!* (1973), *Nightmares* (1980), *Heaven's Burning* (1997), *Maslin Beach* (1997), *Selkie* (2000), *Black and White* (2002) and *Swerve* (2011).

Away from acting, Edmund enjoys cricket, golf and tennis and is a member of Adelaide University Fencing Club. He continues to divide his time between London and Adelaide, South Australia.

Carry On ... *Quotes*

... my only recollection of that shoot was that the guest star Phil Silvers was suitably out of place amongst those English comic actors. He was bombastic in a typical American way and those English actors accepted that he needed to be the centre of attention. Of course it suited the theme of this particular Carry On *movie ... I am surprised that my name was on the cast list as I was really only a glorified extra in the opening sequence as the bowler in the cricket match. I got it because I played cricket for the Stage Cricket Club. It's the only time I've ever seen my bowling action (which alarmed me).*
As for the Carry On *movies as a whole, the success relied heavily on the idiosyncratic comic talents of those actors. No film series is easy to write but the writer had a kind of formula to write by, based on those idiosyncrasies. And I would imagine there would have been a lot of input from the actors themselves. Actors invariably make an indifferent script on the page appear wonderful. You can't write comic timing.*
Edmund Pegge, 2001

Lance Percival

A popular actor, entertainer and personality, Lance Percival played Haines, the eccentric ship's chef, in *Carry On Cruising*.

Lance Percival was born in Sevenoaks, Kent, on 26 July 1933. After entering show business with a Calypso group he achieved fame in the stage revue *One Over the Eight*, with Kenneth Williams and Sheila Hancock (q.v.) in 1960.

The toothy, heavy-jawed actor made his screen debut in *Three Men in a Boat* in 1956 and has since made over thirty film appearances, including *In the Doghouse* (1960), *What a Whopper* (1961), *Raising the Wind* (1962), *Twice Round the Daffodils* (1962), *The V.I.P.s* (1963), *Hide and Seek* (1964), *The Big Job* (1965), *Mrs. Brown, You've Got a Lovely Daughter* (1968), *Up Pompeii* (1971), *Up the Chastity Belt* (1972), *Confessions from a Holiday Camp* (1977), *Rosie Dixon – Night Nurse* (1978), *The Water Babies* (voice only, 1978) and *Jekyll and Hyde* (TV, 1990). Given his involvement in several Peter Rogers films, it is hardly surprising that Lance would be chosen to appear in a *Carry On*, famously as a last-minute replacement for a temperamental Charles Hawtrey.

It is quite possible that Lance Percival would have become a regular member of the *Carry On* team had television not taken priority over film work from 1963. On the small screen Lance is best remembered for his work in the BBC satire programme *That Was the Week That Was* (1962-

63), although he has made a variety of television appearances, both as an actor and as a personality, including *It's a Living* (1962, series as Foxy Flint), *Lance at Large* (1964, series as Alan Day), *Up the Workers* (1974-76, 2 series as Bernard Peck), *The Kenneth Williams Show* (1976), *Happy Families* (1985), *Bluebirds* (1989, series with Barbara Windsor), *Through the Keyhole*, *Noel's House Party* and *Pro-Celebrity Golf*.

In addition to work on television (and radio), Lance has worked as a scriptwriter throughout his career. Most notably, he wrote 105 episodes of the popular 1970s series *Whodunnit?*, the success of which resulted in an invitation for him to write further episodes for the NBC Network in America.

In recent years Lance Percival's work has mainly been as a guest speaker, and in 1998 he received the UK After Dinner Speaker of the Year award. In the same year he returned to Pinewood Studios for the *Carry On* 40th Anniversary reunion and was interviewed for the documentary *What's a Carry On*? He has also provided commentary for the DVD release of *Carry On Cruising*.

Lance Percival, who has one son, Jamie, has written two books: *Well Versed Dogs* (1985) and *Well Versed Cats* (1986). In his CV (written by the actor himself and testament to a brilliant wit) he lists his hobbies as golf and "facing the impossible" every day by doing the *Times* crossword. Lance lives in London with a basset hound and a Burmese cat.

Carry On ... ***Quotes***

I was only in one Carry On *film (*Cruising*) as I then went into the BBC satire show* That Was the Week That Was. *However, I did do several other Peter Rogers films before that.*

I was in a Kenneth Williams revue called One Over the Eight *and that was where I was spotted by Peter Rogers. Therefore I worked with Kenneth Williams a lot and had nothing but admiration for his work – he really did make me laugh, and I can imitate him quite well. I still use his voice and humour in my speeches.*

Kenneth Williams and Kenneth Connor used to compete to see which one could get the most laughs between film takes, so the Carry On *sets were hilarious. But my favourite, as a person, was Sid James – no fuss, knew the lines, did them very well, but was also very helpful to the new guys like me. Sid died in 1976, but if you showed his picture to any kid on the street they would recognise him immediately.*

Lance Percival, 1999

Bill Pertwee MBE (b. William Desmond Anthony Pertwee)

A well-known and popular actor of stage, television and radio as well as a successful author, Bill Pertwee appeared in cameo roles in *Carry On Loving* and *Carry On Girls*.

Born in Amersham on 21 July 1926, Bill Pertwee has a mixed ancestry – his father was English with a French background and his mother was born in Brazil. Notably, Bill is the second cousin of fellow actor Jon Pertwee (q.v.), the playwright Michael Pertwee (1916-91) and Roland Pertwee.

After leaving school at the age of sixteen Bill was employed in a variety of fields, including farming, factory work and even serving as a baggage boy for the Indian cricket team during their test match tour in 1946. Bill would later work as a stock exchange clerk and a salesman and he was employed by a window-cleaning firm for five years.

In 1954, while working as an assistant to Jon Pertwee, Bill was offered comedy material by Beryl Reid (q.v.) and began his acting career with Beryl in *The Watergate Revue*. His early work included variety, summer shows and nearly two years at London's Windmill Theatre. In 1955 Bill made his radio debut and he has now made over 1,000 broadcasts, both as a solo artist and in several series. His career on radio took a step forward when he joined the cast of *Beyond Our Ken* (1960-64), with Kenneth Williams, and its sequel, *Round the Horne* (1965-68).

Bill made his *Carry On* debut as the barman with Sid James and Jacki Piper (q.v.) in *Carry On Loving* and also played the fireman with Kenneth Connor in *Carry On Girls*. In addition, Bill recorded a scene in *Carry On At Your Convenience*, with Julian Holloway and Shirley Stelfox, which sadly hit the cutting room floor. His other screen appearances include the film version of *Dad's Army* (1971), *The Magnificent Seven Deadly Sins* (1971), *Psychomania* (1972), *Love Thy Neighbour* (1973), *Confessions of a Pop Performer* (1975), *What's Up Nurse?* (1978) and *What's Up Superdoc?* (1978).

On the small screen Bill is best known as ARP Warden Hodges in the television classic *Dad's Army*, a role that kept him busy for nine years from 1968. He also appeared in two series of *Two in Clover* (1969) and four series of *You Rang, M'Lord?* (1991-93, as PC Wilson). Bill's numerous guest appearances include episodes of *Beggar My Neighbour*, *Sykes*, *Worzel Gummidge* and *Woof!*, and he was the subject of *This Is Your Life* in 1999.

Bill Pertwee is also the author of six books: *Promenades and Pierrots* (1979), *By Royal Command* (1986), *Dad's Army: The Making of a Television Legend* (1989), *The Station Now Standing: Britain's Colourful Railway Stations* (1991) and *Stars in Battledress* (1993), together with his autobiography, *A Funny Way to Make a Living* (1996).

Bill, who took part in the Queen Mother's 100th Birthday parade in

2000, was present at the *Carry On* 40th Anniversary reunion in 1998 and is also a popular guest at *Dad's Army* celebrations.

Bill Pertwee married former actress and dancer Marion MacLeod (1928-2005) in 1960 and they had one son, Jonathan (James Pertwee, q.v.). Awarded the MBE in 2007, in private Bill Pertwee is an avid cricket fan and also enjoys gardening and swimming. He lives in Surrey.

Carry On ... ***Quotes***

The Carry On's *are a distant memory now. All I can remember is that filming my sequences was carried over only one or two days. When they re-run a film on TV and I happen to be watching I am generally surprised to see myself. In my sequences I only met the people in that scene. I see Jacki Piper quite often and Bernard Cribbins and occasionally Barbara Windsor, although I never had a scene with the latter two folk. I of course knew Ken Williams pretty well when I was in* Beyond Our Ken *and* Round the Horne. *I did a TV series with Sid James and Victor Spinetti called* Two in Clover. *I found Sid and Vic nice people to work with.*
Bill Pertwee MBE, 1997

James Pertwee (aka: Jonathan Pertwee)

Following in the footsteps of his father, James Pertwee played one of the Inquisitors in *Carry On Columbus*. Along with actors such as Toby Dale and Michael Hobbs, James was unrecognisable behind a thick black cloak.

James, who was born in 1966, has made a variety of stage, screen and television appearances. In addition to *Carry On Columbus*, he featured in *The Moscow Connection* (1995) and *Mastermind* (1997). On the small screen he has appeared in comedies such as *'Allo 'Allo* (1992, as a soldier) and *Oh, Doctor Beeching!* (1996, as a photographer).

James accompanied his father, Bill Pertwee (q.v.), to the *Carry On* 40th Anniversary reunion at Pinewood Studios in 1998.

Jon Pertwee (b. John Devon Roland Pertwee)

Jon Pertwee was best known on television as the third Doctor Who and later as the lovable children's character Worzel Gummidge. The immensely talented star of stage, screen, television and radio also brought his talents to four films.

Jon Pertwee was born in Chelsea, London, on 7 July 1919, the younger son of playwright and actor Roland Pertwee (1885-1963) and his first wife Avice. His distinguished family included his brother, writer Michael Pertwee (1916-91) and second cousin Bill Pertwee (q.v.).

After appearing in several school plays Jon auditioned for the Central School of Speech and Drama but failed to gain entrance. He was later accepted to train at RADA (1936), but his time there was short-lived: he was expelled after refusing to play the part of the wind in a Greek play! In 1937 he joined the Arts League of Service Travelling Theatre and went on to gain considerable experience in the theatre. His career was interrupted by active service with the Royal Navy during the Second World War, before returning to the stage in foreign tours in variety and a long run in *A Funny Thing Happened on the Way to the Forum* in the mid-1960s (with Kenneth Connor and Charles Hawtrey). Busy on stage into his seventies, his final credits included appearances in pantomime and *Scrooge: The Musical* (1992-94).

Jon made his screen debut in *A Yank at Oxford* in 1937 and went on to make more than forty film appearances, including *William Comes to Town* (1948), *Helter Skelter* (1949), *Stop Press Girl* (1949), *Will Any Gentleman...?* (1953), *It's a Wonderful World* (1956), *The Ugly Duckling* (1959), *Nearly a Nasty Accident* (1961), *Ladies Who Do* (1963), *A Funny Thing Happened on the Way to the Forum* (1966), *The House That Dripped Blood* (1970), *There's a Girl in My Soup* (1974), *One of Our Dinosaurs Is Missing* (1975) and *The Boys in Blue* (1983). He also provided voices for *Wombling Free* (1977) and *The Water Babies* (1978).

Jon Pertwee made his *Carry On* debut in a superb character role as the Soothsayer in *Carry On Cleo*. He later played Sheriff Albert Earp in *Carry On Cowboy* and the eccentric Scottish Doctor Fettle who meets an unfortunate fate in *Carry On Screaming*. Amazingly, a quarter of a century later Jon was one of the few veteran actors to return to the series when he played the Duke of Costa Brava in *Carry On Columbus*. Sadly, most of Jon's scenes (this being his final film appearance) hit the cutting room floor. He would later admit that he used outrageous accents and disguises in his *Carry On* roles in the hope that he would not be recognised!

A stalwart radio actor, Jon's talent for voices and accents kept him busy throughout his career, most notably in the long-running series *The Navy Lark* (1959-76). He performed on radio from the late 1930s, first coming to prominence with Eric Barker (q.v.) in *Waterlogged Spa* (1948-49), and he was constantly in demand as a voice-over artist.

Jon gained worldwide stardom on television in 1970 when he replaced Patrick Troughton in the title role of *Doctor Who*. The role kept him busy for four years and made him one of television's best-known actors.

Following *Doctor Who* Jon hosted the quiz show *Whodunnit?* (1974) and starred in the title role of the children's series *Worzel Gummidge* (4 series, 1979-81). This hugely successful comedy featured a host of well-known faces, including Una Stubbs, Megs Jenkins, Norman Bird and *Carry On* actors Joan Sims, Barbara Windsor, Bill Maynard and Norman Mitchell. Jon later resurrected the character of the popular scarecrow for *Worzel Gummidge Down Under* (2 series, 1987-89). His additional small-screen credits included *Merry-Go-Round* (1947), *Round the Bend* (1955-56), *Evans Abode* (1956-57), *The Jon Pertwee Show* (1966), *Jackanory*, *Call My Bluff*, *This Is Your Life* (subject, 1971), *The Goodies*, *Virtual Murder* and *Young Indiana Jones* (1995).

In later years Jon's popularity continued as the voice of Spotty in the children's cartoon series *SuperTed* (1983-86). He took part in several *Doctor Who* compilations and also featured as a lively guest on programmes such as *Give Us a Clue*, *Wogan*, *Noel's House Party* and *Countdown*.

Jon Pertwee married actress Jean Marsh in 1955 and following their divorce in 1960 married Ingebourg Rhoesa. They had two children, actors Dariel Pertwee (1961-) and Sean Pertwee (1964-). Jon remained busy until the very end of his life, touring the world to take part in *Doctor Who* conventions and continuing to appear on television and radio as one of Britain's most popular personalities. His autobiography, *I Am the Doctor* (with David J. Howe) was completed shortly before his death.

Jon Pertwee died suddenly in New York (from a heart attack in his sleep) on 20 May 1996, aged seventy-six.

Dorothea Phillips

A distinctive character actress of stage, screen and television, Dorothea Phillips featured in a wordless cameo role as Aunt Beatrice Grubb in *Carry On Loving*. It was her only appearance in the series.

Born in Glamorgan, Wales, in 1928, Dorothea began her acting career in the 1950s. Since then she has featured in a host of minor roles in films, tele-films and television series, most recently as Mrs Mirthless in *102 Dalmatians* (2000) and as a holiday rep in *Goodnight Sweetheart* (1999).

Dorothea's additional screen credits include *Under Milk Wood* (1973), *S.O.S. Titanic* (TV, 1979), *Santa Claus* (1985), *Duet for One* (1986), *Century* (1993) and *The Canterville Ghost* (TV, 1996). Her television guest appearances include episodes of *The Saint*, *Poirot*, *The New Statesman*, *Agony Again* and *She-Wolf of London* (series, 1990, as Aunt Elsa).

Leslie Phillips CBE

A leading man in *Carry On Nurse*, *Teacher* and *Constable*, Leslie Phillips is one of Britain's best-known actors. A key figure in the early years of the *Carry On's*, Leslie returned to the series after an absence of more than thirty years to play King Ferdinand in *Carry On Columbus*.

Leslie Phillips was born in Tottenham, London, on 20 April 1924. He made his first stage appearance – appropriately, as the Wolf – in *Peter Pan* in 1935. After training at the Italia Conti Stage School Leslie appeared in repertory before serving with the Durham Light (as a Lieutenant) during the latter stages of the Second World War.

Returning to the stage in leading roles, the good-looking young actor spent eighteen months in the stage version of *For Better, for Worse* before returning to film roles.

Leslie made his screen debut in *A Lassie from Lancashire* in 1935 and has since made well over sixty film appearances. Usually seen in leading comic roles, his screen credits include *The Galloping Major* (1950), *As long as They're Happy* (1955), *Brother in Law* (1957), *I Was Monty's Double* (1958), *The Man Who Liked Funerals* (1959), *Please Turn Over* (1959), *The Night We Dropped a Clanger* (1959), *The Navy Lark* (1959), *Inn for Trouble* (1960), *Watch Your Stern* (1960), *Raising the Wind* (1961), *In the Doghouse* (1962), *The Magnificent Seven Deadly Sins* (1971), *Don't Just Lie There, Say Something!* (1973) and *Not Now, Comrade* (1976).

Leslie made his *Carry On* debut as Jack Bell in *Carry On Nurse*, and as the handsome leading man he even managed to outshine Terence Longdon (q.v.). In *Carry On Teacher* he played child psychologist Alistair Grigg and in *Carry On Constable* (as PC Potter) his famous 'wolfish' demeanour emerged, particularly opposite a stunning Shirley Eaton (q.v.). Leslie's contribution to the series was that of a bright, bouncy, likeable cad and he is still well remembered for his work in the *Carry On's*. Surprisingly, he returned to the series in 1992 to play King Ferdinand of Spain in *Carry On Columbus*, ironically again seen opposite June Whitfield (q.v.), his co-star in *Carry On Nurse*.

In 1960 Leslie took over from Sir Dirk Bogarde in the lead role of the *Doctor* series of films and went on to appear in *Doctor in Love* (1960), *Doctor in Distress* (1963), *Doctor in Clover* (1966) and *Doctor in Trouble* (1970).

In an attempt to broaden his film range he took on a leading dramatic role in *Maroc 7* in 1967, which was not successful. From the mid-1980s Leslie resumed his film career in leading character roles, notably in *Out of Africa* (1985), *Empire Under the Sun* (1987), *King Ralph* (1991), *August* (1995), *Caught in the Act* (1995), *The Jackal* (1997), *Saving Grace* (2000), *Tomb Raider* (2001), *Collusion* (2003), *Churchill: The Hollywood Years* (2004),

Venus (2006), *Is Anybody There?* (2008) and *Late Bloomers* (2011). He also gained a new generation of fans as the voice of The Sorting Hat in the *Harry Potter* films.

On television, since 1948, Leslie has appeared in a variety of roles. He was familiar to viewers in the 1960s as Rev. Andrew Parker in *Our Man at St Mark's* (1963) and played Henry Newhouse in *Casanova* (1973). More recently Leslie played Lord Montague in *The House of Windsor* (series, 1994) and was reunited with Joan Sims in *The Canterville Ghost* (tele-film, 1996). He has also made guest appearances in *The Bill*, *Dalziel and Pascoe*, *Midsomer Murders: Painted with Blood* (2003), *Heartbeat* (2006) and *Marple: By the Pricking of My Thumbs* (2006).

On radio Leslie played Sub-Lieutenant Phillips in *The Navy Lark* for almost twenty years and also starred in series such as *Would the Last Businessman* (1978-79), *Drop Me Here, Darling* (1982) and *Starring Leslie Willey* (1987).

Now in his late eighties, Leslie Phillips continues to work consistently on stage, latterly in the works of Shakespeare and Chekhov. He has also toured the country in his acclaimed one-man show.

Leslie returned to Pinewood Studios in 1998 for the *Carry On* 40th Anniversary celebrations and unveiled a British Comedy Society plaque in memory of Charles Hawtrey. In the same year he also took part in the television documentary *What's a Carry On?* Leslie was a special guest at the *Carry On Loving* celebrations in 2000 and the Joan Sims Tribute four years later and was also a guest at the 50th Anniversary celebrations in 2008.

Leslie was married to Penelope Bartley for many years and they had two sons, Andrew and Roger, and two daughters, Caroline and Claudia, before their divorce. Leslie married secondly actress Angela Scoular (1945-2011). Leslie, who was awarded the OBE in 1998 and CBE in 2008, released his autobiography, *Hello*, in 2006.

Ambrosine Phillpotts (b. Ambrosine Marie Phillpotts)

A distinguished stage actress, Ambrosine Phillpotts graced the *Carry On*'s as Yoki's owner in *Carry On Regardless* and as the aristocratic lady in *Carry On Cabby*.

Ambrosine Phillpotts was born in London on 13 September 1912. From a distinctly upper-class background – her father was Admiral Edward Montgomery Phillpotts and her uncle the author Eden Phillpotts – Ambrosine studied music in Paris and trained at RADA.

Ambrosine made her stage debut in 1930, as Cora Ann in *The Ringer*. Over the next fifty years she appeared in repertory seasons and well over fifty stage plays, making her one of Britain's busiest and most respected character actresses. Her theatre credits included the roles of Madeline in *No Sleep for the Wicked* (1937), Kitty Cranston in *Sugar Plum* (1939), Wanda Baring in *The Morning Star* (1943), Maggie Cutler in *The Man Who Came to Dinner* (1943), Aunt Cora in *Wonders Never Cease* (1948), Marion Butterworth in *Count Your Blessings* (1951), Mrs Wagstaff in *Dry Rot* (1954), Lucy in *The Edwardians* (1959), Lady Fidget in *The Country Wife* (1964), Mrs Mercy Croft in *The Killing of Sister George* (1967), Mrs Culver in *The Constant Wife* (1971), Lady Matheson in *Separate Tables* (1977) and Lady Hunstanton in *A Woman of No Importance* (1978).

With such a long list of theatre credits, it is hardly surprising that Ambrosine appeared in relatively few films. She was, however, always distinctive, and after making her screen debut in *This Man Is Mine* (1946) she was perhaps most memorable as Lady Spratt in *Doctor in Love* (1960). Her additional film credits included *Happy Go Lovely* (1951), *The Duke Wore Jeans* (1958), *Room at the Top* (1959), *Expresso Bongo* (1959), *Life at the Top* (1965), *Beserk!* (1968), *Ooh ... You Are Awful* (1972) and *The Wildcats of St Trinian's* (1980).

On television Ambrosine was familiar as Lady Helen in *Hadleigh* (1975-76) and also played Lady Cornford in *Doctor in Charge* (1972) and Lady Skerrington-Mallett in *It's Murder But Is It Art* (1972).

Ambrosine Phillpotts, whose marriage to John Anthony Reiss ended in divorce, had two children, actress Amanda Reiss, and a son, Jeremy. Despite suffering from polymyalgia rheumatica in later life she continued to work until the year of her death. She died from heart failure at her home in Ascot, Berkshire, on 12 October 1980, at the age of sixty-eight.

Jacki Piper (b. Jacqueline Crump)

A much-loved leading lady of the *Carry On* series, Jacki Piper appeared in four of the films and such was her popularity that she had the unique privilege of being offered a two-year contract by Peter Rogers.

Jacki Piper was born in Birmingham on 3 August 1946. After studying at business college Jacki auditioned to become an ASM and went on to train at the Birmingham Theatre School. She began her career with four years in repertory at Keswick and York.

A petite, attractive blonde, Jacki made an impressive *Carry On* debut as June (Joan Sims's maid) in *Carry On Up the Jungle*. Almost immediately she was placed under contract and would continue in leading roles: as model Sally Martin in *Carry On Loving* and as Sid James's daughter, canteen worker Myrtle Plummer, in *Carry On At Your Convenience*. Jacki made a fourth (and final) appearance in the *Carry On* series in a supporting role as the hospital sister in *Carry On Matron*. Ironically, she was pregnant at the time! Very much part of the 'next generation' of *Carry On* actors, Jacki (along with contemporaries such as Richard O'Callaghan, q.v.) brought fresh interest to the *Carry On* series as it moved into the 1970s.

In addition to the *Carry On*'s, Jacki has appeared in a handful of other films, namely *The Man Who Haunted Himself* (1970), *Doctor in Trouble* (1970), *The Love Ban* (1972) and *Mr. Love* (1985). She made her television debut as a Welsh girl in an episode of *Z-Cars* and went on to appear in Galton and Simpson's *Don't Dilly Dally* (1969, as Avril). Her later television appearances included *Hogg's Back* (series, 1975, as Pearl), *The Rough with the Smooth* (1975, as Jane) and *The Fall and Rise of Reginald Perrin* (series, 1976, as Esther Pigeon). More recently Jacki has been seen in episodes of *The Bill*, *Dangerfield* (1995, as Margaret Talbot), *The Things You Do for Love* (1997, as Doreen), *Strange But True* (1997), *Take a Girl Like You* (2000), *Doctors* (2002), *Barbara* (2003, as Angela Croft) and *Wire in the Blood* (2003, as Mrs Davis).

After taking six years out of acting following the birth of her second son, Jacki returned to the stage in a tour of *No Sex Please, We're British* in the early 1980s. She went on to tour the world in similar farces, notably *Run for Your Wife*, with Terry Scott (q.v.). In more recent years Jacki has continued to remain busy on stage, her recent work including *Cinderella* (as Fairy Godmother, 1998) and *A Bedfull of Foreigners* (1999-2000, as Helga).

A charming real-life personality, Jacki Piper returned to Pinewood Studios in 1995 for the unveiling of a British Comedy Society plaque in memory of Gerald Thomas. Since then she has supported most *Carry On* celebrations at Pinewood Studios, including the 40th Anniversary celebrations in 1998, the *Carry On* Weekend in 1999 and 2001, the *Carry On Loving* celebrations in 2000 and the 50th Anniversary celebrations in 2008. Jacki also contributed to the 1998 documentary *What's a Carry On*?, and she has provided commentary for DVD releases of the series.

Jacki Piper is married to surveyor Douglas Barrell and they have two sons, Nick and Tim. Away from acting, Jacki enjoys theatre, cinema and playing tennis ("badly!"). When not working, Jacki loves to spend time on the family's old boat on the Thames with her family and their cats. She lives in Richmond.

Carry On ... **Quotes**

The Carry On's *were great fun to do, as you can imagine.* Carry On Up the Jungle *was very exciting and I really did enjoy it. The fact that I started out as a rather prim character, a sort of female version of Charles Hawtrey, and then changed into a very glamorous character, was a great change. I remember being very nervous on the first day of filming. I had done four years in rep. and then I had this huge lead in a film. Both Hattie Jacques and I hated watching ourselves in the rushes and used to hide in the canteen. On the first day of* Up the Jungle *Gerald Thomas came to the canteen to talk to me about the rushes and I assumed they weren't happy with my work. In actual fact I had a bucket of water thrown in my face and it was done with such ferocity that my false eyelashes and hairpiece were literally blown away! They had to do a second take and luckily got it right! The other funny scene is now quite famous and occurred when Terry Scott 'popped' out of his loincloth during one of his scenes. Gerald Thomas said to the make-up lady, "Nora, you haven't made that up!" She was rather prim and didn't really know what he was talking about! I later worked with Terry Scott at the end of his life when he was really quite ill. He was so determined to continue acting that he saved all his strength during the day and only got out of his wheelchair to go to the duty-free shops in the airport - he didn't trust me to pick his whisky! He was a brilliant farcer ….*

Another funny thing happened during the cake fight scene of Carry On Loving. *Bernie Bresslaw threw a cake on my head and I ended up with an ear full of cream! I was on stage later that night and didn't have time to have it syringed out. When I went to my new GP, whom I hadn't seen before (and who didn't know I was an actress), I ended up going very red as he syringed a lot of cream out of my ear which had gone off!*

I auditioned for the part of June and, on the strength of that, was offered a contract - something Peter Rogers told me he had never done for any other actor. I was terribly grateful for the opportunity to work on the films. In fact the strength of my contract enabled us to get a mortgage on our first house. The main team were just incredible and so talented. Joan Sims, for example, is a brilliant, understated actress. In fact they were all just amazing to work with …

After the Carry On's *I found that I became terribly busy with offers of work because I was well known through my involvement with the series, and it was nice that I chose to stop appearing in the series, rather than the other way round!*

The continued interest in the series is amazing - and it's so nice to see so many young people coming to Carry On *events. I was even asked to give a lecture on the series at Sheffield University. I am often so busy that I don't get chance to meet with the other actors from the series, so when we do get together it is always lovely. I saw Patsy Rowlands at the* Carry On Loving *reunion (February 2000) - it was lovely to meet up with her again, as we hadn't seen each other for years. In fact the last time was when I was on stage in Norwich*

and she saw my name outside the theatre and dropped in to see me. Valerie Leon is very sweet and always comes to see me if I'm in a play. I've worked with John Clive a couple of times in the theatre and on a number of occasions with Bill Pertwee. I also toured New Zealand with Robin Askwith and Windsor Davies (1986/87) and Robin and I did a comedy commercial together in Sydney, Australia!
Jacki Piper, 2000

Nigel Planer

An award-winning actor and best-selling writer, Nigel Planer was among many of his contemporaries when he played the Wazir in *Carry On Columbus*.

Born in London on 22 February 1953 (some sources say 1955), Nigel began his career on television in the late 1970s after training at LAMDA. He appeared in the 1981 television special *Boom Boom Out Go the Lights* before gaining cult status on the small screen as Neil, the Gormless hippie, in *The Young Ones* (1982-84).

Nigel has since enjoyed a successful small-screen career, as both a comedian and a dramatic actor. He was especially popular as the asthmatic Lou Lewis in *Shine on Harvey Moon* (3 series, 1982-84), a role he resurrected in 1995. He also played Nigel Cochrane in two series of *Roll Over Beethoven* (1985, with Liza Goddard, Richard Vernon and Desmond McNamara, q.v.) and Ralph Filthy in *Filthy, Rich & Catflap* (series, 1987), and he starred in the lead role of *Nicholas Craig, the Naked Actor* (1990-92). Nigel's dramatic acting appearances include *King & Castle* (series, 1986, as David Castle), the touching 1988 tele-film *Number 27* (with Joyce Carey) and episodes of *The Memoirs of Sherlock Holmes*, *Jonathan Creek*, *The Bill* and *Marple: The Pale Horse* (2010).

A founder member of the *Comic Strip* group, Nigel has appeared in five series of the popular television comedy, directed by Peter Richardson (q.v.), while most recently he has been familiar to television viewers as Baz Grimley in three series of *The Grimleys*.

In addition to *Carry On Columbus*, Nigel has featured in a handful of other films, including *Yellowbeard* (1983), *Brazil* (1985), *The Supergrass* (1985), *Eat the Rich* (1987), *Clockwork Mice* (1995), *The Wind in the Willows* (1996), *Diana & Me* (1997), *The Land Girls* (1998), *Virgin Territory* (2007) and *Flood* (2007).

Nigel's stage credits include *Evita* (original stage production, as Che), *Chicago* (as Amos) and *Feel Good* (as George). He received critical acclaim as Pop in the hit musical *We Will Rock You* (2001-02).

Aside from his successful acting career, Nigel is also a best-selling writer. His books include *Therapy and How to Avoid It* (1996, with Robert Llewellyn), *I, An Actor by Nicholas Craig* (1998, with Christopher Douglas), *The Right Man* (1999) and *Faking It* (2001). He has also narrated many of Terry Pratchett's best-selling novels. In 1991 Nigel formed Elephant Productions, with Jamie Rix and Clive Hedges, and in the same year he narrated their first film, *The Return of the Magic Roundabout*.

Nigel, who has been married twice, has two sons. He lives in London.

Steve Plytas

Steve Plytas, who played the Arabian official in *Carry On Emmannuelle*, had a film career spanning three decades.

Often seen in cameo roles as waiters, minor officials and dubious foreigners, Steve made his screen debut in *Passport to Shame* (1958). He went on to appear in more than twenty films, including *Very Important Person* (1961), *The Spy Who Came in from the Cold* (1965), *Theatre of Death* (1967), *Ooh ... You Are Awful* (1972), *Revenge of the Pink Panther* (1978), *The Bitch* (1979), *Superman IV* (1987) and *Batman* (1989).

On television Steve's credits included guest roles in episodes of *The Avengers*, *Doctor Who*, *Jason King*, *Man About the House*, *Fawlty Towers*, *Robin's Nest* and *Keep It in the Family* (1980).

Born in Istanbul, Turkey, on 9 January 1913, Steve Plytas appears to have died in Surrey in December 1994 (some sources say 1997).

Eric Pohlmann (b. Erich Pollak)

A superb character actor, Eric Pohlmann appeared in cameo roles in two *Carry On* films: as the Sinister Man, requiring a fourth at bridge, in *Carry On Regardless* and as the Fat Man (with Barbara Windsor) in *Carry On Spying*.

Eric Pohlmann was born in Vienna, Austria, on 18 July 1913. He escaped his native country, and the wrath of the Second World War, to take up residency in England in 1939 with his wife, actress Liselotte Goettinger (1904-68).

After several years on the British stage Eric made his screen debut in *Portrait from Life* (1948), going on to make just over a hundred film appearances over the next thirty years. His role in *Carry On Spying* perhaps typified his screen career in Britain, which often saw him cast as foreigners or villainous nightclub owners. The large, balding, mustachioed actor, although usually seen in cameo roles, was always highly distinctive. Throughout the 1950s and 1960s he was kept busy in films such as *Marry Me!* (1950), *His Excellency* (1952), *Venetian Bird* (1952), *Moulin Rouge* (1952), *The Belles of St Trinian's* (1954), *Reach for the Sky*

(1956), *A Tale of Two Cities* (1958), *Upstairs and Downstairs* (1959), *The Navy Lark* (1959), *Curse of the Werewolf* (1961), *The Devil's Agent* (1962), *The Sicilians* (1964), *Night Train to Paris* (1964), *Those Magnificent Men in Their Flying Machines* (1965), *Tiffany Jones* (1973) and *The Return of the Pink Panther* (1975). In his final years he returned to his native Austria (and Germany) and appeared in a further handful of films, culminating in *Tales from the Vienna Woods* in 1979.

In addition to his film credits, Eric worked regularly on television, playing Inspector Hoffmeister in the 1959 series *The Man Who Finally Died* and the Inspector in *Salto Mortale* (series, 1969). He also made guest appearances in programmes such *Danger Man*, *The Avengers* and *Jason King*.

Eric's first marriage ended with Liselotte's death from a heart attack in 1968 and he married secondly in 1976. From his first marriage Eric had two sons, Michael (1942-) and Stephen (1945-).

Eric Pohlmann was appearing at the Salzburg Festival when he died from a heart attack in Bad Reichenhall, Bavaria, Germany, on 25 July 1979. He was sixty-six years old.

Jackie Pool/(e)

Jackie played Betty, one of the schoolgirls, in *Carry On Camping*. It appears to have been her only film appearance.

Adrienne Posta (b. A. Poster)

A light leading lady of the 1970s, invariably seen in comic roles, Adrienne Posta made a guest appearance in *Carry On Behind*, playing ditzy housewife Norma Baxter.

Born on 1 March 1948, Adrienne began her acting career as a child. By the age of nine she had already made her film debut, playing Cathy in *No Time for Tears*. As a teenager and young adult she subsequently went on to appear in *To Sir, with Love* (1967), *Up the Junction* (1968), *Here We Go Round the Mulberry Bush* (1968), *Some Girls Do* (1969), *Spring and Port Wine* (1970), *All the Way Up* (1970), *Percy* (1971), *Up Pompeii* (1971), *The Alf Garnett Saga* (1972, as Rita), *Percy's Progress* (1974), *Three for All* (1974), *Adventures of a Taxi Driver* (1976) and *Adventures of a Private Eye* (1977).

On television one of Adrienne's earliest appearances was with Lance Percival (q.v.) in *It's a Living* (series, 1962, with Jimmy Jewel and Ben Warriss). She was later a regular guest on the *Mike Yarwood Show* and played Renata Green in *Alexander the Greatest* (series, 1971) and Iris in *Moody and Peg* (1975-76).

Although her career since the end of the 1970s has been sporadic, the bubbly actress has continued to turn up occasionally on television in guest roles. Her latter credits have included episodes of *Boon* (1987), *The Bill* (1994) and *Red Dwarf* (1997), and she played Babs in *Real Women* (1998). Most recently Adrienne has been busy with charity work.

Nosher Powell (b. Frederick Bernard Powell)

Former professional boxer turned stuntman Nosher Powell worked on both the *Carry On* films and an episode of *Carry On Laughing* on television. His brother, Dinny Powell, and son, Greg Powell, also worked on the series.

Nosher Powell was born in Camberwell, South London, on 15 August 1928. His nickname of 'Nosher' came from his hearty appetite as a child! After leaving school Nosher worked on the fruit and vegetables stalls of Covent Garden, and it was not until he carried out his National Service that his famous 'Fist of Numbness' was used to its full potential. At 6ft 4in Nosher went on to become a formidable sparring partner for boxing legends such as Sugar Ray Robinson and Muhammad Ali, and in seventy-eight professional fights Nosher was never knocked out.

Nosher entered the film industry as a stuntman in *Henry V* in 1944. He has since worked on over 130 films and "God knows how many TV shows!" Indeed his credits read like a roll call of British (and American) films and include *Oliver Twist* (1948), *Passport to Pimlico* (1949), *Emergency Call* (1952), *Doctor at Sea* (1955), *Ben-Hur* (1959), *The Guns of Navarone* (1961), *Lawrence of Arabia* (1962), *Cleopatra* (1962), *The Day of the Triffids* (1963), *Lord Jim* (1965), *The Sandwich Man* (1966), *Casino Royale* (1967), *Where Eagles Dare* (1968), *The Magic Christian* (1969), *The Alf Garnett Saga* (1972), *Superman* (1978), *Krull* (1982), *Eat the Rich* (1987), *First Knight* (1995) *Legionnaire* (1997) and the majority of the James Bond '007' movies.

In the *Carry On*'s Nosher worked as both an actor and a stuntman. His credits include *Carry On Cowboy*, *Up the Khyber* and *Henry* (as a stuntman) and *Carry On Dick* (as a footpad). He also played a Pikeman in 'One in the Eye for Harold', an episode of *Carry On Laughing*, on television in 1975.

In between stunts and acting Nosher also worked as a bouncer at Isow's famous nightclub, The Jack of Hearts. He has also worked as a minder and personal bodyguard to famous names such as Sammy Davies Jnr, Dean Martin and Shirley MacLaine. In the 1970s Nosher ran the Prince of Wales pub in Wimbledon.

Nosher Powell, who was still working in his seventies, has been married since 1951 and he and his wife Pauline have two sons, stuntmen Greg and Gary. Nosher's best-selling autobiography, *Nosher*, was published in 1999. He lives in Surrey.

Carry On ... ***Quotes***

... the Carry On *films were a twenty-two carat gold giggle from end to end. Sid James and I got on very well, as he was an ex-boxer like myself, but what a tapper. He always seemed to have left his wallet somewhere when he wanted dough (ha!). I had worked with both Hattie Jacques and Joan Sims in the Eric Sykes show and both were lovely people. Jack Douglas was one of the most humane people you could hope to meet, always putting his hand in his pocket for charity ...*
My days grow shorter now, but I have some great memories of some great guys, the likes that will never be seen again. Sure you have stars today – but they are gone tomorrow – my guys went on and on and on for years, I'm afraid they don't make them like that anymore.
Nosher Powell, 2000

Dave/(David) Prowse MBE

Famous throughout the world as Darth Vader – and familiar to British audiences as the Green Cross Code Man – Dave Prowse played Charles Hawtrey's torturer in *Carry On Henry*.

Dave Prowse was born in Bristol on 1 July 1935. A former weightlifting champion and former Mr Universe, he entered the entertainment industry in the early 1960s.

At 6ft 7in tall, Dave's film appearances often made the most of his imposing physical presence, and he was cast as 'monsters' in *The Horror of Frankenstein* (1970) and *Frankenstein and the Monster from Hell* (1974). His additional screen credits include *Casino Royale* (1967), *Hammerhead* (1968), *Crossplot* (1969), *A Clockwork Orange* (1971), *Vampire Circus* (1972), *White Cargo* (1973), *Callan* (1974), *Confessions of a Pop Performer* (1975), *The People That Time Forgot* (1977) and *Jabberwocky* (1977). In addition to *Carry On Henry*, Dave also worked with comic legend Frankie Howerd in *Up Pompeii* (1971) and *Up the Chastity Belt* (1972).

On television from 1962, Dave made guest appearances in an array of programmes, including *Doctor Who*, *The Avengers*, *The Benny Hill Show*, *The Dick Emery Show*, *The Kenneth Williams Show*, *Morecambe and Wise*, *The Two Ronnies* and *The Hitch Hikers Guide to the Galaxy* (1981).

In 1976 Dave became familiar on television as The Green Cross Code

Man. In the following year, after turning down the role of Chewbacca, he was cast as the man in the costume of Darth Vader in *Star Wars* (1977). He also donned the famous black suit in *The Empire Strikes Back* (1980) and *The Return of the Jedi* (1983). Dave's thick West Country accent was not heard in any of the films (the voice of Darth Vader being provided by James Earl Jones), but the role of Vader has ensured a cult status for Dave and he has a legion of fans throughout the world. Until recently Dave ran his own gym in London. He is now heavily involved in charity work, particularly for Action Against Arthritis, and he tours the world attending *Star Wars* conventions. Dave is married to Norma and they have three children.

Dave Prowse was awarded the MBE for services to charity and road safety in 2000. His autobiography, *Straight from the Force's Mouth*, was published in 2011.

Christine Pryor

Christine, who had an uncredited role in *Carry On Don't Lose Your Head*, went on to make minor appearances in a couple of other films. She played the party girl in *The Crimson Altar* (1968), the café waitress in *All Neat in Black Stockings* (1969) and the apartment tenant in *The Adding Machine* (1969).

Jennifer Pyle

Jennifer played Hilda, one of the pupils of Chaste Place, in *Carry On Camping*.

Peter Quince

Peter Quince made his screen debut as Gunner Sharpe in *Carry On England*. His film appearances since have included *A Bridge Too Far* (1977), *Hawk the Slayer* (1980), *Fever Pitch* (1997) and *Christie Malry's Own Double Entry* (2000).

Born in Nottingham in 1944, Peter worked in various professions before becoming an actor. His early work was on stage in repertory before moving into television.

On the small screen Peter's credits over the last twenty-five years have included *Robin's Nest*, *George and Mildred*, *Bergerac*, *London's Burning*, *Minder*, *EastEnders* (as Marco) and several episodes of *The Bill*. He is still a working actor.

*Carry On ... **Quotes***

Carry On England *was shot in five weeks during the very hot summer of 1976. I was told this was the usual timescale for* Carry On's. *Joan Sims, who was in the first* Carry On, *said they offered the cast a smaller fee, with a percentage [of royalties] - no one accepted. They never got the chance again. She also told us of some strange things they did while shooting* Carry On Camping, *which was filmed in winter. There was very little grass in the field so they sprayed the mud green. The following day it snowed. They were supposed to be sunbathing. The director said, "Carry On, it looks just like apple blossom."*
Peter Quince, 2003

Brian Rawlinson

Character actor, writer and director Brian Rawlinson appeared in cameo roles in three *Carry On* films.

Brian was born in Stockport, Cheshire, on 12 November 1931. He trained for acting at RADA, although his time there was interrupted by a term of service in Korea. His early work on stage included repertory and Shakespeare at the Old Vic. He went on to appear in numerous stage plays, receiving a nomination for the MEN Award for Best Supporting Actor for his role as Sir Timothy Farrar in *Hindle Wakes* and a Best Actor Award for his role in *Fragments*.

As well as his many acting credits, Brian was Artistic Director of the Marlow Theatre (Canterbury) and devised and scripted the series *Churchill's People*, for BBC TV.

Brian Rawlinson made his film debut as a feature player in the films of J. Arthur Rank. He played the Steward in *Carry On Cruising*, the Hessian Driver who picks up Kenneth Connor in *Carry On Cleo* and the Stagecoach Driver in *Carry On Cowboy*. Brian also worked for Peters Rogers in *The Iron Maiden* (1962), *Nurse on Wheels* (1963) and *The Big Job* (1965), and his other screen appearances included *Dangerous Exile* (1957), *Sword of Sherwood Forest* (1960), *Far from the Madding Crowd* (1967), *Blind Terror* (1971), *Helen* (1981) and *Fragments* (1992).

Brian's television career spanned forty years and included over 300 appearances, from *The Buccaneers* in 1957 to episodes of *Last of the Summer Wine*. He played Robert Onedin in *The Onedin Line* in the 1970s and also appeared in *Coronation Street*, *Constant Hot Water*, *The Bill* and *Goodnight Sweetheart*.

Brian continued to work until the very end of his life and at the time of his death was appearing at Northcott Theatre as Sir Anthony Absolute in *The Rivals*.

Although he admitted to being a private person who shunned the spotlight associated with his profession, Brian was present for the *Carry On* 40th Anniversary reunion in 1998 and was a special guest at the *Carry On Stuffing* celebrations in November 1999.

Brian Rawlinson, who never married, died suddenly in his sleep at his country home in Lyme Regis on 23 November 2000, aged sixty-nine.

Carry On ... *Quotes*

It is gratifying to know that there is such interest in my work, though I tend to keep a low profile personally and let the many performances and appearances speak for themselves. I have never had much taste for publicity.
I daresay that there are many stories and anecdotes connected with the Carry On *films that I'd be happy to recount if I could remember them. Suffice it to say that I first met Peter Gilmore when I gave him a lift back to the location in my stagecoach while filming* Carry On Cowboy, *and we have been friends ever since. You will recall that we cemented that friendship when we appeared together as the* Onedin Line *brothers in the eponymous series. He and his wife, Anne Stallybrass are still very much in touch.*
Brian Rawlinson, 1999

Andrew Ray (b. Andrew Olden)

The younger son of Ted Ray and brother of Robin Ray (both q.v.), Andrew Ray played Willie in 'And in My Lady's Chamber' and 'Who Needs Kitchener?', two episodes of *Carry On Laughing*. He was also a close real-life friend of *Carry On* legend Kenneth Williams.

Born in London on 31 May 1939, Andrew quickly followed in his father's footsteps and as a child actor appeared in a string of films, including *The Mudlark* (1950), *The Yellow Balloon* (1953), *Escape by Night* (1953) and *Serious Charge* (1959). At the age of twenty-three Andrew played Chris Walker in *Twice Round the Daffodils*, along with many of the *Carry On* team, under the direction of Gerald Thomas. He later moved away from film roles, choosing instead to tour on stage in India and Africa.

On television Andrew was memorable as Herbert Pocket in the 1974 television adaptation of *Great Expectations* and played the Duke of York in the 1979 mini-series *Edward & Mrs. Simpson* and The Duke of Windsor in *Passion and Paradise* (1989). His acting appearances became increasingly sporadic in later years, although he continued to turn up on the small screen into the 1990s, with roles in programmes such as *Inspector Morse* and *Peak Practice*.

Andrew, who featured in television documentaries for some of his famous co-stars (including Kenneth Williams and Diana Dors), was married to actress Susan Burnet (Olden) (1938-2010) from 1959 and they had one daughter, Madeline, and one son, Mark. The couple separated in 1970 but never divorced and remained the best of friends, seeing each other almost every day until Andrew's death.

Andrew Ray died from a heart attack in London on 20 August 2003, aged sixty-four.

Robin Ray (b. Robin Olden)

Having worked for Gerald Thomas in *Watch Your Stern* in 1960, Robin Ray went on to play the Assistant Manager in *Carry On Constable*. The son of Ted Ray and brother of Andrew Ray (both q.v.), he later became a popular radio panellist.

Born in London on 17 September 1934, Robin trained at RADA and made his stage debut in *The Challenging* (1960). He made his film debut in *I'm All Right, Jack* (1959) and also featured in the Beatles' film, *A Hard Day's Night* (1964), as the TV floor manager.

Robin was best known as a long-serving panellist on the BBC 2 quiz show *Face the Music*. A well-regarded expert on classical music, in the early 1970s he hosted his own quiz show on BB1, *Music Quiz*, and was also the Chairman of *Call My Bluff*.

During his career Robin Ray made over a thousand radio and television broadcasts and was one of the founders of Classic FM. He was record reviewer for Capital Radio, London, for seven years and continued to work as an advisor for Classic FM until 1997.

Robin also wrote several books, including *Robin Ray's Music Quiz*, *Favourite Hymns* and *Carols and Words on Music*, and wrote the play *Café Puccini*, which opened at Wyndham's Theatre in 1980.

Robin married actress and presenter Susan Stranks (1939-) in 1960 and they had one son, Rupert. Robin Ray died in Brighton, following a short illness, on 28 November 1998. He was sixty-four years old.

Ted Ray (Charles Olden)

A comedian, variety artist and star of radio, Ted Ray featured in a guest role as Mr Wakefield, the respected headmaster of Maudlin Street School, in *Carry On Teacher*. It was his most memorable film appearance.

Ted Ray was born in Wigan, Lancashire, on 21 November 1905 (some sources say 1909). He made his stage debut in 1927 and in the 1930s was topping the bill as a violin-playing comedian and variety artist, performing under the title of Nedlo the Gypsy Violinist. His subsequent stage career, which continued into the 1960s, included tours of South Africa and four Royal Variety Performances.

Ted Ray made his radio debut in 1939 and ten years later starred in his own series, *Ray's a Laugh*, with a host of popular actors from the time, including Charles Hawtrey and Kenneth Connor. The series spanned twelve years and 250 episodes. As a forerunner to Bob Monkhouse, during the 1950s and 1960s Ted was constantly busy on radio and television as a comedian, MC, singer and personality. From 1955 he starred in his own television series, *The Ted Ray Show*, which ran for six series. He also starred in *Hip Hip Who Ray* (series, 1956) and *It's Saturday Night* (series, 1959) and later featured in *The Jokers* and was a panellist on *New Faces* in the 1970s.

Ted made his film debut in *Elstree Calling* in 1930. He went on to appear in *Radio Parade of 1935* (1934), *A Ray of Sunshine* (1950), *Meet Me Tonight* (1952), *Escape by Night* (1953), *My Wife's Family* (1956), *The Crowning Touch* (1959) and *Please Turn Over* (1959, directed by Gerald Thomas).

Ted released two volumes of autobiography, *Raising the Laughs* (1952) and *My Turn Next* (1963), and a book about his lifelong hobby, *Golf – A Slice of My Life*. He was married to Dorothy Sybil Stevens and they had two sons, Robin and Andrew (both q.v.), both of whom followed their father into the entertainment industry.

In 1975 Ted was seriously injured in a car accident, but he continued to work on radio up until his death from a heart attack on 8 November 1977.

Cyril Raymond MBE

Cyril Raymond had already made over fifty film appearances when he played the Army Officer in *Carry On Regardless*. It was his only *Carry On* film and was one of his last screen roles.

Born on 13 February 1899 (some sources say 1895 or 1897), Cyril began his career on stage in 1915 and he went on to work in the West End in plays such as *Short Story* (with Dame Sybil Thorndike) and *The Constant Wife*. He appeared in several silent films before making the transition to talkies in the early 1930s. Among his many screen credits were *Mixed Doubles* (1933), *Night Alone* (1938), *Goodbye, Mr. Chips* (1939), *Brief Encounter* (1945, as Fred Jesson), *Dunkirk* (1958), *No Kidding* (1960) and *Night Train to Paris* (1964). During the Second World War he served in the RAF and was awarded the MBE for military service.

Cyril Raymond married actress Iris Hoey (1885-1979) in 1922 and they had one son, writer John Raymond (1923-1977). He married secondly actress Gillian Lind (1904-83) in 1937. Cyril retired from acting due to poor health in 1965 and died on 28 July 1973.

Gavin Reed

Gavin Reed played the window dresser, opposite Richard O'Callaghan (and a mannequin!), in *Carry On Loving*.

Born in Liverpool on 3 June 1931, Gavin played the Rev. Alexander Algernon Ford in *The Body Beneath* (1970). He is also credited with roles in *Tattoo* (1981), the Dustin Hoffmann classic *Tootsie* (1982) and *The Return of the Shaggy Dog* (TV, 1987).

Gavin died from respiratory failure in Portland, Maine, on 3 December 1990.

Llewellyn Rees

A distinguished figure in British acting, particularly in the politics of the profession, Llewellyn Rees played the Lord Chief Justice in *Carry On Emmannuelle*.

Born in Dorset on 18 June 1901, Llewellyn trained at RADA. After three years as a private tutor (1923-26) he made his stage debut as Inspector Garrett in *The Joker* in 1928. He subsequently enjoyed a fifty-year career in the theatre as an actor, manager and Hon. President of the International Theatre Institute.

Llewellyn built up his acting experience with two years (1930-32) in repertory in Newcastle. His subsequent stage credits included *The Lake* and *Mrs Nobby Clark*. During the 1940s and 1950s he was heavily involved in the politics of acting, holding numerous positions including General Secretary of Equity (1940-46), Governor of the Old Vic (1945-46) and Member of the British Council Drama Committee (1952-75). He returned to acting on stage, after an absence of seventeen years, in *The Public Prosecutor* (1954) and continued to work on stage well into old age.

Llewellyn's sporadic film credits, beginning in the 1950s, included *You Can't Escape* (1955), *Brothers in Law* (1957), *The Navy Lark* (1959), *The Double* (1963), *Salt and Pepper* (1968), *Cromwell* (1970), *The Ruling Class* (1972), *The Return of the Soldier* (1982), *The Dresser* (1983), *Another Country* (1984) and *A Fish Called Wanda* (1988, as Sir John).

On television Llewellyn took over from Justice Millhouse in *Whose Line Is It Anyway?* and also featured in programmes ranging from *Doctor Who* to *The Comic Strip Presents*.... Active in films and television until his nineties, Llewellyn's later work included *Boon*, *Inspector Morse* and *Jeeves & Wooster (*1992), and he played the Old Major in the Eric Idle film *Splitting Heirs* (1993). His final appearance came with a cameo role as a grumpy patient in the BBC *Screen One* film *Tender Loving Care* (starring Dawn French and Joan Sims) in 1993.

Llewellyn, who was married to Madeleine Newbury, died in Dorset on 7 January 1994, aged ninety-two.

(P.) Kynaston Reeves (b. Philip Arthur Reeves)

Kynaston Reeves, who played the Testy Old Man opposite Sid James in *Carry On Regardless*, had a film career spanning over half a century.

Born on 29 May 1893 in Hammersmith, London, Kynaston made his screen debut in *Last Defence* in 1919, after a short spell in the army. He was kept busy in character roles, latterly often as academic types, for forty years. Tall, slender and highly distinctive, he made well over seventy film appearances, including *The Lodger* (1932), *Vintage Wine* (1935), *Strawberry Roan* (1944), *The Rake's Progress* (1945), *The Winslow Boy* (1948), *The Weaker Sex* (1948), *The Mudlark* (1950), *Fun at St Fanny's* (1956), *School for Scoundrels* (1959), *In the Doghouse* (1961) and *Hide and Seek* (1963).

He also appeared frequently on television, notably as Mr Quelch in *Billy Bunter of Greyfriars School* (1952) and as Uncle Nicholas Forsyte in *The Forsyte Saga* (1967).

Active until the end of his life, Kynaston's final appearances included *Anne of a Thousand Days* (1969) and *The Private Life of Sherlock Holmes* (1970).

Kynaston Reeves died in London on 11 December 1971, aged seventy-eight.

Linda Regan

A busy stage and television actress and successful author, Linda Regan played Private Taylor in *Carry On England* and also featured as an Island Girl in *Carry On Again Christmas* on television in 1970.

Linda Regan was born in London on 5 November 1959. She began her career on stage and has now appeared in more than a hundred plays, ranging from *Macbeth* to *Cinderella*. Linda is perhaps still best remembered for her role as April in the 1980s sit-com *Hi-De-Hi!* (1984-87). Her additional television credits include *Minder* (as Liz), *Dempsey and Makepeace* (as Carla), *C.A.T.S Eyes* (as Amber), *Birds of A Feather* (as Maureen), *Over the Rainbow*, *Hale & Pace*, *Agony* (as Janice), *The Knock* (series, 1994, as June), *The Ghostbusters of East Finchley*, *Harry & Cosh*

(1999), *London's Burning* (2000), several episodes of *The Bill* and most recently *Doctors* and *Holby City*.

As well as *Carry On England*, Linda's film appearances have been *Adolf Hitler – My Part In His Downfall* (1972), *Keep It Up, Jack* (1973), *Confessions of a Pop Performer* (1975), *Hardcore* (1977), *Adventures of a Private Eye* (1977), *Quadrophenia* (1979), *Lost in London* (TV, 1985) and *The Last Horror Movie* (2003).

Linda is the second wife of actor Brian Murphy (1933-), best known for his role as George in the classic TV sit-com *George and Mildred*. Her novels include *Dead Like Her* (2009), *Passion Killers* (2007) and *Behind You!* (2006).

Carry On ... ***Quotes***

Carry On Again Christmas *was one of my very, very young appearances. I was uncredited in it, but am delighted to say I worked with Sidney James and Barbara Windsor.*
Linda Regan, 2010

Beryl Reid OBE (b. Beryl Elizabeth Reid)

One of Britain's leading comediennes, Beryl Reid appeared in a guest role as Mrs Valentine in *Carry On Emmannuelle*. Fittingly, for an actress who loved to shock, Beryl's only *Carry On* appearance was in the most blatant film of the series.

Born in Hereford on 17 June 1919, Beryl Reid was a stage-struck child. She made her first professional stage appearances in 1936 in summer seasons and pantomime and worked in variety for £2 a week.

During her long stage career Beryl appeared in countless pantomime productions (to best effect as an Ugly Sister in *Cinderella*), often in partnership with Jimmy Edwards (1920-87). In the 1950s and early 1960s she was kept busy in revue at the Watergate Theatre, and she toured South Africa in *Something New* in 1962. Beryl also proved capable of more dramatic performances, notably in *Romeo and Juliet* (as the nurse) at the Old Vic in 1973, and she achieved international stardom with her role in *The Killing of Sister George*, in which she played a middle-aged lesbian actress. The play ran in London for over a year before transferring to Broadway, where Beryl won a Tony Award (1967) for this most memorable performance. Beryl later won the SWET Award for Best Comedy Performance in *Born in the Garden* (1979-80) and she remained active on stage well into the 1980s, her final appearances including *The School for Scandal* (1984) and *Gigi* (1985-86).

As a comedy actress Beryl Reid loved to shock audiences. She came to fame via radio, playing Marlene, the dreaded schoolgirl, in *Educating Archie* (1953-57), and later proved that she was not afraid to take part in bawdy film romps, including *Joseph Andrews* (1977), *Rosie Dixon – Night Nurse* (1978) and *Yellowbeard* (1983). She had made her screen debut in *The Belles of St Trinian's* in 1954 and appeared in more than a dozen films, including *Two-Way Stretch* (1960), *The Dock Brief* (1962), *Star!* (1968), *The Killing of Sister George* (1968), *The Assassination Bureau* (1969), *Entertaining Mr. Sloane* (1970), *The Beast in the Cellar* (1970), *Dr. Phibes Rises Again!* (1972), *No Sex Please, We're British* (1973), *The Doctor and the Devils* (1985) and *Duel of Hearts* (TV, 1991).

Beryl's small-screen career spanned forty years. She played Arethusa Wildersin in the 1957 series *The Most Likely Girl* and went on to appear in *Man O'Brass/Bold As Brass* (special and series, 1963-64, as Bessie Briggs), *The Hen House* (1964, with Barbara Windsor), *Wink to Me Only* (series, 1969, as Rene Jelliot) and *Alcock and Gander* (series, 1972, as Marigold Alcock). She also hosted her own television series and specials, including *The Beryl Reid Show*, *Beryl Reid Says Good Evening* (1968), *Beryl Reid Special* (1977) and *Beryl Reid* (1980).

In 1983 Beryl received the BAFTA Award for Best Actress for her role as Connie Sachs in *Smiley's People*. She also received critical acclaim for her role in *The Beiderbecke Tapes* (1983, as Sylvia) and was familiar to audiences as Gran in *The Secret Diary of Adrian Mole Aged 13¾* (series, 1985) and *The Growing Pains of Adrian Mole* (series, 1987). Her countless guest appearances included episodes of *The Goodies*, *Father, Dear Father*, *Doctor Who*, *Worzel Gummidge*, *Minder*, *Bergerac*, *Boon*, *Perfect Scoundrels* and *The Comic Strip Presents....*

Active on television into her seventies, Beryl's final credits included *Bunch of Five* (1992, as Gran), *Cracker* (1993, as Robbie Coltrane's mother), *Blue Heaven* (1994) and *The Stuart Hall Show* (1994).

Beryl Reid married Bill Wolsey in 1950 and secondly musician Derek Franklin in 1954. Both marriages ended in divorce. Away from acting she enjoyed entertaining friends, cooking and gardening. In her final years she lived at Honeypot Cottage, on the river near Staines in Berkshire, surrounded by a large menagerie of cats. Beryl's autobiography, *So Much Love*, was published in 1984 and she also wrote *The Cat's Whiskers* (1986), *Beryl, Food and Friends* (1988) and *The Kingfisher Jump* (1991). She was awarded the OBE in 1986.

Beryl Reid, who suffered from osteoporosis in later years, died in hospital from pneumonia (following surgery on her knee) on 13 October 1996.

Eva Reuber-Staier

Best-known as Miss World (1969), Austrian beauty Eva Reuber-Staier turned up as one of Joan Sims's 'birds of paradise' in *Carry On Dick*. It was her only appearance in the series.

Following *Carry On Dick* Eva played the princess in *The Slipper and the Rose* (1976) and went on to become a minor Bond girl, featuring as Rublevitch in *The Spy Who Loved Me* (1977), *For Your Eyes Only* (1981) and *Octopussy* (1983). Recently she has made appearances at autograph conventions in Britain and America.

Wendy Richard MBE (b. W. Emerton)

Television legend Wendy Richard appeared in two *Carry On* films and a Christmas special, shortly before going on to become an icon as Miss Brahms in *Are You Being Served?*. Latterly she was best known as *EastEnders* 'grande dame' Pauline Fowler.

Wendy Richard was born in Middlesbrough on 20 July 1943. She trained at the Italia Conti Stage School and had her first professional break as a singer, when she recorded the 1962 number one hit 'Come Outside' with Mike Sarne, and she subsequently went on to appear in television programmes such as *The Newcomers, Please Sir!* and *Dad's Army.*

Wendy Richard made her *Carry On* debut as Kate in the 1970 Christmas special. Two years later she played the aptly named Nurse Willing in *Carry On Matron* and was later seen as Ida Downs (from Bristol!) in *Carry On Girls*. Wendy looked back on the *Carry On*'s with happy memories, and although absent from 1990s celebrations she did take part in the 1998 documentary *What's a Carry On*?.

In addition to the *Carry On* films, Wendy featured in *Doctor in Clover* (1966), opposite Joan Sims, *No Blade of Grass* (1970), *Gumshoe* (1971) and the screen versions of *On the Buses* (1971), *Bless This House* (1972) and *Are You Being Served?* (1977).

Following the *Carry On*'s Wendy played sexy Miss Brahms in the classic sitcom *Are You Being Served?*. The role would secure Wendy's reputation as a talented comedienne and kept her busy for twelve years.

In 1985, following the overwhelming success of *Are You Being Served?*, Wendy went on to create another memorable and long-running television character, as matriarch Pauline Fowler in *EastEnders*, for which she is now best remembered. The roles of Miss Brahms and Pauline Fowler could not have been more different, although Wendy later admitted that she enjoyed the change. She did, however, resurrect the character of Miss Brahms for two series of *Grace and Favour* (1991-92). Wendy left *EastEnders* in 2006, after playing Pauline for more than twenty years, and she received a British Soap Lifetime Achievement Award the following year. She went on to display her considerable skills as a character actress with roles in *Benidorm* (2008, as Sylvia) and *Marple: A Pocketful of Rye* (2008, as housekeeper Mrs Crump).

While Wendy achieved great professional success, her personal life was often less than happy. Her first three marriages ended in divorce and it was not until 2008 that she married her long-term partner, John Burns. In 1996 and 2002 she was diagnosed with breast cancer, but during her periods of remission she courageously continued to work. In 2000 Wendy (a staunch royalist) was thrilled to receive the MBE, and in the same year she released her autobiography, *Wendy Richard, No S: My Life Story*.

In private Wendy was a self-confessed collector of ceramic frogs, clowns and condiment sets and she was devoted to her Cairn terrier, Miss Shirley Brahms II. After being diagnosed with terminal cancer in October 2008, Wendy Richard died peacefully at a Harley Street Clinic on 26 February 2009. She was sixty-five years old.

Gordon Richardson

Gordon had a non-speaking cameo role as Jenny's Uncle Ernest Grubb in *Carry On Loving* and appeared in minor film roles for over twenty years. The Scottish-born actor died in December 1994, shortly before his 83rd birthday.

Peter Richardson

An actor, writer and director, Peter Richardson played Bart Columbus in *Carry On Columbus*.

Born in Devon on 15 October 1951, Peter began his career in the mid-1970s and gained fame at London's Comedy Store. Among an elite group of alternative comedians, including his frequent writing partner Nigel Planer (q.v.), Peter has appeared in cult films such as *The Supergrass* (1985), *Eat the Rich* (1987) and *The Pope Must Die* (1991). Over a twenty-year period Peter also appeared in more than thirty episodes of *The Comic Strip Presents…*, as well as writing, producing and directing more than twenty episodes of the series.

Peter's recent work as a writer includes *Stella Street* (2004) and *Churchill: The Hollywood Years* (2004). He is married and has four children.

Arnold Ridley OBE (b. William Arnold Ridley)

Unforgettable as the lovable Private Godfrey in seven series of *Dad's*

Army, Arnold Ridley appeared in a cameo role in *Carry On Girls*, as the ancient Alderman Pratt. The popular actor was also well known as the writer of many plays, including *The Ghost Train*.

Born in Bath, Somerset, on 7 January 1896, Arnold made his stage debut at the Theatre Royal, Bristol, in *Prunella* in 1914 and was educated at Bristol University. He served in the army during the First World War but was wounded and discharged in 1917. His health never fully recovered and his subsequent acting career was often put on hold due to health constraints. Nevertheless, he went on to spend two years with the Birmingham Repertory Company (1918-20) and a further year with the Plymouth Repertory Company (1920-21), appearing in over forty plays.

Although Arnold's stage credits were sporadic – with only a handful of appearances in the theatre between *The Ghost Train* (1927, as Saul Hogdkin) and *Dad's Army* (1975) – he gained fame as the writer of over twenty plays, including *The Brass God* (1921), *The Ghost Train* (1925), *Out She Goes* (1938), *Beggar My Neighbour* (1951) and *High Fidelity* (1960).

Apart from his successful career as a writer, Arnold was best known on television as the incontinent Private Godfrey in ten series of *Dad's Army*. He was seventy-one when the series began in 1967 and over eighty when it finally ended ten years later. He also appeared in the stage version and 1971 feature film. The public took to heart the kindly old soldier, and thanks to constant re-runs of the series Arnold remains a familiar face to television viewers.

In addition to *Carry On Girls*, Arnold appeared in a small selection of other films, including *The Interrupted Journey* (1949), *Green Grow the Rushes* (1951), *A Stolen Face* (1952), *Wings of Mystery* (1963), *Crooks in Cloisters* (1964) and *The Amorous Milkman* (1974). As well as *Dad's Army*, he was also familiar on television as Rev. Guy Atkins in the early years of *Crossroads*.

Arnold Ridley's first two marriages (to Hilda Cooke and Isola Strong) ended in divorce. He married thirdly former actress Althea Parker (1911-2001) in 1947 and they had one son. Away from the stage he enjoyed rugby, cricket and football and he was a life member of the Bath Rugby Football Club. As his health declined, Arnold spent his final years living quietly in London and was awarded the OBE in 1982.

Arnold Ridley died peacefully on 12 March 1984, aged eighty-eight years old.

Douglas Ridley

In addition to playing the 2nd Plotter, opposite Kenneth Connor, in *Carry On Henry*, Douglas appeared in a couple of low-budget 1970s films: *Loot* (1970) and *Cool It Carol!* (1970).

Peter Rigby

Peter played one of King Henry's courtiers in *Carry On Henry*.

Nancy Roberts

Nancy Roberts' uncredited role as the old lady at the train station in *Carry On Regardless* was her final screen appearance. The Welsh-born actress had previously played Mother Dorothea in *Black Narcissus* (1947) and Gran in *Cosh Boy* (1953) and *It's a Great Day* (1955). She also appeared on television in *The Grove Family* (1955, as Gran) and *The Avengers* (1961, as Madame Zenobia).

Nancy died in London on 25 June 1962, aged eighty.

Trevor Roberts

Trevor, along with Peter Rigby and Peter Munt, played one of King Henry's courtiers in *Carry On Henry*.

Dany Robin (b. Danielle Robin)

A heart-throb of a generation of Frenchmen in the late 1940s and 1950s, Dany Robin made a guest appearance in *Carry On Don't Lose Your Head*, playing Jacqueline, Sid James's love interest. It was one of her final screen appearances.

Born in Clamart, Hauts-de-Seine, on 14 April 1927, Dany began her career as a dancer with the Paris Opera troupe. She made her film debut in *Lunegarde* in 1943 and went on to appear in almost fifty films in her native country. She first came to international prominence in *Act of Love* (1953) and among her other English-speaking screen appearances were *Love and the Frenchwoman* (1960), *Waltz of the Toreadors* (1962), *Mysteries of Paris* (1962), *Follow the Boys* (1963) and *The Best House in London* (1968). On the whole, however, the pretty, fair-haired actress preferred to work in her native country. Dany made a final screen appearance in Alfred Hitchcock's *Topaz* in 1969, and following her second marriage in the same year she retired from acting to concentrate on family life.

Dany's first husband was French actor Georges Marchal (1920-97) and she married secondly British theatrical agent Michael Sullivan. Ironically, Sullivan was the agent of several *Carry On* actors, including Sid James.

Dany Robin died tragically, together with her husband, from injuries sustained in a fire at her Paris apartment on 25 May 1995, aged sixty-eight.

Cardew Robinson (b. Douglas John Cardew Robinson)

In a notable guest role Cardew Robinson played the crazy Fakir in *Carry On Up the Khyber*. Although it was his only appearance in the series, it secured him an unforgettable place in *Carry On* history.

Cardew was born in Goodmayes, Essex, on 14 August 1917. He worked in variety upon leaving school, and while in the RAF Gang Shows he invented his most famous character: the evil, delinquent schoolboy Cardew the Cad of St Fanny's – an act he performed in variety and later, to greater success, on radio. He even brought the character to screen in *Fun at St Fanny's* (1956).

The tall, lanky actor made his film debut in *Knight Without Armour* in 1937. He subsequently appeared in scene-stealing roles in thirty films, including *Happy Is the Bride* (1958), *I'm All Right, Jack* (1959), *The Navy Lark* (1959), *Waltz of the Toreadors* (1962), *Alfie* (1966), *The Magnificent Seven Deadly Sins* (1971), *What's Up Nurse?* (1977), *Pirates* (1986) and *Shirley Valentine* (1989, as an English tourist).

On television from 1947 Cardew's appearances ranged from *Hancock's Half Hour* to episodes of *The Avengers*. He also played Hairpin in *Fire Crackers* (1964), Lord Chumpton in *The Small World of Samuel Tweet* (2 series, 1974-75) and Mr Banyard in *The End of the Pier Show* (1981). Cardew's numerous guest appearances included *The Gang Show Gala* (1970) and *Milligan in ...* (1972). Cardew, who was a Brother Rat, also wrote scripts and short stories.

Cardew's only marriage ended in divorce and he had two daughters, Leanne and Lindy. On 18 October 1992 Cardew was present at the unveiling of the British Comedy Society plaque in memory of Sid James, along with *Carry On* actors Jack Douglas, David Lodge, Pat Coombs and Nicholas Parsons (all q.v.).

Cardew Robinson died in London on 27 December 1992, following a short illness (bowel infection). He was seventy-five years old.

Joe Robinson (b. Joseph William Robinson Harle)

Frequently called upon to play a range of 'heavy' characters in films of the 1960s, Joe Robinson played Dynamite Dan, opposite Charles Hawtrey, in *Carry On Regardless*.

Born in Newcastle-upon-Tyne on 31 May 1927, Joe began his acting career in the mid-1950s after training at RADA. His height (6ft 2in) and build saw him cast as muscle men and thugs and he was always guaranteed to stand out. His film credits included the role of Sam in *A Kid for Two Farthings* (1955, with Diana Dors), *Fighting Mad* (1957), *Sea Fury* (1958), *The Bulldog Breed* (1960) and *Doctor in Distress* (1963), and he is best known as Peter Franks in *Diamonds Are Forever* (1971).

Following in the footsteps of his father and grandfather, Joe became a professional wrestler and as 'Tiger Joe Robinson' became a European and world champion. He also gained high black belt grades in both judo and karate.

Now in his eighties, Joe has recently been kept busy as a popular guest at autograph conventions.

*Carry On ... **Quotes***

In Carry On Regardless *I worked with Freddie Mills - ex-world boxing champ. I was also a world champion - at wrestling! My character - Dynamite Dan - was supposedly a coward who was scared to fight the gruesome Boxer in the other corner. In real life I beat him in under 60 seconds. Sid James was also in the film and I worked with him when I played the lead in* A Kid for Two Farthings*; likewise Charles Hawtrey, who was just as funny in real life.*
Joe Robinson, 2006

George Roderick

George Roderick, who played the waiter in *Carry On Again Doctor*, had a film career stretching back to the 1950s.

Invariably seen in bit-part roles, his screen credits included *The Ladykillers* (1955), *Serious Charge* (1959), *Finders Keepers* (1969), *On the Buses* (as the 2nd Policeman, 1971), *That's Your Funeral* (1972) and *Love Thy Neighbour* (1973).

Born in 1913, George also acted on television in series such as *The Love of Mike* (1960), *Three Live Wires* (1961) and *Swallows & Amazons* (1963).

George Roderick died on 10 March 1976.

Anton Rodgers (b. Anthony Rodgers)

Popular television actor Anton Rodgers appeared in two *Carry On* films at the beginning of his career. He played the Young Man in *Carry On Cruising* and Hardy in *Carry On Jack*. He also worked for Gerald Thomas in *The Iron Maiden* in 1962.

Born in Wisbech, Cambridgeshire, on 10 January 1933, Anton trained at the Italia Conti Stage School and later at LAMDA. He made his stage debut at the age of fourteen and during his teens played Pip in a tour of *Great Expectations* (1948) and toured in the title role of *The Winslow Boy* (1949). After a short spell in repertory he went on to appear in numerous stage plays from the late 1950s, including *The Boy Friend* (1957), *Pickwick* (1963, as Jingle, also in New York), *An Italian Straw Hat* (1967), *The Threepenny Opera* (1972, as Macheath) and *Uncle Vanya* (1976). His later stage appearances included *How the Other Half Loves* (1998), *Under the Doctor* (2001) and *Chitty Chitty Bang Bang* (2002, as Grandpa Potts). The Olivier Award-winning actor also directed frequently in the theatre and toured Australia in the mid-1970s for the National Theatre.

Anton made his television debut in *The Skylarks* (1958), as Lieutenant Gilmore. He went on to appear in over forty series, including *Danger Man, Ukridge* (series, 1968, as Stanley), *Upstairs, Downstairs, Zodiac* (series, 1974), *Lillie* (1978, as Edward Langtry), *Disraeli* (1979), *Rumpole of the Bailey, Uprising* (1999), *Midsomer Murders: Market for Murder* (2001), *C.S. Lewis: Beyond Narnia* (2005, as C.S. Lewis) and *Longford* (2006).

Anton's screen credits were equally diverse. They included *Crash Dive* (1959), *Tarnished Heroes* (1961), *Petticoat Pirates* (1961), *The Traitors* (1963), *Rotten to the Core* (1965), *Scrooge* (1970), *The Man Who Haunted Himself* (1970), *The Day of the Jackal* (1973), *The Fourth Protocol* (1987), *Impromptu* (1991), *Son of the Pink Panther* (1993), *Secret Passage* (2004) and *The Last Drop* (2005). He also featured among the all-star cast of the 1984 tele-movie, *Murder with Mirrors*, with Sir John Mills, Bette Davis and Helen Hayes.

In middle age Anton gained success on the small screen as accountant William Fields, in three series of *Fresh Fields* (1984-86), with Julia McKenzie. The pair later appeared together in the equally successful follow-up *French Fields* (1989-91) and reunited shortly before Anton's death in the 2007 tele-movie *You Can Choose Your Friends*. Anton also gained a legion of fans as solicitor Alec Callender in six series of *May to December* (1991-94) and went on to star as vet Noah Kirby in *Noah's Ark* (1997-98), with Angela Thorne.

Anton's first marriage ended in divorce and he married secondly actress Elizabeth Garvie. He had five children: a daughter Thalia and son Adam from his first marriage, and three sons, Barnaby, Dominic and Luke, from his second marriage.

Anton Rodgers died on 1 December 2007, aged seventy-four.

Christine Rodgers

Christine had uncredited roles in *Carry On Cleo* and *Carry On Spying*, playing a hand maiden and Amazon guard respectively.

Gordon Rollings/(Rawlings)

Best known for character roles in a succession of television series,

Gordon Rollings played the night porter in *Carry On Doctor*.

Born in Batley, Yorkshire, on 17 April 1926, Gordon Rollings trained as a clown before making his television debut in *Play School*. He subsequently went on to work consistently on the small screen, with appearances in *Coronation Street* (1964-65, as Charlie Moffit) and a wide variety of sitcoms such as *Room at the Bottom* (series, 1967, as Happy Brazier, with Kenneth Connor, q.v.), *On the House* (series, 1970, as Walter, with Kenneth Connor), *Bright's Boffins* (3 series, 1970-72, as Dogsears Dawson), *Hogg's Back* (2 series, 1975-76, as Mr Diehard), *Life Begins at Forty* (series, 1980, as Horace the milkman), *Big Jim and the Figaro Club* (series, 1981, as Old Ned), *Bootle Saddles* (series, 1984, as Cyril, with Kenneth Cope, q.v.) and *Sharon and Elsie* (series, 1984, as Ike).

Gordon also appeared in a handful of films, including *A Weekend with Lulu* (1961), *The Valiant* (1962), *Just for Fun* (1963), *Press for Time* (1966), *The Bed Sitting Room* (1969), *The Pink Panther Strikes Again* (1976) and *Jabberwocky* (1977). He also had minor roles in *Superman II* and *Superman III* (1980 and 1983).

Gordon's final television appearances included a guest appearance in *The Kenny Everett Show* and the role of Mr Cleat in *Miss Marple: The Moving Finger* (1985).

Gordon became a familiar face to television viewers as Arkwright in the John Smith's Yorkshire bitter commercials shortly before he died from cancer at Bristol Royal Infirmary on 7 June 1985.

Edina Ronay

Now a well-known fashion designer with her own exclusive label, Edina Ronay played Dolores, the saloon girl who ends up in a catfight with Joan Sims and Angela Douglas, in *Carry On Cowboy*. She also worked for Rogers and Thomas in *The Big Job* (1965), playing Sally Gamely.

Edina, the daughter of cookery expert Egon Ronay, was born in 1944. After training at St Martin's School of Acting and RADA she began working as a model before making her film debut in *Night Train to Paris* in 1964. Over the next six years she appeared in decorative roles in a dozen films, including *A Study in Terror* (1965), *Prehistoric Women* (1967) and *Our Mother's House* (1970). She also made occasional television appearances into the 1970s before her final screen appearance in *The Swordsman* in 1974.

Edina launched her own knitwear collection in the late 1960s with Lena Stengard. She launched her own label in 1984, which has since gone from strength to strength. Her daughter is film reviewer and broadcaster, Shebah Ronay.

Barbara Rosenblat

Barbara, who played an ATS in *Carry On England*, is still a working actress. In addition to her solo appearance in the *Carry On* series, she has featured in minor roles in films such as *Turtle Diary* (1985), *Haunted Honeymoon* (1986) and *Little Shop of Horrors* (1986). She has also worked extensively on stage.

Norman Rossington

Norman Rossington provided wonderful performances in three early *Carry On* films, roles that were a small portion of a prodigious career that ranged from Shakespeare to pantomime.

Born in Liverpool on 24 December 1928, Norman began his career at the Theatre Royal, Bristol. He later joined the Old Vic Company and toured the USA as Snout in *A Midsummer Night's Dream*. Norman made his West End debut in *Tiger at the Gate* and in 1963 he was a member of Olivier's original pre-National Theatre Company at Chichester.

Norman also worked in stage musicals for over forty years, and following his debut in *Salad Days* he went on to appear in *Hello, Dolly!*, *Annie Get Your Gun* and Sir Harry Secombe's *Pickwick*. His final stage role was in the Disney version of *Beauty and the Beast* (1997-98). Norman also appeared in two Royal Command Performances and in 1995 performed at the D-Day 50th Anniversary celebrations in Hyde Park.

Norman Rossington made his screen debut in *Keep It Clean* in 1956. He went on to appear in over forty films, including classics such as *Lawrence of Arabia* (1962), *Tobruk* (1967) and *The Charge of the Light Brigade* (1968). He was proud of the fact that he was the only actor to have ever appeared on screen with both Elvis Presley (in *Double Trouble*, 1967) and The Beatles (as their manager, Norm, in *A Hard Day's Night,* 1964). His additional screen appearances included *I Only Arsked!* (1958), *Doctor in Love* (1960), *No Love for Johnnie* (1961), *Nurse on Wheels* (1963), *The Rise and Rise of Michael Rimmer* (1970), *Young Winston* (1972), *Digby, the Biggest Dog in the World* (1973), *Joseph Andrews* (1977), *S.O.S. Titanic* (1979), *Rhubarb, Rhubarb* (short, 1980), *The Krays* (1990) and *Let Him Have It* (1991).

A small, stocky man with a convincing range of accents, from his native Liverpudlian to broad cockney, Norman made his *Carry On* debut as Herbert Brown in *Carry On Sergeant*. He had a brief cameo role as Norm, Kenneth Connor's jelly-brained sparring partner, in *Carry On Nurse* and made a final appearance as the Referee in *Carry On Regardless*. Norman also featured in the 1972 Christmas special, *Carry On Stuffing*, and was particularly memorable as the camp Genie of the Lamp!

On television Norman's roles were as diverse as those on stage and screen. He first came to prominence on the small screen in *The Army Game* (1957-61, as Private 'Cupcake' Cook, with Bernard Bresslaw and Charles Hawtrey). He also worked with several other *Carry On* actors in the 1960 series, *Our House*. Norman's additional television credits included *Curry and Chips* (1969), *Cilla* (1972), *Follow That Dog* (series, 1974, as PC Fogg), *I, Claudius* (1976), *Big Jim and the Figaro Club* (1979-81, as Big Jim), *Spooner's Patch* (1979, as PC Goatman), *The 19th Hole* (1989), *Last of the Summer Wine* (1995, as Mr Microwave), *Sharpe's Regiment* (1996), *Heartbeat* (1996, as Bertie) and *And the Beat Goes On* (1996, as Pop).

Away from acting Norman enjoyed carpentry and was a member of the Crimea War Research Society. He attended the *Carry On* 40th Anniversary reunion in 1998 and in the same year featured in the documentary *What's a Carry On*?.

Norman Rossington married Cindy, his long-term girlfriend, in January 1999. He died in a Manchester hospital, after a six-month battle with cancer, on 21 May 1999, aged seventy.

Jan Rossini

Although her scenes as the 'hoopla girl' in *Carry On At Your Convenience* were deleted from the final film release, Jan Rossini still features in the film's opening credits.

In addition to *Carry On At Your Convenience*, Jan also played a prostitute in *The Oblong Box* (1969), the Rock Girl in *When Dinosaurs Ruled the Earth* (1970, co-starring *Carry On* actors Billy Cornelius, Imogen Hassall and Carol Hawkins, q.v.) and Bess in *Cry of the Banshee* (1970). Her brief acting career ended with her solo *Carry On* appearance.

Patsy Rowlands

(See MAIN TEAM).

Robert Russell

Robert Russell, who played the policeman in *Carry On Loving*, had a long acting career dating back over forty years.

Among Robert's screen appearances were *Shadow of Fear* (1963), *Othello* (1965), *Bedazzled* (1967), *Inspector Clouseau* (1968), *Sudden Terror* (1970), *Man in the Wilderness* (1971), *Sitting Target* (1972) and *Silver Dream Racer* (1980).

On television he featured in numerous series, including *Doctor Who* (several episodes), *Space: 1999*, *Blake's 7* and *Sorry!*. Robert died on 12 May 2008.

Anthony/(Tony) Sagar

A familiar face to fans of the series, Anthony Sagar appeared in seven *Carry On* films, from *Carry On Sergeant* in 1958 to *Carry On Loving* over a decade later.

Anthony was born in Burnley on 19 June 1920. He made his stage debut in 1939 before six years of active war service (with the Royal Navy) interrupted his acting career. During his time with the Navy, as a Leading Telegraphist, he organised shows and entertainment aboard HMS *Victorious*.

Returning to the stage in 1946, Anthony built up his experience with several years in repertory in Birmingham and Wolverhampton and spent one month touring Canada. From 1949 he enjoyed a busy stage career, his numerous theatre appearances including *The Good Sailor* (1956), *The Ring of Truth* (250 performances, 1959-60, with David Tomlinson) and *March Hares* (1964, with Ian Carmichael), and he played Porter for two years in *There's a Girl in My Soup* (1966-68). His last stage appearance was as Percy Elliot in *Epitaph for George Dillon* at the Young Vic Theatre in December 1972.

Anthony made his *Carry On* debut as the Stores Sergeant in *Carry On Sergeant* and in the following year played the First Ambulance Man in *Carry On Nurse*. He then went on to play an 'angry customer' in *Carry On Constable*, the Bus Conductor (opposite Kenneth Williams and a chimpanzee!) in *Carry On Regardless*, the Cook in *Carry On Cruising* and the Policeman in *Carry On Screaming*. Anthony made his final *Carry On* appearance as the man in the hospital bed next to Richard O'Callaghan in *Carry On Loving*. He also filmed scenes for *Carry On Henry* (as a 'heckler') which did not appear in the final film release.

In addition to the *Carry On* films, Anthony's screen credits included appearances in *Barnacle Bill* (1957), *Law and Disorder* (1958), *I Was Monty's Double* (1958), *Jack the Ripper* (1959), *The Bulldog Breed* (1960), *A Pair of Briefs* (1962), *Dad's Army* (1971), *That's Your Funeral* (1972) and *The Offence* (1973). He also worked for Gerald Thomas in *Please Turn Over* (1959).

On television Anthony Sagar appeared in guest roles in *The Avengers, Doomwatch, Dad's Army* and *Spyder's Web* (1972).

Anthony was married to actress Laurel Solash and they had one daughter. He died on 24 January 1973, at the early age of fifty-two.

Nejdet Salih (aka: Carter Ward/ Nej Adamson)

Still best remembered as Ali in *EastEnders*, Nejdet Salih played Fayid, one of the crew members, in *Carry On Columbus*.

Born in London on 23 December 1958, Nejdet trained at Moutview Theatre School for three years.

Prior to gaining national fame in *EastEnders* he appeared on television in *The Brief, Auf Wiedersehen Pet* and *West*. As café owner Ali Osman he was kept busy in the BBC soap for four years until 1989. After spending some time in America in the 1990s Nejdet returned to the UK and could be glimpsed playing the Short Sailor in *Pirates of the Caribbean: The Curse of the Black Pearl* (2003) and its 2006 sequel.

Nejdet's three-year marriage ended in divorce in 1992 and he has one daughter.

Alexei Sayle

One of Britain's best-known contemporary comedians and writers, Alexei Sayle had a leading role as Achmed in *Carry On* Columbus.

Born in Liverpool, on 7 August 1952, Alexei began his career as a stand-up comedian and compère at the Comedy Store, having formerly worked as a teacher.

Alexei's aggressive style, skinhead haircut and tight-fitting suits would become his trademark in a television career now spanning thirty years. He first came to prominence via television as landlord Jerzy Balowski in *The Young Ones* with Rik Mayall (q.v.), Adrian Edmondson and Nigel Planer (q.v.). He was also co-writer for the series, which went on to achieve cult status.

As an actor and writer Alexei was constantly in demand throughout the 1980s and 1990s. In addition to *The Young Ones*, he wrote and starred in *Alexei Sayle's Stuff* (series, 1988), *Itch* (1989), *The All New Alexei Sayle Show* (series, 1994), *Alexei Sayle's Comedy Hour* (series, 1997) and *Alexei Sayle's Merry-Go-Round* (series, 1998). He has also written and starred in a number of episodes of *The Comic Strip Presents*....

Alexei's numerous other television credits (which have also seen him in occasional dramatic roles) include *Doctor Who, Roland Rat: The Series* (1986), *Lovejoy, Common as Muck, Jackanory* (presenter), *You Cannot Be Serious* (presenter, 1999), *Arabian Nights* (2000, as BacBac), *Keen Eddie* (2004) and *Marple: They Do It with Mirrors* (2009).

In addition to his role in *Carry On Columbus*, Alexei has appeared in more than a dozen films ranging from *Gorky Park* (1983) to *Swing* (1999). His other notable screen roles include playing the policeman in *The Supergrass* (1985), the Sultan in *Indiana Jones and the Last Crusade* (1989) and Major Wib in *Reckless Kelly* (1993).

Most recently Alexei has been concentrating on his career as a best-selling writer. His books include *Alexei Sayle's Great Bus Journeys of the World* (1989), *Barcelona Plates* (2000), *The Dog Catcher* (2001), *The Weeping Women Hotel* (2006), *Mister Roberts* (2009) and *Stalin Ate My Homework* (2010).

Alexei and his wife Linda have been married since 1974 and live in London.

Stephanie Schiller

Stephanie played the new nurse in *Carry On Nurse*.

Anne Scott

Anne had an uncredited role as one of the harem girls in *Carry On Follow That Camel* and could later be glimpsed as one of the Khasi's wives in *Carry On Up the Khyber*.

Steven Scott

Steven played a Burpa Guard in *Carry On Up the Khyber*. He is also credited with minor appearances in *Friends and Neighbours* (1959), *The Bombay Strangler* (1960), *Make Mine Mink* (1960), *Guns of Darkness* (1963) and *Sammy Going South* (1963).

Terry Scott

(See MAIN TEAM).

Harry Shacklock

Harry played the lavatory attendant chasing Charles Hawtrey in *Carry On Loving*.

Dino Shafeek

Dino, who played the Immigration Officer in *Carry On Emmannuelle*, also appeared in *The Charge of the Light Brigade* (1968), *Young Winston* (1972, as the Indian servant) and *Stand Up, Virgin Soldiers* (1977). On television he was seen in *It Ain't Half Hot Mum* (1974) and *Mind Your Language* (1977). His final film was *High Road to China* (1983). He died from a heart attack in 1984, aged fifty-four.

Denis Shaw

A plump character actor of stage, screen and television, Denis Shaw played the 2nd Sinister Passenger, opposite Kenneth Connor, in *Carry*

On Regardless. It was just one of over forty films appearances in a twenty-year acting career cut short by his sudden death.

Denis Shaw was born in Dulwich on 7 April 1921. He served in the army from 1939 to 1948 before making his stage debut as Atkins in *Dark of the Moon* at the Lyric Hammersmith Theatre in 1949. He went on to appear in plays such as *Love in a Court Yard* (1950), *The Desperate Hours* (1955, 167 performances, Hippodrome), *Saint Joan of the Stockyard* (1964, Queens), and *Inside Out* (1969, Royal Court).

Denis made his screen debut in *Girdle of Gold* in 1952 and appeared in a range of films, including *The Seekers* (1954), *Forbidden Cargo* (1955), *Blood of the Vampire* (1958), *Passport to Shame* (1959), *Jack the Ripper* (1959), *The Night We Dropped a Clanger* (1959), *Make Mine Mink* (1960), *Curse of the Werewolf* (1961), *A Weekend with Lulu* (1961), *The Day of the Triffids* (1962), *The Viking Queen* (1967) and *The File of the Golden Goose* (1969).

Denis was working on the BBC series *Bright's Boffins* when he died in London, from a heart attack, on 28 February 1971, aged forty-nine.

Richard Shaw

Richard Shaw, who played the Captain of the Soldiers in *Carry On Don't Lose Your Head*, worked as an actor for over thirty years.

Born in 1920 (some sources say 1918), Richard's film credits dating back to the 1950s included *Black Orchid* (1953), *The Hideout* (1956), *The Crooked Sky* (1957), *No Trees in the Street* (1958), *Partners in Crime* (1961), *Attack on the Iron Coast* (1968) and *Give Us Tomorrow* (1978).

On television Richard featured in minor roles in *Doctor Who, The Saint, Robin's Nest* and *George and Mildred*. He retired from acting in 1988 and died on 9 April 2010.

Susan Shaw (b. Patsy Sloots)

One of Britain's leading young actresses of the late 1940s and 1950s, Susan Shaw played Jane Bishop in *Carry On Nurse*. It was notable as her only role in the series as well as one of her final screen appearances.

Susan Shaw was born in West Norwood, London, on 29 August 1929. She began her career on stage and as a model before being 'groomed' for films by the Rank 'charm' school. The stunningly beautiful, blonde-haired actress made her film debut (aged seventeen) in *London Town* (1946). She quickly became a familiar face to cinema-goers of the late 1940s, particularly as the daughter in the Huggett series of films, including *Here Come the Huggetts* (1948) and *The Huggetts Abroad* (1949). From the late 1940s to the mid-1950s Susan was a leading lady, topping the credit list of films such as *London Belongs to Me* (1948), *Marry Me*

(1949), *Waterfront* (1950), *There Is Another Sun* (1951), *The Large Rope* (1953), *The Good Die Young* (1954) and *Fire Maidens from Outer Space* (1956).

Susan's film career was sadly declining by the time she appeared as Kenneth Connor's wife in *Carry On Nurse*. She appears touchingly melancholy in comparison to other characters in the film, and in private she was still grieving for her husband, the American actor Bonar Colleano, who had been killed in a car accident in August 1958, at the age of thirty-four.

Susan had married German actor Albert Lieven (1906-71) in 1949, but the marriage ended in divorce in 1953. In the following year she married Colleano, with whom she had one son, actor Mark Colleano (1955-). Following Colleano's tragic death Susan's personal and professional lives took a downward turn that would continue until her premature death twenty years later.

After *The Switch* (1963) Susan's film work dried up - although she is occasionally credited with a bit-part in *Sitting Target* (1972), and in a notoriously unpredictable profession she found herself in very reduced circumstances when further work was not forthcoming. In later years she worked as a barmaid, nightclub hostess and clerical worker. Her only son was raised by his paternal grandmother.

Susan Shaw died at Middlesex Hospital from cirrhosis of the liver on 27 November 1978, aged forty-nine. By the time of her death the former leading lady was almost penniless and her old benefactors, the Rank Organisation, famously paid her funeral expenses. It was a tragic end for a stunning leading lady.

Carry On ... **Quotes**

Susan Shaw was very tragic ... She went to pieces after Bonar Colleano died. I spoke to her several times when I was the minder at Isow's nightclub, The Jack of Clubs, and even brought her in from the cold one night to have a cup of coffee, but that's life. One minute you're up there with the gods and the next minute you're on the slag heap.
Nosher Powell, 2000

Carole Shelley

Tony Award-winning actress Carole Shelley appeared in delightful cameo roles in *Carry On Regardless* and *Carry On Cabby* shortly before moving to America, where for the past forty years she has been a leading stage actress.

Carole was born in London on 16 August 1939, the daughter of composer Curtis Shelley and singer Deborah Bloomstein. She made her first appearance at the age of three in the film version of *Little Nell* and made her stage debut at the age of eleven in *The Old Curiosity Shop*. Carole attended the Students Art School (1943-56) and went on to train at RADA (1956-57).

Perennially slender with an endearingly girlish voice, Carole Shelley played Helen Delling in *Carry On Regardless*, opposite Liz Fraser and Jimmy Thompson (both q.v.) and was later seen as the 'dumb' GlamCab driver in *Carry On Cabby*.

Following a successful tour on stage in *Mary, Mary* in 1963, Carole Shelley settled permanently in America from 1964. She has since built a reputation there as a prodigious leading lady, and her stage successes have been recognised with numerous awards, including a Tony Award (and several nominations) and nominations for the Outer Critics Circle Award. Her stage credits have ranged from Shakespeare to musicals, and in her early sixties she returned to Britain in a successful run of *Show Boat*, as Parthy Ann. More recently she played Madame Morrible on Broadway in *Wicked* (2003-05) and received a Tony nomination for her role in *Billy Elliot - The Musical* in 2009.

On the small screen Carole appeared in two series of *Dial RIX* (1962-63), *The Dickie Henderson Show* and *The Avengers*. In America she is best known as Gwendolyn Pigeon in *The Odd Couple* (1970-71), a role she also recreated on stage and screen.

In addition to the *Carry On*'s, Carole's screen credits include *It's Great to Be Young!* (1956), *No, My Darling Daughter* (1961), *The Boston Strangler* (1968), *Little Noises* (1992), *Quiz Show* (1994), *Jungle 2 Jungle* (1997), *Labor Pains* (2000) and *Bewitched* (2005, as Aunt Clara). She also provided voices for Disney animated classics such as *The Aristocats* (1970), *Robin Hood* (1973) and *Hercules* (1997).

Now a US citizen, Carole Shelley married Albert G. Woods in 1967 and was widowed in 1971. In private she enjoys needlepoint, dressmaking, cooking and reading.

Valerie Shute

With five *Carry On* films to her credit, Valerie Shute became a familiar member of the supporting cast halfway through the series. She is perhaps best remembered as the insatiable 'girl lover', who is seen in various locations (and positions!) with Mike Grady in *Carry On Loving*.

Valerie Shute was born in London in May 1945 and trained for two years as an actress and dancer at the Aida Foster School. She began her professional career as an understudy and ASM before embarking on a stage career, which included tours with Margaret Lockwood, Dame Cicely Courtneidge, Jack Hulbert and Sir Donald Sinden.

Valerie made her *Carry On* debut as Pat, one of the schoolgirls in *Carry On Camping* and went on to play a nurse in *Carry On Again Doctor*, a maid in *Carry On Henry* and Miss Smethurst in *Carry On Matron*. In addition to the *Carry On*'s, Valerie played the girl in the chemist shop in *Assault* in 1971.

On the small screen Valerie made appearances in *How We Used to Live*, *Emmerdale Farm* (as Sarah James) and *Secret Army*. She began writing in 1979 and has now retired from acting to concentrate on writing stage plays and musicals for children.

Valerie Shute married playwright, screenwriter and novelist Willis Hall (1929-2005) in 1973 and they had one son, who now works in television. Her hobbies include yoga, swimming and tennis and she enjoys films and theatre and belongs to a ladies' book group. Valerie lives in Leeds.

Carry On … **Quotes**

I have a couple of stories to share from my time on the Carry On's. Carry On Camping *was filmed in late October/November in a field next to Pinewood Studios. There had been lots of rain, and with all the activity taking place the ground soon turned to mud and had to be sprayed with green paint to look like grass. We 'girls' were provided with old-fashioned galoshes to wear over our sandals to keep them clean. Although we were quite well looked after, many of the extras who took part in the rock concert scene at the end of the film were most unhappy about the miserable conditions in which they had to hang around. I believe they actually threatened a strike, although you may want to get confirmation of this from another source.*

I recently bumped into Mike Grady and we were reminiscing about our time working on Carry On Loving. *In one particular scene Mike and I were supposed to be snogging under a table while a big party was going on. When director Gerald Thomas – what a nice man – called my name I had to look out from under the tablecloth, whereupon Gerry would then throw a large cream cake full into my face. It landed with quite a smack. After each take I had to be cleaned up, blouse removed, hair washed and blow-dried with a hairdryer and got ready for another take. The cake and all the other food in the scene was for real and by the end of the day it had really started to whiff!*

I only spent the odd day working on the other Carry On's*; arrived, did my*

bit and went home again, so I haven't any stories about them.
Valerie Shute, 2000

Phil Silvers (b. Philip Silver)

In a rare move to 'import' a foreign actor to appear in the *Carry On* series, Peter Rogers and Gerald Thomas cast American comedian Phil Silvers to play the lead role (as Sergeant Nocker) in *Carry On Follow That Camel*.

Phil Silvers was born in New York on 11 May 1911. The youngest of eight children, he began his career as a child in vaudeville. A singer in theatres until his voice broke, Phil subsequently worked hard for many years to make his name as a top comedian. His persistence paid off and he later had a string of hits on Broadway, including *Top Banana* (1951, for which he won a Tony Award), *Do-Re-Mi* (1961) and *A Funny Thing Happened on the Way to the Forum* (1971).

During the Second World War Phil was busy making comic film appearances, including *Tom, Dick & Harry* (1941), *You're in the Army Now* (1941), *Roxie Hart* (1942), *My Gal Sal* (1942), *Cover Girl* (1944), *Something for the Boys* (1944), *Where Do We Go from Here?* (1945) and *If I'm Lucky* (1946). In the late 1940s he returned to the stage in vaudeville before achieving television stardom, as Sergeant Bilko, in *You'll Never Get Rich* (1955-58). The role made the bespectacled, bald-headed comedian a household name and earned him two Emmy Awards. He subsequently starred in his own television series, *The New Phil Silvers Show*, in 1964.

In the 1960s Phil's success continued on screen in *It's a Mad, Mad, Mad, Mad World* (1963) and *A Funny Thing Happened on the Way to the Forum* (1966). He also continued to work on television, notably as Shifty Shafer in *The Beverly Hillbillies* (1969-71). In 1972, however, a massive stroke slowed down his career and his speech was left slurred. Indomitably, he made cameo appearances in a selection of films, including *Won Ton Ton: the Dog Who Saved Hollywood* (1976), *There Goes the Bride* (1980) and *The Happy Hooker Goes Hollywood* (1980). Sadly, his last years were clouded by health problems, although he continued to make very occasional television guest appearances into the early 1980s.

Phil married actress (and Miss America, 1942), Jo-Carroll Dennison in 1945. They divorced five years later and in 1956 he married Evelyn Patrick. This marriage also ended in divorce, in 1966. Phil Silvers had five children, including actress Cathy Silvers (1961-). His autobiography, *The Laugh Is On Me*, was published in 1973.

Phil Silvers died from a heart attack in Century City, California, on 1 November 1985. He was seventy-four years old.

Georgina Simpson

Georgina played the men's ward nurse in *Carry On Again Doctor*. She also featured briefly in a couple of other films: *Otley* (1968), *Walk a Crooked Path* (1969) and *Perfect Friday* (1970).

Joan Sims

(See MAIN TEAM).

Marc Sinden

Actor and artistic director Marc Sinden played Captain Perez in *Carry On Columbus*.

Marc was born in London on 9 May 1954, the son of Sir Donald Sinden. Following in the footsteps of his father, his uncle (actor Leon Sinden) and brother, Jeremy Sinden (1950-96), Marc trained at Bristol Old Vic Theatre School. He has since been most at home in the theatre, appearing in plays such as *Her Royal Highness*, *The School for Scandal* and *Over My Dead Body*. In recent years he has worked as Artistic Director of the Mermaid Theatre.

On television since the late 1970s, Marc's appearances include *Dick Turpin, Never the Twain, Bergerac, All at No. 20, Emmerdale, Against All Odds* (1994) and *The Politician's Wife* (1995).

In addition to *Carry On Columbus*, Marc has appeared in a number of other films, notably *The Wicked Lady* (1983), *White Nights* (1985), *Man Eaters* (1988), *The Mystery of Edwin Drood* (1993) and *The Brylcreem Boys* (1998).

Marc, who was a guest at the *Carry On* 40th Anniversary reunion in 1998 and a 'tour guide' at the *Carry On* Weekend in 1999, is a man with many interests, ranging from zoology to bomb disposal. He has been awarded the Freedom of the City of London and is an Honorary Member of Stunts Incorporated.

Marc Sinden's twenty-year marriage to Jo Gilbert ended in divorce in 1997 and he has two children, Henry (1980-) and Birdie (1990-).

Frank Singuineau (b. Francis Ethlebert Singuineau)

Frank Singuineau, the Trinidad-born actor, played the Riff at Abdul's second tent in *Carry On Follow That Camel* and later had a memorable cameo role as the Native Porter with Jim Dale in *Carry On* Again Doctor.

Frank's additional screen credits included *Simba* (1955), *Safari* (1956), *The Mummy* (1959), *The Nun's Story* (1959), *The Pumpkin Eater* (1964), *The Wrong Box* (1966), *Hot Millions* (1968), *Firepower* (1979), *An American Werewolf in London* (1981) and *Biggles* (1986).

Frank Singuineau died in London on 11 September 1992, aged seventy-nine.

Susan Skipper (b. S. Cook)

Light leading lady Susan Skipper is perhaps best known for her work with Nigel Havers in the long-running sitcom *Don't Wait Up*. She played Mabel in 'Short Knight, Long Daze', an episode of television's *Carry On Laughing*, and thirty-five years after her solo appearance in the series she recalled it as one of three television appearances that marked the start of her small-screen career. Susan remembers the team, and in particular Peter Butterworth and Kenneth Connor, with great affection.

Susan was born in London on 27 January 1951 and spent her childhood years in Dorset and Sussex. She trained at the Central School of Speech and Drama, and since the mid-1970s her TV credits have included *The Cedar Tree* (1976, series as Victoria), *Doctor Who, The Dancing Years, Ladykillers, Sorry!, West End Tales* (1981, series, as Tina) and *Wish You Were Here*, and she played Madeleine Forbes/Latimer in six series of *Don't Wait Up* (1983-90).

In recent years Susan has mainly worked on stage, with appearances in *An Ideal Husband, Say Who You Are*, *Ten Times Table* (2000, as Sophie), *The Odd Couple* and *Murder Hunt*, and she toured in *Fatal Encounter* with Anita Harris (q.v.) in 2010.

Susan has been married to actor Anthony Valentine (1939-) since 1982.

Tony Slattery (b. Anthony Declan James Slattery)

Actor, singer and comedian Tony Slattery appeared in a cameo role as Baba the Messenger in *Carry On Columbus*.

Born in Stonebridge, London, on 9 November 1959, Tony studied Medieval and Modern Languages at Cambridge University. During his time as a student Tony was invited by Stephen Fry to join the Cambridge Footlights, and in 1981 he won the first ever Perrier Comedy Award at the Edinburgh Festival.

During his early career Tony worked as a stand-up comedian in clubs and made various guest appearances on television, including *Behind the Bike Sheds* (1985 and wrote), *The Lenny Henry Show* and *Boon*.

In 1986 Tony gained critical acclaim for his role in the stage musical *Me and My Girl*, and in 1988 he became the host of the popular television series *Whose Line Is It Anyway?*, for which he is still best known. He went on to become team captain of *Going for a Song* (1995-98) and has also featured in quiz shows and panel games such as *The Music Game* (1992), *Just a Minute* (1994) and *Tibs and Fibs* (1997).

As an actor on television Tony played Tristan Beasley in *That's Love* (series, 1988), David Harper in *This Is David Harper* (series, 1990) and Nick Brim in *Just a Gigolo* (1993). In the mid-1990s he took two years out of the entertainment industry, before returning to the small screen with appearances in *Ruby* (with Ruby Wax), *The Christine Hamilton Show* and the 2000 mini-series *Metropolis*. More recently he has turned up for guest appearances in a variety of series from *Bad Girls* to *Coronation Street* and played Sidney Snell in *Kingdom* (2007-09).

In addition to *Carry On Columbus*, Tony has appeared in a selection of other films, including *How to Get Ahead in Advertising* (1989), *Peter's Friends* (1992), *The Crying Game* (1992), *To Die For* (1994) and *The Wedding Tackle* (2000).

Carol Sloan

Carol played a Harem Girl in *Carry On Follow That Camel*.

Patsy Smart (b. Patricia Doris Smart)

Patsy played the Old Hag in 'One in the Eye for Harold', an episode of *Carry On Laughing* on television in 1975.

Born on 14 August 1918, Patsy had a long career on stage, screen and television, usually in bit-part character roles. She made her screen debut in The Flying Scot in 1957 and went on to appear in a range of films, including *Steptoe and Son* (1973), *The Return of the Pink Panther* (1975), *The Pink Panther Strikes Again* (1976), *Tess* (1979), *The Wildcats of St Trinian's* (1980), *The Elephant Man* (1980) and *The Fourth Protocol* (1987).

She was at her busiest on television in the 1970s and 1980s, most notably as Maude Roberts in *Upstairs, Downstairs* (1971-73) and Aunt Mabel in *Rentaghost* (1983-84). She also appeared in television mini-series such as *Great Expectations* (1974, as Mrs Wopsle), *Nicholas Nickleby* (1977, as Miss La Creevy) and *Lace II* (1985).

Among Patsy's final credits were guest appearances in episodes of *Terry and June* (as Miss Dingle), *Miss Marple: The Moving Finger* (1985, as Mrs Cleat), *Hallelujah*, *Up the Elephant*, *Casualty* and *Filthy, Rich and Catflap*.

Patsy Smart died in Northwood, Middlesex on 6 February 1996, aged seventy-seven.

Jack Smethurst

Jack Smethurst is still best known for his role in *Love Thy Neighbour*. Twenty years prior to achieving television stardom in the popular 1970s sitcom, he played Wilson, one of the recruits, in *Carry On Sergeant*.

Jack Smethurst was born in Lancashire on 9 April 1932 and was a gold medal winner at LAMDA.

Jack made his screen debut in *Trial and Error* in 1956 and has since appeared in *Saturday Night & Sunday Morning* (1960), *On the Fiddle* (1961), *A Kind of Loving* (1962), screen versions of *Please Sir!* (1971), *For the Love of Ada* (1971-72), *Love Thy Neighbour* (1973) and *Man About the House* (1974, as himself), *Chariots of Fire* (1981), *King Ralph* (1991) and *La Passione* (1996).

By no means limited to comic roles, Jack has also made countless stage appearances in productions as diverse as *The Taming of the Shrew* and *The Mikado*. He has also appeared in numerous roles in pantomime and has worked with Barbara Windsor in tours of *The Mating Game*.

Jack's best-known role on the small screen was as Eddie Booth in eight series of *Love Thy Neighbour* (1972-76, with Nina Baden-Semper, q.v.). He was, however, already a familiar face to television viewers through his role in four series of *For the Love of Ada* (1970-71, as Leslie Pollitt, with Irene Handl, q.v.). In addition to his celebrated comic roles on television, Jack has appeared in *Coronation Street* (various characters), *All Things Bright and Beautiful* (as Charles) and *Heartbeat* (1996, as Jenkins). He has also been the subject of *This Is Your Life*.

In his sixties Jack took on the role of *Henry Hobson* in Hobson's Choice at the Yorkshire Playhouse and more recently has been seen on television in episodes of *Casualty* and *Doctors*. He lives in Watford.

Madeline Smith

A popular comedy actress of the 1970s Madeline Smith played Mrs. Pullit, a concerned mother, in *Carry On Matron*.

Born in Hartfield, Sussex, on 2 August 1949, Madeline began her career as a model and made her film debut in her late teens. She is still well remembered for work in Hammer Horror films such as *The Vampire Lovers* (1970) and *Taste the Blood of Dracula* (1970), although she later admitted to finding the films 'scary' and 'hated the nudity', and she became a 'Bond' girl when she played the beautiful Miss Caruso in *Live and Let Die* (1973) opposite Sir Roger Moore. Her favourite screen role was as Bella, the simple-minded daughter, in *The Amazing Mr. Blunden* (1972) with the 'fabulous' Diana Dors. Madeline's other film appearances included *The Magnificent Seven Deadly Sins* (1971), *Up Pompeii* (1971) and *Up the Front* (1972), both with Frankie Howerd, *Theatre of Blood* (1973), *Percy's Progress* (1974), *Frankenstein and the Monster From Hell* (1974), *Galileo* (1975), *The Bawdy Adventures of Tom Jones* (1976) and *The Passionate Pilgrim* (1984).

During the 1970s Madeline became a 'foil' on television for some of the country's finest comics and comedy actors. One of her most fondly remembered roles was in *The Two Ronnies* (1971, as Henrietta Beckett), where she gained national recognition as the gormless heroine in the spoof serial 'Hampton Wick'. She also enjoyed playing Arthur Lowe's daughter in five episodes of *Doctor At Large* (1971), recalling the *Dad's Army* star as a 'wonderful wonderful' man. On the small screen Madeline additional credits included *His and Hers* (1971, as Janet Burgess), *Clochmerle* (1972) and Leslie Phillips's (q.v.) series *Casanova '73* (1973). Her guest appearances around the same time ranged from episodes of *The Persuaders* to *All Creatures Great and Small*.

On stage, in addition to numerous tours, Madeline appeared in *Habeas Corpus* (with Sir Alec Guinness) and in 1984 worked with Terry Scott in *The School for Wives*. Her last appearance in the theatre was in *The Mousetrap* in its 38th year.

Madeline continued acting on stage and television well into the 1980s, notably in *Why Didn't They Ask Evans?* (1980), *Eureka* (1982-86) and *The Steam Video Company* (1984). Following the death of her husband, actor David Buck, in 1989, Madeline retired from acting to spend more time with their daughter. In recent years she has been kept busy as a guest at film and autograph conventions and has also contributed to several television documentaries including *Crumpet! A Very British Sex Symbol* (2005) and *British Film Forever* (2007). She returned to Pinewood Studios in 2004 for the Joan Sims Tribute and in 2007 for Jack Douglas' 80th birthday celebrations.

Carry On ... ***Quotes***

I truly loved my 'small part' and one naughty line in Carry On Matron. *The line* ***was*** *longer, but cut by an over-eager censor who thought it too rude!! It took only half a day to film my cameo as Mrs. Pullitt, but the memory has given* ***me*** *a lifetime of enjoyment, and more importantly, the public.*
Peter Rogers wanted to keep me on in his next film, as a member of his team, but unfortunately I was committed to an extensive theatrical tour.
Madeline Smith, 2010

Vicki Smith

Vicki played an Amazon Guard in *Carry On Spying*, a Vestal Virgin in *Carry On Cleo* and a year later was seen in *Carry On Cowboy*, playing Polly, one of the girls in the saloon.

Patsy Snell

Patsy played a Harem Girl in *Carry On Follow That Camel.*

Prudence Solomon

Prudence played Ha Ha in *Carry On Columbus.*

Elke Sommer (E. Schletz)

German actress Elke Sommer made a guest appearance in the *Carry On* series as Russian Professor Anna Vrooshka in *Carry On Behind.* A favourite of Peter Rogers, Elke was reputedly paid £30,000 to appear in the film, making her by far the highest paid *Carry On* actor.

Born in Berlin on 5 November 1940, Elke made her screen debut at the age of eighteen in *Das Totenschiff.* She has since appeared in more than eighty films, both in her native Germany and in France, America and Britain. A truly international film star, the ultra-blonde sex symbol's film credits include *Don't Bother to Knock* (1961), *The Victors* (1963), *The Prize* (1963), *A Shot in the Dark* (1964), *The Money Trap* (1965), *The Oscar* (1966), *Percy* (1971), *The Prisoner of Zenda* (1979), *Dangerous Cargo* (1996) and *Flashback* (2000).

In 1975 Elke was a welcome guest star in *Carry On Behind.* The only previous attempt to 'import' a foreign star (namely Phil Silvers, q.v.) to work in the *Carry On*'s had not been successful. Thankfully, Elke fitted in well with the regular team, even with Kenneth Williams, her notoriously temperamental co-star!

A talented artist, Elke hosted her own television show, *Painting with Elke*, in 1985. Her additional small-screen credits have included The *Love Boat* (1981-84), *Inside the Third Reich* (1982), *Jenny's War* (1985), *St. Elsewhere* (1986) and *Anastasia: The Mystery of Anna* (1986, as Isabel Von Hohenstauffen),

Elke was awarded a Golden Globe Award in 1965 and a Jefferson Award, Merit of Achievement Award in 1990.

Elke Sommer, who speaks seven languages, has been married three times, twice to writer Joe Hyams and since 1993 to Walther Wolf.

David Spenser

David's role as Bunghit Din's servant in *Carry On Up the Khyber* appears to have been his final screen appearance. Previously his credits had ranged from *Conflict of Wings* (1954) to *Battle Beneath the Earth* (1967). After several television appearances in the early 1970s he appears to have left the profession.

Jean St Clair (Jean Margaret A. St Clair)

Jean St Clair made an unforgettable appearance in the *Carry On* series as Mrs Smith, Peter Butterworth's grape-chewing wife, in *Carry On Doctor*. It was her only appearance in the series.

Born on 23 September 1920, Jean St Clair studied acting at the Gate Theatre, Dublin, where she spent seven years. She began her acting career in the mid-1940s on stage in plays such as *A Play for Ronnie* (1946), *Pick Up Girl* (1946), *This Blessed Plot* (1947) and *Present Laughter* (tours, 1947 and 1948).

During the 1950s Jean was kept busy on both stage and screen. In the theatre she went on to distinguish herself in character roles in numerous West End plays, including *Birthday Honours* (1953, with Moira Lister, 288 performances), *Accounting for Love* (Saville, 1954), *Bells Are Ringing* (1957-68, as Sue, Coliseum) and *Finders Keepers* (Arts, 1961).

Jean made her film debut in *The Gentle Gunman* in 1952 and went on to appear in *Eight O'Clock Walk* (1954), *Aunt Clara* (1954), *Impulse* (1954), *John and Julie* (1955), *Doctor at Large* (1957), *The Young and the Guilty* (1958), *Dentist in the Chair* (1960) and *The Great St Trinian's Train Robbery* (1966, as Drunken Dolly).

Carry On Doctor appears to have been Jean's last major acting appearance, although she appeared in an episode of *Dad's Army* (as Miss Meadows) in 1969.

Jean St Clair died in Kensington, London, in 1973.

Charles Stanley

In addition to being credited with the role of a porter in *Carry On Nurse* and playing Geoff in *Carry On Cabby*, Charles also worked for Gerald Thomas in *Raising the Wind* (1961), playing a removal man. His scenes in *Carry On Nurse* appear to have been deleted from the film release and he had an uncredited role (as a newspaper man) in *Carry On Constable*.

Norman Stanley

Norman played a drunk in *Carry On Cowboy*.

Marita Stanton

Marita played Rose Harper in *Carry On Nurse*.

Valerie Stanton

Valerie popped up as Jack Douglas's fantasy in *Carry On Stuffing* on television in 1972. In decorative roles in film and television for over a decade. until the mid-1970s, Valerie also appeared on TV in *The Avengers* and *Up Pompeii*.

Shirley Stelfox

A busy television actress, Shirley Stelfox made a brief appearance in the *Carry On* series and can be seen as the 'bunny girl' serving Jacki Piper and Richard O'Callaghan in *Carry On At Your Convenience*. Sadly, most of her work in the film, which included scenes with Bill Pertwee, hit the cutting room floor.

Shirley Stelfox was born in Dukinfield, Cheshire, on 11 April 1941. Over the past forty years she has worked almost exclusively on television, usually as down-to-earth northern characters. In addition to numerous television guest appearances in programmes such as *Crown Court*, *Coronation Street* and *Brookside*, Shirley played Colette Stevenson in *Andy Capp* (series, 1988), Rose in the first series of *Keeping Up Appearances* (1990) and Helen in *Civvies* (1992).

More recently Shirley received critical acclaim for her role as Vera in *Pat and Margaret* (1994) and played Jean in three series of *Common as Muck* (1994-97). Shirley currently plays Edna Birch in *Emmerdale* (2000-).

Shirley made her film debut in Corruption in 1968 and was also seen in *1984* (1984) and *Personal Services* (1987), playing a prostitute.

Shirley Stelfox married actor Don Henderson (q.v.) in 1979. She has a daughter from her first marriage (which was dissolved) and two stepdaughters from her marriage to Don Henderson. Shirley was widowed in 1997.

Yutte Stensgaard (b. Jytte Stensgaard)

Best known for her work in Hammer Horror films of the early 1970s, Danish-born leading lady Yutte Stensgaard is credited with the role of Trolley Nurse in *Carry On Again Doctor*. She also played a client of Kenneth Williams in *Carry On Loving*, although, sadly, her scenes with Williams (and James Beck, q.v.) were edited from the final film release.

Yutte Stensgaard was born in Thisted, Denmark, on 14 May 1946. She came to Britain as an au pair in the early 1960s before working as a model and training at drama school. Still well remembered for her work in Hammer classics such as *Scream and Scream Again* (1970) and *Lust for a Vampire* (1971), her additional screen credits included *Zeta One* (1969), *Some Girls Do* (1969), *The Buttercup Chain* (1970), *Doctor in Trouble* (1970) and *Burke & Hare* (1972).

During her time in Britain Yutte Stensgaard also appeared on television as Helga in *Doctor in the House* (series, 1969) and made guest appearances in *The Saint, The Persuaders* and *Jason King*.

Twice married and divorced (once to art director Tony Curtis), Yutte has one son. Now a successful businesswoman living in America, Yutte has recently been a popular guest at Hammer Horror conventions in America.

Susan Stephen

A leading lady of the 1950s, Susan Stephen, along with Susan Beaumont and Ann Firbank, formed a trio of actresses who all appeared in just one *Carry On*. Interestingly, it was one of the most popular of the entire series – *Carry On Nurse*.

Susan Stephen was born in London on 16 July 1931. After training at RADA the attractive, faired-haired actress made her film debut, aged twenty, in *His Excellency* (1952). She went on to appear in leading roles in a variety of films, including *Stolen Face* (1952), *For Better, for Worse* (1954), *As Long As They're Happy* (1955), *Value for Money* (1955), *It's Never Too Late* (1956), *The Court Martial of Major Keller* (1961) and *Three Spare Wives* (1962).

Susan married actor Lawrence Ward in 1953 and following their divorce married secondly cinematographer/director Nicolas Roeg CBE (1928-), in 1957. They had four sons before their subsequent divorce in 1977. Nicolas married secondly actress Theresa Russell (1957-).

Susan Stephen retired from acting in her early thirties to concentrate on family life. She spent her final years, in poor health, living in Henfield in Surrey, where she died on 24 April 2000, aged sixty-eight.

Dorinda Stevens

Dorinda Stevens ended her ten-year acting career when she played one of the girls at Dirty Dick's Tavern in *Carry On Jack*. She was previously credited with the role of a girl in *Carry On Constable*.

Dorinda, who was born in Southampton on 16 August 1932, made her film debut at the age of twenty in *Scotland Yard Inspector*. As a minor leading lady she went on to appear in over twenty films, including *The Golden Link* (1954), *Jack the Ripper* (1959), *Make Mine Mink* (1960), *His and Hers* (1961), *Raising the Wind* (1961) and *Night Train to Paris* (1964). She also made occasional appearances on television in programmes such as *The Saint* and *The Avengers*.

Julie Stevens

Best known on television as a presenter of programmes such as *Play School* and *Play Away*, Julie Stevens made just one *Carry On* appearance in what, to date, is her only film role.

Julie Stevens was born in Greater Manchester on 20 December 1936. At the age of eighteen she trained as a nurse at Manchester Royal Infirmary. Deciding that life as a nurse was not for her ("the sadness and the pain, not the actual work"), Julie began her show business career 'by accident' when she entered a talent competition. She quickly secured a television contract when ITV opened their Northern studios. It was on television that Julie gained most of her experience before moving into repertory theatre.

Julie joined the *Carry On* team for a one-off appearance, as Jim Dale's girlfriend Gloria in *Carry On Cleo*. Clad in an eye-catching fur bikini, she contributed a range of one-liners, and for the actress herself *Cleo* remains a very special addition to her CV. Forty years after her solo *Carry On* appearance Julie provided commentary on the DVD release of *Cleo*.

On television Julie spent thirteen years as a presenter of *Play School* and later went on to host *Play Away* for over a decade. Among her acting roles on the small screen are appearances in *The Avengers* and three series of *Girls About Town* (1970-72, as Rosemary).

In the 1980s Julie spent several years working with Sir Harry Secombe, as his secretary and personal manager. In the late 1990s she returned to acting work on stage, most recently in Stephen Hurst's *Giselle* and in pantomime.

Julie has a son and a daughter from her first marriage, which ended in divorce in 1976. In 1980 she married secondly an actor thirteen years her junior. In private Julie enjoys spending time with her grandchildren, knitting, sewing, cooking, learning languages, music, reading, walking and talking! She has travelled extensively and usually visits her son in Sweden throughout the year. Julie, who spent four years living in France in the 1990s, now lives in Barnes, London.

Carry On ... ***Quotes***

I only did one Carry On, *but it was huge fun. To be surrounded by brilliant comics such as Sid James, Charles Hawtrey and Kenneth Williams was amazing. There was lots of messing about, but when it came time to 'do a take', it was usually in the can in one go. I was grateful to Sid, as I was the most junior character in the film and had a large 'chorus' dressing room, on my own, with no bath or shower. I was always plastered in brown make-up, as my costumes were very skimpy, and Sid, who only lived up the road and went home to shower after work, let me use his magnificent bath to sort myself out*

at the end of each day's filming.
Kenneth was a real mixture of academic and lout! He would tell really filthy jokes, and even flash himself (he wore nothing under his toga) when in the mood, and then over lunch would have the most interesting conversations about Shakespeare and world politics. A strange and troubled man, really. The only thing of real interest was that I was supposed to be a girl with huge breasts, and although I had recently had my first child, Daniel, and was breast feeding, I had to have my fur bikini 'stuffed' with cotton wool, which was so crammed in that it kept trying to get out during the scene!
Julie Stevens, 1998

Ronnie Stevens

Although a regular member of the *Doctor* series of films, Ronnie Stevens made just one *Carry On* appearance, playing the affable drunk in *Carry On Cruising*.

Born in London on 2 September 1925, Ronnie trained at PARADA and RADA. He gained initial success in the stage revue *Intimacy at Eight Thirty* in the early 1950s, having made his theatrical debut in 1948. He subsequently appeared in over fifty stage plays, and from the mid-1960s he was closely associated with the Prospect Theatre Company, touring the world in a wide variety of roles.

Ronnie made his film debut in *Top Secret* in 1952, and in more than forty film appearances he was usually seen in comic character roles. Among his most notable screen appearances were *As Long As They're Happy* (1955), *Doctor at Large* (1957), *I'm All Right, Jack* (1959), *Doctor in Love* (1960), *Dentist in the Chair* (1960), *Dentist on the Job* (1961), *Nearly a Nasty Accident* (1961), *A Pair of Briefs* (1962), *Doctor in Distress* (1963), *The Big Job* (1965), *San Ferry Ann* (1965), *Doctor in Clover* (1966), *S.O.S. Titanic* (1979), *Killing Dad* (1989), *Brassed Off* (1996) and finally as Grandpa Charles James in *The Parent Trap* (1998). Given his involvement in the *Doctor* series of films, produced by Betty Box (the wife of Peter Rogers), it was not surprising that Ronnie would turn up for at least one *Carry On* film, in addition to other Peter Rogers comedies.

Having made his television appearance in 1949, Ronnie's small-screen credits spanned fifty years. He continued to act into his seventies, with appearances in *As Time Goes By* (1995, as Eric), *Goodnight Sweetheart* (1995-96, as Sidney Wix), *Hetty Wainthropp Investigates* (1996, as Mr Cullimore) and *Bernard's Watch* (1997).

From 1959 Ronnie was married to Ann Bristow (who died in March 2006) and they had two sons, one of whom died in 1990. In private he enjoyed reading, painting and yoga. Ronnie Stevens lived in East Anglia for many years before moving to Denville Hall, the actors' retirement home in Middlesex, where he died on 11 November 2006, aged eighty-one.

Carry On ... **Quotes**

Carry On Cruising *was the one and only appearance in that series. I didn't have much time to acquaint myself with the regular team – but have no adverse memories.*
Ronnie Stevens, 1997

Graham Stewart

In addition to playing the 2nd Storeman in *Carry On Sergeant* and George Field in *Carry On Nurse*, Scottish-born actor Graham Stewart appeared in *Cockleshell Heroes* (1955), *Stormy Crossing* (1958) and *The Man Upstairs* (1958). Born on 5 September 1927, he trained at RADA before moving into television production in the 1960s (where his credits included *Dr. Finlay*).

Graham Stewart died on 29 July 2003, aged seventy-five.

Roy Stewart

Roy had an uncredited role as a native in *Carry On Up the Jungle*. He featured in a number of films in the 1970s (often as slaves and servants), including *Leo the Last* (1970), *Julius Caesar* (1970), *Lady Caroline Lamb* (1972), *Live and Let Die* (1973), *Stand Up, Virgin Soldiers* (1977) and *Arabian Adventure* (1979).

Born in Jamaica on 15 May 1925, he spent his latter years running a London nightclub and restaurant until his death on 27 October 2008, aged eighty-three.

Sara Stockbridge

Popular screen and television actress and model Sara Stockbridge was just beginning her career when she featured in a minor role in *Carry On Columbus*, playing Nina the Model.

Born on 14 November 1965, Sara, who made her screen debut in *Spilt Second* in 1992, has featured in a range of films, including *Interview with the Vampire* (1994, as Estelle), *Go Now* (1995), *24 Hours in London* (2000), *The Wedding Tackle* (2000), *Bridget Jones's Diary* (2001), *Rag Tale* (2005), *Enter the Void* (2009) and *The Making of Plus One* (2010).

On television Sara is best known as Megan in *Lucy Sullivan Is Getting Married* (series, 1999-2000) and as Midge Palmer in *Days Like These* (series, 1999). She also played Lucy Lastic in *Gone to Seed* (series, 1992) and Louise in *EastEnders* (1996) and has appeared in guest roles in *Red Dwarf, The Comic Strip Presents...* (various episodes), *Casualty, The Bill* (10 episodes) and *Grange Hill* (2002).

David Stoll

David Stoll, who played the Distraught Manager in *Carry On Regardless*, has been 'in the business' for fifty years.

Born in 1922 and the eldest grandson of music hall impresario, Sir Oswald Stoll, David has enjoyed a long and successful stage career. Among his most notable theatre credits are *The Way Things Go* (with Kenneth More and Glynis Johns), *Birthday Honours* (with Moira Lister and Hugh Latimer) and *Quartet for Five* (with Rachel Roberts).

David has also worked on stage with Dame Peggy Ashcroft, Dame Celia Johnson and Sir Ralph Richardson in *Lloyd George Knew My Father*, subsequently touring the USA and Canada in the same play. He also played in *Key for Two* (with Moira Lister and Patrick Cargill, q.v.) and co-starred with Sheila Hancock (q.v.) in *The Bed Before Yesterday*.

In addition to *Carry On Regardless*, David's occasional film credits include *Death of an Angel* (1952), *Private's Progress* (1956), *The Night We Dropped a Clanger* (1959), *Little Dorrit* (1988), *King Ralph* (1991, as the Butler) and *The Secret Garden* (1993, as the grandfather at the dock).

On television David has appeared in numerous sitcoms and series, including *Yus My Dear, The Swish of the Curtain* (as Mr Bell), *Keep It in the Family* and *The Bretts*. His most recent appearances include guest roles in *All at No. 20, The New Statesman, Casualty*, *Mr. Bean* and *Backup*.

In 2001 David recalled that his work on *Carry On Regardless* was filmed in just one day! In recent years David, who is now in his eighties, has slowed down on his acting commitments.

Marianne Stone (b. Mary Haydon Stone)

With an incredible fifty-year acting career, Marianne Stone appeared in nine *Carry On* films throughout almost the entire lifespan of the series.

Born in London on 23 August 1922, Marianne Stone trained at RADA and made her film debut in *Brighton Rock* in 1947. Well over 200 film appearances would follow over the next four decades, giving her a record as one of Britain's most prolific actors. After a brief spell as a leading lady Marianne was invariably seen in minor supporting roles and was especially effective when cast as wives, mothers or nosy neighbours.

Marianne Stone made her *Carry On* debut in *Carry On Nurse*, as Cyril Chamberlain's wife, Alice Able. The pair had previously worked together in *Simon and Laura* (1955) and they were able to give polished performances. Marianne turned up five years later as the owner of Dirty Dick's Tavern in *Carry On Jack* and could be seen as Joan Sims's friend, Mrs Parker, in *Carry On Screaming*. She gave a spirited cameo performance as the Landlady in *Carry On Don't Lose Your Head* and also had cameo roles in *Carry On Doctor* (as the exasperated mother with a problem son) and *Carry On Girls* (as Miss Drew). Her largest *Carry On* role was as the excitable Maud in *Carry On At Your Convenience*, again alongside Joan Sims. Marianne's finest role in the *Carry On* series was as Old Maggie in *Carry On Dick* as she elegantly informed Kenneth Williams and Jack Douglas about Big Dick's curious birthmark. She made a final appearance in the series as Mrs Rowan, one of Windsor Davies's customers, in *Carry On Behind*.

In addition to the *Carry On* films, Marianne was seen in the film version of *Bless This House* (1972) and played Madame Petra in 'The Case of the Screaming Winkles', an episode of *Carry On Laughing*. She also filmed a scene in *Carry On Matron*, which sadly hit the cutting room floor.

Although notable as a *Carry On* 'regular', her nine appearances in the series represent a tiny proportion of an extraordinary film career. A popular addition to the cast, Marianne regrettably admitted to having "nothing to tell" about the series when contacted in 1998.

Marianne Stone retired from acting in the mid-1980s, her final screen appearances having included *The Wicked Lady* (1983) and *Déjà Vu* (1985). She was a surprise guest at the *Carry On* 40th Anniversary reunion at Pinewood Studios in 1998 (but did not appear in the official group photograph) and returned to the studios again in 2004 for the Joan Sims tribute celebrations.

Marianne was married to the show business columnist Peter Noble (1917-97) for over fifty years and they had two daughters, one of whom is journalist Kara Noble.

Marianne Stone died peacefully at her London home on 21 December 2009, aged eighty-seven.

Philip Stone (b. P. Stones)

A distinctive character actor of stage, screen and television, Philip Stone played Robinson, Kenneth Williams's boss, in *Carry On Loving* and was credited with the role of Mr. Bulstrode in *Carry On At Your Convenience* (although the latter was cut from the final film release).

Philip Stone was born in Yorkshire on 14 April 1924. He graduated as an actor through work in provincial repertory theatres, having previously worked as a laminated spring maker. His early career was interrupted at the end of the 1940s by a serious bout of tuberculosis and he was lucky to survive. Returning to the stage, he eventually made it to the West End before moving on to appear in film and television.

Philip's small-screen credits included the first two episodes of *The Avengers* (1961), *Jacks and Knaves* (1961), *The Rat Catchers* (1965-66, as the Brigadier), *Star Maidens* (1976), *Harem* (mini-series, 1986), *Heartbeat* (1994), *Moses* (1996), *A Touch of Frost* (1997), *A Certain Justice* (1998) and *Doomwatch: Winter Angel* (1999).

Philip's film appearances are equally varied and he held the rare distinction of having appeared in three of Stanley Kubrick's films: *A Clockwork Orange* (1971), *Barry Lyndon* (1975) and *The Shining* (1980). Additional appearances included *Fragment of Fear* (1970), *Hitler: The Last Ten Days* (1973), *The Medusa Touch* (1978), *S.O.S. Titanic* (1979), *Flash Gordon* (1980) and *Indiana Jones and the Temple of Doom* (1984).

Philip and his wife Margaret (who died in 1981) had two children, Katie and Matthew. Philip continued to act up until the end of his life and in his late seventies he toured the country with his one-man stage show. His autobiography, *Beginnings and Endings ... An Actor's Way*, was published in 1998.

Philip Stone died in London on 15 June 2003, aged seventy-nine.

Carry On ... ***Quotes***

I don't remember much about my Carry On *experience. I see from my accounts book, I did one day's filming on* Carry On Loving *in May 1970 and one day's filming on* Carry On At Your Convenience *in April 1971. Two fleeting days thirty years ago.*
I remember Kenneth Williams was very easy to work with – we had longish scenes together. He told me he took sleeping tablets in the form of suppositories to give him a good night's sleep – they were more effective in that form he said. He was quite jokey, but I got the impression of a sad man really – in view of what happened I was right! We're not all as we seem.
So, you see, my Carry On *was a brief Carry On!*
Philip Stone, 2000

George Street

George Street, who played the club receptionist in *Carry On Regardless*, had a film career stretching back to the late 1930s. Usually seen in small roles, often as innkeepers, publicans and general workers, his screen credits included *Pastor Hall* (1940), *Pimpernel Smith* (1941), *Old Mother Riley Detective* (1943), *Chance of a Lifetime* (1950), *Gift Horse* (1952) and *Jack the Ripper* (1959). Prior to his solo appearance in the *Carry On* series, George had played the removal man in Gerald Thomas's *Please Turn Over* in 1959.

Eleanor Summerfield

Veteran character comedienne Eleanor Summerfield was cast in a guest role in the all-star production of *Carry On Regardless*. Unfortunately for fans of the popular actress, her scenes with Charles Hawtrey were cut from the final film release.

Eleanor Summerfield was born in London on 7 March 1921. She trained for acting under Lady Benson before going on to become a gold medal winner at RADA. Eleanor made her first stage appearance on tour with ENSA and in 1940 she played the young woman in *Cornelius* at Westminster Theatre. During the Second World War she worked at the War Office before returning to the stage at the end of 1945. Over the next decade Eleanor appeared in over a dozen stage plays, ranging from *A Phoenix Too Frequent* (1946) to *When in Rome* (1959). Thereafter most of her work was in films, television and radio, although she continued to make stage appearances until as late as 1989, when she received critical acclaim for her role as Lady Wishfort in *The Way of the World*.

Blonde-haired with high-arched eyebrows and a natural comedic look, Eleanor made her film debut in *Take My Life* in 1947. She went on to make over forty film appearances, including *London Belongs to Me* (1948), *The Weaker Sex* (1948), *Scrooge* (1951), *Top Secret* (1952), *Street Corner* (1953), *Lost* (1956), *Dentist in the Chair* (1960), *Petticoat Pirates* (1961), *On the Beat* (1962), *The Yellow Hat* (1966), *Some Will, Some Won't* (1970) and *The Watcher in the Woods* (1980).

In addition to her many stage and screen roles, Eleanor Summerfield was also well known as a radio personality, especially in *Many a Slip*, with Roy Plomley. Her early television appearances included *The Amazing Dr. Clitterhouse* (1947), *My Wife's Sister* (1956), *The Two Charlies* (1959, with Charlie Drake), *Night Train to Surbition* (1965) and as Aunt Dahlia in *The World of Wooster* (1965-67). In later years she turned up for guest appearance in programmes such as *Casualty* and *Lovejoy*.

By the mid-1990s Eleanor Summerfield was 'semi-retired' from acting, but towards the end of her life she featured in scene-stealing roles on the small screen, notably in *Jake's Progress* (1995) and as Alice in *Family Money* (1997, with June Whitfield, q.v.). In 1997 she gave a delightful performance opposite Peter Jones (q.v.) in 'Faithful Unto Death', an episode of *Midsomer Murders*. It was her final acting role.

Eleanor was married to actor Leonard Sachs (1911-90) from 1947, and they had two sons, Toby and actor Robin Sachs (1951-). Robin, who has spent the past twenty years of his career working in America, is well known for his work in television series such as *Babylon 5* and *Buffy the Vampire Slayer*.

Eleanor Summerfield died in a London hospital on 13 July 2001, aged eighty.

Carry On ... ***Quotes***

I'm afraid I can't help you much with Carry On *anecdotes. All my scenes were with Charlie Hawtrey and that entire storyline was cut from the final print. I had a charming letter from the producer apologising – they had over-run so much that they had to make a big cut. However, I do remember enjoying the shooting of* Carry On Regardless *very much.*
Eleanor Summerfield, 1998

Derek Sydney

Derek Sydney played the Algerian Gent in *Carry On Spying* and the Major Domo in *Carry On Up the Khyber*.

Derek Sydney was born in Whitechapel, London, on 11 January 1920. He won an Alexander Korda Scholarship and trained for acting at RADA. In addition to the *Carry On* series, his film credits included *Hot Ice* (1952), *The Constant Husband* (1955), *Gentlemen Marry Brunettes* (1955), *Passport to Treason* (1956), *Sands of the Desert* (1960), *Make Mine Mink* (1960) and *Vendetta for the Saint* (1969). He also appeared on television from the late 1950s.

Fully retired from 1990, Derek Sydney divided his final years between London and America, where he undertook charity work. He died in San Marcos, California, after suffering a heart attack, on 18 June 2000. He was eighty years old.

Jonathan Tafler

Jonathan Tafler, along with several other young actors, was unrecognisable in his solo *Carry On* role. He played one of the hooded Inquisitors (number three, for the record!) in *Carry On Columbus*.

Jonathan, who in addition to *Carry On Columbus* appeared in the

Barbra Streisand film *Yentl* (1983, as Jacov), has mainly worked on television, where his credits include *A.D.* (mini-series, 1985), *Paul Merton – Does China Exist* (1997), *London Bridge* (1997, as Terry), *Cadfael III: The Holy Thief* (1997, as Moneylender), *EastEnders* (1998, as David Samuels), *Foyle's War* (2003, as Max Joseph), *Murphy's Law* (2005, as Max Levine) and *Doctors* (2 episodes).

Sydney Tafler

Dark-haired character actor Sydney Tafler featured among the all-star cast of *Carry On Regardless*, playing the strip club manager opposite Charles Hawtrey. It was his only *Carry On* appearance.

Sydney Tafler was born in London on 31 July 1916. He trained for acting at RADA after gaining a scholarship and enjoyed a varied acting career on stage, screen, television and radio.

Sydney made his screen debut in *It Always Rains on Sunday* (1947) and over the next thirty years made more than seventy film appearances. Adept as untrustworthy characters in comic or dramatic roles, his film credits included *London Belongs to Me* (1948), *Passport to Pimlico* (1949), *The Lavender Hill Mob* (1951), *Hotel Sahara* (1951), *Time Gentlemen, Please!* (1952), *Cockleshell Heroes* (1955), *Reach for the Sky* (1956), *Too Many Crooks* (1959), *Make Mine Mink* (1960), *The Bulldog Breed* (1960), *Alfie* (1966), *Danger Point* (1971) and *The Spy Who Loved Me* (1977).

On the small screen from the late 1940s, Sidney was memorable as Charlie Davenport in the 1960 series *Citizen James*, with Sid James and Liz Fraser (both q.v.), and he later made guest appearances in programmes such as *Vienna 1900* (1973), *Some Mother Do 'Ave 'Em* (1973), *The Sweeney* (1975) and *Survivors* (1976).

Sydney was married to leading lady Joy Shelton (1922-2000) and they had a daughter and two sons.

Sydney Tafler was sixty-three when he died in London (from cancer) on 8 November 1979.

Gordon Tanner

Canadian-born actor Gordon Tanner played the 1st Specialist examining Kenneth Connor in *Carry On Sergeant*. It was his only *Carry On* appearance.

Born in Toronto on 17 July 1918, Gordon appeared in films and on television for almost thirty years. Before moving to the UK he made his American screen debut in *Golden Arrow* in 1949. His subsequent appearances ranged from *On the Run* (1958) to *Eskimo Nell* (1975, as Big Dick).

Gordon Tanner died on 3 August 1983, aged sixty-five.

Jack Taylor

Jack Taylor made his film debut in *Robin Hood and His Merry Men* in 1952. In the *Carry On* series he played Cliff in *Carry On Constable*, the Policeman in *Carry On Regardless* and the 1st Thug in *Carry On Spying*. He is believed to have died in 1968.

Larry Taylor

Character actor Larry Taylor appeared in bit-part roles in three *Carry On* films: *Carry On Follow That Camel*, *Carry On Up the Khyber* and *Carry On Dick*.

Larry Taylor was born in Peterborough on 13 July 1918 and began his acting career in 1946. After making his film debut in 1947, Larry spent several years touring the country in repertory.

In his fifty-year career Larry made over eighty screen appearances, mainly in bit parts or cameo roles. Among his film appearances were *Take a Powder* (1953), *Alexander the Great* (1956), *Robbery Under Arms* (1957), *Exodus* (1958), *The Gypsy and the Gentleman* (1958), *Too Hot to Handle* (1960), *Swiss Family Robinson* (1960), *Lawrence of Arabia* (1962), *Cleopatra* (1962), *The Girl Hunters* (1963), *Zulu* (1964), *Judith* (1966), *The Magnificent Two* (1967), *Chitty Chitty Bang Bang* (1968), *Cromwell* (1969), *The Wife Swappers* (1970), *Mary Queen of Scots* (1971), *Ooh … You Are Awful* (1972), *The Creeping Flesh* (1973), *S.P.Y.S.* (1974), *Slavers* (1978) and *Zulu Dawn* (1979).

In the *Carry On*'s Larry can be seen as Riff in *Follow That Camel*, the Burpa at the door-grid in *Up the Khyber* and one of the tough men in *Carry On Dick*. Larry continued to work into his eighties, doing "the odd commercial – to keep active".

Having worked in South Africa in 1963 when filming for *Zulu*, Larry returned there for a holiday in 1974 and remained there until his death. He suffered a heart attack at the age of eighty-five and died on 6 August 2003.

Carry On … **Quotes**

I have got to say everybody who worked on the Carry On *series loved the whole set-up; it was a happy family affair. The pay was rather small for those days. I made three of them and the one I enjoyed the most was* Follow That Camel. *Phil Silvers was wonderful to work with, and we became good pals.*
Larry Taylor, 2000

Thelma Taylor

Thelma played Seneca's servant in *Carry On Cleo*.

Leon Thau

Leon, who was born in Israel in 1926, played Stinghi in *Carry On Up the Khyber*. He also featured in several other films, notably *The Great St Trinian's Train Robbery* (1966, as the Pakistani Porter) and *The Magic Christian* (1969, as the engine room toff).

Leon's television appearances included *All Square* (1966), *The Gnomes of Dulwich* (series, 1969, as Plastic, with Terry Scott and John Clive, both q.v.), *The World of Beachcomber* (1969), *Up Pompeii*, with Frankie Howerd, and the children's series *T-Bag* from 1986 to 1990.

Lisa Thomas

Lisa played Sally in *Carry On Cowboy*. A year later she made a second (and final) film appearance as Sura in *One Million Years B.C.*.

Jimmy Thompson (b. James Edward Thompson)

Jimmy Thompson was perfectly cast for appearances in three *Carry On's*. The dark-haired, cheeky-looking character actor was memorable as Mr Delling (with Liz Fraser and Carole Shelley, both q.v.) in *Carry On Regardless* and as passenger Sam Turner in *Carry On Cruising*. He made a final appearance as Lord Nelson in *Carry On Jack*.

Jimmy Thompson was born in Halifax, Yorkshire, on 30 October 1925. He trained as a construction engineer and spent two years working for his father's company. During his spare time Jimmy worked as an amateur actor at Halifax Playhouse and was accepted as a student member of the Arts Council of West Riding Theatre. During the war he was called up for military service and joined the Durham Light Infantry. He was later transferred to the RAMC, where he entertained the troops in revues and plays.

After being demobbed Jimmy travelled to London, where he was engaged to appear in *Oranges and Lemons*, which ran for 177 performances until 1949. He then went on to pursue one of the busiest stage careers of any *Carry On* actor, with countless theatre credits such as *Penny Plain* (443 performances on tour with Max Adrian and Joyce Grenfell, 1951-52), *For Amusement Only* (revue, 1956), *The Quiz Kid* (title role as Simon Merridew, 1959-60), *Charley's Aunt* (tour, 1964), *The Shooting Party* (1966), *The Clandestine Marriage* (tour, 1971) and *A Funny Thing Happened on the Way to the Forum* (tour, 1973-74).

Jimmy remained busy in the theatre until the early 1990s, his later credits including *Hay Fever* (tour, 1975, with Phyllis Calvert), *Don't Just Lie There, Say Something!* (tour, 1975), *The Mikado* (1983), *No, No, Nanette* (1984) and *Spread a Little Happiness* (1992). From the late 1970s he was also called upon frequently to appear in pantomime and he has also directed on stage.

In addition to the *Carry On* series, Jimmy's film appearances included *The Whole Truth* (1958), *The Man Who Liked Funerals* (1959, co-starring Leslie Phillips and Susan Beaumont, both q.v.) and *Raising the Wind* (1961), for Gerald Thomas. He was later seen in *Those Magnificent Men in Their Flying Machines* (1965) and played the ship's doctor in *Doctor in Trouble* (1970).

On television Jimmy's appearances ranged from *The Benny Hill Show* to *George and Mildred*. He also appeared in *Here and Now* (series, 1956, with Joan Sims), *Faces of Jim – The Face of Wisdom* (1961) and *Pinky and Perky* (1964), and he played Roger in *The Very Merry Widow* (series, 1969). In later years Jimmy concentrated on running his own production company, Marcel Productions.

Jimmy Thompson was married to Nina (who died in 1999) and had two children, Sandra and Roderick. He spent his final years living in York, where he died on 21 April 2005, aged seventy-nine.

Frank Thornton (b. Frank Thornton Ball)

Probably best known as Captain Peacock in the long-running television sitcom *Are You Being Served?* and latterly familiar as Truly in *Last of the Summer Wine*, Frank Thornton played the outraged shop manager in *Carry On Screaming*. It was his only *Carry On* appearance.

Born in London on 15 January 1921, Frank's first job was as an insurance clerk before training at the London School of Dramatic Art from 1940. He made his professional stage debut (on April Fool's Day!) in County Tipperary in *French Without Tears*, with Donald Wolfit. After several stage appearances in London Frank went on to serve with the RAF for almost four years during the Second World War.

From 1946 Frank toured in repertory before moving into West End productions opposite such legendary performers as Ralph Lynn, Robertson Hare and Alfred Drayton. Despite a busy television career Frank has consistently returned to the stage, where his distinguished list of credits includes time with the Royal Shakespeare Company. Well into his seventies he was still treading the boards, his latter appearances including *Hobson's Choice* (1995-96, as Henry Horatio Hobson) and *Cash On Delivery* (1996-97, as Mr Jenkins).

Frank made his screen debut in 1953 and has since made over fifty film appearances, usually in cameo roles. His film career peaked in the 1960s when he turned up for all kinds of roles in films, such as *The Dock Brief* (1962), *The Wild Affair* (1963), *The Comedy Man* (1964), *A Hard Day's Night* (1964), Peter Roger's *The Big Job* (1965), *Gonks Go Beat* (1965), *A Funny Thing Happened on the Way to the Forum* (1966), *Thirty Is a Dangerous Age, Cynthia* (1968), *Till Death Us Do Part* (1969) and *The Magic Christian* (1969). In the 1970s Frank was seen in several low-budget comedies, including *Up the Chastity Belt* (1971), *Bless This House* (1972, again for Rogers and Thomas), *No Sex Please, We're British* (1973), *Our Miss Fred* (1974) and *Vampira* (1974). Frank's most recent screen appearances were as Dame Maggie Smith's butler in *Gosford Park* (2001) and the gardener in *Back in Business* (2007).

On the small screen Frank has chiefly been seen in comic roles, notably in Spike Milligan's *It's a Square World* (1960-64) and *HMS Paradise* (1964, as Commander Fairweather). He gained worldwide recognition as the acidic Captain Peacock in eleven series of *Are You Being Served?* (1972-84) and resurrected the role in the early 1990s in *Grace & Favour* (1992-93). In 1998 Frank continued his long television career, taking on the role of Detective Sergeant Herbert 'Truly' Truelove in *Last of the Summer Wine*. It kept him busy until the series ended in 2010.

Frank's additional television appearances include *Steptoe and Son, The Goodies, The Taming of the Shrew* (1980), *Great Expectations* (mini-series, 1989), *The Upper Hand, The Old Curiosity Shop* (mini-series, 1994), *All Rise for Julian Clary* (1996) and *Casualty* (2001). He was the subject of *This Is Your Life* in 1998.

Frank Thornton returned to Pinewood Studios in 1998 for the *Carry On* 40th Anniversary reunion and three years later was present at the Kenneth Williams celebrations. In 2008 he was once again at the studios for the 50th Anniversary celebrations.

Frank has been married to former actress Beryl Evans since 1945 and they have one daughter, stage manager Jane Thornton. Away from acting Frank enjoys spending time with his family (including his three grandchildren), photography, music and wildlife conservation. He lives in London.

Silvestre Tobias (aka: Selva Rasalingam)

Silvestre played Abdullah in *Carry On Columbus*. It was the beginning of a career that includes appearances in films such as *Son of the Pink Panther* (1993), *Anita and Me* (2002), *Man About Dog* (2004) and *The Devil's Double* (2010) and on television in *Holby City, Jonathan Creek, The Bill, Waking the Dead*, *Coronation Street* and *Torchwood*.

Bob Todd (b. Brian Todd)

A familiar face on television through his long-running role in *The Benny Hill Show*, Bob Todd played the unfortunate man on the breathing apparatus in *Carry On Again Doctor*. He also appeared in the 1970 television special, *Carry On Again Christmas*.

Bob Todd was born in Faversham, Kent, on 15 December 1921. A former cattle breeder, Bob made his first television appearances in *The Channel Swimmer* (1962, as the boat pilot) and *Citizen James* (1963, with Sid James). The plump, bald-headed actor quickly went on to become a top 'foil' for Dick Emery, Marty Feldman and Benny Hill.

Bob's numerous television credits included *The Best Things in Life* (series, 1970, as Mr Pollard), *Cribbins* (1969-70, with Bernard Cribbins), *The Marty Feldman Comedy Machine* (1972) and *Doctor at Sea* (series, 1974, as Entertainments Officer). He was later seen in *Jane* (series, 1984, as Professor Crankshaft), *The Jim Davidson Show* (regular) and *The Steam Video Company* (series, 1984). Bob's only starring role on television was in the 1972 series *In for a Penny*, playing Dan, the lavatory man.

Although best known as a television actor, Bob also appeared in a range of films, including *Hot Millions* (1968), *Scars of Dracula* (1970), *Bachelor of Arts* (1971), *Burke & Hare* (1972), *That's Your Funeral* (1972), *Mutiny on the Buses* (1972), *Adolf Hitler – My Part in His Downfall* (1972), *Digby, The Biggest Dog in the World* (1973), *The Four Musketeers* (1974), *Rosie Dixon Night Nurse* (1978), *Superman III* (1983) and *The Return of the Musketeers* (1989).

On television, in addition to his work with Benny Hill, Bob also worked with comic legend Eric Sykes on numerous occasions, having guest roles in the television series *Sykes* and several specials including *Rhubarb Rhubarb* (1980), *It's Your Move* (1982) and *Mr. H Is Late* (1987).

Bob Todd was married for forty-five years and he and his wife Monica had one daughter, Anne, and two sons, John and Patrick.

Bob died on 21 October 1992, just six months after Benny Hill. He was seventy years old.

Paul Toothill

Paul played Gunner Gale in *Carry On England*.

Harry Towb

A versatile character actor of stage, screen and television, Harry Towb made a cameo appearance in *Carry On At Your Convenience*, as the bespectacled, hot-under-the-collar narrator of the dubious sex film watched by Bernard Bresslaw and Kenneth Cope!

Harry Towb was born in Larne, County Antrim (Ireland) on 27 July 1925. He began his theatrical career at the Guildhall, Londonderry, before making his stage debut in *The Gentle Gunman*. During his long career Harry made numerous stage appearances, ranging from musicals to work with the RSC and National Theatre Company. He made his New York stage debut in *Under the Weather* in 1966 and toured with Patrick Mower (q.v.) and Dennis Waterman in *Bing-Bong* in 1999. In his eighties he was still treading the boards, playing Tiresias in *Antigone* at the Waterfront Hall, Belfast, shortly before his death.

After making his screen debut in *The Quiet Woman* (1950) Harry appeared in over thirty films, including *The Gift Horse* (1952), *Eyewitness* (1956), *The End of the Line* (1957), *All Night Long* (1962), *Thirty Is a Dangerous Age, Cynthia* (1968), *The Bliss of Mrs. Blossom* (1968), *Digby, the Biggest Dog in the World* (1973), *Barry Lyndon* (1975), *Lassister* (1984), *Moll Flanders* (1996), *Conspiracy of Silence* (2003), *Cheeky* (2003), *The 10th Man* (2006) and *Gardens with Red Roses* (2009).

On television Harry featured in countless series over a forty-year period. One of his earliest appearances was as Mike Kelly in two series of *Joan and Leslie* (1956-58) and he later went on to play Private Dooley in *The Army Game* (1959-60). In the 1980s Harry was familiar as butler Henry Compton in four series of *Home James!* (1987-90, with Jim Davidson) and played George Nathan in the 1991 series *So You Think You've Got Troubles*. Harry's innumerable guest appearances on the small screen included episodes of *Doctor Who, The Avengers, Paradise Postponed, The Camomile Lawn* and, latterly, *The Bill* (2001-07, various characters), *Holby City* (2001, as Jack Herrmann) and *Heartbeat* (2005, as Hugo Cummins). His final television role was in two episodes of *EastEnders* (playing David) in 2008.

Harry Towb died at his London home, following a short battle with cancer, on 24 July 2009.

Anthony Trent

Anthony played a Herald in 'One in the Eye for Harold', an episode of *Carry On Laughing* on television in 1975.

Virginia Tyler

Virginia had uncredited roles in two *Carry On* films: as a Funhouse Girl in *Carry On Spying* and as a Hand Maiden in *Carry On Cleo*.

Stanley Unwin

A unique British entertainer celebrated for his 'Unwinese' or gobbledegook, Stanley Unwin had a leading guest role as the Landlord in *Carry On Regardless*. It was a memorable solo appearance in the series.

Stanley Unwin was born in Pretoria, South Africa, on 7 June 1911. He returned to England with his mother in 1914, following the death of his father. After two years' training at nautical school Stanley obtained a first class GPO Wireless Operator's Certificate and went to sea at the age of sixteen as a deckhand. He later spent three years with a wireless business in London's East End before joining the Plessy Company in Ilford, designing and building electronic test equipment. He joined the BBC as an electronics engineer in 1940 and four years later joined the War Reporting Unit. As a sound recorder he covered the D-Day dispatches, the Paris Peace Conference and the 1947 Royal tour of South Africa.

A deep interest in foreign languages led to Stanley's creation of 'Unwinese' (a term coined by Gerald Nethercot of BBC public relations in 1946). After being auditioned by Ted Kavanagh, writer of *ITMA*, Stanley made his first radio broadcasts on *Mirror of the Month* in 1948. While his children were growing up Stanley continued to work for the BBC, making occasional broadcasts on radio.

Stanley officially entered show business in 1961, joining Equity, appearing in cabaret and working as an after dinner speaker. He had already made his film debut in *Fun At St. Fanny's* (1956) and went on to appear in the Frankie Howerd comedy, *Further Up the Creek* (1958). As the Landlord in *Carry On Regardless* Stanley had a recurring role, baffling Sid James and Esma Cannon to the point of desperation! Only in the final stages of the film is Stanley's 'Unwinese' deciphered by Kenneth Williams: "Goodlee byelode". Stanley's additional screen appearances included *Hair of the Dog* (1962) and *Press for Time* (1966), and he played the Chancellor in *Chitty Chitty Bang Bang* (1968).

On television Stanley played Father Stanley Unwin in *The Secret Service*, Gerry Anderson's puppet series, in 1969. He also appeared in *The Laughing Prisoner* (1988), *Lazarus and Dingwall* (1991) and *Inside Victor Lewis-Smith* (1993). He continued to appear as a guest on shows such as *Jim Davidson's Generation Game* and *The Freddie Starr Show* well into his eighties.

Stanley Unwin married in 1939 and he and his wife Frances had a son and two daughters. Stanley was widowed in 1994. His hobbies included listening to music of "all sorts" and "translating philosophical and classical work into Unwinese". Stanley wrote several children's books in addition to his 1985 autobiography, *Deep Joy*.

A survivor from a bygone age of British entertainment, Stanley Unwin died peacefully at the Danetre Hospital in Daventry, Northamptonshire, on 12 January 2002. He was ninety years old.

*Carry On ... **Quotes***

Of my Carry On *associates Kenneth Williams was especially good to work with. He had immediate comprehension of the meaning contained in my nonsense. Sid James too. Always quick to use a good ad lib.*
My choice for the film Carry On Regardless *was suggested by my agent, Johnnie Riscoe, who heard me on radio and insisted I took his telephone number. I knew most of the characters in these films, like Kenneth Connor, Bill Owen, Sid James and especially Kenneth Williams, who was among the best feeds I was lucky enough to work with. Bernard Braden was another great feed, then Ted Ray. Because of my rather late entry into the business I am happy to take on cameo parts in films and ad hoc radio and TV work.*
Stanley Unwin, 1998

Nikki van der Zyl (aka: Monica van der Zyl)

Nikki van der Zyl, who played the messenger girl in *Carry On Don't Lose Your Head* and featured as a stunt actress in *Carry On Cleo*, has enjoyed a varied career and is perhaps best known for her work in nine of the Bond '007' films.

The daughter of Rabi Dr. Werner van der Zyl (founder of the Leo Baeck College), Nikki was born in Berlin, Germany, and moved to England at the age of four. After training at the Central School of Speech and Drama, she worked on stage before embarking on a busy film and television career.

In addition to her post-synchronisation work in the iconic Bond films and her involvement in the *Carry On* series, Nikki also worked on Hammer Horror films and more than fifty other screen favourites including *What A Whopper* (1961), *One Million Years B.C* (1966, as the voice of Raquel Welch), *The Oblong Box* (1969), *Every Home Should Have One* (1970) and *Up the Front* (1972). Nikki's television work included classics such as *The Saint* and *The Persuaders*, revoicing a variety of characters.

Although much of Nikki's work on screen and television was in an uncredited capacity she has nevertheless enjoyed an enviable career having worked closely with great names of the cinema including Sir Sean Connery, Sir Roger Moore and the late Tony Curtis.

After qualifying as a barrister in 1973, Nikki worked in the House of Commons as a political assistant to an MP and then joined the Press Gallery of the House of Commons as a broadcast journalist for a television company. She has many other interests, including singing, song writing and jewellery design, and published a book of poetry, *MPs in Verse* in 1990. Nikki also gives frequent talks and after-dinner speeches, particularly on the Bond films and her time at the House of Commons. In 2010 she was interviewed by Fiona Bruce for an episode of *The Antiques Roadshow*.

Nikki is married and lives in London.

Carry On ... Quotes

I worked on Carry On Cleo *as a stand-in (stunt double) for Cleo and was the girl wrapped up in the carpet when it was rolled out in front of Julius Caesar. Naturally in the first take I rolled out and hit a trestle table with fruit resting on it! Needless to say we had to do a retake!*
Cleopatra's bath water was made with real milk, so you can imagine the smell after the studio lights had been on it for a while .... I had to stand in for Amanda Barrie in the bath and of course Sid James didn't want me to get out. He was full of jokes and that was Sid James being Sid James! I got to know Kenny Williams quite well and really do remember those days as a fun time. I had the chance to meet Peter Rogers again, not long before his death. He was a wonderful gentleman and hadn't changed at all.
Nikki van der Zyl, 2010

John Van Eyssen

John Van Eyssen, who played Stephens in *Carry On Nurse*, was best known as Chief Production Executive for Columbia Pictures in Britain (1969-73).

Born in South Africa on 19 March 1922, John made his film debut in The Angel with the *Trumpet* in 1950. Over the next decade he went on to appear in more than twenty films, including *The Men of Sherwood Forest* (1954, as Will Scarlett), *The Cockleshell Heroes* (1955), *Brothers in Law* (1957), *Dracula* (1958), *I'm All Right, Jack* (1959), *Blind Date* (1959) and *Marriage of Convenience* (1961).

John, who from the mid-1970s worked as a theatrical agent, was the companion of screen legend Ingrid Bergman up until her death from cancer in 1982. John himself succumbed to cancer thirteen years later, dying in London on 13 November 1995, aged seventy-three.

Valerie Van Ost

Glamorous actress Valerie Van Ost appeared in four *Carry On's*. She played a GlamCab driver in *Carry On Cabby*, the 2nd Lady listening to Charles Hawtrey in *Carry On Don't Lose Your Head*, the nurse with Sid James in *Carry On Doctor* and the out-patients nurse (with Patricia Hayes and Jim Dale) in *Carry On Again Doctor*.

Valerie, who was born on 25 July 1944 (some sources say 1942), also appeared in *Corruption* (1967), *School for Unclaimed Girls* (1969) and a couple of Horror Hammer films: *Incense for the Damned* (1972) and *The Satanic Rites of Dracula* (1974). One of her final acting roles was on television in 1976, ironically in the Sid James series *Bless This House*.

Valerie left the acting profession in the 1970s and now runs her own casting agency in London.

Colin Vancao

Colin played Wilberforce Grubb, one of Imogen Hassall's peculiar relatives in *Carry On Loving*. His sporadic acting career included appearances in films and television, ranging from *Charge of the Light Brigade* (1968) to *Minder on the Orient Express* (1985). He moved to Australia in the 1970s, where he continued to act (with roles in series such as *Prisoner: Cell Block H*) up until 1990. He died in 1992.

Sue Vaughan

Sue had an uncredited role as a Hospitality Girl in *Carry On Up the Khyber*.

Wanda Ventham

A striking leading lady, Wanda Ventham appeared in cameo roles in two *Carry On* films. She can be spotted as the attractive bidder at the auction for Jim Dale in *Carry On Cleo* and also played one of the Khasi's wives in *Carry On Up the Khyber*.

Born in Brighton on 5 August 1935 (some sources say 1938 or 1939), Wanda trained at the Central School of Speech and Drama and began her career in films such as *My Teenage Daughter* (1956) and *The Navy Lark* (1959). She went on to become a leading actress, with screen appearances ranging from light comedy to House of Hammer horrors. In addition to the *Carry On's*, Wanda also worked for Peter Rogers in *The Big Job* (1965), and her other film appearances have included *The Spy with the Cold Nose* (1966), *Love Is a Woman* (1967), *The Blood Beast Terror* (1968), *Captain Kronos – Vampire Hunter* (1974), *Mrs Caldicot's Cabbage War* (2000) and *Asylum* (2005).

In the theatre Wanda worked with Esma Cannon (q.v.) in *Watch It, Sailor!* in the early 1960s and more recently has been seen in the works of Ray Cooney.

On television Wanda Ventham is one of the country's busiest actresses. She began her small-screen career in the early 1960s playing Shirley in *The Rag Trade* (1963) and has since appeared in countless series, including *Doctor Who* (1967 & '87), *UFO* (1970-73, as Colonel Virginia Lake), *The Lotus Eaters* (1970-72, as Ann Shepherd), *The Sweeney* (1975), *The Upchat Line* (1977), *Fallen Hero* (1978), *Union Castle* (1982, as Ursula, Lady Thaxted), *Executive Stress* (1986-88, as Sylvia), *Lost Empires* (mini-series, 1986), *Only Fools and Horses* (2 Christmas specials), *Capstick's Law* (series, 1989), *Just a Gigolo* (series, 1993), *Next of Kin* (1995-97, as Rosie), *Heartbeat* (1996-97, as Fiona Weston), *Hetty Wainthropp Investigates* (1997), *Dangerfield* (1998), *Verdict* (1998), *Hope and Glory* (2000), *Coupling* (2001), *Midsomer Murders: Second Sight* (2005) and *Lewis* (2007).

Wanda's first marriage, from which she has a daughter, ended in divorce and in April 1976 she married her second husband, actor Timothy Carlton, with whom she has co-starred in several TV series, including *Next of Kin*. Their son is the award-winning actor Benedict Cumberbatch (1976-).

Carry On ... ***Quotes***

I'm afraid you must forgive me, but I really wasn't involved in my two appearances in Carry On *films for more than a week at a time – and it was 35 years ago! I only had two tiny roles.*
Wanda Ventham, 1997

Vivienne Ventura

Vivienne played the Spanish Secretary in *Carry On Jack*.

James Villiers (b. J. Michael Hyde Villiers)

A character actor of stage, screen and television, James Villiers began his acting career as the 7th Recruit in *Carry On Sergeant*. It was the start of a screen career spanning forty years.

Born in London on 29 September 1933 (some sources say 1929 or 1930), James was a descendant of the Dukes of Rockingham. After training for two years at RADA he spent a season at Stratford-upon-Avon before making his West End stage debut in *Toad of Toad Hall* in 1954. He subsequently spent two years with the Old Vic and a year with the English Stage Company. Among James Villiers's many stage credits were

Henry IV, The White Devil, The Way of the World, Saint Joan and *The Doctor's Dilemma*.

James's film appearances included *Operation Snatch* (1962), *Murder at the Gallop* (1963), *Father Came Too!* (1964), *King & Country* (1964), *Repulsion* (1965), *The Nanny* (1965), *The Alphabet Murders* (1965), *Otley* (1968), *A Nice Girl Like Me* (1969), *Blood from the Mummy's Tomb* (1971), *Asylum* (1972), *Joseph Andrews* (1977), *For Your Eyes Only* (1981), *Mantrap* (1983), *Scandal* (1989), *King Ralph* (1991), *Let Him Have It* (1991), *Uncovered* (1994), *E=mc2* (1996) and *The Tichborne Claimant* (1998).

On the small screen he made guest appearances in a variety of telefilms, mini-series and series, including *The Saint, The Avengers, The First Churchills* (1969, as Charles II), *Lady Windermere's Fan* (1972), *The Marquise* (1980), *Dick Turpin* and *Rumpole of the Bailey*. Although best known for dramatic performances (perhaps not surprisingly in aristocratic roles), James could also turn his hand to comedy, appearing in *Marty Back Together Again* (1974, with Marty Feldman), *Emery Presents* (1983, with Dick Emery) and three series of *The Other 'Arf* (1980-82, as Lord Freddy Apthorpe).

James continued to work on television until the end of his life, with latter appearances in *Lovejoy, Fortunes of War* (mini-series, 1987), *House of Cards* (1990), *The Memoirs of Sherlock Holmes* (1994) and *A Dance to the Music of Time* (1997, as Buster Foxe).

James's eighteen-year marriage to Patricia Donovan ended in divorce in 1984 and he married secondly Lucy Jex. Away from acting he enjoyed collecting antiques and watching sport.

James Villiers died from cancer in Arundel, Sussex, on 18 January 1998. He was sixty-four years old.

Kenneth Waller

A familiar face to television viewers in the 1970s and 1980s and a veteran stage actor, Kenneth Waller played the barman in *Carry On Behind*. It was his only role in the series.

Kenneth Waller was born in Huddersfield, Yorkshire, on 5 November 1927. Following National Service in the RAF he began his career on stage at Huddersfield's Theatre Royal. After serving his apprenticeship with various repertory companies he made his West End debut in *Free as Air* (1957). His subsequent stage appearances included *Salad Days* (686 performances), *Solid Gold Cadillac* (with Sid James) and *Entertaining Mr Sloane* (with Barbara Windsor). He also made appearances in pantomime and continued to work on stage well into the 1990s, his final engagement being a tour of *Beauty and the Beast* in 1998.

Kenneth made his film debut in *Room at the Top* in 1959. His other film appearances were *Chitty Chitty Bang Bang* (1968), *Scrooge* (1970) and *The Love Pill* (1971).

On television Kenneth Waller was probably best known for his roles in two long-running sitcoms: as Mr Grace in *Are You Being Served?* (1978-81) and as the demanding Grandad in *Bread* (1986-91), for which he received the Variety Club BBC Personality of the Year Award in 1988. Kenneth also had guest roles in programmes such as *Boon* and *Coronation Street*.

Kenneth Waller, who never married, died in London on 28 January 2000, aged seventy-two.

Carry On ... Quotes

I was only involved for two days in Carry On Behind *playing a barman. It was all quite painless and the cast (particularly Ian Lavender) very friendly. Kenneth Williams was the only one who was a bit aloof and snooty.*
Kenneth Waller, 1998

Valerie Walsh

A leading lady on stage and television, Valerie Walsh played Lady Ermintrude in 'Under the Round Table', an episode of *Carry On Laughing*. It was her only *Carry On* appearance.

Valerie studied drama, singing and dance in London and Paris and was a member of the famous Joan Littlewood Theatre Workshop (notably on Broadway in *Oh, What a Lovely War!*, with Barbara Windsor). On stage Valerie also appeared in *Belle Star* (with Betty Grable), *Pieces of Eight*, *Gentlemen Prefer Blondes* and more recently *Cabaret* and *Stepping Out*.

Valerie also starred with Danny La Rue in the revue *London's Talk of the Town* for several years and was Bruce Forsyth's leading lady in *The Travelling Music Show*.

On television Valerie Walsh played Molly in the 1976 series *Yus My Dear* and more recently Rita Flanks in *High Street Blues* (1989). She also appeared in two films: *Evidence in Concrete* (1960) and *Strictly for the Birds* (1963).

Valerie, whose hobbies include carpentry, lives in London.

Guy Ward (aka: Merlyn Ward)

Guy, who played the Dandy in *Carry On Emmannuelle*, also featured in a couple of other films of the 1970s: *The Beast in the Cellar* (1970) and *The Stud* (1978).

Haydn Ward

Haydn played the 8th Recruit in *Carry On Sergeant*.

Michael Ward (b. George William Everard Yoe Ward)

An impeccable character actor, Michael Ward turned up for cameo roles in five *Carry On* films. His thirty-year career spent in sophisticated, effete roles was probably best summed up with his unforgettable appearance in *Carry On Cabby* as the Man in Tweeds opposite Kenneth Connor.

Michael Ward, the son of a clergyman, was born in Redruth, Cornwall, on 9 April 1909. From 1930 until the outbreak of the Second World War Michael was engaged as a private tutor, and during the war he worked as an ambulance driver. In 1946 Michael won a scholarship and trained at the Central School of Speech and Drama. He spent two years as an understudy for Vic Oliver and later made West End stage appearances that included *Alice in Wonderland, The Gay Pavilion* and *A Fig for Glory*.

Michael made his screen debut in *An Ideal Husband* (1947) and went on to make over sixty film appearances. By the 1950s, the tall, slender actor had moved into comic roles and proved a useful foil for top comedians, particularly Norman Wisdom in *Trouble in Store* (1953), *Man of the Moment* (1955), *Up in the World* (1956) and *Just My Luck* (1957). He was also memorable with Irene Handl, Joan Sims and Liz Fraser (all q.v.) in *Doctor in Love* (1960), and among his additional screen appearances were *Lost* (1956), *Brothers in Law* (1957), *The Ugly Duckling* (1959), *I'm All Right, Jack* (1959), *A Pair of Briefs* (1962) and *Smashing Time* (1967).

Michael made his *Carry On* debut as the mincing photographer in *Carry On Regardless* with Ian Wilson (q.v.) and Kenneth Williams. His finest moment in the series came when he played the Man in Tweeds opposite Kenneth Connor in *Carry On Cabby*. His perfect delivery of a famous line has gone down in history as a classic moment of British comedy. In *Carry On Cleo*, opposite Kenneth Williams and Sid James, Michael played the flouncing Archimedes, and he was equally successful as the distraught shop assistant, Mr Vivian, in *Carry On Screaming*. Michael's final role in the series was as the teary eyed, ultra camp Henri in *Carry On Don't Lose Your Head*, again with Sid James. Michael also worked for Peter Rogers and Gerald Thomas in their 1965 comedy *The Big Job*, playing an undertaker.

Michael Ward continued to appear in film roles throughout the 1970s. His final credits included *That's Your Funeral* (1972), *Man About the House*

(1974, with Melvyn Hayes, q.v.), *Frankenstein and the Monster from Hell* (1974) and *Revenge of the Pink Panther* (1978).

On television he turned up for guest appearances in *Hancock's Half Hour, Sykes, Steptoe and Son, Rising Damp* and *The Dick Emery Show*, and he played Adrian, Morecambe and Wise's camp neighbour, in their 1978 series.

Michael was forced to quit acting after suffering a stroke shortly before his seventieth birthday. He spent the last twenty years of his life living quietly in retirement, and from 1986 he was confined to a wheelchair. A lifelong bachelor and something of an eccentric, he was well loved by his colleagues.

A qualified statistician and concert pianist, Michael Ward died in hospital on 8 November 1997, at the age of eighty-eight.

Neville Ware

Neville had an uncredited role in *Carry On Emmannuelle*.

Gina Warwick

Gina played one of the Harem Girls in *Carry On Follow That Camel*. She also appeared in the 1969 feature film *Horror House* and made appearances on television in *Department S* and *On the Buses*. Some sources state that Gina died in 2003.

Richard Wattis

In addition to more than a hundred film appearances, character actor Richard Wattis was also well known for his work with Eric Sykes and Hattie Jacques in their long-running television series. The superb comic actor made just one appearance in the *Carry On* series, as the world-weary Cobley in *Carry On Spying*.

Richard Wattis was born in Wednesbury, Staffordshire, on 25 February 1912. He joined an amateur dramatic group after leaving school and worked in his family's electrical company before studying for the stage under J. Baxter Sommerville at Croyden Repertory.

Richard made his stage debut in *The Little Minister* in 1935. After active war service (in the RAMC) he returned to the theatre in 1945. His stage credits over the next four decades included *Dandy Dick* (1948, as Major Tarver), *Ring Round the Moon* (1950-51, 678 performances with Dame Margaret Rutherford and Paul Scofield), *First Person Singular* (1952, with Athene Seyler and Felix Aylmer), *The Sleeping Prince* (1954, 274 performances with Laurence Olivier, Vivien Leigh and Martita Hunt) and *Come Spy with Me* (1966, with Danny La Rue).

Richard made his screen debut in *A Yank at Oxford* in 1938. In 1949, after an absence of over a decade, the tall, bespectacled, stork-like actor returned to screen work and went on to appear in a wide selection of films, including *The Importance of Being Earnest* (1952), *Mother Riley Meets the Vampire* (1952), *Colonel March Investigates* (1953), *Hobson's Choice* (1954), *The Belles of St Trinian's* (1954), *An Alligator Named Daisy* (1955), *The Prince and the Showgirl* (1957), *Blue Murder at St Trinian's* (1957), *The Ugly Duckling* (1959), *Follow a Star* (1959), *Nearly a Nasty Accident* (1961), *The V.I.P.s* (1963), *The Great St Trinian's Train Robbery* (1966) and *Chitty Chitty Bang Bang* (1968). Towards the end of his life Richard appeared in *That's Your Funeral* (1972) and sex comedies such as *The Love Box* (1972) and *Confessions of a Window Cleaner* (1974).

To the public at large, apart from his frequent film appearances, Richard was best known for his role as Mr Brown, the snooty next-door neighbour in the Eric Sykes/Hattie Jacques series *Sykes* (3 series, 1960-61). Richard returned to play Charles Brown for a further three series of *Sykes* in 1972. The role kept him busy until shortly before his death. Richard's additional small-screen credits included *Dick and the Duchess* (series, 1959, as Peter Jamison), *Copper's End* (series, 1971, as PC Eddie Edwards, with Bill Owen, q.v.) and guest appearances in *Father, Dear Father, The Avengers* and *The Goodies*. One of his final television assignments was 'Orgy and Bess', an episode of *Carry On Laughing*. Sadly, his scenes were not shown in the final release.

Richard Wattis died suddenly from a heart attack on 1 February 1975.

Gwendolyn Watts

After making her *Carry On* debut as Charles Hawtrey's heavily pregnant wife, Mrs Barron, in *Carry On Doctor*, character actress Gwendolyn Watts went on to appear in two more 'hospital' *Carry On* films. In *Carry On Again Doctor* (again with Hawtrey) she played the night nurse, and she later appeared as Frances Kemp, the hospital receptionist, in *Carry On Matron*.

In addition to the *Carry On* films, Gwendolyn's screen credits included *Sons and Lovers* (1960), *Billy Liar* (1963, as Rita), *My Fair Lady* (1964, as the cook), *The System* (1964), *Fanatic* (1965), *The Wrong Box* (1966), *All Neat in Black Stockings* (1968) and *The Games* (1970).

On the small screen Gwendolyn was best known as Brenda in the 1967 series *Sorry, I'm Single*, with Elizabeth Knight (q.v.). Her numerous other television appearances included *The Rag Trade, The Avengers, Steptoe and Son, Call It What You Like* (1965, with June Whitfield, q.v.), *Adam Adamant Lives, On the Buses, The Ronnie Barker Playhouse* (1968) and *Justice* (series, 1972).

In later years Gwendolyn continued a consistent acting career, with appearances in *House of Cards* (mini-series, 1990), *The Plant* (feature film, 1994) and *The Final Cut* (mini-series, 1995). In 1997 Gwen toured England in a critically acclaimed role in *Stepping Out*, directed by Julia McKenzie.

Born in Carhampton, Somerset, on 23 September 1932 (some sources say 1937), Gwendolyn Watts was married to actor Gertan Klauber (q.v.) from 1959. They had two children, David and Holly. Gwendolyn died suddenly from a heart attack on 5 February 2000, aged sixty-seven.

Ann Way

A diminutive but highly distinctive character actress, Ann Way appeared in a non-speaking cameo role as Aunt Victoria Grubb in *Carry On Loving*.

Born on 14 November 1915, Ann Way was one of the first students of the Bristol Old Vic Theatre School. During her long acting career she appeared in numerous stage plays, having gained experience in repertory in England and Scotland. After many years working in regional theatres around the country Ann went on to appear in West End productions, including *Mary Rose* (1972), *Grease* (1973, as Miss Lynch), *One Way Pendulum* (1988, Old Vic) and *The Cabinet Minister* (1991, as Lady MacPhail, with Maureen Lipman, q.v.).

Ann made her screen debut in *The Hands of Orlac* in 1960 and subsequently appeared in over twenty films. With her domed forehead and petite frame, she always managed to stand out in films such as *The Prime of Miss Jean Brodie* (1969, as Celia Johnson's secretary), *Twinky* (1970), *Hands of the Ripper* (1971), *Endless Night* (1972), *The Sailor's Return* (1978), *The Dresser* (1983), *Bullshot* (1983), *Brazil* (1985), *Clockwise* (1986, as Mrs Way), *Crystalstone* (1987) and *Killing Dad* (1989). She also appeared with Patsy Rowlands (q.v.) in the 1980 tele-movie *Little Lord Fauntleroy* (as Miss Smith) and played Gertrude Dana in *War and Remembrance* (mini-series, 1989).

On television Ann Way's most memorable role was as Mrs Hall in a 1975 episode of *Fawlty Towers*. In addition, she turned up for guest appearances in a diverse range of programmes, including *Emergency Ward Ten, The Goodies, Basil Brush, Within These Walls, David Copperfield* (1986), *Juliet Bravo, All Creatures Great and Small, Don't Wait Up, Rumpole of the Bailey* (as Dodo Macintosh) and *Jackanory*, reading the Mrs Pepperpot stories.

Ann continued to work until the end of her life, her final appearances including the films *Once Upon a Crime* (1992) and *Anchoress* (1993) and on television in an episode of *Lovejoy* (1993, as Mrs Thomas). In the autumn of 1992 she was forced to give up a role on stage in *The Ghost Train* after

being diagnosed with an inoperable brain tumour.
Ann Way died on 13 March 1993, aged seventy-seven.

Lincoln Webb

Lincoln played the Nosha (with Nina Baden-Semper) who is interrupted at an inconvenient moment by Charles Hawtrey in *Carry On Up the Jungle*. Lincoln went on to appear in the 1974 comedy *Barry McKenzie Holds His Own*.

Malcolm Webster

Malcolm played the 5th Recruit in *Carry On Sergeant*.

Molly Weir (aka: Mary Weir)

A dainty, beaming, fluffy blonde character actress, author and personality, Molly Weir appeared as the Bird Lady with Bill Owen in *Carry On Regardless*. It was to be a memorable appearance in a long and varied acting career.

Born in Glasgow on 17 March 1910, Molly Weir was brought up by her widowed mother and grandmother. She made her first stage appearance at her local cinema at the tender age of five. Passionate about both acting and writing from an early age, Molly had her first article published in the *Glasgow Evening Times* when she was just fifteen and later attended the University of Glasgow. After training as a secretary (with a champion shorthand speed of 300 words per minute!) Molly began her acting career on Scottish radio at the beginning of the Second World War. During the London Blitz Molly was called upon to play in many radio dramas, having to "leap from various wartime jobs to perform from scripts hot from the copying machines". This early experience in "acting live with no time for rehearsal" would hold Molly in good stead for a radio career spanning over fifty years. She was perhaps best known on radio as Aggie MacDonald in *Life with the Lyons* (1950-61) and as Rebecca in *Rebecca of Sunnybrook Farm*, for which she was voted children's radio top personality.

Molly made her screen debut in *2,000 Women* (1944) and went on to act in over twenty films, including *Floodtide* (1949), *Miss Robin Hood* (1951), *Life with the Lyons* (1954), *Value for Money* (1955), *The Bridal Path* (1959), *The Hands of Orlac* (1960), *What a Whopper* (1961), *The Prime of Miss Jean Brodie* (1969), *Scrooge* (1970), *Hands of the Ripper* (1971), *Mr Selkie* (1978) and finally *Captain Jack* (1999). As one of the many unfortunate clients of Helping Hands, Molly's Scottish accent stood out among the all-star cast of *Carry On Regardless*, and a decade later she made another cameo appearance in an 'unofficial' *Carry On* film, playing Patricia Franklin's mother in *Bless This House*. She was also memorable as the Scottish Nanny in *One of Our Dinosaurs Is Missing* (1975), with Joan Sims and Bernard Bresslaw.

On television Molly Weir is best remembered as Hazel McWitch in three series of *Rentaghost* (1980-84). Her additional small-screen credits, dating back to the 1950s, included *Life with the Lyons* (1957 & '61), *Within These Walls, All Creatures Great and Small, This Is Your Life* (subject, 1977), *Great Expectations* (as Miss Havisham), *Uncle Jack and Operation Loch Ness* (1991), *The High Life* (1995, as Professor Wormit), *Flowers of the Forest* (1996, as Annie), *The Peter Principle* (1997) and *Last Respects* (from the American TV series *Tales from the Crypt*).

Molly also worked prodigiously in television commercials and voice-overs and was familiar in the 1970s advertising 'Flash'!

A popular personality and public speaker, Molly Weir wrote seven volumes of autobiography: *Shoes Were for Sunday* (1970), *Best Foot Forward* (1972), *A Toe on the Ladder* (1973), *Stepping into the Spotlight* (1975), *Walking into the Lyon's Den* (1977), *One Small Footprint* (1980) and *Spinning Like a Peerie* (1983). Molly also wrote the best-seller *Molly Weir's Recipes* (1960) and regularly contributed to magazines.

Molly Weir was married to Alexander (Sandy) Hamilton, her childhood sweetheart, until his death in 1997. She continued to act into the late 1990s, until a broken shoulder bone (the result of a fall) forced her to slow down on work and her numerous hobbies, which included gardening, reading, walking and 'homely' pursuits such as knitting and cooking. Molly spent many years living in Pinner, Middlesex, although she remained true to her Scottish roots was named Scotswoman of the Year in 2000. Another bad fall in her nineties forced Molly to move to a nursing home during the last year of her life, and she died on 28 November 2004, aged ninety-four.

Carry On ... ***Quotes***

Carry On Regardless *was great fun to do and I thoroughly enjoyed my part as the Bird Woman opposite Bill Owen. We rehearsed our scene separately in our dressing room, and I amazed him by telling him there were two ways I could play this little character. "Don't confuse them, Molly," he urged, "by giving them a choice! It will only hold up the film. Settle on one and give them that!. Which advice I took and all was well.*

I sat in make-up beside an old friend, Hattie Jacques, with whom I later

worked in the Sykes TV show, and she told me that when he saw the rushes, Kenneth Williams, whom at the time I hadn't met, was quite entranced and kept saying, "Who is she? She's divine." Later I was to work with him in TV pantomime, where no sign was given that he'd ever heard of me in the Carry On *film! And I was in far too much awe of him to mention it!*
The other recollection I have is of a group of Chinese 'extras' who adored being able to hang around and watch us all being filmed, and as they all had dead straight, heavy black hair they found my fine silky hair quite fascinating. Not so the director, who kept wanting my 'crowning glory' to be dulled down and a bit less photogenic!
I also later worked with Barbara Windsor in a radio series, and helping to choose Miss Scotland up in lovely Edinburgh Theatre, and who is always very friendly whenever we meet. She is still as attractive as ever.
Molly Weir, 1997

Jerold Wells (aka: Jerrold Wells)

Best known for his regular appearances over many years in *The Benny Hill Show*, Jerold Wells played Black Cowl in 'One in the Eye for Harold', an episode of *Carry On Laughing*.

Born in Wallington, Hampshire, on 8 August 1908, Jerold came to films relatively late in life, making his screen debut in *High Hell* in 1958. His subsequent film credits, which were mainly cameo roles, included *Frankenstein and the Monster from Hell* (1974), *Jabberwocky* (1977), *Adventures of a Plumber's Mate* (1978), *Time Bandits* (1981) and *Sword of the Valiant* (1984).

Although adept at sinister roles (including an acclaimed performance as Magwitch in a 1957 television production of *Great Expectations*), the bald-headed actor was best known for his work in *The Benny Hill Show*, a role he fulfilled from 1971 until the final series in 1989.

Jerold Wells died in Bath on 19 July 1999.

Gloria West

Gloria played Bridget, one of the saloon girls in *Carry On Cowboy*.

Patrick Westwood

Patrick played the Burpa on the roof in the latter stages of *Carry On Up the Khyber*.

Caroline Whitaker

Caroline played Miss Mary Parker, a beauty contestant, in *Carry On Girls* and also had an uncredited role (as an archaeology student) in *Carry On Behind*.

Carol White (aka: Carole White)

Joining the ranks of Susan Shaw and Imogen Hassall (both q.v.), Carol White was a tragic figure. A child star, whose obvious talent was wasted in Hollywood, the former leading lady – who played Sheila Dale in *Carry On Teacher* – ended her life pitifully in 1991.

Carol White was born in Hammersmith, London, on 1 April 1943 (some sources say 1941 or 1942). She trained at the Corona Stage School and made her film debut as a child in *The Belles of St Trinian's* (1954). Carol subsequently went on to appear in more than thirty films and indeed had already appeared in almost a dozen films, including *Doctor in the House* (1954), *Doctor at Sea* (1955), *An Alligator Named Daisy* (1955) and *Blue Murder at St Trinian's* (1957), when she made her solo appearance in the *Carry On* series as one of the unruly pupils at Maudlin Street School.

In 1966 Carol gained critical acclaim on television for her role as Carol in *Cathy Come Home* (with Ray Brooks, q.v.). Further success followed when she was cast as Joy in *Poor Cow* (1967) and Jody Pringle in *The Man Who Had Power Over Women* (1970).

Sadly, after 1970, despite a move across the Atlantic, her career began to decline and she made only a handful of screen appearances during the remainder of her career, including *Some Call It Loving* (1973), *The Squeeze* (1977) and *Nutcracker* (1982). She made a triumphant return to the London stage in *Steaming* in 1982, but the success was short-lived. Carol's television appearances in America included episodes of *Hawaii Five-O* and *Different Strokes* (1980).

Carol White's three marriages all ended in divorce. Her first husband was singer Michael King, with whom she had two sons. She later married Stuart Lerner and finally Michael Arnold.

By the 1980s drug abuse and alcoholism had rendered Carol's acting career effectively over. In 1982 her autobiography, *Carol Come Home*, revealed a tragic personal life and a string of affairs with many of Hollywood's leading men. Sadly, she never found personal happiness.

Suffering from cirrhosis of the liver, Carol White spent the final four weeks of her life in a coma, and she died in hospital in Miami Beach, Florida, on 16 September 1991, aged forty-eight. Her body was cremated and her ashes returned to London.

Donna White

Donna made her *Carry On* debut as a Vestal Virgin in *Carry On Cleo* and in the following year played Jane, one of the saloon girls, in *Carry On Cowboy*.

Jane White

Jane played Irene, one of the pupils in *Carry On Teacher*. She is not to be confused with the American actress (b.1922) of the same name.

Jenny White

Jenny played the nurse in the bath in *Carry On Doctor*.

Nick White

Nick had an uncredited role in *Carry On Emmannuelle*.

June Whitfield CBE (b. June Rosemary Whitfield)

A much-loved comic actress, June Whitfield's contribution to the *Carry On* series spanned over thirty years, from *Carry On Nurse* in 1959 to *Carry On Columbus* in 1992. The popular television and radio actress proved to be a welcome, and fondly remembered, addition to the series.

Born in Streatham, London, on 11 November 1925, June Whitfield trained at RADA and gained her Diploma in 1944. Her early work was on stage in pantomime, revue and musicals, and she worked with a young Barbara Windsor in *Love from Judy* (1952-54). June then went on to gain lasting success on radio, as Eth Glum, in the long-running *Take It from Here* (1953-61).

In her sixty-year career June has appeared almost exclusively on television and radio. She made her film debut in *Carry On Nurse* as Meg, Leslie Phillips's attractive girlfriend. After an absence of thirteen years she returned to play the sexually repressed Evelyn Blunt in *Carry On Abroad*. Opposite Kenneth Connor she provided a brilliant characterisation as she was transformed into a passionate temptress. In her third (and finest) appearance in the series, June played north-country councillor Augusta Prodworthy in *Carry On Girls*. June was one of the few members of the original team to return to the series in 1992, when she reunited with Leslie Phillips to play Queen Isabella in *Carry On Columbus*. Six years later she summed up the film well with the famous quote: "Perhaps it should have been called Carry *Off* Columbus!" In 1998 June unveiled a British Comedy Society plaque in memory of Hattie Jacques at the *Carry On* 40th Anniversary reunion and also featured in the documentary *What's a Carry On?*. In 2004 she was present at Pinewood Studios to pay tribute to her friend and co-star Joan Sims.

In addition to the *Carry On* films, June appeared on the big screen in

Friends and Neighbours (1959), *The Spy with a Cold Nose* (1966), *The Magnificent Seven Deadly Sins* (1971), *Bless This House* (1972, with Terry Scott, q.v.), *Not Now, Comrade* (1976), *Jude* (1996) and *Innocent* (2010).

On television June remains one of the country's busiest actors. Her first appearances date back to the 1950s and include *Fast and Loose* (1953-54, with Bob Monkhouse), episodes of *Hancock's Half Hour, Faces of Jim* (1962-63, with Jimmy Edwards), *The Frankie Howerd Show* (1966), *Beggar My Neighbour* (1966-68, with Pat Coombs, q.v.) and *Scott On ...* (1969). She is perhaps best known for her long-running association with Terry Scott, notably in *Happy Ever After* (1974-79) and *Terry and June* (1979-87). Their portrayal of husband and wife was so convincing that it led many viewers to believe that they were married in real life!

Since the early 1990s June Whitfield's career has enjoyed a well-deserved renaissance. Her role as Jennifer Saunders' mother in five series of *Absolutely Fabulous* (1992-95, 2001 & '03) and its various spin-offs has brought June a new generation of fans. In her mid-eighties she remains prodigiously busy, her more recent appearances including *Common as Muck* (1997, as Irene), *Tom Jones* (1997, as Mrs Whitfield), *Family Money* (1997), *The Last of the Blonde Bombshells* (TV-film, 2000, with Dame Judi Dench and Joan Sims), Catherine Cookson's *The Secret* (2000), *Mirrorball* (2000), *Doctor Who* (2009) and *Coronation Street* (2010). After making a 2001 guest appearance in *Last of the Summer Wine* almost inevitably she joined the regular cast (as Nellie) in 2005, and she has continued to turn up for the occasional dramatic role, with appearances in *Midsomer Murders: Midsomer Rhapsody* (2005) and *Marple: By the Pricking of My Thumbs* (2006, as Mrs Lancaster).

In addition to her countless television appearances, June is still one of Britain's leading radio actors. In the 1990s she played Miss Marple in adaptations of Agatha Christie's novels and starred with Roy Hudd in the long-running *News Huddlines*. Her recent stage credits have included *Bedroom Farce* (2002) and she played Madam Dilley, an alcoholic singing teacher, in *On the Town* in 2007.

June, who was the subject of *This Is Your Life* in 1976 and 1995, was married to surveyor Tim Aitchison from 1955 until his death in 2001 and they had one daughter, actress Suzy Aitchison (1960-). June Whitfield was made a Freeman of the City of London in 1982 and was awarded the OBE in 1985. As a fitting tribute for fifty years of acting June received a Lifetime Achievement Award at the British Comedy Awards in 1994 and four years later, as a further mark of appreciation, she was awarded the CBE. Her autobiography, *And June Whitfield*, was published in 2000 and was followed by a further pictorial memoir, *At a Glance*, in 2009.

The actress herself remains modest of a talent that has kept her busy for so long, saying, "I realise how lucky I am to still be working!" The lucky ones, undoubtedly, have been the audiences around the world who continue to enjoy her many radio and television performances.

Carry On ... ***Quotes***

In the Carry On's *I was usually involved with Ken Connor, sadly no longer with us like so many of the 'originals'. I was in four of them and usually it was all work and no time for play! But always enjoyable with such a good crowd.*
June Whitfield CBE, 1997

Ian Whittaker

Ian, who is credited with the role of a Medical Corporal in *Carry On Sergeant* and a shop assistant in *Carry On Regardless*, appeared in minor film roles from the early 1950s. He was at his busiest in the first half of the 1960s, with roles in light comedies such as *Nearly a Nasty Accident* (1961), *Dentist on the Job* (1961) and *Operation Snatch* (1962). Born in 1928, he was last seen on screen as Baggott, in the 1986 mini-series *Anastasia: The Mystery of Anna*.

Brian Wilde

Best known for his work in the long–running sitcoms *Porridge* and *Last of the Summer Wine*, television actor Brian Wilde worked on two *Carry On* films.

Born on 13 June 1927 (some sources say 1921 or 1924), Brian Wilde's acting career spanned fifty years. He made his film debut in *Will Any Gentleman...?* in 1953 and went on to make over twenty screen appearances, including *Simon and Laura* (1955), *Tiger in the Smoke* (1956), *Girls at Sea* (1958), *Rattle of a Simple Man* (1964), *Darling* (1965), *The Jokers* (1967), *No Sex Please, We're British* (1973) and *Alfie Darling* (1975). In the *Carry On*'s Brian made a cameo appearance as the man from Cox & Carter measuring Frankie Howerd's bed for rubber sheets in *Carry On Doctor*! Three years later he worked on *Carry On Henry*, although his scenes ended up on the cutting room floor.

Tall and often bespectacled, Brian was best known as dithering characters on television. He gained national recognition as Barrowclough, the mild-mannered prison officer in the Ronnie Barker series *Porridge* (1973-77). Small-screen success for Brian continued with the role of Foggy Dewhurst in *Last of the Summer Wine*, from 1975. Brian's 'difficulties' in the series with co-star Bill Owen (q.v.) were well publicised and he eventually left the series in 1985. Five years later, off-screen friction aside, he returned for a further seven years until 1997.

Brian's numerous other television series included *For the Love of Mike* (1960), *Room at the Bottom* (1967, as Mr Salisbury), two series of *The Dustbinmen* (1970, as Bloody Delilah) and *Wyatt's Watchdogs* (series, 1988, as Major Wyatt). He also made guest appearances in countless series, such as *The Men from Room 13* (1960), *Hancock* (1963), *The Avengers* (1967, as Raven in 'The Fear Merchants'), *Elizabeth R* (1971, as Donald Ramsay), *The Sweeney* and *Wuthering Heights* (1978, as Joseph).

Brian Wilde was married to actress Eva Stuart and had a son and a daughter. He died in his sleep, seven weeks after suffering a fall, on 20 March 2008. He was 80 years old.

Carry On ... ***Quotes***

I do not recall anything about the Carry On *films I was in, or have any anecdotes. I was only on them for a very few days. My opinion on the* Carry On *films as a whole is that they were very good for their kind.*
Brian Wilde, 2001

David Williams

David had three roles in the *Carry On* series: as the 7th Storeman in *Carry On Sergeant*, as Andrew Newman in *Carry On Nurse* and as the Policeman in *Carry On Regardless*. He also appeared in films such as *Time Lock* (1957) and *The Night We Dropped a Clanger* (1958). He is not to be confused with another actor of the same name, who is still in the acting profession.

David Williams died in Australia in 1984, aged sixty-two.

Kenneth Williams

(See MAIN TEAM).

Anna Willoughby

Anna had an uncredited role in *Carry On Don't Lose Your Head*. In the same year she played the boutique attendant in *The Man Outside*. Anna also featured in an uncredited role (as a dancer) in the 1971 film version of *Macbeth*.

Audrey Wilson

Audrey appeared in two *Carry On* films: as an Amazon Guard in *Carry On Spying* and as Jane (one of the girls in the bar) in *Carry On Cowboy*.

Ian Wilson

Despite appearances in over a hundred films, details on the life of character actor Ian Wilson are scarce and he is possibly the most mysterious of the *Carry On* actors. Indeed, even the dates of his birth and death are obscure. What remain clear, however, are his superb cameo appearances in four *Carry On* films, from *Carry On Regardless* to *Carry On Jack*.

Born in 1901 (or 1904), Ian began his career in silent films in the 1920s. After making a successful transition to talkies he quickly became one of those indispensable characters actors who turned up for the tiniest of cameo roles. Between the mid-1930s and the early 1970s the diminutive, often bespectacled actor seemed to appear in just about every British film produced, particularly in comic roles.

Ian made his *Carry On* debut as the advertising man with Kenneth Williams and Michael Ward (q.v.) in *Carry On Regardless*. He later played the clerk in *Carry On Cabby* and the 'ancient carrier', with Jim Dale, in *Carry On Jack*. Ian's final *Carry On* role was his most memorable, when he played the hotfooted messenger in *Carry On Cleo*. Almost thirty years later Tony Slattery (q.v.) paid tribute to this cameo appearance in *Carry On Columbus*. In addition to the *Carry On's*, Ian also worked for Gerald Thomas in *Raising the Wind* (1961) and *The Iron Maiden* (1962).

Among Ian's numerous other screen appearances were roles in *Up in the World* (1956), *Just My Luck* (1957), *I'm All Right, Jack* (1959), *Two Way Stretch* (1960), *Phantom of the Opera* (1962) and *The Day of the Triffids* (1962). His final film appearances included *Help!* (1965), *San Ferry Ann* (1965), *The Sandwich Man* (1966), *The Plank* (1967) and *The Wicker Man* (1973).

The date of Ian Wilson's death, like most of his life history, remains obscure, but is possibly 1980 or 1987.

Richard Wilson OBE (b. Iain Carmichael Wilson)

Scottish character actor Richard Wilson has been immortalised in television history as irascible pensioner Victor Meldrew in ten series of *One Foot in the Grave*. A few years after gaining fame as Meldrew, Richard was called upon to play Don Juan Felipe, opposite Maureen Lipman (q.v.), in *Carry On Columbus*.

Richard Wilson was born in Greenock, Renfrewshire, on 9 July 1936, the son of a shipyard timekeeper. Following National Service in Singapore Richard spent some time as a laboratory technician at Gateside Hospital, Greenock. He moved to London at the end of the 1950s and trained for acting at RADA in the mid-1960s.

Richard made his television debut in an episode of *Dr. Finlay's Casebook* in 1965. He went on to work in repertory theatre, and during the remainder of the 1960s and throughout the 1970s he was kept busy on stage, including a season with the Oxford Playhouse. In addition to acting he also produced and directed in the theatre.

Until the 1980s Richard was relatively unknown to screen and television audiences. Among his early screen appearances were *Not on Your Nellie* (with Hylda Baker), *Virginia Fly Is Drowning*, *The Sweeney*, *Only When I Laugh* (series, 1979, as Dr Gordon Thorpe) and *In Loving Memory*. In the mid-1980s his late flowering began and he came to prominence in films and television, notably as Turton in *A Passage to India* (1984) and as Nigel Lipman in *Whoops Apocalypse* (1988).

By the late 1980s, following roles in a succession of television series that included *High and Dry* (series, 1987, as Richard Talbot), *Tutti Frutti* (series, 1987, as Eddie Clockerty) and *Hot Metal* (series, 1988, as Dicky Lipton), Richard had at last become a familiar face to television audiences. He secured long-term success as Victor Meldrew, one of the most memorable comic characters of all time, in ten series of *One Foot in the Grave* (1990-2000). His superb portrayal of the grumpy pensioner (whose catchphrase "I don't believe it!" quickly caught on) brought Richard, and his co-star Annette Crosbie, a legion of fans.

Since taking on the role of Victor Meldrew Richard has become one of Britain's busiest character actors, having managed successfully to avoid being typecast. Among his most recent appearances have been series such as *Duck Patrol* (1998, as PC Rose), *Other Animals* (1999, as Alex Cameron), *Life Support* (1999, as John Doone), *High Stakes* (2001, as Bruce Morton), *Born and Bred* (2004-05, as Dr Donald Newman) and *Doctor Who* (2005, as Dr Constantine), and he played Gaius in *Merlin* (2008-10).

In addition to *Carry On Columbus* and the above-mentioned film appearances, Richard's screen credits include *Foreign Body* (1986), *How to Get Ahead in Advertising* (1989), *A Dry White Season* (1989), *Soft Top, Hard Shoulder* (1993), *The Man Who Knew Too Little* (1997), *Women Talking Dirty* (1999) and *Gnomeo and Juliet* (voice only, 2011). He has also appeared in several mini-series and tele-movies, notably *Butter* (1994), *In the Red* (1998, as Lord Tone), *Gulliver's Travels* (1996) and *Lord of Misrule* (1996).

A lifelong bachelor, Richard was awarded the OBE in 1994 and was Rector of Glasgow University for three years (1996-99).

Barbara Windsor MBE

(See MAIN TEAM).

Elsie Winsor

Elsie played the cloakroom attendant who interrupts Barbara Windsor and Sid James in *Carry On Girls*.

Barbara Wise

Barbara played Miss Julia Oates in *Carry On Girls*. In the same year she also featured on *The Benny Hill Show*.

Corbett Woodall

Real-life television newsreader Corbett Woodall played the ITV newsreader in *Carry On Emmannuelle*. He played similar roles in several other films and television series, notably numerous episodes of *The Goodies* in the 1970s and 1980s. He died in 1982 at the age of fifty-three.

George Woodbridge

A distinctive, portly character actor with over a hundred films to his credit, George Woodbridge played Ned in *Carry On Jack*. He had previously worked for Peter Rogers and Gerald Thomas in *Raising the Wind* (1961), *The Iron Maiden* (1962) and *Nurse on Wheels* (1963).

Born in Exeter, Devon, on 16 February 1907, George made his film debut in *Young and Innocent* in 1937. Over the next thirty-five years he was kept busy with cameo appearances in films such as *The Life and Death of Colonel Blimp* (1943), *Bonnie Prince Charlie* (1948) and *The Fallen Idol* (1949). During the 1950s he built up his reputation as a stalwart player and gained added familiarity on television as Sergeant Hawker in *Stryker of the Yard* (1957). A quick glimpse through his later screen credits reveals appearances in *Dracula: Prince of Darkness* (1966), *All the Way Up* (1970) and *Up Pompeii* (1971).

George Woodbridge continued to work until the end of his life, his final appearance being as Inigo Pipkin in the 1973 television series *Pipkins*. George died on 31 March 1973, aged sixty-six.

Vicki Woolf

Vicki Woolf, who played one of the Khasi's wives in *Carry On Up the Khyber*, has been acting in films and television since her teens.

Born in Brighton in 1945, Vicki made her screen debut in *The Hands of Orlac* in 1960. She went on to appear in *The Vampire Lovers* (1970), *Hands of the Ripper* (1971) and *Confessions of a Pop Performer* (1975).

On the small screen Vicki played Maria in *Never Mind the Quality, Feel the Width* (1967) and in the 1970s she made guest appearances in programmes such as *The Persuaders* and *Are You Being Served?* In the late 1980s she played Rhonda, Michael Elphick's neighbour, in *Three Up, Two Down*. Vicki is still a working actress.

Martin Wyldeck

Martin Wyldeck appeared in a cameo role in *Carry On Sergeant*, playing Bob Monkhouse's father, Mr Sage.

Born in Birmingham on 11 January 1914, Martin spent his early years living in Austria. He came from a theatrical background – his mother and uncle were both actors and his grandfather was playwright Frank Harvey.

Martin began his acting career on stage in 1935 as a pirate in *Treasure Island*. He then went on to work in repertory at Colchester before his acting career was interrupted by four years of active service during the Second World War.

In addition to *Carry On Sergeant*, Martin made over thirty film appearances, including *Operation Diamond* (1948), *Will Any Gentleman...?* (1953), *Timeslip* (1955), *The Hypnotist* (1957), *A Story of David* (1960), *The Girl on the Boat* (1961), *That Kind of Girl* (1963), *The Oblong Box* (1969), *Cool It Carol!* (1970) and *Tiffany Jones* (1973).

Martin's first major television appearance was in the Dora Bryan/Eleanor Summerfield (both q.v.) series *My Wife's Sister* (1956-57, as Charlie Hackett). In his later years he was kept busy with bit parts in a variety of series, notably episodes of *Dad's Army* and *Fawlty Towers* (1975, as Sir Richard Morris). Martin's final appearances were in the television mini-series *The Scarlet Pimpernel* (1982) and *Squaring the Circle* (1984).

Martin Wyldeck was still a working actor when he died suddenly in Richmond on 29 April 1988, aged seventy-four.

Carol Wyler

Carol played Miss Maureen Darcy, a beauty contestant, in *Carry On Girls*. It was her only film appearance.

Bruce Wyllie

Bruce had an uncredited role in *Carry On Emmannuelle*.

Madame Yang

Madame Yang had an uncredited role as the elderly Chinese lady in *Carry On Regardless*.

Joan Young (b. Joan Cecilia Wragge)

Joan Young's career on stage, screen, television and radio spanned sixty years. In her sole *Carry On* appearance she played the outraged Lady Mayoress accused of shoplifting by Kenneth Williams and Charles Hawtrey in *Carry On Constable*.

Born in Newcastle-upon-Tyne on 1 February 1900, Joan came from a music hall background. She made her stage debut at Woolwich Hippodrome in 1918 and went on to appear in music hall productions as a singer and actress.

From its earliest conception Joan Young was a constant performer on radio, a medium that kept her busy - almost exclusively - into the 1940s. With the outbreak of the Second World War Joan continued to work for BBC light entertainment, broadcasting from Bristol and later Bangor, North Wales. Her fine ear for accents, combined with her abilities as a singer, ensured that she was in constant demand among producers. Among Joan's many radio credits were *Just Kidd-ing* (1941, as the cook), *Hitch Hike* (1942), *Whack-O!* (1961, as Matron) and *Doctor in the House* (1968).

Towards the end of the war Joan returned to the theatre, appearing in numerous plays such as *Our Town, Big Ben, Dandy Dick, Old Chelsea* and *Lady Chatterley*. Near the end of her life she enjoyed great success touring in the play *Big Bad Mouse*, which took her around the world (including tours of Hong Kong and the USA) until 1978.

Joan made her screen debut in *Victoria the Great* in 1937. She subsequently appeared in more than twenty films, often as matronly characters, including *The Lamp Still Burns* (1943), *Strawberry Roan* (1944), *School for Secrets* (1946), *The Small Voice* (1948), *Vice Versa* (1948), *The Fallen Idol* (1948), *Trottie True* (1949), *The Magic Box* (1952), *Time Gentlemen, Please!* (1952), *Fast and Loose* (1954), *An Alligator Named Daisy* (1955), *The Inn of the Sixth Happiness* (1958), *Suddenly, Last Summer* (1959), *In the Doghouse* (1961), *The Plank* (1967), *The Last Shot You Hear* (1969) and *Blood from the Mummy's Tomb* (1971). Her final film appearance was a bit-part role (non-speaking and uncredited) in the opening scenes of *Death on the Nile* (1978).

Joan Young's small-screen appearances included *Dr Finlay's Casebook* (1955), *Maverick* (1957), *Doctor Knock* (1961), *Danger Man* (1964), *Doctor Who* (1966, as Catherine de Medici), *Sinister Street* (1969), *Ours Is a Nice House* (1970), *For the Love of Ada* (1971), *Big Bad Mouse* (1972), *Sykes* (3 episodes, 1972, '73 & '74), *Billy Liar* (1973), *Shades of Green – Root of All Evil* (1975), *The Chiffy Kids* (1978) and *All Creatures Great and Small* (2 episodes, 1980, as Miss Westerman).

Joan married journalist/editor John Young (1901-2004) in 1923. They had one daughter, April Young (the subsequent agent of, among others, June Whitfield and Molly Weir, both q.v.).

Joan Young died in London from heart and kidney failure on 10 October 1984, aged eighty-four.

Karen Young

Karen had uncredited roles in three *Carry On* films: as one of the girls in *Carry On Don't Lose Your Head*, as a Harem Girl in *Carry On Follow That Camel* and as a Hospitality Girl in *Carry On Up the Khyber*.

And Finally ...

During the course of my research several members of the *Carry On* production crew were contacted. Sadly, space does not allow me to include full profiles of these remarkable people, but some of their memories of the series can be found below.

Dave Freeman (1922-2005)

Scriptwriter: *Carry On Behind, Columbus.*
A well-known scriptwriter, Dave also wrote six episodes of *Carry On Laughing* for television in 1975 and *Carry On Laughing's Christmas Classics* (1983). In addition, he is credited with the role of Inquisitor No. 1 in *Carry On Columbus.*

I can't begin to understand the renewed popularity of the series. Ninety per cent of its success was due to the performers; the rest being shared among the camera crew, the set designer, the script and the director. It is of course broad, basic, bawdy comedy, which I hope will always be in demand.
Sadly, today they reported that Joan Sims died. Almost the last of the old team, I first worked with her on radio in 1956 together with Ken Connor in a show called Floggits. *A very nice lady and a first-rate actress.*
Dave Freeman, 2001

Julie Harris (1921-)

Costume Designer: *Carry On Cleo.*
Julie's long and distinguished career in the business saw her win an Oscar for Best Costume Design for the 1965 black-and-white film *Darling*. She retired from the profession in 1992 and became a successful oil painter.

As with all Carry On *productions there was a very small costume budget, but then the company was not renowned for the size of its pay cheques – as is probably commented on by interviews with the actors! The film did look particularly lavishly costumed. I designed all but Sid James's outer bits, which very fortunately were previously made for and worn by Richard Burton – no expense spared! This added to a good wardrobe look. Kenneth Williams had three or four little 'cocktail frocks' as he called them. Oddly, his fittings were*

anything but hilarious. Joan Sims and Amanda Barrie were delightful to work with and good at wearing their Roman/Egyptian costumes. Amanda Barrie's headdresses and jewellery were made by top craftspeople at the time.
Julie Harris, 2000

Norman Hudis (1923-)

Scriptwriter: *Carry On Sergeant, Nurse, Teacher, Constable, Regardless* and *Cruising*.

A former journalist and playwright, Norman moved to America in the mid-1960s, where he has enjoyed a long and successful career. His autobiography, *No Laughing Matter: How I Carried On*, was published in 2008.

Mr Hudis kindly agreed to answer questions via email from his home in America in October 2000. A selection is included here.

Q. What was your reaction at the time to the overwhelming success of Carry On Nurse?
A. I simply revelled in it. But with inner gratitude. This business is so capricious and loaded in the direction of failure and disappointment that anyone who isn't grateful for success in it is asking, in Noel Coward's warning phrase, 'for the Blue Bird of Happiness to shit on me'. Carry On Nurse *was an especial pleasure for me, of course, because so much of its fun came from the real-life experience of my SRN wife, Rita.*

Q. Did you spend much time on the set at Pinewood and do you have any particular memories of the actors involved?
A. I might look in and say hello. But not often. I had spent 10 years in studio publicity, so seeing filming had long since lost any novelty it might once have had for me.

Q. How did the success of the Carry On's *influence your subsequent career in America?*
A. Carry On Nurse *had a freak success in metropolitan areas of the US. As a result I was invited to Hollywood. However, there was no attempt to reproduce the style in American terms. The Pinewood product was indelibly British. So, what wit I have I employed in the normal course of working on all kinds of shows, ranging from* The Man from UNCLE *to the Biblical Special,* The Story of Esther.

Q. Do you have any particular memories of recent reunions?
A. They are extremely pleasant occasions and overall it is gratifying to be

remembered by so many people. Generally: let me conclude by putting on record that the Carry On's *are inescapable in their continuing effect on my life. Example: I've just come back from a Film Festival in Indianapolis where my full-length animation movie* A Monkey's Tale *won its third award so far. At the Gala Dinner I was seated next to an embarrassingly awed lady who told me that she had been "brought up on the* Carry On's *in Dublin, Ireland". I was touched that she distinguished the town from Dublin, Georgia, where, I am fairly certain, this remarkable string of Brit comedies is entirely unknown!*

Alan Hume BSC (1924-2010)

Cameraman: *Carry On Sergeant, Nurse, Teacher and Constable.*

Director of Photography: *Regardless, Cruising, Cabby, Jack, Spying, Cleo, Cowboy, Screaming, Don't Lose Your Head, Follow That Camel, Doctor, Henry, Abroad, Girls, Emmannuelle* and *Columbus.*

Cinematographer Alan Hume had a distinguished career in British films over a period of fifty years. In addition to the majority of the *Carry On* films, he worked on more than a hundred big-screen productions, including many of the Bond films, *Star Wars IV: The Return of the Jedi* (1983), *A Fish Called Wanda* (1988) and *Shirley Valentine* (1989). A modest man and popular with fans, his autobiography, *A Life Through the Lens*, was published in 2004.

All of the Carry On *actors were very nice people to work with and great fun. It was a pleasure to be at work and very often I had to stuff a handkerchief in my mouth to stop me from laughing out loud and ruining the soundtrack. Gerald Thomas, the director, was very clever when editing the films. He had a great feel for timing, often cutting to close-ups so as to accentuate the punchlines.*

Alan Hume, 2000

Larry (aka: Terence Parkes) (1927-2003)

Cartoonist: *Carry On Doctor, Up the Khyber, Camping.*

A cartoonist and illustrator, Larry provided the title sequences for three *Carry On* films. His autobiography, *Larry on Larry*, was published in 1994. He also released a large selection of other books featuring his work.

I remember sitting watching Carry On Up the Khyber *alongside the scriptwriter Talbot Rothwell, Peter Rogers and others. I'm afraid I had to*

pretend to be amused. Carry On *films are not my cup of tea. Will Hay films, Laurel and Hardy, etc., are very much more my kind of thing. However, I'm very much in a minority.* Carry On *films will be forever popular with the masses. Alongside what goes on today they are beginning to look good! Although I never met him, Kenneth Williams chose me to illustrate one of his books. He was a real funny man, more in his element on chat shows.*
Larry (Terence Parkes), 1998

BIBLIOGRAPHY
REFERENCE BOOKS

Bonner, Hilary, *Heartbeat: The Real Life Story*, Boxtree, 1994.

Bright, Morris & Ross, Robert, *Carry On Uncensored: The Exclusive Behind-the-Scenes Story*, Boxtree, 1999.

Cameron-Wilson, James, *Film Review 1997-98*, Virgin, 1997.

Evans, Jeff, *The Guinness Television Encyclopedia*, Guinness Publishing, 1995.

Genower, Peter (Editor-in-Chief), *TV Times Who's Who On Television*, Boxtree, 2000.

Haining, Peter, *Agatha Christie: Murder in Four Acts*, Virgin, 1990.

Harrison, Tony, *The Australian Film and Television Companion*, Simon & Schuster, 1994.

Hayward, Anthony & Deborah, *TV Unforgettables: Over 250 Legends of the Small Screen*, Guinness Publishing, 1993.

Hayward, Anthony, *Who's Who on Television*, Boxtree, 1990 & 1996.

________, *Who's Who of Soap Operas*, Guinness Publishing, 1995.

Herbert, Ian (and others, editor), *Who's Who in the Theatre* (17 editions), Pitman, various dates, 1929-84.

Hibbin, Sally & Hibbin, Nina, *What a Carry On: The Official Story of the Carry On Film Series*, Hamlyn, 1988.

Hudd Roy (with Philip Hindin), *Roy Hudd's Cavalcade of Variety Acts: A Who's Who of Light Entertainment*, Robson Books, 1997.

Kenworthy, Christopher, *Badger: In Drama and Real Life*, BBC

Worldwide, 2000.

Kingsley, Hilary, *Soap Box: The Papermac Guide to Soap Opera*, Papermac, 1988.

Lewisohn, Mark, *Radio Times Guide to TV Comedy*, BBC Worldwide, 1998.

Little, Daran, *The Coronation Street Story: Celebrating Thirty-Five Years of the Street*, Boxtree, 1995.

McFarlane, Brian, *An Autobiography of British Cinema*, Methuen/BFI Publishing, 1997.

________, *The Encyclopedia of British Film*, Methuen/BFI Publishing, 2003.

Massingberd, Hugh, *The Daily Telegraph Fifth Book of Obituaries: Twentieth-Century Lives*, Macmillan, 1999.

Palmer, Scott, *British Film Actors' Credits, 1895-1987*, McFarland, 1988.

Pertwee, Bill, *Dad's Army: The Making of a Television Legend*, PRC Publishing, 1997.

Quinlan, David, *Quinlan's Film Stars*, B.T. Batsford, 1991, 1996 & 2000.

________, *Quinlan's Illustrated Directory of Film Character Actors*, B.T. Batsford, 1995.

________, *Quinlan's Illustrated Directory of Film Comedy Stars*, B.T. Batsford, 1992.

Rigelsford, Adrian, *Carry On Laughing: A Celebration*, Virgin, 1996.

Ross, Robert, *The Carry On Companion*, B.T. Batsford, 1996.

Sheridan, Simon, *Keeping the British End Up: Four Decades of Saucy Cinema*, Reynolds & Hearn, 2001.

Taylor, Rod, *The Guinness Book of Sitcoms*, Guinness Publishing, 1994.

Vahimagi, Tise, *British Television: An Illustrated Guide*, BFI Publishing, 1994.

Walker, John (Editor), *Halliwell's Filmgoer's Companion*, HarperCollins, 1997.

________, *Halliwell's Film & Video Guide*, HarperCollins, 1999 & 2002.

________, *Halliwell's Who's Who in the Movies*, HarperCollins, 1999 & 2001.

Webber, Richard, *Are You Being Served?*, Orion, 1998.

________, *Whatever Happened to the Likely Lads?*, Orion, 1999.

________, *Dad's Army: A Celebration*, Virgin, 1999.

________, *A Celebration of The Good Life*, Orion, 2000.

________, *The Complete A-Z of Everything Carry On*, Harper Collins, 2005.

Upton, Julian, *Fallen Stars: Tragic Lives and Lost Careers*, Critical Vision/Headpress, 2004.

BIOGRAPHIES & AUTOBIOGRAPHIES

Askwith, Robin, *The Confessions of Robin Askwith*, Ebury Press, 1999.

Ball, Vincent, *Buck Jones Where Are You? An Australian Boy's Adventure*, Random House, 1996.

Barrie, Amanda, *It's Not a Rehearsal*, Headline, 2002.

Box, Betty, *Lifting the Lid: The Autobiography of Film Producer Betty Box, OBE*, The Book Guild, 2000.

Bright, Morris & Ross, Robert, *Mr Carry On: The Life and Works of Peter Rogers*, BBC Worldwide, 2000.

Carney, Jessica, *Who's There? The Life and Career of William Hartnell*, Virgin, 1996.

Davies, Russell (Editor), *The Kenneth Williams Diaries*, HarperCollins, 1993.

________, *The Kenneth Williams Letters*, HarperCollins, 1995.

Douglas, Angela, *Swings and Roundabouts*, Elm Tree, 1983.

Eaton, Shirley, *Golden Girl*, B.T. Batsford, 1999.

Goodwin, Cliff, *Sid James*, Century, 1995.

Houston, Renée, *Don't Fence Me In*, Pan, 1974.

Jennings, Teresa (with Patricia Hayes), *A Funny Old Life*, Robson Books, 1990.

Le Mesurier, Joan, *Dear John*, Sidgwick & Jackson, 2001.

Lewis, Roger, *Charles Hawtrey 1914-1988: The Man Who Was Private Widdle*, Faber & Faber, 2001.

Lipman, Maureen, *When's It Coming Out?* Robson Books, 1992.

Logan, Jimmy, *It's a Funny Life*, B&W Publishing, 1998.

Merriman, Andy, *Hattie: The Authorised Biography of Hattie Jacques*, Aurum, 2007.

Mitchell, Norman (with Paul Laffan), *An Actor's Life for Me*, Sims Publications, 2003.

Owen, Bill, *Summer Wine and Vintage Years: A Cluttered Life*, Robson Books, 1994.

Parkes, Terence (with Mark Bryant), *Larry On Larry: My Life in Cartoons*, Grub Street, 1994.

Pertwee, Bill, *A Funny Way to Make a Living!*, Sunburst Books, 1996.

Powell, Nosher, *Nosher*, Blake, 1999.

Richard, Wendy (with Lizzie Wiggins), *Wendy Richard, No 's': My Life Story*, Simon & Schuster, 2000.

Roose-Evans, James, *One Foot on the Stage: The Biography of Richard Wilson*, Orion, 1997.

Sims, Joan, *High Spirits*, Partridge, 2000.

Stone, Philip, *Beginnings and Endings ... An Actor's Way*. Autolycus Press, 1998.

Weir, Molly, *Spinning Like a Peerie*, Gordon Wright, 1983, & Lomond Book, 1999.

Whitfield, June, *... And June Whitfield*, Bantam Press, 2000.

________, *At a Glance: An Absolutely Fabulous Life*, Weidenfeld & Nicolson, 2009.

Williams, Kenneth, *Just Williams*, Fontana, 1985, & HarperCollins, 1993.

________, *Back Drops*, Futura, 1983.

Windsor, Barbara, *Barbara: The Laughter & Tears of a Cockney Sparrow*, Century, 1990, & Arrow, 1991.

________, *All of Me: My Extraordinary Life*, Headline, 2000.

WEBSITES

The following websites have been particularly useful during the course of writing this book;

www.imdb.com

www.britmovie.co.uk/forums/

DVD RELEASES

The entire *Carry On* series, including *Carry On Columbus*, has been released on DVD.

A boxed set* (not including *Columbus*) has been released with numerous 'extra' features including audio commentary by author Robert Ross and the following members of the *Carry On* team:

Sergeant (Dora Bryan, Shirley Eaton and Terence Longdon)
Nurse (Shirley Eaton and Terence Longdon)
Teacher (Paul Cole, Larry Dann and Richard O'Sullivan)
Constable (Leslie Phillips)
Regardless (Liz Fraser and Terence Longdon)
Cruising (Dilys Laye and Lance Percival)
Cabby (Liz Fraser)
Jack (Bernard Cribbins)
Spying (Bernard Cribbins and Dilys Laye)
Cleo (Amanda Barrie and Julie Stevens)
Cowboy (Angela Douglas)
Screaming (Angela Douglas and Fenella Fielding)
Don't Lose Your Head (Jim Dale)
Follow That Camel (Jim Dale)
Doctor (Jim Dale)
Up the Khyber (Peter Rogers)
Camping (Dilys Laye and Sandra Caron)
Again, Doctor (Jim Dale)
Up the Jungle (Valerie Leon and Jacki Piper)
Loving (Jacki Piper and Richard O'Callaghan)
Henry (Alan Hume)
At Your Convenience (Jacki Piper and Richard O'Callaghan)
Matron (Patsy Rowlands, Valerie Leon and Jacki Piper)
Abroad (John Clive, Sally Geeson, Carol Hawkins and David Kernan)
Girls (Jack Douglas, Patsy Rowlands and June Whitfield)
Dick (Jack Douglas)
Behind (Larry Dann, Jack Douglas, Dave Freeman and Patsy Rowlands)
England (Patrick Mower)
That's Carry On (Peter Rogers)

Emmannuelle (Jack Douglas and Larry Dann)

* issued by ITV DVD, Studio Canal, Optimum Classic.

PHOTOGRAPHIC CREDITS

The following photographs are copyright Rex Features and reproduced with permission.

Front/Back Cover:
Barbara Windsor (Stuart Atkins/Rex Features, 2005)
Kenneth Williams (FreemantleMedia Ltd/Rex Features)
Hattie Jacques (ITV/Rex Features, 1975)
Sid James (ITV/Rex Features, 1960s)

Internal photographs:
Jack Douglas (John Fowler/Rex Features, 1982)
Hattie Jacques (ITV/Rex Features, 1967)
Sid James (Granada International/Rex Features, 1949)
Peter Butterworth (ITV/Rex Features, 1970)

Charles Hawtrey (Rex Features, 1973)
Joan Sims & Liz Fraser (Rex Features, 1960)
Sid James (ITV/Rex Features)
Fenella Fielding (ITV/Rex Features, 1964)

Terry Scott & June Whitfield (John Curtis/Rex Features, 1978)
Kenneth Connor (ITV/Rex Features, 1976)
Charles Hawtrey (FreemantleMedia Ltd/Rex Features, 1979)
Hattie Jacques (FreemantleMedia Ltd/Rex Features, 1980)

Kenneth Williams (Peter Brooker/Rex Features, 1985)
Bernard Bresslaw (Nils Jorgensen/Rex Features, 1990)
Kenneth Connor (Nils Jorgensen/Rex Features, 1991)
Barbara Windsor, Terry Scott, Anita Harris, Jack Douglas, Bernard Bresslaw (Paul Fievez/Mail On Sunday/Rex Features, 1987)

Barbara Windsor (Jonathan Hordle/Rex Features, 2009)
Jim Dale (Carolyn Contino/BEI/Rex Features, 2009)
Joan Sims (Clive Limpkin/Daily Mail/Rex Features, 1998)
Patsy Rowlands & Alan Sircom (Steve Back/Daily Mail/Rex Features, 1998)

Additional photographs are from the author's private collection (copyright, Andrew Ross).

Author photograph, copyright Brian Ellwood (Barrett & Co.), 2010.

Author's Note

This book is designed as a reference and affectionate tribute to the actors and production personnel involved in the *Carry On* film series.

It is not the intention of the author to deliberately offend or discredit any person or persons living or dead (and their families) mentioned in this book in any way.

In the event of any grievance being taken by any of the material in this book, the author will, if contacted, gladly edit and/or remove any said references in future editions of the book.

Notes

Notes

Notes

Notes

Notes

Notes

Notes

Notes